Assessment Clear and Simple

BARBARA E. WALVOORD

Foreword by
Trudy W. Banta

Assessment Clear and Simple

A Practical Guide for Institutions, Departments, and General Education

JOSSEY-BASS
A Wiley Imprint
www.josseybass.com

MT

Published by Jossey-Bass
A Wiley Imprint
989 Market Street, San Francisco, CA 94103-1741   www.josseybass.com

Jossey-Bass books and products are available through most bookstores. To contact Jossey-Bass directly call our Customer Care Department within the U.S. at 800-956-7739, outside the U.S. at 317-572-3986 or fax 317-572-4002.

Jossey-Bass also publishes its books in a variety of electronic formats. Some content that appears in print may not be available in electronic books.

Library of Congress Cataloging-in-Publication Data

Walvoord, Barbara E. Fassler, 1941–
   Assessment clear and simple : a practical guide for institutions, departments, and general education / Barbara E. Walvoord.— 1st ed.
      p. cm. — (The Jossey-Bass higher and adult education series)
Includes bibliographical references and index.
   ISBN 0-7879-7311-4 (alk. paper)
  1. Educational evaluation.   I. Title. II. Series.
   LB2822.75.W35 2004
   379.1'5—dc22

                              2003027457

Printed in the United States of America
FIRST EDITION
PB Printing 10 9 8 7 6 5 4 3 2

12/17/04

The Jossey-Bass
Higher and Adult Education Series

To my beloved spouse, partner, and friend,
Judith A. Sturnick

CONTENTS

In our respective travels around the country talking with faculty about assessment, Barbara Walvoord and I have heard this question many times: "How do we get started in assessment?" That is often followed with a plea, "Isn't there a simple step-by-step guide we can follow?" Until this point we have had to say no to that entreaty. But now Barbara has stepped forward to present *Assessment Clear and Simple,* and all of us—the novices who seek help and experienced practitioners who try to provide it—are indebted to her.

In clear, persuasive prose that reflects her grounding in the discipline of English, Barbara brings us a straightforward definition of assessment that emphasizes the use of carefully considered evidence to improve learning. True to her promise in the subtitle to keep her message short, Barbara defines her audience narrowly and then tells each of three groups that they need to read just two of the book's four chapters! There is an introductory chapter for everyone, then a special chapter each for institution-wide planners and administrators, faculty concerned with assessment at the department or program level, and faculty and staff charged with the responsibility of assessing the general education experience.

Despite promising to keep things simple, Barbara Walvoord is never simplistic in her presentation. She acknowledges the complexity of learning and of the assessment that must match its features. While endeavoring to keep assessment "simple, cost efficient, and useful," she encourages faculty to set ambitious goals for student learning, even if they may seem ambiguous in terms of their measurement potential. She urges that we not fall into the trap of discarding goals like preparing students to become ethical decision makers and good citizens just because these abilities seem difficult to measure. Even today we can employ questionnaires and interviews to ask current students and recent graduates if they perceive that they have experienced growth in these areas as a result of their college experiences, and in future years we can operationalize these concepts and develop more direct measures of associated behaviors.

When faculty are confronted with the necessity of creating an assessment initiative to satisfy a state or board of trustees mandate or the requirements of an accreditor, they often respond—quite rightly—"Aren't we already assessing student learning? After all, we evaluate student work and give grades." One of the many features of this work that I admire is Barbara Walvoord's willingness to identify and respond to legitimate concerns about outcomes assessment. In this case, she not only acknowledges that faculty and student affairs staff on every campus are engaged in assessment, but includes in every chapter the vital step of completing an audit of all the assessment activities already in place and asking how the use of the data from these activities to improve student learning could be enhanced. In her prior presentations and publications Barbara has become well known for her advocacy of the use of rubrics to make meaning of grades in the outcomes assessment process. In this volume we are treated to new examples of rubric construction and of the use of classroom assessment techniques in the quest for data that can help us improve instruction and ultimately learning.

In reviewing such a brief work, my greatest concern was related to the limited ability to provide context for the steps to be taken in inaugurating and sustaining an assessment initiative. Assessment approaches are unique, due primarily to the diverse organizational structures and background experiences, expertise, and personalities of instructors and student affairs staff that constitute the environments on different campuses. Barbara has addressed this concern by providing examples and options for proceeding in a variety of contexts, and in the appendices, specific illustrations designed for a variety of institutions.

Barbara Walvoord gives us detailed examples of reporting formats applicable at department and institution-wide levels. She urges that responses to assessment findings be based on the best current theories of student and organizational growth and development, then cites references that can be helpful in the search for such theories.

I could say more, but I am reminded of Barbara's emphasis on brevity. My overview, then, is designed simply to whet your appetite for the rich educational experience that lies in the pages ahead. Happy reading!

Trudy W. Banta

ABOUT THE AUTHOR

BARBARA E. WALVOORD, Ph.D., is Fellow of the Institute for Educational Initiatives and concurrent professor of English at the University of Notre Dame, Indiana. She has coordinated Notre Dame's regional accreditation self-study. As founding director of four college and university faculty development centers, she has also consulted or led workshops on assessment, productivity, effective teaching, and writing across the curriculum at more than 250 institutions of higher education. In addition to this book, her publications include *Effective Grading: A Tool for Learning and Assessment* (Jossey-Bass, 1998). She is the 1987 Maryland English Teacher of the Year for Higher Education.

CHAPTER 1

For Everyone:
The Basics of Assessment

You probably are reading this book because you have been asked to "do assessment" or to carry forward a previous assessment plan for a regional or discipline-based accreditor or for a legislative or trustee mandate. You may be an administrator, department chair, assessment director, general education committee member, or faculty member involved in assessment. I wrote this book after serving in several of those administrative and faculty roles myself, and having been engaged as a consultant on assessment by institutions both public and private, large and small, traditional and nontraditional. I saw that what people needed was a short, clear, no-nonsense guide to assessment. They needed to know how assessment could serve departmental and institutional goals—not merely external mandates—and how assessment could be conducted effectively and efficiently with the time, expertise, and resources that were available.

The Purpose of This Book

This book aims to make assessment simple, cost efficient, and useful to the institution, while meeting the assessment requirements of accreditation agencies, legislatures, review boards, and others.

The Organization of This Book

This book is organized in the following way:

- This chapter, which everyone should read

- Chapters especially for
  - Institution-wide planners and administrators
  - Departments
  - General education

Defining Assessment of Student Learning

Assessment of student learning can be defined as *the systematic collection of information about student learning, using the time, knowledge, expertise, and resources available, in order to inform decisions about how to improve learning.*

- Assessment is a kind of "action research," intended not so much to generate broad theories as to inform local action.
- Educational situations contain too many variables to make "proof" possible. Therefore, assessment gathers indicators that will be useful for decision making.
- Assessment does not limit itself only to learning that can be objectively tested. It need not be a reductive exercise. Rather, a department can state its highest goals, including goals such as students' ethical development, understanding of diversity, and the like. Then it can seek the best available indicators about whether those goals are being met.
- Assessment does not require standardized tests or "objective" measures. Faculty regularly assess complex work in their fields and make judgments about its quality; in assessment of learning, faculty make informed professional judgments about critical thinking, scientific reasoning, or other qualities in student work, and then use those judgments to inform departmental and institutional decisions.
- Assessment means basing decisions about curriculum, pedagogy, staffing, advising, and student support upon the best possible data about student learning and the factors that affect it.
- A great deal of assessment is already occurring in responsible classrooms, departments, and institutions, though we have not always called it that.
- Assessment can move beyond the classroom to become program assessment:

  Classroom assessment: The teacher of the senior capstone course evaluates her students' final projects, assigns grades, and uses the information for her own improvement next semester.

Program assessment: The faculty teaching the senior capstone report annually to the department, outlining the strengths and weaknesses of the students' work in relation to departmental learning goals. The department uses these and other data, such as student and alumni questionnaires, to inform decisions about curriculum, pedagogy, and other factors that affect student learning.

The Three Steps of Assessment

1. Articulate your goals for student learning ("When they complete our program, students will be able to . . .").

2. Gather evidence about how well students are meeting the goals.

   Direct measures directly evaluate student work. Examples of direct measures include exams, papers, projects, computer programs, interaction with a client, or musical performances.

   Indirect measures include asking students or alumni how well they thought they learned, tracking their graduate school or job placement rates, and so on.

   Evidence includes qualitative as well as quantitative information. No one forces you to use standardized tests.

3. Use the information for improvement.

Can Assessment Be Applied to Complex Liberal Learning?

Yes. Learning goals, such as the inclination to question assumptions, sensitivity to poverty and injustice, scientific literacy, the ability to work effectively with people of diverse backgrounds and cultures, the development of ethical values, or, for faith-based institutions, the development of spiritual qualities, are difficult to assess. Yet they are among the goals that faculty and institutions hold most dear, and they may be the most important qualities that higher education can nurture in the citizens of the future. To make good choices about how to nurture those qualities, educators need indicators of how well students are achieving them. A combination of direct and indirect measures can be useful:

- Student journals and essays can be evaluated by criteria that address the qualities the institution hopes to nurture, such as recognition of alternative points of view; evidence that the student is constructing her own value system rather than unquestioningly adopting values of home, church, or the larger society; demonstration of a humble stance toward the truth, even when the student states firm moral conviction; commitment to uphold freedom of speech while rejecting racism, sexism, and other biases; evidence that the student seeks to learn from those she disagrees with, even when she believe she must oppose their beliefs and practices. (Some of this language is adapted from a set of criteria used to evaluate student essays by faculty at Bluffton College, a Mennonite institution in Bluffton, Ohio. Edited by Gerald Schlabach. Copyright 1999, Bluffton College. Used by permission.)

- Student and alumni questionnaires can ask students how well they believe they have learned to function independently, be aware of social problems, identify moral and ethical issues, place current problems in perspective, relate to different races and religions, evaluate and choose courses of action, or formulate original ideas and solutions. Nationally normed instruments can provide comparison with peer institutions.

- Alumni and student questionnaires can also identify behaviors such as volunteer service, civic participation, or lifetime learning practices that exemplify the values the institution hopes to instill.

Such indicators are not proof, but they reveal whether students show any of the signs we would expect if they are learning what we hope. The indicators help keep us honest, rather than allowing us to go on composing blue-sky mission statements with no anchor to the reality of what is happening with our students.

Can Assessment Be Applied to Distance Learning and Accelerated Learning?

Yes. Assessment gathers information about student learning. Once one sees where students are weak, then one examines pedagogy, technology, learning format, and other factors to see what is going wrong and how it may be addressed. That process is the same whether the pedagogy uses the old blackboard and chalk or the latest computer technology, whether the course is offered during traditional classroom hours or in an accelerated format, whether the course has met face-to-face three times a week or is conducted entirely online. If students are weak in grasping a certain concept, the remedy may be somewhat different in an online course than in a face-to-face course, but the basic assessment process is the same.

The Context: Assessment in the United States Today _____

The current assessment movement has arisen primarily from outside the academy: from legislators, employers, governors, and other constituents who were disappointed with the quality of college graduates and the rising costs of higher education. Thus the assessment movement wants change. It is suspicious of the status quo, or of those who say, "We're already doing it." Other forces driving assessment are educational reform movements such as writing across the curriculum, learning communities, and problem-based learning, which rely on data about learning as the basis for meaningful reform. Assessment has been driven, too, by the increased competition among institutions of higher education, with up-and-comers using data about learning to market themselves and to challenge traditional institutions. Finally, in a consumerist era, public media are, as Ewell (2002) notes, "far more performance-conscious and data-hungry than they were two decades ago" (p. 22). The result is that "assessment has become an unavoidable condition of doing business; institutions can no more abandon assessment than they can do without a development office" (p. 22). Educators often believe that the higher types of learning they care about are not capable of being measured well enough to be useful and that therefore it is better to concentrate on the input: curriculum, resources, faculty qualifications, and classroom teaching strategies. Academics are also rightly wary of external interference with faculty control over curriculum, testing, and graduation—rights that are basic to a free society. Assessment has gathered a jargon and become an industry. For all these reasons, the national "assessment movement" elicits strong emotions and lively controversy. The challenge is to identify what is healthy and productive about assessment and use it to improve the institution as well as to meet the requirements of accreditors and other external audiences.

The Scholarly Questions of Assessment _____

Despite these aspects of the assessment movement, the basic questions of assessment are scholarly in the best sense:

- We're spending time and resources trying to achieve student learning—is it working?
- When we claim to be graduating students with qualities like "critical thinking" or "scientific literacy," do we have evidence of our claims?
- We have the impression that our students are weak in area X—would more systematic research back up this impression and help us understand the weakness more thoroughly?

- When we identify a weakness in our students' learning, how can we best address the problem?
- How can we improve learning most effectively in a time of tight resources?

The Benefits of Assessment

Assessment need not be complicated, and rightly used it can be a powerful instrument for improvement. Good information in the right hands is potentially the best lever for change. If assessment is done properly, it can provide a basis for wiser planning, budgeting, and change in curriculum, pedagogy, staffing, programming, and student support, rather than wasting resources on the latest educational fad or on vague notions about what might be effective. Astin (1993a) calls assessment a "technology" for enhancing the feedback concerning the impact of educational policies and practices. He compares it to a dancer's mirror, which enhances and makes more systematic the dancer's ability to critique and correct her own performance (p. 130). Further, careful attention to students' learning by departments and the institution can help create a climate of caring and engagement that supports students' own commitment to their learning.

We've Been Doing Assessment All Along

Every good teacher continually examines student work not just to give a grade but to improve teaching. Looking over the final exams, the teacher may say to herself, "Hmmm, they did better on X this semester, but Y is still a problem. I wonder if they could learn it better if I . . ." This is assessment, but it has been confined to the individual classroom. For example, whatever the teacher learns in a capstone course about the strengths and weaknesses of the department's graduating seniors may not be systematically used for department-level decision making. Whatever the general education teachers learn about students' development may not be systematically aggregated and fed back to the general education program as a whole.

So we've all been doing "stealth assessment" for limited audiences. Many of us have been doing more than that. We have conducted student and alumni surveys to ask students what they thought they learned; we have examined student portfolios; we have evaluated student writing; we have asked businesspeople to review senior student projects; we have sat on committees that looked at doctoral theses; we have appointed student advisory committees; and we have used this information to inform our curriculum revisions and our decisions about pedagogy and staffing—in other words, we have conducted assessment. Not perfect assessment, as we would be the first to admit, but assessment.

Many institutions have constructed formal "assessment plans," either for their own benefit or because an accrediting agency or legislature required it. They may have collected assessment plans from every department or instituted a portfolio system for general education assessment. Some of these plans are practical and useful; some are so complicated or time consuming that, after the accreditation team visits or the report is submitted, they sink of their own weight.

Whatever your own situation, this book assumes that assessment is happening at your institution and that you want to refine and improve it. A major focus of each succeeding chapter is the "assessment audit," which helps you identify the assessment already taking place in your department or institution and build on that assessment in sensible ways, changing or simplifying as needed, and moving forward.

Assessment as Cross-Cultural Communication

Because we've been doing assessment all along, but not necessarily calling it that, part of the task of "doing assessment" for an audience of external reviewers or accreditors is to identify what the department or institution is already doing, make plans to improve it, and explain it in terms the accreditors will understand. Assessment is an exercise in cross-cultural communication between the academy and those it serves.

Bergquist's book *The Four Cultures of the Academy* (1992) provides a useful perspective here, because it reflects the four cultures that coexist on most campuses and that influence how "assessment" is named, perceived, and used. Two of the cultures are most relevant here: the assessment movement lies primarily within the "Managerial" culture, which values specification of desired outcomes and objectives, use of data, and hierarchical systems in which overall goals inform goals at lower levels, and everyone works in tandem toward these well-specified outcomes. Many faculty, on the other hand, are part of the "Collegial" culture, marked by high value on faculty independence and autonomy, as well as suspicion of any systematic procedure that supposedly can be applied to what they view as the subtle art of teaching. Yet each culture has aspects that overlap the other, and both care about student learning.

To find out what kinds of assessment are occurring, in all campus cultures, and to document assessment for external audiences, each chapter of this book recommends beginning with an "assessment audit" to uncover the assessment already occurring in the institution or department, even though people may not be calling it assessment. The task of the assessment audit is to discover what is really happening, to interpret one culture to the other, to promote mutual understanding and collaboration, and to serve as the basis for actions that can gain widespread campus support to improve student learning.

Concerns About Assessment

Academic Freedom

Assessment rightly conducted does not ask faculty to repress their knowledge or judgments. Rather, it asks faculty to work together as colleagues to assess student work fairly by criteria respected in the field and to share their knowledge of student strengths and weaknesses, in order to improve curriculum, pedagogy, and other factors that affect learning. No one has ever had the right to teach a course just as she pleases; we always are bound by the rules of responsible interaction with students, by departmental agreement about what a course will cover, and by the requirement that we assign each student a grade that is public to limited audiences. We hand out a syllabus or put it on the Web. We establish goals for the course and share them with colleagues and students. We share problems in student learning and plans for a course whenever we submit a course to the curriculum committee for approval, ask for new resources, come up for tenure, or engage in a departmental discussion about improving our teaching. Assessment asks for an extension of this collegial work. It asks us to gather information about student learning and use it for decision making at the departmental and institutional level. It asks us to build on and improve the assessment we are already conducting.

Student Privacy

Assessment sometimes requires that student work, anonymously, be shared in the aggregate with colleagues beyond the classroom. For a faculty member to say to her department at a department meeting, "Forty-three percent of the capstone students scored lower than I would like on research design," is not a violation of an individual student's privacy and does not require student permission.

However, if individual student classroom work is to be evaluated by those outside the classroom, you may need to inform students about these audiences and perhaps also to get their informed consent. This is time consuming but not impossible. Social scientists have standard procedures that can be followed.

The Real Goals of Higher Education Cannot Be Measured

True, they cannot be fully or "objectively" measured. However, as professionals, we assess our own, our students', and our colleagues' work all the time. When we publish in our fields, we often critique the work of others—that's how the field advances. We're trained to develop sound criteria and apply our professional judgment to complex work in the field. Assessing students' work is part of that responsibility. We are not caught between "objectivity" (in the sense that all judges of a student performance will agree on its quality) and "subjectivity" in the sense of individual whim. In between those two poles stands informed judgment of student work using explicit criteria. In assessing student work, not all judges of a single piece of student work will agree on its quality, but social science researchers have established ways to handle that: take the average score, ask another rater to break the tie, or have raters discuss the student work to see whether they can come to agreement.

Evaluation of Faculty

Assessment is an evaluation of student learning in order to determine what faculty as a whole can do to improve that learning. A wise institution keeps the focus on collective action, not on individual blame. However, if students are learning well in a class, a faculty member may find that information highly useful at renewal, promotion, or tenure time. Evidence of learning can balance low student evaluations, for example. But the opposite is also true. Evidence of inadequate student learning in one's class ought to galvanize the teacher and the department for appropriate action. That action must be collegial and supportive, just as it optimally is when a faculty member is not producing sufficient research. The truth is that assessment brings to teaching a level of accountability that was not always present before and that can be used to benefit the students, the faculty, and the institution.

Student Learning Is Affected by Factors Beyond Faculty Control

True, it is. But faculty, departmental, and institutional decisions do affect learning. A wise assessment program focuses on those factors you can control. For some publics, you may also want to gather information about factors beyond your control, such as students' reasons for coming to college or the literacy practices in their homes, in order to present a fair picture of the context for student learning in your institution.

Assessment is not a panacea; it is a complex activity with many facets, and it is part of the contemporary higher education scene, with all its problems and possibilities. The concerns listed here must be handled thoughtfully, but they need not be roadblocks to effective assessment.

What Does an Assessment Report or Plan Look Like?

A *report* tells what you have done and are doing. A *plan* tells what you will do in the future. Most documents about assessment contain both, though the terminology may be one or the other.

An assessment plan or report may do one or both of these two things:

1. Report assessment mechanisms and strategies already in place and describe plans or make recommendations to *improve assessment*
2. Report outcomes of assessment measures and describe plans or make recommendations to *improve student learning*

Here is a common outline for a report or plan that does both. If your task is only to recommend improvements in assessment procedures, use numbers 1–6.

1. Oversight for assessment
2. Resources and structures for assessment
3. Learning goals: how they are constructed and used for assessment
4. Measures of student achievement of the goals: what the measures are, why these measures were chosen, how the choice relates to the goals, and how the measures are administered
5. How assessment data are used for improvement of learning
6. Recommended changes to improve assessment mechanisms
7. Goals for learning: list the goals
8. Data from assessment measures and what they suggest about student achievement of the learning goals
9. Recommended changes to improve student learning

How to Build an Assessment Plan or Report _____

When an institution, department, program, or general education body is called upon to write an assessment report or plan, it may follow this process:

1. Embed assessment in high-stakes and high-energy processes.
2. Consider audiences and purposes.
3. Arrange oversight and resources.
4. Articulate learning goals.
5. Conduct an "assessment audit" of assessment measures already in place and how the data are used for decision making.
6. Take steps to improve the assessment process.
7. Take steps to improve student learning.
8. Write the report or plan.

Timeline

The first four steps may take between a month and a year or more, depending on the level of planning already in place. If you already have well-articulated learning goals, Step 4 is quick; if not, it may take up to a year, depending on whether you need to make formal changes or seek the approval of governing bodies for changes in mission or goals. The assessment audit (Step 5, above) will take between a month and six months, depending on how quickly you can schedule the necessary interviews and collect the information. Actions to improve assessment and/or student learning may be quite apparent to everyone once you have completed Steps 1–5, or you may need a few months to seek campuswide input and deliberation. Throughout all the steps, you should be keeping notes, outlining, and even drafting, so that writing the final report or plan is fairly straightforward. Allow enough time throughout for unexpected delays and for democratic and collegial processes that get everyone on board. Regional accreditors recommend that you begin planning three years ahead for an accreditation visit, including the assessment aspect. But in fact, assessment is not like climbing Mt. Everest, where everything focuses on the one big moment of supreme effort and then it's all over. Instead, assessment is an ongoing process that should be embedded in the institution's most basic processes and cultures. Whenever you start, you need to follow the steps listed, taking enough time to do them well. When the report is due, you write honestly what you've done so far and what you plan to do.

Assessment as Part of a Broader Initiative

A common pattern for institutions that are asked to "do assessment" is to ask every department or program to submit an assessment plan by October 15. The goal of "doing assessment" becomes an end in itself. Big mistake. Doing assessment by itself, with no link to anything else, has little reward, support, or motivation. For departments, being required to do an assessment report in a vacuum can produce resentment, mere compliance, and waste of resources.

> People don't want to "do assessment"; they want to realize a dream, improve what they're doing, or be excited by a new initiative.

So when you are asked to "do assessment," link it to institutional dreams, goals, and processes that are important to the campus. Rather than simply ask people for an assessment report due October 15, embed assessment as a necessary step in compelling, powerful, and consequential processes such as departmental review, strategic planning, and curriculum revision, or initiatives such as retention, learning communities, distance learning, or enhancing productivity. For the accreditor who needs an assessment report, highlight the assessment aspect, but keep the institution's eyes fixed on the compelling vision.

Assessment in General Education

Some audiences for accreditation may ask for separate information about "general education" assessment. "General education" is a slippery term. When applied to *goals*, the term sometimes includes all general institution-wide goals except those that focus on specialized disciplinary knowledge. The general goals may be addressed not only by the curriculum (including the curriculum for majors and graduate students), but also by units such as Student Affairs, Athletics, Service Learning, or the library.

When applied to *curriculum*, the term "general education" generally means all the courses that are required of all students in the institution, as well as any courses that can be used by students to satisfy a distributive course requirement. These courses will have their own goals, derived from the institution-wide goals, and faculty will conduct assessment of how well students are meeting those goals, using the information to improve general education course curricula, class size, pedagogy, and the like. Be clear about what your accreditor and other audiences want.

If assessment of general goals is required, no matter where they are addressed, include them in the work of the institution-wide assessment committee described in Chapter Two. For assessment in the general education curriculum, you may appoint a committee or subcommittee (see Chapter Four).

Building Assessment on the Grading Process

One of the most important principles for building a sensible and feasible assessment plan is to build on the grading process. Grading is a "direct" measure of learning because it directly evaluates student work such as an exam, assignment, work-related task, interaction with a client, or musical performance.

A direct measure requires

- A student performance such as an exam or project
- A set of criteria by which to evaluate the performance
- Analysis and interpretation of the results
- A feedback loop into department, gen ed, and/or institutional decision-making processes

Any of these can be generated at the instructor, department, gen ed, or institutional level, or by an external body such as the constructors of a standardized test.

In grading, the first three factors listed—the student performance, the criteria, and the analysis/interpretation—are all in the professor's hands (influenced of course by departmental and disciplinary norms). The feedback loop for grading has traditionally been limited to students, the instructor, and prospective employers or admissions offices. An enormous amount of time, effort, energy, and faculty expertise goes into the grading process. Grading is already accepted within the culture of higher education. It is a pervasive system by which the institution communicates to various audiences about individual student learning. It makes great sense, therefore, to build an institutional or departmental assessment plan on the grading process.

Assessment agencies have sometimes said, "You can't use grades for assessment." What they mean is that you can't just say, "Seventy-three percent of our students get grades of A or B in the major, so we are doing okay." A letter grade by itself does not give enough information about the learning that was tested or the criteria that were used. However, if the performance and criteria are made explicit, and the feedback loop includes the institution or department, then the grading process is an excellent basis for direct assessment of learning at the departmental, general education, and institutional levels.

Figure 1.1.   The Simplest Form of Direct Assessment: Expanding the Grading Process

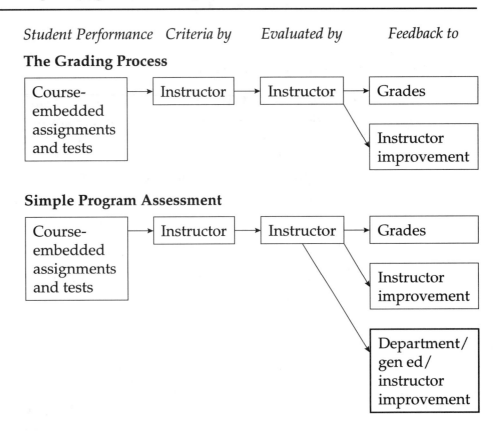

Student Performance   Criteria by   Evaluated by   Feedback to

The Grading Process

Simple Program Assessment

Making the Grading Process Useful for Program Assessment

To use the grading process for assessment, one must:

- Ensure that the classroom exam or assignment actually measures the learning goals
- State explicitly in writing the criteria for evaluating student work in sufficient detail to identify students' strengths and weaknesses
- Develop systematic ways of feeding information about student strengths and weaknesses back to decision makers at the departmental, general education, and institutional levels, and using that information for programmatic improvement

The Simplest Assessment Model Using the Grading Process

The simplest model for program assessment based on the grading process is diagrammed in Figure 1.1.

Examples: The Simplest Model

Departmental   A biology department has as one of its learning goals that graduating seniors will be able to conduct original scientific research and present it in writing and orally to a scientific audience. Their senior capstone course requires students to do exactly that. The teacher of the capstone course has developed an explicit set of criteria by which she assesses the students' scientific reports (Appendix A). She uses this rubric to help determine the grade and also to prepare her end-of-year annual report to the department, in which she shares her students' strengths and weaknesses in the aggregate. At the department meeting, this capstone faculty member distributes copies of her assignment, her written criteria, and the class's aggregate scores compared to previous years. She might say something like, "Students' scores on 'research design' were low two years ago. I made some changes in how I teach it, and the scores were better these last two years, but I'm still not satisfied. Here's what I plan to try next year. . . ." Colleagues express support and offer suggestions and help for her plan. It is very important that they not turn this session into an evaluation of her teaching, but only express support for her efforts to assess and improve student learning. Then she goes on to recommend departmental action: "I'm concerned that these senior students are so ignorant of basic graphing skills. I don't think I should have to teach graphing at the capstone level. Can we look at the curriculum to see whether we can do better on teaching graphing skills earlier?" The department now examines where in the curriculum students are being taught graphing skills. Perhaps Profs. Maldin and Washington agree to give more time to graphing in the intro course. Perhaps the department can arrange with the mathematics department for graphing to be more heavily emphasized in the required math course that all biology majors take. Throughout this meeting, someone is taking minutes as a base for departmental action and any needed reports to outsiders. The department may approach the administration for funding as needed, and/or submit a report to the university's assessment committee about the assessment that is taking place, so that the committee can fulfill its role in monitoring assessment on campus or in reporting to the accrediting agency. The department's role thus is threefold:

1. To encourage and support the faculty member
2. To address problems that require department-level solutions
3. To record and report to administrators and external audiences

General Education A general education assessment committee needs to assess students' "critical thinking and quantitative reasoning." They ask that in each general education course, faculty members define "critical thinking or quantitative reasoning" in terms that make sense within the discipline, and then give at least one major assignment or exam that measures it. Also, each faculty member is asked to construct written criteria for evaluating student work on that assignment or exam, using the format modeled in Appendix A. Each department conducts an annual department meeting at which each teacher of a gen ed course shares his or her assignment, criteria, and evaluation of student work. The department then encourages each faculty member, takes whatever actions seem appropriate at the department level, and reports to the general education committee, which in turn reports to the chief academic officer, the principal faculty-administrative-student decision-making body, and the accrediting agency. (See Cooper-Freytag, Walvoord, and Denton, 1998, for an example of this plan in action.)

Expanding the Simplest Model

The diagram in Figure 1.1 and the examples mentioned show the simplest plan, in which the department relies on faculty members' own reports of student strengths and weaknesses. This mode is the easiest and least time consuming because no one else takes the time to evaluate individual pieces of student work. The objectivity of the teacher's judgment is monitored in a limited way by the department as the teacher shares written copies of the assignment and the criteria. However, the obvious question about this method is whether the department or general education committee wants to rely solely on the teacher's judgment of students' strengths and weaknesses.

If the department, institution, or general education committee wishes, it can bring in other players to expand the number of voices evaluating the quality of student work. Figure 1.2 shows how the most simple pattern—asking the instructor to report students' strengths and weaknesses—can be expanded to bring other players into the mix.

Examples: Expansions of the Model

Here are some examples of how departments and general education committees might expand the group of players using the schemes diagramed in Figure 1.2. These procedures help the department to get information from someone other than the professor, but they also take more time, so it's a matter of balancing benefits against costs.

**Figure 1.2.   Expanding the Players
for Classroom-Based Direct Assessment**

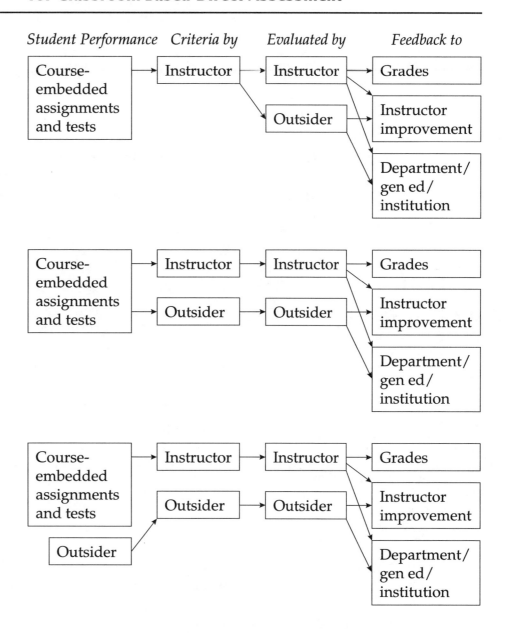

- An instructor might construct the exam or project and its criteria herself but ask a colleague or two from her own or a neighboring institution's department to evaluate the students' classroom work using her rubric, so that there are multiple raters, thereby adding to the reliability of the ratings of student work (Anderson and Walvoord, 1990, is one example).

- A committee of faculty might examine a portfolio of student work taken from across the curriculum, or such a portfolio might be collected as part of a capstone course. The committee then develops its own rubric expressing the criteria it is seeking in student work; it evaluates the portfolios and reports its findings to the department or general education committee.

- External evaluators might examine student senior projects or student portfolios, giving feedback not only to the student and instructor but also to the department.

- A general education committee might ask all gen ed courses to include an assignment that calls for students to construct and support an argument. Faculty would agree to use three criteria in common to evaluate student work on that assignment (such as stating a debatable position, supporting the position with evidence, and addressing counterarguments). When these teachers each report, there is a common ground, and data from all the teachers can be aggregated to show students' strengths and weaknesses on the three criteria.

- A department might decide to construct, as a department, some common parts of the introductory course exam that will be taken by students in all sections. Then the department aggregates those results to determine how well students as a whole are mastering basic skills and information by the end of the introductory course.

- A Ph.D. program might ask all faculty who sit on dissertation committees to meet once a year to evaluate student performance on the dissertation and make changes in graduate student preparation as needed.

Standardized Exams

A national standardized exam is a direct measure that places the goals, performance, criteria, and evaluation with an external source, not the instructor. The advantage is that you have a national standard against which to measure your own students. The disadvantage is that the exam may not measure what your instructors are teaching or are willing to teach. If a national standardized exam is to be workable, instructors must teach the skills and knowledge it measures. Otherwise, if your students score low on the standardized exam, you have no way to motivate the faculty to work to improve the scores. One way to use a national standardized exam effectively is to integrate it as part of students' classroom work, reporting results back to the department and comparing students' performance on the standardized test with their performance on other teacher-constructed classroom work. For example, an introductory political science course used a national exam of students' political science knowledge as part of students' coursework, in addition to the instructor-constructed exam. The faculty teaching the course then compared students' scores on the national exam with scores on their own exam and found a high correlation. They decided henceforth to use their own exam only, and to report those scores to the department annually. They might also have decided to use only the national exam, in which case they would have had a national benchmark annually.

If you lack instructor buy-in to the national exam, don't waste your resources on it, because you have no way to address the student weaknesses it reveals.

Making Criteria Explicit

An important key to direct assessment based on classroom work is making criteria very clear and explicit in writing. This does not drive you back to only "objective measures"; it simply means that the judgments a trained professional makes about her students' work now must be captured as clearly as possible in explicit language. In short, you need what is often called a "rubric." A rubric articulates in writing the various criteria and standards that a faculty member uses to evaluate student work. It translates informed professional judgment into numerical ratings on a scale. Something is always lost in the translation, but the advantage is that these ratings can now be communicated and compared. Appendix A contains examples of rubrics in a variety of disciplines, including rubrics that measure complex learning.

You are trying to construct a rubric that will allow professionals in your field to evaluate student work in reasonably similar ways. Of course, professionals will disagree somewhat in their evaluation of the same piece of student work, just as they disagree somewhat on their evaluation of their colleagues' work in the field. However, a rubric makes explicit the criteria that are being applied to this work at this time, and it brings judgments closer together.

A rubric can be constructed by:

- The faculty member, who uses it to evaluate student work and then reports to the department or the gen ed committee

- A group of faculty (or teaching assistants) all teaching the same course, who evaluate their own students' work using the common rubric and then report to the department or general education committee

- A department or gen ed committee that is establishing criteria for evaluating samples of student work or that wants all faculty teaching a certain course to use the same rubric

The rubric that will be used for program-level assessment does not have to cover all the criteria that will be used for grading student work. You may want to select one, two, or three criteria that are most important to departmental or general education goals.

Constructing a rubric may seem difficult at first, but it gets easier as you gain practice. Here are steps to construct a rubric:

1. Choose a test or assignment that tests what you want to evaluate. Make clear your objectives for the assignment.

2. Collect any grading criteria you have handed out to students in the past as well as sample student papers with your comments, if you have them. These will be useful in the steps that follow.

3. Identify the "traits" that will count in the evaluation. These are nouns or noun phrases without any implication of judgment: for example, "thesis," "eye contact with client," "costume design," or "control of variables."

4. For each trait, construct a scale describing each level of student performance from the least skillful to the most skillful. You may use three levels for basic distinctions between poor, competent, and excellent, or use four or five levels for finer distinctions, depending on what you need. The scales use descriptive statements. For example, "A thesis that receives a score of '5' is limited enough for the writer to support within the scope of the essay and is clear to the reader; it intelligently enters the dialogue of the discipline as reflected in the students' sources, and it does so at a level that shows synthesis and original thought; it neither exactly repeats any of the student's sources nor states the obvious."

5. Try out the scale with actual student work. Revise the scale as needed.

6. Have a colleague in your discipline use your scale to evaluate actual student work. Revise the scale as needed.

Walvoord and Anderson (1998, Chapter Five and Appendix C) provide more instruction about how to construct rubrics.

Building an Array of Assessment Measures

In addition to direct assessment through classroom-based work or standardized tests, an institution will want to make strategic use of indirect data that can provide a check on direct data, offer assessment data where direct measures are difficult or impossible, and address additional issues. As you decide on a mix of assessment data, focus on how they will be used by the faculty, staff, and administrators who have the power and responsibility to institute changes. This chapter earlier listed some common types of indirect data: student or alumni questionnaires, placement and career development data, retention rates, and the like. I would suggest beginning with Pike (2002), who presents a sixteen-page, practical, and sensible guide to the choice of assessment instruments and suggests a wide range of other, more detailed resources. Pike overviews issues such as the research approach to be adopted, qualitative versus quantitative methods, sampling, and issues of validity and reliability. More broadly, he emphasizes that an institution's mix of assessment measures must address that institution's own mission and goals, investigate factors the institution can change, suggest interventions that can affect students' achievement of the goals, and be effectively communicated to decision makers.

Deciding How to Improve Learning, Based on Assessment Data

An issue that is crucial to any assessment effort is how to use assessment data for change. You have data on students' strengths and weaknesses, but what can you do about it? To answer that question, you need two things:

1. *Research and theories of student learning that suggest what steps might work to improve student learning in a given situation. Sources that may help:*

- Chickering, A. W., and Gamson, Z. F. "Seven Principles of Good Practice in Undergraduate Education." *AAHE Bulletin,* 1987, *39* (7), 3–7. Seven research-based teaching strategies that have been shown to enhance learning in undergraduate higher education and are still a viable guide, despite their publication date. For emphasis on the role of technology, see Chickering, A. W., and Ehrmann, S. C. "Implementing the Seven Principles: Technology as Lever." *AAHE Bulletin,* 1996, *49* (2), 3–6.

- Pascarella, E. T., and Terenzini, P. T. *How College Affects Students.* San Francisco: Jossey-Bass, 1991. Summarizes research on the factors that lead to college outcomes, including student learning and retention.

- Astin, A. W. *What Matters in College: Four Critical Years Revisited.* San Francisco: Jossey-Bass, 1993. Emphasizes "involvement" as a key factor in learning. Article-length summary and update: "Involvement in Learning Revisited: Lessons We Have Learned." *Journal of College Student Development*, 1996, *37* (2), 123–134.

- For specific disciplines, search the database ERIC, which indexes education literature, including teaching-focused journals in various disciplines (for example, *Teaching Sociology*). Your librarian can help with descriptors and search strategies.

2. *Data on the factors that may be affecting learning for your students in particular.*

There are two ways to gather data on factors that may be affecting your students' learning:

1. *Ask them.* The most feasible and often the best way to discover what factors are affecting students' learning is to ask them.

- Madan Batra, in his international marketing class at Indiana University of Pennsylvania, identified nine teaching strategies he used to help students complete a major group project. Some strategies were, for example, a project outline guide given to students early in the course, a work-allocation sheet the groups completed in the third week of the project, and opportunity for draft response from the instructor. He asked students to rate each strategy in terms of how helpful it was to them in achieving various pedagogical goals: for example, students were asked to mark various levels of agreement or disagreement with the statement that draft response "contributed substantially to the overall quality of the final group project" and that it "helped me to become involved in the project" (Batra, Walvoord, and Krishnan, 1987). He found that some strategies were rated very helpful by almost all his students, so he retained them. Some were not helpful, so he could jettison them. Some were helpful to some students and less helpful to others, so he tried to improve them or to focus them toward the students who needed them.

- Student or alumni questionnaires that ask students to suggest how the department or institution could do better are another strategy.

2. *Compare them.* As Pike (2002) points out, true experimental designs with random assignment of subjects to treatment and control groups are not feasible in assessment research; however, com-

parison groups are often available. Palomba and Banta (1999) explain briefly and in simple terms the issues involved in comparing one group of students to another or comparing the same group of students at an early point and a later point (pp. 107–110). The issues concern the selection of groups that are as much alike as possible, and ways of accounting for differences between the groups and for the presence of multiple variables. Data from comparison groups or longitudinal studies must be used with appropriate recognition of their limitations. If you are unfamiliar with these types of research designs, a consultant from a sociology or education department or from a social science research institute may be helpful. The examples following reflect the work of ordinary departments and faculty conducting feasible studies to inform their own practices, not necessarily for formal publication in a research journal.

- For example, faculty members with whom I worked in a department of mathematics at a large research university were divided about the best methods to teach calculus; about half were using traditional pedagogies and half were using a new pedagogy pioneered at Harvard. They all used a set of common questions/problems within their individual final exams for the course. This was a fine setup for comparing the two groups because there were multiple sections of the same course yet a common test of student learning. The department invited a social science researcher from their university's research institute to design and conduct a study comparing the traditional sections with the new pedagogy sections. The researcher reported that, using regression analysis, there was little difference in learning attributable to pedagogy; instead, the greatest variance in students' test scores was attributable to the differences in instructor and to the student's scores on a pre-calculus test. So the department stopped worrying about which pedagogy instructors were using and instituted workshops and individual coaching to help them become better teachers using whatever pedagogy they chose. It also tightened its tracking system, so that students with low calculus-readiness scores were more reliably placed in pre-calculus.

- For an example of a multisection comparison in a literature class, see MacDonald and Cooper (1992). For examples of pre-post designs implemented by faculty and departments, see the work of chemistry professor Dennis Jacobs and his department at Notre Dame, described in Hutchings (2000) and McClanahan and McClanahan (2002).

Pitfalls of Assessment

The most common pitfalls of assessment include

- Mere compliance with external demands
- Triggering resistance and hostility of faculty
- Gathering data no one will use
- Letting administrators do it
- Making the process too complicated

The Themes of the Book

The following themes recur throughout this book (each chapter also ends with a chapter summary).

- Assessment may seem alien, but it can actually be scholarly in the best sense.
- Assessment rightly used can provide a basis for wiser planning, budgeting, and change across the institution. It can move you from "seat of the pants" planning to information-based planning for student learning.
- Don't just "do assessment"; embed assessment into visions, processes, and reforms that people care about.
- Assessment can be applied to complex liberal learning goals as well as to distance and accelerated learning.
- Assessment is composed of three simple steps.
- Build on what you're already doing, including grading.
- Articulate the criteria for evaluating student work.
- It is not enough to gather data about student strengths and weaknesses; you need information and hypotheses about the causes of student weaknesses.
- Keep it simple!

Summary

This chapter has outlined the basics of assessment common to institutional, departmental, and general education settings, and it has suggested strategies for conducting assessment. It has emphasized several pitfalls and introduced several themes that will be common throughout the succeeding chapters.

CHAPTER 2

For Institution-Wide Planners

You are probably consulting this chapter because you are a provost, president, dean, assessment director, or member of a university-wide or collegewide planning committee, and you have been asked to "do assessment" at the institution, perhaps by a regional accreditor, perhaps by a board or legislature. Whether or not you have an assessment plan from the past, this chapter will help you to build on what you are already doing and to construct a simple, direct, and cost-efficient assessment process that will benefit your institution as well as satisfying accreditors, legislators, or other external audiences.

This chapter assumes that you have already read Chapter One.

Embed Assessment into High-Energy and High-Stakes Processes

Chapter One emphasized the importance of embedding assessment as a necessary step in realizing the goals, dreams, initiatives, and processes that attract energy and commitment within the institution. Here are some examples:

- Require assessment as part of cyclical review of departments and programs by the provost and/or by external reviewers (sample guidelines are in Appendix B).

- Begin strategic planning with assessment, both at the institutional and the unit levels.

- Embed assessment of learning into a new institutional initiative such as retention, technology, distance learning, or learning communities.

- Embed assessment of student learning into evaluation of teaching (see Appendix C).

- Embed assessment into general education curriculum reform, requiring that each course accepted for fulfillment of the gen ed requirement incorporate assessment of student learning.

- Require assessment as part of departmental requests for new money or new faculty or staff lines.

If you embed assessment in these ways, you may not need to ask each department for a separate assessment plan. Rather, your effort goes toward revising the structures listed so they embed assessment, and then offering guidance, support, and resources to help departments conduct high-quality assessment as they come up for provostial review, prepare to submit their strategic plans, ask for new monies, or participate in institutional initiatives.

For example, one institution with which I worked embedded assessment into the cyclical review of departments by the provost and into its strategic planning process. Its report to the regional accreditor stated that by year X, all departments will have submitted assessment plans as they come up for their cyclical review by the provost and that the departments and the institution will have conducted thorough assessment of learning as part of the current strategic planning process. Other assessment strategies were part of the report as well, but these two embedded strategies helped the institution avoid having to require each department to submit a separate assessment plan by October 15.

If your institution in the past collected assessment plans from every unit, you need to determine how people feel about these plans, whether and how they are being followed, how they may need to change, and whether you want now to embed assessment into other processes and initiatives. You can use what worked in the past, discard or change what did not, and move forward.

Appoint a Coordinator and a Committee

Though assessment should be embedded into wider institutional initiatives, you will need a structure and a line of responsibility to focus on assessment and to ensure that, wherever it is embedded, it is working. If you have been asked to do assessment for an external audience, you will need people to gather the information and write the report. For these purposes, most institutions operate with an assessment coordinator and committee. The coordinator should report to the provost, perhaps through an associate provost.

The coordinator may be an associate or assistant provost, a faculty member with released time for this task, or a recent retiree who still knows the institution well. I have seen all three options work smoothly. The coordinator should possess:

- Thorough knowledge of the institution
- The respect of faculty and administrators
- Excellent communication skills
- Excellent organizational and leadership skills

These qualities are more important than quantitative research skills, statistical knowledge, a background in education, or previous familiarity with the assessment movement.

The coordinator's tasks are to:

- Become thoroughly knowledgeable about assessment and use that knowledge to inform others and to shape the institutional effort
- Take the lead in planning and implementing the actions described in this chapter
- Chair the assessment committee

The committee should report to the chief academic officer. Its tasks are to:

- Understand what is being asked by the external audiences
- Conduct a campus audit to discover what assessment is already taking place
- Recommend actions to enhance assessment and student learning
- Recommend the ongoing bodies that will be needed to implement those actions
- Write the report to the external agency and other audiences
- Continue to monitor the quality of the assessment of learning that is embedded in campus structures and processes

On the committee, you need people like these:

- Someone who is good at "big picture" thinking and planning, and good at analysis of campus politics
- A good ethnographer or social science researcher who understands how to gather information about cultures
- Someone from Institutional Research or whatever office is collecting institution-wide data on your campus, who is familiar with the instruments, data, and methods of analysis being used

- Representatives from Student Affairs as well as the academic side
- A representative sample of powerful, well-respected, knowledgeable faculty who know the campus culture well and who represent the major colleges, schools, or other faculty units
- Someone who has been involved in professional accreditation such as nursing, architecture, engineering, or business
- Representative graduate and undergraduate students who have been active in gathering the data and evidence that supported student requests for change

You may want to engage a consultant to work with the committee. Be sure that the consultant shares your philosophy of embedded assessment and is not going to advise you into a separate assessment bureaucracy.

If you already have an assessment committee, now is the time to ensure that its membership and reporting lines are serving you well. Has the committee rotated its membership according to written guidelines? If not, construct those guidelines. Is the current committee tired and discouraged? Maybe now is the time to change the name or structure of the committee, let the previous members retire in honor, and begin again. If the committee is unwieldy, can you place more responsibility with a small steering committee formed from the larger group?

The committee may appoint a subcommittee or a separate committee to analyze assessment within the general education curriculum (see Chapter Four) and/or a subcommittee to focus on assessment within departments (Chapter Three).

Analyze Task, Audiences, and Purposes

Being time efficient about assessment means clearly understanding the task, as well as the audiences and purposes.

Understanding Your Task

The assessment committee's first task is to understand exactly what you are being asked to do and what you are *not* being asked to do by the accrediting agency or other external audiences. The first item to clarify is whether you are being asked to report and recommend strategies to improve assessment mechanisms or whether you are also being asked to analyze assessment data and recommend ways to improve student learning.

One of the most common mistakes is to believe that the regional accreditors asking for assessment are primarily interested in the *content of your data,* in how well your students are doing. For some purposes, that may be true, but when they are examining your assessment report, their primary goal is to be sure that you have in place solid, ongoing *structures and processes* to gather and use your assessment data. In other words, they're not so much interested in how well your students are doing as in whether *you know* how well your students are doing. It is possible that your students will be weak in critical thinking, but if you have good structures in place to discover that weakness and you use your assessment data to try to improve the situation, you will get an *A* in assessment.

An accrediting agency may require an interim report or visit with a focus on assessment. In that case, you probably have specific feedback from the accreditors, citing the weaknesses in your past efforts and requesting specific changes. Read those with great care and consult with representatives of the agency to be sure you understand what is being asked. What points are most important to address? Are there other requirements besides those noted in the suggestions? Have new approaches arisen since your review was written? How should you organize your interim report or visit?

Analyzing Audiences and Purposes

Make a chart of all potential audiences for the assessment information you gather. Even though your assessment efforts are primarily driven by the requirements of an external accreditor, it may be possible to serve other audiences. Ask, "Who needs to know what, for what?" Don't neglect your own internal audiences, who may be among the most important. Appendix D is an example of a chart that will help you analyze multiple audiences and purposes for assessment information.

Articulate University-Wide Learning Goals

After analyzing task, audiences, and purposes, the assessment committee should begin analyzing how the campus implements the three steps of assessment outlined in Chapter One: articulating learning goals, using appropriate measures to gather data, and using data for improvement. Your committee's work can begin by analyzing your written institutional mission and goal statements and making any needed adjustments to allow them to serve as the basis for assessment.

Gathering Mission and Goal Statements

The first task is to locate institution-wide statements of mission and goals. Don't neglect statements that may have emerged from previous self-studies, fund-raising campaigns, reports to a board or legislature, or other recent events that may provide greater sharpness or detail than the mission and goals in your catalog. Here are guidelines for the kinds of goal statements you need:

Format   "When students graduate from our institution, we want them to be able to . . ."

The following are *not* learning goals, but strategies by which the institution hopes to achieve the learning goals:

- "The curriculum emphasizes *X, Y,* and *Z.*"
- "Students will be exposed to . . ." or "Students will participate in . . ."

Some of these kinds of statements imply learning goals and can be reframed in the "Students will . . ." format.

Your Highest Goals   Include your highest goals, for example, critical thinking, scientific intuition, development of thoughtful ethical principles, or ability to work with people of diverse backgrounds, even if the goals cannot be fully "measured." Do not let assessment become an exercise in reduction. You don't have to measure every single goal this year or even next year, and you may choose not to list all of them in a particular assessment report, but for internal planning purposes and for most external audiences, you should appropriately represent your institution's highest mission.

Goals at Different Levels   Goals will have to be stated at different levels of generality. *Examples:*

Institution: "Students will be able to communicate appropriately orally and in writing."

- *The College of Science:* "Students will be able to communicate about science, in writing and orally, to scientific and lay audiences."
  - *Biology department:* "Senior majors will conduct original biological research and write up their results in the scientific report format typically required by a journal in that field, and they will present their results orally to classmates as if presenting to an audience of biologists at a conference." When the measure gets that specific, it leads to criteria by which evaluators can make judgments about strengths and weaknesses in the student work (for a set of explicit criteria for senior biology research projects, see the first example in Appendix A).

- *The School of Business:* "Students will be able to communicate orally and in writing to business audiences, including colleagues, supervisors, and clients, in appropriate ways about business issues."

  - *Marketing department:* "Students will construct a marketing plan and prepare written and oral communications appropriate to a client firm."

Institution: "Students will appreciate their social and moral responsibilities."

- *Required composition class:* "Students will be able to describe in writing and will use in their own papers ethical practices of integrating source materials and collaborating with other writers."

- *Biology department:* "Doctoral students will be able to describe in writing and to follow in their own research the ethical standards of the discipline for treatment of human and animal subjects, environmental protection, and collaboration with other researchers."

Choosing Workable Goals for Assessment

If formally stated goals are too general or are not appropriately framed for use as the basis of assessment, you have two options. The first option, formally changing the institution's mission statement or goals, may be worthwhile if the institution needs to recast its mission or goals. However, the process may require a long period of time and involve extensive governance procedures. An alternative is for the committee to write explanatory statements, more detailed statements, or simply select those goals it can work with—all steps that a committee can take on its own or after focus groups with faculty. Do not try to change formal mission and goal statements on an official level unless there is very good reason to do so for the institution's own benefit. Otherwise, use other methods to establish workable goals as the basis for assessment.

For example, here is part of the mission statement for a public, two-year, open-admissions college, printed in the college bulletin and on the Web page:

> Ultimately, the college works toward the creation of an informed citizenry with the ability to think critically, communicate effectively, and solve problems. The college strives to provide a general education that promotes tolerance, lifelong learning, and devotion to free inquiry and free expression to ensure that its graduates are individuals of character, more competent to contribute to society, and more civil in habits of thought, speech, and action.

There is nothing wrong with that mission statement except that it was written without any notion that the college would ever be asked to produce evidence that students were achieving these goals. The rhetorical purpose of that language is to inspire and to encourage high ideals, not to serve as the basis for assessment. To try formally to alter the statement, though, might involve the college in a yearlong (if they're lucky) struggle over their mission in which every campus tension would emerge, neighboring community colleges would arm their borders, and the state regulatory agencies would go on red alert. In this small college, the assessment committee was large, representative, and composed of highly regarded faculty. They simply took it upon themselves to derive from the mission statement three specific goals as the basis for their initial assessment program—goals they considered important, that the college was already assessing in some ways, and that they thought would be relatively easy starting places for assessment:

1. Upon graduation, students will demonstrate effective writing skills.

2. Upon graduation, students will demonstrate effective quantitative reasoning skills.

3. Upon graduation, students will demonstrate that they can think critically about issues and arguments presented in the humanities and the behavioral sciences.

These goals are more specific and also selective. They omit for the time being an assessment of "character," "competence to contribute to society," or "civility." Those qualities may play an important role in the mission statement, but assessment of them will be addressed later, once assessment of writing, quantitative reasoning, and critical thinking is working reasonably well.

When the institution does tackle them, it will have to interpret "character" more specifically, with a set of attributes about which some indications can be gathered. For example, they may decide to take one aspect of character—a person acts ethically in professional and personal situations—a statement that implies one could assess students' ethical reasoning in papers for certain courses, could gather statistics on instances of cheating, or could query alumni about whether they thought their education contributed to their ability to act ethically. None of these types of data would cover all of "character" or even all of "acting ethically," but would provide *indications* of whether one's students were acting ethically in certain ways.

With a highly idealistic mission statement, then, one proceeds by rephrasing, narrowing, and finding indicators, selecting the easier aspects first, then later the more difficult goals.

The institution just described decided to handle the process right in the committee. Another option is to go beyond committee action to university-wide action. For example, a private, Catholic national research university's mission statement reads in part:

> The University prides itself on being an environment of teaching and learning that fosters the development in its students of those disciplined habits of mind, body, and spirit that characterize educated, skilled, and free human beings. In addition, the University seeks to cultivate in its students not only an appreciation for the great achievements of human beings but also a disciplined sensibility of the poverty, injustice, and oppression that burden the lives of so many. The aim is to create a sense of human solidarity and concern for the common good that will bear fruit as learning becomes service to justice.

The assessment committee in this case decided not simply to select and articulate more specific learning goals by itself, as the community college did, but to seek campuswide accord. With leadership from the provost's office, the committee drafted a set of four goals that were then passed by each of the college councils and by the main faculty-administrative-student governance body (it took a year). These read as follows:

> The University seeks to develop students who:
> 1. Pursue knowledge and evaluate its consequences
>   a. Think critically, abstractly, and logically to evaluate and solve problems
>   b. Integrate new information to formulate principles and theories and display an openness to different viewpoints
>   c. Share the desire for intellectual creativity and the acquisition of knowledge
> 2. Communicate clearly and effectively in both written and oral forms
> 3. Demonstrate knowledge and abilities in chosen areas of study
>   a. Develop an understanding of resources and procedures of fields and the ability to use them
>   b. Possess an appropriate core of knowledge in chosen fields
> 4. Appreciate their social and moral responsibilities
>   a. Reflect upon the spiritual, moral, and ethical dimensions of life
>   b. Display the moral dimensions of their decisions and actions
>   c. Contribute to society as an active member

Once passed by the appropriate internal governance bodies, these goals were placed on the university's Web page along with the mission statement and were used as the basis for assessment. They were commended in two successive reviews by regional accrediting teams.

The verbs in 4a, b, and c suggest assessment measures that could yield indicators. For example, senior student and alumni surveys could ask whether respondents believe they have learned these qualities. Students' journals and papers in relevant courses or internships might be examined for reflection on spiritual, moral, and ethical dimensions. Rates of plagiarism, vandalism, binge drinking, and other behaviors could provide indications of students' ability to display the moral dimensions of their decisions. Records of student and alumni volunteer service and participation in religious organizations would give some indication of whether students and alumni are contributing to society. Well-stated goals at the institutional level should be broad enough to reflect the full aspirations of the institution yet specific enough to suggest measures that will give at least some indication of whether the learning is being achieved.

Conduct an Assessment Audit

Now that the institution-wide learning goals have been shaped to serve as the basis for assessment, the next step is to find out as fully as possible what assessment is already occurring, or being planned and desired, in your institution. Don't assume that assessment is a brand-new initiative you can add to what people are already doing. Rather, assessment is already happening, whether or not you have an assessment plan by that name. Your task is to discover it, improve it, and translate it for various audiences. I call this the "assessment audit," but it is also social science research, closely allied to ethnography and other disciplines that study cultures. The purpose of the audit is to tease out from your culture the activities that the external accreditor calls "assessment," but that the faculty may not be labeling in that way at all.

The audit is time consuming, but do not skip it! You need it whether you have a previous assessment plan in place or whether you are just beginning formal assessment. The knowledge of current campus assessment practices, dreams, and plans must inform everything you do from here on. Without that knowledge, you run the risk of costly mistakes.

Listing the Sites of Assessment

First, list all the places in your institution where you think assessment may be happening, even if people are not calling it assessment, and even if it is being collected for a variety of purposes—to recruit students, attract donors, enhance the institution's reputation, comply with external demands from granting agencies, adhere to federal regulations, ease administrative tasks, certify students and programs, or inform budgeting and planning for student learning. Here is one assessment committee's brainstormed list: it includes both processes such as strategic planning and structural units such as the Writing Program.

- Departments as they review data and make decisions about curriculum, staffing, equipment, and the like
- Professional accreditation in disciplines such as engineering and business
- Program review of departments every eight years on a rolling basis
- Current university-wide strategic planning process
- Student Affairs office
- Writing Program
- Office of Institutional Research
- Centers for women, multicultural, gay/lesbian, international, and other groups
- Career placement
- Graduate school
- Student government
- Teaching/Learning Center
- Administrators of required core courses, learning communities, or similar programs
- Service learning center
- Office of Information Technology
- Residence halls
- Commuter Student office
- International Studies
- First-year student support services
- Counseling services
- Grant-funded projects
- Faculty evaluation for reappointment, promotion, and tenure
- Governance bodies such as faculty senate and academic council
- Advancement/Development office
- Alumni Affairs

Gathering and Analyzing Data About Assessment

Now you must find out what kind of assessment is occurring, how it is being used, how it might be used, and what kinds of assessment people want in each of these places.

Institution-Wide Data   Begin by finding out what *institution-wide* data on student learning are being collected and how they are being distributed and used. Common sites for such collection are Institutional Research, Career Placement, the graduate school, Writing Across the Curriculum, tutoring centers, counseling centers, residence halls, and the like. Appendix E is one research university's analysis of the data that were being collected to assess each of its four broad goals for student learning. The analysis evolved from interviews with Institutional Research, the graduate school, student government, the service learning center, first-year students' office, Student Affairs, career center, and the like. Some smaller institutions may have significantly less data.

As you collect this information, be sure to get specific details about exactly what data goes where, in what form, and for what audiences and purposes. Collect samples of the data reports that are sent. You'll need these to analyze how assessment data flows in your institution. Most institutions are gathering more data than they are effectively using, so some of the committee's eventual recommendations may concern more effective aggregation, distribution, and use of data.

Departmental Data   Once you know what centralized data are being collected, you need to know how assessment is occurring in departments, in units that have gen ed responsibility such as composition or the humanities core, and in Student Affairs, the library, and other units directly concerned with student learning. You will be completing a matrix, showing each unit's goals for learning, the measures it employs to assess student achievement of the goals, and how it uses the data (Appendix H). The top of the matrix should contain the categories you or the assessor need to analyze.

It is my experience that just asking unit heads to fill out a report telling you what they do for assessment does not work. People are resentful of the time, they find the forms daunting, they may misperceive in some way what is going on, and they fail to tell you all the assessment that is happening because they don't think of it as assessment.

Therefore, I recommend conducting hour-long interviews individually with each department or program chair, dean, and director of programs that contribute to the student learning you want to assess. This is time consuming, but it pays off in the quality of information you get and in the collegial spirit that arises in face-to-face discussion. This book's chapter for departments is intended to help department chairs prepare for such an interview, thus making your task easier.

In the interview, you will be ferreting out the assessment that is occurring as part of other initiatives, such as department review, retention efforts, curriculum revision, or just ongoing analysis that the department conducts to make sure it's on track. Departments will not necessarily name all these processes as assessment. It is your job to:

- Identify what internal and external audiences need to know about assessment

- Help department chairs to examine the assessment aspects of what they do and to strengthen those aspects as needed

- Identify assessment needs that can best be addressed at the institutional level

The tone of the interview should be friendly and supportive. You are not the assessment police, trying to find out how inadequate the department is. Rather, the department chair is a colleague, and the two of you are gathered for a collegial discussion. There may be an "aha!" factor for one or both of you, as together you work to make the chair's leadership more effective and more efficient.

The first step of assessment is to state goals. If the department is familiar with assessment terminology and processes, you may begin by asking whether they have stated, written learning goals and proceed from there to ask about measures for assessing those goals and use of the data for decision making.

However, if the department is not very knowledgeable about assessment terminology, or is hostile to it, you may begin the interview by asking the chair what changes the department has undertaken recently to improve student learning. I have found that chairs talk easily about the changes that have occurred and are proud of them. They'll tell you that they're undertaking a review of the undergraduate curriculum, that they have introduced a new course, or that they have provided better training for graduate assistants. Then ask what information led the department to make those changes. Often, that question elicits the assessment measures, even if they are informal. The chair may say something like, "Well, our students just weren't able to . . ." Ask, then, how they knew the students weren't able to do X. You may have to pursue the issue through several rounds, because the underlying assessment information, especially if it is informal, may not easily be visible to the chair.

In conducting such interviews, I have found that a great deal of assessment goes on, even in departments that are defensive or hostile to the term "assessment." For example, one chemistry department annually held a meeting of faculty in which those who taught courses in a sequence told each other what the students in the follow-on courses needed, and they decided on changes for the following year. This is responsible, sensible, and useful assessment, even though the chair would not have listed it on a questionnaire and even though he expounded vigorously on how useless "assessment" is.

Throughout the interview, be thinking how you can translate what the chair is saying for your external audiences. For example, when you write a report for accreditors about the chemistry department mentioned, you will say that each course gives exams and tests to assess the learning goals, faculty evaluate the student work to discover classwide strengths and weaknesses, and they meet annually to exchange information and make changes in sequenced courses. Collect or note the location of the minutes of these meetings, copies of the exams, or any written guidelines that faculty use to evaluate student work—all helpful as documentation.

Look for opportunities to elicit changes the chair wants or would entertain. For example, when you find that faculty evaluation of the strengths and weaknesses of student work is informal, not written, one of your questions should be whether the review by faculty of test and exam results would be more useful if it were more systematic. Would the department be well served by a written checklist or rubric that would guide the faculty evaluation (Appendix A)?

I have emerged from a set of department chair interviews with a fine list of improvements recommended by department chairs themselves. For example, several chairs suggested that new chairs be better informed about available centralized data. One chair who was about to conduct a series of brown-bag lunches for departmental faculty on teaching realized in the interview that these conversations would be much richer if informed by data on learning, and he planned how to collect the data from Institutional Research and his own files. These ground-level needs and ideas can be the basis of the assessment committee's and/or the institution's initiatives to improve assessment.

As you conduct the interviews, gather documents generated by assessment practices and take copious notes in a common format so that you can aggregate the data for analysis. If, in the interview itself, you cannot complete the matrix (Appendix F) showing how each assessment measure maps to the relevant goals, you may have to take looser notes, in the order of the conversation, and complete the grid later. If the department has no explicit learning goals, or incomplete goals, you may simply have to list the measures they are using and then work with the department over time on explicit goals.

As you interview departments and deans in disciplines such as health sciences, engineering, business, or architecture, find out what professional accreditations they are conducting, when they are due, and what they require. It is often possible for, say, a College of Engineering to extract an assessment report for regional accreditation right from its most recent ABET accreditation report. Be careful, though, about terminology that differs. For example, direct assessment in ABET may have a different meaning than for a regional accreditor. Appendix G presents a grid that might be helpful for an institution-wide picture of assessment embedded within professional accreditation. Palomba and Banta (2001) is a useful general guide to professional assessment.

Once you complete your data gathering in departments, you need a way of organizing and interpreting the data. Begin by constructing a master matrix that will show the progress of all the departments and general education units. Across the top, list the main aspects the accreditors need or you yourself want to track. Decide on these categories before you conduct the interviews, so you can anticipate what you need to ask. Down the left side, list each unit or process on which you have data (Appendix H).

Next, ponder your matrix (referring back as needed to the fuller notes on individual departments) to analyze what is going on and what you think the institution ought to be doing for its own benefit and for compliance with external requirements. It may be helpful to take the master matrix to a representative group of good faculty and administrative "big picture" analyzers on your campus and let them sit around and comment on what they see. Appendix I is an example of one institution's analysis.

Recommend Actions to Strengthen Assessment

The audit process helps you examine all your ongoing institutional processes with an eye to the role of assessment within them and to take steps to strengthen assessment as part of these vital processes. You do not necessarily need to create a brand-new assessment superstructure on campus nor require each department to submit a separate assessment plan by October 15. Rather, you are using the assessment mandate to examine and strengthen the assessment component of all your institutional structures and processes. For example, the institution whose analysis occurs in Appendix I has not created an assessment program, nor does it plan to ask each department for an assessment plan. Rather, the recommendations concern the integration of assessment of student learning into the processes that are currently capturing the energy and the high-stakes attention on campus: provostial review of departments and the current strategic planning process with the initiatives that will emerge from it. As you shape your own recommendations for enhancing assessment, begin by shaping recommendations for gathering and using institution-wide data.

Institution-Wide Data

First ask, "What questions about your students' learning are most important to the institution and to your constituencies, and what institution-wide data should we be gathering to address those questions?" Here are possibilities:

- Retention and graduation statistics.
- Graduate student publications, fellowships, post-docs.
- Placement in jobs or further schooling. (Future plans surveys of graduating students will work for some institutions. For others, especially community colleges where most students enter employment or further schooling in the geographical area, records of student enrollment in further schooling may be gathered directly from the institutions in the area.)
- Student perceptions of their own learning. These have been shown to have some correlation with student learning as measured by tests, so they can serve as a useful but not infallible indirect measure of student learning. Student course evaluations such as the IDEA (www.idea.ksu.edu) stress students' perception of their learning as well as of the quality of instruction. Senior surveys such as COFHE's Senior Survey, the Higher Education Research Institute (HERI) College Student Survey developed at UCLA, and the National Survey of Student Engagement (NSSE) developed at Indiana University contain questions about students' perceptions of their learning.
- Student scores on a standardized test of critical thinking or some other quality. These tests present many problems. If the faculty are not willing to teach to the test, then you have no way of influencing the outcomes, so it's useless to collect the data. At one two-year college with which I have worked, faculty on the assessment committee themselves took a national standardized test of critical thinking and decided that it tested things or used language they did not teach and

did not want to teach, it was too general for the discipline-specific kinds of critical thinking they taught, and they could not see themselves teaching so as to raise student scores on the test. National standardized tests have their place in an assessment plan, but they are more useful at the unit level where, for example, dental hygiene students' scores on the national and state board exams are a relevant and necessary assessment measure for which faculty accept responsibility.

- Measures of the behaviors of faculty and students that research has shown to be linked to learning. The National Survey of Student Engagement (NSSE) developed at Indiana University (www.indiana.edu/~nsse) is a recent instrument increasingly employed. National senior student surveys such as the College Student Survey (CSE) and first-year student surveys such as Your First College Year (YFCY), both administered by the Higher Education Research Institute at UCLA (www.gseis.ucla.edu/heri/), also contain questions about behaviors such as student-faculty collaboration in research, student out-of-class contact with faculty, and students' study hours, which have been shown to affect learning.

- Data on campuswide teaching practices or attitudes that research has shown may be linked to greater student learning: practices such as active learning, the amount of writing that teachers assign and comment on, or the percentage of students involved in faculty research. These may be self-reported by students or by faculty, or they may be inferred from an examination of syllabi or other records. For a summary of research-supported good teaching practices that is accepted as a standard in the field, see Chickering and Gamson (1987).

- Portfolios of student work evaluated by faculty give a sense of the types of work students are being asked to do and the types of thinking that are involved, as well as a sense of the students' development over time. See Palomba and Banta (1999, Chapter Five) for a sensible discussion of the pros and cons of portfolio assessment.

- Random samples of student work collected from a selection of classes in a given semester and evaluated by a set of criteria give a snapshot of student work at a particular moment, including strengths and weaknesses.

- Faculty surveys asking faculty members to reflect their observations of students' strengths and weaknesses. Institution-wide surveys of this type are not common, but they should be, because faculty are in the trenches observing student work every day; why not tap this knowledge? You can hear it informally around the coffeepots and in committee meetings; a well-constructed faculty survey form would capture it for action, not just grousing.

Next ask, "How are institution-wide data distributed and used?" It is better to have a few institution-wide measures that are well managed, and where data are well distributed and well used, than to proliferate expensive measures to produce data that no one uses.

If I had to choose three institution-wide measures I would recommend to any institution, I would choose the following and make sure the data were very well used:

- Retention and graduation rates.

- A national student survey.

- A very tight, manageable portfolio sample evaluated by a large number of faculty, according to criteria that faculty have generated, to enhance faculty knowledge of the kinds of work students are doing across the campus, and thus inform faculty teaching and deliberations about curriculum and pedagogy.

- For community colleges, I would add a study of the grades and retention of students in further schooling. One institution that tracks these data is Raymond Walters College, a two-year branch campus of the University of Cincinnati, which has collected information about its students who go on to enroll for four-year work at nearby campuses. Their research has suggested that Raymond Walters students do better in terms of junior-senior grades and degree completion than students who took their first two years on the four-year school's own campus—a statistic that has been of inestimable value to the community college.

Program Review Processes

Appendix B is a sample of guidelines for assessment embedded in the guidelines for program review of departments. If you have such guidelines within program review, you may not need to ask departments for separate assessment plans—all you need is to provide good guidance and resources for departments to conduct assessment as they come up cyclically for review. In your report to the accreditors, samples of these reviews demonstrate departmental assessment processes.

Strategic Planning Processes

Any institution-wide strategic planning ought to begin with a review of all available data on student learning, both at the institution-wide and at the unit level, with units reporting to the strategic planning committee the strengths and weaknesses of their students' learning as their data indicate.

Budgeting and Fund-Raising

- Like the strategic planning process, annual budgeting and fund-raising processes can begin with a thorough review of data on student learning and the establishment of relevant priorities based on those data.

- Budget hearings can require those who are asking for new money to show how they are assessing learning and how their plans will impact student learning.

- One chief academic officer keeps a special line in her budget to support initiatives arising from the assessment activities of faculty and departments. For example, a department that has conducted an assessment may come and say, "We found some things that need careful thought; could you fund a day-long retreat for the department to consider these assessment results and plan our actions for the future?"

Evaluation of Faculty and Administrators

Is student learning appropriately considered when teaching is evaluated for reappointment, promotion, and tenure? Appendix C is one research university's document showing the role of assessment of learning in evaluation of teaching.

Student Support

- How do student support systems assess student learning? What data are collected by offices such as student affairs, counseling, residence hall staff, service learning, international studies, and the like?

- How are these data used within the unit and, as relevant, within the university as a whole?

Departmental Decision Making

Is assessment appropriately embedded in the processes by which departments make decisions about curriculum, pedagogy, and staffing?

- Within departments, what data are available and how are they used? The common pattern for departments is for the chair and perhaps a relevant committee or director to review the data on learning and then either take action or recommend action to the department. How well is this system working? Are chairs and committees getting the information they need? Do they understand its uses and limitations? Are they using it effectively to inform action? On what basis do departments institute changes in curriculum, advising, staffing, or pedagogy? Are assessment data well used in these decisions? How can the institution help improve these departmental processes?

- Is assessment embedded in processes and initiatives that have rewards and meaning for units?

- What incentives would be meaningful to departments?

- Can you help reduce departmental workload connected to assessment?

- Do departments need methodological guidance for assessment?

- Can you build on what the departments are already doing?

- Are departments getting the support they need to address issues of academic freedom, student privacy, and so on?

- How do departmental data influence departmental, college, and institutional decision making?

General Education Curriculum

- Is good assessment taking place at all gen ed sites?

  - Departments that offer gen ed courses
  - Gen ed courses such as composition, humanities core
  - Student Affairs
  - Advising
  - Other initiatives such as service learning or learning communities

- Is assessment embedded into relevant processes?

  - Curriculum review
  - General education curriculum reform
  - Approval of courses for general education credit

- Faculty development for general education
- Grants to support general education

- Are there effective committees and directors to conduct assessment in gen ed?

Establish Oversight for Assessment Processes

When the assessment committee has shaped a set of recommendations about assessment processes and these have been shared with relevant administrators or decision-making bodies, it will be necessary to assign responsibility for them to an oversight person or body. For example, if assessment is to be stronger within the upcoming general education curriculum reform, responsibility should ideally be placed with the gen ed planning committee, which may appoint a subcommittee to shepherd the assessment piece of the task. The original assessment committee may continue as a resource group and as an advisory body to the provost that continues to analyze how assessment is being conducted university-wide. Members may also serve as assessment experts on bodies such as the gen ed committee.

Recommend Actions for Student Learning

In addition to recommendations for improving the assessment processes themselves, some institution-wide assessment initiatives also review actual assessment data and recommend steps to enhance student learning. This latter is a complex and difficult task, and I recommend that it be added to the assessment committee's task only in certain circumstances and only after exploring some crucial questions.

The first question is, "What will happen to the committee's recommendations about student learning and how will they fit into the institution's life?" It is imperative that a review of assessment data be connected to ongoing strategic planning, budgeting, and unit review. If the institution already has a full plate of initiatives and a strategic plan under way, the assessment committee will do far better to ensure that assessment data are an integral part of those processes than to come in from left field with its own set of recommendations for improving student learning.

A second question is, "Who will review the data and at what level?" The assessment committee is likely to have uncovered a large amount of assessment data being collected at many sites. Reviewing all of it is a huge task. Further, if the assessment committee is in charge of reviewing all the data, the end result may be that the committee members are the only ones on campus invested in the resulting recommendations. Thus a review of assessment data might better begin with a request for each unit to review its own assessment data and forward recommendations to a central committee and/or to the chief academic officer. This begins to have the dimensions of an institution-wide strategic planning initiative, and so it should. My point is that an assessment committee cannot simply sit down in a short time, review data, and come up with recommendations that will really change things.

There may be assessment data that no one is adequately reviewing. For example, in some institutions, the Office of Institutional Research administers national senior student surveys, but no one really carefully reviews the data and feeds it into the decision-making process. The problem is systemic; it concerns the ongoing flow of data in the institution. In that case, the committee may be better off making sure that relevant data are reviewed periodically by appropriate decision makers rather than a one-shot review of the data by the assessment committee.

In short, the only situation where an institution-wide assessment committee might be wise to conduct a review of actual data and make recommendations for student learning is when that committee is part of a larger strategic planning, budgeting, or fundraising initiative, and when it is logically connected to other bodies participating in the planning process.

Write the Assessment Report

The assessment committee will write whatever reports are required by the regional accreditor, legislature, or other external body. Here are some guidelines:

- Review the agency's requirements carefully and follow them.
- If possible, ask the agency to recommend some sample reports it thinks are outstanding.
- Be honest about the strengths and weaknesses of your assessment processes.
- Select an outline. Two options are:

  - The sample outline in Chapter One that builds on the three steps.

- If you are responding to a critique by an accrediting agency, you may want to organize your report around the recommendations or requirements they have made specifically for you.

Before you choose any outline, check with the agency to be sure that this is the most effective mode of organization.

In a regional accreditation self-study, there is likely to be a section that describes assessment processes, and then multiple sections that address the institution's strengths and weaknesses in research, student learning, community outreach, and other institutional goals. Assessment data will be thoroughly integrated within all those sections. For example, in one institution's full review for reaccreditation, a chapter dealt with the assessment processes in place and recommendations for improving them. The chapter on student learning presented the actual assessment data showing student strengths and weaknesses and recommendations for changes in curriculum, pedagogy, and other aspects intended to improve student learning. The chapter on the institution's research mission likewise gave statistics on research achievements and made recommendations to improve.

Summary

This chapter has emphasized the importance of:

- Knowing the audiences and purposes for assessment
- Clarifying the tasks of the assessment committee, especially distinguishing between recommendations about assessment processes and recommendations for student learning
- Embedding assessment into the most important planning and budgeting processes of the institution
- Building on the assessment already taking place, including the grading process

Members of the assessment committee, officers, and planners may want now to read or at least skim the other two chapters—on departments and general education—to be familiar with what those leaders will be reading.

CHAPTER 3

For Departments and Programs

The following people will find this chapter most relevant:

- Department chairs
- Department assessment or accreditation committees
- Department faculty
- Planners and administrators responsible for supporting departmental assessment

This chapter assumes you have read Chapter One.

This chapter is addressed to "departments" as a generic term, including "divisions," "colleges," or "schools." Some such units will have common goals and assessment measures for all subunits and may also need to generate separate goals and measures for individual subunits or tracks.

The Purposes of This Chapter

Your department, division, college, or school is already doing assessment, as Chapter One emphasizes. You are probably turning to this chapter because you have been asked to improve your assessment and report it for one or several of these purposes:

- Regional accreditation for the institution as a whole
- Professional accreditation in disciplines such as engineering, business, health sciences, or architecture

- A board or legislative mandate to the institution for assessment

- Assessment as part of an institutional initiative such as retention, distance learning, or technology upgrade

- Assessment as part of a departmental initiative such as curriculum review or hiring

This chapter will help you make assessment:

- Time efficient
- Useful for the department's own goals
- Consonant with external accreditation requirements

Analyze Task, Audiences, and Purposes

Understanding precisely what you are being asked to do and what you are not being asked to do as well as identifying your audiences and purposes will help you gather only the data that you need, in the form that will be most useful.

Understanding Your Task

Be very clear about which of the following tasks you are undertaking:

- Reviewing the department's current assessment practices and recommending changes in how the department conducts assessment

- Reviewing the assessment data about student learning and recommending changes in curriculum, pedagogy, and other aspects to improve learning

For the first task, you will report, for example, that a senior survey is administered annually by Institutional Research, with an 80–90 percent return, and that relevant findings from these data are distributed regularly to Student Affairs, the provost, and the strategic planning committee, but departments find these data hard to use. You recommend that reports be disaggregated by students' major and results made available to each department for its own majors. For the second task, you will report that 41 percent of your undergraduate majors respond on the senior questionnaire that your university greatly or moderately enhanced their ability to function effectively as a member of a team and that this is lower than a group of your peer institutions. You institute a workshop in your department, school, or college to help faculty use teams more effectively in their classes and a review of the curriculum to consider incorporating more team projects.

Analyzing Audiences and Purposes

A single audience may be the immediate driver for your attention to assessment, but you may be able to serve other audiences and purposes at the same time. For example, data on the percentage of students involved with faculty in research may be useful as a recruitment tool, as well as part of your assessment report to accreditors. The most important audience is the department itself; you must conduct assessment so that it serves the department and its students. The matrix in Appendix D may be helpful in identifying your audiences and their needs.

Exactly what kind of report are you being asked to submit, and to whom? If your institution is using interviews or questionnaires with department chairs as part of its information collection for regional or legislature- or board-mandated assessment, what questions will the institution ask of you? If you are asked to submit a written report, what is the format and content, and how will the collectors use it? If you are preparing for a professional accreditation visit in your discipline, what will the self-study require, and what will the visiting team look for?

Envision the Departmental Assessment Report or Plan

A departmental assessment report or plan may be written for a variety of audiences using formats that make sense to those audiences. You can be most efficient if you envision, early in the process, what your final report will need. Examples of department reports and plans are in Appendix F.

Plan Carefully for Departmental Collaboration in Assessment

Assessment can be divisive and unnecessarily time consuming or it can be productive, inspiring, and thought-provoking for the department, helping the department to be more clear about its aims and more effective and cost efficient in achieving them. The challenge is to manage your departmental culture so as to achieve these desired outcomes. This chapter offers sequential steps to implement successful assessment. However, you will need to follow these steps within the context of your own departmental culture. Before you begin any new moves in assessment, gather a group of the wisest heads in your department to discuss Chapters One and Three and then to brainstorm—not yet to make recommendations about your assessment structures but to plan how best to manage the assessment discussions you are about to have. Here is a guide for this discussion:

- What exactly is the department being asked to do and *not* asked to do about assessment, and why? How can we communicate these requirements accurately to everyone?

- Is there a difficult departmental issue we have managed well in the past that can teach us how to manage these discussions well? Is there a difficult issue we have managed badly? How can we avoid similar pitfalls?

- What fears do our department members have about assessment? Are there ways we can address those fears?

- What does each department member stand to gain from participating in assessment or at least not actively blocking it? How can we enhance those rewards?

If beginning a discussion about assessment with the entire department seems too difficult, sometimes it is possible to begin assessment within a subset of the department. In my experience, units such as the composition and rhetoric program in English, language instruction in departments of language and literature, or master's degrees that serve the needs of practicing professionals (such as Master of Divinity in theology or Executive MBA in business) may be most open to assessment. Look for a subsection of the department that already is familiar with assessment or that sees the benefit of it. Let them begin analyzing assessment practices in their track or program.

If a department is marked by serious mistrust, conflict, or tension, these issues may need to be addressed first before you can make much progress on assessment.

Establish Responsibility for Assessment

To conduct the assessment review, the chair may appoint an assistant chair, a faculty point person, or a committee, but the chair should remain involved and publicly supportive. Follow your own departmental culture and decision-making practices in determining what will work best. If you work by committee, include representative adjunct and non-tenure-line faculty, as well as students if that is your department's practice, but be sure that the committee membership demonstrates the investment and commitment of full-time, tenure-line faculty.

Articulate Departmental Learning Goals

As Chapter One explains, the assessment process is built on articulation of the departments' learning goals. Appendices F and J contain examples of departmental learning goals. Goals should be stated in this format: "When students complete our program (e.g., major, doctorate, program, or core course), they should be able to . . ."

- Statements such as "The Department will do *XYZ*" or "The students will be exposed to *XYZ*" are fine goals in their place, but they are not learning goals. They are goals for action the department hopes will lead to learning.
- You may have somewhat different goals for general education students, nonmajors in service courses, graduate programs, undergraduate majors, or different tracks within the major.

If your disciplinary accrediting agency dictates the learning goals, as, for example, in engineering and architecture, you can skip this step unless you want to add, for your own benefit, goals for assessment that the accreditors do not require. For example, some institutions want to aim higher than the basic accreditation goals, including more complex kinds of thinking and problem solving. Faith-based institutions may want to expand the discipline's goals with learning goals that fit their own missions.

The first task of your assessment review is to determine whether and in what ways you have already stated department-level goals for student learning and to move the department toward effective goal statements.

- Identify your distinct student populations with somewhat different learning goals.
- Collect already existing goal statements, such as:

  - Goals completed for past accreditations or other purposes
  - Goals generated by curriculum review committees
  - Goals emerging from departmental retreats
  - Goals accompanying budgetary requests
  - Goals established by your disciplinary society or in the literature of your discipline
  - Goals established with the help of your industry advisory group

- Work from the mission and goal statements of the university and the school or college. Accrediting agencies often want you to make explicit the link between your departmental goals and the goals of your college or school and university.
- For departmental purposes, goals will need to be made sufficiently specific so that they imply student performances

and criteria for evaluating those performances. For example, the university-wide goal might be related to critical thinking. The history department might interpret that goal as "Students will be able to write historical arguments in which they define a debatable issue in the field, take a position, defend the position with appropriate historical evidence, and address counterarguments." Such a statement implies that students in a senior history course could be asked to write a historical argument and that faculty could evaluate it by the criteria implied in the goal statement.

- If you have no usable statements of learning goals, try these strategies for generating them:

  - Ask faculty to contribute their course goals (taken from their own knowledge of what they are aiming for and/or from statements on their syllabi). Then let one or two people from the department work from those goals to draft a coherent statement and bring it back to the department for revision. You can do this exercise even if a few faculty do not contribute their goals; simply ask them to react to the draft statement. If they don't do that either, just move forward with those in the department who are willing to participate.

  - Investigate whether your scholarly or professional society has published goals or standards for undergraduate student majors. If so, use these as a draft for discussion and emendation in the department.

  - In a department meeting, brainstorm goals, writing down on newsprint what each person contributes, without judgment or selection. Then ask a departmental committee to work from these brainstormed statements to draft student learning goals for departmental discussion and emendation.

- If the department cannot agree on a comprehensive list of all its learning goals, do not spend a lot of time trying to get a comprehensive list. Instead, take one or two goals on which the department *does* agree and begin to find out how well students are achieving those goals and how the curriculum and pedagogy of the department serves those goals. For example, one biology department, in their initial conversations, could agree on only one thing: that biology majors ought to be able to use the microscope. So they instituted a microscope exam for all exiting seniors, in which the senior had to come into the lab, set up the microscope, and identify an organism on a slide. About one-third of their graduating seniors failed this test. That gave the department plenty to work on; they could focus on improving this one aspect without getting bogged down in an attempt to reach consensus on a full set of goals.

The important point is to get a set of goals you can use as the basis for assessment, without spending more time on them than necessary to for the department's own needs.

Conduct an Assessment Audit

The next step is to identify the assessment of the learning goals that is already occurring in your department. Wherever you are gathering information about student learning, even if it is informal, even if it is not written down, even if it is not being used very well, even if no one has called it assessment, include it now, because it is a potential site or building block for assessment. Your goal at the end of this audit is to construct an analysis similar to those in Appendix F.

Identifying Classroom Assessment

Begin your audit by identifying where in your classrooms the departmental goals are being taught and assessed. Appendix K presents matrices that each faculty member can complete for the courses that he or she teaches, showing how he or she teaches and assesses department-level goals and, in the final example, identifying strengths and weaknesses the faculty member perceives in student work. This information on classroom assessment eventually will be included in the complete report on all assessment in the department (Appendix F).

Identifying Assessment Beyond the Individual Classroom

For the second part of your audit, make a list of departmental assessment measures beyond the individual classroom, both direct and indirect (see Chapter One for definitions of these terms). Identify how each measure is used for departmental decision making. You may be able to link the assessment measures immediately to your goals on the matrix (as in the first three examples in Appendix F), or you may at this stage simply have to list the assessment measures and decide later how they relate to the goals. Following is a list of some of the assessment measures you may have in place.

Direct Measures

- Review of senior projects by external evaluators. Are criteria for their judgments written down? Could they be? Do the evaluators merely give awards or feedback to the individual students, or do they also give feedback to the department as a whole? If they don't now give feedback to the department, could they?

- A national or state exam that your students must take (for example, national or state boards or certification exams). From what percentage of your student test takers do you get information? For example, dental hygiene departments generally get information on all their students who attempt the board exams, but law schools may not know how many of their graduates attempted the bar and who passed. Does your information include strengths and weaknesses or only pass rates? How is this information used in the department?

- Where in your curriculum do multiple faculty members examine student work, as, for example, senior projects in the major, or Ph.D. qualifying exams or dissertations. Are there written criteria that faculty use? Would such criteria help make evaluation more accurate or systematic? Does faculty knowledge of the weaknesses and strengths of student work in the aggregate get fed back systematically to the department? Could it be?

- Some departments have an entering, noncredit exam that tests students' knowledge as they begin a particular course within a sequence of courses. The exam helps the professor understand what students have and what they need coming into the course. When shared with the department and/or with instructors of prerequisite courses, the exam serves as a benchmark of students' knowledge at a certain point in the curriculum. Would this work for your department? Could the results be shared with the department?

Indirect Measures

- *Retention and Graduation Statistics:* Does the department keep track of retention data, such as how many of the students who take its introductory course go on to declare and/or complete the program or major? Would such information be useful? Could it be collected with available resources?

- *Placement:* Does the department collect information from exiting students about their plans or placement in jobs or further education? If this gathering is informal, would it be helpful to make it more systematic? If you are not gathering this information, is the alumni office or Institutional Research gathering it? Can they aggregate or break out and report their information in ways that would be useful to you?

- *Career Development:* Does the department gather information about the career progress of its alumni over time? If faculty gather this information informally by keeping in touch with students, is there a way to make the information more systematic and to feed it back into decision making? Does the career placement office, alumni office, or Institutional Research gather the information, and could they aggregate it or break it out in ways that would be useful?

- *Student Evaluations:* Does the department or any of its courses gather student evaluations? Could these be aggregated for department-wide analysis? If the student evaluations ask only about the quality of instruction, would it be useful to add questions that ask students how well they thought they achieved the learning goals of the course? Do you, or could you, convene student focus groups, a student advisory group to the chair, or a student club or committee that would systematically give feedback?

- *Alumni Surveys:* Do you conduct formal or informal surveys of alumni about their perceptions of their own learning or their suggestions for improvement in the department? If these are informal, would it be useful to make them more systematic? Is Institutional Research or the alumni office collecting this information?

- *Student Activities:* Do you or your Institutional Research office collect information about students' activities that might indicate their learning—for example, their participation in research or internships, their volunteer service, and the like? If this information is collected on an institution-wide basis, could it be broken out for your own majors?

- *Teaching Strategies:* Do you have information about the use of teaching strategies that research has suggested can enhance learning—for example, the amount of writing assigned and the ways faculty respond to writing in your department or the amount of involvement by students in professors' research?

- *Program Review*: Does the department undergo periodic review by the provost, external bodies, or others? What kinds of data are collected—does the review team interview students? Examine student work?

Identifying How Data Are Used

For each of the types of data you list, describe how they are used, as in the departmental assessment plans in Appendix F. Here are some possibilities:

- The chair and/or departmental committees or directors of undergraduate studies, graduate studies, curricula, or other aspects review data and make recommendations to the department. Are they reviewing all relevant data? Is the review sufficiently systematic? Do they have all the information they need for good decision making? Does the department have the appropriate committees in place for addressing student learning? Are centralized data from Institutional Research, career placement, and similar offices appropriately used in the department?

- Periodically, as the department undergoes academic review or professional accreditation, a team of external reviewers analyzes all relevant data and makes recommendations to the department. Do they have the data they need for good recommendations? Is the review process fruitful for the department?

- An industry or alumni advisory body reviews relevant data and makes recommendations to the department. Do they review the right data for their level of understanding about the department? Does the review process effectively tap their particular expertise?

Putting It All Together

Now you have information about the assessment being conducted in individual classrooms (from Part One of the audit) and about other assessment measures (from Part Two). You are ready to put it all together into a coherent picture. The examples in Appendix F show completed departmental reports, including explicit links between learning goals and assessment measures.

You may have assessment measures that do not map to any stated goal. If so, that becomes part of your report to the department and your consideration of the department's total assessment picture.

Strengthen the Department's Assessment Processes _____

Once you have completed your matrix showing the assessment being conducted, you are ready to recommend how the department can improve its assessment procedures. Appendix F contains examples of recommendations that are part of departmental assessment reports. Here are some factors to consider:

Are Learning Goals Well Stated?

At the beginning of the process, you constructed departmental learning goals. Now that you have collected information about the assessment measures in place, do the goals still seem appropriate? Do you have measures for goals you did not state or measures that imply a different phrasing of goals? If so, do you want to revise your learning goals?

Are All Learning Goals Being Taught in a Sensible Sequence?

From the matrix in Part One of the audit showing classroom assessment (Appendix K), are each of your goals being taught? Are they being taught in a sensible sequence? Are skills and knowledge being developed progressively throughout the curriculum? If not, this is the first item you should address. It's hard for learning goals to be achieved if they are not being taught.

What About Goal Disparity by Course Section?

You may find that some sections of a course have different learning goals than other sections (Appendix K). The department may want to work together to achieve greater unanimity. However, assessment need not impose a cookie-cutter uniformity. There may be very good reasons in your department to allow faculty discretion about goals and assessment measures within different sections of the same course. If so, you need to ensure that all students, no matter what their sections, are experiencing a sensible sequence of learning goals within the curriculum. Track their paths: If a student takes Prof. Andring's section of 201, what will be the student's sequence of learning goals? If a student takes Prof. Chu's section of 201, what will be the student's sequence of learning goals?

It is possible to bring sections of a course closer together in terms of *learning goals* and still have a wide variety of *course content and teaching methods,* according to each teacher's choice. Thus a department might say, for example, that in the first course of the

British literature survey, faculty will aim for goals *X*, *Y*, and *Z*. But faculty can individually decide what literary works to teach, how many to teach, what kinds of writing assignments, and how to mix lecture, discussion, and small-group work.

Can You Build on the Grading Process?

As Chapter One explains, one of the most effective yet least time-consuming modes of assessment is to use a classroom assignment that is being conducted for grading purposes and feed back the information to the department. Where in your classroom assessment grid is an assignment whose results yield evidence of how well students have reached one or more of the departmental goals and would be useful to the department in decisions about curriculum, pedagogy, staffing, and the like? Here are some examples:

- In a community college statistics course, taken by all students in the mathematics and physics program, the faculty member assigned a statistical project in which students gathered data, made statistical computations, and wrote up their reports. For grading, he used multiple criteria, but three of them were especially important for departmental learning goals. The department asked him to report annually to them about students' strengths and weaknesses in these three areas.

- In a political science department at a four-year institution, all seniors completed a thesis, under the guidance of an individual faculty member. The department instituted an annual meeting at which the faculty thesis advisors met with the department to report, in a systematic way, the strengths and weaknesses they saw in student work and to recommend to the department what needed to be done. For example, they reported that students entering the thesis process often did not know how to formulate an appropriate question for inquiry in the field. The department revised courses earlier in the curriculum to place more emphasis on building that skill.

- In a major national research university, all doctoral theses were read by at least three faculty members in the department. This store of knowledge about student work was not being systematically fed back into departmental deliberations. A department that wished to do so asked its faculty to keep written records of the strengths and weaknesses of student dissertations, related to their learning goals for Ph.D.

students. Annually, all dissertation advisors reported to the department the strengths and weaknesses they had observed, and the department discussed how its curriculum, advising, or other actions could help students more effectively.

Can You Use Student Evaluations?

If your department has a common student course evaluation, you may be able to aggregate the returns to get a department-wide picture. For example, at one national research university, a standard student evaluation form is used for all classes. Institutional Research sends individual reports to faculty for their own improvement, and it also aggregates data by department. Thus the department chair in history, for example, can see how history students' perceptions of the quality of their own learning and the quality of instruction compare to the student perceptions in other departments in Arts and Letters and other departments in the institution. Departments that score low in relation to their peers are urged to gather further information and address the problems. Student evaluations are most useful if they ask questions both about students' perceptions of how well they met the learning goals of the course and also about the quality of instruction. A fine national questionnaire that does both is IDEA (www.idea.ksu.edu), which can be adopted by a single class, subset of classes, or a department.

Are You Using Institutional Data Effectively?

It is common for institutions to be gathering data that are potentially useful to departments but not aggregated, formatted, or distributed to departments in ways that are maximally useful to them. Offices to check include Institutional Research, career placement, alumni, Student Affairs, student government, and Multicultural Affairs. Are these data broken out by department, or could they be broken out, to show how *your* majors perceive their learning, how *your* majors progress in their careers, or how *your* minority students perceive their learning experience?

What Are Your Structures and Processes for Feedback?

It is useful to define who in your department makes decisions about the following issues that may affect student learning and how each of these processes uses assessment data:

- Curriculum: overall course content and sequence
- Specific course content
- Pedagogy
- Testing, exams, and projects: shaping their content, helping students prepare
- Availability of labs, computers, library resources, and other aids to learning
- Tutoring
- Extra curricula such as department clubs, internships, and the like
- Out-of-class interaction between faculty and students, such as faculty having meals with students or talking with students
- Physical facilities
- Course staffing: Who teaches what?
- Inclusion of students in faculty research
- Course scheduling
- Class size
- Systems for student advising
- Systems for helping students who are having difficulty
- Other factors you believe may affect learning

What information about student learning is relevant to each of these decisions, and how is such information fed into the appropriate decision-making process?

How to Link Data and Action?

Chapter One discusses the need for data and hypotheses about the causes of student weaknesses in learning. In your department, when people have data about student weaknesses in learning, how do they decide what steps might improve the situation? Can you improve their access to the literature about learning in the field and their ease in using that literature? Can you improve the data-gathering process so as to yield information about *why* certain weaknesses in student learning are occurring and what actions might most effectively address the problem?

How Do Resources Support Change?

What is the relationship between data on student learning and the department's budgeting processes? When the department or some faculty within the department have good ideas for improving student learning, what avenues are open to get their colleagues' support and appropriate funding?

How Is the Effectiveness of Change Assessed?

When the department makes a change intended to enhance student learning, what measures and processes are used to explore whether the change is working?

In sum, as a result of analyzing your departmental assessment audit and with the help of the questions listed, you will generate recommendations for improving your assessment processes and structures (see Appendix F). As these structures and processes become more effective, the department will feel the effects of the new information throughout all its decision making. Your primary focus should be not on onetime assessment or onetime fixes for whatever problems in learning turn up, but on building the structures and processes for ongoing assessment that yield good decision making in all areas consistently across time.

Recommend Actions to Improve Student Learning

In addition to recommendations for improving the assessment process, a department may also review assessment data and recommend actions to enhance student learning. The final example in Appendix F is the report of an economics department at a Research I university, which describes their assessment measures, summarizes what the data reveal, and goes on to recommend changes to enhance student learning.

If you undertake such recommendations, be sure that they can be heard, owned, and acted upon. For example, if assessment data show the department has a number of weaknesses, including student advising, it may be wise to focus just on advising. Make sure the entire department is familiar with the data and buys into the goal of improving it. Delegate responsibility for recommending changes to the best possible people in the department (those most capable of improving advising may be different from those on the assessment committee).

Construct Records and Reports

The committee will write whatever assessment report is necessary, following the guidelines of the accreditors or other audiences. In the best scenario, reports and recommendations about assessment and learning are fed smoothly into departmental and institutional planning and budgeting (sample departmental reports are in Appendix F). In addition, the committee should review the department's Web site and brochures to be sure that departmental learning goals and assessment procedures are appropriately visible.

Establish Ongoing Oversight for Assessment

The goal is that assessment becomes a way of doing business for the department, integral to all its decisions about curriculum, pedagogy, staffing, budgeting, and other factors that affect learning. If assessment processes are well embedded into ongoing committees such as curriculum, undergraduate studies, and the like, the assessment committee may safely disband. However, in many cases, the committee may continue with ongoing responsibilities for tracking how well assessment is working in all the structures and processes of the department.

Additional Resources

If I were to compile a very small collection of resources on departmental assessment, I would include the following:

- Lucas and Associates (2000). Essays by various authors. Gardiner and Angelo are most helpful on assessment.
- Nichols (1995a, 1995b, and 1995c). Guides a detailed and extensive departmental assessment process, including cases.
- Banta, Lund, Black, and Oblander (1996). Contains a number of two- to four-page cases of department-level assessment.
- Walvoord and others (2000). How to understand and change departmental cultures.

Summary

In sum, this chapter has emphasized that a department should:

- Know its task, audiences, and purposes.
- Plan carefully for departmental discussion and collaboration.
- Articulate learning goals.

- Conduct an audit to discover where, within the curriculum, learning goals are being addressed and/or assessed and what measures are being used outside individual classrooms.

- Shape recommendations for improving the assessment mechanisms.

- Analyze assessment data to recommend changes in curriculum, pedagogy, or other aspects intended to improve student learning. The goal is to keep it simple and to use the assessment process for better decision making.

CHAPTER 4

For General Education

This chapter is intended for the following readers:

- General education committees charged with assessment
- Faculty involved in assessment of general education
- Central administrators or institutional assessment committees charged with oversight for general education assessment

This chapter assumes you have read Chapter One.

Define General Education

"General education" is a slippery term, as Chapter One explains. This chapter guides those who are responsible for assessment of the learning goals within the general education curriculum. Usually this means both:

1. Courses, such as composition or a humanities core, that are required for all undergraduate students or the majority of them (students in certain specialized programs may be exempt)

2. Courses that can be used to satisfy a distribution requirement

   - In some cases, a single course satisfies the distribution requirement. For example, at one institution, all students must take a literature course; the English department offers a course titled "World Literature," in multiple sections, which virtually all students use to satisfy this requirement.

   - In some cases, a wide range of courses is used to satisfy a requirement. For example, at one institution, students are required to take a course in the social sciences. The departments of psychology, sociology, economics, and political science all offer introductory courses that can be used to satisfy this requirement, and those courses also serve as introductions to the major.

In community colleges, the courses that normally make up the general education curriculum for all baccalaureate students in a four-year institution may comprise much of the curriculum of the two-year associate degree students who will transfer to four-year institutions. Outside of the associate degree program, there may be few, if any, courses required of all other students. If this is your situation, you have two choices:

1. Define your committee's responsibility as measuring student achievement of learning goals only within the associate degree program and any other courses, such as composition, that are required of all students.

2. Define your committee's responsibility as measuring student achievement of the college's general goals (except specialized disciplinary knowledge) within each of your departments and programs, no matter what courses are required of students. If this is your goal, read Chapter Two, as well as this chapter, and work closely with the collegewide assessment committee and administrators.

Understand Task, Audiences, and Purposes

If your task is to focus on the general education curriculum, your goal is to make sure that the faculty and administrative units managing that curriculum have clear learning goals linked to institution-wide goals, that they are conducting effective assessment or receiving assessment data, and that they are using the data in the best possible way to inform decisions about their curriculum, pedagogy, and related issues.

First, clarify whether you are responsible for one or both of these tasks:

1. Reviewing assessment processes for the general education curriculum and recommending improvements in these processes

2. Reviewing data on student learning and recommending improvements in curriculum, pedagogy, or related factors intended to improve learning in the general education courses

Next, identify all potential audiences and purposes. Though an accrediting body may be the first audience, assessment data may have other audiences as well. The most important audience is the institution itself; assessment must help it enhance student learning. Appendix D will help you identify potential audiences and purposes for your work.

Articulate General Education Goals

Once your task, purposes, and audiences are clear, make sure that you have well-formulated learning goals for the general education curriculum—goals that can serve as the basis for assessment. The format for goals is, "When students graduate, they will be able to . . ." Examples are in Appendix L.

First, find out what goals you already have. Search not only the institution's catalog, faculty handbook, and Web page, but also goal statements arising from past general education curriculum reforms, rationales that departments have submitted as they proposed courses for general education credit, course objectives that appear on syllabi, and exams and assignments in general education courses. You may have goals at any or all of these four levels:

1. The institution's mission statement.
2. The institution's general learning goals. You may assume that all of them except specialized knowledge in a discipline are "general education" goals.
3. The institution's statements of general education goals that the entire gen ed curriculum should address (these may be the same as, or more specific than, the institution's general learning goals).
4. Learning goals for specific gen ed courses and assignments.

Here are examples of how several goal levels may interrelate:

Institutional: Students will communicate effectively orally and in writing.

- *General education curriculum:* Students will write essays in which they select and defend a position on a debatable issue, analyze a text, propose research, or define a problem and suggest solutions.

  - *Composition course:* Students will write a five- to seven-page argumentative essay in which they select and defend a position on a debatable issue, support their position with evidence from their readings, and address counterarguments.

- *Writing-intensive gen ed psychology course:* Students will accurately review the psychology literature accessible to them and will propose a research question and outline a research project that might move the field forward.

Institutional: Students will be sensitive to issues of poverty and injustice.

- *General education curriculum:* The same.

    - *Humanities core course:* In their journals and essays for this course, students demonstrate understanding that poverty has multiple causes, some of which are societal, not just personal; they show familiarity with the definitions of a "just society" in their readings and with the assumptions and implications behind that concept; they show evidence of having considered for themselves the concept of a "just society"; and they express a sense of their own responsibility to address issues of poverty and injustice in their society.

Those two examples, showing clearly articulated goals at several levels, are the ideal. In actual fact, you may have an institutional mission statement and/or general institutional goals for qualities like good citizenship and ethical development, plus a vague assumption that the general education curriculum addresses these goals, and nothing more. If your institution has not clearly articulated learning goals for the general education curriculum and for specific courses and assignments within it, you have two options:

1. *Top-Down—Major Formal Gen Ed Review and Reform:* Work with your institution-wide assessment committee, your administrators, and your faculty governance body to construct and approve a set of formal general education curriculum goals that the entire general education curriculum should serve. Then the assessment audit described below records how each gen ed course or program serves one or more of the general education goals and how it assesses those goals. Then revise the general education curriculum, if necessary, to address all the goals and assess them effectively. This option obviously will take a great deal of time and raise complex issues, so undertake it only if you see clear benefits from the broad buy-in and official status that this step, at its best, can achieve; if you have institutional support strong enough to support general education reform at this point in the institution's history; and if your institutional culture is comfortable with this type of process.

2. *Bottom-Up—Building on Goals Already in Place:* Use the audit process described below to discover course-level goals and assessments already in place. Aggregate these to construct, in the committee, a statement of the general education goals that are being served by one or more courses. If you wish, at this point, you can include only those goals addressed by general education courses that are also stated or implied by the university's mission and/or general learning goals. These are your gen ed goals. You may want to make recommendations for a better fit between goals-in-place and the institutional mission or goals, but you do not expend the time and effort needed for a top-down formal construction of general education goals. Rather, you accept the goals-in-place and focus your efforts on ensuring that those goals are being assessed as responsibly as possible and that the assessment data are being used effectively to improve students' achievement of the goals-in-place.

Conduct the Assessment Audit

You need to know how general education goals are already being assessed, even if people have not been using the term "assessment." Without such knowledge, you run the risk of offending the very people whose cooperation you most need, duplicating effort unnecessarily, or making costly mistakes. Thus, although the assessment audit takes time and effort, don't skip it.

The assessment audit for the general education curriculum has these parts:

- Discover the learning goals being served in the general education courses. If you are following the top-down model, you will discover how each course serves the official gen ed goals. If you are following the bottom-up method, you will discover each course's own goals.

- Identify classroom assessment (assignments, exams) that tests the learning goals in gen ed courses.

- Identify institution-wide *direct* measures of student learning that test what the gen ed curriculum is supposed to teach: for example, an institution-wide test of writing or critical thinking. These goals may need to be addressed by the entire institution, including departments, Student Affairs, and others, but you will be focusing on how the general education curriculum uses these data for improvement.

- Identify institution-wide *indirect* measures, such as student or alumni surveys that assess the general education goals *and that have implications for the general education curriculum goals*. For example, your students and alumni may be responding to questions about how well they believed their general education courses helped them learn, or how well they achieved the learning goals toward which your general education curriculum aims. In the latter case, the entire institution, including departments and Student Affairs, will need to address the results of the student or alumni questionnaires, but you will focus on how the gen ed curriculum can do its part.

Identifying Classroom-Based Gen Ed Goals and Assessment

Your first step is to identify classroom-based goals and assignments (the first two items above in "Conduct the Assessment Audit"). An example of an assessment matrix for a departmental gen ed course is in Appendix F, Example 2. You will have a similar matrix for each gen ed course offered in departments, as well as gen ed programs such as composition or Introduction to the University. An institution-wide assessment committee (Chapter Two) may already have gathered the information for these matrices, along with those for departmental majors and graduate programs. If so, simply ask the committee to share the gen ed matrices with you and go on to the next step. If not, read the section of Chapter Two that describes the assessment audit and construct a matrix for each gen ed course or program.

Identifying Institution-Wide Gen Ed Goals and Assessment

Your next step is to identify the *institution-wide* assessment procedures (items 3 and 4 in "Conduct the Assessment Audit"), but you need a list of the general education goals if you are to investigate the institution-wide measures that address them. If you have a formal set of general education goals, use those. If you are using the bottom-up, goals-in-place approach described, you now use your matrices to compile a list of the goals actually being addressed by one or more courses. You will need to find a common terminology for goals that may be expressed in different language, and you may want to aggregate some lower-level goals under higher-level ones. You might end up with five to ten general education goals.

Now you need to discover institution-wide assessment procedures that are addressing the gen ed goals. Your matrix will resemble the matrix in Appendix E, but without Goal 3 (knowledge and abilities in chosen area of study). If the institutional assessment committee has already done such a matrix, you need only extract those measures that concern general education goals. Here are some possible measures:

Indirect measures

- Student or alumni questionnaires that ask students how well they believe they have achieved the general education goals or how they evaluate the general education curriculum or pedagogy
- Measures of student or alumni behaviors, such as volunteer service, that reflect the values the institution wants to nurture

Direct measures

- Examination of student work in general education classes, evaluated by a faculty committee using criteria linked to the general education goals. This may be done by:

  - Asking a random sample of faculty in a given semester to submit student work that addresses one or more gen ed goals and then evaluating that work by a central set of criteria linked to the gen ed goals.
  - Asking a random sample of students to submit work they have completed in gen ed courses and then evaluating that work by a central set of criteria linked to gen ed goals.

- An institution-wide test administered to all students—for example, a test of writing or of critical thinking. The test may be administered at the beginning and at the end of the students' college career to assess what the institution added to their learning, or only at one point within it to assess whether they achieved a certain standard.

Bringing It All Together

When you have completed the information gathering about both course-based and institution-wide gen ed assessment measures, bring it all together into a matrix that shows each gen ed assessment measure, whether classroom-based or institution-wide, the goals being assessed, and how the information is being used. Appendix L contains examples.

Recommend Improvement in Gen Ed Assessment Procedures

Once you know what general education assessment procedures are already in place, the next step is to recommend improvements. It may be helpful to gather a group of the most thoughtful people from various general education sites, show them the matrix (as well as other supporting information as needed), and ask them to brainstorm about improvements. Appendix L shows some examples.

As you consider how to improve your assessment processes in the general education curriculum, consider these aspects:

Embedding General Education Assessment in Meaningful Processes and Initiatives

As Chapter One emphasized, to "do assessment" in a vacuum has little appeal to faculty or units. Look for ways to embed assessment into these processes:

- General education curriculum reform
- Provostial or external review of general education programs
- Approval of courses for general education credit
- Faculty development for general education
- Grants to support general education

A good way to embed general education assessment into the life of the institution is to integrate it with program review by the provost, so that in addition to being asked to assess learning in their majors and graduate programs, a department is also accountable for assessment in its general education courses. Appendix B is an example of departmental review guidelines that call for general education assessment.

Another mechanism for working with departments is the process by which departments propose courses for general education credit. Some institutions have a committee that approves such proposals. The committee can require that each course proposal contain a description of how student learning of the general education goals will be assessed and how that information will be used for improvement. A department might say, for example, that a final essay in each of their general education courses assesses learning goals X, Y, and Z, that each general education faculty member constructs a rubric for evaluating those three goals in the essays, and that the general education instructors report once a year to the department and/or to the general education committee the strengths and weaknesses of student learning, the instructor's plans for improvement of the course, and any recommendations the instructor makes for departmental or institutional action.

Some institutions have no committee that approves courses for general education credit, but simply require that students take one course in each of several disciplines, leaving it to the department to decide what those courses should be. At one large research university in this situation, the ad hoc general education committee that had convened for strategic planning and regional accreditation decided that its first step was to get a standing general education curriculum committee in place, which members accomplished by a vote of the faculty-administrative governance body. The only language that the faculty body would accept for such a committee addressed assessment only in the most general terms, asking each department to submit to the committee a rationale for each of its general education courses, specifying the "knowledge, skills, experiences, etc., that students should acquire through the course," and thereafter, every three years, to demonstrate that the course was fulfilling its purposes. Once the committee was in place under this very general mandate, it could then establish specific guidelines for the rationale and for the ways in which departments could demonstrate that general education goals were being assessed in the courses.

Using Standardized Tests

If you use a standardized test of a goal such as critical thinking, you must have faculty who are willing to teach so as to help students do well on the test. Faculty will resist "teaching to the test," and for good reason. However, it is possible to teach to the *criteria* that will be used to evaluate student work. In other words, you don't teach students what to say about a certain topic, you teach them how to argue effectively about any debatable topic. If you are using or considering a standardized test, all the faculty who will teach to it should take the test. You will need a great deal of faculty development to discuss the test, address peoples' concerns or misconceptions, and suggest effective curricula and pedagogies. If you cannot achieve the cooperation of the majority of the general education faculty, do not use the standardized test, because you have no way to address the weaknesses it may reveal. If you are mandated to use the standardized test, then you must work to get buy-in from as many general education faculty as possible.

The best way to handle a standardized test is to embed it into regular classroom work for which students receive credit. If students get no credit, they may not be willing to take the time or care to do well on the test. Ideally, all relevant general education courses will form a sensible sequence of skills development for critical thinking, and the test itself will be embedded as a major credit-bearing exam within one general education course, with preparatory assignments that help students build the necessary knowledge and skills.

Building on Classroom Work

One of the best forms of general education assessment is regular classroom work, with results reported to the relevant programs and administrators for action. Chapter One presents several models for building assessment on the grading process. In general education courses, faculty may report their results to the department, which then takes action at the department level and also reports results to the general education assessment committee. Alternately, faculty may report their results in a group of general education faculty. If faculty are adjuncts, are located on different campuses, or otherwise find it hard to get together, make the groups very small. For example, the composition program at the University of Cincinnati has gathered composition instructors into groups of three who meet twice a semester at their own convenience to examine a selection of one another's student papers, discuss ways of addressing students' weaknesses, and report common problems to the composition program directors for program-level action. Before small groups meet on their own, a large-group meeting or two will be necessary for initial instruction, orientation, and some sample evaluations of student papers, using the common rubric (Roemer, Schultz, and Durst, 1991).

Using Portfolios and Samples of Student Work

Some institutions attempt to gather portfolios of student work over time, or samples of student work from various classes, to assess how well students have achieved the general education learning goals. These can be strong assessment techniques, or they can expend a great deal of energy for little gain. To make them effective, you must be realistic about the time and resources it will take to gather student work, create a rubric, and have someone besides the professor reevaluate it. Select a very small sample first, to try out your methods and your rubric. Even the main study should have a limited sample. For example, at one research university with many students and many resources, the writing program, which has a staff of five full-time people and a number of part-timers, received funding for a study of just twenty-nine students, across four years, collecting their papers from all their classes, with teacher comments, and interviewing them each semester, to understand what kinds of writing and thinking they were being asked to do in their courses across the curriculum, from first year to senior year. Just twenty-nine students comprised a huge amount of work. Portfolios must be used more like case studies than like large samples. Their purpose is to bore a deep but narrow hole, to give richer texture and depth to the institution's understanding of how students learn.

Recommend Actions to Enhance Student Learning

The general education assessment committee may or may not assume responsibility for actually analyzing data on student learning and recommending changes in curriculum, pedagogy, or other factors designed to enhance student learning within the general education courses. If the committee does assume this responsibility, here are some guidelines.

- Be sure that the committee's suggestions will be considered and funded. All too often, recommendations about curriculum, pedagogy, or other factors, forwarded by assessment committees, do not have the power or place in the institution to make a real difference. The assessment committee might do better to devote its energy to ensuring that good assessment data makes its way into the institution's strategic planning processes or provostial review of departments.

- Compile suggestions from general education faculty and departments, based on their assessment of classroom work. Appendix K, Example 3, contains a questionnaire that could be used for general education faculty, asking them to identify the general education goals they teach, tell how they assess those goals, and then analyze the students' strengths and weaknesses they see and make recommendations for their own action and for institutional action to improve student learning in their general education courses. General education faculty may respond to a mailed questionnaire in sufficient numbers to yield a useful sample, or you may choose to interview a sample of general education faculty, using the questionnaire as an interview outline.

- Analyze all available data to identify one or two student weaknesses that arise again and again. That may be all you need for effective action.

- You must have data and theories about the causes of those student weaknesses, or you may spend time and energy on a remedy that won't address the problem. You may need to gather additional data before you propose remedies. For example, at one institution, faculty teaching general education courses, as well as residence hall advisors and student surveys, reflected that students did not often talk with each other outside of class about the great ideas and literature they were studying in their general education courses. The institution wanted to focus on integrating students' intellectual experiences with their out-of-class lives—but how to do that? The committee cannot simply suggest remedies it believes to be helpful, nor can it merely copy the latest educational fad. Taking action that has a reasonable chance of achieving the goal will require a faculty committee to review the research literature thoroughly, to gather additional data such as student surveys and systematic observations of their interactions, and then to make recommendations, together with ways of determining whether the new initiatives are working.

Write the General Education Assessment Report

The general education assessment committee will usually be writing a part of a larger report on institution-wide assessment, perhaps for regional accreditation. Thus the committee will work closely with the institutional assessment committee. A matrix such as those in Appendix L may be a useful guide for your report.

Additional Resources

- Palomba and Banta (1999, Chapter Nine) address the assessment of general education, including various views of the goals of general education and various approaches to assessing it. They include an overview of the various kinds of assessment instruments, how they may be implemented, and how findings can effectively be used.
- Banta, Lund, Black, and Oblander (1996) include a section of two- to four-page case studies showing how various institutions have assessed general education.

Summary

This chapter for committees and administrators charged with assessment in the general education curriculum has emphasized these steps:

- Define "general education" very clearly.
- Know your audiences and purposes.
- Undertake major construction or revision of formal general education goals only for very good reasons; otherwise, work more locally in committee to select or construct general education curriculum goals.
- Conduct an assessment audit to discover the assessment already taking place.
- Build on the grading system.
- Recognize that portfolios and standardized tests are useful in their place, but they are more complicated and more work than most people realize. Proceed carefully.
- To make recommendations about assessment procedures, consider how to embed assessment in meaningful processes and initiatives and build on classroom work.
- To make recommendations about student learning, ensure that the committee's suggestions will be taken seriously. Once you identify student weaknesses you want to address, get the best information, literature, and learning theories you can as the basis for action.

Sample Rubrics for Evaluating Student Classroom Work

The best way to explain a rubric is to show one. Glance over the following examples. A rubric, for our purposes, is a matrix that explicitly states the criteria and standards for student work. It identifies the traits that are important ("research design" or "originality") and describes levels of performance within each of the traits. A rubric may lead to a grade or be part of the grading process. However, it is more specific, detailed, and disaggregated than a grade. Thus it can show strengths and weaknesses in student work.

Teachers can construct rubrics for their students' work. Some of the language for the rubric can be found in the teacher's assignment, stated grading criteria, comments on students' papers, or handouts intended to help students complete an assignment. If the teacher wants an outside view, she can ask one or more colleagues to use the rubric independently to score student work.

The rubric can be shared with students before they begin work on the assignment, so they will know the criteria on which they will be evaluated, learn the qualities of good work in the field, and consciously strive for those qualities.

For other examples of rubrics in various disciples, see Barbara Walvoord and Virginia Anderson, *Effective Grading: A Tool for Learning and Assessment* (Jossey-Bass, 1998).

Rubric Showing Criteria for Biology Research Reports* _____

Assignment: Semester-long assignment to design an original experiment, carry it out, and write it up in scientific report format.

The teacher identifies these aspects to measure:

Title

Introduction

Scientific Format

Materials and Methods

Nonexperimental Information

Experimental Design

Operational Definitions

Control of Variables

Data Collection and Display

Interpretation of Data

Under each, she constructs a scale describing levels of student performance. Examples:

Methods and Materials Section

5   Report contains effective, quantifiable, concisely organized information that allows the experiment to be replicated; is written so that all information inherent to the document can be related back to this section; identifies sources of all data to be collected; identifies sequential information in an appropriate chronology; does not contain unnecessary, wordy descriptions of procedures.

4   As 5 above, but report contains unnecessary information and/or wordy descriptions within the section.

3   Report presents an experiment that is definitely replicable; all information in document may be related to this section; however, fails to identify some sources of data and/or presents sequential information in a disorganized, difficult pattern.

2   Report presents an experiment that is marginally replicable; parts of the basic design must be inferred by the reader; procedures not quantitatively described; some information in Results or Conclusions cannot be anticipated by reading the Methods and Materials section.

1   Report describes the experiment so poorly or in such a nonscientific way that it cannot be replicated.

---

*By Virginia Anderson, Department of Biology, Towson University, Towson, Maryland.

Controlling Variables

5   Student demonstrates, by written statement, the ability to control variables by experimental control and by randomization; student makes reference to, or implies, factors to be disregarded by reference to pilot or experience; superior overall control of variables.

4   As 5 above, but student demonstrates an adequate control of variables.

3   Student demonstrates the ability to control important variables experimentally; Methods and Materials section does not indicate knowledge of randomization and/or selected disregard of variables.

2   Student demonstrates the ability to control some, but not all, of the important variables experimentally.

1   Student demonstrates a lack of understanding about controlling variables.

Collecting Data and Communicating Results

5   Student selects quantifiable experimental factors and/or defines and establishes quantitative units of comparison; measures the quantifiable factors and/or units in appropriate quantities or intervals; student selects appropriate statistical information to be utilized in the results; when effective, student displays results in graphs with correctly labeled axes; data are presented to the reader in text as well as graphic forms; tables or graphs have self-contained headings.

4   As 5 above, but the student did not prepare self-contained headings for tables or graphs.

3   As 4 above, but data reported in graphs or tables contain materials that are irrelevant and/or not statistically appropriate.

2   Student selects quantifiable experimental factors and/or defines and establishes quantitative units of comparison; fails to select appropriate quantities or intervals and/or fails to display information graphically when appropriate.

1   Student does not select, collect, and/or communicate quantifiable results.

Interpreting Data: Drawing Conclusions/Implications

5   Student summarizes the purpose and findings of the research; student draws inferences that are consistent with the data and scientific reasoning and relates these to interested audiences; student explains expected results and offers explanations and/or suggestions for further research for unexpected results; student presents data

Table A.1. Sample Data

Trait	Class Mean, Year #1	Class Mean, Year #2
Title	2.95	3.22
Introduction	3.18	3.64
Scientific Format	3.09	3.32
Methods and Materials	3.00	3.55
Nonexperimental Information	3.18	3.50
Designing the Experiment	2.68	3.32
Defining Operationally	2.68	3.50
Controlling Variables	2.73	3.18
Collecting Data	2.86	3.36
Interpreting Data	2.90	3.59
Overall	2.93	3.42

honestly, distinguishes between fact and implication, and avoids overgeneralizing; student organizes nonexperimental information to support conclusion; student accepts or rejects the hypothesis.

4   As 5 above, but student does not accept or reject the hypothesis.

3   As 4 above, but the student overgeneralizes and/or fails to organize nonexperimental information to support conclusions.

2   Student summarizes the purpose and findings of the research; student explains expected results, but ignores unexpected results.

1   Student may or may not summarize the results, but fails to interpret their significance to interested audiences.

Rubric Showing Criteria for Writing Assignment in Economics 101*

Assignment: For your employer, a congresswoman, research and analyze a proposed law to raise the minimum wage.

*By Philip Way, Department of Economics, University of Cincinnati.

Executive Summary

5 Clearly states the position of the researcher; summarizes the main reasons for this conclusion.

4 Clearly states the position of the researcher; provides some information as to why this conclusion was reached.

3 Clearly states the position of the researcher.

2 Position of the researcher is present in the summary, but must be identified by the reader.

1 Fails to identify the position of the researcher.

Criteria

3 Student clearly (correctly) defines the criteria used to assess the implications of the research question.

2 Student provides definitions of the criteria used to assess the implications of the research question, but the presentation is unclear or at least one definition is not factually correct.

1 Student fails to correctly define criteria used.

Relative Weighting of the Criteria

3 Student indicates the relative weighting (importance) of the criteria.

2 Student's weighting scheme, although present, is unclear.

1 Student fails to identify the relative weighting (importance) of the criteria.

Production Possibility Diagram

5 Student clearly presents and fully explains the impact of the proposed change in terms of a production possibility frontier (PPF) diagram. Graph is appropriately drawn and labeled. Discussion is in terms of identified criteria.

4 Student presents and explains the impact of the proposed change in terms of a PPF diagram. Either the explanation or the graph is less than clear, although they do not contain factual errors.

3 Student presents and explains the impact of the proposed change in terms of a PPF diagram, although presentation contains some factual errors.

2 Student presents and explains the impact of the proposed change in terms of a PPF diagram. Presentation contains serious factual errors.

1 Student does not present the impact of the proposed change in terms of a PPF diagram.

Supply and Demand Diagram

5 Student clearly presents and fully explains the impact of the proposed change in terms of a supply and demand

diagram. Graph is appropriately drawn and labeled. Discussion is in terms of identified criteria.

4   Student presents and explains the impact of the proposed change in terms of a supply and demand diagram. Either the explanation or the graph is less than clear, although they do not contain factual errors.

3   Student presents and explains the impact of the proposed change in terms of a supply and demand diagram, although presentation contains some factual errors.

2   Student presents and explains the impact of the proposed change in terms of a supply and demand diagram. Presentation contains serious factual errors.

1   Student does not present the impact of the proposed change in terms of a supply and demand diagram.

Production Costs/Supply Diagram

5   Student clearly presents and fully explains the impact of the proposed change in terms of a production costs/supply diagram. Graph is appropriately drawn and labeled. Discussion is in terms of identified criteria.

4   Student presents and explains the impact of the proposed change in terms of a supply and demand production costs/supply diagram. Either the explanation or the graph is less than clear, although they do not contain factual errors.

3   Student presents and explains the impact of the proposed change in terms of a production costs/supply diagram, although presentation contains some factual errors.

2   Student presents and explains the impact of the proposed change in terms of a production costs/supply diagram. Presentation contains serious factual errors.

1   Student does not present the impact of the proposed change in terms of a production costs/supply diagram.

Supporting Data

5   Student provides an analysis of economic data that support the student's position. Quantitative and qualitative information concerning the effect of the increase are presented accurately; differences of opinion are noted where they exist.

4   Student provides an analysis of economic data that support the student's position. Either quantitative *or* qualitative information concerning the effect of the increase is presented accurately; differences of opinion are noted where they exist.

3   Student provides an analysis of economic data that support his or her position. However, the discussion is unclear or contains some factual errors.

2   Student provides an analysis of economic data that support the student's position. However, the discussion is very unclear or contains serious factual errors.

1   Student fails to provide an analysis of economic data that supports the student's position.

Integration

3   Student provides a clear link between the theoretical and empirical analyses and the assessment criteria.

2   Student provides some link between the theoretical and empirical analyses and the assessment criteria.

1   Student does not provide a link between the theoretical and empirical analyses and the assessment criteria.

Conclusions

3   Student's conclusion is fully consistent with his or her analysis.

2   Student's conclusion is generally consistent with his or her analysis.

1   Student's conclusion is not consistent with his or her analysis.

Original Thought

3   Paper shows evidence of original thought: that is, analysis is not simply a summary of others' opinions or analyses, but rather an evaluation of the proposals in light of the criteria and weighting scheme chosen by the student.

2   Paper shows some evidence of original thought but is mostly a summary of others' opinions or analyses, rather than an evaluation of the proposals in light of the criteria and weighting scheme chosen by the student.

1   Student's paper fails to show evidence of original thought.

Miscellaneous

5   Student appropriately cites sources. The paper is typewritten, neat, and easy to read.

4   The student's paper is generally professional and includes citations; however, it contains minor stylistic errors.

3   The paper is legible and includes some citations. However, it contains serious stylistic errors.

2   The student's paper lacks citations, is sloppy, or is otherwise unprofessional.

1   The student's work is not professionally presented.

Rubric Showing Criteria for a Take-Home Essay Exam in Literature*

Assignment: This take-home exam asked students to take a position on a debatable issue concerning the interpretation of the literature they had studied.

Position

5   Student takes a defensible position on the issue posed in the exam question and states the position clearly. Position does not merely state the obvious or parrot one of the readings, but shows a creative mind at work.

4   Student takes a defensible position on the issue posed in the exam and states the position clearly. Position may be somewhat obvious or closely parallel one of the readings.

3   Student takes a defensible position on the issue posed in the exam and states the position clearly, but the position may state the obvious or simply paraphrase one of the readings.

2   Student takes a defensible position on the issue posed in the exam, but the statement is ambiguous, carelessly stated, or must be inferred.

1   Student does not clearly state a defensible position, or position is not defensible, or position is irrelevant to the question posed in the exam.

Support

5   Support for the position is imaginative, thorough, relevant, and clearly stated. Shows a thorough knowledge of the readings and ability to use material from readings as evidence. Evidence is accurately stated. Writer smoothly integrates evidence from various parts of the texts. Makes clear how the textual references support the writer's point. Includes all important relevant evidence found in the readings.

4   Support for the position is thorough, though perhaps somewhat prosaic. Shows a thorough knowledge of the readings. Evidence is accurately stated. Makes clear how

*By Barbara E. Walvoord, Department of English, University of Notre Dame.

the textual references support the writer's point. May not smoothly integrate evidence from various parts of the texts. Includes most of the important relevant evidence found in the readings.

3   Support for the position is adequate. Shows a thorough knowledge of the readings. Evidence is substantially accurate, though may have some distortion or inaccuracies. Mostly clear about how the textual references support the writer's point. May not smoothly integrate evidence from various parts of the texts. May omit some relevant evidence found in the readings.

2   As for 3 above, but support for the position is barely adequate and/or may omit major relevant evidence found in the readings.

1   Support is absent or slim, and/or textual references are substantially inaccurate and/or not related to the writer's point.

Acknowledgment of Alternative Points of View

5   Acknowledges all reasonable alternative points of view found in the readings or raised in class. Accurately and respectfully summarizes these points of view. Responds to alternative points of view thoroughly and creatively, showing why the writer has chosen his or her own point of view rather than these.

4   Acknowledges most reasonable alternative points of view found in the readings or raised in class. Summary of these points of view is substantially accurate. Responds adequately to alternative points of view, showing why the writer has chosen his or her own point of view rather than these.

3   Acknowledges at least one reasonable alternative point of view found in the readings or raised in class. Summary of this point of view is substantially accurate.

2   Acknowledges at least one reasonable alternative point of view found in the readings or raised in class. Summary of this point of view is substantially inaccurate.

1   Acknowledges no alternative points of view.

Guidelines for Program Review of Departments, Incorporating Assessment

This example comes from a university that conducts a program review of departments every six to eight years on a rolling basis. To incorporate assessment more clearly into the program review process, the university revised its guidelines for departmental self-study. Departments are asked to present their mission statements, then their resources, including faculty qualifications, faculty output, teaching load, curriculum, students, and any external rankings of the department. Next comes this section, which explicitly addresses assessment of learning:

Assessment: Undergraduate Degree Programs

1. *State the department's goals for student learning in the under-graduate major.*

These should be goals upon which the department has agreed. The department does not need to state all possible goals, but it should try to articulate its most important ones. If the department cannot agree on goals, select those on which there is some agreement. If the department serves two or more distinct types of students, some goals may apply only to one type of student.

It is important to focus on the skills, knowledge, and/or traits a students should acquire through the course of instruction in the major, not on the action of the department. Consequently, the department goals should be stated in the form, "Upon completion of the major, students will be able to . . ." or "Students will acquire a virtue or habit to act such-and-such a way," rather than "The department will teach such-and-such a course or offer such-and-such a program."

2. *By what methods does the department evaluate the quality of student learning in the undergraduate major?*

Evaluation may include a combination of direct and indirect indications.

    a. Direct indications include immediate evaluation of a student performance, such as a test, paper, project, laboratory procedure, musical performance, and so on. (These may be classroom-based activities such as papers and exams evaluated by the professor's own criteria and then reported to the department, they may be exams and projects defined by the department as a whole, or they may be standardized exams as relevant to the field.) It is important that such performances are measured against a set of explicit criteria that are drawn from the departmental goals for student learning.

    b. Indirect indications are less immediate, but nonetheless relevant evidence of student learning. They include, for example, student reports about what they learned (from the questions about learning on the student evaluations or exit interviews of graduating students or alumni) or the record of job placement, graduate school admissions, or fellowships and prizes won by graduating majors.

3. *How is information about the quality of learning shared and used for departmental decision making in areas such as curriculum, pedagogy, and other aspects that affect learning?*

An example of a mode of generating and sharing this information is to use senior capstone projects, evaluated by the faculty members teaching the capstone, according to specific written criteria, and then shared with the department, along with other relevant indirect information such as alumni surveys and the like.

4. *What departmental changes in curriculum, pedagogy, or other aspects have resulted from this evaluation process?*

5. *What are the department's plans for improving student learning in the major?*

(The same set of questions is posed for nonmajors and gen ed courses offered by the department and for graduate programs.)

Guidelines for the Evaluation of Teaching, Incorporating Assessment of Learning

This table is part of a four-page document, constructed and passed by the faculty-student-administrative governance body at a research university, to guide the evaluation of faculty for promotion and tenure. The heart of the document is a chart showing three questions that need to be addressed in evaluating teaching (including the question of student learning) and suggesting types of evidence for each question.

Table C.1. Three Questions for Evaluating Teaching

Three Basic Questions for Evaluating Teaching	*Instruments of Evaluation*
1. Are the learning objectives of the course being met? Are students being inspired and motivated to think analytically and creatively and to develop habits of mind appropriate to the discipline?	▪ Measures of student learning based on students' in-course papers, projects, or exams evaluated by the faculty member's explicit standards and criteria ▪ Students' performance on standardized tests ▪ Students' performance in subsequent courses
2. Are the course material, concepts, and activities rigorous, current, relevant for students' needs, and consonant with the announced course description?	▪ Colleague examination of course syllabus, exams, and other material
3. Do students perceive themselves to be well taught?	▪ Student course evaluations, surveys, focus groups ▪ Alumni surveys

Sample Analysis of Audiences and Purposes for Assessment

This matrix can be used by an assessment committee to analyze audiences and purposes. This example illustrates how a hypothetical institution might complete the matrix.

Who?	Needs to Know What?	For What?
Institution/ Department	How well do our strategies for student learning work? What can we do to improve?	Make improvements
Assessment Committee	What assessment strategies do we have in place? What do we need/plan for successful assessment in the future?	Recommend changes for improvement of assessment Report to regional accreditor or other external audience
Accreditor	What assessment strategies does the institution have in place? What does it plan for the future? Does the institution meet our standards?	Accreditation review
Prospective Students	How good is this institution in helping me reach my learning, professional, and personal educational goals?	Enrollment
Donors	How well is this institution doing by objective measures and external reviewers? Are they able to exercise appropriate accountability for using my money well?	Giving
Trustees, Legislature	What assessment strategies are in place? What do we need to do to strengthen assessment? How well are the institution's students doing? Does the institution meet accreditation standards?	Funding, oversight, interpreting university to potential businesses wanting to locate in the state, voters, employers, and others

Institution-Wide Data to Assess Institution-Wide Goals

The following table shows how an assessment committee might analyze university-wide assessment measures in relation to university-wide goals. This example, based on the work of an assessment committee at a large research university, identifies various university-wide assessment measures that transcend a single department's students; shows where the data were generated; links the measures to the university's four broad, university-wide learning goals; and shows how each type of data is used.

Institution-Wide Learning Goals

Students will be able to:

1. Pursue knowledge and evaluate its consequences

   - Think critically, abstractly, and logically to evaluate and solve problems

   - Integrate new information to formulate principles and theories and display an openness to different viewpoints

   - Share the desire for intellectual creativity and the acquisition of knowledge

2. Communicate clearly and effectively in both written and oral forms

3. Demonstrate knowledge and abilities in chosen areas of study

- Develop an understanding of resources and procedures of fields and the ability to use them
- Possess an appropriate core of knowledge in chosen fields

4. Appreciate their social and moral responsibilities

- Reflect upon the spiritual, moral, and ethical dimensions of life
- Display the moral dimensions of their decisions and actions
- Contribute to society as active members

Table E.1. University-Wide Measures to Assess University-Wide Learning Goals

University-Wide Measures That Transcend a Single Department's Students (Site Where Data Are Generated)	Goal 1 Pursue Knowledge	Goal 2 Communicate	Goal 3 Chosen Area	Goal 4 Social, Moral	How Data Are Used for Improvement
Direct: Study of Writing and Thinking in Composition and Across Curriculum calculates the types of thinking and writing required in papers written by a sample of 29 students, in all their courses, across all four years (Writing Program). One time	X	X			Study not yet complete. Will be distributed to university community. Preliminary results already used by committee to help departments adhere to "intensive writing" requirements.
Faculty surveys on teaching, student learning, climate, and faculty development, including faculty perception of whether student learning increased after changes in teaching (Teaching/Learning Center; Institutional Research). One time	X	X	X	X	Data informed major changes in Center direction, especially attention to departments. Also presented to officers, deans, department chairs, and board to inform decisions at those levels.
Student evaluations administered in every course, every semester, about quality of instruction and students' perception of their achievement of course learning goals: data aggregated by department, college, and for entire institution (Institutional Research). Ongoing	X	X	X	X	Data reported twice annually to departments and colleges and to provost and university promotion-tenure committee. Used for institution-wide decisions and budgeting on quality of teaching and learning. Used by departments and colleges for personnel decisions, course assignment, and unit policies.
Interviews with all first-year students, including difficulties in learning; also tutoring and collaborative study groups, which reveal problems (First-Year Studies). Ongoing	X	X		X	Data inform First-Year Studies policy and is shared with officers, academic council, and departments as appropriate for action to improve first-year student learning.

Table E.1. (continued)

University-Wide Measures That Transcend a Single Department's Students (Site Where Data Are Generated)	Goal 1 Pursue Knowledge	Goal 2 Communicate	Goal 3 Chosen Area	Goal 4 Social, Moral	How Data Are Used for Improvement
Enrollment, retention, placement, and time-to-degree data for graduate and undergraduate students (Institutional Research; graduate school)			X		Shared regularly with graduate council and departmental directors of graduate study for their action.
National Science Foundation Survey of Earned Doctorates (graduate school). Ongoing			X		Shared regularly with graduate council and departmental directors of graduate study for their action.
Graduate students' professional activities and impact on their field (graduate school)	X	X	X		Shared regularly with graduate council and departmental directors of graduate study for their action.
Information technology surveys of faculty and students, including how technology helps or hinders learning (Office of Information Technology). Ongoing	X	X	X	X	Data informs OIT consultations and grants to faculty for technology; also reported to provost and chief information officer/vice president to inform decisions.
Student-conducted surveys of students, including factors that affect learning (student government and Graduate Student Union)	X	X	X	X	Annual report by students to board of trustees and campus to inform decisions at all levels.
Senior student surveys of perceptions of learning and factors affecting learning, using HERI, CIRP, and NSSE national surveys (Institutional Research). Ongoing	X	X	X	X	Shared regularly with deans, department chairs, officers. Regular reports from OIR to entire campus.
Your First Year of College survey administered to all first-year students (Institutional Research). Ongoing	X	X		X	Shared with First-Year Studies, reported to officers and campus.

Activity					Use of Results
Alumni surveys of perceptions of learning and factors affecting learning (Institutional Research). Ongoing	X	X	X	X	Shared regularly with deans, department chairs, officers. Regular reports from OIR to entire campus.
Survey and focus groups of students on meaning of student-evaluation question whether the course "stimulates creative and analytical thinking" (Scholarship of Teaching and Learning; Institutional Research). One time	X			X	Use by IR in presentations to faculty and promotion/tenure committees on evaluation of teaching.
Student alcohol use, using national instrument from Harvard. (Student Affairs). Ongoing				X	Data shared with academic council, university-wide in special reports, and with Student Affairs staff and officers to inform decisions.
Student participation in volunteer service, service learning, and for-credit community-based learning (Institutional Research; Center for Service Learning, Student Affairs)				X	Shared with campus community and with organizations involved, especially Student Affairs and Service Learning Center.
Student participation in internships, faculty-sponsored research (Institutional Research, Service Learning). Ongoing			X		Used by departments and colleges for decision making.
Graduation rates for groups such as minorities, athletes (Institutional Research). Ongoing		X	X	X	Shared with campus community and with organizations involved, especially academic council, athletics, Student Affairs.
Student self-reports on aspects of extracurricular life, for example, drinking, participation in service, life in residence hall (Student Affairs)				X	Used by Student Affairs for improvement; shared with campus, officers, trustees.
Four-year longitudinal study of how students' spirituality, personality, and attitude are associated with adjustment to college environments, satisfaction with college life, and psychological well-being (Student Affairs). One time				X	Study is in process. Results will be used by Student Affairs and entire campus.

Departmental Assessment Reports

The examples following show how departments can construct assessment reports for various graduate and undergraduate tracks or programs.

Example 1: Majors, Department of Biology

This hypothetical example is based on assessment reports of several departments at various types of institutions. It shows how the biology department assesses learning goals for its undergraduate majors. Similar matrices would be produced for general education and graduate programs in the department.

Profile

Number of majors: ___
Number of faculty: ___full-time ___part-time ___teaching assistants
Departmental factors that affect assessment and learning (for example, department is growing or shrinking rapidly, job market changing for graduates, field changing rapidly, large percentage of faculty retiring in next three years):

_____

_____

Learning Goals for Majors

1. Describe and apply basic biological information and concepts

2. Conduct original biological research and report results orally and in writing to scientific audiences

3. Apply ethical principles of the discipline in regard to human and animal subjects, environmental protection, use of sources, and collaboration with colleagues

Are these on the Web or otherwise readily available to students and faculty? _____

Assessment Measures

Examples of Changes Based on Assessment

- Two years ago, an advisory council of regional employers noted that our majors had a good level of biological knowledge but needed stronger skills in conducting biological research. Data from the alumni survey also supported this need. We instituted the required capstone course, which requires students to conduct original scientific research, and we asked the instructor annually to report to the department on student research and communication skills demonstrated by their capstone projects. In three years, when several cohorts of majors have passed through the capstone, we will again survey alumni and employers to see whether student skills have increased, and we will review data from all years of the capstone projects.

- The capstone instructor last year reported her impression of low graphing skills in seniors; we arranged with the mathematics department for greater emphasis on graphing in the required math course and for assessment of graphing skills during that course, working closely with the capstone instructor(s). The capstone instructor(s) will report next year whether graphing skills are stronger. Prof. Brody is currently developing a rubric to assess graphing skills more accurately.

Recommendation for Improving Assessment Processes

- Standardized national test is costly and time consuming to administer, has low student motivation in its current format, and results are difficult to map to our curriculum. Committee should review usefulness of the national test.

Table F.1. Assessment for Biology Majors

Measures	Goal 1	Goal 2	Goal 3	Use of Information
Standardized test is given to all seniors, and final exams are administered in three basic biology courses.	X			Data are reported to the department annually by the standardized exam committee and the instructors of the three basic courses. The department supports and encourages the instructors, takes any appropriate department-level actions, and reports meeting outcomes to dean or other body that has resources to address problems.
In senior capstone course, students complete an original scientific experiment, write it up in scientific report format, and make an oral report to the class. The teacher uses a set of explicit criteria to evaluate their work.	X	X	X	Annually, the senior capstone teachers share students' scores with the department. The department takes action, as above.
Alumni survey asks how well alums thought they learned to conduct and communicate scientific research.		X	X	Data reviewed annually by department for action, as above.
Sample of regional employers gathered two years ago to reflect how well our majors are doing and give advice to department.	X	X	X	Data reviewed by department for action, as above.

Example 2: General Education Literature Course, Department of English

This hypothetical example is a report for a general education or core literature class taught by the English department. Similar reports would be submitted for other required general education courses.

Profile

Number of core lit students per year: _____ Average section size: _____

Percentage of sections taught by full-time faculty: _____
by part-time faculty: _____ by T.A.: _____

Departmental factors that affect core lit assessment and learning (for example, changes in university-wide gen ed requirements, core lit newly being offered online, student numbers growing or shrinking rapidly, large percentage of faculty are retiring in next three years):

_____

_____

Learning Goals Course

1. During and after the course, students will read literature for pleasure.

2. Students will write a literary-critical essay demonstrating ability to use the techniques of literary analysis they have been taught in the class and to acknowledge alternative interpretations.

3. Students will reflect thoughtfully on their own ideas and values in response to works of literature.

Are these on the Web or otherwise readily available to faculty and students? _____

Assessment Measures

Examples of Changes Based on Assessment

- Minutes from the meetings on journals show that instructors express their intentions to adopt strategies they have heard in the meetings and report having done so. Percentage of journals that make thoughtful links has risen in the past three years from 47 percent to 68 percent.

Recommendation for Improving Assessment Processes

- Our goal is that students will form a lifelong habit of reading literature for pleasure. Yet we have data only on the core lit course and senior students. High rates of student employment and family responsibility at our institution mean that students' discretionary reading time is exceptionally limited during the college years. Could Institutional Research add a question to the next alumni survey asking whether alums have, in the past year, read a novel, poem, or short story, or attended a live drama performance, not required for academic credit?

Table F.2. Assessment for Core Literature Students

Measures	Goal 1	Goal 2	Goal 3	Use of Information
In all core lit courses, instructors assign an essay requiring students to apply literary critical methods to literature and to acknowledge alternative interpretations. They evaluate students' essays by explicit written criteria.	X			In annual meeting, core lit instructors report student scores to their colleagues who: ■ Collegially support the instructor's plans for improvement ■ Take appropriate action if needed at the department level ■ Report results of the meeting to dean or other body with budgetary resources if needed
Each core lit course requires at least three two- to four-page journal entries in which students reflect the impact of the literature they read on their own thinking and values. Instructors evaluate the journals using a rubric that identifies those journal entries that merely summarize the literature, those that merely reflect on students' lives and values with little connection to the literature, and those that make thoughtful links between the literature and their own thinking. Instructors report the percentage of student journals that make thoughtful links.		X		In an annual meeting, instructors share their evaluations of the journals and strategies for encouraging more reflective and thoughtful journals.
Survey administered to students at the end of each core lit class, asking whether, during that semester, they have read literature not required in class. Student survey administered by Institutional Research to all seniors asking whether they have read books not required in class.			X	Results reported annually to the department for discussion and action.

Example 3: Ph.D. Program, Department of Sociology _____

This hypothetical example is based on assessment reports of several departments at research universities. Following is the report for doctoral students. The department would also report its assessment for undergraduate majors and for other departmental programs or tracks.

Profile

Number of Ph.D. students: _____

Number of graduate faculty: _____

Departmental factors that affect graduate assessment and learning (for example, changes in job market, student numbers growing or shrinking rapidly, large percentage of graduate faculty are retiring in next three years): _____

_____

Assessment Measures

Learning Goals for Ph.D. Students

1. Produce publishable research in the field

2. Follow ethical principles of the discipline for citing sources, using human subjects, and working with colleagues

3. For those bound for college teaching: teach effectively

Examples of Changes Based on Assessment

- Based on departmental dissatisfaction with the publication rate of graduate students, a new graduate course, "Publishing in Sociology," was added three years ago, which has resulted in a threefold increase in the number of graduate student publications in refereed journals.

- In response to graduate student exit interviews requesting teaching experience with different kinds of students, two teaching internships per year were developed for students to teach sociology in a nearby community college and a small liberal arts college.

Recommendation for Improving Assessment Processes

- Faculty visitation to T.A. classes is not happening as regularly as it should. Faculty complain that the rubric is not adequate. Committee should review this entire assessment procedure and recommend changes by next fall.

Table F.3. Assessment for Sociology Doctoral Students

Measures	Goal 1	Goal 2	Goal 3	Use of Information
Graduate student publications (collected by graduate school and by departmental advisors)	X			Reviewed annually by director of graduate studies and presented to graduate faculty for action as needed.
Job placement (collected as above)	X	X	X	Reviewed annually by director of graduate studies and presented to graduate faculty for action as needed.
501, Research Methods: Exam questions test students' knowledge of ethical principles and application to sample cases		X		501 Instructor(s) report results to director of graduate studies, who presents to graduate faculty for action as needed.
630, Teaching Sociology: Students prepare syllabi, give lectures, lead discussions. Instructor evaluates these with a rubric			X	630 Instructor(s) report results to director of graduate studies, who presents to graduate faculty for action as needed.
Student exit interviews conducted by graduate school	X	X	X	Graduate school reports results for sociology students to director of graduate studies, who presents to graduate faculty for action as needed.
A faculty member visits the classroom of every teaching assistant at least twice a semester and prepares a written analysis of the quality of teaching, using a departmental rubric			X	Faculty visitors report annually to the department for action as needed.

Example 4: Economics Department Undergraduate Majors _____

Note: This report, unlike those above, includes actual data on student learning. The assessment committee thus undertook *both* of the possible tasks: analyzing assessment processes for recommendations about improving those processes *and* analyzing assessment data for recommendations about student learning. Because the department presents actual data, they use a slightly different format. They list each learning goal, then show the assessment method and the data that each method produced. This report is adapted from an assessment report prepared by Prof. Philip Way for the Department of Economics at the University of Cincinnati.

Measures of Student Learning for B.A. in Economics, B.A. in Business Economics

- Survey of alumni, conducted with help of the Office of Institutional Research
- Focus groups of current students, who met for an hour with the assistant chair
- Analysis of the senior capstone research projects evaluated according to the faculty members' criteria
- Audit of transcripts of majors to determine which courses they took and in which sequences

Goals, Assessment Methods, and Findings

1. *Critical thinking (analytical) and communication skills to enable undergraduate students to think and communicate like economists (in other words, to become skilled in the logic and rhetoric of economics).*

A. To use mathematical methods to represent economic concepts and to analyze economic issues

Surveys: Average rating of 4.33 (helped somewhat) on a five-point scale (1–5). Achievement of this objective is rated 4 out of 12 objectives.

Focus Groups: Amount of math varies among classes—maybe calculus should be required.

Capstone: Papers and presentations: none included math.

B. To represent economic relationships in terms of theoretical models

Surveys: Average rating of 4.33 (helped somewhat). Ranked 4 of 12.

Focus Groups: Achievement is aided by having T.A. sessions. Good foundation if taken before other courses.

Capstone: Models used in papers and presentations with reasonable success.

C. To gather economic data pertinent to economic theories in order to analyze economic questions

Surveys: Average rating of 4.17 (helped somewhat). Ranked 7 of 12.

Focus Groups: Library research used in a few classes only.

Capstone: Students showed an ability to collect data but overrelied on the Web.

D. To use statistical methods to analyze economic questions

Surveys: Average rating of 3.83 (helped somewhat). Ranked 10 of 12.

Focus Groups: Limited exposure. Complaint about book used.

Capstone: Little evidence of statistical methods.

E. To use statistical computer software to analyze economic issues

Surveys: Average rating of 3.33 (no effect one way or the other). Ranked 12 of 12.

Focus Groups: Concern that software used in career will be different.

Capstone: Little evidence of use.

F. To express economic ideas succinctly and professionally in writing

Surveys: Average rating of 4.17 (helped somewhat). Ranked 7 of 12.

Focus Groups: Writing required more than speaking. In particular, research papers required in 558 and 575.

Capstone: Writing skills in economics generally acceptable, but not "very good" or "excellent."

G. To express economic ideas succinctly and professionally orally

Surveys: Average rating of 4.5 (helped somewhat/significantly). Ranked 2 of 12.

Focus Groups: Most courses do not involve oral communication, although it would be useful after graduation in the workforce. One idea was a sequence of courses in communication as part of the Arts and Science college requirements. More discussion and presentations were advised.

Capstone: Presentations revealed a lack of training in how to present as well as nerves.

2. *Content:* To master key economic concepts and fields and to understand how the field works in practice and what economists do.

A. To master key economics concepts

Surveys: Average rating of 4.5 (helped significantly). Ranked 2 of 12.

Focus Groups: No complaints.

B. To understand economics in general, and at least two fields of economics in depth (one field for Business Economics)

Surveys: Average rating of 4.33 (helped somewhat). Ranked 4 of 12.

Focus Groups: Students like being able to choose what interests them. Exposure to variety was said to be helpful. Business Economics students appear to have more diverse training.

Audits: [Report presents the courses actually taken by majors and their sequence]

C. To understand international economics and economic development

Surveys: Average rating of 4.0 (helped somewhat). Ranked 9 of 12.

Focus Groups: Students like this recommendation—useful.

Audits: The average student completes 2.3 courses in international/development.

D. To understand how the economy works in practice and what economists do

Surveys: Average ratings of 4.67 (helped significantly) and 3.67 (helped somewhat). Ranked 1 of 12 and 11 of 12.

Focus Groups: Students like having guest speakers in class. At present, few think they know what economists do. Some advocated a broader co-op program.

Capstone: Students exposed to several speakers who are economists. Learned what they do.

Recommendations for Student Learning

Main weaknesses are in:

- Achievement of learning goals related to statistical methods and software

- Knowledge about what economists do

Survey indicated that the program did not facilitate exposure to international and development economics, but data from focus groups and course audits showed otherwise. No changes were therefore made.

Steps taken:

- Last year introduced premajor course (Computer and Data Resources in Economics) for better preparation in statistical methods and software

- Capstone course changed to provide more information about what economists do

Recommendations for Assessment Processes

- *Surveys of Recent Graduates:* A low response rate (20 percent) continues to be a concern. While we prefer to delay sending out the surveys because we wish to learn of students' new positions, it may be better to mandate that students complete them before graduation.

- *Focus Groups:* These have proven to be a source of rich, detailed data. The time cost is small. We will continue them.

- *Course Audits:* These are easy to do because we have graduation checklists in place that we use for verifying eligibility for graduation. We will continue to do these audits. Limitation: they tell us what students were exposed to, not necessarily what they learned or remember.

- *Capstone:* The capstone is intended to achieve many of the program goals. It is easy to rate student work products in terms of the objectives. Limitation: the students are not graded on whether they achieve all the program goals—for example, they do not have to use statistical software, but they might choose to.

Matrix for Analyzing Professional Accreditation

This matrix can be used by the assessment committee to overview and integrate the various professional and regional accrediting processes within the institution. The hypothetical example shows how one institution might complete the matrix.

Disciplines/ Departments	Accrediting Body	What Assessment Is Required?	Dates of Most Recent Review and Next Review	How Can Professional Assessment Be Useful for Regional Accreditation?
Engineering	ABET	Required to assess student performance on ABET-stated learning goals	Recent: 2004, Next: 2009	Dean Xiu wants to combine processes and data collection as much as possible. Caution: use of term "direct assessment" is different than for regional accreditation. Associate Dean Hendricks is point person for both.

Matrix for Analyzing Institution-Wide Departmental Assessment Information

This matrix can be used by the assessment committee to analyze the assessment being conducted in departments. It allows the committee to determine how each department's assessment practices meet certain criteria that may be needed for regional accreditation or other purposes. For example, the matrix might show that 87 percent of departments are using some type of direct measure or that 28 percent of departments are using their own departmental alumni survey.

Department/Program, General Education Unit	Written Learning Goals	Goals Readily Accessible to Students and Faculty	Direct Measures	Dept. Student Survey/Focus Groups	Use Institutional Research (IR) Student Survey	Dept. Alumni Survey	IR Alumni Survey	Dept. Placement Data	IR Placement Data	Chair, Committee Review	Other
College of Arts and Letters											
American Studies	X				X		X		X	X	
Anthropology			X	X		X				X	

Analysis of Assessment in Institution, Departments, and General Education

This example shows how an assessment committee, having completed its audit, might analyze the strengths and weaknesses of assessment processes at the institution-wide, departmental, and general education levels and recommend specific actions. This hypothetical report illustrates how one institution might complete the analysis.

Institution-Wide Assessment

Strengths

- The institution is generating a large amount of good indirect data on student learning, including three national surveys.

- The Writing Program is conducting direct assessment—a well-designed study of the writing being done by a sample of students across all disciplines and all four years.

- A number of different offices generate the data, including Institutional Research, Graduate School, Student Government, Career Center, Student Affairs, and the like. Assessment is thus part of the culture and structures of the university.

Weaknesses

- Chairs report that centralized data are sometimes not reported to departments in formats that chairs and department committees can easily understand or use.

- As department chairs change, new chairs are not always well oriented to the centralized data available to them.

Departmental Assessment

Strengths

- 73 percent of departments have some kind of department-wide statement of learning goals.

- All departments use at least some data on student learning, whether they collect it or get it from a centralized source.

- 58 percent of departments use direct measures.

- 100 percent of departments use some type of indirect evidence. The most common types are IR data on student perception of their learning (63 percent), IR placement data (46 percent), and departmentally conducted senior student exit interviews (27 percent).

- All departments undergo program review on an eight-year cycle, with certain requirements for gathering data.

- All departments must participate in the current strategic planning process.

Weaknesses

- 27 percent of departments have no stated learning goals.

- Stated goals are very vague.

- Some goals are not readily available but exist in committee documents or the like.

- Program review and strategic planning documents do not clearly specify assessment of learning as the basis for departmental review, analysis, and planning.

General Education Assessment

Strengths

- The Writing Program conducts direct assessment of portfolios of a sample of students for writing across the curriculum.

- General institutional data provide information on student and alumni perception of such qualities as their moral and civic development, critical thinking, writing and speaking skills, and so on.

- Humanities core faculty meet once a month for discussions of pedagogy.

Weaknesses

- The Writing Program data are not well known on campus.

- General institutional data are not well known or well used by the campus as a whole.

- Humanities core monthly meetings do not focus as clearly as they might on assessing student learning as the basis for pedagogical decisions.

- Departments that offer gen ed course options for the distribution requirement do not generally conduct effective assessment linked to gen ed goals.

Recommendations

- Change program review guidelines to require assessment of majors, gen ed courses, and graduate programs. Then provide rich support for departments (resource persons, funding) to conduct assessment in preparation for provostial review.

- Embed assessment into the new initiatives that emerge from the current strategic planning process.

- As part of new department chairs orientation in the fall, introduce new chairs to the available centralized data, including Writing Program data and its appropriate use.

- Appoint a committee of chairs to work with IR and appropriate vice president to make data more readily usable by the chairs.

Departmental Learning Goals

These examples illustrate how departments in various disciplines might construct their learning goals. They are adapted from learning goals in a variety of departments at different types of institutions. Additional examples appear in Appendix F.

A Theology Department

Theology undergraduate majors will:

- Demonstrate awareness of the religious nature of the human person
- View theology as a science
- Conduct theological inquiry
- Describe and analyze the central areas and key issues of theology, especially in the Roman Catholic tradition

Students preparing for church vocations will:

- Demonstrate the skills necessary for service to the church in ministry and teaching

A Chemistry Department

Chemistry undergraduate majors will:

- View science as questions that are continually being reframed and investigated

- Possess the chemical tools to build further knowledge
- View chemistry problems as unique, requiring problem-solving skills
- Be interested and confident enough to read and explore independently

A Political Science Department

Undergraduate majors will demonstrate learning at these levels:

- Understand basic historical, institutional, informational, and conceptual frameworks for studies within the department's four subfields
- Master vocabulary, concepts, information, and ideas to understand politics and world affairs

300–400-level students will:

- Use tools and methods of research appropriate to subfields
- Use journals and scholarly books

491–492: Writing seminar students will:

- Conduct a more intense and focused investigation of one subarea
- Write extended assignments in a research rather than narrative mode
- Think for themselves

495–496: Senior honors thesis students will:

- Identify a problem, situate it within an appropriate literature, pose a particular hypothesis or intellectual puzzle, then use original sources to test the hypothesis or solve the puzzle

500-level (for most talented undergrads) will:

- Hone research skills in preparation for graduate work

Identifying Classroom Assessment in the Department

The examples demonstrate various ways, both simple and complex, for departments to gather information about the assessment being conducted by faculty in departmental courses.

Example 1: The Simplest Matrix for Identifying Classroom Assessment of Goals

This matrix represents the simplest way for a department to gather information about assessment being conducted in its courses. Each instructor fills out the matrix for his or her own courses. Then the department aggregates the data.

When all or most instructors have submitted the matrix, the department aggregates the data, showing what percentage of all instructors assess a particular goal in a particular course. For example, the department may find that 100 percent of the instructors of course 101 assess Goal 1, but only 45 percent assess Goal 2. The matrix allows the department to see where it has disparate goals within the same course, whether all of its goals are being assessed somewhere in the curriculum, whether the goals are being assessed frequently over time, and where in the curriculum might be a good place for assessment results to be reported to the department.

Completed by Each Instructor for His/Her Own Course

Name of Instructor: *Kolodny*
Departmental Learning Goals [listed and numbered]:
To the Instructor: For each course that you taught last year or are teaching in the current year, place a check mark under every goal that you significantly assess in a major exam or project. Leave the other cells blank.

Course	Goal 1	Goal 2	Goal 3	Goal 4	Goal 5
101	X	X			
102					
103					
104					
201					
230	X	X	X		
231					
300					
314			X	X	
(and so on)					

Department-Wide Summary

Course	Goal 1	Goal 2	Goal 3	Goal 4	Goal 5
101	100%	45%			
102	100%		100%		
103		84%	45%	59%	5%
104		37%	58%	100%	
201	100%	100%	100%		
(and so on)					

Example 2: Departmental Matrix Gathering— More Information

This matrix is more complex than the one above, but it allows the department to gather fuller data about how its goals are being taught and assessed in its courses. The example is adapted from a matrix used by the Lake Forest (Illinois) Graduate School of Management. It shows how the instructor for one course, Marketing 730, might complete the form. The department could then aggregate the data from all courses to show how its goals were being addressed throughout the curriculum.

Content (What)	Impact (Why)	Hierarchy (Where)	Sequence (When)	Delivery (How)	Measurement (How Much)
What are the most important learnings in the course? Knowledge Attitude Skill Habit Identify applicable KASH component	*Why are these core learnings significant in business?*	*Where in future courses are these core learnings applied? Expanded?*	*To master these core learnings, do students need prerequisites? Prior knowledge?*	*What teaching method(s) are used to teach these core learnings?*	*What measurement is used to ascertain mastery of these core learnings*
Understand marketing in a global environment and its integrative role in organizations (KA)	A broad perspective of marketing and its role enhances the effectiveness of the marketing process	*Applied:* 865 Strategic Management; 784-B-B Marketing; 792-New Venture Creation	*Prereq:* 770-International Management	Readings/ discussion; case analysis; video	Individual: Class participation (2)
Assess the marketing environment as a foundation for marketing strategy development (KS)	Marketing decision making must be based on a clear understanding of environmental factors	*Applied:* 784-B-B Marketing; 792-New Venture Creation *Expanded:* 865-Strategic Management	*Prereq:* 835-Research Methods; 726-Business Economics	Readings/ discussion; case analysis; video; final project preparation; Internet	Individual: Class participation (2); Case analysis (2)
Construct an effective marketing strategy based on competitive advantages and sound market positioning (KS)	Competing effectively in today's turbulent business environment requires a sound marketing strategy	*Expanded:* 865-Strategic Management; 784-B-B Marketing		Readings/ discussion; case analysis; video; final project preparation	Individual: Class participation (2); Case analysis (2)
Develop tactical marketing mix components that drive an overall marketing program, including integrated marketing communications and e-business (KS)	Tactical tools are what marketers need to implement strategic marketing plans	*Applied:* 784-B-B Marketing; 792-New Venture Creation; 865-Strategic Management	*Prereq:* 726-Business Economics	Readings/ discussion; case analysis; video; final project preparation	Individual: Class participation (2); Case analysis (2)

Content (What)	Impact (Why)	Hierarchy (Where)	Sequence (When)	Delivery (How)	Measurement (How Much)
Identify, evaluate, and formulate solutions to marketing problems utilizing critical thinking skills (KASH)	Optimal solutions to marketing problems result from critical thinking	*Applied:* 784-B-B Marketing; 755-Operations Management *Expanded:* 865-Strategic Management; 792-New Venture Creation	*Prereq:* 910-Critical Thinking Through Case Analysis; 750-Managerial Accounting	Readings/ discussion; case analysis and role play; video; final project preparation	Individual: Class participation (2); Case analysis (2); Connections assignment (2/3)
Integrate marketing decisions into a real-world marketing plan for a product or service (KS)	The plan is the critical "road map" that logically integrates environmental assessment, strategy decisions, tactical choices, implementation methods, and controls to guide business activity	*Applied:* 784-B-B Marketing; 865-Strategic Management; 792-New Venture Creation	*Prereq:* 750 Managerial Accounting *Prior knowledge:* Projected financial statements	Final project preparation	Group: Marketing plan project (2–4)

Example 3: Departmental Matrix Gathering Assessment Methods and Results

In this example, faculty complete a matrix for each of their courses, both before the semester begins and again after it ends. This method allows the department to identify not only where various learning goals are being assessed but also each teacher's findings concerning students' strengths and weaknesses. The example is adapted from a matrix developed by Professor Steven Skaarfor in the Department of Aerospace and Mechanical Engineering at the University of Notre Dame.

Completed by Each Instructor *Before* the Semester Begins

Learning Outcome # (refer to Learning Outcomes List)	Brief description of how learning outcome is addressed in the course materials and information provided to students (for example, readings, lecture, multimedia, field trips)	Brief description of work performed by students that will demonstrate or assess the learning outcome (for example, exams, homework, projects, laboratories)	List of material that will be collected to evidence the learning outcome
[faculty member fills in]	[faculty member fills in]	[faculty member fills in]	[faculty member fills in]

Completed by Each Instructor *After* the Semester Begins

Learning Outcome # (should correspond with presemester form you submitted)	Identify strengths and weaknesses in your teaching methods for course materials related to this goal	Indicate strengths and weaknesses in student achievement of the learning outcome	What changes, if any, do you plan for the next time you teach this course to improve student learning?	What actions can the department take to improve student weaknesses you identified?
[faculty member fills in]	[faculty member fills in]	[faculty member fills in]	[faculty member fills in]	[faculty member fills in]

Sample General Education Assessment Matrix

Example 1: A Large Catholic University with a Substantial General Education Requirement

This hypothetical example has been compiled from documents of several large Catholic universities.

General Education Learning Goals

1. To demonstrate the habit of reflective self-assessment aimed at developing self-knowledge, taking responsibility for one's own learning, monitoring one's intellectual and personal growth, and acting thoughtfully on one's beliefs

2. To participate competently in academic and civic discourse by writing and speaking effectively, by thinking critically and imaginatively, by conducting purposeful inquiry, and by using appropriate technological tools for research and analysis

3. To understand key concepts, perspectives, and methods in philosophy, religious studies, and mathematics and in representative disciplines in the natural sciences, the social sciences, and the humanities

4. To integrate and consolidate knowledge and learning from various core courses, cocurricular experiences, and courses

in the major into a worldview that is open to new ideas and persons, understands diversity and multicultural perspectives, and tolerates ambiguity

5. To articulate one's vision of social and environmental justice, to assess one's own personal commitment to justice, and to demonstrate actions taken to ameliorate injustice and to promote a better world

6. To demonstrate the ability to work with and for others; to translate beliefs, thoughts, values, and commitments into action, thereby becoming responsibly empowered in the world

General Education Curriculum

Phase 1: Foundations of Wisdom

- Introductory courses in philosophy, literature, history, fine arts, mathematics, laboratory science, and composition

- *Goals:* Develop foundational habits of academic life and cultural literacy; disciplinary ways of knowing and posing questions; conducting inquiry; making arguments; close reading, analysis, and critical thinking; numerical analysis and scientific method; effective writing and speaking; library and Internet research; systematic problem solving; empathic listening; rigorous study

Phase 2: Persons in Society

- Juxtaposes two social science courses with Philosophy of the Human Person and a religious studies course; creates opportunities for service learning

- *Goals:* Develop and refine skills of Phase 1; encounter and examine issues of multiculturalism, diversity, social justice, and citizenship

Phase 3: Responsibility and Service

- Four advanced courses, taken during junior and senior years, that help students develop and apply their knowledge and skills to contemporary problems and integrate their undergraduate learning: Ethics, Religious Studies, Interdisciplinary course, and Senior Synthesis

- *Goals:* Integrate learning; apply knowledge and skills to contemporary problems and ethical quandaries; self-reflective projects and narratives; connect past with future

Table L.1. Assessment of Gen Ed Goals

Assessment Measure (Office Where Data Originate)	Goal 1	Goal 2	Goal 3	Goal 4	Goal 5	Goal 6	How Data Are Used for Improvement
Senior student questionnaire (Institutional Research)	X	X		X		X	Not being well used at present, because questions related to core goals are not separately collected or reported to core instructors or committees.
Alumni questionnaire (Institutional Research)	X	X	X	X	X	X	As above.
Core goals questionnaire annually to all students in Senior Synthesis (Core Assessment Committee)	X	X	X	X	X	X	Reviewed annually by Core Assessment Committee and Senior Synthesis faculty.
Analysis of a sample of Senior Synthesis reflective narratives, using a rubric based on goals of Senior Synthesis (Core Assessment Committee)	X	X		X	X		Not working well at present because only about half the Senior Synthesis courses assign reflective narratives, and students often will not give permission for their narratives to be read by the committee.
Analysis of one student assignment in each core curriculum class, using an instructor-generated rubric based on core goals	X	X	X	X	X	X	Annual meetings by discipline of all faculty teaching core curriculum to share instructor analysis of students' strengths and weaknesses. Followed by discussion of pedagogical strategies. Written report and recommendations sent to Core Assessment Committee. Has been implemented only in composition so far.

**Recommendations for Improvement
in Assessment Processes**

1. Work with departments to achieve greater uniformity for Senior Synthesis courses, in working toward general education goals

2. Work with Institutional Research to determine whether student and alumni survey data, if disaggregated, could be useful to gen ed departments and faculty, and if so, how to manage and fund the disaggregation and distribution of those data

3. Expand the instructor reports from composition incrementally into other gen ed courses

4. Fund an annual workshop for gen ed faculty, especially new faculty, to reaffirm gen ed goals and discuss appropriate course design and pedagogy. Every four years, fund a week-long summer workshop, with stipends to the faculty, for an expanded version of the same purpose

Example 2: A Public, Two-Year, Open-Admissions College

Note: This hypothetical example has been compiled from documents of several community colleges

General Education Curriculum

One semester of composition must be taken by all students (about one-third of the students test out or enter with college-level composition credit gained in high school). Virtually all composition instructors are adjuncts.

General Education Curriculum Goals

Note that the college may have many other goals, but the general education curriculum consists of one course, and the assessment committee has decided, given the complexities of an adjunct faculty and a diverse student body, to address only these two goals:

1. Students will be able to write an essay in which they take a position on a debatable issue, support their position with evidence, and address counterarguments.

2. In small-group discussion, students will demonstrate respect for ideas, cultures, and values different from their own, while at the same time being clear about their own ideas and values and the evidence and reasoning behind them.

Table L.2. Assessment of Gen Ed Goals

Assessment Measure	Goal 1	Goal 2	How the Data Are Used for Improvement
Each faculty member annually submits two representative student argumentative essays at each grade level (A-F). The Composition Committee evaluates these, using the committee's rubric (which is shared with the instructors and students)	X		Committee works with any instructor from whom the committee's evaluation differs substantially. Overall results are aggregated for list of students' strengths and weaknesses, and these are discussed at composition faculty meetings, held twice a semester, with actions as needed to address pedagogy and curriculum.
Annual questionnaire to all students, asking students how well the institution so far has helped them learn to write well and to respect different races, cultures, and points of view (Institutional Research)	X	X	Institutional Research selects those students who have already taken a composition course and those who have not and reports the raw scores and the comparative scores to the Composition Committee, which shares them in faculty meetings for appropriate discussion and action.
Teaching mentors (experienced faculty chosen for their high teaching skills) will work with an instructor at his/her request, analyzing student work and/or discussions in his/her classroom and helping the instructor to achieve better student writing and discussion	X	X	The feedback loop goes directly from the Teaching Mentor to the instructor to be used for pedagogical change. To create a safe environment for the faculty member, free from influence of evaluation for reappointment, the information is not shared with the Composition Committee. A survey of faculty two years ago, inquiring about the effectiveness of faculty development for composition, asked whether the respondent had worked with a Teaching Mentor, and if so whether the work had been helpful.

Recommendations for Improvement in Assessment Processes

The rubric is problematic. Not all instructors submit their sample essays in a timely way. The committee's evaluation of the essays differs significantly from the instructor's in about 20 percent of the cases. Often the problems these instructors face are larger than just the evaluation of student work. The question then is, Who works with the instructor? The committee members, all volunteers, do not have the time or in some cases the expertise to work with the instructor whose assessments are off-base. The program chair also does not have the time. Teaching mentors have traditionally done their work confidentially, only at the faculty member's request, not at the behest of the committee, triggered by a disparity between the committee's and the instructor's evaluation of student work.

We recommend that a committee be formed to study and make recommendations about the evaluation rubric, its use by instructors and their students, and the process for helping instructors whose evaluations are disparate from those of the committee.

A Short List

The Really Short List

If I were to select just a few resources to augment this one, I would choose:

- Palomba, C. A., and Banta, T. W. (eds.). *Assessing Student Competence in Accredited Disciplines: Pioneering Approaches to Assessment in Higher Education.* Sterling, VA: Stylus, 2001. At 350 pages, it gives more extensive details on many of the subjects covered in this volume, and it is organized as a manual of advice to practitioners. The single most useful reference as an accompaniment to this short guide.

- Banta, T. W., Lund, J. P., Black, K. E., and Oblander, F. W. *Assessment in Practice: Putting Principles to Work on College Campuses.* San Francisco: Jossey-Bass, 1996. Contains 82 case studies of best practice, each in 2–3 pages—a wealth of practical ideas. 350 pages.

- Banta, T. W., and Associates. *Building a Scholarship of Assessment.* San Francisco: Jossey-Bass, 2002. Essays by leaders in the field, addressing practical issues, but focusing on developing a "scholarship of assessment." Bibliography provides recent references to more specialized works on designing and selecting assessment instruments and other topics. 300 pages.

- Subscribe to *Assessment Update* for the most recent examples and developments in assessment. Published monthly, it contains brief case studies of successful practice, updates on new developments, and reflections on issues of theory and practice. Order from the Web (www.josseybass.com) or by phone, 888–481–2665. Back issues are available.

- The American Association for Higher Education (AAHE) is the premier national higher education organization helping higher education institutions with assessment. Their conferences, web resources, and publications are an ongoing source of good information (www.aahe.org).

- Web pages and publications of your regional accreditor

- Conferences:

  - AAHE annual conference on assessment (www.aahe.org)

  - National Assessment Institute, held in Indianapolis at the conference center of the Indiana University-Purdue University Indianapolis, organized by Trudy Banta, one of the leading experts in assessment (www.planning.iupui.edu. Click on conferences).

  - Annual conferences of your regional or disciplinary accreditor

Additional, More Specialized Resources

- Astin, A. W. *Assessment for Excellence: The Philosophy and Practice of Assessment and Evaluation in Higher Education.* American Council on Education Series on Higher Education. Phoenix: Oryx, 1993. A thoughtful treatment of the values and theoretical frameworks behind various assessment practices, as well as very practical advice about gathering and interpreting data, from one of the most respected higher education researchers.

- Huba, M. E., and Freed, J. E. *Learner-Centered Assessment on College Campuses: Shifting the Focus from Teaching to Learning.* Needham Heights, MA: Allyn & Bacon, 2000.

- Lucas, A. F., and Associates. *Leading Academic Change: Essential Roles for Department Chairs.* San Francisco: Jossey-Bass, 2000. Collection of essays on leading change in departments. Essays by Gardiner and Angelo are especially valuable for guiding assessment.

- Messick, S. J. (ed.). *Assessment in Higher Education: Issues of Access, Quality, Student Development, and Public Policy.* Mahwah, NJ: Erlbaum, 1999. Places assessment in broader social and political contexts.

- Nichols, J. L. *Assessment Case Studies: Common Issues in Implementation with Various Campus Approaches to Resolution.* New York: Agathon Press, 1995; Nichols, J. O. *The Departmental Guide and Record Book for Student Outcomes Assessment and Institutional Effectiveness.* (2nd ed.) New York: Agathon Press, 1995; Nichols, J. O. *A Practitioner's Handbook for Institutional Effectiveness and Student Outcomes Assessment Implementation.* (3rd ed.) New York: Agathon Press, 1995. These are practical guides to an extensive assessment process, with illustrative case studies.

- Peterson, M. S., Augustine, C. H., Einarson, M. K., and Vaughan, D. S. *Designing Student Assessment to Strengthen Institutional Performance in Associate of Arts Institutions.* Stanford, CA: Stanford University, National Center for Postsecondary Improvement, 1999. Similar volumes, also 1999, on baccalaureate, comprehensive, and doctoral/research universities.

- Upcraft, M. L., and Schuh, J. H. *Assessment in Student Affairs: A Guide for Practitioners.* San Francisco: Jossey-Bass, 1996.

- Walvoord, B. E., and Anderson, V. J. *Effective Grading: A Tool for Learning and Assessment.* San Francisco: Jossey-Bass, 1998. Shows how the classroom grading process can be enhanced and how it can be used for assessment. Contains a case study of how a community college used the grading process for general-education assessment.

- Walvoord, B. E. "Assessment in Accelerated Learning Programs." In R. J. Wlodkowski and C. E. Kasworm (eds.), *Accelerated Learning for Adults: The Promise and Practice of Intensive Educational Formats.* New Directions for Adult and Continuing Education, no. 97. San Francisco: Jossey-Bass, 2003. An eleven-page summary of the approach of this volume, applicable not only to accelerated learning but also to traditional higher education.

- http://ericae.net provides links to what the sponsors consider some of the best full-text books, reports, journal articles, newsletter articles, and papers on the Internet that address educational measurement, evaluation, and learning theory

- http://ts.mivu.org. The online journal, *The Technology Source,* sponsored by Michigan Virtual University, contains an online index; look under "assessment—past articles." Practical ideas for classroom and institutional assessment of online courses as well as other computer-based applications such as online testing.

REFERENCES

Anderson, V. J., and Walvoord, B. E. "Conducting and Reporting Original Scientific Research: Anderson's Biology Class." In B. E. Walvoord and L. P. McCarthy, *Thinking and Writing in College*. Urbana, IL: National Council of Teachers of English, 1990.

Astin, A. W. *Assessment for Excellence: The Philosophy and Practice of Assessment and Evaluation in Higher Education*. American Council on Education Series on Higher Education. Phoenix: Oryx Press, 1993a.

Astin, A. W. *What Matters in College: Four Critical Years Revisited*. San Francisco: Jossey-Bass, 1993.

Astin, A. W. "Involvement in Learning Revisited: Lessons We Have Learned." *Journal of College Student Development*. 1996, 37(2), 123–134.

Banta, T. W., and Associates. *Building a Scholarship of Assessment*. San Francisco: Jossey-Bass, 2002.

Banta, T. W., Lund, J. P., Black, K. E., and Oblander, F. W. *Assessment in Practice: Putting Principles to Work on College Campuses*. San Francisco: Jossey-Bass, 1996.

Batra, M. M., Walvoord, B. E., and Krishnan, K. S. "Effective Pedagogy for Student Team Projects." *Journal of Marketing Education*, 1987, 9(2), 26–42.

Bergquist, W. H. *The Four Cultures of the Academy*. San Francisco: Jossey-Bass, 1992.

Chickering, A. W., and Ehrmann, S. C. "Implementing the Seven Principles: Technology as Lever." *AAHE Bulletin*, 1996, 49(2), 3–6.

Chickering, A. W., and Gamson, Z. F. "Seven Principles of Good Practice in Undergraduate Education." *AAHE Bulletin*, 1987, 39(7), 3–7.

Cooper-Freytag, L., Walvoord, B. E., and Denton, J. "A Case Study of Grading as a Tool for Assessment: One College's Story." In B. E. Walvoord and V. J. Anderson, *Effective Grading: A Tool for Learning and Assessment*. San Francisco: Jossey-Bass, 1998.

Ewell, P. T. "An Emerging Scholarship: A Brief History of Assessment." In T. W. Banta and Associates, *Building a Scholarship of Assessment*. San Francisco: Jossey-Bass, 2002.

Huba, M. E., and Freed, J. E. *Learner-Centered Assessment on College Campuses: Shifting the Focus from Teaching to Learning*. Needham Heights, MA: Allyn & Bacon, 2000.

Hutchings, P. (ed.). *Opening Lines: Approaches to the Scholarship of Teaching and Learning*. Menlo Park, CA: The Carnegie Foundation for the Advancement of Teaching, 2000.

Lucas, A. F., and Associates. *Leading Academic Change: Essential Roles for Department Chairs*. San Francisco: Jossey-Bass, 2000.

MacDonald, S. P., and Cooper, C. R. "Contributions of Academic and Dialogic Journals to Writing About Literature." In A. Herrington and C. Moran (eds.), *Writing, Teaching, and Learning in the Disciplines*. New York: Modern Language Association, 1992.

McClanahan, E. G., and McClanahan, L. L. "Active Learning in a Non-Majors Biology Class." *College Teaching*, 2002, 50(3), 92–96.

Messick, S. J. (ed.). *Assessment in Higher Education: Issues of Access, Quality, Student Development, and Public Policy.* Mahwah, NJ: Erlbaum, 1999.

Nichols, J. L. *Assessment Case Studies: Common Issues in Implementation with Various Campus Approaches to Resolution.* New York: Agathon Press, 1995a.

Nichols, J. O. *The Departmental Guide and Record Book for Student Outcomes Assessment and Institutional Effectiveness.* (2nd ed.) New York: Agathon Press, 1995b.

Nichols, J. O. *A Practitioner's Handbook for Institutional Effectiveness and Student Outcomes Assessment Implementation.* (3rd ed.) New York: Agathon Press, 1995c.

Palomba, C. A., and Banta, T. W. *Assessment Essentials: Planning, Implementing, and Improving Assessment in Higher Education.* San Francisco: Jossey-Bass, 1999.

Palomba, C. A., and Banta, T. W. (eds.) *Assessing Student Competence in Accredited Disciplines: Pioneering Approaches to Assessment in Higher Education.* Sterling, VA: Stylus, 2001.

Pascarella, E. T., and Terenzini, P. T. *How College Affects Students.* San Francisco: Jossey-Bass, 1991.

Peterson, M. S., Augustine, C. H., Einarson, M. K., and Vaughan, D. S. *Designing Student Assessment to Strengthen Institutional Performance in Associate of Arts Institutions.* Stanford, CA: Stanford University, National Center for Postsecondary Improvement, 1999.

Peterson, M. S., Augustine, C. H., Einarson, M. K., and Vaughan, D. S. *Designing Student Assessment to Strengthen Institutional Performance in Baccalaureate Institutions.* Stanford, CA: Stanford University, National Center for Postsecondary Improvement, 1999.

Peterson, M. S., Augustine, C. H., Einarson, M. K., and Vaughan, D. S. *Designing Student Assessment to Strengthen Institutional Performance in Comprehensive Institutions.* Stanford, CA: Stanford University, National Center for Postsecondary Improvement, 1999.

Peterson, M. S., Augustine, C. H., Einarson, M. K., and Vaughan, D. S. *Designing Student Assessment to Strengthen Institutional Performance in Doctoral and Research Institutions.* Stanford, CA: Stanford University, National Center for Postsecondary Improvement, 1999.

Pike, G. R. "Measurement Issues in Outcomes Assessment." In T. W. Banta and Associates, *Building a Scholarship of Assessment.* San Francisco: Jossey-Bass, 2002.

Roemer, M., Schultz, L., and Durst, R. "Portfolios and the Process of Change." *College Composition and Communication*, 1991, 42(4), 455–469.

Upcraft, M. L., and Schuh, J. H. *Assessment in Student Affairs: A Guide for Practitioners.* San Francisco: Jossey-Bass, 1996.

Walvoord, B. E., and others. *Academic Departments: How They Work, How They Change.* ASHE-ERIC Higher Education Reports, vol. 27, no. 8. San Francisco: Jossey-Bass, 2000.

Walvoord, B. E. "Assessment in Accelerated Learning Programs." In R. J. Wlodkowski and C. E. Kasworm (eds.), *Accelerated Learning for Adults: The Promise and Practice of Intensive Educational Formats.* New Directions for Adult and Continuing Education, no. 97. San Francisco: Jossey-Bass, 2003.

Walvoord, B. E., and Anderson, V. J. *Effective Grading: A Tool for Learning and Assessment.* San Francisco: Jossey-Bass, 1998.

INDEX

Cultures in Contention

Cultures in Contention

Judith Francisca Baca

Albert J. Camigliano

Ernesto Cardenal

Peter Dunn

Honor Ford-Smith

Martha Gever

Hans Haacke

DeeDee Halleck

Abbie Hoffman

Ross Kidd

Peter King

Tetsuo Kogawa

Leslie Labowitz

Suzanne Lacy

Loraine Leeson

Lucy R. Lippard

Fred Lonidier

Gabriel Garcia Marquez

Holly Near

Richie Perez

Arlene Raven

Bernice Johnson Reagon

Archie Shepp

Klaus Staeck

Günter Wallraff

Tom Ward

Douglas Kahn and Diane Neumaier, Editors

THE REAL COMET PRESS

Seattle  1985

Copyeditor: Elizabeth Gjelten.

Design: Nancy D. Roberts.

Manufactured in the United States of America.

First printing, 1985.

Library of Congress Cataloging-in-Publication Data

Main entry under title:

Cultures in contention.

Bibliography: p.
1. Arts and society—Addresses, essays, lectures. I. Kahn, Douglas, 1951-
II. Neumaier, Diane, 1946-
NX180.S6C86 1984 700'.1'03 84-16074
ISBN 0-941104-06-0 (pbk.)

85 86 87 88 89 90 10 9 8 7 6 5 4 3 2 1

CONTENTS

INTRODUCTION

CULTURES IN CONTENTION PRESENTS A
collection of articles detailing a broad range of
cultural activities that are motivated by the pursuit of
liberatory social and political change. By bringing
these articles together, we are arguing for an
understanding of cultural work different from, and
certainly preferable to, prevailing notions.

Contrary to conventional wisdom, culture is inex-
tricably bound up with larger social and political
realities. The practice, in concept or in action, of
isolating culture from these realities necessarily leads
to its impoverishment.

It's relatively easy to see the cultural-political link
when "culture" (that is, "cultures") is used in its
anthropological sense, because anthropology is more
apt to see these links as part of the totality of society.
However, when "culture" is used to designate "the
arts," people are suddenly reluctant even to entertain
the possibility that politics and culture are connected.
Such reluctance is difficult to maintain in light of the
type of work described in this collection—because the
"culture" here is situated between or, rather, amid
the anthropological and artistic senses. It is more
specific than the anthropological because it deals with
products and performances usually associated with
the arts; at the same time, it is more general than the
arts because it is conceived from the very beginning
in social and political frameworks.

Cultures in Contention seeks to reinstate an
understanding of the preeminently social character of
all cultural action. Most often, cultural products and
performances are cordoned off categorically accord-

ing to media or discipline and examined from the perspective of the individual practitioner. An emphasis on the *objects* of culture diminishes the real value of human *subjects*, and the emphasis on the individual artist all but denies the collective dimension of cultural production. A vicious cycle is set up when artists develop within an environment saturated with such notions—in a capitalist system which has this valorization of things over humans at its root—and go on to produce work alienated from social realities, thus providing confirmation for the original bias.

In contrast, the following pages chronicle the contributions of people who have so thoroughly integrated social realities into their work that the work itself is a means of acting on those realities. All of the authors are directly or closely associated with the activities they describe. These activities take place in differing social arenas: clandestine, community, small group, institutional, mass culture. Some are rooted in long, regenerative traditions; others have arisen in response to recent forms of encroaching technology and commodification into culture and daily life. They are carried out within capitalist or capitalist-dominated societies; even Nicaragua, the exception, is seeking to construct and reconstruct its culture in the face of protracted intervention from the United States. Although most take place in the U.S.A., work from Latin America and the Caribbean, West Germany, England, Kenya, Japan and Australia is also included. Yet national distinctions often break down, as issues and arenas are internationalized. West German-born, New York City-based artist Hans

Haacke exhibits his works on South Africa in England, while Washington, D.C.-based Sweet Honey in the Rock sings songs of Soweto in West Berlin.

Throughout this collection culture is understood in light of contending social forces—and for the understanding to be complete, those forces must be named. This process of *naming* stretches from stating and restating the (unstated) obvious to investigating and identifying realities that have been hidden. The process can be broken down into two approaches, based on whether the focus is on the dominated or dominating social group.

The first approach is self-naming, actively assuming an identity which has been suppressed, ending silence in a process of individual and collective empowerment. This approach is typified by Honor Ford-Smith in the opening sentences of her article on the Jamaican women's theater, Sistren:

> There exists among the women of the Caribbean a need for naming of experience and a need for communal support of that process. In the past, silence has surrounded our experience. We have not been named in literature or in history. The discovery through dialogue, through encounter with others, of the possibilities of our power can help us to shape the forces which, at present, still shape us.

She cites Paulo Freire for the conceptualization of this process, as does Ross Kidd in his contribution on the Kamīrīĩthu Community Educational and Cultural Center. (Freire outlines the concept in the third chapter of his *Pedagogy of the Oppressed*.)

9

Some practitioners refer to this approach as affirmative culture, because it affirms the collective empowering of a subjugated social group; they in turn reject the term "oppositional culture," because they have no desire to define cultural activity in reaction to, and therefore within the framework of, the oppressors. Yet, to be truly affirmative, there must be a continual recognition of the source of subjugation and identification of that source as part of a system that subjugates others as well. In other words, in order to be truly affirmative, it must be ultimately oppositional.

The naming of one's own reality is crucial because cultural self-representation is inseparable from political self-determination. Activists in the South Bronx at one point found their efforts on behalf of the community threatened by *Fort Apache, the Bronx*, a movie being made by Time-Life Films that painted a degrading picture of the people of the South Bronx, blaming them for causing the barbaric conditions it depicted. In his article on the organizing work of the Committee Against Fort Apache, Richie Perez points out that CAFA's demonstrations and critiques not only *opposed* the film's attempted naming of the community, but also *affirmed* its culture and the struggle of its people for their own betterment.

This type of dual program can also be seen in Suzanne Lacy and Leslie Labowitz's feminist media performance, *In Mourning and in Rage*. In order to counter the media sensationalism surrounding the Hillside Strangler case in Los Angeles, which delivered the message that women somehow deserved to be victims, Lacy and Labowitz structured an event to garner press coverage of their message: not simply mourning the victims but affirming women's power and capacity for resistance. In this way, *In Mourning and in Rage* and CAFA's work, along with similar efforts discussed in this collection, may be understood to incorporate both self-naming and the second approach to the naming process.

This approach has to do with those who, as ruling elites, have the resources and wherewithall to acknowledge their multifarious incursions into everybody's lives but are exceedingly reluctant to do so. In his book *Mythologies*, Roland Barthes discusses this phenomenon in terms of class.

> . . .[A]s an economic fact, the bourgeoisie is *named* without any difficulty: capitalism is openly professed. As a political fact, the bourgeoisie has some difficulty in acknowledging itself: there are no "bourgeois" parties in the Chamber. As an ideological fact, it completely disappears: the bourgeoisie has obliterated its name in passing from reality to representation, from economic man to mental man. It comes to an agreement with the facts, but does not compromise about values, it makes its status undergo a real *ex-nominating* operation: the bourgeoisie is defined as *the social class which does not want to be named*. (Emphasis in original.)

The task in the second approach, therefore, is to name those who do not want to be named. Yet those individuals, groups, corporations or even systems that have the luxury of choosing to be silent also have the means to counter and even prosecute those who effectively blow their cover. Thus, attempts to do so must be backed by thorough investigation and proof. Both Günter Wallraff and Klaus Staeck have been prosecuted in West Germany for their work; Staeck is sued so often that it's fortunate he's a lawyer. In certain circumstances, law itself can be dealt with as yet another unnamed representation of social domination. The Australian aboveground organization of underground billboard rectifiers, BUGA UP (described in Peter King's article), has countered this representation through protracted transgression of the law, to name the private concerns that have legal privilege over public spaces.

A particularly powerful form of this approach is to arrange for those who don't want to be named to name themselves—a public confession of sorts. This has always been the source of power for parody, but it has also taken on some contemporary variations, as in Abbie Hoffman's Wall Street action (where money changers were transformed suddenly into money grabbers) and in the French Situationists' concept of *détournement*, discussed in Tom Ward's article. Günter Wallraff provided a dramatic example (described in his article reprinted here) when he posed as a West German operative for a "sting," in which General Spinola revealed, among other things, his plans for a right-wing coup in Portugal.

There are many other frameworks within which we could discuss the activities presented in this collection, and there are many other such activities to consider. *Cultures in Contention* is a modest sampling;

it is obviously neither comprehensive nor fully representative. Some areas were deliberately underrepresented. We veered away from work—often a part of the "art world"—that may address sociopolitical themes but shows little understanding or concern for the social context in which it is engaged or exhibited; certain visual and performance art carried on outside the confines of the art world, as well as the work of artists such as Hans Haacke within it, demonstrates that this need not be the case. We also avoided other work, such as film, that has long been the subject of informative, critical and theoretical discussions in generally accessible publications. Similarly, we did not include a discussion of the visual and performance art associated with the international nuclear freeze movement, because its success has already created a good degree of popular awareness.

Some exclusions, however, were not deliberate. In a number of cases, we attempted unsuccessfully to solicit a contribution. (We still wonder how those who did write found time to do so.) We were unable to track down some interesting projects and, of course, were unaware of many others. Finally, practical necessity required that we reduce the collection to a manageable size.

The type of activities described in *Cultures in Contention* do not enjoy social visibility. They have been dealt with in a variety of small publications which, unfortunately, are often fleeting or difficult to locate. Like the activities they chronicle, these publications deserve greater support from progressives and the political Left. The larger leftist publications also need to give contentious culture its due; presently, their cultural reporting is narrowed down to mainstream art and film and then relegated to the "culture hole" in the back pages. In the opening comments to his article, Fred Lonidier broaches this problem and its counterpart: the glaring lack of critical and theoretical discourse among radical artists and intellectuals. One goal in publishing *Cultures in Contention* is to help build a basis for such discourse.

As a result of limited exposure to the kind of information offered in this collection, many cultural practitioners have had to reinvent and redevelop the wheels which propel their work. By bringing together the experience of many of them, we are trying to help alleviate this situation. We hope the following articles will serve as inspirations, provocations and even practical guides in promoting an increased level of cultural activism countering the vacuities and repressions of contemporary capitalist society.

Cultures in Contention had its beginnings at the ArtPolitik conference held in Seattle at and/or gallery in June 1981. We would like to acknowledge the support of Anne Focke, and/or, and our initial Board of Advisors: Suzanne Lacy, Lucy Lippard, Catherine Lord, and Martha Rosler. As the project grew in scope and ambition, we received invaluable assistance from many people, including contributors Judy Baca, Martha Gever, Hans Haacke, DeeDee Halleck, Fred Lonidier, Holly Near, and Tom Ward.

We also received crucial guidance from Eva Cockcroft, Jane Creighton, Felipe Ehrenberg, Stuart Ewen, Jill Hartman, and Roberto Vargas.

Unlike other anthologies in which most articles are reprints, the majority of these were written especially for this volume. In editing the submitted drafts, we received invaluable assistance from our copy editor Elizabeth Gjelten. It was her skillful attention and work with each writer, with the help of proofreader Pam Meidell, that brought the manuscripts to their present form. We would also like to thank Nancy Roberts, who did a superb job of designing the book; this was no easy task, given the diversity of materials.

We can hardly begin to thank our families—Doug's parents Sam and Ruby and Diane's parents Virginia and John—for their longstanding support, which preceded even the earliest notion of this book. To Diane's son Jed Lewison, who provided word processing skills, blind faith and patience with this project that constantly took attention away from him, and to Tom Abrams, whose insightful and practical input was only one part of his inexhaustible support, no thank you's will ever express full appreciation.

Lastly, we would like to heap infinite gratitude on Cathy Hillenbrand, who propelled this project—from its shaky beginnings as a glorified pamphlet to the present book—with her enthusiasm, support, and tolerance. If this anthology in fact belongs among the activities it anthologizes, it is due to her.

Douglas Kahn and Diane Neumaier

DANGER
KEEP OUT
DEEP WATER

WHAT
WHAT
GOING
BEHIN
OUR BAC

LONDON DOCKLANDS STRATEGIC PLAN

London Borough of New

Docklands

DOCKLANDS

ISLE OF DOGS 1980
A Consultation Report

Help Plan and Docklands
Housing

Help Plan Docklands

Help Plan Docklands

LOCAL LEGACY WORKS

Help Plan Docklands

The
Changing
Picture
Of
Docklands

by Peter Dunn
with
Loraine Leeson

The Changing Picture

We began working with trade unions and activist groups in 1977 in the belief that cultural production has a strategic role in social change. But the question of how it may act as a progressive or reactionary force is not simple or clear-cut; "good intentions" may be misdirected, and contradictions are endemic.

This essay is partly a description of progress to date, but its emphasis is on problems encountered, issues raised and glimpses at possible ways forward.

Photographs by Peter Dunn & Loraine Leeson

Of Docklands

IN ROW UPON ROW, LIKE BANKS OF HUGE SHINY MIRRORS, advertising billboards bounce back our self-image, refracted through the shimmering surface of consumer capitalism. Similarly in the movies, on television, in the images on buses and in the subway, our society's values, norms and goals are reflected, grinning, back at us. Like

by Peter Dunn with Loraine Leeson

the mirror behind the bar, they give the illusion of more social space, more glitter. Just as the billboards themselves hide the environmental blight behind them, so their looking-glass world obscures the underlying social, economic and emotional conditions of life under capitalism. But so what? Few people believe that these images present a true picture, any more than they do when they see their laterally inverted twin in the barroom mirror. Why then does the Left seem so obsessed with them? Each year, millions of words go into print which are devoted to these images: analyzing them, explaining their illusions, demonstrating how they work, and seemingly concluding what most people already know by experience. This is not to devalue such work; on the contrary, it is simply to point out that, in itself, such analysis does not diminish the ideological power that these images possess. It cannot perform a simple (or even a complex) exorcism merely by revealing the process of their construction; neither can it decrease any pleasure derived from their consumption. On the contrary, it serves to enhance this pleasure by adding another dimension to the reading of such images and actually may *create* pleasure, via a metadiscourse, even though the original material is regarded as distasteful or offensive on primary impact.

Where, then, does the power of these images lie, and how can the analysis of them be of use in the development of a socialist visual practice? Obviously these are large questions, and we shall not attempt to address all their ramifications here. However, if we are to describe our own practice, which operates in the public domain alongside these dominant representations, we should at least sketch some of the wider terrain before moving onto our specific site of struggle.

The question of power is crucial. Part of the power of dominant representations is clearly economic: their saturation of visual space enables them to appear widely diverse while preserving a subtextual consensus. They may often be stereotyped, formularized and exaggerated. Many of the goals with which they entice us are often clearly, and deliberately, unobtainable—and, as fantasy, that is part of their attraction. Yet they appeal to, and are grounded in, the values and norms which lubricate and regulate the social, economic and emotional transactions of life under capitalism. That is their consensus, their "truth." Of course this consensus is partly self-validating and self-reinforcing because of the pervasiveness of these representations. Nevertheless it has as its touchstone the lived experience: the economic and ideological transactions they refer to are all around us; the humor they draw upon, the racism and sexism, is all there. Yet clearly it *is* a distortion. And this is perceived more explicitly in the representation of goals—we "better ourselves by being good" at capitalist transactions, by going with the system rather than fighting it. There is a carrot and a stick. It is an *inversion* of how the majority of us could truly better ourselves.

Dunn/Leeson: *The Changing Picture of Docklands*

SIMPLE INVERSION

It is clear that the power of these dominant representations does not reside in creating a credible illusion, a simplistic "false consciousness." If this were so, it would be a relatively simple matter—armed with semiology—to shatter this illusion. The scales would fall from people's eyes and "reality" would be clearly visible. The motivation for change would be a natural outcome, and organizing to bring it about would be a simple matter of logistics—revolution as easy as A-B-C. That approach, and all its more convoluted variants, is no more than scientist idealism.

It is also not enough for a socialist cultural practice to be a crude mirror image of its capitalist counterparts—a kind of advertising agency for the Left, using easy slogans which gloss over the complexity of the issues. Knowledge is power, and the capitalist media deprives us of this power by giving us a lot of sensation, the hard sell in soft packaging, but very little hard information. That is why you cannot "sell" socialism like Brand X (or the Conservative Party),[1] because it only reinforces capitalist modes of representation and reduces socialism to just another promise or offer within the system.

Information, counterinformation, is therefore crucial to the struggle. A socialist practice should not obscure but rather reveal underlying social and economic conditions; it should expose ideology rather than mask it. (As we have already pointed out, this is not as simple as exposing "false consciousness.") This function is an element of the inversion process that cuts across all levels of socialist activity, not just the cultural. Another part of this process specific to the cultural, and particularly to the visual, is to throw into question the modes of representation themselves—the visual forms which act as vehicles for the passive, semi-conscious induction of ideology—the "consensus builders." But again, as we have stressed, this is not just a matter of making the process of construction visible or of illustrating semiological theory.[2] The politics of representation is not confined just to what lies within the frame of an image, its decoding and analysis. It concerns the wider questions of a total working process—its structure and context, who it represents and engages, and who—ultimately—it serves.

THESE QUESTIONS, AND THE contradictions inherent in attempting to develop a socialist practice within a capitalist society, certainly are not resolved easily. But they can at least be addressed. The process of building an alternative cultural practice is a cumulative and collective task: there is no single route, nor should there be if we are to develop the richness and variation necessary both to engage the many existing forms of bourgeois culture and to create the building blocks for the wide range of cultural expression that a truly democratic society would require. We do not believe our concerns to be the only concerns, nor our site of struggle the only site. We do, however, believe that working with trade unions and tenants' and activist groups is an important site.

This area is often neglected by cultural workers because of the real difficulties of winning trust and acceptance by these groups, who have learned by bitter experience to beware of middle-class do-gooders. But more often it is because many cultural workers fear that such acceptance can only be achieved either by compromising their "creative freedom" or by becoming ensnared in "parochial" concerns. On the other side of the coin, there is a lot of "romance of the worker" that needs to be demystified.

By discussing some of these questions and our attempts to resolve them—the mistakes and failures, as well as the steps forward—we hope to be of use to those striving in similar directions; we also hope that some of the more general issues raised will find an echo in others operating in very different contexts from our own. Before moving on to describe the work in more detail—how and, more importantly, why we arrived at our present orientation—we would like first to give a single example of what we mean by an inversion process that extends beyond the frame of the image; an example concrete enough to be descriptive but also metaphoric enough for a general approach.

Our current work uses billboards as one of its vehicles, a vehicle most commonly associated with capitalist forms of representation. Beyond the frame, what do they normally represent? They represent authority from above; on many levels, but fundamentally, and indeed physically, this is expressed by their imposition upon a community without any consultation or consent (except nominally through the

official planning process). In contrast, we began with the community. First, we were invited by local activists—because they knew our work and our approach—to address the issues surrounding redevelopment in London's Docklands. From there we held extensive discussions with local tenants' and activist groups to decide what was needed, what form the work should take, what strategies would be best for expressing their views, and what structure was required to ensure that these views represented them. (We will go into detail later about what this means in practice.)

In order to move these discussions into a formally constituted body capable of making decisions, a steering committee was formed comprising representatives from the tenants' and activist groups. Initially, members came from the groups with whom we had preliminary discussions, but others joined as interest grew and the project expanded; all the main areas of Docklands are now represented. The committee decides the main issues to be tackled, establishes priorities, and formulates strategy. Visualization of the issues is our contribution, and knowledge of the issues is the contribution of those on the front line, the people who live with their effects; but the dialogue between the politics of representation and the representation of politics is the essential dynamic. It is a two-way education process. The decision to use custom-made billboards and the general location came out of these discussions. However, the appropriate local tenants' organization chooses the specific sites. Apart from the many other ways in which these billboards are different from advertising ones (which we shall describe later), they are a direct result of community initiative, consultation and consent on a fundamental level—in their physical existence, in their structures and in their images. This is a total inversion of ideology and practice in both the role and use of billboards.

CONTEXT

One cannot arrive at such an approach overnight. Rarely does any established network exist with which one can easily link; one has to create new spaces and build new bridges. Even when a reasonably established political or community network exists, cultural struggle is always at the bottom of the agenda—if it is on the agenda at all. And the only way of giving cultural struggle credibility in such circumstances is to demonstrate tangibly that it is useful. That has to be established before any of its more subtle and indirect values can be argued successfully. Art school does not prepare you for this. On the contrary, one is taught to develop work which is useless in those terms. This is compounded by the pervasive ideology—those who are not involved in cultural production have a low expectation of its use value.

How then can one begin to change these expectations, both in oneself and in others, to develop useful cultural strategies and gain the experience to understand where they can be effective? Any socialist cultural practice operating within capitalism must, by its very position, have a questioning of its context as a baseline. But this seldom begins as a critique of the total system; it usually starts with a response to a directly felt contradiction between expectations and the lived experience—a perception of what should be against what is. Of course this happens all the time, but the point at which a pattern of behavior or practice shifts into a wider critique and translates into politicized action is crucial. It might therefore be useful at this point to describe briefly how we first embarked upon the direction that led to our present position and to note some of the major turning points along the way.

At art college in the early seventies, issues of "art and politics" were in the air, but, from the little one could find out about practices, they seemed rather remote and more metaphysical than dialectical. What was real, however, was the contradiction of being trained (sic) for a system that was rapidly becoming merely the nostalgia of our tutors—the booming art market and gallery network of the sixties. The work that had mushroomed during that period was still being pushed at art schools, and its naive "formalist-revolutionary" hedonism[3] seemed hollow, superficial and so inward looking that communication was difficult between different studios—those of the "hard edge" or "soft edge"—let alone outside the

department. This was set against a background of education cuts, of the miners' confrontation with the government and the "three-day week,"[4] of student demonstrations and occupations—all of which seemed more vital than the listless art world and its stylistic squabbles.

We had arrived at a position where we believed there had to be a better way to produce and use art but had only a sketchy analysis of the existing structures and even less knowledge of how to change it. We began working together, probably for mutual support rather than for ideological reasons, doing group works which sometimes involved students from other faculties and colleges. These works began by questioning the role of art but soon moved on to take in the education system and its ideology. However, these early works never really extended beyond the immediate educational or art context; they were as incestuous in their way as the work we criticized, and we still saw them as peripheral to our individual work, our "real" work. They had, however, served as an arena where we could make useful mistakes and had provided indications for ways forward. We resolved when we left college to try and develop a practice outside the traditional art network—a "social practice."

Once outside the protective womb of the art world, its network and discourse, we quickly discovered that any naive "art and society" notions were worse than useless: it is not a question of making a relationship between "art" and "society"—that already exists—the point is to change them both. We learned that artists, as individuals, cannot hope to contribute to such change merely by presenting a visual drop in an ocean of bourgeois perceptions. We realized it was necessary to work collectively, in collaboration with those striving for similar goals. This may not mean physically working together; the main thing is solidarity. A socialist cultural practice within a capitalist society cannot exist in isolation. It needs support; it needs roots in the struggle of the working class and the dispossessed.

Of course there are many sites of struggle, many levels of racial and sexual dispossession that cannot be reduced to simple economic analysis, and there are as many ways of tackling them and creating bonds of solidarity. Probably the best way of describing our route is to discuss some of the problems and contradictions which earlier works brought out, along with our attempted solutions. Because the theoretical base was developed out of this process

19

Dunn/Leeson: *The Changing Picture*

rather than imposed on it, and because it has been discussed at length elsewhere,[5] we shall confine ourselves to those issues which arose directly from the work and its context.

The Present Day Creates History (1977) was a series of exhibitions in two towns, one in the Northeast of England and one in the Southeast, which examined their development from the turn of the century to the present day. Comprising predominantly image and text, it contrasted the future projected by generations of planners, developers, commercial interests and advertisers with the lived reality—using people's recollections, diaries, snapshots, family albums, medical records, and so forth. It was based upon Brecht's idea of taking the ordinary, the familiar, the "given," and shifting the ideological perception of it: "The audience no longer takes refuge from the present day in history—*the present day becomes history.*"[6] (Emphasis added.) The intention was that the familiar and "given"—the houses, streets, facilities and institutions—would be shown within a perspective of change and, by implication, seen as a site of future change and intervention. We wanted the body of work eventually to become a cultural resource which might also act as a political tool: a kind of people's history on one side—of struggles to unionize, organize or just survive—and on the other an analysis of capitalist organization and its development in those towns from an early capitalist structure at the turn of the century to the multinationalism of today. It was incredibly ambitious and, apart from the visual and design problems (which we will not go into here),[7] it raised a number of fundamental contradictions about our approach.

Let us begin with the economic base. As is normal in art practice, we were doing the work "free of strings;" that is to say we saw ourselves as free agents, not allied to any organization, initiating the work ourselves on our perception of its value, scratching together material costs from our own meager resources and applying for grant aid from arts bodies (which was not forthcoming). Apart from the limitations that lack of money imposed, this approach hampered the collaborative element which was essential to the intended catalytic role of the work. People were confused and sometimes suspicious because they did not understand our motives or who we were representing: Were we doing it for charity? Who were the beneficiaries? What was the purpose? Did we see ourselves as cultural missionaries or political cadres? The final results reflected this lack of clarity in our motives.

This is not to deny that some good things came out of it: it generated some interest at the time and is now a permanent resource housed in a library in one of the towns. But its position, as an archive, makes it a more likely haunt of middle-class researchers and local historians than a political tool of working-class people, our initial intention. As such, the work has some value in presenting an alternative interpretation of the history, if only to those researchers, but it must also be acknowledged that the format—of seductive sepia images and dense text—placed more emphasis on visual nostalgia. Our intention was reversed: many members of our audience appeared to "take refuge from the present day in history." In retrospect, the impetus for change this work represented probably pointed more to our approach than to the social and political questions it tried to engage.

This realization, together with the particular demands of a campaign, made our next piece of work very different. The Bethnal Green Hospital was about to be closed as a result of government spending cuts. The opposition to this threat was one of the first campaigns of resistance against government attacks on services that had been achieved through a century of working-class struggle. In this case we were no longer trying to be "instigators" but were simply part of a whole range of forces with a common purpose which was clear and concrete: it was obvious what we were doing and why. We were already working in the area on a Regional Arts Association Film/Video Fellowship, running workshops for adults and children. We were also funded for other activities of our own choosing; one of these was to produce a video tape for the hospital campaign. We then began making posters, paid for out of campaign funds, followed by an exhibition/resource that was housed in the hospital entrance during the

***Passing the Buck*. Full-color montage, published as a poster (A2) by East London Health Project and as a postcard by Leeds Postcards.**

THE TRANSFER PRICE GAME
1. Take a product like Valium (original price £20 per kilo),
2. Pass it through your subsidiaries, preferably using tax havens,
3. Raise the price substantially at each transfer,
4. But ensure final transaction only shows a "reasonable profit,"
5. Sell your product to the NHS at £370 per kilo,
6. Collect 1,850% profit, avoiding DHSS scrutiny on excessive profits.
OBJECT: to prove your firm "operates and may be expected to operate against the public interest" (Monopolies Commission report on Roche's activities).

THE THIRD WORLD GAME
1. Take an untried drug like injectable steroid contraceptives,
2. Get "consent" for testing from illiterate or low income groups,
3. Usual test groups: 75% black, 25% coloured—no whites!,
4. If drug works, sell expensively in developed countries,
5. If not, or too many side effects, sell to third world,
6. If dangerous, do not release test results—hush it up.
OBJECT: to maximise profits at lowest possible outlay whilst maintaining a reputation for high standards of safety.

THE CONTROL GAME
1. Ensure the drug companies are not nationalized,
2. Send each GP 1cwt of advertising per month, plus lots of "free gifts,"
3. Ensure doctors prescribe by brand name, not by generic name,
4. Maintain and exploit patent rights as long as possible,
5. Only list possible side effects if required by law,
6. Keep all your activities as secret as possible.
OBJECT: to put greed before need—winner takes all.

Dunn/Leeson: *The Changing Picture of Docklands*

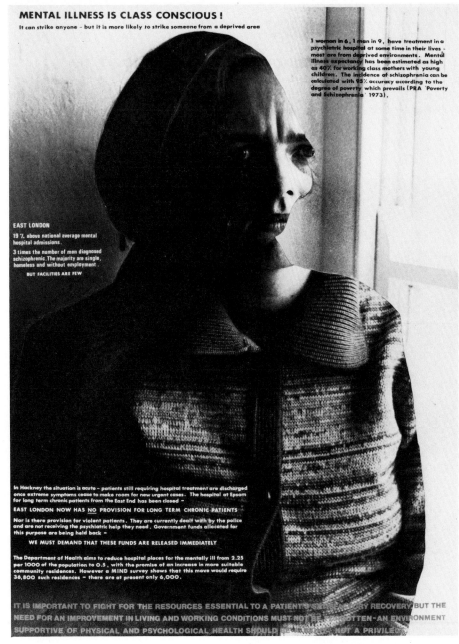

MENTAL ILLNESS IS CLASS CONSCIOUS!
It can strike anyone – but it is more likely to strike someone from a deprived area

1 woman in 6, 1 man in 9, have treatment in a psychiatric hospital at some time in their lives – most are from deprived environments. Mental illness expectancy has been estimated as high as 40% for working class mothers with young children. The incidence of schizophrenia can be calculated with 95% accuracy according to the degree of poverty which prevails (PRA 'Poverty and Schizophrenia' 1973).

EAST LONDON
19% above national average mental hospital admissions.
3 times the number of men diagnosed schizophrenic. The majority are single, homeless and without employment.
BUT FACILITIES ARE FEW

In Hackney the situation is acute – patients still requiring hospital treatment are discharged once extreme symptoms cease to make room for new urgent cases. The hospital at Epsom for long term chronic patients from the East End has been closed –
EAST LONDON NOW HAS <u>NO</u> PROVISION FOR LONG TERM CHRONIC PATIENTS
Nor is there provision for violent patients. They are currently dealt with by the police and are not receiving the psychiatric help they need. Government funds allocated for this purpose are being held back –
WE MUST DEMAND THAT THESE FUNDS ARE RELEASED IMMEDIATELY
The Department of Health aims to reduce hospital places for the mentally ill from 2.25 per 1000 of the population to 0.5, with the promise of an increase in more suitable community residences. However a MIND survey shows that this move would require 36,800 such residences – there are at present only 6,000.

IT IS IMPORTANT TO FIGHT FOR THE RESOURCES ESSENTIAL TO A PATIENT'S RECOVERY BUT THE NEED FOR AN IMPROVEMENT IN LIVING AND WORKING CONDITIONS MUST NOT BE FORGOTTEN-AN ENVIRONMENT SUPPORTIVE OF PHYSICAL AND PSYCHOLOGICAL HEALTH SHOULD NOT BE A PRIVILEGE

Mental Illness is Class Conscious.
Two-color poster (A2), published by the East London Health Project.

campaign. This presented the broader context of the campaign—the "economic crisis"—and, in collaboration with other campaigns, provided information on issues such as the authorities' dirty tricks, information gathering, mobilization and public support. This work was subsequently used by other campaigns and by Fightback, the national campaigning organization that emerged from those early struggles.

This exhibition continued the resource idea begun in *The Present Day Creates History*, but its focus was clearer, its content more militant and its use overtly one of struggle and implicitly one of reflection.

The form of the work had also clarified. In the previous work, text and image were separate and linear, complementary narratives. For example, there would be a chronological arrangement of images from one town accompanied by text; below, a parallel arrangement represented the development of the other town. The text did not necessarily refer directly to an accompanying image but might refer to something else happening at the same time; it was used in a more oblique way to reestablish a context for the images, to reinsert the photographs—those "frozen instants"—back into the changing flow of events from which they were torn. However, this relied on a very complex reading. It was necessary to keep in mind the horizontal development—the additive chronology of both image and text—and at the same time to make vertical comparisons and juxtapositions between the visual and textual representations of both towns. Given the density and the amount of material involved, it was difficult to maintain a focus.

In the Bethnal Green Hospital campaign, however, rapid and direct communication of information was necessary. The more deliberately *constructed* form of montage allowed us to deal with complex issues with closer juxtaposition and to use image and text in a more symbiotic relationship. This work fell basically into two categories: that produced to be used directly as tools for enlisting support—the outgoing active element—and that produced to document the continuing experience of the struggle as it progressed—the reflective element. These elements did not exist independently but were dialectically linked and acted upon one another during the campaign; however, their function changed once the campaign was over. The more immediate and specific work had only a limited span of usefulness, and the exhibition/resource could only be shown in one location at a time. For this reason we resolved to expand this idea into large edition prints that could be widely distributed. This formed the basis of the *East London Health Project*.

The impetus for this project, begun in 1979, came from the East London Trades Councils. These councils comprise representatives from the trade unions active in a given area, usually corresponding with the boundaries of borough councils (local government). However, their activities are centered on the wider social and political issues of the area rather than on the traditional concerns of the workplace. They also serve to coordinate interunion activity where necessary. As a result of the Bethnal Green Hospital campaign (which won a limited victory), the trades councils decided that the scope of campaigning should be broadened to encompass the wider health issues of the area, using some of the visual means we had deployed in defense of the hospital. They were particularly interested in our device of combining the visual impact of a poster with the more in-depth information a pamphlet might contain—a kind of visual pamphlet rather than just simple slogans. Following discussion with the trades councils about how the project should proceed, a steering committee—comprising the relevant unions, tenants' groups and ourselves—was set up to discuss themes, investigate further contacts for research, and carry out other activities. We were left more or less to our own devices on the synthesis of information and visual decisions, though designs and drafts were discussed and approved before anything went into print. Later, as a result of response from the first edition, stronger links were developed with other groups such as Radical Statistics, Politics of Health, and Science for People, who helped not only with compiling information and research but also with distribution and making suggestions for issues.

This not only gave us a much firmer economic base—the trades councils provided initial funds, and sales of posters provided ongoing finances—but also created a stronger network of solidarity. That network expanded as the posters extended beyond East London, both in

terms of content and distribution, to encompass both national and, in certain cases, international perspectives. The work is still going on, but because of the nature of its economic base—we have to wait for money to come in from a previous batch of posters before producing the next batch—it operates on a stop-and-go basis. However, as a result of this work and the lessons learned, we could begin to develop the context of our current work to extend the politics of representation beyond the frame of the images.

***Women Beware of Man Made Medicine*.** **Two-color poster (A2), published by the East London Health Project in conjunction with the Women's Health Centre Information Collective.**

Dunn/Leeson: *The Changing Picture of Docklands*

THE CHANGING PICTURE OF DOCKLANDS

As stated earlier, our current work—the *Docklands Community Poster Project*—has a steering committee made up of representatives from the trades councils and local tenants' and activist groups in London's Docklands. The issues surrounding Docklands redevelopment are highly complex, and it is possible to give only the briefest of sketches here. The area has a history of social deprivation and militant struggle, not only by the dockworkers but also by the communities surrounding the docks; the local women have their own tradition of activism, and it was here that the early suffragette movement enlisted most of its working-class support.

The most recent chain of events, however, began in the late sixties when the dockworkers had just won the battle to establish security of employment. Containerization of cargo, however, allowed the employers to change the rules of the game: new docks were built at the Thames estuary, making the old docks, as well as the industry and communities built around them, redundant. Some of the dockworkers moved, but because the new cargoes required less labor many people were still left unemployed. A downward spiral developed rapidly as dock-related industry and upriver transport declined, leading to increased rates for remaining industries and thus forcing them either to move or face economic difficulties.

By the mid-seventies the situation was becoming desperate, and redevelopment was seen as the only solution. However, the proximity of Docklands to the City of London (the center of finance), along with the policies of a then-Conservative government, led to all kinds of laissez-faire land speculation. Although nothing was built, land prices escalated to the point where real development became uneconomic—the oil crisis and accompanying economic uncertainty put the last nail in the coffin of this approach. A subsequent Labour government limited this kind of speculation by introducing a law tying the purchase of land more closely to genuine use. It also gave power and money for redevelopment to the labor-controlled Docklands borough councils. In consultation with local tenants' and activist groups, the councils devised a plan to introduce a mix of small manufacturing industry, some office development, and high quality public housing (low rise with gardens and parkland)—which was desperately needed to relieve the long waiting lists for housing and to transfer many of the people in high-rise and very old and decaying accommodations.

This plan was just getting under way as the Thatcher government came to power. By special act of parliament, the Conservatives removed powers from the democratically elected local councils and instituted a Development Corporation answerable directly to the central government. All public housing has been halted, and the contradictory policy of state-aided "market forces" has been introduced: selling off land to the highest bidder by offering incentives such as rate-free periods, grants and relaxation of all kinds of regulations within an "Enterprise Zone." Basically Docklands is being used as a test bed for Thatcherist policies of restructuring capital and smashing resistance; the Enterprise Zone concept and the strategy of removing local democracy has now been introduced throughout other parts of Britain (especially in areas of labor control). The local communities of Docklands are not taking this lying down, however; their history has taught them valuable lessons in organization and resistance. With the growing realization that they have nothing to lose, that it is a question of fight or go under, the momentum is building and the struggle for Docklands is on.

The nature and complexity of these issues are crucial factors in determining the form of the work. We cannot discuss the complexities here, as we have said, but suffice it to say that we are dealing with change, not only of the social and physical environment imposed by the Development Corporation and developers, but also the shifts in attitude and action taking place in the communities as a result of the struggle. This complexity must be unfolded over a period of time, both to deal with the issues in the depth required and to accommodate new developments as they arise. It also requires different levels of response to tackle the long-term general questions on one hand and, on the other, the immediate, specific and localized issues (in such a large area, different locales have different problems).[8]

The billboard images, therefore, are not designed in the usual format in which a static single image attempts to "sum up" an issue. They are giant photomontages made up from portable sections which are changed piecemeal, transforming the images gradually—rather like a slow animation process—to reveal different aspects of the same issue or relationships between issues. The sequence unfolds by means of a visual metaphor: the billboard becomes literally "The Changing Picture of Docklands."

The idea of using portable sections is not only a means of creating a more dialectical relationship between the form and content; it is also an economic question. We cannot afford to make these large images as multiple prints, disposable after use on a single site like advertising posters. By mounting them and sealing them against the weather, however, we are able to use them on a series of sites. As each section is taken down from one site, it is moved to the next, eventually following a circuit throughout Docklands; each site will display a different stage in the sequence at any given time. Underneath each billboard, a smaller panel is used to display photographs of the previous changes. This "predella" is to ensure that any single image or stage in the sequence is seen in the context of its history, even for the casual visitor to the site.

The images are photographically enlarged in black and white, also for economic reasons. This limitation, however, has served to make us much more discerning in our use of color, which is applied by hand. In advertising, full-color imagery is the norm, partly because it is an easy way of providing the slick glossy presentation which confers status on both product and advertisers, but mainly because of its seductive qualities—and seduction is the name of the game. In this context, a black-and-white image has more impact precisely because it does not conform to the norm. And often the stark black and white is more appropriate to the subject—not seduction but alienation. (Article text continued on page 29)

The Changing Picture of Docklands. **Actual size 18 x 12 feet, photomontage and applied color. Seven from a series sited on billboards in London's Docklands, by Peter Dunn and Loraine Leeson.**

BIG MONEY IS MOVING IN

BIG MONEY IS MOVING IN

Massive luxury riverside
development
— public housing cut to nil
Large enterprises moving in

Dockland boroughs unemployment 80000+
Planned public housing scrapped 5000+
Housing waiting lists—
Tower Hamlets 9500+
Southwark 9000+
Newham 6700+

If you had £10 for each person on the waiting lists you might just be able to buy a penthouse flat in St. Johns Wharf

THE SCRAP HEAP

WHARVES

Is this the way to draw the community into planning?

Dockland boroughs unemployment 80000+
Planned public housing scrapped 5000+
Housing waiting lists—
Tower Hamlets 9500+
Southwark 9000+
Newham 6700+

If you had £10 for each person on the waiting lists you might just be able to buy a penthouse flat in St. Johns Wharf

THE SCRAP HEAP

SHATTERING THE DEVELOPERS' ILLUSIONS

There has been a lot of talk about land – the planning of land, land for this, land for that. But Docklands is not about land, it's about people. And the birthright of the people is being sold off. Although the people have never owned the land, they've lived on it, worked on it and died on it. It is their heritage – it should be their future.

Pat Hanshaw, Association of Wapping Organisations

However, color is useful on a number of levels, and we tend to apply it to create emphasis, enhance juxtaposition, and extend the process of distancing by moving in and out of, and sometimes violently interrupting, illusions of the "real." The process of stretching and challenging the illusion of photographic "truth" is implicit as a baseline for political photomontage, but this use of color, occasional shallow relief, and changes in scale are opening up new opportunities for extending the process.

To date, the images on the billboards—which we have titled photomurals as another way of marking their difference from advertising billboards—have begun by raising questions and dealing with a general scenario. The first cycle of eight changes opens with an image of corrugated iron, symbolizing the dereliction of vast areas of Docklands. On one side it is covered with posters from the many campaigns waged in Docklands over the past decade; on the other side stands a dustbin stuffed with the consultation documents of the previous administration. Across the center a scrawled graffiti caption reads: "What's Going On Behind Our Backs?" In stages, the corrugated iron is taken down to reveal the "City" skyline;[9] as further exposure takes place, one realizes that the buildings are really stacks of money. As the foreground is revealed, the money is seen to be crushing people and pushing them over the edge of an abyss. The money is in naturalistic color; everything else is in black and white. When the bottom section of this image is changed, the perspective shifts and the viewpoint is from down in the abyss, looking up. As people pour over the edge, they fall down to join the remnants of scrapped housing and industry. Throughout this transition the image has gradually transformed from photomontage to drawing; viewed from further down in the scrap heap, a developer's hand (in color) is shown executing this drawing with a gold pen. The changing text throughout this sequence deals with how luxury development has proliferated whilst all council housing has been scrapped, how one of the highest unemployment levels in Southeast England is rising because high profit/low employment schemes are pushing out remaining local employers; and how public land and resources are being used to benefit profiteering developers whilst the needs of the local community are ignored. How-

ever, this image, the "developers' illusion," is then shattered by another set of representations showing the community fighting back: they literally burst through the "scrap heap," which falls away to reveal an image of a community conscious of its heritage of struggle and united in the fight for its future. Full color is applied here, not in a photo realist way but to enhance the mood of celebration.

The methods for making these changes are also evolving as we become more experienced. For example, in the first set of four changes, we used a simple rectangular panel structure, which also corresponded with the way corrugated iron fences are constructed; but as we progressed, different-shaped structures were introduced, like a jigsaw, and shallow relief was employed in the shattering sequence to further extend the photographic perspective.

The siting of the billboards is a key element in this gradual unfolding of the issues. Unlike the conventional advertising approach, which seeks maximum exposure with the minimum of content—just enough to arrest the fleeting glance of a passing motorist on a busy highway—our billboards are located where people are likely to congregate regularly: near where they live, where they will be on foot and are able to spend more time looking at the images. For example, our first site in Wapping is adjacent to the only shopping center in the area, opposite the health center and an open space with seating facing the billboard.

The billboard structures are custom-made for a number of reasons. First, as mentioned earlier, commercial sites are aimed mainly at passing motorists; working-class residential areas are usually off the beaten track as far as commercial advertising is concerned. Second, it is cheaper in the long run to build a billboard than to rent one; commercial billboards are, after all, profit-making products in themselves. Third, it allows us to construct them in such a way as to distinguish them from advertisements—by format, color, title board, form and content of the images. Finally, because the project technically owns these structures, they can be turned over for a variety of other community uses once the project ceases to function in its present form. Community groups could use them directly, or schools and youth centers could produce panels for them; a whole range of possibilities opens up once they have been established.

Dunn/Leeson: *The Changing Picture*

COUNTERATTACK

At the time of writing we have four operational sites and a further four planned for construction over the next few months; we will have two in each of the Docklands boroughs and two at strategic locations outside the area. These sites are not acquired without a struggle, and counterattacks from the opposition are an ever-present fact of life.

This began right at the outset at the fund-raising stage. Our main funding comes from the Greater London Council (GLC), which is at present under the control of a radical left administration (whose policies we shall describe later). They of course were very supportive, but the Conservative opposition members of the council and the nonelected, supposedly nonpolitical officers were so outraged that they took the rare precedent of referring the application to full council instead of handling it in the normal way at the committee level. Funding was eventually approved, but not without considerable delay and a battle at each stage of the process. Then with the announcement of funding came attacks from the right-wing press. In both cases our steering committee was invaluable: they wrote letters of support, rallied political allies, gave television interviews and generally countered all accusations of "extremist outsiders" which the opposition used in an attempt to discredit us.

Our first site, in Wapping, was approved before the Development Corporation took power in Docklands, but subsequent sites came under their jurisdiction. Our next site, not surprisingly, was refused planning permission on grounds that it was "too prominent" and "detrimental to the amenity of the local residents." As we said earlier, local residents had chosen this site precisely because of its prominence. The corporation, following its normal practice, had not consulted residents since it knows best what residents want—whether they like it or not. Interestingly, they were so eager to process our application—which they did in record time—that they even broke a courtesy arrangement for allowing the local council to comment on the application. (Not that this matters much; they have no obligation to consult with local councils and, more often than not, ignore their wishes.) We appealed the decision to the Department of Environment—the very government department which set up the corporation in the first place. We lost in spite of having a good legal case, but they were embarrassed by the ensuing publicity and approved our next site. Unfortunately, that is certainly not the end of the matter; each site has to be fought tooth and nail.

Our most serious setback happened on 31 March 1983. Late in the afternoon preceding the Easter bank holiday weekend, a team of demolition contractors went to Wapping and smashed our first photomural. They left the remains, sharp pieces of steel and jagged wooden splinters, half-balanced across some unused swings in an exposed position next to a children's playground, to "make it safe." Why was this photomural dangerous? Differing accounts of the incident from the various official departments involved were contradictory to say the least, but they all closed ranks around the assertion that it had nothing to do with the content of the images—it was a matter of "crossed wires."

Before we examine what they meant by this, let us explain something about the timing of the demolition. Most controversial demolitions, such as those to listed buildings,[10] happen just before bank holiday weekends when all official channels close down for several days. There are also a number of interesting coincidences which have no bearing on the matter; however, paranoia bids me record them: the project's continued funding was up for review at the time and the Wapping photomural was our only operational site; the "Plan for Wapping"[11] had just been published, and a campaign by the Association of Wapping Organizations—represented on our steering committee—was about to be launched; and a Select Committee of Parliament was about to visit the area.

Now to the technicalities. The photomural had all the necessary licenses and planning consent. It had, however, suffered some distortion due to exceptionally high winds, as had other nearby structures used by commercial advertisers (which were not demolished). Unlike these other billboards, our photomural was being reinforced by the construction firm that had built it. The firm was in contact with the borough surveyor, who had inspected the site on the very morning of the day in question and was satisfied with the action being taken. Hours later, without warning

or any communication with us, the building contractor or the borough surveyor, the district surveyor used his "powers of discretion" and ordered the demolition team in. The portable panels could have been removed easily and at short notice if there had been any indication of such action, but they were smashed along with the structure and strewn all around the site. Furthermore, the demolition itself was unorthodox: instead of the normal practice of unbolting the backing board from its supports and lowering it to the ground, they sawed through the supports and toppled it. The final irony is that the district surveyor is employed by the GLC, which funds the project, although he does have the power to act on his own discretion and on information or complaints by other parties. (We have never managed to establish who this may have been, though we have our suspicions.) The matter was raised at the full council of the GLC, where the district surveyor's action was described as "high-handed, totally unnecessary and wholly unacceptable." Investigations are continuing, but in the meantime the photomural has been rebuilt with funding by the GLC.

There have also been other incidents, perpetrated by persons unknown, such as the theft of an eighteen-by-twelve-foot paste-up board and other items from the project's workshop; this would have required a lot of effort, not to mention a very large vehicle, for what could have only been a very small economic gain. But in an area where, over the past decade, an unusually high number of listed buildings on prime development sites have "accidentally" caught fire, such incidents are no longer surprising.

We will not be put off by such setbacks. After all, if you are trying to do work which exposes the raw nerves of the powerful forces in society, then you should not be surprised by reflex action. Indeed such incidents only serve to harden our resolve, to give further impetus to erect more photomurals—even if they have to be sited on the borders of Docklands, outside the corporation's jurisdiction—and to underline the necessity of presenting the obverse side of the shiny new Docklands coin presented by the public relations of the government and its Development Corporation.

Demolished photomural (31 March 1983).

Dunn/Leeson: *The Changing Picture of Docklands*

FLEXIBILITY

The billboards, however, are only one aspect of the project's activities. Immediate and localized struggles tend to arise quickly and require swift action. The large billboard images, by the nature of their production and planned sequences, cannot meet these needs. The production of artwork for leaflets, publications, small-scale single-issue posters, and photo-documentation work are therefore an important part of the project's work. This work is crucial, not only as a means of directly contributing to the struggle at hand, but as an umbilical cord which maintains contact with the nitty gritty. It is, after all, through these struggles that the issues become crystallized and are made concrete. It is the tenants' and activist groups who are on the front line: they have the deepest knowledge of the issues and the experience of tactics and timing. If we lose contact with this and concentrate solely on the images and longer-term strategies, our work could degenerate into a once-removed and rarefied activity, out of touch with the day-to-day facts of life in Docklands. Flexibility is crucial if we are to be able to respond to the demands which are constantly growing and changing.

Beginning almost as a by-product of this work, an archive of negatives and visual materials that document key events in Docklands now serves as an image bank both for ourselves and the activist groups. We also hope to use this material as the basis for a future touring exhibition and have already made a start with a series of five laminated exhibition panels called "Community Action WINS" (an acronym for the four main districts of Docklands: Wapping, Isle of Dogs, Newham, Southwark). The panels document successful struggles by the riverside communities over the last decade.

Another recent project is the People's Plan, a local alternative to redevelopment for the Royal Docks in Newham. Funded by the Popular Planning Unit of the GLC, a locally run center has been set up to gather research and present the plan to a public inquiry into the future of the Royals. Drawing on the experience of dock workers, tenants' organizations, trade unionists and others, it aims to establish an integrated economic and social struc-

"**Single Issue**" **poster from the Docklands Community Poster Project, A2 silkscreen print; red, white and black.**

ture based upon the real needs and aspirations of the community. We provide the visual materials for discussions, publications and presentation of proposals. We hope eventually to supplement this kind of material with an historical perspective reaching back to the dock workers' struggles early in the century, and to keep adding contemporary material to bring it up to date. Besides touring in Docklands, such an exhibition could be used to place the current situation in context for those living outside the area and could travel to such places as Liverpool, where similar developments are taking place. It also has an international dimension in the sense that it shows a model of Thatcher/Reagan policies of "restructuring" at work and offers some lessons of resistance.

As the intentions of the government and its Development Corporation are made explicit by their actions—as the smoke screen clears—the communities of Docklands are forced more and more into confrontation. The immediate issues become less about differences in ideology and approach, as it was in the "honeymoon period," and more about struggles for basic survival. The demand for quick-response material is therefore increasing so rapidly that our present resources are stretched to their limits. However, the project has recently taken on another full-time worker, Sandra Buchanan, and two part-time workers, Belinda Kidd and Tony Minnion.

FUNDING

Initial funding for the project came from Tower Hamlets Arts Committee. This committee, formally an advisory body of the borough council's amenity committee, is unique in both its actual powers and its composition. Members are elected at the Annual General Meeting, and anyone living or working in the borough may stand. Specialized knowledge of the arts is not a condition of membership; besides local cultural workers, the constitution ensures representation from tenants, community and education groups in the borough. This composition—unique for borough councils in the U.K.—obviously influences policy on the kind of work which is funded (a matter to which we shall return later). This seed funding enabled the project to develop sufficiently to approach other funding bodies for

further expansion. Fortunately, Greater London Arts Association had a progressive panel at the right moment. Even more fortunate was the timely election of a radical left administration to the GLC, which provided the major contribution to establishing the project realistically—with adequate funding for premises, billboard sites and wages for the five workers (who are paid equally).

This funding was due entirely to historical "accident;" better to say, it was very unlikely—especially in the present political climate—that all three funding bodies were in progressive hands at the same time, and it will also be very short-lived. This circumstance also highlights our vulnerability: if, as the government intends, the GLC is abolished, then we fold along with it. Of course, this is part of a much wider struggle over the government's right to abolish a democratically elected tier of local government. But for cultural workers in London, and especially those on the Left, it will be a major disaster. At least we might say that we have had our short but productive moment, but for those outside London the situation is even worse. Cultural workers on the Left are permanently crippled and marginalized through lack of funds. But we do not mean to moan; we are, after all, living in a capitalist society and cannot expect to be rewarded for our opposition. The real point is what it implies about a long-term socialist cultural strategy and, more importantly, the Left's slowness in recognizing the significance of the ideological battle and the role cultural struggle plays in it.

Capitalism has for a long time been expanding and refining its ideological weapons, to such a degree that they are interwoven almost seamlessly into the fabric of our culture—so much so that they often seem natural, harmless and unworthy of serious attention. This is especially true of specialist cultural production (or "high art"), which is seen as transcending ideology and politics—it is of another world and therefore "neutral" territory. The Trades Union Congress document on the arts, and to some extent the last Labour Party document, saw the only problem as one of distribution: to make *consumption* of high art less elitist and more widely available. Such an approach simply tinkers with the periphery. The status quo remains unchallenged, and it is precisely this status quo which effectively excludes socialist cultural production. The same status quo, with its ramifications in education and distribution of resources, excludes the working class and discriminates against women and blacks.[12] The labor movement, at the executive level, has in effect colluded with capitalism, by its inaction, in excluding its own potential allies—or rather, in keeping them at the fringes of the struggle and thus preventing them from engaging in mainstream cultural arenas. In fact, it is doing capitalism a favor: opposition is fine as long as it is not effective, because it proves how liberal and democratic the system is without challenging it.

Why have previous Labour governments failed to grasp the nettle of establishment control of culture, both specialist and mass culture? Apart from elements within the Labour Party who never really wanted socialism, just a more acceptable face of capitalism (as the recent Social Democratic defections clearly show), the reason rests in the power of the neutrality myth and its progeny—the "arm's length" policy. State control of British culture is considerable, with nearly all funding for "high culture" channelled through the Arts Council of Great Britain (independent and business sponsorship is virtually nonexistent, and even the Regional Arts Associations are dependent on the good will of the Arts Council for their continued existence.[13] In mass media, the British Broadcasing Corporation corners a considerable portion of the market, and there are many semi-independent bodies such as the British Film Institute which rely heavily on government subsidy. These major bodies are nonelected and protected by Royal Charter against "political interference" by elected governments. In practice, however, their overall budgets are decided by parliament, and appointments to the executive operate on the old boy network. Indeed, the appointment of the new Secretary General of the Arts Council, Luke Rittner (who is said to be a personal favorite of Margaret Thatcher), was made against considerble opposition within the council itself. They have the best ideological weapon of all: they claim that political control of cultural institutions is totalitarian (even when exercised by elected representatives) and thus ensure that real control stays in the hands of nonelected mandarins of the establishment. If you move against it, popular ideology puts you in the wrong; if you do not, you can never hope

to break the monopoly which sustains the myths of this ideology—and a good deal more besides.

The present radical Greater London Council has taken courageous steps to deal with this issue—and has paid the price in extensive media abuse. The council has significantly increased the budget of its Arts and Recreation Committee, which not only indicates their recognition of the significance of cultural production but also breaks the monopoly of other funding bodies in London—shattering the apparent consensus on funding criteria. The effect of this has been to expose the tokenism of these other bodies, particularly with respect to community and ethnic arts, thus forcing them to redress the balance to maintain their credibility. The GLC has openly declared that its policy of *positive discrimination*, in favor of those who have previously been excluded, is a political act—a socialist strategy. This kind of action is long overdue, and we can only hope that it will serve as a guide to others on the left, especially a future Socialist government in Britain, which could implement such policies on a national basis (and, we hope, would abolish the London Docklands Development Corporation). That would be a major step for cultural production in this country and a sign that we were moving away from the entrenched state capitalism which both Labour and Conservative parties have pursued, with minor differences in emphasis. A beginning.

Unless we recognize and act upon the political and ideological dimension of culture today, we will fail to create the socialist society of tomorrow. The capitalist ideology which is embedded in our culture—arriving incognito into our homes through our television screens, bombarding us daily on the streets, in buses and on the subway—cannot go unchallenged. Wherever we go it surrounds us, cajoles and entices us, insidiously implanting the message that we can only better ourselves by joining the system, and by implication not fighting it. Socialism must break the monopoly of these "mirrors of capitalism" if it is to win the ideological battle. If it loses this battle then it has lost the war.△

NOTES

1. The Thatcher government used an advertising agency, Saachi & Saachi, in its election campaign and continues to do so to maintain its public image. More recently, there has been talk of using this company to promote the introduction of cruise missiles into Britain. The same company owns a substantial collection of, and plays a large part in promoting, the works of the so-called New Image Expressionist movement; it is certainly not ignorant of the role cultural production plays in the ideological battle.

2. Just to ensure there is no misunderstanding: we do not intend here to implicate the work of Vic Burgin and others which, although deeply embedded in semiology, cannot be said to be merely illustrative of theory. His is a developed and pioneering practice which we respect, though some of his imitators—misunderstanding his aims—do fall into this trap.

3. By this we mean a whole range of art activity at that time which saw the transformation in the form of art as revolutionary in itself. Some were clearly only interested in aesthetic revolution, but many others made claims of wider social and political ramifications. For example, many of those who revolted against the art object (performance art, happenings, conceptual, art pouvre, body art, postal art, etc.) did so in the belief that they were attacking the commodity fetishism of the art market. The ease with which this was accommodated within the system, along with the benefit of hindsight, indicates that this was a fairly logical extension of avant-gardism which placed more and more emphasis on the mythologized personality of the artist as the essential commodity fetish. As the evidence of pre- or non-capitalist societies shows, it is not the object which is the problem but the system which emphasizes commodity value above use value.

4. The miners' strike caused a rationing of energy resources, resulting in a three-day week for all industrial output, and power blackouts across large areas of the country. The resulting crisis brought down the Conservative government of Edward Heath.

5. In *Block* (U.K.) 1 and more briefly in *Camerawork* (U.K.) 21.

6. Bertolt Brecht, "Messinghauf Dialogues" (Methuen), 76.

7. Discussed in *Block* 2 and *Camerawork* 21.

8. Beginning at the very heart of London, Docklands stretches from Tower Bridge eastwards on both sides of the river for about nine miles. The London Docklands Development Zone covers 5,101 acres of land.

9. The "City" refers specifically to what was once the original walled city (one square mile) on the east side, which is now the center of high finance. Local people refer to the "City marching eastwards" into Docklands.

10. Listed buildings are those which are officially recognized as having special architectural or historical merit and cannot be demolished without a special inquiry, unless they are unsafe and constitute a danger to the public.

11. The "Plan for Wapping" was published by the Development Corporation reallocating land previously zoned for public housing to private developers. Much public money had already been spent preparing this land, including filling in docks. It is the only large area left in the borough for public housing—the waiting list for such housing stands at over 9,500.

12. The term "black" in Britain is often used by groups other than those of Afro–West Indian origin, such as Asians, because it is a way of presenting the problems of racism as a unified struggle. There are also other generalized terms like "ethnic minorities," but these are regarded by the more militant black groups as a category imposed by a dominant white society—the implication being that it intends to remain dominant.

13. Around the time of the 1981 riots in Liverpool, the Merseyside Regional Arts Association was dissolved by the Arts Council because it had not been conducting its business in a "proper manner." It is no accident that just previously there had been a lot of publicity about their funding of "militant politically motivated groups." The association was reconstituted, but only after changes were made in its staffing and organization.

Paper Tiger Television

by *DeeDee Halleck*

Smashing the myths of the information industry every week on public access cable.

Public Access

Most of the cable systems in the United States have a few channels which must be made available free to community members. These public access channels are the bane of the cable corporations, who see their space as so much fallow land. The corporations would rather program a twenty-four-hour, advertiser-based weather channel or yet another subscription movie channel. That they haven't done so has nothing to do with their sense of public service; rather, it is the *law*, in the form of franchise agreements made with the local municipalities. Most cities and towns have negotiated contracts that exact public access channel space in exchange for the right to run cables through city streets and sewers. Franchise agreements vary from city to city and depend on both the level of activism on the part of local access enthusiasts and the level of competition for the franchise on the part of corporations. When both are high, cable systems provide well-stocked public access studios and portable video equipment for free loan on a first-come, first-served basis.

The access movement took root at a moment of maximum disillusionment with network television. Residual political optimism from the sixties combined with the flush of infatuation with small-format video to generate hope that cable would offer a genuine alternative to the vast television wasteland. A National Federation of Local Cable Programmers, under the tutelage of New York University professor and access pioneer, George Stoney, helped to organize access committees wherever franchise agreements were being negotiated. Pragmatic city officials, far from discouraging access, used this pressure to increase the bribes which they lapped up from cable advance men. As a result of this confluence of circumstances, a rare opportunity now exists in many communities for authentic participatory media. How long this will continue depends on how large a constituency the access activists and programmers can muster.

It may be difficult to create a unified political force among users of public access (both makers and watchers). Access at its best has been *narrow-casting*: covering specific local issues and directed to a specific local audience. Some ethnic and religious groups have successfully networked groups of shows to loyal adherents in many cities, but there have been few programs on access that offer a progressive political perspective to a wider community. With few exceptions, the American Left has ignored the cable potential—an indication of the media mystification that exists on all levels of this society.[1]

Herb Schiller reads *The New York Times #4. Foreign Correspondents in Consumer Capitals: Information about the world as we glean it from our daily and Sunday* New York Times *is minimal, trivial and diverting. It is loaded with the viewpoints of the ruling cliques with whom the foreign correspondents have their daily contact. It would be nice if we could say that we had a window on the world. In reality what we have is a window on a very special portion of a very special privileged group. All the news that's fit to print, indeed.*

Halleck: Paper Tiger Television

Paper Tiger

Paper Tiger is one of the nearly 200 weekly series transmitted on access channels to subscribers of Manhattan Cable in New York City. These regularly scheduled programs range from astrology call-ins to film reviews by thirteen-year-olds. Many immigrant groups have programs of music and dancing—Bulgarian, Greek, Spanish flamenco. Several of the religious cults have weekly slots—Rajneesh, Krishna-murti, Scientology. The Boy Scouts, the League of Women Voters, and the National Organization for Women of New York have all done series. *Potato Wolf*, *Communications Update* and *Artists Television Network* are program series that are produced by progressive artists using a wide variety of styles and formats.

Paper Tiger began as a special series on *Communications Update* with Herbert Schiller reading *The New York Times*, a task he has habitually done with students as a warm-up exercise in his communications theory classes. I had visited Schiller's classes at Hunter College and had been amazed at both the insight and humor he was able to glean from those venerable pages. "Herb," I said, "that would make a great TV show." It could join a sparse but memorable tradition of "readings": New York City Mayor Fiorello LaGuardia reading the funny papers on the radio in the thirties; Julius Lester's sardonic readings of *The New York Times* on morning radio in the sixties; and Mattleart and Dorfman's analysis of Disney's role in the ideological penetration of the Third World in *How to Read Donald Duck*.[2]

Schiller began with an explanation of how *The Times* serves as the "steering mechanism of the ruling class" and went on for five other programs to cover the Washington Talk page, the foreign correspondents in the consumer capitals of the world, the annual search for the hundred neediest cases, the conflict of interest in the way they cover communications issues, and how their Sunday Book Review section serves as a gatekeeper of Western ideas.

The shows were very popular, especially with the group that had assembled to make them, and we realized that this was a format that could be used for other programs. Since that time we have done over fifty "readings"—from "Teresa Costa Reads *Biker Life Style*" to "Archie Singham Reads *Foreign Policy*."

AFTER IMAGE VISUAL STUDIES WORKSHOP

Mary Feaster reads *Time* on the Murray Bookchin show: Time *makes time disappear. Everything is the same. There is no history. . . . The essence of* Time *is that it destroys the present, the past, and the future. Just like the hands of a clock keep turning around and around and give you no message, no perspective, no coordinates, no sense of direction. What* Time *does is relax you in time.*

Content

Each week Paper Tiger offers a critical reading of one publication. In addition to looking at the content and language of specific articles, the programs include basic information on the economic structure of the corporation that produces the publication. Many programs also look at the demographics: who the readers are, what products they consume (for example, *U.S. News and World Report* readers buy wine by the *case*), and how much a full-page color ad costs. Sometimes we examine the board of directors or the background of the editors and reporters. Although the specific focus each week is on one publication, it is the intention of the series to provide an accumulative view of the culture industry as a whole. With the expansion of all sectors of the economy into the information business, it is important to keep track of how this is played out in the vehicles of mass culture. More and more of the Manhattan population works either directly or peripherally in the information industry. *Paper Tiger* gives them some economic and historical perspective with which to view their own participation in the cultural apparatus. Employees of the featured publication make up the best audience for each show. (During the Schiller series, we leafleted the *Times* building during shift change.)

The programs begin with the words: "It's 8:30. Do you know where your brains are?"—a nice joke from a Tuli Kupferberg cartoon that serves several functions. First of all, it implants the time slot in people's minds. Second, it's a stock opening, one which we can vary in innumerable ways, but which will always have a kind of familiarity about it. Finally, it inverts a familiar phrase used by Group W News in New York—"It's 10:00 P.M. Do you know where your children are?"—to tweak up the anxiety levels of all parents in the audience, so that they will continue to watch the news. By using Tuli's inversion, we hope to tweak up the level of critical consciousness with our own anxiety-producing question, one which we hope can raise the consciousness of the viewer as well.

We hope that much of *Paper Tiger* works in the same way. Although most people are cynical about the media and are aware of being manipulated, most are unaware of *how* this manipulation is worked out issue by issue, ad by ad. Many people think of the media as a form of journalism, distinct from other areas of economic life. By going over a publication in detail, by examining how it is enmeshed in the transnational corporate work and by pointing out exactly how and why certain information appears, a good critical reading can *invert* the media so that they work against themselves. The next time a viewer reads a publication that was covered on *Paper Tiger,* each ad and each article becomes a reinforcement of the critical reading.

Formal Strategies

There are certain practical requirements for public access programming, the first of which is that it has to be regular. Since there is little hope of access programs being included in *TV Guide*'s schedule, or being listed in local papers, the main way of building an audience is to make it a *habit*: the show must be on every week at the same time. Most television viewing is habitual; that is, people are home on certain nights and turn on the tube at certain times. However, if they switch the dial around during the breaks between shows, they might linger on something that looks different. Ergo, another strategy is to look different, to have an immediately discernable distinctive quality, without being intimidating or alienating. *Paper Tiger* uses brightly painted sets to help leaven the heavy subject matter. There are no pompous "director" chairs, no stuffed couches, no glittery curtains. It looks homey, but very colorful, like the funny papers on Sunday. The guest, sitting on a yellow kitchen chair, is projected into the foreground with pizzazz. We sometimes use actors to provide simultaneous nonverbal translations of the text. For instance, during the discussion of *TV Guide* by Brian Winston, we placed a young woman in the corner of the frame. She was watching television (the actual shows being aired at that time). As Brian pointed out the lack of real choice on network and cable, she switched channels sporadically, pored over a copy of *TV Guide*, and eventually fell asleep in her easy chair. On the *Sports Illustrated* show, a bubble gum–chewing fan leafed through a collection of baseball cards, while Tuli Kupferberg pointed out the connections between sport and the military.

If there is a specific look to the series, it is *handmade*: a comfortable, nontechnocratic look that says *friendly* and low budget. The seams show: we often use overview wide-angle shots to give the

Joan Braderman reads the *National Enquirer*. *Welcome to the world of the* National Enquirer. *This is it. The contemporary eighties locus of the Great American Contradiction. It's a fucking veil of tears for most of us folks, but the* Enquirer, *like the* Reader's Digest, *is upbeat.*

viewers a sense of the people who are making the show and the types of equipment we use. We often use charts and graphics, but they are hand lettered or cut and pasted rather than created by elaborate video effects. Sometimes we even make them with magic markers and scissors a few minutes before the show begins. The graphics are not fed into a mechanical graphic holder but are held in place so that the fingers show. At the end of the program, along with the credits, we usually disclose the budget—including everything from magic markers to studio rental. The total can vary from $19 for one show with a black-and-white camera to $150 for a two-camera color set-up that includes a switcher, audio mixer and two video recording decks. By showing the seams and the price tags, we hope to demystify the process of live television and to prove that making programs isn't all that prohibitively expensive.

Organization

The group that works on *Paper Tiger* is a loose affiliation of interested, committed and talented people. Since there is no pay for the work, most have to hold full-time jobs in the media industry. These jobs are often high-pressured and draining. That we can pull a show together after a long day of work is some kind of miracle. We meet in a coffee shop for a half an hour and do some rough planning, then run to the studio where we have only thirty minutes to hang the set, test the mikes, adjust the lights, cue up the tape for the breaks, put the graphic cards in order, reassure and cue our guest and maybe, just maybe, have a minute to do a quick run-through of the opening transition. It can be rough. Equipment problems alone often account for missed cues and ragged taping. We sometimes spend the breaks madly repairing a set mike or replacing an audio cassette deck that has malfunctioned. "For eighty-five dollars, what do you expect?" is the oft-repeated answer to our many complaints to the studio owner. The shows are done without run-throughs and often with new crew members who need to be briefed during the precious set-up time. When the beginning works well, we're off and running, and the show is spontaneous and fresh. When we flub the opening, it sets everything off, and the momentum is hard to regain.

One of our hardest challenges is to maintain the spontaneous excitement of

Halleck: Paper Tiger Television

the first programs, while at the same time improving the "tech." The goal is to make the shows not slick and polished but at least snappy and fast moving. "Clean," as John Lennon said. Many of the people who work on the show do so because it is one of the few places to gain hands-on experience with live television. There is something about going out to audiences live that sets the adrenalin pumping. However, it's hard to put together a show on short notice, using a large crew, all with their ante upped. Most television is not made with collaborative or nonauthoritarian structure. Achieving unity and strength while maintaining maximum participation, imagination and humanism is an old structural problem. Subtlety and tolerance are difficult to achieve in the supercharged tension of a television studio, about to go on the air in three-and-a-half minutes.

Spontaneity Aside

This is not to say that the shows are instantaneous slapdash affairs that are easily replicable. Every show requires many hours of research on the political economy of the various publications. In addition, each one reflects years of commitment, often a lifetime of work and reflection, on the part of the guest. The budget of the program is also deceptive, because one major expense is missing: salaries. The level of talent, experience and expertise donated to the series would be hard to match anywhere.

The live shows are taped for distribution, and this enables us to clean up things like missed close-ups of articles and tardy music for sound cues, and we can sometimes add additional reference material as superimposed text. This post-production phase greatly increases both the out-of-pocket costs and the time demands on the group. Meeting once a week to do live shows is one thing; reconvening the next day to clean up the tape is another.

Distribution

For better or for worse, after fifty shows the studio organization has remained loose and receptive to spontaneous input (and mistakes). The interest and demand for the taped shows, however, is forcing a

AFTER IMAGE VISUAL STUDIES WORKSHOP

Alex Cockburn reads the *Washington Post*: The Washington Post *covers very little of the business of government. . . . Their editorials are unvaryingly reactionary, buttressed by columns that are equally reactionary. . . . They use the word 'pragmatist' a lot. That's a terrific word for journalists. It usually means someone who has no principles at all. . . . The Washington Post *is part of the Iron Triangle. You have the political correspondents who order the discussion, the consultants who run the campaign and the pollsters who ask the questions that people like David Broder (Washington Post *columnist) want asked. Thus is the political discourse of the nation's capital ordered.

more organized structure. We have tried to make *Paper Tiger* a model for cheap, imaginative access programming. As such, it is important that the programs be distributed to other access systems and to schools and community groups. At the present time, they are being cablecast in Madison, Wisconsin; Woodstock, New York; and on both cable systems in Manhattan. Individual programs have been shown on occasion in Austin, Texas; Fairfield, Connecticut; Saint Louis, Missouri; and Buffalo, New York. Requests for shows have come from many other communities, but our limited resources for making dupes and buying postage have not allowed broader distribution.

Seize the Time

Perhaps the only auspicious aspect of the relentless technological developments in the communications industries is the fact that the cost per image has plummeted. Lightweight, high quality, portable equipment can produce programming for a cost that is within the reach of individuals and groups in the "developed" world. Many of these new images are produced outside the traditional networks of media concentration. However, the bulk of this production is being used to increase repression (surveillance systems, for example) or to reinforce cultural penetration (cassette distribution of Hollywood films and old television programs). But no historical development is one-sided. The last decade has seen the growth of small-format media as organizing tools for progressive change. The alternative media community has created networks that have greatly increased the production, distribution and use of media products from sources other than the transnational corporations. Certainly the many films, tapes and radio programs on the situation in Central America have given U.S. citizens a level of information more profound than that which leaked through the cracks of network news during the Vietnam War. Cable has rarely been a forum for these alternative views. Organizational work in cable tended to focus on increasing the availability of channels and making access centers responsive to community needs. Very little attention has been paid to the programs themselves or to the possible use of access channels for distribution. The opportunity that public access provides for wide dissemination of progressive issue-oriented media is an emancipatory moment yet to be realized.

Paper Tiger is a mostly live public access television show. It is made by: Diana Agosta, Pennee Bender, Alison Morse, DeeDee Halleck, Martin Lopez, Dominique Chausse, Vesna Kulasinovic, Alan Steinheimer, Caryn Rogoff, Daniel Brooks, David Shulman, Shu Lea Cheang, Esti Marpet, Leann Mella, Mary Feaster, Melissa Leo, William Bodde, Fusun Atesar, Barry Malitzer, Roger Politzer, Martha Wallner, Roy Wilson, Preacher, Ezra Halleck, Hilery Kipnis, Ellen Windmuth, Linda Cranor, Adam Merims, Daniel Del Solar, and many others.

It is supported through contributions, distribution fees and small grants from the New York State Council on the Arts and The Film Fund.△

Notes

1. *Alternative Views* is the longest running exception. Doug Kellner and others at the University of Texas at Austin have produced more than 200 public access programs, reaching an audience of over 12,000 each week. The series uses documentaries on social issues and interviews with guests (Helen Caldicott, Daniel Ellsberg and ex-CIA agent John Stockwell, for example). For a catalogue write: Alternative Views, Box 7279, Department 55, Austin, Texas 78712.

2. *How to Read Donald Duck*, by Armand Mattleart and Ariel Dorfman. International General, Box 350, New York, New York 10013.

All of the *Paper Tiger Television* shows end with information about the production, including the budget. One of the functions of the show is to offer imaginative examples of cheap public access formats.

Diana Agosta winds the "crankie" at the end of the show.

Democratization of Culture In Nicaragua

by Ernesto Cardenal

PART ONE

The community of Mesquite Indians, a very poor population situated on a river-bank, had been gathered together so that I could talk to them. While the interpreter was translating my words, I observed disinterest, indifference, and boredom in their faces. I told them that I was the Minister of Culture who came to visit them (and I noted that this interested none of them) and I commenced to explain that this new Ministry was created by the Revolution for dance (there I noticed their sudden interest), for music, for ancestral traditions (and the interest in their faces was more noticeable), for the different languages we spoke (since their language is something we must preserve and defend), for crafts. I had to explain that this meant using our hands to make beautiful things more useful. As examples, I showed them some very primitive drawings which they had carved in some maracas, I showed them a "tuno" which they had just given me, a canvas which they take from the bark of a tree, and I explained to them how they could paint these canvases. I have recounted this story before speaking of political culture in Nicaragua. Why is it important? For me, its importance is that these people, who were exploited over several centuries and did not have anything except their culture and their own language (and what they had, they were also about to lose), had just realized that the Ministry of Culture was especially for them; and the Ministry was especially there to oppose cultural ethnocide of all those segregated like them.

The destruction of indigenous culture and language is attempted in other American countries. The people are killed, hunted on the plains like deer, sent donations of sugar laced with arsenic, of clothing contaminated with cholera. But we have made them literate in their languages. We believe that they enrich our cultural identity. And we want them to progress within their culture, without remaining stagnant in it, but also without losing it. A language that is lost is an irreparable loss for humanity, since it is a people's particular vision of the world which is lost.

I founded a small community on Nicaragua Lake in the archipelago of Solentiname inhabited by poor and isolated peasants. We developed crafts, primitive painting, and poetry with them. The crafts and painting were greatly appreciated abroad, and were sold in Paris, Switzerland, Germany, New York. Much later, the community joined the Sandinista Front's struggle for liberation. As a consequence, the Somozan forces destroyed all of the community's installations, the great library we had, archaeological pieces, records, pictures, kilns full of ceramics and enamel, everything. And peasants all over the archipelago were repressed because of us. And the police prohibited them from painting. And peasant girls went up into the mountains to paint in secret. If a policeman saw a picture inside a hut he broke it with his bayonet. Why do I tell you this? Because I want to present an image to you of how Nicaraguan culture was repressed. Literature, music, and theater were repressed—because we had

This article is an edited version of a speech delivered by Ernesto Cardenal, Nicaragua's Minister of Culture, at the UNESCO Conference in Paris on 24 April 1982. The original Spanish version was first published in the Nicaraguan cultural weekly Barricada Cultural Ventana 60, 70, and 71 (1, 8, 15 May 1982). *The translation from the Spanish is by Amy Edelman of the Peoples Translation Service in Oakland, California.*

an eminent literature of protest, a politically committed music, a popular street theater that stirred things up and yet had to be at times clandestine. And they banned books. First it was certain books that were considered most dangerous, finally it was all books, since all books were considered subversive.

The Culture of Liberation

When the Revolution triumphed there was a great thirst for reading in our nation. A mobile bookseller, who previously sold books in the street at great risk, began to sell his books in the pavilion of the Ministry of Culture. Such street vendors appeared all over, until there was one that set up his booth in the Transit Headquarters, in front of the police! The many copies which were published—very many for our means—sold very rapidly. A street vendor, who once sold 300 pesos a day, was selling 2,500 daily. And a student exclaimed enthusiastically, "Now we are definitely free. Now we can read what we like. Before it was so difficult."

And the police who banned those books were so feared that the people closed their doors and did not even want to show their heads when the police passed. Their green uniforms and green helmets were symbols of terror and death. Now policemen, and soldiers in the army, and members of State Security forces in the Ministry of the Interior are writing poetry—and very fine poetry.

A young woman in an infantry batallion wrote this poem:

To the Soldier Juan Bustamente of the Southern Front

It was six in the afternoon the 17th of
    February 1980
when I fell in love with you, Juan.
With your camouflage uniform
and your GALIL on top of the desk
completing your twenty-four hours of duty
I approached you
and touched your chocolate-colored skin.

A police officer wrote this poem:

As Free as the Birds

Looking through the barred window
at the front of my room
I see how the sun rises

and its light between the leaves of the
    guanabana tree.
On the floor it forms figures.

A zanate alights and sings in the branch
    of a jocote.
It jumps. It jumps.
It returns to the same branch singing.
I think about that bird
                    of Nicaragua.
The Salvadoreans, the Guatemalans,
    the Belicians,
                    all Latin America
will be free as that bird.

The second point which I wanted to express is that, in the past, we had a culture of oppression, and now we have one of freedom. There was oppression in everything, so also in the culture. One cannot have oppression of a people without oppression of their culture as well. Now we have freedom in culture, and in everything.

An Answer to Imperialism: Corn

Last year the United States government brusquely refused us the purchase of wheat. Our people were to be without bread. The Ministry of Culture planned a Corn Fair, with the theme, "The Corn, Our Roots," the idea being to promote all the national dishes made from corn. The Fair was celebrated in local villages all over the country, and culminated in a national gathering in the indigenous settlement of Monimbo, legendary for its heroism in the battle against Somoza. The plaza and street of Monimbo were not big enough for the 250,000 people who came to sample Nicaraguan food and drink made from corn. Members of the Junta, Commanders of the Revolution, Ministers, and heads of famous restaurants made up the jury that awarded the best *tortilla* (our corn bread), *tamales* (corn mash wrapped up in leaves which one eats with cheese), *indio-viejo* (an Indian dish that is a stew of corn with meat and many condiments and lard), *cosas-de-horno* (different biscuits made of corn), *pinol*, our national drink (cornmeal with water), *cusuza* (a very strong corn liquor), *chicha* (Indian wine made from fermented corn), and innumerable desserts and tidbits made from corn. Dishes arrived from some remote regions

of the country which not even we knew and which now we have discovered.

We named the Fair "Xilonem," after the Indian goddess of tender corn. According to the myth, she sacrificed herself for her people and with her blood she produced a great crop of corn in a year of drought. For us this was also a symbol of all the martyrs of the Revolution who sacrificed themselves for the well-being of their people. One of our top researchers, who had studied this myth of Xilonem, Dr. Alejandro Davila Bolanos, was one of those who spilled his blood in the struggle for liberation.

Our culture and that of all Central America has been a culture of corn. According to Popol-Vuh, the Biblical Mayan, the Gods created man from corn. The truth is that man created corn. From a wild ear of corn two or three inches in length—as one can see in the Museum of Anthropology in Mexico—Central American man was able to cultivate the ear of corn we know today, since, unlike other grains, like wheat, which is dispersed by the wind, the ear of corn falls to the earth covered by a strong wrapper, and in order to germinate must be unwrapped by human hands. Man created corn and corn created our culture, and we are THE CORN PEOPLE/THE MEN OF CORN. An old Nahualtl poem says that "the tender, blond ear of corn is a light to us." And the great Corn Fair allowed our people to reaffirm their national identity, their cultural identity, and their defense of the Revolution, and to reject imperialist aggression.

Furthermore, this gave our people their own food, something part of their own culture. And after the triumph of the Revolution Nicaraguan food has been much more appreciated, together with everything else that originates from our own Nicaraguan past: a native past, a Spanish colonial past, an English past on our Caribbean coast, and above all, a culturally integrated past.

"A people with a kitchen is a people with culture" is a French saying. And I have come to talk of the kitchen because this is a third point that I wanted to present to you: our Revolutionary culture has been a re-exploration of origins. And this re-exploration has involved the creation of a new kind of life. This was already indicated in the name of the Corn Goddess that, according to the ancient

Nahuas, meant "delicate and tender, like a tender and fresh ear of corn."

But beside the French saying that a people with a kitchen is a people with culture, I want to add the words of our great poet, Jose Coronel Urtecho, who says that a good society and a good kitchen always walk hand-in-hand, and that decadence of the kitchen is a product of the dissolution of the society: it is a reference to the extremely bad nourishment in great masses of the population in the impoverished and underdeveloped countries, all victims of capitalism. Our present culture, embodying the rediscovery of our origins, and the rescue of our own identity, of our food and our myths, is a soldier of liberation.

People's Culture

These different things which I have recounted serve as an introduction to the subject that I come to discuss here at UNESCO, that of the Democratization of Culture in Nicaragua. Why do I come to you to talk of some practical and theoretical aspects of a small country like Nicaragua, which was until recently very dependent? Because Nicaragua is one of those countries in Latin America, Africa, and Asia, recently liberated or in the process of liberation, which contain more than half of the world's population. Countries in which powerful social transformations occur that embrace all spheres of life. The terrible problems of ignorance, sickness, hunger, and misery can only be solved by our countries quickly developing their economies and creating new social structures. This is an eminently cultural matter, since our country is effecting rapid change not only of traditional social structures, but also of cultural values and cultural needs. I believe it is useful to become acquainted with our experience.

I also have come to talk to you of Nicaragua's cultural tasks because in our political development and our immense effort to take leave of economic underdevelopment, we have united cultural transformations with the idea of creating a society free of violence, and now this is seriously threatened.

In Nicaragua, cultural liberation has been part of the national struggle for liberation. This past February, on the anniversary of his birth, our great poet, Ruben Dario, was proclaimed Hero of Cultural Independence, and that day was named Day of Cultural Independence. The cultural heritage, actually the anti-cultural heritage, left by a dictatorship imposed and maintained by the United States since mid-century, could not have been more catastrophic. When the Revolution triumphed on 19 July 1979, more than half of all Nicaraguans were illiterate. And the dominant classes considered their cultural center to be Miami.

Our Revolution is concerned with the present, and is above all concerned with the future, but is also concerned with the past. Our past has been revolutionary, too. In the first place there was a resurrection of the dead (in our people's consciousness). Our history immediately was different. Our heritage, which before was not visible, was declared publicly. National traditions flourished. The entire nation was always united with the liberation movement, but liberation has been the precondition under which the nation becomes a good community.

Artistic skills had been decaying more and more during the long Somozan reign; at the end, Nicaragua was a country of very poor craftsmanship, and it was seen as something irretrievably lost. The Revolution came to its rescue, and in very little time, the ancient lost arts have reappeared in many parts of the country, and there is a new popular art, as well. It is an expression more of our identity, of the Nicaraguan nature, of our own selves, because it struggled against foreign domination, and it was achieved with the triumph of the Popular Sandinista Revolution.

The hammock is the cradle of the Nicaraguan, and the cradle of American mankind. In the city of Masaya where the war ended, the hammock is woven tirelessly in gay colors, and in Europe it is said that it is the best hammock in the world; sometimes our hammocks have been presented as gifts to heads of State. They are works of art—these tapestries of sisal fiber from Masaya and Camoapa, woven in luminous colors and pre-Colombian and modern designs. In San Juan de Oriente, a small village that has traditionally done pottery, replicas of pre-Colombian ceramics or new inspired creations are produced. In Matagalpa and Jinotega a very delicate black pottery is crafted, the clay made black by pine smoke. The only ones who still made it when the Revolution triumphed were two families, and the Revolution, through the Ministry of Culture, saved the craft from extinction. Only an old woman still knew how to carve the fine designs delicately into the white mugs. We have saved the millinery craft, producing students who have learned to carve the intricate mosaic of birds, butterflies, and flowers. In Masatepe and Granada the ancient art of making furniture out of fresh mimbre (a plant) has been revived, its delicate and resistant tiling so well adapted to our tropical climate. And an important change is no longer to prefer furniture from Miami over Nicaraguan furniture. In the northern part of the country there is a mountain of soft rock of various tones and veined like marble, which the local peasant population converts into birds, fish, women's bodies. We have sent the best sculptor and professor of sculpture in Nicaragua to them and now San Juan de Limay is a village of sculptors. Much of what they produce is not folkcraft, but a modern sculpture. On the Atlantic Coast, site of our gold mines, we have revived the lost art of goldwork. And our Caribbean coast becomes a virtual jewelry store, with marine turtle shells, black coral, shark skeletons, and pearls. The Mesquite Indians carve precious wood, converting it into figures which, like their dances, represent their work: fishing, hunting, and farming. The most advanced Indians now have returned to making drawings with brown, yellow, and red plant dyes on the "tuno" canvas, which they make from the bark of a tree.

For all this rich and varied and previously unknown art, the Ministry of Culture has established different stores, and the best samples are exhibited in what we call "The Gallery for the People's Art" in Managua, which previously was the branch office of a bank.

PART TWO

The craftperson's hardships are due to cultural, economic, and political reasons. Because of this we have forged our own road—not capitalist—leaving out the intermediaries, and having the state financially support its artists. It is a fact that in our countries the penetration of capitalist civilization converts crafts into business; it takes it from the plaza to the marketplace, it strips it of its traditional functions, converts it to the product of a "boutique." The peasants, deprived of their pottery craft, eat from plastic plates; the sisal fiber is no longer used; and the craftperson depends more and more on money for his or her work. In Nicaragua, we seek out another, completely different, route. The destiny of our masks is not only to hang from the walls as adornments; the masks continue to live, and the craftpeople organize themselves into cooperatives.

The masks continue to live. One day the indigenous population of Monimbo, a population of craftpeople, rose up against Somoza. They fought with pistols and .22 rifles, with machetes, sticks, and stones. With iron rods used for construction they made lances, with pipes they made bazookas, with gunpowder from their festivals they invented an extremely powerful bomb. They launched the rockets from their festivals against the helicopters, their marimbas playing war songs from the Black Dance, and they gave press conferences with festival masks on, so that they would not be recognized. (From this the soldiers in the cities got the idea of fighting with a handkerchief over their faces.) And the festival masks are the pink and red faces of the Spanish conquerors; they danced with masks from the Spanish conquest in order to ridicule the conqueror. Those masks showed that they were a people that had never been defeated by domination. They invented an entire craft out of war. And an army could not bend them with machine guns, tanks, planes, and helicopters.

The enemies of the Revolution, from within and without, try to oppose religion. But popular religious traditions are encouraged by the Revolution. Thus it has become accustomed to "La Purisima," and "La Griteria," which are Marian traditions deeply rooted in our nation; the Patron festivals, some of which are widely celebrated, like that of Santo Domingo of

Managua and San Jeronimo of Masaya; and Christmas. In 1980, the Junta, stating "that along with the changes in fundamental structure effected by our Revolution, the Christmas celebration must recover its true popular and Christian feeling," decreed: "All kinds of advertisements and commercial promotions that are broadcast by printed media, television, and radio and by whatever other form of public instruments that use or invoke Christmas and everything that is related to the date of the birth of Christ in order to encourage the sale of good or services, are prohibited."

Vices that previously were fomented in Patron Festivals by Somoza and his followers, like prostitution, gambling, and drinking, have been prohibited. As a result, the festivals have been made more sane, more pleasurable, furthermore, more Christian, and fit better with the more genuine cultural efforts of our nation.

At our festivals one can sample the many native dishes. The festivals also provide the opportunity to tighten our bonds with each other, to reaffirm the importance of community, as incarnated in a Patron Saint. The festival is like a real utopia where all the needs of the community and of those who pull it together seem for one time to be fulfilled.

To us, culture does not occupy a separate sphere from social development. Furthermore, it is inconceivable to have economic development without cultural development in Nicaragua.

In Solentiname, a group of peasants gathered together with me once a week, bringing their poems. It was a Poetry Workshop. Children came also. One time a ten-year-old boy brought this brief poem:

I saw a turtle in the lake.
It was swimming
and I was in a sailboat.

It seems to me to illustrate nicely that definition of culture proposed by UNESCO: that it is everything that man adds to nature. Apollinaire said: When man wanted to move more quickly, he did not create a third foot, he invented the wheel. The boy here had a cultural consciousness: The turtle and I swim in Nicaragua Lake, it swims with its paws, and I go in a boat. I am like the turtle, but I am different from the turtle.

But we must develop the concept of culture more. I think of another poem from the workshop, this written by a peasant of Solentiname:

I go away to the dark green guabo tree, that is at the beach,
to wash the corn for tortillas.

I take off my clothes to feel more comfortable
and have remained only in my red pants.

I scrub the corn until it is white.
I finish, I wash my pink cotona, I bathe, and I come back.

A reflection about the everyday peasant life, a great harmony with nature, a consciousness of the self and of the language, a desire for communication. Those elements, which involve a development defended against exploitation, ignorance, and alienation, made it possible for that peasant girl, after she was a guerrilla, to write a poem so classical and so free.

Culture:
The Right of the Masses

Culture within any given society depends on the capacity the members of that society have to develop their potential. If the members of a society are not given this opportunity, then there can be no democratization of culture. There can be no culture, nor democracy.

Not too long ago, an article in *The Wall Street Journal* denounced that in the U.S. works of art and literature have become mere decorative pieces to be preserved as bonds or fiduciary funds. Society does not expect a secretary of state to have any deeper knowledge of history than that required for a sixth-grade exam. The article added: "The U.S. has made a business of its culture and a culture of its business."

In Nicaragua, on the other hand, we now have a new understanding of culture. The Nicaraguan writer, Sergio Ramírez, who is a member of the Government Junta, has said: "If culture was formerly the exclusive domain of a minority, now it will be the privilege of the masses, the right of the masses."

We also have a new understanding of the intellectual. Colonel Santos López, who fought alongside Sandino and later became one of the founders of the Sandinista Front in a jungle region, did not know how to read. Yet one of the Commanders of our Revolution, Victor Tirado López, has called him an intellectual. He considers that not having known how to read was one of this man's highest virtues

because, as he had once told him, you had to have a clean mind and a sensitive heart in order to understand what was happening in Nicaragua as a result of U.S. intervention. Commander Tirado then added, "The reason for his great success lies precisely in the fact that he did not go to school to learn to read his first words." This reminds me of what Gramsci once said, that culture is the critique of exploitation. This is the same as Socrates' famous maxim 'know thyself,' which means that the plebians should know that they have the same human nature as the nobles who exploit them.

So for this very reason all of the Nicaraguan people were taught to read immediately after the triumph of the Revolution. The literacy campaign was started with the aim of producing liberated citizens. It was like a second liberation war against *Somocismo*, i.e. against the ignorance left behind by *Somocismo* (what Julio Cortázar called "the strategy of ignorance"). More than half of the high school students in the country became literacy teachers. This was voluntary and without pay. They were divided into brigades, columns and squadrons. The country itself was divided into various war fronts, the same ones that had existed in the liberation struggle: the Northern Front, Southern Front, Western Front, etc.... Each place in which the battle was won, was declared "Victorious over Illiteracy." As in the other war, there was also a Final Offensive. And thousands of victorious youths entered Managua in endless lines of trucks, just as the Sandinistas had entered Managua triumphantly, acclaimed by all the people.

With our democratization of the alphabet, the *campesinos* not only learned the alphabet but they learned about their reality and themselves as well. Edmundo, a sixteen-year-old literacy teacher says that "they learned quickly because we spoke of their reality, of exploitation, of the Revolution, and not about topics that were irrelevant to them."

To these young literacy teachers, the experience was also a school for learning about the Revolution. Oscar, a sixteen-year-old, said: "For me it was the best school, the best workshop, the best study session we've ever had, because we weren't just told about the life of the *campesino*, we actually went to see and experience the conditions in which *campesinos* live. We understood the moral obligation we had, as young people, to help remedy all the harm done by

Cardenal: *Democratization of Culture in Nicaragua*

previous governments. Since then I am committed to trying to consolidate the Revolution."

They had the experience of peasant work. Ligia, seventeen years old, says: "It was very beautiful because I did not know how to do farmwork." Another young woman recounts that she returned with the desire to study medicine immediately, and that this time would pass quickly, because those peasants needed her. A young sixteen-year-old says: "After the Crusade the collective spirit has impregnated many of us students." And a fifteen-year-old from a rich family says: "After the Crusade I found in my parents my political friends."

A Revolutionary Education

Teachers of literacy have continued receiving education. There has been a great growth in the quantity of scholars and universities. The University costs six dollars per semester, practically free. Also there has been a qualitative change in education; now Nicaragua is the subject of education and research.

As an example I will speak of the new kind of museums that we are creating with the help of UNESCO and the Organization of American States. The museums always have been elitist in the eyes of the people. The French Revolution opened the Louvre to the people, so that they could appreciate the works of art that previously were restricted only to the aristocracy. And this was an advance. But the people always have seen in the museums a mummified culture. And they have been passive spectators there. During Somoza's reign, our National Museum was not even this way; it was totally abandoned. A woman had been volunteer director of it all her life without salary. A little before she died we took her there in her wheel chair so that she could see the remodeling that we had done, and she was surprised to see how the Pharomachus moccino or the Momotus moto, which she herself had dissected, now were exhibited, and she said: "It seems to me that I am in another country." They have created more museums and remodeled others. But the new type of museums of which I speak will be like cultural centers; they will be created with the participation of the entire community, and cared for by it; they will

offer courses, will gain an audience for art. They will be a medium for popular culture for all ages and cultural levels. The museums will be like schools for the whole community. To make up for our insufficient schools, the museums will be a true medium for cultural socialization—and informal education, not academic, perhaps unconscious. The subjects addressed by the museums will be: health, agricultural technology, ecology, crafts, education, archaeology—whatever the community wants. The museums will not only be there to portray records of the past, but the needs of the present and the dreams of the future. In this way, the people will get their culture from the museums. The man in the community will have a consciousness of himself as a cultured being and a social being. We believe that if a village was capable of making a Revolution, it is capable of making its own museums. Theodore Law said, speaking of the museums: "Democracy and popular culture are synonyms." We already inaugurated the first of these museums in a small village, and a group of the more important Latin American writers and artists that were at a gathering in Managua traveled a long and dusty road to the inauguration of that humble museum. We can perhaps say that this is a type of museum that contradicts the traditional concept of museums.

PART THREE

The Poetry Workshops have been created in crowded inner city neighborhoods, in humble populations, in the indigenous communities of Monimbo and Subtiava, in the Armed Forces. Here, workers, peasants, police, soldiers learn to write poetry and very fine poetry. Before I spoke of the Poetry of the Armed Forces. At Harvard, where I gave the closing address at a convention about Peace and Disarmament, I said that our army would be able to give technical advice to other armies about poetry. The Venezuelan writer Joaquin Marta Sosa has written of these workshops: "We can say that the Sandinista Revolution, for the first time, has socialized the means of poetic production." He explained it further, adding, "The people have begun to become masters of poetry in Nicaragua: not because they read more and from expensive editions, but because they produce it."

I read last week in *Time* magazine that poetry books in the United States "do not usually pile up next to the cash register." In Nicaragua, poetry publications printed by the Ministry of Culture disappear rapidly; our magazine *Poesia Libre*, which is made up exclusively of poetry, and is published on kraft paper, sells widely at the popular level. We have re-issued the first editions because they continue to be demanded.

Our music has been able to have a social use along with its aesthetic value. UNICEF's means to measure the health of a village (number of doctors, paramedics, etc.) reveal that Nicaragua is faulty in this area. As in the literacy crusade, the entire population is mobilized in a health campaign to eradicate malaria or vaccinate all the children in the country. And music has been a part of that. During the war, our great composer Carlos Mejia Godoy wrote lyrics to go with the mazurka, teaching to arm and disarm a Fal and a Falil. The same thing happens with popular theater. Without worrying about action, time, or space, which play a great part in contemporary theater, our peasants, workers, and students use scenes to dramatize their daily life or their social or psychological conflicts. Nicaraguan cinema had its birth during the war, when battle fields were filmed. Now films portray all the aspects of the new society that is being created, basically like a documentary.

Sports are part of the Ministry of Culture, and the Revolution has a sporting politic: it looks toward total participation by the masses in sports; sports as a part of daily village life; people as not simply spectators (as they were under Somoza), but as participants; sports for the whole society, all classes, without distinction by age or sex.

We desire mass participation in sport, not for the sake of sport itself, but for a strategic objective: what sport produces—improvement, emulation, collective work, brotherhood, health. Mass participation in sports strengthens competence, and this leads to selection with an eye towards excellence. The goal of excellence is common to all spheres of the Revolution. We cannot have inferior goals; we can have a gradual process, but the ultimate goal, in all things, is excellence. And the athlete who reaches the ranks of excellence is living proof of what the Revolution can and must achieve, and is an example for others. And the best will be able to compete in international events.

The People's Answer

Due to problems with foreign currency and the difficulty of importing many articles, we produced a fair, "La Piñata," which was a huge national exposition and sale of Nicaraguan goods—crafts and products of small industry. By the thousands, people attended this large sale of toys, clothing, furniture, books, records, nutritious products and ornamental plants. Children came to break the many piñatas. Along with the fair there was a circus. There were booths with typical foods. There was music and singing.

Its purpose was to create a consciousness of the value of native products; before it was believed that only the foreign was worthwhile. Its purpose was not to promote a consumer society in the sense of useless consumption or waste. Yes, we want good consumption for our people. And this is also within the sphere of culture, not just of economics, in the sphere of a poor nation's culture. Our economic-cultural-political condition was defined very well by a toymaker crippled in the war in heroic Monimbo, who said when the fair occurred: "The question, comrades, is to make each time a toy more beautiful and durable because a wheelbarrow with a rotary on top is something with which the children can play for years." The great volume of vendors showed that this was a stimulus without precedent for Nicaraguan craft and small industry. And it was a political answer and an alternative by which to break dependence on other countries.

In Nicaragua, the bourgeoisie dressed itself in the stores of Miami. Bridal furnishings were bought in Miami (before in Paris). The Revolution has revived the popular Nicaraguan dress. It is not merely for its colorfulness; it is for its beauty and furthermore for its usefulness in this climate. The cotona, this white shirt that I wear, has been the traditional shirt of the Nicaraguan peasant; at one time it had practically disappeared; now it is the most popular shirt in Nicaragua. As a peasant shirt, it is a symbol of work, of struggle, of freedom, of the Revolution. The cotona was the uniform of the literacy teachers. When thousands of those young people triumphantly entered Managua, they had the commanders of the Revolution put on those cotonas—the commanders who presided over the great public event were scarcely older than those young people.

Nicaragua is also beginning to change relations between men and women. But this is a long-term cultural transformation. "Before, I was an insupportable machista," says a sixteen-year-old youth, "and the Sandinista Youth movement has made me radically change my position with respect to women. Now I treat them differently." This indicates to us that the change we begin now will principally involve the future generations. There is now a law of publicity, prohibiting the use of commercial ads presenting women as sexual objects.

Our relationship with nature is also beginning to change. The contraband of wild animals and indiscriminate deforestation have been stopped. We begin to learn a new harmony with nature.△

Popular Theater &

The story of the Kamĩrĩĩthu Community Educational and Cultural Center.

Popular Struggle in Kenya

by *Ross Kidd*

In March 1982, Kenyan authorities banned for the second time a popular theater performance created by a community organization of peasants and workers, withdrew their license, and battered down the open-air theater which the community had built. The following article gives some of the background.

POPULAR THEATER IN THE THIRD World often claims to be a tool of protest and struggle and a means of social transformation, but rarely does it challenge the status quo in a significant way. Too often it becomes as marginal as the peasants and workers it represents, with little real impact on the society as a whole.

One significant exception has been the popular theater work of the Kamĩrĩĩthu Community Educational and Cultural Center (KCECC),[1] a peasant- and worker-controlled organization in rural Kenya. Its voicing of protest against injustice and corruption and its championing of workers' rights and popular expression have made the center a major target for official repression.

In 1977 the performance of its first drama, a community production in which over two hundred villagers participated, was stopped and one of the organizers, Ngũgĩ wa Thiong'o, imprisoned. Early in 1982 its second drama was stopped, its license as a community organization withdrawn, and the community-built two thousand–seat theater smashed to the ground.

Why would peasant-produced dramas call down the wrath of the Kenyan government? Why has a program which has significantly reduced illiteracy and alcoholism, increased employment opportunities, fostered a people's culture, and raised the awareness and participation of villagers been suppressed? Why has Kamĩrĩĩthu had such a powerful effect on Kenyan society, whereas popular theater in other parts of Africa has remained ephemeral and insignificant? To understand this we must take a look at Kamĩrĩĩthu's history.

History of Domination and Resistance

Although KCECC was formed in 1976, it is an outgrowth of the resistance by peasants and workers against foreign domination which has continued for the last five centuries. It is an extension of their struggle against invasion, slavery, forced labor, alienation of their land, heavy taxation with only token representation, exploitive working conditions, and cultural genocide.

This struggle started back in the 1500s with the invasions of Arab slave traders and later Portuguese colonizers. Each of these invasions was beaten back, and it took four centuries of fighting before colonialism prevailed under the British. Once the military conquest was complete, the colonial authorities seized 8.5 million acres of the most fertile land in the central highlands of Kenya, turned it over to white settlers, and herded the displaced Africans onto reserves. Through forced labor (initially), taxation, and a ban on African production of certain cash crops, they forced the Africans to work (and squat) on the European estates. They also introduced a labor control system requiring every African to carry a pass.

Corralled in the reserves, deprived of their land, forced into working for the settlers, and humiliated through racial discrimination, the Africans fought back. They formed nationalist organizations to pressure for reforms through petitions, marches, and demonstrations. Each of these challenges was suppressed, often brutally, the organizations banned and the

Kidd: Popular Theater & Popular Struggle

leaders detained, but new movements arose to take their place. In the thirties and forties, much of the nationalist energies went into supporting direct lobbying by Jomo Kenyatta in Britain.[2]

In the late forties and early fifties it became increasingly clear that the reformist option was closed. For a while educational work and strikes replaced petitions and appeals, but even these challenges were suppressed and the leaders imprisoned. A militant group of workers and peasants—the Forty Group, which later came to be known as Mau Mau—took over the nationalist initiative. Eschewing the reformist or constitutional approach of the middle-class nationalists, they developed a broad-based mass organization and launched an armed struggle with revolutionary aims. Through an oath of commitment and dedication they bound each freedom fighter to the goals of driving the British out of Kenya and overturning the system of foreign domination and capitalist exploitation.[3]

The landless laborers, small farmers, squatters, and urban workers who made up the ranks of the guerrilla army stood the most to gain from a real revolution—one which gave them back their land, basic rights, decent working conditions, and a greater say in the running of their country. As the war developed, it took on the form of a civil war, with much of the fighting pitting the uneducated and landless peasants (the forest fighters) against the educated, landowning classes (the "home guards" and "loyalists")—many of whom sided with the colonialists.

This landed class had developed through mission education and the colonial civil service, through the benefits derived by chiefs who collaborated with the colonial regime, and through the economic opportunities which opened up in the forties and fifties for a minority of the African population on the reserves. Once the colonial regime recognized the power of the peasants' and workers' movements, it moved quickly to strengthen the position of the landed middle class as a buffer against the radicalism of the popular movements. In the late fifties (while the freedom fighters were in detention), a land consolidation and registration program legitimized the occupation and ownership of large blocks of land by the richer African farmers, many of whom were colonial collaborators. As a result, over half

of all Kikuyus became landless, and more than half of the land was given to less than two percent of the population.[4]

By the end of the decade many of the forest fighters had been arrested and detained and their leaders killed. However, their determined resistance had made an impact: the pressure forced the British to accept constitutional or "flag" independence—that is, African political but not economic control. Working with the bourgeois nationalists who, under Kenyatta, returned to lead the constitutional process, the colonial regime worked out a formula for independence which reassured foreign capital and the European settlers and betrayed the peasants and workers who had fought for revolutionary change.

On 12 December 1963, Kenya got its constitutional independence. In spite of a decade of armed struggle and two centuries of militant resistance to colonial invasion and rule, the political settlement left the economy firmly under foreign control. The new ruling class entered into an alliance with foreign capital as the junior partner in a neocolonial arrangement. Multinational capital moved into Kenya in a big way, taking the dominant economic position formerly occupied by the white settlers. Power and wealth became more and more concentrated in the hands of a small ruling clique of Kenyans. As a member of parliament, Jaime Kariuki, put it, Kenya became a country of "ten millionaires and ten million beggars." (Soon after making this statement in March 1975, Kariuki was shot dead in the streets of Nairobi.)

The richer farmers, the only ones with access to credit, reaped the benefits of the schemes to buy back land from the European settlers. This landed middle class also used their newly acquired power to gain control over the agricultural sector, trade, and small business.

The peasants and workers, who had done all the fighting in the forests, lost out. They remained on the whole landless, poor, subject to the same exploitative working conditions, and without an effective means of political expression and participation. Trade unions lost their right to strike and their independence of state control. The opposition party was harassed and finally banned. Those who spoke out publicly against the ruling clique's unbridled corruption and concentration of wealth were detained or, in a few cases, assassinated. Ethnic loyalties were manipulated to build division within the working class. (The most cynical example of this was the reintroduction of oathing on an ethnic basis.) Symbols of traditional culture such as *Harambee* ("All pull together") were used to divert peasant energies into ethnic concerns, to diffuse class tensions, and to paper over the destruction of the peasants' and workers' movements. This is the context in which the KCECC came into being.

Kamīrīīthu: A Place of Struggle, a Labor Reserve and a Rural Slum

The Kamīrīīthu Community Educational and Cultural Center was started in a place with a long tradition of struggle. In fact, its existence as a village was a direct result of the liberation struggle.

Kamīrīīthu lay in the middle of the area of greatest conflict during the liberation war, and many people from the area had joined the forest fighters. Because of its strategic location, the British decided to use the site as an "emergency village," one of a number of fortified concentration villages.[5] Their own homes burnt down, people from the area were driven into Kamīrīīthu and expected to do forced labor. Later in 1957 the village was made into a permanent settlement. While the forest fighters languished in colonial detention camps, the land was deeded mainly to the richer farmers—many of whom were colonial collaborators. Kamīrīīthu became a labor reserve, supplying workers to the tea and coffee plantations in the nearby area (the former white highlands) and to the industries in Limuru and Nairobi (thirty-two kilometers away).[6]

Today Kamīrīīthu has a population of over ten thousand people. It is partly a "dormitory village," from which residents commute each day to their workplaces. Some villagers live on plantations or industrial estates but are forced to move back to Kamīrīīthu once they are fired. Those who are not employed in the plantations or the Limuru factories eke out a living through self-employment and/or casual labor, working for richer farmers, selling vegetables at the Limuru market, brewing and selling beer, and in some cases engaging in petty crime or prostitution. There is no security of employment: each worker competes with many others for the few jobs available. Even when they get

work, the wages are kept very low because of the large pool of unemployed workers.

Many of the villagers are squatters who lost their land through white settlement or through the land consolidation process. Some have been forced to sell their small plots because, without adequate income, they were unable to repay bank loans. Those without their own land live in temporary structures built on footpaths and are constantly faced with the threat of eviction.

The village is a rural slum: it bears all of the costs of reproducing and supporting the work force with minimal help from the state or the corporations who profit from their labor.[7] Villagers have to cope on their own without basic services—water, medical facilities, sanitation, street lighting, and so forth. Whenever peasants make demands for these services they are told to organize their own self-help effort or *Harambee*, in effect an exercise in collecting contributions from and praising Kenyan businessmen and rich farmers who have benefited from exploiting the peasants. (It also represents an attempt to channel peasant energies into acceptable avenues, diffusing class struggle and promoting class collaboration.)

Starting KCECC, a People's Organization

The only token service to this community of ten thousand people was a community center, and even that had been built through community effort. During the liberation war, the colonial authorities set aside a four-acre plot of land for "social purposes." When no assistance from the colonial government materialized, the village youth built a shelter and used it to meet, talk, and perform traditional dances.

After independence in 1963, the site was converted into a vocational training center for young people. With the help of the Kīambu Area Council, the villagers built a three-room wooden building in which carpentry classes were held. However, this training program was abandoned in 1973 when the area councils were abolished. Funds available for village-level social services dried up, and the center fell into disuse.

As bureaucratic neglect, unemployment and insecurity deepened, the villagers decided to revive the center and use it to do something about their worsening situa-

tion.[8] This initiative represented a convergence of interests. On one hand there were the peasants and workers who had seen their hopes go up in smoke as the real meaning of *Uhuru* became transparent. In spite of independence the conditions of their life remained the same: no land to cultivate or on which to build a house; insecurity of employment and exploitation in their workplaces; their own culture denigrated, tokenized, and supplanted by the new foreign consumer culture.

On the other hand there were a number of intellectuals—teachers, university staff, civil servants, and so forth—who lived in the Kamīrīīthu area and shared the feeling of betrayal about the nationalist struggle. Many of them had been involved in protests against foreign control of Kenya's economic, political and cultural life and had begun to recognize the importance of working with the peasants and workers in this struggle. Foremost among them was novelist and playwright Ngũgĩ wa Thiong'o, the head of the University of Nairobi's literature department. He had played a leading role in popularizing Kenya's history of resistance and had organized a number of struggles against the foreign monopoly of culture in Kenya, as seen in the dominance of Broadway musicals and West End plays at the national theater and the preeminence given to English rather than African languages at the University of Nairobi. In his writings he had made a powerful case for developing a national culture out of the creative energies of peasants and workers.[9] When he took a traveling university theater group to Kamīrīīthu in 1976, he recognized the possibilities for putting this idea into practice.

Ngũgĩ wa Mirii also emerged as a key organizer and supporter of the KCECC. An adult educator and research worker employed by the University of Nairobi, he had become fed up with the subservient role played by adult education in the Kenyan social system and had developed a deep interest in the radical teaching methodology of Paulo Freire as a means of transforming society.[10]

There was enthusiastic response at the initial community meeting, and after a few more planning meetings the participants agreed on a program and established an organizing structure. They formed a central committee along with subcommittees for activities such as fund-raising, adult education, and cultural activity. Ngũgĩ wa Thiong'o was elected chairman

Kidd: Popular Theater & Popular Struggle

of the cultural committee and Ngũgĩ wa Mirii chairman of the adult education committee.

The KCECC started with what seemed like conventional aims: to provide a meeting place for the villagers and a program of integrated rural development, including adult education, study groups, cultural activity, economic production, and health. What distinguished it, however, was its structure and process: the peasants and workers were in control (rather than government bureaucrats or the middle class), and it was run in a highly collective fashion. The villagers made the decisions on the basis of extensive discussions; as one member put it: "Nobody can make a decision without consulting the people because every decision affects the people."[11] Even academic writing on the Kamĩrĩĩthu experience had to be cleared first with the executive committee. As a result of this collective approach, agreements represented real commitments, and the villagers regarded the center as their own organization.

The committee work itself was an educational process: peasants and workers examined ways of working together to solve their problems and reach their aspirations. Each decision was discussed on the basis of frank criticism and in terms of its overall effect—whether it served the interests of the membership, whether it countered or reinforced negative aspects of Kenyan society, and so forth. For example, members decided to demand that people be sober when coming to the center and to ban photographs during performances, since they felt they had been exploited by camera-clicking tourists in the past.[12]

Learning to Read the World

The first activity taken up was adult literacy, a priority for many of the peasants who felt humiliated by their inability to read. Ngũgĩ wa Mirii offered to teach one of the classes as well as to train other teachers in the Freirean literacy approach. Two hundred people came to participate in the classes, but in the first phase it was only possible to accommodate those with no previous education (fifty-six in all).

Unlike traditional literacy work, which conditions people to accept the structure of inequality and their compliant role in it, the Kamĩrĩĩthu program encouraged people to question what was happening to them, to overcome the rationalizations and myths provided by society, and to begin to understand why they were landless and poor. In Freire's terms, they learned "to read the world."

Instead of depending on the teachers to plan and run the program, the students made all the decisions, recruited teachers, and set the rate of pay. They also designed their own study plan. The literacy committee analyzed the situation in Kamĩrĩĩthu—its problems and underlying causes—and examined the history of changes in Kenya. With this as a context, they looked at the curricula and primers distributed by development agencies—and found them wanting.

These "functional literacy" primers provided technical information on agriculture, health, nutrition and family planning but failed to address the key issues of the villagers. Knowing how to use modern methods of agriculture seemed pointless when the peasants had no land and couldn't afford the fertilizer, insecticides, and other supplies; reading slogans about health and nutrition seemed equally futile when they had neither land on which to grow food nor access to water and sanitation facilities. These texts not only ignored the peasants' own knowledge and experience of surviving in a difficult environment, but they blamed the peasants for their poverty, rather than exposing the political and economic structures which produced the inequality, landlessness, and impoverishment.[13]

The literacy committee decided it needed totally new curricula and materials, designed not by outside "experts" but by the villagers themselves. (In Ngũgĩ's view this represented an advance on Freire's curriculum approach, which depended on the skills of a team of professionals to make the analysis and prepare the codifications.) The peasants and workers based their curriculum on the fundamental problems of the village: landlessness, unemployment, low wages, insecurity of tenure, lack of services, lack of access to firewood and water, high prices for food and transport, and the effects of poverty—heavy drinking, prostitution, crime, and

more. For each of these problems they prepared a "code"—a picture, a story, a song, or a short skit which could be used to stimulate discussion on the problem.

These discussions made up the heart of the literacy sessions and provided the content for the reading and writing exercises which followed. People explored the roots of their problems and discovered the connections between them. In a discussion on alcoholism, for example, people said that although drinking is a source of income for Kenyan business, for the squatters it is a way of dealing with the frustrations and insecurity of landlessness and unemployment. The peasants also began to recognize how their history of domination and struggle shaped their present set of circumstances.

The results were equally unconventional. Unlike most such projects, in which there is heavy attrition and minimal learning, the Kamĩrĩĩthu program had no dropouts, and by the end of the six-month period all of the participants could read and write. Many of the students had even started to write their life histories, in a few cases running to ten thousand words in length!

From Peasant Autobiography to Community Scriptwriting

The interest created through the literacy program spurred the center to its next step. The villagers wanted to continue with adult education, but in a medium which would involve everyone in the community. Drama suited their purpose: the new literates were familiar with it, having used it in the form of role-playing and short skits in their classes and having seen the plays put on by the university's traveling theater group. Moreover, the script would provide an excellent text for follow-up reading. The process of creating a play would also create a forum for community discussion and might provide a source of employment and income for the center.

The literacy and cultural committees held several meetings to discuss the content for a play. The two Ngũgĩs were commissioned to write a draft script, drawing on committee and class discussions as well as student autobiographies; it was to "reflect the people's experiences, concerns, aspirations, grievances, etc., and the problems and contradictions in the village, using the words and expressions of the people."[14]

Once the draft was produced, it was reviewed and amended by the students and the executive committee, then discussed and criticized at a number of public readings which went on for two months. Villagers suggested changes when they felt the analysis was inadequate. In one case, for example, they demanded "a more rigorous questioning of the acquisitive values which had come with Western culture."[15] In effect it became the community's play: "This play was not a one-man's act. It was the result of cooperation among many people. For instance, the whole *Gitiiro* opera sequence in the play was written word-for-word at the dictation of an illiterate peasant woman at Kamīriīthu."[16] The villagers were able to reappropriate their own culture through the process. "People saw that the script or content of the play reflected their lives and history, and so they appropriated it—they added to it, altered it, until when they came to perform it, *Ngaahika Ndeenda* was part of their lives."[17]

The People's Play

The play *Ngaahika Ndeenda* ("I Will Marry When I Want") talks about the people of Kamīriīthu—their lives, history, struggles, songs, experiences, hopes, and concerns. It exposes through satire the manipulation of religion, the greed and corruption of the ruling classes, the treachery of colonial collaborators, and the exploitative practices of multinational corporations. The central character of the play (Kigunda) is a poor farm laborer who is swindled out of his small plot of land by his employer, a rich farmer and former colonial collaborator (Kioi). Kigunda's daughter, impregnated by Kioi's son, is forced to drop out of school and start working on a coffee plantation. She falls in love with a worker from the Bata Shoe Company and resists the men who come to seduce her by asserting, "I will marry when I want." At the end of the play the worker organizes a strike at the Bata factory, and the daughter leads a struggle against the multinational owner of the coffee plantation.

One particular strength of the play comes from the songs, which are resurrected from the Mau Mau struggle.[18] They reinforce the central message of the play: the peasants and workers must work together to transform their country and free it from foreign domination. The songs also help bridge the generations in the community, providing a chance for the older people to teach the younger about the liberation struggle, a period of tremendous cultural activity.[19]

Participatory Play Making and Building a Sense of Community

Once the script was final, rehearsals started with actors selected by the community. Sometimes as many as three hundred people came to the open clearing in the village that served as the rehearsal space—to take part in the acting and singing, to join in the discussion, to suggest songs that reinforced the message, to direct the dance movements, to watch and enjoy. It was a powerful experience of collective community effort. A women's choir was formed, and a group of young unemployed men and workers from the Bata Shoe Company created an orchestra to provide songs for the play and music for the interval. Other groups prepared costumes and props and made food for the participants. In the end about two hundred villagers took part.

Outside the rehearsals, people took on the identities of their characters and referred to situations in the play in arguments and conversations. As Ngũgĩ wa Thiong'o wrote, they rediscovered "their collective strength—that they could accomplish anything—even transform the whole village and their lives without a single *Harambee* of charity." Their self-confidence grew and there was a significant decline in drinking and crime:

> By the time we came to perform it was generally understood and accepted that drunkenness was not allowed at the centre. For a village which was known for drunken brawls, it was a remarkable achievement of our collective self-discipline that we never had a single incident of fighting or a single drunken disruption for all the six months of public rehearsals and performances.[20]

The whole effort unleashed a wealth of talent and demystified the creative process. Some of the examples of this burst of creativity and self-awareness were given by Ngũgĩ wa Thiong'o:

> Before the play was over we

received three scripts of plays in the Gĩkũyũ language, two written by a worker, and one by a primary school teacher. One unemployed youth, who had tried to commit suicide four times because he thought his life was useless, now suddenly discovered that he had a tremendous voice which, when raised in song kept its listeners on dramatic tenterhooks.[21]

The *Harambee* of Sweat: Building the People's National Theater

Perhaps the biggest achievement of the community was the construction of a huge open-air theater. During the initial public readings of the play the idea was raised, and the community decided to go ahead with it. Although expensive to build, it was seen as important to the presentation of the play and a way of making money for the KCECC.

The question then was, how to pay for it? People spoke vehemently against the idea of holding a *Harambee* rally in which "big people" pledged contributions to the project. They felt this was a vulgarization of the real *Harambee*—in which the whole community joined in a collective physical effort—and was just a platform for self-praise and a chance for the *wabenzi*[22] to show off their wealth, which had been stolen from the peasants and workers in the first place. They also rejected the idea of applying for funds from an overseas donor, which they felt might compromise them and introduce another form of dependence.

They proposed instead a "*Harambee* of Sweat": every villager would contribute ideas, labor and materials to building the theater.[23] Weekends were set aside for this project, and a team of young men was selected to take the lead in the design and construction. Working from a matchstick model and using local materials, they constructed a two-thousand seat theater on the plot beside the community center. When finished, it was favorably compared with the National Theater in Nairobi and praised as the true national theater of Kenya—one built by the people, accessible to the people, dealing with their issues and speaking to them in their language and idiom.[24]

Repression and Resistance

On 2 October 1977, the play opened, attracting immediate attention. People came from neighboring villages and, once the word spread, from all over the country. Peasants and workers sat alongside Nairobi businessmen and civil servants; however, according to one correspondent, it was the peasants and workers who laughed and enjoyed themselves the most. It was their lives, their story being enacted on the stage—the first time in Kenya's history that "a play of the people *was* being acted for the people by the people."[25]

After seven weeks of extremely popular performances, with audiences of up to two thousand, the inevitable happened: it was banned. The district commissioner announced that he was withdrawing the play's license on grounds that it fomented strife between classes. The production was too threatening; the ruling class was "mortally scared of peasants and workers who showed no fear in their eyes; workers and peasants who showed no submissiveness in their bearing; workers and peasants who proclaimed their history with unashamed pride and who denounced its betrayal with courage."[26]

The KCECC fought back through their supporters in the press and the middle class, who turned it into a national issue. People flooded the newspapers with protest letters and widened the debate to include the issue of foreign control of Kenyan cultural institutions. When the government saw that the KCECC and its supporters were not backing down, they struck again. On December 31, Ngũgĩ wa Thiong'o was detained. During his detention, he was fired by the university (as was Ngũgĩ wa Mirii).

The resulting tension and fear did have an effect. For a number of weeks villagers stopped coming to the center and waited to see what would happen. But even though their spirits temporarily sagged, they remained convinced of the importance of what they were doing and proud of their achievement. The repression clarified the nature of the class forces involved—those who supported the villagers' struggle (for survival, political rights and freedom of expression) versus those who worked to undermine it—and increased their determination to continue. The authorities underestimated the vil-

lagers' strength, failing to understand the broad-based nature of their organization. They thought that by detaining Ngũgĩ they would break the KCECC. Instead of falling apart, however, the center increased its activities, showing that it was not dependent on any single individual.

Fresh literacy classes were started with new participants, and the enrollment increased to 150 people. The orchestra and choir, which had been created for *Ngaahika Ndeenda*, continued to meet regularly and produced two records: *Ndinguri na Murimi* ("The Rich Man and the Poor Peasant") and *Mwiku Mwiku?* ("Where are you people?"). The women's group became very active, working together to improve family incomes and support each other. Before, when the women had struggled individually to find work, they had been more easily exploited. Now they formed a production group and took on contract work, demanding fair wages and distributing the money among the members. This collective approach made them stronger.

The real effect of the repression was seen elsewhere: the banning and detention stopped a groundswell of peasant-initiated cultural activity in other villages which had been inspired by the Kamĩrĩĩthu experience. As one committee member put it, "If our efforts had not been clubbed down so suddenly there is no telling how many other centers of its kind would now be in existence."[27]

The Second Drama and Further Repression

A year after Ngũgĩ's detention Kenyatta died, and the new regime released him along with other political prisoners. He returned home to Kamĩrĩĩthu, where he started to work with the villagers on a new play, *Maitu Njugira* ("Mother, Sing to Me"). They assumed that by using a historical setting they could avoid provoking the authorities. This play focuses on the colonial system of control, including brutal suppression and apartheid-type legislation; it also shows the Kenyans' determined resistance against colonial rule and exploitation by the settlers. *Maitu Njugira* centers around the resistance songs of various Kenyan nationalities which are sung by the mother to the daughter.

When the rehearsals started, four hundred people auditioned for the fifty parts. Ngũgĩ was thrilled by the turnout. "After the problems we had over the first play I thought people might be scared off, but this time they came knowing exactly what the problems might be—very conscious."[28]

This time the KCECC proposed to perform the play in the National Theater in Nairobi, partly as a challenge to its neocolonial practices.[29] In the fall of 1981 they wrote for permission but never received a reply. The government used "ping pong tactics," passing their letter from department to department. In February 1982, when the theater group showed up at the National Theater for final rehearsals, the doors were locked. They switched their rehearsals to the university, where they performed for ten nights to a packed theater of over a thousand people each night before the university closed the play under pressure from the government. A few days later KCECC's license was withdrawn and its executive committee sacked. The theater group was told it could no longer use the center because the government was taking it over as an adult education study center. To reinforce the message, a squad of police destroyed the theater.[30]

Assessing the Work to Date

The struggle by the peasants and workers of Kamīrīīthu will continue. They may have been silenced, their center taken over and their theater destroyed, but their awareness, commitment, and organization will produce new struggles and new forms of protest. What remains in the interim is to assess the work done so far. The significance of the Kamīrīīthu experience has been largely obscured by the repression and needs to be spelled out so that others can learn from it. This truly popular theater, linked to community organizing and struggle, represented a major advance over other attempts at popular theater in Africa, including:
—Urban-based "political" theater, which is often aimed at a small, privileged English-speaking minority;
—University traveling theater (in Kenya and Zambia), which takes plays to rural villagers but rarely involves them in the creative process;
—"Populist" drama of West Africa (such as Yoruba opera and concert party), which involves working-class performers and audiences but fails to advance working-class interests;

—"Theater for development" (in Botswana and Zambia), which takes plays on development themes to the villages but keeps the control of the process outside the community; and
—Farmers' workshops in northern Nigeria organized by the Ahmadu Bello University Popular Drama Collective, which involve the farmers in the drama-making process and critical analysis but lack an ongoing organizational base.

Popular Participation and Control

What is unique about Kamīrīīthu? To begin with, it is "theater *by* the people." It has emerged organically from the masses rather than being imposed by outsiders. The peasants and workers analyze their situation and act out their own understanding of it, rather than respond passively to the thinking and analysis of others. The high level of participation has helped to demystify theater, to show that ordinary villagers can do it, can "rise to heights hitherto unknown and undreamt of in the area of modern performing arts."[31] It represents a reappropriation of culture by the people; they have taken back what the ruling class has denigrated as "traditional" or converted into a tourist commodity, a means of glorifying the political leadership, or a tool of partisan politics.

But it is more than mere participation. As Williams has shown, participation can be a sham; people can "participate in their own domestication," i.e., be drawn into a process in which they take part but have no control, in which they are manipulated through their involvement to accept the status quo.[32] The Kamīrīīthu villagers are not just actors or a cheap source of labor for a community project shaped by others; they *control* the process and shape it through their participation and ideas. Having started the KCECC, they continue to make all the decisions, control the finances, and determine its direction. No individual or group is allowed to dominate or appropriate the decision-making process. No one is indispensable. As one villager put it: "We cannot close the centre if the Ngũgĩ's are not here. If they stopped writing, we would come together and write something. . . . These two individuals are not the centre; the centre is the members."[33]

The two Ngũgĩs have no special status or privileges. They take part in the physical work, are held responsible by the villagers for their actions, defer completely to the collective structure, and consult the committee on every decision. In effect, they are the "organic intellectuals" which Gramsci talked about; they live in the community, have close long-term contacts with peasants and workers and have have a deep commitment to the village and to their fellow villagers. The relationship is not a one-sided exercise in paternalism or charity; they learn a great deal from the peasants about "music and dance and drama—and the meaning of sheer selfless dedication to a communal effort."[34] When things get rough they face the same victimization as the the villagers.[35]

Villager control accounts for the high level of participation in KCECC activity. People feel they are working for a project which is theirs, a project which they have helped to shape. Through running the KCECC, they begin to feel more in control of their lives. As Ngũgĩ wa Mirii commented in analyzing the literacy work, "The poor will never change as long as the pivot upon which their cultural life is governed is not under their control."[36]

People's Organization

Kamĩrĩĩthu's organization has been the vehicle for popular control. It gives the work continuity, even in the face of repression. The creation of the KCECC has also made it possible to link drama with a process which transforms the community; it becomes one part of a larger ongoing experience rather than simply an on-off event.

In other African popular theater experiences the problem has always been, what happens next? An individual performance may spark a lot of discussion, participation and critical insight, but if there is no organizational vehicle to take it further, all the interest and momentum stops. Kamĩrĩĩthu has shown that people come to a critical class consciousness, not in an abstract intellectual exercise, but in the process of building an organization and struggling for their rights. In this context drama is neither the primary mobilizing agent for community action nor the main source of learning; it is "drama-within-a-process"—one of a number of interconnected activities which serve a broader aim of building a people's organization and struggling against oppression.

Of course this kind of work doesn't go on without a reaction from the ruling class. They can ignore the one-time theater experiments or the theater of political rhetoric for the middle class, but a theater that is rooted in and organized by the peasantry is more threatening. It isn't just the play and the exposure of corruption which concerns them; it is the organization which lies behind the play—the fact that peasants and workers can develop things without bourgeois patronage or bureaucratic influence, that this kind of independent organization can spread to other areas and challenge the roots of the neocolonial structure.

Popular Content

Another strength of the Kamĩrĩĩthu theater is that it advances popular interests. It is not a propagandist theater promoting the dogmatic slogans of modernization and teaching subservience to the dominant structure; rather, it "represents the most progressive section of the people in such a way that they can take over the leadership. . . ."[37] As the outcome of a process which is both collective and critical, a process which is controlled by the people, it is a genuine expression of popular interests and advances the consciousness and organization of the peasants and workers. This popular content accounts for the extraordinarily high level of participation. "Landless peasants can easily participate in a programme which discusses issues related to land. . . just as in the struggle for Independence peasants joined in with a will because it was also a struggle for land."[38]

The content is critical as well as populist. It not only starts with people's experience of poverty but also reveals how they have been made poor and challenges the proverbial, victim-blaming rationalizations. It shows that poverty is created by the political-economic system rather than people's habits, knowledge, and attitudes. Rather than indoctrinating people with modernizing information and techniques, thus reinforcing dependence on outside experts, it encourages the growth of their own analysis, self-confidence, and fighting spirit. It makes people question the political-economic structures which shape their oppression and develop the will to transform these structures.

Although rooted in tradition, the Kamĩrĩĩthu theater does not accept it uncritically but develops it in a progressive way, attempting to overcome the contradictions within the traditional culture. It identifies those aspects of traditional culture which strengthen the people's identity and resistance (such as the songs of struggle) while rooting out those elements which reinforce submission to domination. The best example is the traditional practice of *Harambee*, whose distortions by the ruling class have been exposed by the peasants and workers of Kamĩrĩĩthu.

Popular Theater as Resistance

Having been humiliated, manipulated and victimized, the villagers have discovered in drama a powerful tool for fighting back: rebuilding a sense of community, voicing their concerns and aspirations, clarifying the nature of poverty, raising political consciousness, poking fun at their oppressors, and protesting the abuses of the dominant class. The resignation and alienation of the past has given way to a spirit of questioning, of combativeness, of challenge. One sign of this growing confidence and involvement has been the reduced dependence on drinking.

People's Drama as National Culture

Kamĩrĩĩthu has provided an alternative vision for developing national culture in Kenya, one which incorporates the notion of popular centers in every village rather than elitist and neocolonial cultural institutions in the capital. The Kamĩrĩĩthu community theater has a significance far beyond its own village; it is a concrete example of what a people's national theater should be: accessible to and controlled by the masses, performed in their languages, adopting their forms of cultural expression, and addressing their issues. In this sense it is a direct attack on and a clear alternative to Kenya's existing institutions of national culture which are inaccessible to the masses, controlled by foreigners, in foreign languages, and a reflection of foreign interests and themes. It is an assertion of the peasants' and workers' right to "creative efforts in their own backyards...to a theatre which correctly reflects their lives, fears, hopes, dreams, and history of struggle."[39]

At the same time it is a clear demonstration of the validity of building a national theater and a dynamic national culture out of "the lives of peasants and workers, the languages they speak, the rhythms of their speech and gait and daily work and homely chores...[and] the conflicts in their lives...." The peasants and workers proved that "out of their own internal resources and the passions born of their unique experience of history, they can outshine the best that can be produced by parroting foreigners, and by following submissively the trodden paths of foreign education, foreign theatres, foreign cultures, foreign initiatives, foreign languages."[40]

For Ngũgĩ wa Thiong'o, the Kamĩrĩĩthu experience has been a breakthrough. Before working with the KCECC, his creative expression was an individual effort which reached a very limited audience of people who could read English. Now his efforts are collective, couched in the people's language, and accessible to and influenced by the peasants and workers. He represents a bridge between the literary theater of committed intellectuals and the theater of the people. As Victoria Brittain summarizes in her article on Kenya:

Nairobi's privileged classes live in a world where their cultural alternatives range from French and German theatre to a National Theatre which puts on "Oklahoma," "Carmen," "The King and I." Our rural people can choose between the bar and the church. Kamĩrĩĩthu showed that by writing in one of our national languages and using ordinary people there is a cultural life in Kenya just waiting to be allowed out. Their own Kenyan cultural life is what Kenyans want, instead of being second-class Americans watching "Oklahoma."[41]△

Kidd: Popular Theater & Popular Struggle

NOTES

1. In Gĩkũyũ it is known as *Mucii wa Muingi Mugi.*

2. Resistance also took a cultural form. As a defense against the colonial conditioning and cultural repression of the mission schools, Kenyans developed with their own resources a whole movement of independent schools in which their own history and cultural heritage was taught. (In the fifties the population of these schools numbered as many as 62,000 students.) Songs, dances, drama and poetry on nationalist themes were used as a vehicle of protest and a means of organizing. See Ngũgĩ wa Thiong'o, *Detained: A Writer's Prison Diary* (London: Heinemann, 1981); and Maina wa Kinyatti, *Thunder from the Mountains: Mau Mau Patriotic Songs* (London: Heinemann, 1980). While the Europeans created an escapist, enclave culture in the segregated theater houses of Nairobi, the young Dedan Kimathi, later to become the leader of the liberation struggle, started the open-air Gichamu theater movement as a means of rallying support for the nationalist cause.

3. Maina wa Kinyatti, "Mau Mau: The Peak of African Political Organization in Colonial Kenya," *Kenya Historical Review* 5 (2): 287–311.

4. D. Mukaru Ng'ang'a, "Mau Mau, Loyalists and Politics in Murang'a 1952–1970," *Kenya Historical Review,* 5 (2): 365–384.

5. The object of this mass incarceration was to instill a "culture of fear" and to break the freedom fighters' base of support. See Ngũgĩ wa Thiong'o, "Education for a National Culture." This was one of the earliest uses of the "protected hamlet" or "villagization" strategy later employed in attempting to contain anticolonial struggles in Vietnam and Zimbabwe.

6. The plantations and industries are largely owned by multinationals, the most prominent being Brooke Bond (which runs the large tea estates) and Bata (which owns Limuru's largest industry, the shoe factory).

7. To underline the precariousness of their existence, these rural slums were called *Shauri Yako* ("It's up to you"). Here again the slogan of self-reliance is used to blame the slum dwellers for their poverty and landlessness; to absolve the state and the foreign corporations (which benefit from this cheap pool of labor) from the responsibility to provide adequate services and jobs; and to promote the ideology of competitive individualism, that "getting ahead" is a matter of individual effort.

8. The initial driving force behind the revitalization of the center was Njeeri wa Aamoni, the area's community development assistant, who encouraged everyone in the village to come to the initial planning meetings.

9. Ngũgĩ wa Thiong'o, "Towards a National Culture," in *Home-Coming: Essays on African Literature, Culture and Politics* (London: Heinemann, 1972).

10. Paulo Freire is a Brazilian educator who popularized an innovative approach to adult education and literacy tailored to the needs and psychological conditioning of oppressed people. The aim of his methodology is to enable them to develop the confidence, critical consciousness and organizing capacity to challenge oppressive structures and practices. It is based on discussion rather than formal instruction, active participation and critical reflection rather than passive rote learning, subject matter determined by the participants rather than imposed by the teacher, and learning linked to action rather than mere classroom study.

11. Miriam Kahiga, "Theatre by the People for the People and of the People," *Sunday Nation* (Nairobi), November 6, 1977, 30.

12. George Gitau, "Indigenous Production at People's Theatre," *The Anvil* (University of Nairobi), October 24, 1977.

13. For a detailed critique of "victim-blaming" development work, see Ngũgĩ wa Mirii, "Literacy for and by the People: Kenya's Kamĩrĩĩthu Project," *Convergence* 13 (4): 55–62; R. Kidd and K. Kumar, "Co-opting Freire: A Critical Analysis of Pseudo-Freirean Adult Education," *Economic and Political Weekly* (Bombay), 3–10 January 1981; and R. Kidd and M. Byram, "A Fresh Look at Popular Theatre in Botswana: Demystifying Pseudo-Participatory Non-Formal Education," *Rural Development Participation Review* 3 (1): 19–24.

14. Ngũgĩ wa Mirii, "People's Theatre and Popular Education: The Kamĩrĩĩthu Experience," in R. Kidd, ed., *Third World Popular Theatre* (Toronto: International Popular Theatre Alliance, 1984).

15. Chris Wanjala, "The Silenced Satirist," *Guardian Weekly* (Manchester), 6 March 1978.

16. M. Gacheru, "Ngũgĩ wa Thiong'o still bitter over his detention" (interview), *The Weekly Review* (Nairobi), 5 January 1979, 30–32.

17. Ngũgĩ wa Thiong'o, "The Making of a Rebel: An Interview," *Index on Censorship* 9 (3): 20—24.

18. The process of collecting these songs was a form of oral history research–not the usual one-to-one encounters of interviewer and informant, but the whole community collectively rediscovering their past, each person reinforcing or correcting the views of others.

19. Read, for example, Ngũgĩ wa Thiong'o, *Detained: A Writer's Prison Diary* or Maina wa Kinyatti, *Thunder from the Mountains*, about the explosion of creativity by the peasants and workers during the liberation war.

20. Ngũgĩ wa Thiong'o, *Detained: A Writer's Prison Diary.*

21. Ngũgĩ wa Thiong'o, *Detained: A Writer's Prison Diary.*

22. A pejorative term for the Kenyan bourgeoisie, alluding to the way in which they flaunt their wealth with expensive cars such as the Mercedes Benz.

23. The main source of funding for the theater came from the script, which the East African Literature Bureau agreed to publish in Gĩkũyũ. (All the other publishers turned it down on grounds that it was not in English.) When the issue of selling the script was debated by the community, people said this was a legitimate form of *Harambee*. Everyone in the village had participated in it, turning up at the play readings and community rehearsals to give comments and suggest changes. The script was the community's property, the product of their labor—a *"Harambee* of Sweat."

24. Miriam Kahiga, "Novel Experiment in Theatre is a Big Success," *Sunday Nation*, 6 November 1977, 30.

25. Ibid. The use of Gĩkũyũ rather than English represented a radical shift in Ngũgĩ's writing and commitment from addressing a small, English-speaking audience to working with and being influenced by the peasants and workers.

26. Ngũgĩ wa Thiong'o, *Detained: A Writer's Prison Diary*.

27. Miriam Kahiga, "Kamĩrĩĩthu Revisited," *Daily Nation*(Nairobi), 29 January 1979, 11.

28. Victoria Brittain, "How the Kikuyu Play Brought the House Down," *Guardian Weekly*, 14 April 1982.

29. This theatre is only national in name. Its policies (including a high rental fee) discourage African theatre groups from using it. It serves a small elite with a repertory of plays such as *Oklahoma, The King and I, Gulliver*, and *Carmen*, performed by foreign groups.

30. Both Ngũgĩs left Kenya in the period of escalating repression and political detention before the abortive coup in August 1982. Since then, Ngũgĩ wa Mirii and Kamani Gecau (a former University of Nairobi lecturer who also worked on the Kamĩrĩĩthu project) have been working for the Zimbabwe government, helping to set up a network of community theatre groups in rural Zimbabwe. See Kimani Gecau, "Zimbabwe's New Theatre of the People," *Moto* (Harare) 9:38–39, and Dorothy Kweyu Munyakho, "Theatre: Zimbabwe Snaps Up What Kenyans Rejected," *Daily Nation*, 31 January 1983.

31. Ngũgĩ wa Thiong'o, *Detained: A Writer's Prison Diary*.

32. Rick Williams, "Towards a Pedagogy of Oppressed Youth," *Convergence* 4 (2): 80–82. For a view of "pseudo-participation," see the discussion of the Botswana experience in Kidd and Byram, "A Fresh Look at Popular Theatre in Botswana."

33. Wahome Mutahi, "Kamĩrĩĩthu: Drama Behind the Drama," *Daily Nation*, 22 January 1982.

34. Ngũgĩ wa Thiong'o, *Detained: A Writer's Prison Diary*.

35. In fact, they've been singled out for rougher treatment because, as Ngũgĩ ironically puts it, "detaining a whole village would severely drain a necessary reservoir of cheap labour. Who would now pick the tea leaves and coffee beans—for a pittance?" Ngũgĩ wa Thiong'o, "Education for a National Culture."

36. Ngũgĩ wa Mirii, "On Literary Content." *Working Paper* No. 340 (Nairobi: Institute of Development Studies, University of Nairobi, 1979).

37. Bertolt Brecht, *Brecht on Theatre: The Development of an Aesthetic*, trans. John Willett (London: Eyre Methuen, 1964).

38. Ngũgĩ wa Mirii, "On Literary Content."

39. Ngũgĩ wa Thiong'o, *Detained: A Writer's Prison Diary*.

40. Ibid.

41. Victoria Brittain, "African Reflections from a Prison Cell," *Guardian Weekly*, 14 January 1979.

JUDY BACA

From an interview with the Chicana muralist Judy Baca, by Diane Neumaier in June 1981. With a brief history of the Social and Public Art Resource Center by Nancy Angelo. Photographs by Linda Eber.

OUR PEOPLE ARE THE INTERNAL EXILES. TO AFFIRM THAT AS A valid experience, when all other things are working against it, is a political act. That's the time we stop being Mexican-Americans and start being Chicanos. When you deny a people's culture you can make them disappear, you can control them.

The people coming over the border from Mexico are the most difficult to organize. Even though they are the most exploited in the Los Angeles sweatshops, even though they are providing a very low-cost labor force, supporting the economy in a very substantial way and using very few social services—they are the people who are being shot at the border, raped at the border, beaten at the border, followed by helicopters with infrared, etc. They don't want to hassle anything; it's too dangerous. They will not resist because they want to have this little bit of money and work. They just want to

blend in and be Americans. My point simply is: if you deny the presence of another people and their culture and you deny them their traditions, you are basically committing cultural genocide.

I was born at a time when everybody was working very hard at just being American. In the early fifties, the prevailing idea was that we should all blend in. All separate ethnic groups should disappear and become American. I never did figure out what "American" was. I thought American was hot dogs and Wonderbread. When I went into the school system, I was *forbidden* to speak Spanish.

OUR PEOPLE ARE THE INTERNAL EXILES

BACA: OUR PEOPLE ARE THE INTERNAL EXILES

I did not speak English. I remember being in rooms with people speaking this other language. I didn't understand the words they were saying, but I knew clearly that they were saying I was less than they were because I didn't speak their language. In elementary school, most of the Spanish-speaking kids were treated like they were retarded and held back. I thought to myself, they're not going to be able to do this to me. I'm going to learn what they're saying.

And I learned very quickly. My mother worked on getting me to speak English without an accent. That was real important to her because that accent was an identification. She would have liked me to blend in if I could have, although at this point in her life she's very proud that I didn't. Like a lot of immigrant people, she felt that education was the key if I was to avoid suffering the kind of things that she had suffered.

I was encouraged to be fairly independent—very contrary to the socialization most Latin women are given. However, I also had all those other messages: get married, have children, do all that stuff. But I wanted to be an artist. My family didn't want me to be an artist because it was a crazy thing to be. What impact does your art have on real life? I think a lot of the ethic seeped into me: it's not good enough just to be an artist. How will you support yourself? What does it mean to the people you live around? All those questions got to me. So in college I also minored in history and in education. I developed back-up systems, which have proven very valuable in my work.

I went to school in the sixties at the state university in Northridge, California, in the part of the San Fernando Valley which was all white. Looking across that campus I would never see a Mexican or a black person or anybody of color. This was before the EEOP program, during the time when we were beginning to agitate for African-American studies, Chicano studies, American Indian studies. There were groups of people saying, "We're losing thousands of Chicano young men in the Vietnamese War." And clearly, in the university system Chicanos had no presence. So the sixties had a very powerful influence on me. I had had all these feelings but no place to hang them. The *Movemiento* gave me a place to focus them and affirm the fact that I wasn't crazy.

I was thrown right in the middle of all that struggle but was very much isolated. The moment I left my community to go to college, I was isolated from my own people because not that many of them went to college, and I was isolated from any sense of my own culture in the university system.

When I got out of school, I brought what I had learned back to my family and listened to their responses. When I showed her my work, my grandmother said to me, "What is this? What's it for?" It was clear to me that somehow I had been encouraged not to be who I was, to use Western European art as my model. I hadn't even learned about *Los Tres Grandes*, the three great muralists. I even had no idea about murals. In fact, I had been doing mural work for a year before I even heard of the Mexican muralists.

My grandmother was no dummy. She knew a lot about healing and had been influenced by the Indians in her understanding of religion. It wasn't straight Catholicism because if you hang an *amuleta* (a little pouch with special herbs and things in it) around somebody's neck to heal them and keep the spirits away, that's not Catholicism in the strictist sense. She, along with my mother, had raised me, and I saw her as an extremely powerful person—spiritually powerful—and I respected her. I thought, these are the people I really know and care about. I love these people, and I really want to make them understand, make them be part of this process I'm going through. If I'm supposed to be interested in communicating, if my work is supposed to elevate the spirit of human beings, have I decided these people are not human beings? It seemed crazy to use Western European models, to be completely inundated by that kind of culture, when in fact we were sitting in southern California—which my grandmother always referred to as Mexico. She used to say things to me like, "English? Why do you want to speak English? English is a language which people spit, spit out words." It is true: in Spanish you can say things in ways you can't in English. It's a much more poetic, musical, lovely kind of language.

Title page illustration (previous page): *The Great Wall of Los Angeles*, detail 1980 section. 1930s: The "Okies," refugees from the dust bowl, their fields destroyed by drought, provide a new source of cheap farm labor.

MY IDEAS ABOUT HOW I would make art never began with a political analysis. I am moved in the heart. I see an issue, something I can care about, and then I go about finding solutions in the way I can as an artist. If I were a carpenter, I'd go out and rebuild things. If I were an architect, I would redesign the architecture. But I have other skills. I simply use what tools I have at hand to address what I care about.

I got the idea that making art was probably one of the most important human activities that anyone could engage in. Everywhere I looked, all around me I saw people being asked to dehumanize. Crap is pumped into the air so you can't breathe. The streets are overloaded with so many images that you can't see one of them. The sound level is so high that you have to block your sense of hearing. Every aspect of the sensuality and sensibilities of human beings is decreasing. I always had the feeling that art was the celebration of the senses, that it was a place we kept asking people to make a leap, keep it all together, and just let something happen to themselves in a *real* sensual way. A friend of mine, a Mexican muralist, used to tell me, "A painting should be what it is when you stand back from it, just what it is: a painting. But when you get up to it," he said, "when you get up to it, it should be good enough to eat." So I thought to myself, yeah, that's really what it's about. I want to do that. I want to make art that will ask people to use all of their senses. It's an important human endeavor.

I had, of course, the choice of making art and putting it into galleries, seeing if I could shuffle my things around from place to place and get them shown. Artists, especially students, plug into that system as it exists without ever analyzing for whom they make art—the audience they hope to communicate with through their work. In my case, my people and their images had been made to disappear. Images I grew up with in my home had no representation in that world. There was no aesthetic I knew—a certain exuberance for color, for example—that was validated in the art world. I thought to myself, if I get my work into galleries, who will go there? People in my family had never been to a gallery in their entire lives. My neighbors never went to galleries. All the people I knew didn't go to galleries.

But I thought if I took my work to galleries—and if I was lucky—somebody might buy it. Now what does buying something mean? It means limiting people's access to it. That's what ownership is about. Essentially, you buy something, you own it, and you can let people see it or not. And it didn't make sense to me at the time to put art behind some guarded wall.

So for me, then, there wasn't really any choice. How many ethnic artists do you know whose works are being shown, even now? I had no way to apply my work to that structure. You couldn't take an aesthetic that wasn't mainstream into the galleries and have it accepted—especially as a woman, and especially as a Chicana.

From 1969 through roughly 1974, I worked specifically within the Chicano and Mexicano community. That was an interesting process for me, discovering what I could use to address that culture. It was different from my own upbringing, because things change in the streets. The economic and political circumstances change how people can live in those areas. So I had to learn another language—street language. I had to learn what things were impacting that community at that time. I had to deal with gang warfare in a completely different way than when I was a kid, because the barrios that I grew up in didn't have that kind of *organized* gang warfare.

WHEN I GOT OUT OF COLlege I started teaching at a Catholic high school—in fact, the same school I went to—in a program called Allied Arts, an innovative teaching program which I designed to celebrate the different senses. The kids wrote music, learned basic drama, wrote poetry. We interrelated all the arts. It was a fabulous course for me to teach, because it pulled a lot of things together and helped me understand how to use different techniques to get a desired product. People made presentations using three art forms to express one idea. It took over the whole school and became an incredible event. Kids drove up in a hearse, opened the back door and pulled out coffins to do a presentation on death. There were bands, choral readings, all fabulous stuff that really worked as motivation. We asked these kids to draw up out of themselves something that no one else was requesting of them.

I did my first mural there. I was trying to get team cooperation because there was a problem of division among kids coming from different neighborhoods. So I asked them to draw something together. We took a human figure, divided it up into parts, blew it up ten times its size, reconnected the parts, then dropped it out of a second-story window. Here was a sixty-foot person. It caused an amazing uproar. I saw that you could do an incredible amount of teaching with scale transformation. Changing scale in that way makes people perceive things differently.

Then I got hired in a program for the city with twenty artists. We were supposed to teach at parks all over the city. They looked at us and sent the black people to Watts and the Mexican people to East Los Angeles. So I ended up in East L.A.

I was given two classes, one at ten in the morning and another one at three in the afternoon. It was twenty-six miles from my home, so I would do my morning class and then hang out in the parks. I began to really watch street life. I saw young people, teenagers, adolescents, the throw-away people. Nobody wanted them in the parks; the Recreation and Parks Department had no programs planned for them because they were vandals, because they were involved in gang warfare. So they would play dominoes, drink wine, smoke dope, hang out in various corners. There was always this constant battle. The police would be called to get rid of them, and the kids would come back, like a flock of pigeons that fly up and land again. So I made friends with a lot of them. I met some kids who were involved in tattoo work. Of course, they were also writing all over the walls.

Visual symbols, calligraphy basically, were a focal point in their life on the street. You could read a wall and learn everything you needed to know about that community, about the guys or girls who hung out in the street—who they were, who they hung out with, what generation they were, how many of them had the same nickname—all in what they call *placayasos*.

I became something of an expert reader of street writing. I knew who was who in four or five different neighborhoods because I taught at different places. I realized *I* was moving from one part to the next, but they couldn't. They could not go five blocks without being in danger from other gangs. Some of the feuds were fifty or sixty years old.

That was my constituency. It's certainly not the whole of the Chicano community—I have to say that I get very perturbed when people perceive the Chicano community as being people who write all over the

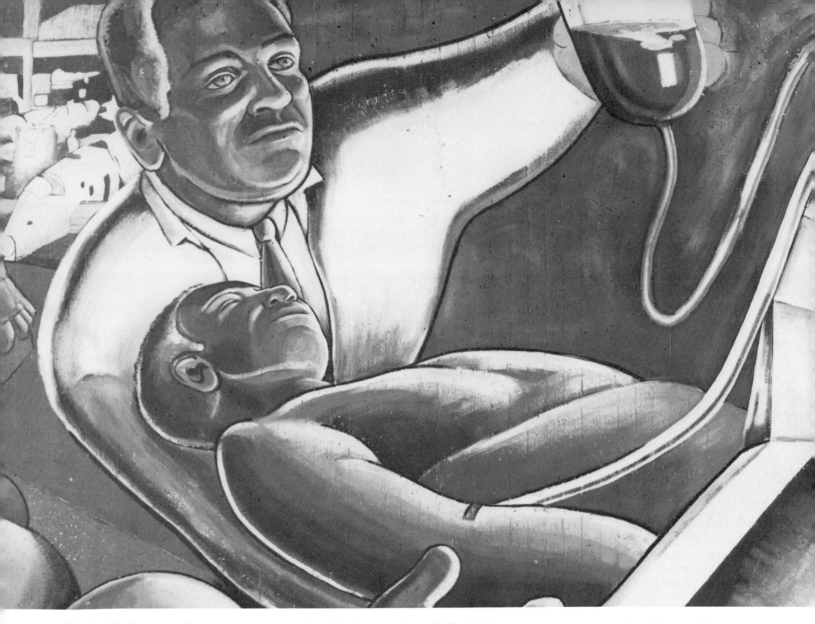

walls—but this is a street phenomenon that has been on the increase. In the sixties, it was more political slogans; now, it's about territory. It has to do with people saying, "Listen, I own nothing here. So I own your wall. Here's who I am." The tattoos are a whole thing, too. Kids with tattooed tears on their cheeks! What does that say about how the kids feel about themselves? What's going on for them is pretty rough, and it's reflected in the highest dropout rate in the entire nation.

I said I wanted to form a mural team. Pretty soon I had a number of people who began to hang with me, who trusted me and would do something I asked them to do. At that point nobody knew what a mural was; it wasn't the phenomenon it is now. I had to explain that we were going

to do a big picture on the wall. But I had to figure out how to get the wall back. It was marked. Who do I have to talk to to get permission to use this wall? So I said to the kids, "Listen, I'm going to take off your *placayasos*. Here's what we're going to do. Do you want to work with us?" It was like negotiating treaties.

The most important skill that I've had to develop in this work is to be able to deal with people in City Hall, then jump in my car, drive ten miles to the East Side, change into boots and jeans, and go sit on the curb with the kids. There are people who are bridge people, and my ability to move between those great extremes has made it possible for me to do what I do. Possibly, because I had a university education, because I became Anglicized to a certain degree, I was able to come back

to my own community with more information and make things happen.

I formed my first mural team of twenty kids from four different neighborhoods. It was the first time in recent history that they had been able to put aside their differences and work together. That was in 1970. We did three pieces that summer, including *Mi Abuelita*, a giant three-sided bandshell with a grandmother image in it— my grandmother, actually. I had to do it on a volunteer basis, but I got the kids paid.

Vandalism in the city park system is in the millions of dollars. The Recreation and Parks Department paints the walls white and dates them; that way, even if they're marked again, the public will know the department took care of its responsibility. Judging by the way the city spent its dollars, property damage was the concern,

The Great Wall of Los Angeles, detail 1981 section. 1940s: Dr. Charles Drew, the inventor of blood plasma, is shown cradling himself in his arms as he dies unnecessarily after a southern hospital refused to treat him for loss of blood. The iron hand, symbol of the dehumanization that racial discrimination brings, is shown cutting off the flow of blood, cutting off life.

not the fact that kids literally die in the parks, overdosing. That's of little significance. What is of significance is that before these kids fall over they write on the walls.

It was distressing to me to see kids die, to see that human beings were not as important as property. I would go to the people in the Recreation and Parks Department thinking that *obviously* if they could see the values their appropriation of money reflected, they would be more responsive to the community. I would say, "Why is it that in East L.A. you have a park built in 1923 with the smallest acreage per capita, when it has one of the largest usages in the city? Why can't you expand this park? Why don't you put in tennis courts?" When they started saying shit to me like, "Mexicans don't like to play tennis," I started getting the picture. I knew that there was racism, but I didn't understand how it was institutionalized.

People were amazed at our work. The *Los Angeles Times* ran sensational articles like "Teenage Youth Gangs Put Down Knives for Brushes." Terrible. The head of Rec and Parks came down to the site— the kids thought he was a narc, and he's lucky he got in and out of there—and said to me, simply, "How can we bottle and package what you do?" I began to understand that I was becoming to the City of Los Angeles a wonderful instrument of graffiti abatement. But I was accomplishing my goals at the same time by doing my own work in the street— which for me was clearly *not* graffiti abatement.

The group of people I was working with was very connected to and influenced by visual symbols—in tattoos, in the kind of writing that went on in the street—but there was no visible reflection of themselves in the larger community. Nothing of the architecture or visual symbols reflected the presence of the people—other than the graffiti. First it was a Jewish community, then Mexican people moved in. What I could see was that any population could move through the place without being reflected in it.

Symbols already had significance in this community, and it made sense to create another set of symbols acknowledging the people's commonality, the fact that they came from the same place and had a common culture. It seemed to me this could break down the divisions among these people, give them information, and change their environment. The murals have been clear forms of expression,

reflecting the issues and needs as they see them. I think decorative murals are a waste of time in urban areas. They're urban decoration, Band-Aids on cancer.

IN THE FIRST YEARS OF THIS work people came by and brought us food and beer, anything we needed. They would volunteer to help us. It was interesting, because there was a real division between the young people from the street and their families; their parents hated them for not being good Mexican kids and thought they had gotten completely out of control. It's that old country–new country stuff. I remember one community meeting when some boys from the White Fence gang were showing their designs. (We always do this to give people a chance to become involved in the process. Then there are no surprises— community people hate surprises.) A woman in the back of the room said, "All you ever do is ruin everything in the community. You write all over everything. You're just worthless. Why should we help you?" I thought, "My, what an outburst of hostility." I thought the kids were doing wonderfully to get up in front of a crowd like that and speak—this from people who were not essentially verbal. I asked, "Who is that?" One of the kids said it was his mother. But when the parents saw their kids doing something positive, connections among the family members began to develop again.

Few girls participated during that time. It was much easier organizing among the young men because girls were not allowed the same mobility. It has been a long process drawing the young girls in, but it's equal. It's taken this many years for that to happen. You see, Latin women are not supposed to be doing things like climbing on scaffolding, being in the public eye.

FROM 1970 TO 1974, THERE WAS an incredible outgrowth of murals in East Los Angeles. It wasn't just me—other people were doing it, too. The East Side of Los Angeles was becoming fairly well known for mural imagery. Suddenly there was an upheaval in the barrios; you could drive through them and see giant pieces all over the place. They were powerful, and they were strong, and they were political. They talked about who those people were, what they cared about, and what they were mad about. They talked about the issues

BACA: OUR PEOPLE ARE THE INTERNAL EXILES

in their community from police brutality to drug abuse.

By taking a small object and transforming it into a giant image, you teach people to look at it in a different way. Claus Oldenberg knew about that. When your whole body fits into the eye of a monumentally rendered head, you are going to look at it in a way you never looked at the eye before. The same thing is true of the issues included in the mural.

Take a piece of historical information: 350,000 Mexican people were deported from the California region in the thirties, 75,000 from Los Angeles. (It was similar to what's going on now; with the economic recession people are concerned that Mexican people are taking their jobs, and again they're talking about another Bracero program.) But you may not care much about history. That's the attitude you get from a lot of people. "Who cares about that fact?" But then, after four days rendering each person who's getting on the train, and standing next to the oversized face of someone who's feeling the agony of that deportation, there's no way not to identify with that feeling. As the light changes you see them in a different way. You make them real. You make it happen again. Or take a concept: the illusion of prosperity. Make some kind of image that will speak to that. Then have people transform the scale to four times natural size. At the end of that process, they can perceive the concept in a substantially different way.

I N 1974 I THOUGHT: WELL, GEE this is really interesting. I think anybody could make a mural. Certainly it's *bleak* in this city. Let's see what we can do about all the grey concrete walls. There were a lot of artists out of work and a lot of people in different communities who could use the opportunity to let the walls speak for them.

I had become fairly friendly with a number of political figures at that point because they had come to the site, seen what I was doing, helped me with the police who were bothering us, and so forth. I wrote a plan to get the city council to help us pay for an East Side brigade. There wasn't one Mexican representative on the whole council, not one in fifteen—even though the population was around forty percent Chicano (not including an uncounted population of probably one or two million undocumented workers). One of the council members told me, "You'll never get this because they don't care about the East Side. They'd like to see it drop off into the ocean." I thought, "He's right. There are fifteen council members, and I have to get it passed by all these votes."

I began to understand a whole lot about the political process. I went before a committee and got slaughtered. I was just devastated. The member from the San Fernando Valley said, "We don't have any gangs in our area. We don't have any youth that need this kind of stuff. Besides, I think we should put them all in jail." A lot of racist stuff came out *that* directly. I couldn't believe it! He said, "What is this, Mexican art?" I had to endure all kinds of abuse.

I went back very discouraged to this black council member who had been friendly with me. He told me, "Judy, you dream too small." I pored over that in my head for days and thought, "He's fuckin' right!" So I wrote a proposal, a very grandiose idea for a citywide mural program. It would incorporate forty murals a year covering a radius of over a hundred miles in every ethnic community of the city. And would cost in the area of $150,000 a year. They gave it to me.

It was a struggle for about six months. I had to appear in front of all types of committees. I would give my spiels over and over again about what it would do for senior citizens, children, professional artists, the black community, the Chicano community, the Asian community, the Korean community, the Thai community, the Chinese community. Then I spent the next three years of my life doing it—a real ordeal. They might give you the money, but they're not going to help you. In fact, they're going to get in your way at every turn. For example, suddenly they would say, "All people hired from now on must have tuberculosis tests." Try getting a thousand people tuberculosis tests who don't have transportation. Or, "All payments will take four to six weeks." The mural would be done in three or four weeks, then you'd get whole gangs of kids coming after you because you haven't paid them. Crazy stuff. That's when I learned administrative skills.

I also learned how to work in a multi-ethnic situation. I no longer was working solely in the Chicano community. I learned that organizing in the Chinese community is *radically* different than organizing in the Chicano community or in the black community. I realized that the Chicano staff was absolutely racist against blacks and saw how the black style of coming in and being able to articulate what's in their mural just turned off my staff, who wanted to veto every black mural that came through.

A LOT OF THE MURALS DONE in that program were cultural kinds of pieces; even the tame ones were, in fact, important statements to announce—for example, the presence of Filipinos in a community where no one would acknowledge them. There was a piece on the landing of Filipinos in the Philippine islands, which was very similar to the Mexican legend of the Aztecs arriving in Tenochtitlan. This is what gave me the idea about overlapping legends. I thought that was a wonderful thing; people could see how they all connected in some ways.

Some of the pieces were about police brutality and the open warfare that goes on between the police and the people in the communities. Some were about immigration, what the immigration authorities were doing, and the exploitation of illegal workers. Others were about drug abuse, including the government-supported influx of drugs into the communities and the *Los Tres* issue in Los Angeles, where three people were imprisoned for shooting a narcotics agent who was bringing narcotics into the community.

A lot of pieces were on gentrification and urban renewal, on how the developers' interests are taking people's homes away from them. One of the most controversial was a piece that showed, on one side, an idyllic scene in the Venice community done in the style of a Persian miniature; on the other side were bulldozers wiping out the folks, knocking down the small wooden houses on the canals to make room for a plush condo city. In the corner was a little guy spraying, "Stop the pigs. Save Venice." Before the mural was put up, these words had been scrawled on the wall in four-foot red letters. The guy who had done that came to our community meeting and said, "My graffiti is more important than your mural." People thought that he had something there and decided to incorporate it into the mural. So the mural was sort of an illustration of his graffiti. The realtors picked up on it and tried to stop us. In

The Great Wall of Los Angeles, detail 1981 section. 1940s: "We Fight Fascism at Home and Abroad" commemorates the struggle by Mrs. Laws against the covenant laws that denied blacks access to equal housing in South Central Los Angeles.

fact, just recently they painted half of it out before the community found out. To keep the mural up, I had to go to about twenty meetings, all the way up to Chief Ed Davis, and explain that in this case "pig" meant greed, not police.

It was truly an *amazing* experience. We were dealing with problems that are manifested in the whole society, going out into these communities and seeing how artists are treated. We did 250 murals (I probably directed around 150) and hired over 1,000 people. It wore me out—to death.

We were putting these pieces up all over the city, which was all fine and good. But at some point, because of the sun and the pollution, and because the murals were in poor communities that were subject to redevelopment, the murals would be torn down. Then the people would get up in arms. For example, somebody would start

to paint out a mural when a building owner had changed, and fifty people would be out there with sticks wanting to beat up the guy. We had organized well in the communities, so they protected their murals. But we couldn't get money for maintenance, and it was very difficult to make building owners keep the pieces up.

I also saw artists do just *awful* things in the communities, like coming into an ethnically mixed community and, because the artist was Chicano, painting a Chicano piece with only Chicano kids. Sometimes they would incite people to attack a police officer; everybody would be beaten up and taken to jail—except the artist. Terrible things!

I couldn't handle it anymore. I couldn't control the quality of the pieces. I was tired of supporting other people, breaking my ass and killing myself, and being in

BACA: OUR PEOPLE ARE THE INTERNAL EXILES

this no-man's land position between the community and the city. The community perceived me as being part of the city bureaucracy, while the officials perceived me as being a flaming radical from the community!

It was very hard, and I was very exhausted by the end of it. I decided to start a nonprofit corporation. I had a support group operating for the Citywide Mural Project because I knew at some point the city would withdraw its support. Some of these pieces were *very* political, and I expected that at some point they would want to stop me. In fact, they tried to kill the mural program twice. There were huge battles, letter campaigns, "Citizens to Save the Murals" committees. I didn't want to continue that type of struggle all the time and not get to do my own work—especially since I actually did it better than a lot of people I was supporting to do it. So in 1977 I left the mural project to do *The Great Wall*.

I'd done a number of other big pieces by that time—the Venice murals, the East L.A. murals. I did a 400-foot-long piece and another couple that were about 300–400 feet long. I decided I would pull together all the stuff I had learned into one place and address the issue of having people work together. I had also seen the ghetto-ization of the work, like wonderful pieces done by black artists that were only seen in the black community. They weren't getting the exposure that they deserved. In some ways, murals began to acquire a connotation as "ghetto art." Middle-class and upper-middle-class areas began to resist them in their neighborhoods because they saw them as a ghetto phenomenon. I figured I had to get on that fast. That's why I began SPARC. I formed it with a friend who's an independent filmmaker and another woman who was a printmaker. We began *The Great Wall* as our first project.

I thought that we could generate additional funding to expand the concept of community murals into other art forms. The concept of working in public art or monumental kinds of public pieces with the community could be the basis of the work that we did, the bottom line being to create social change in whatever environment we were working in. I wanted to see other artists be able to address a community with an idea that they had, whatever the form. That's what happened.

In 1977, through a lot of political maneuvering, we got the old Venice Jail for free. I wanted to be able to work within an institution. We have to create our own institutions that are sort of deinstitutionalized. It gave me a vehicle through which to have an ongoing connection with the community, not be isolated from other people in my studio.

I originally began the mural thinking that with each artist given the responsibility for a segment of the wall, a wonderful piece would come together in some way. But, in fact, the artists were not as willing to work with each other in the composition of an overall piece as I thought they would be. They created a series of easel paintings. I don't feel that the first thousand feet is a mural. Each hundred-foot segment is different and reflects the personal style of the artist and the people in the artist's crew. Now we're doing it with an overall design.

Probably one of the hardest things for me to do is to recognize my leadership ability because I've always been wanting to give it away whenever possible. I think it's part of my cultural thing that comes up. In the Chicano community, leaders are wiped out. People hate leaders. It's not a good position to be in. Also, it's very hard to acknowledge that I have to say "No," "Yes," "You do what I tell you to do," or "I have leadership on this." Yet I would always take all the responsibility: I would raise all the money; I would do all the preparatory work; I would be the one who would ultimately answer to everyone and see to it that everyone was paid—but I submitted to a collective process all the decision-making power over the planning of the mural. By 1978 I realized I couldn't do that again. I really had to decide whether I wanted the piece to go past what it had been in that first summer. I had a vision for it that I thought was much more encompassing, and I realized if I really wanted to see that happen I had to trust my idea and trust myself to know that it was going to be better for me to make those decisions. And it was.

The thing about muralism, particularly in monumental pieces, is that collaboration is a requirement. It isn't like other art forms you might be able to accomplish by yourself. I've seen a lot of men in Los Angeles do monumental pieces on a two-story or eight-story building, by them-
(Interview text continued on page 73)

A BRIEF HISTORY OF S.P.A.R.C.

by NANCY ANGELO

The Great Wall of Los Angeles, 1981 mural crew.

ORIGINALLY AN ADVISORY committee to the Citywide Mural Project, the Social and Public Art Resource Center (SPARC) was founded in the late seventies by muralist Judy Baca, filmmaker Donna Deitch and painter and printmaker Christina Schlesinger, who dreamed of an organization that could expand the vision of public art and reestablish the artist as a visual spokesperson for the community.

Dedicated to the production, exhibition, distribution, and preservation of public art, SPARC has been noted for its passionate commitment to social change issues, innovative approaches, and active involvement of audiences never reached by traditional arts organizations. The organization places special emphasis on artworks that reflect the history, concerns, and aspirations of America's many different races and ethnic groups; it has also particularly sought to serve youth, senior citizens, women, and working people. Here art meets human needs by empowering people to learn skills and enlarge their sense of the world.

SPARC has received funding from government agencies and social service programs as well as traditional art sources. Its organization and staff size has varied over the years with the level of this funding. Currently SPARC's programs fall into six areas:

—The Old Venice Jail Gallery provides a showcase for public and social art. Shows have included *Anti–World War III*, a collection of political posters by the San Francisco Poster Brigade; *The No-Nuke Show* by Artists for Survival; *Changing Venice*, a visual and oral survey showing the impact of gentrification on the local area; *Three Views of LA*, with works by Black, Chicano, and Asian artists; *Portable Murals*, which originated at San Francisco's Galeria de la Raza; and *The NY-LA Urban Activist Show*.

—The Outdoor Gallery is a collection of publicly and SPARC-commissioned murals in the greater Los Angeles area, including *The Great Wall of Los Angeles* and works by Jose Bravo, Roberto Delgado, Rip Cronk, and David Russell.

—The Mural Taller (Spanish for "workshop"), modeled on that of Mexican master Sigueiros, provides training in the technical, artistic, and business aspects of mural-making; it also functions as a production studio.

—The Media Resource Center houses a collection of 12,000 slides which document the history of murals internationally, nationally, and locally—including a special collection of California Chicano murals. The center also distributes slides, filmstrips, videotapes, postcards, mural maps, and publications.

—The Literary Arts Program provides access to the public—through weekly readings and the Venice Poetry Workshop—to writers who have been overlooked and underserved by many traditional literary organizations because of their age, gender, ethnic origin, or political orientation.

—Special projects, sponsored in response to community concerns, have included the "Anti-PCP Dustmobile," a multimedia exhibition produced by the SPARC staff in conjunction with community youth and representatives of drug rehabilitation programs; a hanging put together by Leiko Yamamoto from small pieces woven by schoolchildren; and a series of issue-oriented billboards done by Jose Bravo with ten local youth.

SPARC's largest project is *The Great Wall of Los Angeles*, which began when the Army Corps of Engineers asked Judy Baca to help "beautify" a flood control channel in the San Fernando Valley. The longest mural in the world, this depiction

BACA: OUR PEOPLE ARE THE INTERNAL EXILES

MURAL MAKERS

TODD ABLESER
STEVE ALVARA
OLEG BERSON
ANGEL CHAVEZ
JOHN FLORES
YVONNE FLORE
DARLENE FREE
MIKE GALVAN
FERNANDO GAR
MARIA GARCIA
HILBERT GURALI

Overview of *The Great Wall of Los Angeles*, 1981.

of California's multicultural history from prehistoric to contemporary times runs over one-third mile. Throughout the five summers from 1976 to 1983, over 250 youth and seventy artists, historians and other resource people worked on the wall with Baca, who is artistic director.

Just as the breakdown of institutional racism requires the commitment and involvement of huge numbers of diverse groups and individuals, so does *The Great Wall*. Among the participants orchestrating this massive project, along with SPARC staff, are:
−A myriad of government agencies that have granted permits and funds, cut red tape, lent equipment, volunteered staff to work on the project, and provided needed services.
−Many community organizations that have contributed advice and expertise, funding for youth and supervisors' wages, lunches, publicity, and community contacts.
−Members of local business, industry, unions and arts councils that have provided everything from orange juice and scaffolding to direct funding for a theater component of the project.
−Skilled artists and community youth from different ethnic groups and neighborhoods who are hired to work on the project.
−Historians, anthropologists, folklorists,

and people who lived in the periods depicted in the mural, all of whom contribute to the research each year.

The San Fernando Valley has a long history of racial strife and cultural isolation. Most public spaces in the area are occupied by young people but are not designed to meet their needs. *The Great Wall* enables participants, most of whom have little contact with kids from other cultural backgrounds, to learn about and develop deep relationships with each other. By paying them, it not only gives them sorely needed income but also tells them that their work is valuable to the community. Those who take on more responsibility in subsequent years are paid more. They learn about their cultural heritage and gain important reading, math, research and other skills as a by-product of their work on the project.

The Great Wall provides a context in which change, both social and personal, is not only possible—it has to happen. Working on the mural, the youth learn that they can aspire to something grandiose and see it accomplished through cooperation and struggle. They come to understand that they are not their own and one another's enemies, and their whole concept of the world expands as they learn about other possibilities and solutions.△

The Great Wall of Los Angeles, detail
1980 section. 1940s: Japanese
being forcibly taken to internment
camps during World War II.

selves. But *The Great Wall* is based on a
different conception of what art is for. The
mural is not just a big picture on a wall.
The focus is on cooperation in the process
underlying its creation. I could probably go
into my studio for a year in advance and
design it; but, for one, there's not that
kind of funding to support my work for a
year, and, two, the process that we use
really works in with the overall plan. With
what the historians bring in we develop
images to put back into public consciousness information that has been lost. It's
really incredibly stimulating and exciting.
The mural is a conceptual art piece all
along, and the finished painting is only one
part of it.

To bring talented young people into the
design crew fits the goals of the project.
It's part of the leadership development
aspect of the program, giving kids more
and more power to meet and enhance
their growth. Also, I think the mural is
better because it has a number of minds
working on it. The hardest part is making
the design work as a unified piece, but the
collaboration on ideas really is wonderful.

We sit with the historians and do a
"talk-through." We write out a story:
"First there was this period in which
people thought everything was fine; it was
an 'illusion of prosperity.' What was really

going on was Prohibition, the whole
flapper image, the coming Crash. . . ." It
goes like that. You talk it through in a
literal way, which develops an attitude that
comes from people hashing it out together.
In that way, people who are not the best
at drawing don't have to be relied on for
that. It's orchestrating people's best skills,
using their better abilities, putting them
together where they match. It's geometric
in proportion. It multiplies the power that
you have by taking the best of other
people and putting it all together in one
thing. However, one person must have the
overall vision for it to become a whole.

When we get hung up, it's my job to
push things forward to set up a situation
in which people can be creative. At this
point I have the ultimate veto power when
I think something is not working. I have
to trust my judgment. The people who
work with me understand that I have to
be able to say, "I just think this is not
working." Although the conceptualization
takes place in a group, I approve every
image idea before it goes to thumbnail.

After we develop the thumbnails, I may
do as many as twenty different drawing
studies of the woman carrying a child in
the Dust Bowl scene. Then I take all the
thumbnails and submit them to an overall
discipline of a musical division of space—

The Great Wall of Los Angeles, detail
1981 section. 1940s: Taxis bring
servicemen into Los Angeles for the
"Zoot Suit Riots" in which Mexican-
American boys were stripped and
beaten by marines with the consent
of the police.

ratio development, musical time 3:5, etc.
That's basically how I deal with the
overall composition. I also do corrections
on everyone's drawings if things are not
anatomically correct or whatever. This
way there are many minds working on the
concepts and one artistic vision pulling it
all together.

I THINK I ORIGINALLY HAD THE
idea that leadership meant for me to be
the person who created an environment
in which other people could be creative.
Now I acknowledge the fact that I usually
have more experience than anyone else in
my group, more mural experience. I've
done a tremendous amount of work at this
point. I've also watched a whole lot of
other people do a tremendous amount of
work. And I've made a lot of mistakes.
Now, leadership means trusting my
intuition, which I think is fairly highly
developed, about how to deal with people.

I didn't like any hierarchy. I just thought
that we should all be equal. But for now, I
really can't say that's possible. I think if I
worked in a situation where everybody
raised the money, everybody had responsibility, and eveybody had the same level of
experience, it would be fine. But even
then, the world outside would not relate to
a collective answering a question. There's
got to be one person who ultimately takes
it on the chin. Maybe I'm getting tired,

but I no longer want to take it for
anybody else's mistakes besides my own.
Also, when I don't listen to what I think, I
screw up.

Of course, if a woman takes this on
she's a bitch, a dyke, a macha, a demanding, difficult-to-work-with person—all those
kinds of things. Those are stereotypes
about what a woman is if she's a leader.
I'm conscious all the time of my own
body, of what it says to people when I'm
talking to them, of the way that I use my
words to communicate. I try to use all
those parts and pull them together in a
way that communicates from a soft place
in myself—not the defense/fear place—
what I think and what I care about, what I
want other people to do and think and
care about. They may not care, but at
least I'm communicating my attitudes to
them. That's how I feel I'm a leader. A lot
of times I can plug into the psychology of
a group, the overriding feeling, what
they're creating for themselves—and pull it
out and say, "Let's define it. What is it?"
That's part of my role as a leader. So
much of it is really being a good teacher.
So much of it is drama, being some kind
of theater person. But the other part of it
is that although I take the consequences
for the decisions, I often don't make a
decision totally by myself. A lot of times I
really am a catalyst, a facilitator. But the
other part of it is, I often have to take the
responsibility for making decisions myself.

The whole business of learning to be responsible is hard. I have gotten myself in a position a number of times where I've made myself sick. I had acute acrylic poisoning two years ago from mural paint. I was in intensive care with cardiac arrhythmia. I couldn't breathe. It's a little known fact that the metals in acrylic paint are as dangerous as, and in fact are the same as, those in oil paint. Because artists have no power in this country, they don't get any of the safety hazard information that other workers get. I have had a hard time acknowledging that I have to take care of myself. I say all the time in group meetings with my staff at SPARC, "I am one resource. If you use me up we're all in trouble." That means that I have to see myself as a valuable natural resource that has to be preserved in the same way that a river or a tree has to be preserved. I've got to take care of myself. I'm working at it, but I find myself not doing it a lot of the time. It frightens me. That's part of being willful, pushing yourself when your body is telling you something else. We are not taught to be nurturing of ourselves. We're taught to sacrifice, particularly in my culture. The women put on the black mantilla, and they are the mourners and the producers and the nurturers. They make them and they bury them.

People who do this kind of work are in such danger of burnout, or absolutely destroying themselves. We have all those people who have wonderful capabilities out there, people who've been real instrumental in making things happen, and they all get beat up, literally beat up! There's something wrong with how we are perceiving ourselves. That's critical information.

I THINK THE WORLD IS BECOMING interested in what political artists are doing. Political art is now perceived as "avant-garde" or something, and I see people trying to get recognition in this way. I'm not focusing on that, yet some of it happens. For example, a museum is going to be taking *The Great Wall* and blowing it up, doing a whole thing on all the sketches and studies we do to make it happen.

I don't feel that the mainstream art world is something I either want to attack or court. Certainly, it is another kind of audience, and I believe in audience development. But there's a difference between public and personal art, and I'm a public artist.

If I decided now to take the time to do personal work I could pursue putting it in different places, finding a group of my friends who would like it or finding another audience that would respond to it. That's not invalid. But so far, I've been trying to have the public at large relate to my work. I think this has also been happening in other areas like artists' books and performance art, which has had the capacity for organizing large groups of people and bringing them to a different state of consciousness very quickly.

I see myself as an urban artist, using the entire environment that I work in, which includes the people in that environment. If I'm talking about transforming an environment—changing, enhancing, making it more beautiful—then I am also talking about changing the people who live in that environment as well. Accepting the whole reality of the space means working with who populates the area and seeing what I can do to better the whole situation. The reason I work with adolescents is not simply because I'm interested in teaching, but because they are the people who populate those public areas. I'm also interested in working with all the power structures—the local authorities, local municipalities, the Army Corps of Engineers, Teamsters' Union—because they are part of the reality of that area. That's how I would define myself as an urban artist. The elements of my designing are not just line, form and color but all the environmental and social factors that are inherent in the space and that cannot be separated from it. That's changing everything and not just the facade.△

Smile beneath your Tears

by Holly Near

I AM A SONGWRITER, I DO NOT JUST write about my own life, yet I do write from my own experience, for it is the only one I know. Therefore, it is in my best interest to stretch the boundaries of that experience—through the top of my head, out the bottom of my feet, miles and miles wider than my shoulders and deep in the center of my heart.

Writing is seldom a detached act or an intellectual exercise. Need is often the best inspiration for a song. However, it takes a willingness to know more truth than you bargained for. Because of the nature of everyday life, there is no shortage of subject matter. The limitations come from thinking there are some things we cannot write about. I start out to write a song about child abuse, and it becomes a wrenching journey into the gut of a loved one. I start out to write a song about gay liberation or a lesbian mother, and it turns into the realization of my own sexuality, leading to a new relationship to self and to a powerful love. One must be careful what one says to a songwriter. It might end up in a song. It might end up in her life, for growth and change enhance artistry. Consciousness-raising is a stepping stone to creativity, and life itself must be seen as an intrusion.

Ana Clara, will you tell me about Uruguay? I took a friend with me who understands Spanish better than I do. We drove past familiar trees and gardens, winding up the hill to Cedric and Mary Belfrage's house. I had been falling in love with Mexico (and them) for several weeks now. Ana Clara was becoming a part of that love.

We sat around a big, wooden table . . . it felt like a symbol of the help the Belfrages offer to many refugees and exiles from Latin America and the hand they offer to travelers who visit and experience their busy household. Cedric and Mary have made Cuernavaca their home since Cedric was deported from the United States during the cold war witch-hunts of the 1950s.

The big wooden table, Cedric and Mary, three North Americans who teach in a small town nearby, Ana Clara's family—which included her husband, her former husband, and their children (all exiles from Uruguay)—and Ana Clara herself. I will never forget her or this day.

Ana Clara began by talking joyfully about the music of Uruguay, naming composers such as Daniel Viglietti and Alfredo Zitarrosa. Daniel now lives in exile in Paris and Alfredo in Mexico. She played a song by Zitarrosa called *"Mi Pais"* ("My Country"). There was love in the room—love for Uruguay and for those who struggle for liberation, whether in Paris, Cuernavaca, or Montevideo—love brought to us on the strong wings of the songs. The songs! Always the songs.

Then Ana Clara spoke of the new song movement in Uruguay, the *canto nuevo*—old sounds and rhythms with new lyrics written carefully so as to speak the truth without saying the words, for specific words carry the threat of prison.

Women's Song and Resistance in Uruguay

I think of other international "music lessons" I have had. I think of the time in the Philippines when, at a casual group meeting with revolutionaries, I sang, "I'm gonna lay down my sword and shield and study war no more," and a woman cried and quietly said, "What a privilege to sing such words!" The day when she would be able to lay down her sword and shield was far away.

I think of Saigon. I sat in a small room with a woman who had been in a "tiger cage" prison cell. Bombs were dropping fifty miles outside the city. She spoke quietly to me, for Thieu's police were always outside the door. She gave me a drawing smuggled out of prison, then sang me a song in "poet's code," where the true meaning takes cover between the lines.

I think of a village north of Hanoi. Two young women were sitting in a doorway of the workers' housing. It was very early. I couldn't sleep so I was out walking. I smiled to them. They smiled. They knew who I was. I'd been on TV the day before and was probably the only redhead in North Vietnam! Moments later, they were unbraiding my long red hair. They each had a single braid; I wore mine in two. They took the bands of their braids and traded them for mine, and tenderly rebraided my hair. They sang me a Vietnamese folk song and the "Internationale" in Vietnamese. I sang for them as well, "Birthday Children" and "Wedding Song." We hugged goodbye.

In the early seventies. I went to a concert of lesbian music and slowly realized how much the world, and even the Left, hated the fact that women loved each other—the level of my discomfort becoming a barometer. It took many songs before I could understand that women were feared and hated not only by the fascists but by the Left as well. Several years later, after Harvey Milk was murdered, I wrote "Singing for Our Lives."

Someone told me that women in Ireland were singing "Mountain Song" in their struggle against British occupation. Someone else told me he heard "It Could Have Been Me" sung in a Latin American prison. It was the frustrating experience of not being able to understand the songs of Cuban singer Sara Gonzales that finally encouraged me to study Spanish. I often go to sleep to the songs of Inti-Illimani, Mercedes Sosa, and Norma Gadea—lullabies that produce complex dreams. The songs are sung, regardless. The songs. The songs!

Our meeting is hard. I don't understand enough Spanish to listen and get all the details, the images. I want Ana Clara's words, but I can't write and feel at the same time. I decide to write. My friends help with the translation. I put feeling on the back burner. Ana Clara makes it difficult to refrain from feeling. She brings her story—this woman with a set jaw that softens with the presence of her children, with dark eyes that have seen what I do not want to know, and hands that speak

like a guitarist's hands, accentuating the lyric of a song. Her little daughter plays quietly, never leaving her mother's hip. I wonder how often this child has heard what we are about to hear. I wonder, what does she think? How old do you have to be to know that your mother is alive only by chance and courage?

Ana Clara Trinidad speaks.

"My country is a small country. By 1975, more than seven thousand of us had disappeared into the hands of the fascists. Today, one quarter of the people have fled the country. There is hardly anyone left who has not been attacked in one way or another. Everyone has been affected. What is incredible is the human ability of my people to continue intensive resistance, and to maintain the spirit in the struggle ever since the coup. That was in 1973. At that time, I remember the workers occupied seventy factories for two weeks in what was possibly the greatest organized resistance to a fascist takeover. But we could not hold on. Soon, repression became more horrendous than ever, and all leftist publications went underground.

"I want to tell you about one woman I know. Her name is Chicha. She is sixty-four years old. She has been part of the struggle for liberation all her life. Chicha has a great voice." Ana Clara's eyes twinkle. I assume it is because she is imagining how much I would enjoy hearing Chicha sing. I think of Malvina Reynolds, Aunt Molly Jackson, and others. I smile.

Near: *Smile Beneath Your Tears*

"Chicha is in prison. She has been at the women's prison, *Penal de Punta de Rieles*, for about eight years. Her crime? It is hard to point to one crime when a person is part of resisting fascism. One's very life is a crime. Chicha was editor of the magazine, *Nosotras*, and editorial secretary of the review, *Estudios*. She was arrested in October of 1975. There were massive arrests of alleged members of the Uruguayan Communist Party.

"When Eduardo Bleier was arrested, they buried him alive while Chicha watched. She ran to save him, throwing off the dirt, knowing that they could kill her, too. She dug him up, in front of the bayonets, and for this she received twenty days of *special punishment*.

"For six months, Chicha was held in a prison called *El Infierno* ("hell")—a warehouse made over into a torture· chamber. The prisoners are kept on the ground floor. They are forced to wear hoods so they cannot see. Often they are not allowed clothing. They are nude. Each person has a number. When your number is called, you must walk up the stairs to the mezzanine, the torture area, where you are hung nude by your arms, which are tied behind your back, or by your hair. No one below knows who is being tortured. There are no names. There is no night or day. Loud music is played to drown out the screams...music!...twisted into a brutal psychological weapon."

I remember hearing that in the tiger cages of Saigon they played loud rock and roll while people were being tortured, and they would say to the victims, "Where are your peace movement friends now?" I must not drift...I am missing Ana Clara's story.

"Sometimes a doctor in a white coat stands by—an accomplice—who notifies the torturer when to stop before the prisoner dies. He is trained to know how far torture can go before it kills. Lighted cigarettes and matches are used to burn people like Chicha...applied to sensitive parts of the body. Limbs stretched away from the body. Hands crushed in iron frames. Electrodes attached to fingers, to the head, to the genitals."

My head leaps again to Saigon...where they used live eels to terrorize women prisoners, stuffing them up into women's vaginas...I have never been able to free myself from that story. Why do we need to hear such stories? Because if it is

happening, we must know it is happening, and we must see that it does not happen...it must not keep happening.

Ana Clara's voice comes back to me. "Then you are sent back downstairs to recover. The next number is called. This goes on and on.

"Chicha was held there for six months before being sent to another prison, the Punta Rieles prison for women, where she is presently serving her sentence. We are told Chicha sang all the time. Against the orders of the guard, she would sing. She sang to identify herself. She sang to break down the psychological warfare as well as to sustain her courage during torture. She sang to make contact with other prisoners. She sang to fight alienation and insanity. She began to get the women organized. They did clandestine art, pulling threads out of what little clothing was available. They did an embroidery on a potato sack which was then smuggled out of prison. The women were forced to wear hoods, so they had to sit very straight and look down in order to see their message: '*Despues de la tormenta siempre sale el sol*' ('After the torture, the sun always comes out')."

Why didn't they kill Chicha when she was so defiant and so inspirational to other prisoners? Because to kill her is to make her a martyred heroine. But there is another reason.

Ana Clara continues: "Torture is extremely hard on anyone and a repressive threat to the population. Eduardo Bleier was a party leader, very charismatic, full of life, dearly beloved, Jewish, and because of this he was tortured worse than others. His daughter, who lives in Israel, tried to get help for her father but to no avail. We do not know if he is alive or dead. Jaime Perez, another party leader, was turned into a vegetable by the brutal beatings he suffered. He cannot speak or concentrate. One more year in prison and he will have served half his sentence.

"Torture is even more difficult for women because there is also rape by men, by dogs, and sometimes by other women—for there are women torturers, too. And women prisoners have the special fear for the lives of their children.

"I want to tell you about another woman. Her name is Selva. She has been in prison for seven years. Her husband, Uruguay—yes, that is his real name—has been in prison for seven years, also. He has developed cancer. The children are with the grandparents.

"Selva has been raped many times in prison. Selva says the women in the prison are incredibly strong, and although they have been raped and tortured many times, she has never seen one woman break down and give names or information. Their endurance is beyond imagination. The women talk together about their guilty feelings for having chosen revolution and struggle, knowing this choice would affect their children. Do we have the right to choose such a path? Selva wrote to her child, trying to explain. The grandparents printed the letter and handed it around, hoping it would help others to understand."

Ana Clara tries to remember parts of the letter. At this point in her story, the fire in her eyes has turned to a storm and her hands, moving with a fury, check to feel her child still close by. We all watch, trying to keep our own tears inside a while longer, for the story must not stop. I must keep writing. I must not cry yet—I am so grateful that Ana Clara can still cry. She remembers the letter.

Look at the years I have spent in prison, in the struggle. I miss you so. It is so lonely to not know about your life, to not share life with you. What music do you listen to? What do you think about? All I have to give you is my life as a revolutionary to make a world where children don't have to visit their parents through prison bars. I hope you think this is enough. This is all I have to give you.

There is silence around the table. Now there is room for tears. Ana Clara cries out, "The best of our people! Thousands of children growing up with fear and hate. They do not know what parents are!"

Ana Clara does not speak much of her own life, but I have gathered from conversations with her friends that there is an Ana Clara story, along with that of Chicha and Selva and Eduardo and Uruguay and Jaime and thousands of others, including Daniel Viglietti and Alfredo Zitarrosa. We know that Ana Clara was a teacher at the secondary and university levels. We know she was in prison and that she was tortured. Somehow, she and her family escaped. Her brother disappeared into government hands in Argentina, but his child still writes to Ana Clara. After the coup, when

Mary and Cedric Belfrage were trying to find friends they had met in Uruguay, they were told of a woman and her family, ready with visas to leave the country. She needed only money to escape. Mary heard of this on a Wednesday morning. The woman needed the money by Thursday to leave on Friday. The Belfrages had $200. By noon, they had collected $200 more from their guests. At 3:30, an unexpected visitor arrived, a conservative man they had not seen for years. He noticed Mary's concerned face, asked what was wrong and then, without much more than a brief explanation, wrote out a check. Now they had the necessary $800. Ana Clara and her tired children walked off the plane in Mexico City, Friday night.

Mary did not want to meet Ana Clara. In the past, the refugees she had been able to help felt so grateful for a freedom that Mary believed was their birthright. These meetings were uncomfortable. But the benefactor did want to meet the family he had helped. Mary set up a meeting.

It was not long before Mary and Ana Clara recognized the revolutionary in each other. Theirs was not a "savior" and "the saved" relationship. They became close friends. One time, Mary went to pick up Ana's three-year-old at day care. The child had a little friend who was crying because her mother had not come yet. Ana's daughter said, "Maybe your mother has been arrested." Such is the awareness of children who have survived fascism.

So. . .my people. . .I am trying to tell you. I am trying to tell myself. It takes a willingness to know more truth than you bargained for...the limitations come from thinking there are some things we cannot write about. I am faced with those limitations now. I have tried to write a song about torture. . .for ten years I have tried. I can speak of it and then follow the story with a song, but I cannot put the words to song. I cannot put *those* words to song. It is also that I do not want to give you the nightmares I have. I do not want to put horrendous images into tender minds. And yet, if it is being inflicted on people, we must know about it so that we have the freedom to stop it. And so I write a song that calls for your courage. We will have to sing for Chicha and Selva on the outside. . .joining her voice as it defies the walls of the prison cell.

Sing to soothe the nightmares of those who have been endlessly awake for so long, and sing in hope that we can wake up those who sleep.

Near: *Smile Beneath Your Tears*

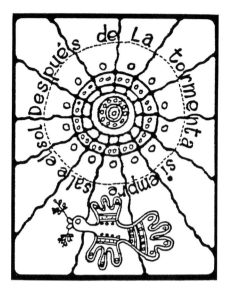

Drawing by Holly Near

Oh Come Smile

Take my hand
Or I may have to leave the room
Please end your story soon
It's not like me to run away
But I don't think that I can stay
To hear your story

Knowing your name
Ties my heart around each tortured cry
And you didn't die
Let me keep looking deep in your eyes
So I have no chance to break the ties
Though the cage is locked the spirit flies
The prison song escapes—the truth defies

Chorus:
Oh come smile with us
It helps to make the days seem less
like years
Oh come smile with us
Smile beneath your tears

Don't turn away
There are things in life my heart must know
Though feelings tell me go hurry go
Words that startle my waking dreams
But if you have lived it then it seems that I
must hear it
Feeling your hand resting on my shoulder
to ease the pain
To ease my shame
Have we forgotten or is it just too hard
to feel
Protecting tenderness with steel
And with the rarest kind of smile
You help me heal

Postscript: March 1984

On my way back from an inspirational visit in Nicaragua, I stopped to see Ana Clara, who had much new news to share about Uruguay. She told me that Chicha had been released from prison and was on her way to Belgium to be reunited with her exiled husband and to have a much-needed coronary operation.

Ana Clara showed me a videotape of an interview with Chicha shortly after her release. Such a face and a smile—even after eight years in prison! Chicha is a beautiful, strong woman with a profound look of dignity and wisdom. In the interview, she talked about how important the news of international solidarity was to her and the other women in the prison. Every time they received a smuggled-in piece of information about international work being done on their behalf, they felt relief and love and support—not only for them personally but for the Uruguayan resistance.

She stressed how important solidarity work is—how it concretely helped her get out of prison—and she wants everyone to know international solidarity work is effective. Each letter, each song, each rally directly affects their lives.

I was astonished to learn that in order for political prisoners to be released when their term is up, they must pay the equivalent of $3 for every day they were in prison. That's more than $1,000 a year. Many of the families of prisoners can't afford that, especially because relatives of political prisoners are blacklisted and cannot find employment. Those who can't afford to pay must stay in prison until they can pay, and their bill goes up each day. Part of the solidarity work with the political prisoners is to raise money to help them get out of prison.

Ana Clara also told me about some important and exciting events that had happened in Uruguay over the past few months. On 27 November 1983, more than 400,000 people (in a tiny country whose total population is 3.5 million) filled the streets of Montevideo demanding an end to the dictatorship and the restoration of democracy: "*Se va a acabar la dictadura militar!*" ("The military dictatorship will end!") It was the largest demonstration in Uruguay in the ten years since the dictatorship took power, and the result of organizing that had begun with a few people banging pots and pans in their houses with the lights out, then spreading through the neighborhoods with people making noise with their lights turned on. It spread as more people stood in open doorways, greeting each other with shouts of protest until they finally took to the streets in such large numbers that the police were ordered to stay away.

One of the victories won through the long, hard organizing was the right to hold *canto nuevo* festivals in the large auditoriums as long as the songs to be sung were approved first by the censor. The songwriters were already rehearsed for this limitation. The censors had no grounds, for example, to ban songs celebrating the "opening of the windows," but the audience knew the true meaning, of course.

Three weeks after the big demonstration, several international organizations staged "*la llegada de los niños*" ("the arrival of the children"). One hundred fifty-six children of Uruguayan political prisoners were allowed to return from exile in Europe for a short visit to see their parents in prison, some of them for the first time since they were infants. About 400,000 people turned out spontaneously to greet the children, lining the streets from the airport to the center of Montevideo. The fifteen-minute drive took over three hours through the crowds.

The government imposed restrictions on the children's visits. Children under ten years were allowed to kiss their parents once, and only once, while those over ten could not have any physical contact but had to talk with their parents on telephones through glass partitions. Despite these cruel restrictions, *la llegada de los niños* was an extremely significant event for a country where more than ten percent of its population lives in exile and hundreds, maybe even thousands, are in prison.

The November 27 demonstration and *la llegada de los niños* clearly point to the strength of the movement for democracy in Uruguay. At the time of this writing (March 1984), the dictatorship announced that there would be elections in November 1984. All of the opposition parties have announced that their platform will include the right of exiles to return to Uruguay. Whether the elections will happen is still a question, but for Ana Clara, exiled in Mexico without a passport, it gives hope that she will someday be able to return to her home.

Towards the end of the evening, I played a tape of "Oh Come Smile" for Ana Clara. She sat very still, with tears in her eyes, as she listened and read the Spanish translation of the lyrics. She was moved by the song and commented that the role and the power of political cultural work is that it should move the listener to have compassion and therefore to take action rather than simply to evoke pity, since pity soon fades.

It would make me very proud as a songwriter if my song somehow contributes to the work of freeing another political prisoner from the torture chambers in Uruguay. A song is a small act—yet it is the accumulation of thousands of small acts that effects change. Perhaps the songs help us to remember our own power.△

For more information on political prisoners in Uruguay and what you can do to help, contact Amnesty International, Uruguay Coordination Group, 2701 Connecticut Avenue Northwest, #702, Washington, D.C. 20008. Telephone: 202-483-4838.

Alsino y el Condor

The story behind the Nicaraguan film

BY GABRIEL GARCIA MARQUEZ

AMONG THE MANY COMPETITORS FOR 1983'S "OSCAR" AWARDED TO the best foreign film, four came very close to being chosen: the Turkish film *Yol*, which shared the Golden Palm of the Cannes Festival last year with *Missing* by Costa Gavras, *Fitzcarraldo* by the German Werner Herzog, which won the prize for best direction at that same festival; the Italian production *Night of San Lorenzo* by the Taviani brothers, which was awarded the special jury prize in Cannes; and *Alsino and the Condor* from Nicaragua, directed by the Chilean exiled in Mexico, Miguel Littin, which was just making its first appearances throughout the world. I was very familiar with the first three films since I had to discuss them as a member of the jury at Cannes. All of them are of such high quality that at one point, they all contended for the Golden Palm.

On the other hand, I had received very good references by friends who had seen *Alsino and the Condor* in private showings, but I had not had the chance to see it. I have just seen it now, surprised by the news that it was chosen in Los Angeles as nominee for the best foreign film award, amid such well-qualified competitors. It is indeed very good.

However, its excellent quality is perhaps not its greatest merit, but rather the fact that this quality was achieved in spite of

82

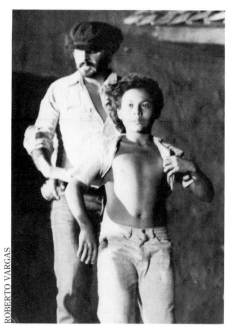

ROBERTO VARGAS

On the set of *Alsino and the Condor*, Miguel Littin directs Alan Esquivel who plays the boy, Alsino.

the almost incredible conditions under which it was produced. In the beginning there was neither a plot nor money. But the Nicaraguan Film Institute wanted Miguel Littin to make a film for them, and Miguel Littin wanted to do so. He had an old and not very promising idea, inspired by a short story by the Chilean Pedro Prado, about a child in the countryside who jumped from trees because he wanted to fly.

It was a good example of Miguel Littin's lyrical obsession, which is the most vulnerable aspect of his films, but to which he always surrenders as if to an illusory lover, in spite of the harsh criticisms by the reviewers and the still harsher, though secret ones, by his friends who love him. Fortunately, the most hard-headed teacher is reality. While traveling through Nicaragua's countryside looking for a setting for his flying boy, looking for trees from which to fly, looking for social justifications that would lend credibility to the adventures of his tropical Icarus, Miguel Littin discovered in the collective memory recollection from the liberation war in Nicaragua that had never been told. All of a sudden — perhaps without realizing it — he found a different but much more real and touching film than the one he was looking for. There is nothing new or strange about this: art has always been this way.

The circumstances under which the film was made could be the subject of another

film. The Nicaraguan government provided all kinds of resources — civilian and military, material and moral — but after adding up all the funds that could be pooled, there was no more than $60,000 U.S., which was much less than what would be charged by an American actor, indispensable for the drama. Cuba contributed technical equipment and even one of its most qualified photography directors — fifty-six-year-old Jorge Herrera — who had earned his prestige with *Lucia* and *La primera carga al machete*. Mexico contributed three actors, and others offered to act on a volunteer basis. Nicaragua made the most substantial contribution with armed troops, combat vehicles, the only tank they had, and a helicopter which was destined to be the star of the film. Its glory was short-lived: after two weeks of filming it suffered a mortal accident with fourteen people aboard while carrying out rescue work in a flood area; all the footage filmed up to then had to be redone.

The replacement, the only Bell helicopter which the Nicaraguan government owns, fulfilled its artistic mission to the end, but with indulgences that no producer would have allowed of his most treasured star. When least expected, it had to be transferred to conflict zones along the border with Honduras, and the filming was suspended until the helicopter was available again. In general, no definite plans could be made. The very troops in the film had to be mobilized when least expected to defend the borders, and when they returned, there were new faces, different weapons and sometimes even a different attitude. Many shots had to be refilmed to avoid visual contradictions. On one occasion, after returning from a battle, the troops enacted a scene using real projectiles, without the director realizing it, because they had run out of blanks. Another time, the townspeople wanted to set fire to a tank — as they had done during the liberation war — because it had allowed the Somocistas in the film to win the battle, as called for in the script. A Nicaraguan actor played the role of one of Somoza's sergeants so well that he awakened suspicions in the town that he might be an ex-member of the National Guard who had infiltrated the movie. One bad day, while filming aboard the helicopter, the photographer Jorge Herrera pressed his hands against his temples and became immobile with an astonished look on his face. "It was as if he were looking at something that only he could see," says

Miguel Littin. He had died of a stroke.

The result of so many setbacks and uncertainties was this movie in which a child who wants to fly is only a circumstantial element. The child was played by Alan Esquivel, a construction worker's son who, at age thirteen, did not know how to read. He learned his parts from an assistant who read them to him. Without a doubt, he is a born actor and Miguel Littin himself says that after a few days he only needed to give him the same directions he would have given a professional actor. However, in my personal opinion, the true drama of this exemplary film, what convinces and moves the viewer most, is that of Captain Frank, a United States advisor played formidably by Dean Stockwell. Although he is not a very well-known actor, those with good memories for film names will recall that he played the role of Peter in *The Boy with Green Hair*. Stockwell not only agreed to act in the film for a ridiculously low fee, but he also stoically and good-humoredly put up with the countless setbacks and seriously resisted political pressures put on him from many sides. There is no doubt that he is a very intelligent man who knew quite well what he was doing.

In reality, Captain Frank, who throughout the film is more lonely than anyone else in his solitary helicopter, does not do it for money, or for the spirit of adventure, but rather out of the conviction and the belief that his mission — even his sacrifice — is a tribute to the triumph of justice and truth. That is precisely the most pathetic aspect of those who are mistaken. It is even more so in the case of Captain Frank because he is a perfect example, lucid and human, of the third generation that the United States sends to die in its filthy wars since the last World War. A whole crop of priceless young men like him were sent to the slaughterhouse of Korea, another to Vietnam and now a third to the hell of Central America, where Mr. Reagan's government is once again showing that the most powerful and fascinating country in the world has not learned from the terrible lessons of its own history. Dean Stockwell cannot possibly be unaware that the humane and slightly messianic Captain that he portrayed had fallen into a trap without escape, where the least serious aspect is that no one loves him. I'm sure he knows it, and this is the great service he has paid his country: placing its people before a mirror that reveals their own strange and undeserved destiny. △

"Sistren" means sisters. First employed in a special make-work program which created jobs such as street cleaning for thousands of women, Sistren collected together around a common interest in drama and its use for social change. The group, thirteen women, first performed publicly in April 1977 at the Workers' Week Concert in Kingston.

Sistren's theater is energetic, fast-paced, humorous yet never loses its analytic purpose—for every effect there's a cause. Whether presented in workshop, where each scene is followed by a group discussion with the audience, or in the full spectacle of theatrical production, Sistren's work gives voice to the experience of poverty without ever submitting to a feeling of powerlessness. It is theater of action with workshops turning into group problem-solving sessions and major productions becoming complete acts of cultural reclamation.

The women of Sistren are: Beverly Elliott, Cerene Stephenson, Beverly Hanson, Jasmine Smith, Rebecca Knowles, Jerline Todd, Vivette Lewis, Lana Finikin, Lorna Burrell, May Thompson, Lillian Foster, Pauline Crawford and Jennifer Williams. Musicians performing with the group are Joy Erskine and Calvin Mitchell. Costumes are designed by Beti Campbell. Sistren also runs a silk-screen textile project which is led by Cerene Stephenson and Jasmine Smith. Joan French directs the group's workshop program, and Jenny Jones coordinates it.

Along with a workshop production of Domestick, *Sistren's* QPH *was performed for the first time in North America in Toronto, 21–27 September 1981.* QPH *was directed by Hertencer Lindsay, and* Domestick *was directed by Honor Ford-Smith, who has guided Sistren from a part-time drama group in 1977 to a full-time theater collective in 1981.*

—Editors of *Fuse* magazine.

SISTREN

Jamaican

Women's

Theater

by Honor Ford-Smith

Photographs by Isobel Harry

THERE EXISTS AMONG THE women of the Caribbean a need for naming of experience and a need for communal support of that process. In the past, silence has surrounded our experience. We have not been named in literature or in history. The discovery through dialogue, through encounter with others, of the possibilities of our power can help us to shape the forces which, at present, still shape us.

Dialogue creates reflection, which in turn creates analysis. Through analysis one moves from being object to becoming subject, from victim to creator. One is able to identify the problems that surround one's experience, objectives, to come forward from the margins of society, to intervene in reality.[1]

Only through supportive exchange is this possible. Only in a special environment is it possible to move forward from the perception of oneself as passive, as separate from the totality of whole experience, and to develop the confidence in oneself to act on one's own wisdom. By creating for ourselves our own institutions of leisure and discussion, our own sense of teamwork and bonding, we insure the confident functioning of our womanhood in a world that we have named.

WOMEN IN JAMAICA

Currently in Jamaica approximately fifty percent of women are unemployed—double the number of unemployed men.[2] Seventy percent of women between seventeen and twenty-four years old are out of work, and these are women with children. Sixty-eight percent of employed women are doing very low status forms of wage work and are earning under the minimum wage. This situation is bad enough, but add this to the fact that one-third of women are heads of households (I think this is a very conservative estimate) and the gravity of the picture emerges. Women dominate the service sector, and many work as domestic servants—without access to unions or even labor associations. There tends to be a lower level of union activity in small factories exploiting women's work such as garment and textile factories, which as late as 1972 were paying wages of $7–10 per week.

Additionally, the level of broadbased autonomous organization of women around questions or problems of direct concern to them is low. Most of the women's organizations are based on social welfare concerns aimed at further domesticating women. Handicraft and domestic schemes exist, offering little chance to analyze whose interests these schemes serve. Much of the problem is complicated by the fact that the subordination of women has not been seen as an issue serious enough to warrant raising embarrassing questions about the unequal sexual division of labor or sexual harrassment, for example. Often, the participation of women in the so-called informal sector of the economy and their work in farming and seasonal wage work is cited as evidence of the "emancipated" Jamaican woman. This blind spot has meant that much of the basic information about the condition of working-class women simply does not exist.

We have to put all our educational resources into resolving these problems if women are to have a future that is at all positive. At the same time, the resolving of these issues, or even the fact that they exist, should not obscure our awareness of the fact that women as a gender have a particular relationship to the issue of class. The issues for us, then (and for women in much of the Third World), are how to create a balance between the solutions to the class questions we face, while at the same time dealing with the specificity of women's oppression in what is still a sexist society; and how to create a new

Ford-Smith: *SISTREN, Jamaican Women's Theater*

society without losing touch with the particular needs of women.

Historically, unlike women in Europe and North America, there is little evidence of autonomous organization of Caribbean women for emancipation as a gender. The social gains that the women of the region have made accompanied the national movements for increased sovereignty and greater social justice. Although women made important gains in the areas of legislation between 1972 and 1980, these do not deal with the material bases or the root questions of control of reproduction and control of production—or the difficult problem of the sexual division of labor.

The preserving of African tradition through the last 300 years has, to a great extent, been facilitated by women. It is they who have kept alive and communicated the customs of an uprooted people—much of this legacy has been denied by the wider society and has been submerged beneath the official character of the country. Its emergence into the open requires different methods of communication than those that survived in the past. It demands a reexamination of the past, with all its taboos and restrictions, in the language of the *present*. It requires that women, hitherto the preservers, become the authors.

thing special, but rather a technique most ordinary people regularly employ as a way of coping with new or unsettling experience."[4]

The process of rehearsing oneself into a significant situation beforehand is an example of this. "In drama, students live 'in advance of themselves' as it were: they face challenge and crisis in imagination before they find themselves overwhelmed by it in real life. They gain the feeling of mastery over events, the sense that they are equal to life . . . ."

Theater, on the other hand, is an artistic product. It is the process of shaping discoveries and presenting them to an audience. The emphasis here is on presentation, on performance, on the expertise of the actors and the production team.

THE PROCESS OF NAMING

Sistren[5] is a collective/cooperative structure within which its members educate themselves through drama, and later, through drama and theater, share their experiences with others. It is a small group of women exploring their understanding through drama, naming it, and presenting that naming in a product—theater. The core collective also works to organize other groups of women in Jamaica. The active relationship between the investigative base (drama workshops) and the more objective completed statement (theater) gives the educational process a tangible goal. The drama workshops aim at a constant process of consciousness-raising. The production of plays necessitates the training of the women in a particular professional skill (acting). A group like Sistren need not choose theater as the end product of its educational process. The drama can be used for consciousness-raising and skill training in any field, because it offers a way of approaching and investigating problems.

The educational process in Sistren addresses itself to the problems of the women with whom we work, as they are articulated by women from the laboring poor. It introduces these problems back into the wider society for discussion, for analysis, for solution. It suggests alternatives. Both drama and theater provide a public forum for the voices of poor women. This is a part of the process of awakening which must take place if

Sistren Theater Collective's production of *QPH* in Toronto, 1981.

Maternity leave and minimum wage were important pieces of legislation. In the 1970s an equal pay for equal work law was passed—along with a maternity leave law guaranteeing women leave with pay for six weeks. The minimum wage law currently sets the minimum weekly earnings at $40 Jamaican (about $10 U.S.) per week. However, in a situation where women do not do and cannot get work that is considered to be equal, an equal pay for equal work law is a bit like putting a Band-Aid on a cancer.

Also, Jamaica is still defining its cultural identity—overcoming a legacy of self-doubt and insecurity which was part of the colonial heritage. Building confidence in traditions is an important process, one in which women have played an important part.

A DRAMA-IN-EDUCATION PROJECT

The experience of Sistren, a theater collective for working-class women, in forming and creating a workplace for women, is a useful case study. Drama is without question an effective means of breaking silence, of stimulating discussion, of posing problems and experimenting with solutions. Drama here is by definition different from theater. Drama is an exploratory process that uses games, role play and narration to bring about self-discovery, "to bring out what (people) already know but don't yet know they know."[3] As Dorothy Heathcote, the English educator has demonstrated: "Drama is not some-

changes in the system that create these problems are to occur.

Sistren's program consists of workshops taken and performances given. Workshops include both research work and special skill workshops in movement, silk-screen printing, and current affairs. Performances include both workshops in Drama for Problem-Solving, which are presented to community organizations and women's groups around the country, and major productions, which are presented commercially, usually composed from group experience, research and improvisation. Four have been presented since 1977: *Belly-woman Bangarang, Bandooloo Version, Nanah Yah* and *QPH* (Queenie, Pearlie and Hopie).

All thirteen members of Sistren were urban street cleaners in a special make-work program called Impact under the Democratic Socialist government of 1972–1980. The program was much criticized by middle-class interests in Jamaica at the time. Later the women who became Sistren were selected for training as teacher aides in a program for women organized by the Women's Bureau and the Council for Voluntary Social Services. There were approximately 10,000 women employed by this special employment program, and although their jobs were unquestionably low status and temporary, the program offered a chance to women to organize around their own concerns.

This coincided with the start of the U.N.

Sistren Theater Collective, *QPH*, Old Women in the Yard of the Alms House, in Kingston, Jamaica. From left to right: Beverly Elliott, Rebecca Knowles, and Vivette Lewis.

GIVING WOMEN OPPORTUNITIES TO ORGANIZE

The ideas about adult education behind the work of Sistren have developed gradually and have stretched themselves as the group's ideas of its identity and its role grew. The work began spontaneously in 1977, the result of a climate of reform and increased worker participation in all areas of the life in the country at that time.

World Decade of Women, which resulted in Women's Bureaus being set up all over the Third World. The effectiveness of these government-led initiatives toward "development, equality and peace" for women depended on the over-all political context—in whose interests governments were acting on and whose they were protecting. In Jamaica in 1977, the context was one of mild socialism. For the first time in the lives of many of us, people from the laboring poor were analyzing, making demands and being openly critical of the forces holding them back. So when the Women's Bureau at that time selected some of the women in the special employment program for training as teacher aides there was a feeling of optimism.

These are some of the reasons why the women of Sistren spoke to me as they did in 1977, when I first met them in an old broken-down schoolhouse in Swallowfield. The group had expressed an interest in drama and sought a director from the Jamaica School of Drama. We met to discuss the performance they wanted to do for a Workers' Week concert. I asked them, "What do you want to do a play about?" and they said, "We want to do plays about how we suffer as women. We want to do plays about how the men treat us bad." Somehow, the employment program had offered them a chance to recognize that they shared something in common. Two years later, in a film about Sistren, Bev Hanson defined the commonality: "In the first place we are all impact workers. . . . In the second place all of us live in the ghetto. . . ." Sistren's consciousness had always been of themselves as *representatives* of working class women. So when we met for the first time, I asked them to tell me how they suffered as women, and this began an exchange of experience, which resulted in our first piece, *Downpression Get a Blow*—a piece about women organizing in a textile factory and achieving their demands as workers.

RESEARCH WORKSHOP 1979-1980

The research workshop in reading skills was set up as a solution to the problem of the lack of formal education not only within the group, but also within the society. The workshop had as its objective the creating of dramatic exercises that would teach comprehension and reading skills, and develop the critical consciousness of the student. This was the first research workshop in which Sistren participated. It attempted to balance skills with a consciousness of class and gender.

The history of the workshop is briefly this. During the group's first major production, *Bellywoman Bangarang*, the women were asked to script scenes they had created from their own experiences. At this point, I learned that some of the

women in the project had more developed reading skills than others. These actresses were able to help others script their scenes, and by the end of the production, interest in reading about their personal experiences motivated many to practice their new skills. By the time we got to our second major production everyone could read their own script.

The research workshop investigated what took place in this process more carefully. In workshop, a wide range of work was done. Physical exercises were based on the shape of the letters. Calisthenics were developed based on the alphabet and, in one case, a dance created from the spelling of the letters of words. Rhythmic sounds and games accompanied these so that letters and sounds were

Sistren Theater Collective's production of *Domestick* in Toronto, 1981.

identified. Writing exercises were linked to exercises in conflict resolution, personal awareness and group development. A great many of the exercises have been developed from Augosto Boal's method of problem-solving skits. In these, the group develops to a climax a skit on a particular theme. They then stop and ask the rest of the group how the problem should be solved. After a discussion, the solution is enacted.

Reading exercises were often taken from the newspaper. The study of articles in the paper and their accompanying pictures is another example of the type of exercise the group used. After looking at a picture, the women acted out what went before and after the moment captured in

the scene. They then read, in character, the newspaper report and commented in discussion on its truthfulness.

The results of these workshops were recorded by members of Sistren and some of the scenes scripted. All writing was done in creole, since the creole language is the women's main medium of communication. The creole was then translated into English. Writing in dialect, with its improvised spelling and immediate flavor, the women learned to write a form of English that had previously been considered "bad, coarse and vulgar." In fact, Jamaican Creole is a variation of English with its own strict rules of grammar, a language which retains much of the Twi construction of its creators. By writing a language that had hitherto been that of a nonliterate people, the women broke silence.

By translating their work into English, the women create an equal relationship between their idiom and the language of the powerful—one they mostly understand but do not speak. It is the official language of the country, and they must learn it if they are to understand the world view of its speakers, if they are not to remain isolated. They must learn it if they are to communicate their needs and demands to the powerful. But for Sistren, as for many other women, it remains a second language.

CREATING PLAYS: THE USE OF FOLK FORMS

The use of the creole language in workshop and performance is only one method of using the cultural tradition of the Caribbean. Sistren's first two major productions were created from forms suggested by the oral and ritual traditions of the country. This tradition, African in origin, is by its nature far more participatory than that of a literary tradition. It evokes a communal response from both audience and actor. The images and symbols contained within the ritual tradition evoke immediate responses from the audience, because they come loaded with overtones from past and present. They echo in the subconscious of the viewer. Dramatic forms originating from ritual demand a supportive relationship between audience and actor. In ritual, the viewer must help the possessed in his or her journey through a reality of the spirit. In workshop the passive participator must be prepared to be drawn in to support the actress who is making discoveries through the medium of drama.

Oral literature and music are a particularly important part of the cultural experience of the women in Sistren. Stories, songs for all occasions, riddles, rhymes and proverbs are among some of the forms that are still used very actively. Oral literature, as Ruth Finnegan has pointed out, has certain techniques built into its structure that demand the attention of the listeners. These devices include onomatopaeia, repetition of a phrase or expression, questions, and songs. Proverbs and riddles depend on metaphors from daily life and the listener's knowledge of folk heroes and heroines to make subtle comments on the life around us.

Bellywomen Bangarang, the group's first major production, was developed using a method almost completely based on folk traditions. In the beginning, each member of the group was asked to go into the center of a circle and sing a folk song from her childhood. She was asked to keep singing until the song evoked either an action or an incident in her memory. When this happened she was to tell the story or act it out. Observers were required to look for ways in which they could identify with her story. If anyone felt that the experience being described aroused a memory of a similar experience in her own life she joined in by telling her story or by linking, through action, her experience to the one that had been acted out. From these simple exercises, the theme of teenage pregnancy and the rites of passage from girlhood to adulthood emerged.

THE GAME STRUCTURE

The wealth of information that emerged demanded to be structured around dramatic images suitable to the theme. We chose to use folk games. The entire narrative structure of *Bellywoman Bangarang* finally rested on the structure of the games and on the resolution of the conflict in the game structure. Most games have a metaphorical content and often suggest a line of narrative action based on the game's objective. An example of this is the game "Bull in the Pen." Here the main player stands in the center of a circle of people whose arms are linked. She asks, by touching each arm, what the pen is made of. She then has to try and break out of it. Dramatically, this game can be used in several ways. In *Bellywoman* it functioned as a means of commenting on a scene that had gone before. The pen became the situation itself and the arms of the players symbolized the problems of the situation. The players then try to improvise a means of breaking out of the pen.

Riddles and proverbs were another form of oral literature used in *Bellywoman*. They were used as a means of stimulating the audience to think about taboo areas of experience. The riddles introduced themes that the audience was afraid to deal with openly, or unused to dealing with at all. Menstruation and illness during pregnancy were dealt with like this. The riddles were presented to the audience as choreopoems. The audience had to figure out the answers.

The structures of riddles and proverbs also help to evoke and suggest structures for group poems, which, if they have enough emphasis on word play and rhythm, communicate with great immediacy to an audience. These kinds of poems connect to the audience's background in ritual chanting and rhythmic bible reading. The content of the poem, or choral statement, juxtaposed with the anticipated content of the familiar form, arouses a questioning interest on the part of the viewer. Poetry like this does not have the connotations of abstraction that it carries in many other societies. It is an extremely direct way of reaching an audience through conscious use of rhythm. The use of other forms of oral and ritual tradition such as choruses and storytelling has informed our work in a continuous way. The use of craftwork is also beginning to be an important part of the group's total program.

Ford-Smith: *SISTREN, Jamaican Women's Theater*

RITUAL AS VEHICLE

"And some there be who have no memorial, who are buried as though they had never been...."

On the night of 20 May 1980, fire broke out in the overcrowded women's ward of Kingston's Alms House, killing 167 destitute women. A year later, an official inquest found no one criminally responsible. *QPH* is about three women from different backgrounds who by chance met and lived at the Alms House—women who struggled bravely in an uncaring society.

put on the tip of the tongue. The drummers on the Ire drum and Achata (kerosene tin) control the proceedings. The Queen controls the dancers and "shawls" each soloist, who represents a family with its own song and dance patterns. Movements are centered on the pelvic area, symbol of fertility, birth and rebirth.

As Queenie says, it is the old women who have the key to the future because they hold the secrets of the past. The production is dedicated to all the women who have struggled for independence in spite of being oppressed. *QPH* attempts to make "their names live for evermore."

Sistren Theater Collective's production of *QPH* in Toronto, 1981.

Developed by Sistren through improvisation and after a great deal of research with the women at the Kingston Alms House, the play is structured around the Etu Ritual—a celebration for the dead. Etu is used in *QPH* to honor the three women and provide a vehicle for them to play out their different routes to Alms House (where two of them died): Queenie, a preacher who is removed from her church; Pearlie, who is banished from her family and driven to prostitution after becoming pregnant by the gardener; Hopie, a servant who, after thirty years of service to one family, is left destitute when her employers move.

An African retention, Etu is now only practiced in western Jamaica. The ritual contains singing, dancing and feasting. A table is laid with white rum, foo-foo, okra stew, and soft drinks for the ancestors. Blood from a goat is used to make a cross on the forehead of the players, and bisi is

LIFE DEMYSTIFIED

The process of working in drama for women involves the creating of a community in which some of the hidden or taboo subjects about women can be exposed and the audience confronted with them. As such, drama is not a reflection of life but a demystification of it, by the full exploration of these realities. Sistren brings to the public the voices of women from the laboring poor and in so doing helps to pressure for change. By confronting what has been considered indecent, irrelevant or accepted, we have begun to make a recorded refusal of ways in which our lives have been thwarted and restricted. We have begun to refuse the forces behind those ways.

Methods and techniques are not very important. It's where they take you that matters. What becomes of the work is determined by the content and the consciousness one brings to the theme. Work of this kind can perpetuate oppressive structures as well as it can help to change them. The form is only important in so far as it structures and analyzes the content and in so far as it leads to new understandings, new knowledge and new collective action.

POSTSCRIPT 1984

Last night we performed to about six hundred people in a backyard high up in the mountains. After the show, I asked one young woman what her reaction was. "I get plenty from it," she said. "It teach me not to be licky-licky." "Subservient" is the standard English word for "licky-licky."

The Sistren Theater Collective in Toronto, 1981.

Since this article was written, our work, along with that of others in popular theater and education, has acquired a particular urgency. The recent response of the U.S. government to events in Central America and Grenada will have far-reaching consequences for us. One of the immediate consequences is that much-needed money is to be spent on maintaining armies on islands that previously had none. In Jamaica, the restrictions of the International Monetary Fund have resulted in massive cuts in public spending, lay-offs, and countless devaluations. The immediate effect of these actions on women is to intensify the burden of housework and child care and also to increase the level of unemployment. The reported incidence of rape and sexual violence has risen too.

Predictions that present political and economic policies would attract foreign capital to create employment and support services have simply not come to pass.

In the last four years, Sistren has begun to create sister groups. We have offered many workshops to women on sugar estates and in factories, to market women, and to unemployed women in Kingston and the rural areas. Slowly we have begun to build a small network among the most marginalized women. We have continued to build on the method of taking in material for our plays and forum theater presentations from the people with whom we work. In 1982, we made a film, *Sweet Sugar Rage*, about our work in the sugar belt of Jamaica. We also created a theater-in-education workshop for adults about one particular violation of our equal pay for equal work law. *The Case of Iris Armstrong* demonstrates and throws open for debate the question of women's position in the hierarchy of production and the relationship between that and their position in the home.

We have also begun to develop a documentation and research project to support our work in popular education.

We hope that our work will continue to grow while remaining fresh and immediate, that we will continue to create a space in which people can link their specific experience of oppression to broader political and economic issues and gain the courage to act on their own insights.△

NOTES

1. The process of conscientization is fully described in Paulo Friere's *Pedagogy of the Oppressed*, Penguin, 1970.

2. "PNP Women's Movement Political Education Programme," 1980, 17–18.

3. *Dorothy Heathcote: Drama as a Learning Medium*, Betty Jane Wagner, National Education Association, 1976, 13.

4. Ibid., 16.

5. In discussing the work of Sistren, I want to stress that what I am writing here are my words. I write "my words" because I want to make clear that my way of working with Sistren is conditioned by my own position on certain issues, by my own class background, and by my skills in theater. All women are oppressed, but we experienced that oppression differently in both extent and form. To ignore the difference between the actresses who make up Sistren and myself is to pass over the important question of class as it affects relations between women. Second, my position on certain questions has changed in three years or so of work with the collective as outside influences on our work has altered or become stronger and as the women in Sistren have studied and taught me more about their situation. Together we evolved certain techniques which I am writing now, here without them—in words they would not use. These techniques are not necessarily the same ones that Sistren would use if they were working on their own or with another director. What I describe has grown out of the conflicts/ mistakes and solutions to problems of the last years' work. They cannot be randomly applied because they aim at bringing about a certain process and a certain end. That end is a greater consciousness of the conditions facing women in the Caribbean. That end is the possibility of changing the structure that creates those conditions.

Video Politics

HISTORICALLY, WOMEN HAVE HAD a difficult relation to facts. Scientifically gathered information has often been interpreted as proof of women's social, psychological and physical inferiority; or the data collectors have ignored us entirely. At the same time, realist or documentary representations, which depend on a factual base, have predictably maintained the same bias. Perhaps because social realism, documentary,[1] posits a correspondence with truth, it has also been the form chosen for many contemporary feminists' critiques of the status quo and for attempts to counter old oppressive patterns. These feminist documentaries generally rely on established codes of realism but employ them to create new social meanings. As such, the works are direct descendants of the nineteenth-century fusion of social realist art and scientific socialist philosophies (Marxism et al.) and, more recently, the radical left-wing cinema and photography of the twenties and the thirties.[2] For feminist artists, then, making documentary films, photographs, and now videotapes (not to mention realist paintings, theater, and all types of literary realism) usually proposes a redefinition of "reality" by asserting the validity of women's existence and experiences, by challenging accepted ideas about those experiences, or by a combination of both strategies.[3]

This article is limited to a discussion of feminist *video* documentaries in the United States in an attempt to narrow a potentially vast subject. This is not an arbitrary choice. It is based on the coincidence of two important political and cultural phenomena: the renaissance of the feminist movement and the proliferation of alternative, progressive media in the late sixties. Among other effects, this overlap (not to be confused with a causal relationship á la McLuhan) led to the involvement of a number of women in video production and in the video groups which emerged throughout the United States in the early seventies. During this period several women's video collectives formed[4] and an annual women's video festival was organized,[5] all this in addition to various women video artists working more or less individually. Although the tapes produced by these women are not uniform in any sense, many reflect feminist concerns and documentaries prevail.

The four videotapes I have chosen to represent the genre of feminist video documentaries for the purposes of this analysis are works which have variously affected my thinking about political documentary, but I do not intend to valorize these four tapes as masterpieces. Indeed, one of my main theses is that they are tentative examples of the convergence of a popular political movement, a form of cultural production and distribution, and an aesthetic approach. Collectively, they belong to a genre generally neglected by video historians and critics and unknown to many feminist historians and critics. It is a genre now virtually in eclipse but one, I would argue, which has hardly been exhausted. First, however, without regressing much beyond 1968, let me sketch some of the relevant political, technical, and aesthetic influences which shaped this genre and these four tapes.

Early Feminist Projects

by *Martha Gever*

When relatively low-cost portable video equipment ($1,500–$2,000 for portable recorder, black-and-white camera, and monitor) became widely available in the United States in the late sixties, portapaks and lightweight cameras were quickly assimilated as tools of the "counterculture." The annals of these early years of independent video are filled with optimistic rhetoric on the revolutionary potential of alternative television. For example, Michael Shamberg, a propagandist for what he called "guerrilla television," borrowed language from the New Left vocabulary: "Survival in an information environment demands information tools.... [There is] potential in Guerrilla Television [as] an information infrastructure for Media America, a grassroots network of indigenous media activity."[6] These projections for the future of video, afterwards seriously modified by experience and a shrinking economy, were sometimes colored by entrepreneurial ambitions but were more often founded on genuine, if naive, visions of democratic and decentralized communications networks. The names which various early video groups gave themselves are indicative: Video Free America, People's Video Theater, Videofreex, Global Village, Media Access Center, etc. All revolutionary allusions aside, however, the prominent figures among the first generation of video activists were almost all white, middle-class, and male, with most women, Blacks, Latinos, Asian-Americans, etc. playing supporting roles.[7]

When independent video made its debut, media-consciousness was extremely high. The politically engaged arm of the alternative television movement set about recording events and issues of the day: antiwar organizing, prison reform, rock music, Black Panthers, Native American activists, ecology, and women's liberation. The tapes which resulted borrowed heavily from two different traditions: television journalism and cinema verité. These politically committed documentarians hoped to give attention to subjects and viewpoints which they felt commercial television ignored or opposed. Cinema verité, U.S. style,[8] provided an aesthetic model for many of these tapes since this form allowed personal, emotional elements to structure presentations of social reality. These documentarians preferred the economic advantage of video as compared to 16mm film, defending this choice with aesthetic arguments for the enhanced intimacy of the small-screen image. The chief *political* claims of these tapemakers, however, hinged on potential systems for video distribution. Community viewing centers, the public television network (PBS) and its affiliated stations, public access channels on cable TV, even communications satellites, promised decentralization and an audience for independent video. Some projects, most notably the National Film Board of Canada's "Challenge for Change," were practical experiments in community-based media production where the process of making tapes and films was integrated with other programs for community self-definition.[9] Most media activists in the U.S. lacked the generous financial support of a government agency like the Film

Gever: Video Politics, Early Feminist Projects

Board (or compensatory fund-raising skills) and had to settle for more modest community involvements. With a few exceptions, their revolutionary fervor faded by the late seventies, when the complexities of financing community media centers became apparent and the "so simple anyone can do it"[10] approach resulted in hours of out-of-focus, badly lit, and not very compelling tapes. At that point many tapemakers either changed tactics or abandoned the field.

Against this scenario of energetic video activity in the early and mid-seventies, let me superimpose the more familiar recent history of the women's liberation movement. As issues like women's health, sexuality, marriage, gender roles, rape and other kinds of physical abuse were claimed and defined as feminist concerns, a steady stream of books, periodicals, films, and videotapes appeared within the feminist arena. The tapes which I will analyze here must be considered as part of that movement.

I N 1968 ANNE KOEDT published the first version of "The Myth of the Vaginal Orgasm,"[11] a short but widely circulated and influential feminist essay on the implications of Masters and Johnson's research on sexuality. In 1972 Dr. Mary Jane Sherfey published her book, *The Nature and Evolution of Female Sexuality*,[12] a detailed biological and physiological refutation of standard beliefs about female sexuality, which also drew on the work of Masters and Johnson. Both works added to and were part of feminist conversations which identified the female body as a site of political struggle.

Julie Gustafson's videotape *The Politics of Intimacy* (1972–1973) is predicated on these and other debates on sexual politics at the most personal level; indeed, it is a tape constructed from pieces of such conversations. The tape is almost entirely talking heads. The women who speak could belong to some ideal consciousness-raising (c-r) group, though this is unlikely.[13]

They vary in age, color (one woman is black), sexual experience and orientation (there is one obvious lesbian), and marital status (some mention husbands). All, however, seem to be middle-class North Americans. Brief lectures in physiology by Dr. Sherfey are the only exceptions to the predominant tone of subjective, personal testimony. The c-r temper of the tape is enhanced by its structure; the ten women seem to be commenting and building on each other's statements, but the changing backgrounds soon reveal this as artificial. Not that Gustafson was trying to deceive anyone. Consciously or unconsciously, she chose a form which reflected the feminist sources of her tape.

The impression of the tape as a polyphonous discussion among trusted friends is furthered by several devices beyond the participation of diverse women. First, facial close-ups are frequent. The reiteration of closely framed, animated faces telling intimate truths puts the audience in the position of a trusted friend. Several times the camera reveals that two of the women are actually talking to each other, although this only becomes clear midway through the fifty-minute tape. In general, the listener is off-screen and silent. Second, the conversations which comprise the tape's raw material have been cut and spliced to construct plausible conversational sequences around six topics such as "power" and "self-love."

These techniques establish a sense of continuity and direct the viewer's attention in predictable ways, but it is the editing of *Politics of Intimacy* which most clearly shapes its meaning. Oddly, the choice and ordering of material results in two distinct and essentially contradictory meanings. As I have suggested, the basic reference for the tape is the c-r group, where accounts of personal experience contribute to analyses of the operations of political power. A plurality of views is necessary to ensure collective accuracy, and Gustafson provides variety. Some of the women enjoy sexual activities; some don't. Some like to masturbate; others think it's stupid. Some want to please their husbands; others think that men are a waste of time, that women are invariably better lovers. One woman declares, with resignation, "I think it's just a lot of hard work."

In addition to plurality, Gustafson also gives us a moral. For some of the women, speaking about sex is difficult, even

painful, whereas others easily recall private desires and experiences. Consequently, the ones for whom language is an acute problem, the ones who talk with hesitant, quiet voices, fall into the stereotyped characters of "repressed women." Watching them becomes embarrassing. Meanwhile, a desirable standard is set by the relaxed, multiorgasmic woman or the cheerful, uninhibited lesbian.

These hierarchical relationships, antithetical to the democratic principles of c-r, can be attributed, I think, to the reliance on a fairly conventional documentary format. If speech (confession) is the primary method of developing a theme and the major building block in the editing process, as it is here, performance ability, not honesty or accuracy, will control the tape's effect. Certain characters are more appealing, more attractive, than others; hence their words are more convincing.

This critical evaluation can be turned around, however, since Gustafson introduces several variants into the verbal documentary formula. Women doing all the talking on substantive topics like sexuality is still unusual. Women talking freely about sex and their own pleasure is even more uncommon. While several of the women are sexually naive or confused they are not typecast in familar media terms. None of the women, save Dr. Sherfey, are presented as extraordinary, and no authoritative voice frames their conversations. Ultimately the technical flaws and even the moralistic layer is neutralized by the power of women speaking for themselves. That this tape was not produced for broadcast TV, but was intended to be shown to small groups (of women, mainly) in closed-circuit situations, also needs to be factored into any evaluation of its meaning.

Intimacy is not only a topic for discussion in *Politics of Intimacy*; it is also the precondition for most of the conversations which supplied Gustafson's raw material. It is not incidental, then, that Gustafson's mother and sister appear in the tape, though they are not identified as such to the audience. Nonetheless, this information underlines the basic role of family relationships, especially female kinship, in many women's lives. In *Ama l'Uomo Tuo* ("Always Love Your Man," 1974), an easy rapport between the tapemaker, Cara de Vito, and her grandmother Adeline Lejudas similarly depends on an atmosphere of familiarity which encourages personal disclosure. The tape is based on Adeline's life, but it relates only a partial

From the "Power" Section of *Politics of Intimacy* (1972–1973), by Julie Gustafson

It's important for me to have sexual satisfaction, but I think that I'd much rather make sure that my husband has sexual satisfaction, you know. In other words, if he is reaching the point of coming to a climax, I don't want to say, "Wait," and put him off. I want to see my husband sexually satisfied.

I was seventeen when I met him, and I come from a family that's very strict. My mother never let me do anything. The biggest thing to me was to turn him on. . . . We went to the beach once and, boy, did he get—oh, wow, it's incredible—he got hot, hot, hot. And there was nothing he could do, and my defense on him, to keep him from doing anything was, "My mother knows where I am. . . ."

During Mezolithic times, before civilization began, the women would have been much freer. They would have been much more sexually available. . . . However, with the onset of animal husbandry. . . and the onset of agriculture, which required settled homes and the presence of many children . . . it became necessary for laws of inheritance to come into being, and women's sexual activity had to be curtailed.

My first sexual relationship with a man was initiated by him but completely dependent on me, because I knew what I was doing and he didn't. But I didn't know what I was doing in that I had no idea about what it was that a woman could enjoy, even though I had been masturbating since I was little. I didn't even know that I was masturbating. It just felt good and I did it. And so I did what he wanted me to do, and just never learned a lot of things about myself. That relationship ended in a disaster. I got pregnant and didn't have another relationship with a man for a long time. And I also became terrified of sexuality. . .

Gever: Video Politics, Early Feminist Projects

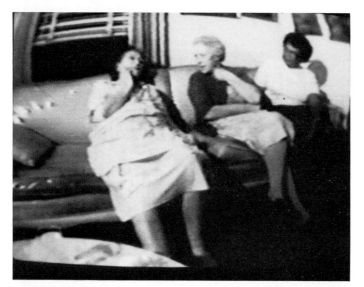

Anybody. . . if you live with a little dog fifty years, one year, two years, you get so attached that when anything happen to the dog, you're lost. Imagine if you live fifty years with the same man, that you see him every night, come home in the morning, go out, give him a coffee, prepare, wash. People don't understand, Cara, it's not because I lost him, because I know that I have to go, too. But to come home into such large house, alone, nobody to share work and if you feel sick you can say, "Oh, gee, I don't feel good today." To who you tell? To the wall?

Now you ask why I married him? I told you. I used to live with my brother and my sister-in-law who was very mean to me. She was very, very mean. And one day I says, "If there comes a horse with a head on and a pair of pants, I'm going to marry him, and long as I get out from here." So I says, "He's a business man, I'm sure that a piece of bread I'll never miss it; if I raise a child I'm sure that he's not going to miss anything." The best things in my life they were my son and my daughter. . . .

biography centered on her fifty-year marriage and her husband's violence toward her. Again, as with Gustafson's work, de Vito produced this tape using simple production methods and low-cost equipment. *Ama l'Uomo Tuo* was, for the most part, shown for small groups at video screenings and in video classes, not on TV.

The narrative line which structures *Ama l'Uomo Tuo* begins with a recollection from Adeline's childhood in Italy—her mother's suggestion of a possible fiancé and her response, "Married? Me?" It ends with a gruesome account of her near-death following a botched, illegal abortion which she didn't want but which her husband, Benny, insisted she have. In between, she recalls Benny's authoritarian attitudes and

several beatings. A few times de Vito interrupts the sequence of bad memories (Benny is now dead) with scenes in the present tense depicting Adeline as a capable, active person. Early on, for instance, a series of brief vignettes show her cleaning, gardening, visiting with friends, edited to the cadence of an Italian ballad. The upbeat tempo and mood of these scenes relieves somewhat the intensity of Adeline's vivid descriptions of Benny's brutal behavior.

What would attract and hold a woman like Adeline to a man like Benny? The question seems obvious, the answer less so. Adeline understands her own motivation and answers unapologetically: she opted for financial security for herself and

her children in a culture where not marrying, even divorce, was unthinkable. Her concluding words (de Vito's chosen finale for the tape) betray another, less rational factor governing such relationships. "*Ama l'uomo tuo.* Always love your man, no matter what," she intones. When all the parts of de Vito's composite portrait of her grandmother are added up, the impression of Adeline as a victim—of her husband and of social codes—persists.

Just like Gustafson's ambiguous use of established documentary forms, de Vito's tape subverts and is subverted by assumptions about depictions of reality. In this tape, too, unaffected, personal observations about fairly ordinary (though in this case, terrible) experiences manage to break time-honored taboos—not proscribing behavior as much as speech. Another strategy de Vito uses to avoid condescension is her obvious but unobtrusive presence behind the camera, which establishes her relationship with her grandmother. Even more effective is de Vito's attention to the mundane details of housework and Adeline's domestic environment. The enclosing interior views produced by de Vito's wide-angle lens place Adeline in her familiar space and establish her as the central figure here.

Still, the pathos of Adeline's reminiscences risks turning *Ama l'Uomo Tuo* into a "human interest story." While a documentary profile of an individual often doubles as a sociological case study, an opposite movement also occurs: the conversion of social phenomena into personal conflict can defuse arguments for political action. No one could accuse de Vito of exploiting Adeline's trust; the respect and love between the two is quite evident. But, there is a voyeuristic flavor here, perhaps because no substantial exchange between them takes place on screen. And, in contrast to the rather crude technique of *Politics of Intimacy*, de Vito's more sophisticated camera work, sound mixing, and editing tend to enhance entertainment at the expense of concentrating on issues. That is, the audience is led to empathize with Adeline, not analyze her experiences. I don't mean to deny the need for technical and conceptual precision, but to consider the complacency that an easy-flowing and emotionally gripping narrative can create.

This tape was made when the widespread incidence of rape and woman-battering was first being publicized and politicized by feminists.[14] Difficult and as yet unresolved debates about the portrayal of victimized women arose from the conflicting needs to describe the nature and degree of these forms of terrorism and the considerably tougher problem of changing social relations. Seen in this context, *Ama l'Uomo Tuo* describes more than it analyzes or even agitates—remaining, therefore, well within the domain of documentary portraiture. De Vito, however, does not seem unconscious of the dilemmas she proposes. Even the title, which sounds like a motto for defeated women, must be reinterpreted. Recited by Adeline as a kind of postscript to her history of marital violence, the phrase brings home the power of ideology. De Vito concludes, then, with an obvious contradiction which lays bare the social foundations of her grandmother's individual experience.

Housework and child care, for centuries termed "women's work," have naturally been subjects of much feminist theoretical discourse.[15] In the past, the question, "Does your mother work?" might have been answered, "No, she's just a housewife." Now those conscious of the fallacy of that statement ask, "Does your mother work outside the home?" But, in most cases, the changes thus registered remain superficial. Adeline in *Ama l'Uomo Tuo* argues for the dignity of housework, but she undermines her plea by her acceptance of the double standard of the concept "women's work." *Harriet* (1973), a documentary tape by Nancy Cain, also portrays a woman whose work is housework but who doesn't share Adeline's unquestioning acceptance of it.

Cain follows Harriet Benjamin, her neighbor in the rural Catskill Mountain town of Lanesville, New York, through her daily chores. The tape opens with a long shot of Harriet seeing her older children off at the school bus stop. She washes the dishes, hangs out the laundry, prepares lunch, watches the soap operas—the familiar paces of domestic life. All these actions are recorded in a straightforward direct style, i.e., with no overt intervention by Cain. The frequent wide-angle views and skewed camera angles accentuate the crowded, claustrophic space of the Benjamins' trailer home but don't render it grotesque. Cain relies mainly on camera movement, emphatic sounds, and dramatic editing to make ordinary activity interesting.

Like hints of an anarchist rebellion, flashes from a different scenario momentarily invade Harriet's domestic routines: Harriet throwing a suitcase in a car, Harriet getting behind the wheel, Harriet driving away laughing. These recur irrationally, and eventually these events are played out. The tape concludes with a long sequence of Harriet driving down the highway away from Lanesville singing, "Roll out the barrel, we'll have a barrel of fun." This escape from domestic responsibilities is transparently fictitious, but the dramatization of her desire for autonomy rings true nevertheless. Like other feminist artists who have stretched definitions of reality to encompass resistance to accepted and expected female behavior, Cain uses the realistic connotations of documentary to describe actual experience *and* to indicate dissatisfaction with the status quo.

Harriet is not only Cain's portrait of her

Gever: Video Politics, Early Feminist Projects

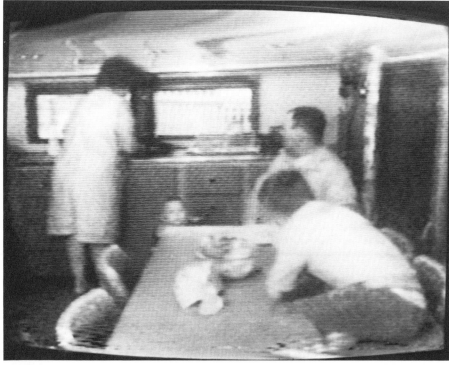

Harriet (1973), by Nancy Cain [no transcription]

neighbor presented as a feminist fable, though. It was made within a specific social context for a specific audience. In 1971, Cain and other members of the Videofreex, later renamed Media Bus, migrated from New York City to the small town of Lanesville. The group brought with them a low-power television transmitter with a broadcasting radius of about three miles, and established "the world's smallest TV station" without a license. For six years they broadcast a weekly program, live and taped, from their farmhouse headquarters; *Harriet* was one of many videotapes produced by Media Bus artists about and for their immediate community.

It is not too presumptuous, I think, to propose that Cain's video portrait would be seen differently by an audience of her neighbors than by strangers. For instance, aired in the impersonal context of nationally broadcast TV,[16] *Harriet* easily becomes a symbolic, charismatic character—though not in the TV star mold—since her spontaneous and good-natured personality is very attractive. In the process, social issues become individualized, identified with the main character. To a Lanesville audience, *Harriet* is likely to appear as a less abstract character, and, therefore, the feminist questions raised in the tape will be more pointed precisely because the people and situations depicted are close to home.

A common premise circulating among video groups in the mid-seventies was that independent documentaries were ideal vehicles for progressive political interventions in mass media territory. Public television seemed the most attractive outlet for this work, and those able to secure the support of a local station were considered exemplary. Though both de Vito and Cain's tapes were aired on WNET's "Video Tape Review" (VTR) series, neither was produced for that purpose. In contrast, *Fifty Wonderful Years* (1973)—a tape produced by the San Francisco video collective Optic Nerve and edited by members Lynn Adler, Sherrie Rabinowitz, and nonmember Bill Bradbury for PBS-affiliate KQED—bears all the marks of television journalism. The producers of this tape about the 1973 Miss California pageant appear neutral; the tape is less personal, less engaged with its characters than the first three works discussed here.

As in *Harriet*, the producers of *Fifty Wonderful Years* remain practically invisible. I'd argue that anonymity is more pronounced here since the camera work

From *Fifty Wonderful Years* (1973) by Optic Nerve

—*What do you think of the women's liberation movement in general?*
—*Well, that's their own thing, and my thing is Sea Scouts.*

—*Do you think women are oppressed?*
—*Are what?*

—*I mean these girls are so ugly they couldn't run for Miss Anything.*

Spend your time this week creating memories, the kind that you will love and cherish for the rest of your life. Because they will be important for the rest of your life. How you act this week will be how you look back upon yourself and how you'll be in the future. Be proud of what you do. Now, the most important day in your life should be the day you walk down the aisle with that special man. Your most important career should be marriage.

and audio techniques are essentially the same as those used in network public affairs products like *60 Minutes.* The difference is that there is no narrator/reporter to guide us through the pageant, and the camera, microphone and editing assume this function. Whereas a documentary videotape about a beauty contest will not necessarily reflect feminist concerns, one made by an alternative collective in 1973 probably will. Superficially, no critique of homogenized feminine beauty as glorified in such contests is made by Optic Nerve. As a result, an audience of beauty contestants and their mothers would probably not be offended or threatened by this tape. The few scenes of a feminist demonstration protesting the Miss California competition might seem an irritating but undeniably real part of the

whole event. Only the concluding sequence, where the winner confronts a group of media men who act like birds of prey, might appear unusual and slightly unsettling.

Closely examined, Optic Nerve's treatment of the subject implies an understated but definite critical position.[17] A great deal of tape is devoted to pageant organizers, supervisors, and chaperones—in other words, the ideologues of standardized, contrived beauty. Often these women (they're all women) are heavily made-up (ex-Miss Something?) and are shown in unflattering close-up shots. Camera zooms bring the sprayed hair and mascarared lashes into even closer range as if to reveal greater truths. This visual device is merely rhetorical, though, borrowed from the repertoire of TV news. On the other hand,

the young women are generally shown without voyeuristic delight. A further critical comment is added through shots of a male judge juxtaposed with the presumed objects of his fixed gaze—the pretty young ladies in evening gowns. From these few but not uncharacteristic examples, we might deduce that beauty contests are cultural institutions perpetuated by mothers and fathers (the pageant functionaries and the judges) with various rewards for compliant daughters. Though I wouldn't dispute this position, which is similar to that taken by the ad hoc feminist group that organized the legendary protest against the 1968 Miss America contest, the expressed political attitude of the producers of *Fifty Wonderful Years* is never enunciated. Instead, the ironic attitude displayed in the tape can only be perceived by those pre-disposed to agree.

The producers of *Fifty Wonderful Years* may have hoped to disguise their unortho-dox views using conventional formats and techniques and, thereby, bring their message to a wider audience. In doing so, they sacrificed political analysis for the look of objectivity: all data has been coolly collected, the relevant facts extracted and presented, and any conclusions are, therefore, informed and reasonable. That such conclusions are intended to be feminist is strongly implied, but the tape so closely resembles the network norm that any subversion remains subtle. The result of this infiltration is bland at best.

I HAVE WRITTEN about these four tapes as if they were contempo-rary work. Though Gustafson, de Vito, Cain, Adler, and Rabinowitz are still active producers, the questions posed by these and other experiments in feminist political video have not been pursued. Tracing the causes for this can be easily as complicated as the original project of analyzing the genre, but I will be succinct.

—The economic position of most women in relation to men has deteriorated in the past decade. Inflation and rising unemploy-ment add to the overall economic inequity. Therefore, the expense of video produc-tion makes it a less attractive artistic option for women.

—Many of the feminist analyses arrived at in the late sixties and the seventies remain viable, but the women's liberation move-ment has dropped the word "liberation," and the tenor of feminist political action has become subdued.

—Broadcast television, the outlet for many social documentaries, is not known for fi-nancing or airing truly radical videotapes. As in the case of *Fifty Wonderful Years*, work made with backing from public tele-vision tends to be oblique or insipid in order to pass inspection by station and network censors.

—Other distribution systems, like the educational and library circuits for 16mm films, do not exist for video.

—Within the field of video art, where radical documentaries might expect to find support, such work is often regarded as a variety of television journalism,[18] and therefore thrown back into the compro-mised embrace of public television or into the back alley of public access channels on cable TV.[19]

—The criteria used to evaluate proposed video art projects and those designed for public TV demand ever-increasing tech-nical sophistication and the attendant funds needed to achieve those production values, thus circling back to women's economic disadvantages.

—In the art world, feminism is supposedly taken for granted, while women's ad-vances are quietly being reversed.

In sum, power and money have as-sumed virtual control of independent video within its fifteen-year life span. Elaborate, flashy, and expensive tapes of the eighties make the black-and-white, cheaply made feminist documentaries of the seventies look crude, even primitive. Clearly, the factors which have led to the effective demise of this genre are highly political: the politics of job segregation and income distribution which reflect sexist social structures, the politics of broadcast TV, and the politics of art are all implicated. At the same time, feminist documentary ex-periments, like those described here, challenge definitions of video art that exclude outspoken, political work, social realism that excludes experimentation, and video histories that credit only singular artists—mostly men. Above all, feminist documentary videotapes contribute to a social history, already recorded, which should be studied and understood, not denigrated or discarded. Otherwise, the mechanisms of forgetting, already set in motion, will deny that the work *and* the history ever existed.△

1. The use of the word "documentary" has been persistently problematic in discussions of what John Grierson more accurately, but also more awkwardly, termed "creative interpretations of actuality." Theories and practices of the field of documentary, camera-based media—photography, film, and video—vary widely, and my use of the term here is intended as broad and vernacular.

Various histories of documentary are especially relevant to a full consideration of the evolution of that form in the United States and as background to this essay: Eric Barnouw, *Documentary: A History of the Non-Fiction Film* (New York: Oxford University Press, 1974); Lewis Jacobs, ed., *The Documentary Tradition: From Nanook to Woodstock* (New York: Hopkinson and Blake, 1971); Stephen Mamber, *Cinema Verité in America: Studies in Uncontrolled Documentary* (Cambridge, Mass.: MIT Press, 1974); William Stott, *Documentary Expression and Thirties America* (New York: Oxford University Press, 1973); and Martha Rosler, "In, Around and After-thoughts (On Documentary)," in *Martha Rosler: 3 Works* (Halifax, N.S.: The Press of the Nova Scotia College of Art and Design, 1981). To date, no history of independent video documentary has been published.

2. Again, a thorough description of the relation between art and progressive political movements—the legacy of con-temporary social documentarians—must be sought in other texts. Linda Nochlin, *Realism* (New York: Penguin Books, 1971) describes nineteenth-century precedents. Russell Campbell, *Cinema Strikes Back: Radical Filmmaking in the United States, 1930–1942* (Ann Arbor, Mich.: UMI Research Press, 1982) is an excellent history of the Workers Film and Photo League, Nykino, and Frontier Films, three left-wing film organizations in the U.S. Campbell's introduction, tracing the roots of this documentary work, was useful to me in my conceptualization of more recent developments. William Alexander, *Film on the Left: American Documentary from 1931 to 1942* (Princetown, N.J.: Princeton University Press, 1981) covers much of the same territory as Campbell's book but is less rigorous and less radical, though more easily available. Ann Tucker, ed., *Photo Notes and Film Front* (Rochester, N.Y.: Visual Studies Workshop Press,

1977) is a collection of newsletters published by the Workers Film and Photo League and its successor, the Photo League, between 1934 and 1950.

3. In "The Political Aesthetics of the Feminist Documentary Film," in *Quarterly Review of Film Studies* 3 (4) (Fall 1978): 507–523, Julia Lesage defines feminist documentary films as a genre. I have borrowed her formulation and taken her work as a starting point for this discussion of the related feminist documentary videotapes. These two media depart mainly where technology and attendant cultural institutions differ.

4. Many of these women's video groups have disbanded without any record. Two I had personal contact with were the Women's Video Collective in Rochester, New York, and the Women's Video Project at the Women's Building in Los Angeles. In 1976 women's video groups in fourteen cities exchanged tapes in a system of "Videoletters." Groups like Women in Focus in Vancouver, B.C. and Iris Video in Minneapolis continue this tradition.

5. From 1972 to 1976 Susan Milano and various other women in New York City organized the Women's Video Festival, first at The Kitchen and later at the Women's Interart Center.

6. Michael Shamberg and Raindance Corporation, *Guerrilla Television* (New York: Holt, Rinehart and Winston, 1971), 8–9.

7. See Beryl Korot's letter to Shamberg, on page 13 of *Guerrilla Television*, in reponse to Shamberg's "personalized history" of independent video on pages 10–19. Shamberg mentions no women other than Korot and Phyllis Gershuny, the founders of *Radical Software*.

8. In a 1982 CBC radio series, "Styles of Truth: Decoding Documentary," produced by Seth Feldman, Brian Winston differentiates the United States brand of cinema verité, *direct cinema*—the fly-on-the-wall approach developed by Robert Drew, Donn Pennebaker, Richard Leacock, Al Maysles, Fred Wiseman, et al.—from the French interventionist cinema pioneered by Jean Rouch and Edgar Morin. Also see Mamber, *Cinema Verité in America*.

9. An extensive study of the ideas and accomplishments of the NFBC's Challenge for Change project has yet to be written. For now, the record exists in the film and tapes produced, in the issues of the project's publication *Challenge for Change Newsletter*, in the files of the Film Board, and in the recollections of the various filmmakers, videomakers, and community residents involved.

10. This expression of media idealism, a quote from the tape *Video: The New Wave*, produced by Fred Barzyk for WGBH in 1973, exemplified the democratic impulses behind many early independent documentary projects and tapes. These iconoclastic tapes, however, were rarely allowed airtime by public TV stations, least of all by WGBH.

11. In *Notes from the First Year*, New York Radical Women, June 1968, 11. Reprinted and expanded in Anne Koedt, Ellen Levine and Anita Rapone, eds., *Radical Feminism* (New York: Quadrangle Books, 1973), 198–207.

12. Mary Jane Sherfey, *The Nature and Evolution of Female Sexuality* (New York: Random House, 1972).

13. See Lesage, "Political Aesthetics of Feminist Documentary Film," 514–517, for her analogy between 1970s feminist documentary films and c-r groups.

14. Concurrent feminist publications included Erin Pizzey, *Scream Quietly or the Neighbors Will Hear* (London: If Books, 1974) and Andra Medea and Kathleen Thompson, *Against Rape* (New York: Farrar, Straus and Giroux, 1974), along with numerous magazine articles which analyzed the everyday physical abuse of women in feminist terms.

15. See Ann Oakley, *The Sociology of Housework* (New York: Pantheon Books, 1975); Pat Mainardi, "The Politics of Housework," in *Sisterhood is Powerful*, ed. Robin Morgan (New York: Vintage Books, 1970), 447–454; and Betsy Warrior, "Housework: Slavery or a Labor of Love," in *Radical Feminism*, 208–212.

16. *Harriet* was aired on WNET-TV's nationally broadcast series "Video Television Review," as part of the composite tape *Lanesville TV*, on June 26, 1975.

17. My interpretation of *Fifty Wonderful Years* as a feminist critique is confirmed in Optic Nerve's synopsis of the tape which appeared in the catalogue for the American Film Institute's 1981 Video Festival: "'Fifty Wonderful Years' reveals the people responsible for the pageant and [for] perpetuating the images of women which are so oppressive to us all." (63).

18. The 1982 media panel at the National Endowment for the Arts, the arbiters of $200,000 in fellowships for video artists, decided to deny support for "video journalism" but rather award grants for documentaries on the basis of artistic merit. No precise criteria for either "journalism" or "artistic merit" were defined, however.

19. Public access cable TV, I should add, is where experimental political video seems to be flourishing.

20. The work that immediately comes to mind is that of Martha Rosler, most recently her tape *A Simple Case for Torture, or How to Sleep at Night*.

Distributors

Politics of Intimacy: Global Village, 454 Broome Street, New York, New York 10013.

Ama l'Uomo Tuo (Always Love Your Man): Electronic Arts Intermix, 84 Fifth Avenue, New York, New York 10011.

Harriet and *Fifty Wonderful Years* are no longer in distribution.

Working With Unions

by *Fred Lonidier*

Prologue

I want to state at the outset that there are enormous limitations on an anthology like this, which are primarily a result of the marginal terrain most radical art occupies. This in turn results from the marginal position of radicals in society, especially in North America, and the consequent lack of resources to compete in the major arenas of the mass media and high art (which has to a great extent been industrialized). Radical art is a small-shop home industry taking on the multinational conglomerates for the allegiance of the masses.

The outcome of this marginalization is that most oppositional cultural practice is largely invisible even to those of us who are obsessed with it. By necessity, if not by choice, we work fairly locally, and it takes almost all we've got to do what we're doing. Therefore, our work must be collected by someone else and made broadly available. But this is only a step toward a real discourse presenting real choices to the reader. Choice in this case—if most readers weren't already predisposed to certain ideas, practices and forms—is probably overwhelming without some critical evaluation that is informed enough and has a clear enough perspective. Choice should be based upon judgment, and the description, discussion and illustration of our often complex, socially specific and extensive works are rarely adequate to the task.

What we need more and more, as oppositional work achieves wider dissemination, is writing which itself compares and contrasts and interrogates our works. When we are invited to group shows and anthologies, the host must see to it that the political and formal issues are laid out in some way; otherwise we have lettuce and tomatoes but no salad. This is no small problem. It can only be done by those who can take the time to actually observe our works in the contexts in which they are intended and do (or don't) work. Furthermore, the apprehending mind must have some ideas about which things work and which don't, about which jobs need to be done and for whom. However successful any of us are in our scene with what we do, we are floundering as a movement of cultural contenders and have much less meaningful contention with each other than the political Left has within itself.

Photo-Text Analysis

On the positive side, though, is the surfacing awareness—on a national and international level—of the vitality and viability of oppositional cultural practice. There are now fledgling networks that transcend our localization, and many of us artists are aware of the need to connect left intellectuals with our burgeoning practice.[1] These latter writers are largely trained and working in academia (when a job can be found) and are heavily steeped in the traditions of critical theory. By and large they have remained aloof from contemporary art-in-struggle unless they are discovering the past (1920s and 1930s) or the work is being done in the Third World or, to a small extent, by ethnic minorities.

I.

My work addresses the growing inability of the U.S. labor movement to *protect* its interests and attempts to point toward the unnameable socialist program that can *advance* the working class to its full political potential. I have to say "attempts" because since 1975 I have been carrying on a slow, uneven, thin, in short, difficult task with just enough support, encouragement and "success" to keep going. This is not a complaint but an acknowledgment that this goal, for all of us committed to it, demands the tenacious resolve of the long run. I must also say that when I began making artwork about and for the labor movement I had hoped things would move much faster. I especially hoped that the unions and their federation, the AFL-CIO, would embrace my first project, *The Health and Safety Game* (H&SG), and commit resources to its wide distribution. On the other hand, I feared that the way I chose to work would not go over at all. I have been working in this way long enough now to evaluate what has happened and point to future directions.

II.

The artworks I am discussing here—*The Health and Safety Game* (1976),[2] *L.A. Public Workers Point to Some Problems* (1979),[3] and *I Like Everything Nothing But Union* (1983)—have a dual social role, in the art world and in the unions, but tend to play one or the other depending on the place shown. They originate from and continue to be a part of the avant-garde high art world, where they challenge and contradict that sacrosanct bourgeois cultural institution. Along with other radical artists who have the requisite credentials, I work to prevent high culture from going on with its business and hypocrisies (art for art's sake) without having to answer occasionally (and sometimes even concede) to criticism. We rally those artists, students, and critics who are inside the art world but who share few of its benefits and who potentially can be encouraged to view their alienation and discontent as related to problems of the society at large. Legitimacy in the art world has been traditionally claimed on the basis of a work's theoretical contribution to the cultural-formal questions raised: what is the nature and boundary of art? In spite of the degeneration of modernism's own theory and practice, there is still some knee-jerk acceptance of serious attempts to raise these questions—and political art often looks very serious to those still concerned about upholding art's intellectual respectability.

In the labor unions, the work is legitimized by its "artness" as well as by the seriousness of the social issues involved. Because organized labor and its concerns have been relatively marginalized—in spite of an overall membership that makes the art world look like a game of solitaire in comparison—unions may welcome an outsider (or in my case, a member of the American Federation of Teachers) who speaks on their behalf to a public audience within prestigious social institutions. As for my work, it doesn't look like anything they'd usually consider art except that they know that modern art often takes unusual forms. This is not a satisfactory understanding of what I do, but it allows me to develop my photo/text pieces until both the workers and I can afford the time and energy needed to discuss all manner of cultural issues. If there is any other legitimate justification for separating art of this nature into high or low categories, it is not on the basis of status but in the acceptance of a vanguard role in the experimental sense. In the same way that the political economy must continuously reassess and test its theory and practice, so must any subarena, such as cultural work. I have the greatest affinity, then, with those who see their work as offering something fundamentally new to the long traditions of oppositional cultural practice. I hope this does not sound pretentious and stuffy. I genuinely believe there is a need for a theoretical distinction in our activities, even if we have not yet worked out completely non-elitist ways of using them.

(Article text continued on page 106)

Photographs by Fred Lonidier

Lonidier: Working with Unions, Photo-Text Analysis

The Health and Safety Game

- The original format had many pieces and sizes of panels. The new format is twenty-six panels, 35 x 40 inches (see below).

- Twenty minute b/w video tape.

- Poster/essay (Allan Sekula).

- Mini version, 48 x 52 inches.

Whitney Museum of American Art, New York, 1977.

San Diego/Imperial Counties Labor Council Occupational Health and Safety Conference, 1982.

The Health and Safety Game: fictions based on fact

Really about the political economy of occupational health, the *H&SG* was my first photo/text artwork for and about the labor movement. It puts a number of photo-narrative "case histories" into the context of the winning political strategies and tactics of management (capital). I include, but downplay, the significance of technical-medical answers to the horren-dous slaughter in the workplace because, although these remedies are in many cases already available, the political unity of the workers needed to force their implementation is not. Of this kind of work that I have done, *The Health and Safety Game* is by far the most shown and reviewed in both the art circuit and the unions. When it has been exhibited for a sufficient time, I think it has proven very effective in its intent to provoke discussion about labor's strategies and tactics.

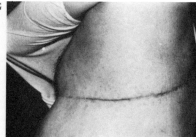

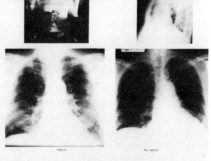

CONSTRUCTION SUPERVISOR'S NECK

I. 1. Damages left knee on a construction job.

II. 2. Commercial garage doors fall on his shoulder.

3. Begins to have back pains and headaches.

4. X-rays reveal severely bent neck column.

5. Goes into retirement on his pension.

6. The state demands a hearing on his injury.

7. Starts seeing a specialist to get relief from pain.

8. Decides to press claim for compensation.

PROLOGUE

Management speaks to labor and offers what amounts to a double bind:

If we spend the kind of money you're talking about for prevention and compensation, we won't have the profits we need for investment, and that will eventually lead to greater unemployment. We will also have to raise the prices of our products, which will reduce demand and therefore sales, which will lead to cutbacks in production and greater unemployment. Thus, at most we can increase our investment in prevention only up to the amount of money that it saves us in compensation payments and workers' lost time. Labor just has to accept a certain amount of illness and injury for the good of us all.

LABOR decides to

Capitulate
(Illness, injury, and death rates rise)
We accept your argument. We'll have to sacrifice some of us at an increasing rate in order to take care of the needs of the rest of us. In any case, we are powerless to act.

Defend itself
(Illness, injury, and death rates level off)
We accept your argument only in part. We know you could do more to keep the injury and disability rates from rising, and we will fight to see that you do. We don't have the resources or the will to press the issue beyond that.

Take the offensive
(Ilness, injury, and death rates fall)
We don't accept your argument. You are hiding your waste and mismanagement. Shape up or get out of Management. If you can't bring the rates down your way, we'll have to find some other way. We are mobilizing ourselves to force action on health and safety.

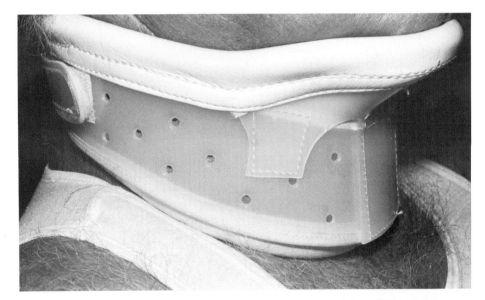

History

2. Of course it happened so quick that you really don't know what happened.

2. It's a normal thing contractors do; if they can cut the cost, they will.

6. Well, I really didn't want to be bothered with going through all this hassle, you know. I really didn't. 'Cause I know what you have to go through. You have to go down to the insurance doctor and the attorney's doctor has to be into it. And then they don't think anything's wrong with you. Then they don't know whether there is or not, so you're in a hassle, back and forth. . . .It disrupts your trend of life because you don't know what's happening and, really, I didn't want to get mixed up with it in the first place.

Herstory

Now we have two retired people, right? Unexpectedly.

Not only is he attempting to cope with his own physical disabilities, which, say, he chose to either ignore or continue in spite of, now he's having to focus on them.

Now you have his self-esteem shattered.

It just threw both of our lives into a state of utter chaos for several months. Not able to solve anything in a practical way. Reacting very illogically with frustration and anxiety, on both our parts.

There's a whole mystique around heavy construction, you know. Like the cigarette ads, you know. Certain kind of maleness.

These muscle spasms, they hit him, and you know there's nothing that's going to deplete your ability to perform any faster than, I suppose, a zigzagging pain down your back, or down your leg, or down your shoulder, and in any position that he gets in, the poor guy just goes berserk.

His sex life has just been shot to hell in just this short time because of the drugs.

Lonidier: Working with Unions, Photo-Text Analysis

Photo/text documentary has evolved as an answer to humanist photography's commitment to singular, dramatic images. I am arguing not that the issue is one of style, but that the artwork needs to be more ambitious in representing the issues and in keeping an audience's attention fixed on the camera's subject rather than on the heroism and virtuosity of the photographer. I support a self-reflexive mode that reveals the documentarian and the tools for scrutiny as long as the balance is maintained between looking inward and outward. Also, the dependence of photographs on context for their meaning makes a demand upon those of us who want to say what we think needs to be said—and not something else—to control as much of the viewing environment as possible. Like in film, where it is now unthinkable that the images and sound/text would not be shaped to create a whole "statement," the documentary photographer produces a complete thing. I am talking about autonomous, self-contained artworks and am not, of course, ruling out other more limited or dependent uses of the medium (like illustration).

There is so much history lost to people and so much reorientation necessary that I resort to rather lengthy texts. There are always interviews with workers that tell what is experienced, seen, thought and felt about the situation from their perspectives. This commentary runs the full range from the specifics of their experience to the long-run historical context, but for the most part the former dominates. The big picture is not well developed, for political reasons, among the U.S. rank and file. Because of this I provide an overview that is historically derived and more global in reach: "How has this issue developed through time? What does it look like in other places?" Usually I also provide some kind of outline for the text in order to make it more accessible. This gives the reader an opportunity to choose which panel(s) to pursue in depth.

I am frequently asked if union members in particular read the entirety of my pieces. (This is often said in response to the widely known rise in illiteracy among us; I don't know why people who bemoan this fact encourage it by arguing for less literature.) *The reason workers can't, won't, don't read has political roots.*

Based on the experience I now have, and on what I have learned from other kinds of extensive works, it is clear that people will make an effort to get through something if the following conditions prevail:

—First, and most important, is the choice of subject matter. I always look for the submerged, missed, or forgotten labor issue—or for an issue that is about to emerge. In hand with this choice is the particular way the issue is treated, the point of view. I look to the absences, inadequacies or invisibilities of the available discourse. In fact, much of what I have to say is already known and discussed or suspected by workers themselves. It may only be a question of legitimizing or distilling certain ideas rather than teaching in the one-way sense.

—Second, the language must be visually well organized and widely understandable.

—Third, the artwork should be installed in a place frequented by workers for lengthy periods of time. If possible, parts of the work should be reproduced in the union's or labor council's literature. It must be publicized. This third requirement causes the most problems for works like mine since so often it is just not possible for one reason or another.

My long-winded strategy may not always be necessary. If the issues are being discussed elsewhere, they won't have to be included in such depth within the artworks.

One other major issue I will only touch on is the active/passive role of the documentarian. I do not believe that any phenomenon necessarily speaks for itself well. For example, workers who are not class conscious speak differently than do those who are. In my editorial choices I give emphasis to the more conscious expressions out of proportion to their occurrence among U.S. workers. I am concerned with what *is* in order to move my audience to consider what *ought* to be. To represent things as they are without indicating *why* they are this way—that is, how they came about—is to reify causation and reinforce the contention that the status quo is immutable. My own contribution to the pieces (such as the "Management" section of the *Health and Safety Game* or the "Crisis of Western Capital" in *L.A. Public Workers. . .*) are efforts to intervene in the discourse of the trade unions (and art world) and insert that which is needed but absent.

(Article text continued on page 115)

San Diego Federation of Teachers, AFT, Local 370, 1982.

L.A. Public Workers Point to Some Problems: sketches of the present for some, point to the future for all?

Produced for the Social Works show at the Los Angeles Institute for Contemporary Art, I tried to use this piece as the hub of an expanded exhibition idea. Since it is very difficult to get labor to come to galleries, editions of the artwork were hung simultaneously in the unions involved and in the Los Angeles County Federation of Labor. The public worker issue was selected, with the help of the federation, because of the timely impact of Proposition 13.[5] Speaking from the perspective of city and county workers about the consequences of this widely supported initiative, this piece addresses several questions:
–Was there "fat" in government? (Some.)
–Did the new law cut the fat? (No, fat is in administration, which can protect itself.)
–What about government services? (Declining.)

–And working conditions? (Bad to worse.)
Another major change from *The Health and Safety Game* was to place the fiscal crises of Los Angeles into an international, national, and regional context by outlining certain facts (surplus industrial capacity has produced a glut of many commodities on world markets, causing a drop in overall profits and a consequent shrinking of the tax base) and quoting contradictory authorities from the business press. Formally, this work was less successful than the *H&SG*. The images are more interesting, I think, but less shocking than scars and burns. More significantly, I gave a lot of space to an outline that was too long to work as such and tended to overload each panel with type. I received generally favorable feedback from the unions but virtually no response from the art establishment reviewers. I don't think a single one went to any of the unions to see how it might look and work there or to talk to officers and members.

Lonidier: Working with Unions, Photo-Text Analysis

San Francisco Labor Council, AFL-CIO.

L.A. Workers Point to Some Problems

– Ten panels, 32 x 50 inches.

– Seven panels published by the Los Angeles County Federation of Labor's paper, *The L.A. Citizen*, in conjunction with the LAICA show, September 14-28, 1979.

– The Focus Gallery was the hub of an exhibit in labor spaces in San Francisco in 1980.

San Francisco Federation of Teachers, AFT, Local 61.

Service Employees International Union.

Focus Gallery and map of installations in the city.

ANNA ACOSTA
TENANT RELATIONS ASSISTANT
AFSCME 143

American Federation of State, County and Municipal Employees

1 *Everybody comes in, you know, on emergency basis, "I don't have anywhere to go," and been put on the street or the landlord sold the house . . . or the rent has gone up and they can't afford it, or they don't want kids . . . But we don't have anywhere to put 'em. Our places are packed and our people don't move . . . But for each apartment we have vacant we have maybe 200 to 300 applications waiting for them.*

6 *Now it's getting a little frustrating but before it was like a family because the projects, there were only 22 and there weren't so many employees as there are now. Everybody kind of knew each other and you kind of moved around from one development to another. It really was a nice place to work.*

6 *They don't even give me a pat on the back, "You're doing a good job and we appreciate it." Yeah, they take it for granted.*

6 *I have found myself really disgusted at times. Before I didn't. I still enjoy my job but I feel that I can't really do as much as I used to be able to before. And the morale in the Authority is very, very low.*

6 *And then you get the attitude, "Well hey," you know, "I'm going to do what I have to do and I'm not going to bend over backwards to help here." And that's a terrible attitude to take but there are people that feel the same way I do.*

7 *I think it's a really good place to work far as fringes and pay.*

8 *It came out to about $75 and out of that if I saw $20 I was lucky. Of course, with the cost of living and the gas situation, that didn't help me.*

9 *This year with the budget and everything, every time we went in there, "No money, no money."*

9 *"We can't promise anything in the future but," you know, "Just keep up the good work. You get less people but keep doing it."*

10 *I think the union has been very effective in getting us a lot of our fringe benefits.*

11 *As far as promotions are concerned, I think that there's been a lot of people, that have been with the Authority and have grown with the Authority, by-passed.*

19 *Oh, I think it's substantial. In fact, I think they could do away with some management positions.*

20 *In the position where I'm in, if you don't have a person that's really capable and good and knows what they're doing your Manager's going to work hard. In fact, a lot of weak Managers are carried by people in my position.*

2 *It's put a little more pressure on us as employees because we're thin, we're thinly spread now. We lose a person and we don't get a person to replace them.*

3 *There were two of us doing what I'm doing now.*

Lonidier: Working with Unions, Photo-Text Analysis

I Like Everything Nothing But Union

This work was requested by the head of my own San Diego-Imperial Counties Labor Council (AFL-CIO) and, after over two years of photographing and interviewing, was installed in the council. Additional editions will travel locally and nationally. It sums up two broad but critical questions for organized labor today: Who are we? Where should we go from here? We begin with the point that the crises of occupational health and the public sector are symptomatic of deeper issues and that the labor movement will have to thoroughly examine itself before it can move ahead. The primary role of the photos is to present the diversity of occupation, ethnic background and sex among workers who must be unified. Lengthy quotations, in question-and-answer format, address the issues as rank-and-file workers see them. The council's interest in the project springs from a desire to raise these concerns both within the unions and before the public at large. This is a significant first step away from the cold war years (under George Meany), when public silence was kept on a lot of big questions about the role of unions in society by containing them within the top levels of the unions and their federation, the AFL-CIO.

Lonidier: Working with Unions, Photo-Text Analysis

International Association of Bridge, Structural and Ornamental Ironworkers Shopmen's Local 627.

San Diego Federation of Teachers, Local 370.

Ola Hosley.

Richard Townsand.

"I Like Everything Nothing But Union"

Workers' Thoughts On:

Management

The reason we have labor unions is because big business took advantage of the worker. And, you know, you can't get away from that.

I tried to tell the guy there when I was working in the safety department on light duty...I said, "You know, a lota the accidents is caused over, is brought on by the supervision," I say. It's the way they fit a person up and they'll find 'em a job and by the time they get started on them, they do this, that and the other to 'em and not much time passes, you know, they get the person frustrated and upset and then there's a accident! I say, if everything is calm and some kind of communication between your supervision, then a person feels better, because they can communicate.

If you speak up, *if* you speak out, *if* you stand up for your rights, hey, you got trouble on your hands.

Every time you turn around, management cries, "Foul," when you go ask for something, and yet management is still making, you know, a lot more money than they were some time ago.

If there was ever a time to break the unions the time is now.... The business people realize this is their golden opportunity. So there's a race who can get their heaviest artillery in there quickest.

When we were hired years ago, we were more or less screened, and I always said that they knew more about me when I went to work than I knew about myself! Yeah, the company. And how they get their information or anything else, I don't know!

Union Protection and Benefits

I think [unions] are to, well, to protect the rights of people that essentially have no rights. And those are, are working-class people. I think a lot of times, the kind of system that we live under, the class system, is people believ[ing] that working people just don't need to have rights, that we don't really require any rights...that we are there for a purpose, to provide something rather than to be given anything.... Well, again, I think that if [unions] didn't exist, the people, working

people would just essentially be exploited. We would just essentially be there like before there were any unions for the purpose of providing cheap labor to a small percentage of the people that would make a profit off of us.

The largest majority goes in favor with the union representation when you *do* have a grievance. Right, you can count on them when you need 'em to represent you in a grievance or a problem area. They'll be there.

Well, yes, I've worked in non-union shops before I joined a union, and I mean there's no question about it: the kind of rights you enjoy on the job and the kind of working conditions you enjoy on the job and the things you can enforce, your job security alone. The employer could not hire and fire at will, at whim. And these are [the] main things. I would have had to accept a rather subservient attitude toward the foreman which we don't have to do, though, [I'd] say they're getting back into the saddle again.

Well, I'd probably be in debt up to my hilt on 'count of my wife. She's had several operations which the union insurance has paid for and, well, about four of my kids, they paid for their delivery. And, like I say, I think it is one of the greatest things that they have ever came up with and I hope they keep it.

I have a good job situation because my union protects me. There are certain rules and regulations in my union that union members abide by, which are a protection for themselves and their fellow workers. You don't go in and take another man's job while he is still hired on that job.... If this was not a union area, I probably would not have been paid for many, many jobs that I've done. So, my job situation is better because I'm in a union and I think that my skills—what I actually have learned in the past five years as a member of the local, is immeasurable. It has so greatly enhanced me by being in the local because I am surrounded by very high quality workers because of the union standards.

The Economy

Unions are tied into the corporate structure. When unionization was recognized or

when unions were recognized as legitimate [legalized], they were being institutionalized in the economy. They became legitimate, but the price that was paid for that recognition was that the parameters would be set by the system for what would be negotiated: being wages, working conditions, benefits. That was all set within, you know, the collective bargaining unit. That's fine; that's a start. Certainly, people have been helped a great deal but, at the same time, fundamental structural problems are not broached. For starters, I think, the union has to attempt to expand or break the parameters from which they operate now, being namely bargaining units. You know, we have to take active, what I would call political action within the corporations by use of our tremendous, you know, the revenue or the investments that we have in these companies through the pension funds. We have an opportunity to even dominate the decision-making process.

The economy is so dominated by the large, "mega," corporations....

The Government and Politics

I think the Labor Council, when they recommend folks for different offices of government, should look seriously and try to get somebody from the unions who really have all the people of the United States, the poor especially, in mind. In other words, who is really sincere about that to run for office.

[What] we found in the thirties is that the government, in *spite* of the liberal administration itself...that whenever there was a rank-and-file fight against the employers, the government agencies always, *always* collaborated with the employers.... I mean, even at the height of the Roosevelt administration, where the F.B.I., as an intimidating agency, was harassing unions, employing labor spies...despite laws on the books, the government agencies like the F.B.I., and so forth, [were] *always, always* cracking down on the unions and disrupting unions and doing everything else. *And* including complicity in murder, and I am not saying this loosely....

Maybe the best thing that ever happened to the labor movement in the last few years is the Reagan administration.

Lonidier: Working with Unions, Photo-Text Analysis

It's taken us from being very passive and thinking, well, you know, things are going along fine [to] where we're starting to get more aggressive...and that's what I mean by the fact that I think it's good. I see some good things coming from this administration, because it's gonna make us, you know, get in and do some hard work. 'Cause we're getting very passive. Labor is getting very passive. And I think this is gonna make us really get together. I really do!

Union Participation

I think that the people that are, that work in the union and that have their heart on the union, do everything they can.

It's the people that don't take an interest in the union, the ones that pull the other direction. So, the thing we have to do is to try to get the people to recognize a union as a great part of our living lives. That's right, educate the people more about what unions, unionism is.

I, I just think that, well gosh, I'm included in the people that don't do enough I think. I think I would just suggest that, well, that people become more and more involved [in their unions].

Union Education

I think those are sort of hard for me to answer because, I guess, I haven't really...I sort of see things so generally without really studying them specifically. I don't really, I haven't really kept up enough [on the labor movement], which is really shameful! Now that we're talking I realize how little I know. And so, you know, I wish I could say more on that...

I feel we're fighting a losing battle and that our membership needs to be made aware of the situation here in San Diego as far as labor versus politics. We have a younger generation coming in, and I think that we need to train them with a little bit of history as far as unions go and what their fathers and their grandfathers fought for.

As I don't think they've been made aware of this, and I know they don't teach very much of it in the schools, I'd like to see more of that.

The Unions

I think we're not working hard enough. We're not working as hard as we used to. I see that around me, you know, that we're just not together like we should be. We're pulling apart instead of pulling together.

Getting people to work together, to me, I think this is the key of the whole thing. Unionism is the best of your ideas, the best of mine, put together, and all the other garbage thrown out and forgotten. There are so many politics within, and so many people trying to get ahead, that they lose sight of this.

I think that organized labor is one of the most, one of the potentially strongest forces for social good in this nation. And, I think that they are falling down terribly right now, and I think they should stand back and take a good look at themselves and get into it or there is gonna be no labor left, no organized labor left.

In my own union we've always been a very proud craft union.... Anytime anybody said, "Why don't you go out and organize across the board? No, all we want is the people we're entitled to." So, we were loath to organize on a broad basis. And no we are. I mean, we'll go into a plant now and take 'em from door to door.

Race and Sex

We have blacks. Not a lot. It's a white trade. No, the union doesn't say anything about it. I don't think it's thought about. I don't think it's discussed. I don't think it's a point anybody cares about.

There's this one woman, every time she goes to her doctor, her blood pressure's up. And there's this one foreman, I keep trying to show her to the point that, "Hey, you can't continue to live like this because this man, he thrives on this kind of stuff, you know. And you gotta think of your health." But she tells me how she can't sleep at night knowing that she got to go in there and have to deal with this man. And I said, "You shouldn't have to live that way. You need your job. Don't quit your job. You *don't* have a husband. You got seven children to support." And, she's been going to counseling and therapy.

However, anticommunism is still a prevailing sanction against the explicit expression of certain political ideas within U.S. unions and the working class itself, although socialism has become a little less threatening as a few major and visible unionists have come out as socialists in recent years.[4] This raises a problem faced by all leftists working with the unions today and especially with their leadership. Some groups in the seventies thought they could go directly to the rank and file with revolutionary politics and unite with them to replace the centrist labor officials. All of those groups, that I know of, now find themselves on the margins of the unions or out altogether. The only alternative remaining for those who favor a socialist program is to enter through the muddy waters of reformism. Many of my choices of issue and of perspective, then, are attempts to push the limits of discourse (liberalism) in order to open the way toward a new working-class politic in this country.

A final consideration of cultural work in the unions is that there are few outlets for these artworks. However, there is great potential because the unions already have members, spaces and newspapers. (Cable TV opens up possibilities I cannot go into here.) The problem is getting some of these resources committed and adapted to cultural work. Just because a union has a hall does not necessarily mean that there is a reasonable space inside for exhibits. Unions also sometimes have money. Direct funding for projects is always a possibility, and each year unions and federations support a number of varied things (mostly films, slide shows, pamphlets, posters and calendars, and occasionally theater and art exhibits). Naturally, it usually takes a lot of time and energy to get an allocation of scarce monies, especially from a movement that is under attack. The issue of patronage control enters here too. Personally, because of my art world/university base, I have been able to draw support from outside labor through grants. I have also used a lot of my university salary for this work (and can take tax deductions for this as a research/education expense). However, labor's political clout must be used to expand government support for the arts as aid for cultural work. In the English-speaking world, the U.S. has the smallest per capita public art endowment; art here is privately owned or controlled, a consequence of political factors.

One way to work with limited resources is to form a group to divide up the efforts. Filmmakers are used to collective modes of working. Eventually I want to work with my fellow unionists from start to finish, but now they participate only as the objects of consideration and have minimal input in the artworks as a whole. Poetry, music, literature, and murals once flowed from the labor temples. Our goal should be to revive, and renew, the cultural side of the labor movement. In short, a lot of work has yet to be done in order to create a broad viable support system.△

Notes

1. In *Praxis* #6, I expand on the thesis that the theoretical and formal underdevelopment of much of our work is partly a result of the left intelligentsia's neglect. However, we need to go beyond the scope of the critical community that is available for left filmmakers. The problem there is that the critics write largely to each other and for the *viewers*; it is not very evident that the critical circle is closed with the *makers* of films. It is a full-circle ideal that I point toward for all our work.

2. *Red-Herring* #2, *Praxis* #6 and *Proceedings of the Marxist Caucus of the College Art Association*, Los Angeles, January 1979.

3. *Obscura* (5) and *Photography/Politics: 2* (forthcoming).

4. Mainly by membership in the Democratic Socialists of America (DSA). It is a well-kept secret from the general public that much of the top leadership of the AFL-CIO belongs to the Social Democrats U.S.A. (SDUSA) which, along with DSA, is a member of the Socialist International.

5. This California ballot initiative was successfully promoted as a property tax reform in 1978, at a time when these taxes for residential property were doubling and nearly tripling within a few years. The actual outcome was significant relief from residential taxes, a tremendous windfall tax break for commercial property owners (the initiative's unstated purpose), and a substantial reduction of the tax base for local public services.

Free Radio In Japan

by Tetsuo Kogawa

SINCE BERT BRECHT PROPOSED THE "democratization of radio" in 1927, the idea of free radio has been placed on the agenda for those involved in social change.[1] During World War II, free radio stations were set up to counter Nazi propaganda, and in the Algerian war, Free Radio-Algeria was an important tool of the National Liberation Front.[2]

However, free radio as we mean it was not launched until the 1970s, when a small number of pirate radio and television stations started operating in Italy. Although these stations risked being shut down by the police, they survived and grew gradually—supported by listeners who had tired of the conventional programs broadcast by the RAI (Radio Audizioni Italia), the government-supervised public broadcasting corporation. After World War II, when the Christian Democratic party replaced Mussolini's fascist regime, the new ruling party soon dominated the RAI. In 1968, however, the Socialist party entered the government coalition and began demanding their slice of airtime along with the other parties. Eventually, after the 1976 elections in which the Communist party elbowed out a part in the government, the Constitutional Court handed down Verdict 202, which held that the RAI monopoly of local broadcasting was unconstitutional.

Within a few months, roughly a thousand private radio stations and a hundred private television stations emerged, among them the "radios of movement" such as Radio Alice (Bologna), Radio Popolare (Milan), Radio Città Futura, Radio Onda Rossa, and Radio Radicale (all in Rome). They played an important role in the *Autonomia* (autonomous left) movement during the late seventies,[3] and their media experiments led up to a radical change in individual self-expression, community relationships, and the meaning of communications.[4]

Before long, the free radio movement in Italy stimulated parallel developments in France and later in other Western European countries. Toward the end of 1980, an estimated 2,500 illegal free radio stations were operating in France; the movement was booming to such a degree that Parisian radio shops began to sell broadcasting devices. When François Mitterand established the new Socialist government in 1981, it was assumed that he would totally legitimize these illegal stations—after all, he had been involved in a free radio station called Radio Riposte where, three years prior to his election, he

of "transmission transversal" suggests that, unlike conventional radio, free radio does not impose programs on a mass audience, whose numbers have been forecast, but freely comes across to a "molecular" public, so that it changes the nature of communication between those who speak and those who listen.[7] The service area should be relatively small, because free radio does not *broadcast* (scatter) information but *communicates* (co-unites) messages to a concrete audience.[8] In order to overthrow the passivity of the audience, Hans Magnus Enzensberger already noted that radio receivers could easily be trans-

Studio-store of the station Setagaya MaMa.

had broadcast political speeches. To the great disappointment of free radio advocates, however, his last word was to accept the proposals of a national commission that called for a state monopoly on the AM dial and restricted licenses for FM stations. Fierce competition for these licenses ensued, with only eighteen granted by mid-July 1982. The remaining stations have continued to broadcast illegally.[5]

In Japan, the idea of free radio was introduced by Félix Guattari, who had been involved in the movement both in Italy during the high tide of *Autonomia* and in France. In November 1980, I interviewed him for the radical journal *Nippon Dokusho Shinbun*.[6] In discussing this new form of communication, Guattari stressed the radically different function of free radio from conventional mass media. His notion

formed into transmitters.[9] However, the problem is not only with the technology but also with the culture of both receiving and transmitting. Nothing would be changed if radio receivers are only technologically transformed into new broadcasters. The concept of receiving and transmitting itself must be changed. Thus, Guattari's idea gave a flash of hope to those of us attempting to cope with the present terrible state of Japanese mass media.

The first radio broadcasts in Japan began in 1924, with television broadcasts following in 1953. In 1969, over 90 percent of Japanese households owned a black-and-white television set; by 1977, 97.7 percent had a color set. At the same time, most middle-class people had at least two personal radio-cassette recorders. Thus, a complete system connecting the population's personal milieu with govern-

Kogawa: Free Radio in Japan

mental or corporate media institutions had been established. If these media outlets provided diverse programs which met people's specific interests, this system could act as an effective network in which people could find indirect self-expression. However, in contrast to the affluence of radio and television sets, there is a poverty of variety and quality in programming. Even in Tokyo, there are only two FM and six AM channels, including three public broadcasting stations operated by NHK, the equivalent of the BBC. (The Far East Network, or FEN—a special broadcast service for U.S. troops stationed in East Asia—is also received on the AM dial.)

Even the few private commercial stations are indirectly controlled by the government through the restriction of licenses and the influence of the Ministry of Post and Telecommunications in the appointment of station executives. Although hundreds of institutions—including advertising agencies and political and religious organizations—have continued to apply to the Ministry of Posts and Telecommunications since 1945, only a few AM licenses were granted. In spite of the availability on the radio spectrum, no AM or FM station has been approved in Tokyo during the past ten years, a period of increasing cultural diversity in the context of economic development. This abnormal situation fits well with the government's policies: those private stations already operating are willing to submit to governmental supervision in order to monopolize the market and avoid competition with newcomers. Thus the government, headed by the Liberal Democratic party, has balked at dismantling this intervention in the private sector.

However, as the Japanese capitalist system has proceeded—accompanied by U.S.-style hyperconsumption—the centralized cultural apparatus has been dismantled to some extent in order to promote consumers' needs, to segment consumers into diverse groups, and to legitimize the rise of people's sociocritical consciousness. In this context, the advanced sectors of the economy, represented by big corporations, find the current state of Japanese media too backward for their needs. They keenly recognize the necessity of innovating mass communications; in fact, the Nippon Telegraph and Telephone Public Corporation is in the process of pursuing the Information Network System project, which will set up a glass-fiber cable network in every private house across the country. However, innovation in technology will not solve the problem without a simultaneous innovation in programming.

The confusion of this transitional period in Japanese mass media is evident in the large qualitative gap between regular television programs and short advertising spots for commodities. Indeed, today's spots on Japanese television have become more and more "artistic"; the better ones are a kind of "short-short" with sophisticated film techniques and original ideas. This is partly because the budget is usually much higher for a twenty-second spot than for thirty minutes of regular soap opera. Many (mostly male) international actors—such as Alain Delon, Marcello Mastroianni, Orson Welles, Sean Connery, Paul Newman, Woody Allen, Sophia Loren, Candice Bergen and Faye Dunaway—are featured. Therefore, the spots are more interesting than the regular programs, and they enable the viewer to endure the "interval" between advertising.

As an example of a similar distortion in radio, many audiences prefer the FEN (although their programs are not as sophisticated as the television spots). FEN's English programs, which stress current American popular music, are so welcomed by Japanese audiences that a special magazine, *FEN Club* (in Japanese), has recently started publishing; there are also several books on the network. However, there are many more listeners who are dissatisfied with Japanese radio but don't care for FEN and can't find alternatives. They prefer watching television for amusement and use radio only for a "speaking clock."

It was in this context that the idea of free radio came to us. In August 1981, some friends and I started investigating the details of what was happening in the free radio movement in Italy and France. While we were studying the Japanese Radio Law, to see if we could legally open a free radio station, we came across an interesting article which suggested that "a station whose broadcasting wave is in a very low power needs no licenses" (Article 3). According to Article 6 of the Enforcement Regulations, this "very low power" means the wave must be "below 15 microvolts per meter at the distance of 100 meters from the transmitter." This unknown "public access" to air waves, which are otherwise very strictly regulated, is intended for wireless microphones, television remote control devices, garage-door openers, model airplanes, and so on.

At first, this seemed to have nothing to do with free radio. However, when we happened to examine a tiny FM transmitter, it turned out that this "toy" should not be despised; its broadcasting wave theoretically could cover a 0.3-mile radius of the city—which in a dense population area contains 20,000 residents, all potential listeners. Also, we realized that the cost of such a transmitter would be low, now that Japanese industry overproduces various kinds of electronic gadgets.

It was not easy to find an appropriate transmitter that could come up to full functioning within the legal power allowance; all of the ones we examined were too weak for our purpose. Major electronic manufacturers limit the transmitting power because they are afraid that even such a tiny toy might violate the law. Under pressure from the government, they maintain a consensus on this conservative policy through the intermediate organization, Nippon Denshikiki Kogyokai (Organization of Japan Electronic Machinery Industries). However, in July 1982 we found an underground company which sold a transmitter with power at the legal maximum. Although this FM transmitter for seventy-six to ninety megahertz was basically sold for car-to-car communication at close distance, it was most appropriate for our purpose: besides the broadcasting capability, it was so cheap that anyone could buy it and join a large network of tiny stations.

After we repeated our broadcasting experiments with this device in the center of Tokyo, students of mine established a station called Radio Polybucket at Wako University (where I work). In the meantime, other people became interested in opening up legal FM stations using this type of transmitter. One of the most ambitious groups was KIDS (opened in August 1982), whose members had been initially interested in establishing an independent commercial recording company to sell their music cassettes. Shrewdly tying up with mass media—thus totally neglecting the radical idea of free radio—they succeeded in stirring up public curiosity.

Young people have followed the KIDS example, and by the spring of 1983, over one hundred stations had opened; by June of the same year, an estimated seven hundred "ministations" were operating across the country. It is true that, without KIDS such a large number of stations would not have appeared in such a short period. However, it is also true that KIDS has laid a wrong track—which, to a certain extent, has emasculated the very idea of free radio. Its operators don't care about the audience or the needs of the neighborhood but broadcast only what they want—so far, childish monologues with American pops. Thus, few people listen to their programs. Interestingly enough, it is well

FUMIO TAKASHIMA

A radio store in Tokyo dealing in various kinds of small transmitters.

known that KIDS and some similar stations are strongly backed by major advertising agencies and media industries, who intend to use this "boom" to prod the stubborn government to change its radio policy.

Not all of the ministations practice the idea of free radio or intend to be *free* from conventional mass media. Many of them want to be subsidiaries to existing big stations or, if at all possible, open up a new big station. However, the very limitation of the service area ensures the continued viability of the Japanese free radio movement. It would be ridiculous

Kogawa: Free Radio in Japan

from the perspective of the conventional concept of mass media, which aims for as large a service area as possible, to be restricted to a 0.3-mile radius. When people within walking distance want to communicate, it would seem easier to come together rather than to broadcast to each other. Mass media used to function as an electronic substitute for direct "oral" contact. However, too much dependence on highly advanced media technology causes serious problems—including media "perversions" such as in Jerzy Kosinski's *Being There*, where Chance, the antihero of this novel, substitutes the world of television for the "real" world.[10]

FUMIO TAKASHIMA

Daikanyama Two & Half in the studio.

Paradoxically, limitations can always transform negative elements into positive ones. In our experience, listeners frequently visited our station, which consequently became a gathering place. Given its essential difference from mass media, this should be the most positive function of free radio. In January 1983, two housewives under the influence of this idea opened Setagaya MaMa. Located in one of the middle-class areas of South Tokyo, the studio is housed in a small shack serving both as a gathering place for neighbors and as an alternative retail store carrying natural foods and other daily necessities. This station is radically free from professional programming and has been open to anyone who wants to talk by radio. Even babblings, clatters, and slams in this store-station are on the air. One time, when several people began talk-ing about community politics, some listen-ers rushed to the station and joined in the discussion.

In sharp contrast to the mass media, whose broadcasting function is *centrifugal*, stations like Setagaya MaMa have a *centri-petal* function. Their relevance as an alternative medium largely depends on the already existing mutual relationships between community members, which they reactivate through their centripetal radio. People in metropolitan areas are isolated, not only as residents but also as consumer *flaneurs*, or metropolitan "nomads."[11] It is very difficult to create bridges between such people, and the centrifugal power of mass media accelerates their estrange-ment. The more they come together in metropolitan areas, the more they lose their "home." Street entertainers and peddlers used to create a provisional home on the sidewalks for *flaneurs*. However, the street administration is much stricter than the Radio Law: since the urban revolts in the late sixties and the early seventies, the Road Traffic Control Law and the Public Security Regulations pro-hibit people from *stopping* on the pavement for long without police permission.

In this context, Radio Contemporain has opened a new direction. On 12 March 1983, on Shinjuku, a crowded street in Tokyo, the operators of this guerrilla station performed and broadcast political rock-and-roll music and protests against the nuclear-powered U.S. aircraft carrier *Enterprise*, which was scheduled to stop at Sasebo. The street event had been pre-viously announced by posters and hand-bills. Their facilities were set up in trucks with a power supply; until the police squad seized their trucks, they were temporarily creating a free space of live sounds and air waves, in which otherwise isolated *flaneurs* came together for something other than shopping. Even apolitical young nomads listened to the music and messages on their portable radios.

Although there are many difficulties in developing Japan's radical free radio movement, stations are still growing on the campus, in the community, and on the street. Free radio is already a social phenomenon, and it has revealed many social contradictions within the present administration.[12] Moreover, it seems to suggest viable directions for a social movement in the eighties. On 25 March 1983, the Ministry of Posts and Telecom-munications referred the matter of mushrooming tiny FM stations to the Air Wave Technology Council for reconsidera-tion of the regulations. Who knows what's happening with the new administration? And how would it be possible to confiscate such a tiny transmitter and receiver? In order to exterminate every facet of this movement, the authorities would have to introduce a most reactionary administra-tion—which would be impossible to the extent that the system wants to maintain the present trends of technological development, economic stability, and a relatively democratic order. This is the point on which the free radio movement in Japan has a radical opportunity to under-mine the dominant system from within.△

Notes

1. Bertolt Brecht, "Vorschläge für den Intendanten des Rundfunks," *Berliner Börsen-Courier,* 25 December 1927. "The Radio as an Apparatus of Communication," *Brecht on Theatre,* ed. and trans. John Willett (New York: Hill and Wang, 1964), 51–53. See also Brecht, "Radio as a Means of Communication: A Talk of the Function of Radio," in *Screen* (London) 20 (3/4); or in *Liberation, Socialism,* Vol. 2 of *Communication and Class Struggle,* ed. Armand Mattelart and Seth Siegelaub (New York: International General, 1983).

2. Frantz Fanon, "Ici la voix de l'Algérie . . ." *Sociologie d'une révolution* (Paris: François Maspero, 1975), 51–82. See also Fanon, *A Dying Colonialism,* trans. Haakon Chevalier (New York: Monthly Review, 1965).

3. For a general discussion of the *Autonomia* movement, see *Italy: Autonomia—Post-Political Politics*, the special issue of *Semiotext(e)* 3 (3) (New York: Columbia University, 1980). For more detailed information, see *Italy 1977-78: Living with an Earthquake* (London: Red Notes, 1982).

4. See Sophi Ghirardi and Jean-Luc Pouthier, "les radios libres en Italie," *Le Debat* 9 (February 1981). John Downing, "Socialist Media II: Italy," *The Media Machine* (London: Pluto Press Limited, 1980) is one of the few materials in English that provides relevant descriptions of the free radio movement in Italy.

5. Free radio in France during the illegal period is discussed in many chapters of Félix Guattari, *La révolution moléculaire* (Paris: Editions Recherches, 1979). The 19 August 1981 issue of *Liberation* comments on the enthusiasm over free radio in Paris immediately after the birth of the Mitterand regime. On aftermaths of the "anarchy," see *Liberation* after September 1981 and Lisa Seidenberg, "Radio Free Paree," *Alternative Media* 14 (1) (Fall 1982): 12–13.

6. See the issue of 10 November 1980. After this, I have continued to write about Italian and French free radio, and about my work on Japanese free radio, for Japanese magazines and newspapers. Those articles up to the end of 1982, as well as interviews with Félix Guattari, are contained in my book, *This is Free Radio* (Tokyo: Shobunsha, 1983).

7. The concepts of "transversality" and "molecular" have a special connotation in the *Autonomia* movement. Guattari differentiates "molecular" from "molar." "Molecular" collectivity consists of independent autonomous individuals, while "molar" collectivity is homogenized and one-dimensional. "The politics of transversality" provoked a lot of interesting debates. See Meaghn Morris. "Eurocommunism vs. Semiological Deliquency," in *Language, Sexuality and Subversion* (Sydney: Feral Publications, 1978). Guattari elaborated this concept in his *Psychanalyse et transversalité* (Paris: Francois Maspero, 1972) and *La révolution moléculaire* (Paris: Union Générale d'Editions).

8. Maurice Merleau-Ponty redefines communication as a "communion" in his *Phenomenology of Perception,* trans. Colin Smith (New York: Humanities Press, 1962), 370. Also, Paulo Freire emphasizes that communication is not an "extension" of one to another but a mutual relationship between "conscious bodies." See his "Extension or Communication," in *Education for Critical Consciousness* (New York: Seabury Press, 1973).

9. "Every transistor radio is, by the nature of its construction, at the same time a potential transmitter; it can interact with other receivers by circuit reversal. The development from a mere distribution medium to a communications medium is . . . consciously prevented for understandable political reasons. The technical distinction between receivers and transmitters reflects the social division of labor into producers and consumers. . . ." Hans Magnus Enzensberger, "Constituents of a Theory of the Media," in *The Consciousness Industry* (New York: Seabury Press, 1974).

10. For a discussion of the "media perversions" syndrome, see Frank Mankiewicz and Joel Swerdlow, *Remote Control: Television and the Manipulation of American Life* (New York: Ballantine Books, 1979), 211.

11. See Walter Benjamin, "Paris, Capital of the Nineteenth Century," in *Reflections* (New York: Harcourt Brace Jovanovich, 1978); or Benjamin, *Charles Baudelaire: A Lyric Poet in the Era of High Capitalism* (London: New Left Books, 1983).

12. Radio Japan, the overseas broadcasting service of NHK in twenty-one languages, aired a fifteen-minute program on free radio in Japan including an interview with me ("Japan Today: My Broadcasting Station") on 7 September 1983; strangely enough, the English and Italian versions were not broadcast.

Feminist Media Strategies For Political Performance

It was violence—

by
Suzanne Lacy
and
Leslie Labowitz

in the media and in society—that gave birth to feminist media art. By 1977 feminists had brought the subject of sexual violence into cultural dialogue; at the same time, an increased social permissiveness allowed more obviously violent and pornographic imagery to "leak" into the dominant culture through media. Across the country women formed groups to protest snuff films, one of the most shocking manifestations of glamourized violence. These groups did not focus on direct services to victims, as did rape centers formed earlier, but on the social effects of popular imagery. A natural liaison developed between activists who criticized violent images and artists who worked to expand their audience base with critical issues.

In 1978 we formed Ariadne: A Social Art Network, an exchange between women in the arts, governmental politics, women's politics, and media. The focus was sex-violent images in popular culture. Through Ariadne we developed a media strategy for performance artists, one applicable to a wide range of experiences, expertise and needs. For the three years of Ariadne's existence, we produced seven major public performance events dealing with advertising, news media, and pornography. From its inception, our work together combined performance and conceptual art ideas with feminist theory, community organizing techniques, media analysis, and activist strategies. The first of these was *Three Weeks in May* (1977), a performance that laid the groundwork for a form we called the public informa-

tional campaign. Two other works followed quickly on its heels, each one developing our ideas about one-time media events (*Record Companies Drag Their Feet*, August 1977; *In Mourning and In Rage*, December 1977). In 1978 Ariadne took on San Francisco's Tenderloin district (*Take Back the Night*) and Las Vegas (*From Reverence to Rape to Respect*) with works that exercised but did not radically transform the strategies. In 1979 we worked independently of each other with core groups of women on two artworks that extended over long periods (*Making It Safe* and *The Incest Awareness Project*) in order to accomplish more than we could with a one-time media event. After Ariadne disbanded in 1980, we continued to use these media strategies in our individual performances.

In the past several years, activists among the Right and Left alike have become more sophisticated about obtaining media coverage, and corporations such as Mobil Oil have gone to great lengths to improve their public image through media manipulation. To the uninitiated, media intervention may appear overwhelming, a result in part of the mystification that surrounds mass communications. Although such work is time-consuming and often chancy (you compete with the unexpected for coverage), it is possible to learn certain basics of media strategy and, more important, to learn how to think creatively about media art. The following ideas on the application of such strategies to performance art should be taken as points of departure—not recipes—for artists who want to make media performances.

Lacy/Labowitz: *Feminist Media Strategies for Political Performance*

ANNE GAULDEN

ROB BLALACK

ROB BLALACK

LOS ANGELES

SUZANNE LACY

Three Weeks in May
**With assistance from the Women's
Building and its artists
Los Angeles, May 1977**

Each day the red stain spread further
over the bright yellow map of Los
Angeles. One red-stamped "rape" marked
occurrences reported to the police department; around each of these, nine fainter
markings represented unreported sexual
assaults. Installed in the City Hall Mall,
the twenty-five-foot map sat next to an
identical one that listed where victims and
their families could go for help.

This performance focused attention on
the pervasiveness of sexual assault
through a city-wide series of thirty events.
Performances, speak-outs, art exhibits and
demonstrations were amplified by media
coverage. In one particularly striking
series of street performances, Leslie
Labowitz focused on myths of rape, men's
role conditioning, and self-defense. Lacy's
performance *She Who Would Fly* provided
a ritual exorcism. Other artists included
Barbara Smith, Cheri Gaulke, Anne
Gaulden, Melissa Hoffman and Laurel
Klick. *Three Weeks* brought together
normally disparate groups—including artists, self-defense instructors, activists and
city officials—in a temporary community
that suggested future collaborative
possibilities.

If You're Considering Media Actions...

The first and most important question to ask is whether or not media coverage is even appropriate for your artwork (action). If so, what kind is most suited to your goals? The seductive power of publicity can overshadow the goals of social change, particularly among artists who have not had much direct political experience. We who understand so well the potential impact of images tend to forget that our particular artwork, placed before a mass audience, might not necessarily be the most effective way to evoke a change in viewers' attitudes, much less provoke them to responsible action on behalf of our issue. However, some performances need to be in the media by virtue of their subject matter and goals. For example, in the history of West Coast media artwork, feminist and otherwise, the most politically and aesthetically potent works have been those that critiqued or parodied media coverage itself; those that commented upon conventions maintained by the media (such as elections and economic forecasting); or those that addressed an issue of direct concern to a mass audience.

If you feel your issues as well as your art ideas demand a mass media format, clarify your goals to help decide what kinds of communication forms to use. Media can serve as an extended voice for politically powerless people and can, as well, be part of a networking effort that brings together various groups with an awareness of shared concerns. It can also be used to reveal information *about* oppression to a larger audience. However, you might find that posting a handbill, passing out leaflets door to door, holding a meeting, organizing a participatory ritual or a street theater piece, or planning a potluck may be better ways to reach your audience. One form of communication is not necessarily better for artists than another; it all depends on what you want to accomplish.

Though the media would like to make "stars" out of a select few, art for the media in the service of political goals is generally a collaborative effort. Artists who enter the political arena are advised to include political activists in their planning. Organizations that work with the same issues you will address can provide an analytical framework, information, and often resources for your project. In the case of antiviolence feminist performance, Women Against Violence Against Women (WAVAW) and Women Against Violence and Pornography in the Media (WAVPM) provided us with a larger social context for our performances and the ongoing community organizing that would extend our effectiveness.

To UNDERSTAND HOW media operates, observe it—with detachment—and be pragmatic. It doesn't matter what you think the media *should* cover, the object of the game (and it is a game) is to get them to play it your way. Mass media time is not a public service; it is a highly valuable commodity that is purchased by corporations and individuals who promote products, ideas, attitudes and images. The stakes of this game are high, and as artists the best we can hope for is a kind of guerrilla foray into that system.

In your own community, learn everything you can about radio and television stations and the printed press. Who owns them? Are they local residents or part of a large network? What are the politics of the owners and managers, and how accessible are they to the public? Information about the points of view of news assignment editors and reporters, which can be gleaned from observation of their work, is invaluable in knowing who to approach when you want coverage.

A reporter in New Orleans once told me their news items had to be geared to the understanding of a seventh grader—or was it a seven-year-old? Reporters and their editors will spend very little time deciphering complicated messages; when you are depending upon news formats, in particular, it's important to be simple and clear. (This isn't the easiest thing to do; presenting new or countercultural ideas can't depend upon tried and true conventions.)

Never transgress the self-image of objectivity shared almost universally by reporters and documentary journalists.

Lacy/Labowitz: *Feminist Media Strategies for Political Performance*

Whether you believe in this professional stance or not, act as if you do! Recently I was orchestrating a performance of 150 older women who were about to release helium balloons. Before giving the signal I asked a photojournalist if he would be able to capture the effect of all the balloons as they flew out of the women's hands. When he said the women were too spread out for that, I asked, "Should I group them closer together?" He looked at me in horror. "I can't tell you what to do!" I quickly agreed with him, then grouped them together for a stronger visual effect.

As YOU BEGIN TO LOOK more closely at the media, its effectiveness in generating emotional responses and states of desire will become apparent. Once you have demystified the image-making process—how the messages one gets depend upon the arrangement of color, form, and content—you will be able to respond more objectively and critically to the bombardment of visual media in your daily life. Sensitivity to this is important for your analysis; once you pierce the manner in which meaning is conveyed through media, you can begin to generate your own meaning.

How are the images, narratives, and forms supportive of ideology? In the case of violent advertising, for example, how are colors, shapes, and sounds employed to seduce sexual response and/or fascination, dulling normal reactions to violence and establishing violation as an appropriate response to women? How do such attitudes tie into existing cultural mythology about the proper treatment of women? Which images instill passivity and which inspire participation and action? Pay as much attention to the form of your message as to its content, compromising between, on the one hand, the best way to capture the attention of both reporters and the public and, on the other, a newer way to educate people through participatory, rather than authoritarian, communication.

This isn't a simple matter, because there are few examples of this use of media. Our notion of what is suitable for television and newspapers is often shaped by the very forms that have manipulated our consciousness for so long. To introduce a more complex social analysis we need to defy certain conventions of news coverage.

For example, using the most obvious ideas and simplistic techniques of advertising may make coverage of your events more likely, but you may inadvertantly generate meaning beyond your intentions, meaning directly at cross purposes to your goals. Graphics designer Sheila de Bretteville first called our attention to this issue by pointing out the coercive nature of billboard advertising. Because it is geared to split-second comprehension, it doesn't allow for design formats that reveal several points of view simultaneously, that share layered and complicated information about more complex subjects, and that allow participation from its viewers. In media performance, as well, the most convincing images with the most impact need to be monitored for implicit attitudes toward audiences: can viewers participate with the imagery and information, or are they being preached to and commanded?

Information about current events in the media is generally disconnected from potential analysis or action on the part of the viewers. Reporters discussing sexual violence, for example, present it as an unsolvable aberration of human nature and explain it in ways that mystify rather than promote understanding. In the case of the Hillside Strangler, for example, reporters keenly scrutinized the particular background of each victim, speculated wildly upon the history of the killer (speculations which were disturbingly similar to social mythology about men, women and sex), and never made the connections between these and other forms of sexual violence. Such connections, of course, are the basis for forming a political analysis. The questions we should have been asking were: How are these killings similar to the other mass murders of women? How are these murders related to entertainment violence? To our attitudes about the innate nature of male sexuality? To our expectations about women as victims? Even, how does sexual violence relate to the status of the economy?

Finally, monitor your own response to media imagery to determine which images and ideas motive you. Only when you are objective about your own conditioning can you walk the line between images that reveal important information and images that overwhelm their viewers. During the airing and public controversy of "The Day After," a fictionalized television broadcast with graphic depictions of the horrors of nuclear holocaust, many activists criticized such imagery as inducing passivity. At what point do people throw up their hands in despair rather than take to the streets or the legislatures? Be aware of this point when creating images about problems that weigh heavily upon the lives of your viewers. You want to motivate people, not dull them further.

MICHELLE CONWAY

Record Companies Drag Their Feet
Leslie Labowitz
In collaboration with Women Against Violence Against Women and the National Organization for Women
Los Angeles, August 1977

How do you bring attention to a national boycott? Working with Women Against Violence Against Women (WAVAW), Leslie Labowitz designed a performance specifically for television news coverage. A parody of the recording industry's greed, which enables it to ignore the effects of its violent advertising on women's lives, this performance was held on Sunset Boulevard, the symbolic heart of the industry. A mock executive's office was set up under a huge billboard for the latest album by the rock group KISS, along with a counter-billboard announcing rape statistics. Three record company moguls—portrayed by women dressed as roosters—arrived in a gold Cadillac, strutted into their "office" and began to count their "blood money." Women pleaded against, the protested their exploitation to no avail. The performance ended when twenty women draped the set with a banner that read, "Don't Support Violence—Boycott!"

Covered by all major television stations in the city and by *Variety*, a trade journal for the entertainment industry, the event launched a successful campaign against the record companies Warner, Atlantic and Electra for their use of violated images of women in their advertising. This performance was not only powerful as a one-time media event, but it also provides one example of how artists can collaborate effectively with an activist organization.

IN MEMORY OF OUR SISTERS·
WOMEN FIGHT BACK

In Mourning and In Rage
Suzanne Lacy and Leslie Labowitz
With assistance from Biba Lowe
Los Angeles, December 1977

Ten seven-foot-tall, heavily veiled women stepped silently from a hearse. As reporters announced to cameras, "We are at City Hall to witness a dramatic commemoration for the ten victims of the Hillside Strangler," the women in black delivered an unexpected message. They did not simply grieve but attacked the sensationalized media coverage that contributes to the climate of violence against women. One at a time, the actresses broke their ominous silence to link these murders with *all* forms of sexual violence (an analysis missing from the media) and to demand concrete solutions.

City council members promised support to activists, Holly Near sang "Fight Back" (written especially for the performance), and news programs across the state carried reports of the performance and its activist message. *In Mourning and In Rage* was perhaps our most compelling example of a one-time media performance, staged as a guerrilla intervention to the conventions of sex crime reportage. Follow-up talk show appearances and activities by local rape hot line advocates created a much broader discussion of the issues than could be covered at the performance itself.

How to Do a
Media Performance

To create an effective media performance, you first need to ask yourselves three questions:

What is the problem? When communicating through the media, time is of the essence. The subtleties of your analysis simply won't be respected or recorded, and you must take great care to present your information in the clearest, most coherent fashion. The *art* is in making it compelling; the *politics* is in making it clear. To do this, you must first clarify your issue.

What is your goal? Simply getting people to *see* your art is not enough when you are working with serious and confrontational issues. What do you want to have happen as a result of your media campaign or event? This, perhaps the most difficult part of your analysis, needs to embody your best and most realistic projections. (Try not to fall into the self-delusive artist's stance about the "tremendous but unidentifiable impact" of your work!)

Who is your audience? Once you clarify who you want to reach, you may decide that the media form you have chosen is not appropriate to that audience. You probably won't reach children on the eleven o'clock news or working people on middle-of-the-afternoon talk shows. In a small community like Watts, California, word-of-mouth could be more effective than the *Los Angeles Times*, depending on your message. What does your audience already know about the topic at hand, and what do you want them to know? What is their attitude on the subject and how would you like to see them respond to your event?

Our media artworks fell into two categories: the media event and the public informational campaign. The first is a one-time event designed specifically for TV newscasts, choreographed to control the content as it is distributed through the media. These events cannot take the place of person-to-person contact through community organizing or long-term media education, but they serve as a very exciting and useful way to identify an issue or point of view about an issue for a large audience. A successful media event is one part of an overall strategy to influence public opinion, but it needs to be followed up with the in-depth information people will need to make knowledgeable choices.

The public informational campaign, a term used by public relations people, can do just that. Several different kinds of media coverage about a specific issue are placed over an extended period of time. More than a one-time media event, this kind of campaign can educate and organize a constituency. During such projects (*Three Weeks in May, Reverence to Rape to Respect, Making It Safe*, and *The Incest Awareness Project*) we reinforced radio interviews, talk shows, TV newscasts, and feature articles with activities that put us in direct contact with the public, such as street performances, lectures, demonstrations, and art exhibitions. Conceiving of the entire campaign as a conceptual performance, we paired art with informative events, designed talk show appearances as mini-performances, and used media opportunities to talk about performance art as well as the issues.

When you are staging a media event:

–The coordinating committee of your group should select the key images and the message. At least one member of this committee should be an artist who can design a format, create the visual images, and assist in the artistic production. Sometimes everyone's imagination will be captured by an exciting image that is evoked automatically or created by an individual in your group; other times a brainstorming session is needed. Your first images may be cliches accumulated from popular culture. Keep exploring your consciousness until strong and original ones come up. If you need a push, look at mythological images; in the case of women, for example, many images reflect positive expressions of power, even though they have accrued negative connotations in this culture. These images need to be reclaimed, and their continued existence in our collective mythology indicates a potentially strong audience response. For instance, *In Mourning and In Rage* took this culture's trivialized images of mourners as old, powerless women and transformed them into commanding seven-foot-tall figures angrily demanding an end to violence against women.

–To get the press to cover your event, establish its timeliness. Reporters come out for issues they think are current and topical; relate to news items already given airplay (if they don't feel the topic has burned out); have an element of sensationalism, high drama, or risk; and on an otherwise slow news day, have a "human interest" angle (although predicting what an assignment editor will deem to be humanly interesting is not always easy). It is important to determine whether your performance will fit preconceptions of what is newsworthy and at the same time maintain its integrity as art and as political action. For example, the media's dramatization of the Hillside Strangler murders ensured coverage of our memorial performance by major local newscasters at the time. As a result, we were asked to appear on TV talk shows to discuss our alternatives to the media's highly sensationalized coverage of the murders.

–Don't fall into the trap of creating media gimmickry. Superficial images that don't go deep into the cultural symbols of society have less impact, particularly when compared to sophisticated and high-impact commercial images. News reporters react negatively to cute tricks aimed at obtaining coverage; they may manipulate, but they don't like to be manipulated. Events designed to express gut-level feelings and real community concerns do not come across as manipulation.

–Avoid overworked images. Activists fall into their own conventions, which may have the opposite effect than desired. For example, picket lines may establish such preconceptions in the mind of viewers that your meaning would be overlooked.

–Do your best to control the media's interpretation of your information, particularly when it is counter to prevailing attitudes. The press release, which will frame the media's perception of your planned action, is an art form in itself. It must be written simply, with enticing descriptions of visual opportunities and a clear political perspective on the issue. It should also include names of participating government officials and celebrities, if there are any, and give the impression that this will be the most important event of the day. Once your event is assigned to a reporter, that person becomes the next key in making sure your message remains relatively undistorted. To prepare for your contact with reporters, analyze television newscasts in your area: find out who the reporters are, how much time is allotted to your kind of issue, and, most important, how news footage is edited. How long is the average news slot? Does the news-caster stand in front of the image while describing the action? What is the ratio of visual-to-verbal information? Design your event to fit the normal newscast format in order to control its coverage as much as possible.

–Arrange the time of day, the day of the week, and the location to suit reporters' schedules. In Los Angeles, Tuesday or Wednesday morning (when news is usually slow) is considered the best time to call a press conference. Weekend news has already broken, and there is a better chance of getting on the evening news the same day. A strategic location will have effective "visuals" or provide a good background, be familiar to reporters, and have electrical outlets, parking, and other facilities. For example, Los Angeles City Hall was chosen as the site for *In Mourning and In Rage* because we were presenting demands to members of the city council, in session at that hour; we also knew the media would be likely to cover the session that day.

–Keep your event under twenty minutes and provide at least one high-impact visual image that is emblematic of your message. Both words and images should be easy to understand; anything ambiguous should be clarified by a speech during the performance or by a simply worded press release. The performance should be confined to a limited area so that the camera can frame the whole set without losing information. Sequences should be clear, logically connected, and few in number.

–Have one director for the performance and another for the reporters. Since the performers in these events are usually not professionals, an artist should supportively guide them through the piece and control the timing. The media director should greet reporters as they arrive, sign them in, hand out press kits and press statements (explaining the symbolism of each image), and give shot sheets (which break down the event's sequences) to the camera people. This director is also responsible for keeping reporters at the site for the entire event. Don't give out interviews or explicit information before the event is over, and brief everyone involved not to give out information but to direct all questions to the media director. Reporters love to "get the scoop" and leave for their next assignment.

Rape is Everybody's Concern, **media performance in Las Vegas, June 1977.**

Las Vegas, glitter capital of the United States—with its high incidence of violent rape and its global image as the epitome of female objectification—was the perfect setting for a performance demonstrating the continuum between idolization and degradation of women. Modeled on *Three Weeks in May*, this campaign/performance created an exchange between women in Las Vegas and Los Angeles.

Ten days of events—including a talk by Margo St. James (founder of the prosti-tute's union COYOTE), an exchange exhibition on violence sponsored by women of Los Angeles and Las Vegas, a performance brought from Los Angeles by the Feminist Art Workers, and other collaborations between artists, humanist scholars, and women from the commu-nity—broke down the myth that Las Vegas has few rapes because sex is so available. Performances (by Suzanne Lacy, Kathy Kauffman, Nancy Buchanan and Leslie Labowitz) were held in galleries and on the streets. Two billboards, coverage in the local media, and a half-hour PBS docu-mentary on rape created broad public exposure for the performance.

Lacy/Labowitz: *Feminist Media Strategies for Political Performance*

POSTER DESIGNED BY BIA LOWE

**Once upon a time she thought incest was something
she had to carry around all by herself.**

The Incest Awareness Project
**Cosponsored by Ariadne and the
Gay and Lesbian Community
Service Center**
**Coordinated by Leslie Labowitz,
Nancy Angelo and Nancy Taylor
Los Angeles, 1979–1981**

The Incest Awareness Project's goal was
to break the silence that surrounded the
subject of incest, create positive images of
women moving out of victimization, and
effect social change through the development of prevention and recovery
programs.

The year-long event included *Bedtime
Stories*, an exhibition of performance and
static artwork by women who had experi-

enced incest; art therapy workshops for
children; and a media campaign. In Nancy
Angelo's *Equal Time and Equal Space*, the
audience sat in a circle with video
monitors, from which women who had
been incest victims spoke to each other as
if they were in a consciousness-raising
session. Afterward, an experienced
counselor led the audience in a discussion.
The prevention and recovery components—conceptualized by members of the
art project with members of the Gay and
Lesbian Community Service Center, and
carried out by counselors there—included
a telephone referral service, counseling, a
speakers bureau, and self-help groups.
Many of these programs are still in
existence.

**When you are planning a public
informational campaign:**

–Form a media committee to think
through strategy, determine the overall
image, build relationships with the press,
develop press kits and write releases. The
press kit should contain a general description, a schedule of events, background
information on your issues and the people
involved in your effort, press releases for
each event, and photos and story-angle
suggestions for feature articles. This
information packet is sent out to contacts
in the media, government, and community
six weeks before the project begins.
Separate releases are sent out several days
before each individual event to news desks
at local television and radio stations and
newspapers.
–Follow up the press release with phone
calls on the day of an important action. If
coverage is still not confirmed, ask to
speak to the station manager. Persist until
you know at least two news teams are
coming out. If they don't show up, reconsider your strategy and then make complaints to stations by phone or letter. In
certain smaller communities, however, it is
more effective to continue to alert reporters before and after the event rather than
make complaints. One significant
advantage of long-term campaigns is that
media interest will build as people become
more aware of your activities. In a sense
you are developing your own history and
context, something reporters look for.
–Develop a permanent log of media
contacts: which reporters have covered
past events and which reporters, feature
writers, programs and columns you would
like to involve in your project. Keep
accurate records of your communications
with media people to build trust and to
plan your media strategy in a systematic
manner. One person, or two in close communication, should be in charge of this.
–Choose individuals for media appearances who are accessible by phone, articulate, well informed, and who think quickly
when confronted by reporters. Moderators
have many ways of steering a dialogue in
their own, often uninformed, direction.
Your representative must know how to
control the situation. Ask the moderator
before the show what questions will be
discussed, and prepare your answers
accordingly. Some interviewers even like
you to suggest questions to them, but be

cautious as some take offense at such a suggestion. Rehearse to prepare for negative as well as positive situations, decide which points you want to get across in the time allotted, and experiment with ways of turning every question to your advantage.

—Go in pairs to media presentations whenever possible, and see each appearance as an opportunity to train members of your group to speak out. It takes courage to speak publicly from one's experience as a woman, a minority or a supporter of a not-yet-popular cause, and those who do it need emotional support from the group. Moreover, by training each other you not only avoid the media's tendency to create stars, but you also empower each other.

Y OUR FINAL STEPS ARE to document and evaluate your artwork. Documentation, an essential tool for performance artists in general, takes on greater implications in media art. You can use it to analyze the success of your own strategies and to demonstrate approaches to others. Some museums and cable stations provide free to low-cost public access to equipment, and students in university broadcast departments will often record events for you. News stations will frequently release or sell their slips if you provide them with a blank videotape, although there are copyright restrictions on the use of this material.

Evaluating the results is your most important post-performance activity. Simply getting coverage is not an unqualified sign of your success; analyze the coverage and try to understand the message it actually communicated to its audience—not just the actual words that were spoken, but the slant given by the reporter's attitudes, the camera's focus, and the general appearance of your images. What makes it successful as art? As political action? What action did you inspire? What new perspectives did you reveal? Is there follow up needed, either in the community or in the media? Although the long-term effects on people's attitudes can only be projected, attempt to make these projections to keep your strategy evolving.

Media work has three ultimate purposes: first, to interrupt the incessant flow of images that supports the established social order with alternative ways of thinking and acting; second, to organize and activate viewers (media is not the only, nor necessarily most effective, way to do this); third, to create artful and original imagery that follows in the tradition of fine art, to help viewers see the world in a new way and learn something about themselves in relation to it. Long after reporters have lost interest in media art, long after our access is truncated due either to our effectiveness or lack thereof, our power to crystallize collective aspirations through art will continue, with or without television. As guerrilla media artists we must be fast on our feet, responding to the vicissitudes of media coverage, and ready to move on when we can no longer see the social change resulting from our efforts there.△

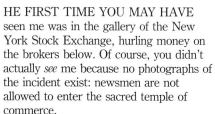

by Abbie Hoffman

THE FIRST TIME YOU MAY HAVE seen me was in the gallery of the New York Stock Exchange, hurling money on the brokers below. Of course, you didn't actually *see* me because no photographs of the incident exist: newsmen are not allowed to enter the sacred temple of commerce.

It all began with a simple telephone call to the Stock Exchange. I arranged for a tour, giving one of my favorite pseudonyms, George Metesky, the notorious mad bomber of Manhattan. Then I scraped together three hundred dollars which I changed into crispy one-dollar bills, rounded up fifteen free spirits, which in those days just took a few phone calls, and off we went to Wall Street.

We didn't call the press; at that time we really had no notion of anything called a media event. (And to make one very important point, I *never* performed for the media. I tried to reach people. It was *not* acting. It was not some media muppet show. That is a cynical interpretation of history.) We just took our places in line with the tourists, although our manner of dress did make us a little conspicuous. The line moved its way past glassed-in exhibits depicting the rise of the industrial revolution and the glorification of the world of commerce. Then the line turned the corner. Suddenly, we saw hordes of reporters and cameras. Somebody must have realized a story was in the making and rung up one of the wire services. In New York the press can mobilize in a matter of minutes. Faster than the police, sometimes.

We started clowning, kissing and hugging, and eating money. Next, some stock exchange bureaucrats appeared and we argued until they allowed us in the gallery, but the guards kept the press out. I passed out money to freaks and tourists alike, then all at once we ran to the railing and began tossing out the bills. Pandemonium. The sacred electronic ticker tape, the heartbeat of the Western world, stopped cold. Stock brokers scrambled over the floor like worried mice, scurrying after the money. Greed had burst through the business-as-usual facade.

It lasted five minutes at the most. The guards quickly ushered us out with a stern warning and the ticker tape started up again.

The reporters and cameramen were waiting for us outside:

"Who are you?"

"I'm Cardinal Spellman."

"Where did you get the money?"

"What are you saying? You don't ask Cardinal Spellman where he gets his money!"

"How much did you throw?"

"Thousands."

"How many are you?"

"Hundreds—three—two—we don't exist! We don't even exist!" As the cameras whirred awway we danced, burned greenbacks and declared the end of money.
BYSTANDER: "This is a disgusting display."
ME: "You're right. These people are nothing but a bunch of filthy commies."

The story was on the air waves that night and our message went around the world, but because the press didn't actually witness the event they had to create their own fantasies of what had happened inside the money temple. One

MUSEUM
Of The Streets

version was we threw Monopoly money, another network called it hundred-dollar bills, a third shredded money. A tourist from Missouri was interviewed who said he had joined in the money-throwing because he'd been throwing away his money all over New York for several days anyway and our way was quicker and more fun. From start to finish the event was a perfect myth. Even the newspeople had to elaborate on what had happened.

A spark had been ignited. The system cracked a little. Not a drop of blood had been spilled, not a bone broken, but on that day, with that gesture, an image war had begun. In the minds of millions of teenagers the stock market had just crashed.

Guerrilla theater is probably the oldest form of political commentary. The ideas just keep getting recycled. Showering money on the Wall Street brokers was the TV-age version of driving the money changers from the temple. The symbols, the spirit, and the lesson were identical. Was it a real threat to the Empire? Two weeks after our band of mind-terrorists raided the stock exchange, twenty thousand dollars was spent to enclose the gallery with bullet-proof glass. Someone out there had read the ticker tape.

In *The Theatre and Its Double*, Antonin Artaud called for a new "poetry of festivals and crowds, with people pouring into the streets." No need to build a stage, it was all around us. Props would be simple and obvious. We would hurl ourselves across the canvas of society like streaks of splattered paint. Highly visual images would become news, and rumor-mongers would rush to spread the excited word.

Newscasters unconsciously began all reports of our actions with the compelling phrase "Did ya hear about ———."

For us, protest as theater came natural. We were already in costume. If we went above Fourteenth Street we were suddenly semi-Indians in a semi-alien culture. Our whole experience was theater—playing the flute on the street corner, panhandling, walking, living protest signs. Our theatricality was not adopted from the outside world. We didn't buy or read about it. It was not a style like disco dressing that you could see in ads and imitate. Once we acknowledged the universe as theater and accepted the war of symbols, the rest was easy. All it took was a little elbow grease, a little hustle.

At meetings people would divide up in groups to work on one theatrical action or another. Some took only a few participants and others were more elaborate. Some had to be planned like bank robberies and others like free-for-all-be-ins.

One night we decided to do something that would express the neighborhood's dismay over increased traffic and thought for the first time about using mobile tactics—people running around and creating a little chaos rather than just standing still. To get everyone assembled and disbursed we put out an anonymous leaflet telling people to gather at St. Mark's Place at 9 P.M., wait for a signal from God, then scatter through the streets. Two thousand people responded.

One of us (guess which one) had gone to a chemist's shop and bought two pounds of magnesium which we packed in coffee tins and put on the roofs around St. Mark's Place. Then we rigged the cans

with delay fuses by shoving lighted cigarettes in match packs. Once done, we raced down to the streets where people were milling around, waiting for God. All of a sudden the whole sky lit up with a huge blast of exploding magnesium. People started running all over. Fire trucks poured into the area. Sometimes chaos makes a good point.

In incense-filled rooms we gather cross-legged on the rugs, conspiring dastardly deeds. The Jokers would show Gotham City no mercy:

"We've just got to end this tourist gawking," complained provo agitator Dana Beal.

"Hey, how's this for the tourist problem?" said Radio Bob Fass. "Wavy Gravy gets dressed up real straight and buys a ticket to go on one of the tours. We all get dressed up as cowboys and hold up the bus when it turns the corner into Second Avenue. We board it, pull Wavy off and hang him from the lamp post."

"Hang him?"

"Well, not really. We rig up one of those harnesses under his jacket just like they do in the movies."

The major event that spring was the be-in in Central Park. That's when I really got hooked in to the whole idea. I was at Liberty House when Lynn House and Jim Fouratt came by and said, "We're going to put on this be-in."

I went on the air to promote the event and Bob Fass at radio station WBAI interviewed me. I started to fantasize about what the be-in was going to be about—no speakers, platform, leaders, no clearly defined format so people could define it

Hoffman: *Museum of the Streets*

for themselves. Folks would just come to the park on Easter Sunday dressed for the occasion and exchange things, balloons, acid, jelly beans, Easter eggs; do Druid dances, or whatever their hearts desired.

Thirty-five thousand people showed up. The traditional Fifth Avenue Easter Parade, our competition, drew less than half that. After the be-in, Anita and I walked out of the park and joined the Fifth Avenue Parade, singing "In Your Easter Bonnet." Our faces were painted silver and I was carrying a huge Easter bunny. In front of St. Patrick's Cathedral the loudspeakers blared, "Come in, come in and worship." Why not? But as soon as we mounted the steps we were stopped by a line of cops.

"You can't go in there looking line that."

"What do you mean, we can't come in? Don't you see who we're with? We're with the Easter bunny."

"The Cardinal says no hippies on Easter Sunday."

A crowd began to gather. We continued to "play the dozens" with the cops. The confrontation heated up so we staged a strategical withdrawal, already plotting a sequel: "We'll come back next Christmas. We'll rent a mule and get some dude with long hair, dress him up in a white robe and sandals, and have him ride right up to the door of St. Patrick's with people waving palm branches, and Cardinal Spellman will come out and say, 'You can't come in here...'"

It's so easy. All you need is a little nerve and a willingness to be considered an embarrassment. Then you just keep pushing it, repeating what they say: "You *mean* the Cardinal *says*..."

IF OBSERVERS OF THE drama are allowed to interpret the act, they will become participants themselves. Too much analysis kills direct theatrical experience. The put-on allows you to circumvent the trap. Smashing conventional mores becomes essential. The concept of mass spectacle, everyday language, and easily recognized symbols was important to get public involvement.

Artists, the vanguard of communication, had grown weary of decades of abstract shapes. Modern art was already institutionalized; ersatz Kandinskys hung in dentists' offices. Andy Warhol broke through the abstraction and let us see the raw stuff of art in supermarkets, on TV, in magazines, and at the garbage dump. Allan Kaprow and other artists were experimenting with a new form called "happenings"—half-scripted, half-chance public exhibitions—3-D art, with people as paint.

"Happenings" were an extension of abstract art and as such were designed for the ruling class. I thought we could improve on that. Perhaps the audience that appreciated *All in the Family* did not approve of our "message" but they *did* understand it. It was public and popular. If we were not accepted by the Archie Bunkers of America, then perhaps by the children of Archie themselves. That the Museum of Modern (sic) Art honored "happenings" and "pop art" while ignoring our brand of political theater just proves the connection between successful artists and the rich.

Lenin once wrote that art was counter-revolutionary because it showed beauty in the *present*, while revolution promised beauty in the future. It's true that art-for-art's sake leads to performing modern dance for Shahs and Sheiks or discussing sculpture at afternoon tea with the Rockefellers. Yet creativity is needed to reach people snowed under by ruling-class images, and only artists can manage the breakthrough. Artists are the collective eyes of the future. One of the worst mistakes any revolution can make is to become boring. It leads to rituals as opposed to games, cults as opposed to community and denial of human rights as opposed to freedom.

In organizing a movement around art we not only allowed people to participate without a sense of guilt but also with a sense of enjoyment. The use of fun in struggle was a new notion. Even in Mississippi where we were truly frightened most of the time with people shooting at us, living with the constant thought that we might lose our lives, it seemed like people enjoyed their "work." All I did was admit it felt good. There's no incongruity in conducting serious business and having fun. This pissed off the straight left no end.

One of the principles of good theater is not to overburden the audience with foot-

Yippie cartoon from "L'Echo des Savanes," #30. Copyright © 1977 by Y. Fremian and M. Trublin. Reprinted by permission of the artists and Anarchy Comics, c/o Last Gasp, 2180 Bryant Street, San Francisco, California, 94110.

noted explanations of what they are seeing. In 1967 a picket sign saying END THE ———was far more involving than one that said END THE WAR. People love filling in the blanks and you could always count on straight people to stick to the core message. A populist movement must allow people to define their own space, their own motives, to be their own critics. A good explanation is no explanation, keeping your mouth shut a correct response. There was, however, an even higher form of communication, since "no response" sounds the same as the bureaucracy's "no comment." Street players have nothing to hide. The solution lies in the zen axiom: say everything by saying nothing, remain silent by telling all. Any good Jewish comedian from Hillel to Don Rickles knows what I'm talking about. Partly truth, partly fiction, the "put-on" gets the job done.

GUARD: Sorry, hippies are not allowed in the Stock Exchange.

ACTOR: But we're not hippies, we're Jewish. Should we tell the press you kept Jews out of Wall Street?

Theater of protest, for me, was a marriage of circumstances and personality. After a while I couldn't keep it a secret who I was. At first, my identity was a bit of a mystery. I often wrote under weird aliases: George Metesky the bomber, Jim Metesky, which was a cross between him and Jim Piersall, a Red Sox ball player I liked, Frankie Abbott, a figure in the Amboy Dukes (dutifully reported in *The New York Times* as Mr. Frank Abbott), Free, The Digger, or just A. Hippie. (The period after A made it me.) After I became well known I couldn't continue the pretense, even if the attitude was right. It was all part of a reluctance (maybe an inability) to define. Definition always seemed to contain an element of control.

On 15 April 1967, the largest demonstration in the country's history, 700,000 people, marched to the United Nations to protest the escalation of the war in Vietnam. Our Lower East Side contingent assembled at Tompkins Square Park and marched north, gathering more people along the way. The artists all turned out, so naturally our form of presentation was pretty colorful: Ginsberg's bells and chants, the Bread and Puppet Theater group, gaily dressed and stoned, a Yellow Submarine, and a lot of people who looked like they had posed for the Sergeant

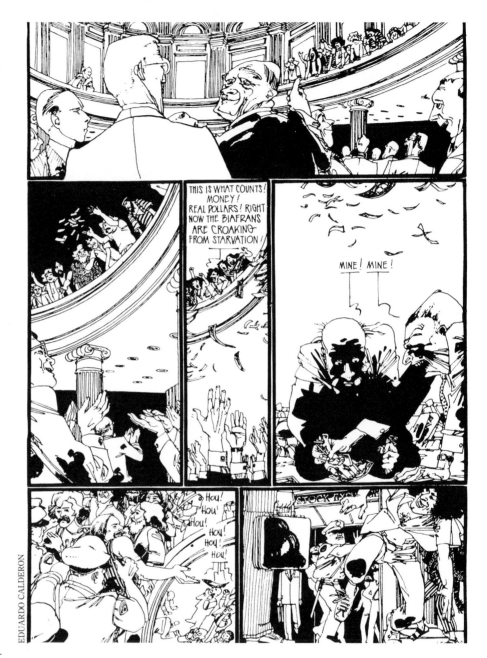

EDUARDO CALDERON

Pepper album cover. (One of the first examples of a masterpiece entering the Supermarket.)

A month later the right-wingers responded with a Support Our Boys rally, and we organized a "flower brigade" to march in their parade. There were about twenty of us with flowers and banners that read "Support Our Boys—Bring Them Home," and we all carried little American flags. I wore a multi-colored cape with the word "Freedom" on it. Anita was all decked out in red, white,

KING AROUND THE ROSEY!

NO! NOT THAT! NO!

THEY'RE CRAZY!

NO! NO!

TOO LATE!

THREE WEEKS LATER...
LAST NIGHT THE STOCK EXCHANGE INSTALLED BULLETPROOF GLASS AND METAL GRILLES AROUND THE VISITOR'S GALLERY. A SPOKESMAN FOR THE EXCHANGE EXPLAINED THAT THIS WAS DONE FOR "SECURITY REASONS."

The New York Times

OOOH!

EDUARDO CALDERON

came at us with fists, feet, beer, spit, red paint. They even ripped up our American flags. Then a flying wedge of cops appeared out of nowhere and escorted us, bleeding and limping, all the way back to St. Mark's Place.

UNDAUNTED, WE marched again, this time to Lincoln Center for a cultural exchange program. "March to Lincoln Center. Bring Your Own Garbage. Let's Trade It for Their Garbage—Even Steven," read the leaflets. About thirty of us walked from our neighborhood through the streets of Manhattan to newly-opened Lincoln Center with our bags of garbage and dumped them in the courtyard fountain, scattering in every direction when the cops chased us. The media got hold of it, turning the event into the potent image we had intended. "Oh, those hippies—they went up and threw garbage at Lincoln Center." That's enough, that was the message. The press didn't yet realize that these images were disruptive to society and they were quickly caught up in the excitement and fashion. Later, editors became more sophisticated.

Once you get the right image the details aren't that important. Over-analyzing reduced the myth. A big insight we learned during this period was that you didn't have to explain why. That's what advertising was all about. "Why" was for the critics.

Radical theater burst onto the streets with a passion. Our guerrilla band attacked Con Edison, New York's utility company. On cue, soot bombs exploded in offices, smudge pots billowed thick smoke into lobbies, black crepe paper encircled the building, and a huge banner hung across the front door: BREATHING IS BAD FOR YOUR HEALTH. Cops and firemen appeared on the scene. We ran in all directions, losing ourselves in the crowds. The six o'clock news opened with clouds of smoke, a pan shot of the banner, and strange-looking guttersnipes running amok. An official from the power company wearing a suit and tie explained Con Ed's position. As he spoke he nervously touched his face. Self-inflicted black spot marks appeared on his cheeks: the vaude-

and blue. Joe Flaherty of *The Village Voice* came by and told us we were asking for trouble. Even the cops tried to talk us out of marching and wouldn't give us an escort for protection. But we saw the "Support Our Boys" stickers on their windshields and we knew we were better off without them.

For a while everything went fine. We marched behind some Boy Scouts from Queens ("Oh, look, they're kissing!" they'd squeal and break formation) and then walked straight into trouble. They

ville show was completed by unwitting self-ridicule. The fatter they are, the harder they fall.

The Army recruiting center in Times Square was plastered with stickers: SEE CANADA NOW. Stop signs on street corners now read STOP WAR. Witches in black robes, bearing roses, exorcised the FBI building of its evil spirits. Hundreds crowded the lobby of the *Daily News* smoking grass and passing out leaflets to employees that began, "Dear Fellow Members of the Communist Conspiracy." A tree was planted in the center of St. Marx Place (we took the liberty of changing the spelling) while 5,000 celebrators danced to rock music. Midnight artists snuck into subway stations and painted huge murals on the walls. Naked people ran through churches. Panhandlers worked the streets for hours, took the change they collected to the nearest bank and scattered it on the floor. A giant Yellow Submarine mysteriously kept appearing in tow-away zones. Tourist buses, now detouring to watch the hippies cavort, were greeted by freaks holding up huge mirrors, screaming, "dig thyself!" All this and more Anita and I got high doing.

Some events grew out of unexpected donations. A person called up, "I've got 10,000 flowers you can have." I have an idea: wouldn't it be great to have these flowers come showering down over the be-in in Central Park? We had to get hold of a head who knew how to fly a plane and was ready to risk arrest. I found one in New Jersey and told him to act fast. He raced to the airport on his motorcycle, smashed-up, left his bike on the street, called a cab and arrived just in time. All the connections were made perfectly except the last one—he dropped all 10,000 flowers blocks away on an empty side street.

If street theater is to avoid growing tedious, it benefits from an edge of menace—a touch of potential violence. When Secretary of State Dean Rusk came to town to speak to some war hawk assemblage at the Waldorf-Astoria, we rallied at Fifty-Seventh Street and Seventh Avenue, ready to "bring the war home." Plastic bags filled with cow's blood flew through the night air. Tape recordings of battle sounds screamed above the crowds. Urban monkeys (not yet guerrillas) with painted faces and water pistols attacked tuxedoed enemy collaborators. Fire alarms were pulled and swarms of angry demonstrators shouting, "Hey, hey, LBJ, how many kids did you kill today?" surged through midtown.

A couple observing the melee said, "What's going on?" "There's a war on, can't you see?" I answered as the police on horseback began to attack. We scattered the sidewalk with marbles and the horses slipped and stumbled. Innocent bystanders (no bystander is innocent) were caught between the clashing armies. The cops waded right into the crowds of people, clubbing away. Crunch! I got carted off to jail.

The head of a pig was delivered to Hubert Humphrey on a silver platter before a shocked throng of liberals. Shelley Winters, that pompous phony, denounced us. Mice were released at a Dow Chemical stockholders' meeting. Cardinal (Pass-the-Lord-and-Praise-the-Ammunition) Spellman, who went to Vietnam and posed behind a machine gun, was confronted by angry Catholics during a church service.

When all else failed, we simply declared the war over. Five thousand of us romped through the streets, hugging people in stores and buses. 'The war is over! Hip-hip-hurray!! It's over!!" Balloons, confetti, singing, dancing. If you don't like the news, we reasoned, make up your own.△

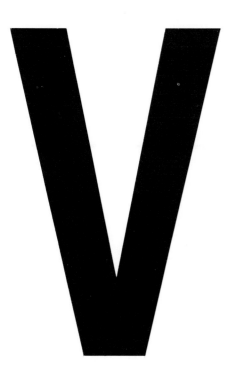

ALENTINE'S DAY HAD SPECIAL significance. For its celebration I concocted a gift of love, compliments of the counterculture. Three thousand persons selected at random from the phone book were sent a well-rolled marijuana cigarette with a card saying: "Happy Valentine's Day. This cigarette contains no harmful cancer-causing ingredients. It is made from 100 percent pure marijuana." Directions followed on how to smoke it, so the recipients could cut through all the baloney and make up their own minds. A postscript warned: "Oh, by the way, possession of the item you now hold in your hand can bring up to five years in prison. It matters not how or from whom you got it."

The press reacted as if a plague of killer-weeds had descended on the defenseless Big Apple. Special squads of narcotics agents, they reported, had been dispatched from Washington to ferret out the perpetrators. Newscaster Bill Jorgensen, then of Channel Five, played the perfect straight guy. Midshot: "Good evening, this is Bill Jorgensen with the evening news. This (*dramatic pause*) is a reefer. It is made from an illegal substance, marijuana. Thousands of unsuspecting citizens of New York received them today with the following Valentine message," he said, straight-faced. "The police have set up a special number to process complaints" (the number flashed across the screen). "We are now going to call that number." News and commercials filled the next twenty minutes while much of New York waited with bated breath. Near the end of the show, the announcer invited two trench-coated men, playing "Dragnet" clones, to come onto the set:

ANNOUNCER: You're the police?
POLICE: That's right.
ANNOUNCER: I received this in the mail.
POLICE: Approximately what time of day was that?
ANNOUNCER: It came in the morning mail.
POLICE: What's your name and address?
ANNOUNCER: Bill Jorgensen.
POLICE: Do you have any identification?
ANNOUNCER (*puzzled*): Why, I'm Bill Jorgensen. See the sign? This is the Bill Jorgensen news show.
POLICE: We'll still have to see some I.D.
ANNOUNCER: What about what it says here (*pointing*) about me—holding this reefer could earn me a prison sentence? Is that true?
POLICE: That's not our department.

AMERICA

HAS

MORE

TELEVISION

SETS

THAN

TOILETS

Hoffman: *America Has More Televisions Than Toilets*

You'll have to ask the D.A.'s office.
ANNOUNCER (*even more puzzled, faces the camera*): Well, that's all we have time for on the news tonight.

All this actually took place on New York television. A New Jersey radio station went so far as to report Bill Jorgensen had been arrested for possession of marijuana while delivering the evening news. Of course no one, including sourpuss Bill, took a fall on the prank, but for days the most amazing stories circulated. Trying to separate news from gossip has been a lifetime endeavor and I'm unconvinced there's any difference. All is subjective, all is information molded by distortion, selection, exaggeration, emphasis, omission, and every other variable of communication. Walter Cronkite just leans over the country's back fence and tells his stories. There's a lot of bias.

Broadcasters report "news," the enemy engages in "propaganda." Our "soldiers" and allies must kill to defend freedom, their "terrorists" kill for criminal reasons. (Remember, no terrorist bombs from a jet plane, therefore only enemies of imperialism can earn that label.) Unions are to blame for strikes, never management. Murders are newsworthy, corporate price-fixing too "abstract." Even the newscaster I most respect, Cronkite, is prone to using cold-war imagery. In covering the Vietnam War, for years he described it as "our American way of life" or "the Free World battling Communism." Home-grown culture versus foreign ideology. No U.S. broadcaster or reporter can ever speak of "capitalism" or "imperialism" being "our way of life," with "cooperation" being the social dynamic of communist countries. It's our "leaders" against their "rulers." Our "free press" compared with their "party-line." Our government, their regime.

On domestic news, I heard of many cases where an editor would tell a reporter, "Ten thousand at that rally? That's too many. Make it three thousand." The reporter would say, "Sure," then go out and get drunk. When you turn on the telly or pick up a newspaper you are tuning in on the boss's gossip and propaganda. If you believe America has a free press it just means you haven't thought about it enough. Everyone who makes and reports the news knows what I'm talking about. (In case you're curious, Jimi Hendrix financed the entire marijuana mailing.)

THEATER OF PROTEST expanded from the streets to the television studio and into the home. Keep in mind, there was a television rule that they only invited a person with any kind of radical ideas on a show for ridicule. Knowing that, I approached talk shows as you would enter a war zone. I brought every conceivable kind of verbal ammunition, prepared for any situation, and before every appearance I spent hours studying the show's format.

It was very tricky business. What I lost by going on these shows was a reinforcement of the idea that America is a free and open society. One of the first questions I'd be asked would be, "If you're so censored how come you're sitting here with me on nationwide TV?" I was also allowing myself to be edited, to fulfill a personality role in a play designed by the producers of American society. "He's just another pretty face." Keeping all these pitfalls in mind, television was nevertheless an enormously successful vehicle for making statements to a mass audience, and I used it as a form of theatrical warfare. Readers should understand television interviews are edited to make the interviewer, not the interviewee, look good. They are "based" on reality, just as all other fiction in the media.

Invited on the David Susskind Show, we were ready for America's star performing intellectual's attempt to neutralize us by forcing explanations. "How do you eat?" queried the Skeptic, and we passed out sandwiches to the audience. "But what *is* a hippie?" pressed the emissary of New York's literati. A box opened as if by magic. "Why don't you ask him, David, he's a hippie?" I said and a duck flew out of the box. Around its neck was a sign saying I AM A HIPPIE. Susskind exploded, "Catch that damn duck!" The duck, scared out of its wits, kept flying into the klieg lights. Chaos, the intellectual's nightmare, broke loose. Staff hands tried to grab the elusive duck. Each time the duck took off he crapped in midflight. Hippie-duck shit-bombs fell on the audience.

"That duck goes," screamed Susskind. "Hold the cameras!"

"David, you're television's worst C-E-N-S-O-R" (a particularly low blow). "No duck, no hippies," we shot back. Negotiations. The duck will stay, the duck shit goes. Later, when the show was aired, Susskind reneged and cut the entire scene. For a week he got late night calls: "Quack, quack, quack!"

THE GOAL OF THIS NAME—less art form—part vaudeville, part insurrection, part communal recreation—was to shatter the pretense of objectivity. The calm, patriarchal voice of reason, embodied in an Eric Sevareid or a David Susskind, could be a greater danger than shrill Red-baiting. We learned to sneak onto the airwaves with Conceptual Art pieces that roused viewers from their video stupor.

To do that, we had to study the medium of television. At first we aimed at the human-interest slot near the end of each news program called the "Happy Talk" segment, offering some freaky tableau to contrast with the nightly news blur. We infiltrated news by entering through the back door and slowly worked our way up to the lead items. To find us in *Time* and *Newsweek* you had to turn to the back pages. Of course, any clever student of mass communication knew most people read those two magazines backwards anyway. Everyone paid attention to Happy Talk because in being personal it deviated from the prepared script.

The things about television you weren't supposed to take seriously I took very seriously, and vice versa. Everybody knows that studio audiences are primed to laugh, applaud like crazy, and look generally ecstatic, but it's easy to forget how contrived and manipulated the situation is. I used this distortion of reality to my own advantage on the David Frost Show, pumping reverse responses out of the studio audience.

During the commercial break I got out of my seat, already creating a little chaos because guests aren't supposed to get out of their seats on talk shows unless the host tells them to get up ("How 'bout a song?" "Yes, sir."). I walked right up to the audience and started conducting them:

"Come on, you're not angry enough! I'm a gook. I'm a nigger, I'm a kike—come on, get it off your chest!" They started yelling and getting up out of their seats, enraged and shaking their fists at me. It was a symphony of hate. By the time the commercial break was over I was back in my seat, smiling like an innocent lamb, while Frost worked me over and the audience roared and snarled. Then I jumped up and played hate conductor again. It came off very effectively.

On the same Frost Show I waited until the camera was on me while I was talking, and near the end of my rap I mouthed some words soundlessly, putting in the word "fuck" for those who were up to a little lip reading. People watching said, "Oh, my God. They've censored him. They blipped him right there! I saw it!"

To practice this reverse manipulation you had to be very much in control. People weren't supposed to do these things in the television studio. The point was to give the home audience a different message, one closer to reality. I mean, who really gives a fuck about how hard it is for actors to get up at 5 A.M. to powder their noses?

RADIO NEEDED another frame of mind. I studied how it was different, always preferred it to TV, and felt I was better on the radio because the listener couldn't see what was going on and respond to certain visual images I had to create. One night I was being interviewed by a hostile host live on New York radio station WNEW. I picked up my host's pack of cancerettes and said, "Can I have a cigarette?"

"Sure, help yourself," he said, and I took one and dragged on it slurpily. "Hey, this is really good stuff here, man," I said, imitating the stereotyped stoned musician. The host got all flustered and announced, "Ladies and gentlemen, he's just smoking a plain Marlboro cigarette." "Tell them that—tell them it's just a cigarette, man," I agreed, then apologized profusely. "Oh my God, ah shoudna done it. . . . I'm sorry, I don't wanna blow your gig. So cool, though, man disguisin it as a cigarette." There was no way the host could get out of the little trap with just words. He completely lost his composure, but he had me back.

On another talk show, I got a call-in death threat. I said over the air that I'd be leaving the studio at 5 o'clock and went on

to describe myself, only using the appearance of the host. "I got horn-rimmed glasses and a brown and white-checkered sports jacket." Most of the time I'd talk about the war or other social issues, using humor as a hook. I would use the opportunities to advertise upcoming demonstrations. It was free space and effective. Before Disco, people actually talked on radio. Now it seems like everyone, disc jockeys, broadcasters, newsmen, are all hopping to the same monotonous beat. One-two-three. One-two-three.

I practiced talk shows and press conferences just as singers and comedians practice their routines. You train to improvise. Most TV dialogue is canned, but I never read prepared lines. Talk show questions are sometimes given, often requested, from guests. Press conferences by politicians are carefully orchestrated. What viewers are led to believe is that all is "totally unrehearsed." Yet most, if not "rehearsed," is certainly "arranged." For example, take a presidential press conference. Only mainstream (controllable) reporters are allowed in the White House press corps. The safest, most controllable (TV commentators) are recognized for the first questions. Jumping from reporter to reporter, from question to question, lends the appearance that a free and open exchange is taking place. As one who has played both sides of the Q and A, I know that no format lends itself more to burying the truth beneath public relations gloss. Everyone on TV works on a media "presence." From the White House briefings to *The Gong Show*, entertainment rules the tube. The similarities between Rona Barrett and Walter Cronkite are far more interesting than the differences. And, if we are talking of accuracy, Ms. Rona is far ahead of most so-called news reporters. Obviously there is *some* freedom in the U.S. media, but rather than pay it unbending homage is it not better to educate the public in the ways it is *not* free? Like not being free to suggest an alternative to our economic system.

My television act was close to my everyday life. Close, in fact, to my unconscious world. I personalized the audience. I think aloud. Recognizing the limited time span of someone staring at a lighted square in their living room, I trained for the one-liner, the retort jab, or sudden knock-out put-ons. I practiced with friends, waiters, people on the street, cab drivers, mayors, movie stars, cops, reporters, and relatives. When no one was around to practice with, I turned on the

TV set and played each character, internalizing their questions and answers. What I'm trying to say was I didn't practice at *all*;, that all communication is the same—face-to-face or face-to-camera.

I read *Variety, Show Business, Billboard*, and other trade papers far more probably than any radical organizer in history. It would be little problem for me to recite the ten top-rated TV shows or movies of the week. I tried to study things such as the effect of looking at the camera as opposed to the host (it depends) or whether or not to wear makeup. No makeup, although visually handicapping, gave me a bottom-line edge; if I was accused of being a phony I could respond: "It's funny, Dick, people who say that to me are always wearing makeup." Immediately the audience at home could "see" the difference between us and have their consciousness raised about television information. There is nothing more radical you can talk about on TV than TV itself.

In analyzing word communication, I've arranged a list of the ten most acceptable words. The most popular word in the American language is "free," "new" is second. The word "less" is more acceptable than "more." The potential customer is suspicious of "more"; he knows the maxim—you pay more, get less. Television advertising is the height of fantasy manipulation. I tried writing commercials for revolution to learn the medium.

MY WORK IN TV was a long way from accepting its format. I entered the world of television to expose its wasteland. The top one hundred corporations control eighty percent of all network air time. Robert Hutchins once said: "We can put television in its proper light by supposing that Gutenberg's great invention had been directed at printing only comic books."

Later a group of us performed a guerrilla theater piece which adequately summed up our attitude toward television. While Nixon addressed the nation on the need for invading Cambodia, we set a twenty-four-inch receiver on a pedestal and before twenty thousand angry protesters pick-axed the flickering image. Electronic voodoo. Sometimes the proper intellectual argument is "FUCK YOU!"△

**T**HOSE IN THE ENGLISH-SPEAKING WORLD WHO KNOW of the Situationist International (henceforth S.I.) generally relegate them to the status of a sixties period piece. Some even admire them as the most fascinating by-product of the international New Left but see them as hopelessly bound to a bygone era.

My own enthusiasm for the S.I., like that of erstwhile collaborators, hit its peak in the early seventies, the more we became aware of these formidable Frenchmen. Their scandalous methods, wicked humor, intriguing graphics—backed up, we learned, with a well-stocked theoretical arsenal—rang true in "modern" California and zapped many a jaded veteran of a Movement-gone-stale like piercing light through a dense fog. (St. Paul notwithstanding, this *was* epiphany.) So the San Francisco Bay Area then witnessed a considerable flurry of S.I.-influenced activity,[1] including what were by far the most trenchant post-mortems on the waning New Left and counterculture.

Yet by 1975, largely because of a *seemingly* old-fashioned economic crisis that was so unlike the S.I.'s prognosis (along with subtler reasons I'll examine later), the effusion of our posters, pamphlets, graffiti, etc., had slowed to a trickle. Since then, *faute de mieux* (for lack of anything better) would about sum up anyone's lingering loyalty to those yellowing texts.

Still, if I may leap abruptly into the present, into the social climate of the Reagan/Thatcher backlash, a menacing new Cold War, and the worst worldwide economic quagmire since the thirties, then I can state the case for the S.I.'s continued pertinence more sharply. For if this grim backdrop roughly resembles former times, it is also, in even more ways, so unprecedented as to confound *all* our inherited analytical frameworks. Up against such a challenge, the floundering responses of the Democratic Party, the U.K.'s Labour Party, and what's left of the Left appear all the more pitiable. Above all, it is the appalling intellectual bankruptcy of so many who haven't had a fresh idea in fifty years— yet who scurry to regroup even as they refuse to *rethink*—which makes *faute de mieux* a perfectly excellent reason to start advancing further where the S.I. stopped short. And without delay!

In the essay that follows,[2] I address myself to those who want to fight effectively in our nearly paralyzing times, and to those who just as surely do *not* want what the S.I. so dreaded: "a world where the guarantee of not dying of hunger is purchased at the price of dying of boredom."

The Situationists *Reconsidered*

ANTECEDENTS: ADVENTURES OF THE DIALECTIC

To be youthful means being able to forget.   —Benito Mussolini

We Marxists live in traditions, and have not ceased being revolutionists because of it.   —Leon Trotsky

To be sure, only a redeemed mankind receives the fullness of its past. . . . The historical materialist leaves it to others to be drained by the whore called "Once upon a time."   —Walter Benjamin

Too bad it didn't work.
  —Ronald Reagan, after a private screening of *Reds*

by **Tom Ward**

Ms. Susan Sontag, who is to the politics of culture what Gloria Vanderbilt is to jeans, decided, a couple of fashion cycles ago, to dabble awhile in surrealism, Walter Benjamin, etc. So we got her book *On Photography* (1977), with its chapter "Melancholy Objects," that pontifically sets us straight: "Surrealists, who aspire to be cultural radicals, even revolutionaries, have often been under the well-intentioned illusion that they could be, indeed should be, Marxists. But Surrealist aestheticism is too suffused with irony to be compatible with [Marxism], the twentieth century's most seductive form of moralism." From this we are to deduce: (1) that surrealism (along with all of modern irony) and dour old Marxism are the twain that ne'er shall meet: (2) that the entire surrealist project was admirable but silly (thus placing Sontag solidly in Reagan's "too bad it didn't work" camp—not the only ground they share these days); (3) that Marx was a "moralist." (This last is big news to me—have I read too much Marx?) So

many misrepresentations to squeeze into two medium-sized sentences! Prizes should be awarded!

I won't make it to the awards ceremony, but let me here extend my gratitude to Sontag for having so condensed two of the oldest and most tiresome traditions of the conformist intelligentsia: the one that wants modern art to be innocuous and cute; and the one that wants Marx to be unattractive and misunderstood. As Benjamin wrote shortly before his suicide: "In every era the attempt must be made anew to wrest tradition away from a conformism that is about to overpower it . . . *even the dead* will not be safe from the enemy if he wins. And this enemy has not ceased to be victorious."[3]

In other words, it's hard to let sleeping dogs lie when rabid dogs are lying through their teeth.

The S.I. undertook "the correction of the past" by reactivating the dormant potential in two traditions: the (anti-)artistic modernism of the 1910–1925 period, and the libertarian working-class movement that came to maturity—and defeat—around the same time. (This explicit reference to historical antecedents can be easily distinguished from born-yesterday hippies or punks—who acted as if they had *invented* the derivative postures they recycled—and a Left which fancied itself "New" only because it dared not learn enough history to find out which mistakes it was repeating.) Against the linear, cumulative depiction of history (shared by bourgeois historicists and leftist "progressives"), the S.I. staked all on the forgotten "moments" of interrupted revolutions. Between such moments, history is a drag, held on a virtual freeze-frame, or as the dissident Hungarian film posed it, *Time Stands Still*.

The S.I. emerged from Europe's radical artist milieu in 1957, as an offshoot from several prior groupings: Lettrists, Imaginist Bauhaus, Cobra group, etc. Though already resolved *not* to go the way of failed avant-gardes, they moved only gradually beyond these naive origins. Ken Knabb's superb *Situationist International Anthology* (1981)[4] devotes ample attention to pre-S.I. documents and this formative phase, so I'll concentrate instead on three areas: (1) some core themes of the older avant-garde; (2) why the S.I. is *not* part of the Left; (3) the inseparable unity of aesthetics and politics in a genuine radical praxis.

Modern Art

Guy Debord, the S.I.'s foremost theoretician, wrote: "Dadaism and surrealism are the two currents which mark the end of modern art. . . . Dadaism wanted to *suppress art without realizing it*; surrealism wanted to *realize art without suppressing it*. . . . [T]he S.I. has shown that these . . . are inseparable aspects of a single *supersession of art*."[5]

Quite succinct. Quite true. But such a nutshell summary will do little to help a new generation sense the ambitious scope and political seriousness of the earlier avant-garde. And one fears for callow youths, left at the mercy of popularizers like Tom Wolfe or Robert Hughes.[6]

The S.I. viewed the old modernism as a set of related, but only partially successful, syntheses: (1) art/politics; (2) art/technology; (3) art/everyday life. Of course, each

of these topics has since been discussed to death, such that the great breakthroughs of the European twenties are, by now, terribly commonplace. Still, a few comments are in order:

1. Post-representational art developed in a contemporaneous, semiconscious interaction with post-representational politics (that is, the 1917–1923 movements for proletarian *direct* democracy). At the time, this connection was made tenuously at best.[7] Still, the S.I. saw splendid prospects in such a link, through applying more stringent criteria to both the art and the politics in question.

2. The technological "threat" to Art, and (not quite the same) of mass culture to High Culture, was never so dreaded in the U.S. as in Europe, where highbrow revulsion from modernity has persisted as an ideology among archaic social classes. More in line with Brecht, *Neue Sachlichkeit*, Russian Futurism, etc., the S.I.'s strategy was to confront and master the new media, then turn them to advantage. Sensible, for sure, but rather elementary.[8] How one *does* so is the only point of interest (see below).

3. The "realization of art in everyday life"—that is, by ending the separation between the two—was certainly part of the Bauhaus and surrealist projects and, before that, the goal of William Morris, the 1980s Aesthetes, et alia. The S.I. refined on these predecessors only by giving this desideratum pride of place, as well as the most careful exploration it has yet received.

Politics

The S.I. came of age in a Europe where the best and brightest were already bored to tears with "Marxism," where Communist Parties and unions were as tediously familiar as our Democratic Party and AFL-CIO, and where old men spoke of The New Man like he'd already gone out of style.

Yet some on the Left like to see the S.I. as merely "extremist" or "ultra-left," in the sense of: an extreme case of what the Left already is. Such people assume that the S.I. criticized others for not going far enough, fast enough; i.e., because the Left was taking only small steps in the right direction. On the contrary, it had taken long, lumbering strides in the *wrong* direction, with results that were all too evident. In the East, a travesty calling itself "Marxist" had implanted its leaden feet over much of the land area of the globe. In the West, palsied imagination could offer only an infinite horizon of Welfare Statism so dreary it scarcely earned the spittle of contempt.

As Debord wrote: "The historical moment when Bolshevism triumphed *for itself* in Russia and when social-democracy fought *for the old world* marks the inauguration of the state of affairs which is at the

S.I. resumed and elaborated on the original Marxian[10] critique of a global, generalized system in which *everyone*, East and West, was implicated: consumers, Party bureaucrats, lumpen marginals, leftist professors, and all the rest.

So with some validity, one might say that the S.I. derived its *descriptive method* from Marx and its *prescriptive vision* from anarchism (along with utopians like Charles Fourier and artists of social vision). But not quite. First, much of anarchism is moralistic, antitechnological, and so backward-looking that it would

Marx, crows and Toyota (by Jay Kinney and Adam Cornford).

heart of the modern spectacle's domination."[9] Note this well: "At the heart." The Left is not a sideshow to be dealt with later, not an insufficient solution. It is "at the heart" of the problem.

Yet, far from joining the anti-Communist Right, the S.I. formulated a critique of capitalism (including its State-managed variants) that went far deeper than the Left's. Where the Left, in pandering to populism (while retreating ever further from the kind of integral analysis that set the standard in the days of Lenin and Luxembourg), clamored tritely against Big Business, The Rich, imperialism, etc., the

subordinate the individual not to the State (which its fuzzy "analysis" abstractly abhors), but to some primitivist or neomedieval "communitarian" ideal.[11] All such anarchism fears and loathes modernity, while the S.I. sought to be "absolutely modern."

As for Marx, the volumes of exegesis could now fill up several massive libraries, and most could be shredded at no great loss to humanity. The S.I. was interested only in the lost "unitary" scope of Marx's vision[12] but never hesitated to pick apart the corpus of his ideas. The critical notions of "reification" and "commodity fetishism," along with the positive project of "the total man," could be updated and reformulated; but Marx's vacillations on the actual form of communist society, and the strategy to get there, were mercilessly reassessed.

Moreover, it was not theory, Marxian *or* libertarian, which created "the highest reality of the proletarian movements in the first quarter of this century."[13] This was an improvised popular form, the workers' councils, as they emerged in Russia, Germany, Hungary, and elsewhere. But this "spontaneous" form of direct democracy *did* necessitate drastic rethinking on all sides. Unfortunately, very few rose to it. Only those anarchists who overcame their aversion to urban, industrial reality, and those Marxians who broke with every statist of Party-oriented model or organization, could be counted among the exceptions.[14]

Towards Synthesis

Yet even those with newly attained insights into the practical *form* of the new society were usually hobbled by shallow perceptions of its human *content*. Hence, they were ill-equipped to explain the failure and defeat of so many doomed attempts at proletarian self-organization, and to contend with deeper realities: fear of freedom, masochistic craving for strong leaders, or the simple fact that "the man in the street is... bored with socialism."[15]

So we must turn again to the "subjective" side: to psychology, and to what Marcuse called "the aesthetic dimension."

A friend once whimsically suggested that if Wilhelm Reich, André Breton, and the "council-communists"—all of whom were contemporaries—had gotten together during the twenties, the S.I.'s "project" would have commenced some thirty years sooner. As it was, they worked at cross purposes: Reich a party member, Breton a Trotskyist, while the council-communists relied on a prosaic "political economy" that was faithful only to the narrowest reading of Marx. When Debord observed: "They are contemporaries, though only in a relatively conscious manner,"[16] he put it much too mildly. How *could* Dada originators Tzara and Heartfield end up as Stalinists, while the surrealist Aragon became so much of one that he damned

the rebels of May '68? On the flip side, how did Reich and Karl Korsch come to endorse the Americans in the Cold War?

But now let me place one item on the agenda for the project that still lies ahead of us. I suggest that one key to the needed synthesis of aesthetics and politics could be found in the formulation of a *thorough-going hedonistic ethics*. Of course, like most crucial terms, each of these is heavily laden with the presuppositions and bogus associations that official ideology inculcates in everyone: "politics" as the circumscribed realm of parties, statecraft, macropolitical (daily life) and the entire *polis* (public realm); "aesthetics"[17] as a contemplative, antiutilitarian attitude toward art and life—i.e., not life-as-art which must be actively *realized*. And especially so long as "hedonism" is understood through the debased usages of the present commodity-spectacle, then the comprehensive post-Christian ethics I propose will be *completely* misunderstood.

The dominant images of "pleasure" and "play" are the direct outgrowth of our division of labor and strict separation of life activities. Since the time at work demands alienated *activity*, then off-work time (hardly "leisure") is devoted to the pursuit of maximum *passivity*: idle "pleasure" and inconsequential "play." But the kinds of pleasure and play that the S.I., like great hedonists before them, advocated, require both *risk* and sustained *exertion* (not to say "sacrifice"). It is this robust, daring, active pleasure—and this *serious* play—that characterize the hedonism I refer to here.

Once this clarification of terms is achieved, one can posit radical praxis as: libertarian communist politics subsumed within aesthetics, and both subsumed within hedonistic ethics.

Meanwhile, a subdialectical mind like Sontag's will maintain that the aesthetic sensibility (irony, play, etc.) and political seriousness are eternally incompatible. But in fact, quite contrary to Sontag, André Breton was far more moralistic than Marx ever was,[18] which is why Breton's politics were often flaky, and why he succumbed to the duty-bound slogan: "Poetry in the service of revolution!" The S.I. corrected this to read: "Revolution in the service of poetry!" This seems a simple enough reversal, yet it opens up vistas one could take volumes to fill, not to mention the history of the next thousand years....

THE S.I. AGAINST ITS TIME

Man is most fully human when he plays.   —F. Schiller

To be Stirner than Max without failing Marx.   —B. Black

Birds are singing, and the children are playing
There's plenty of work, and the bosses are paying
Not a sad word should a young heart be saying
But fun is a bore, and with money I'm poor.   —'Smokey' Robinson

It is now capitalist abundance which has failed.   —Guy Debord

The world had come to a pretty pass by the late fifties. Two superpowers, commanded by Eisenhower and Khrushchev (two roly-poly dimwits who even *looked* like each other), had imprinted their massified image and likeness on the rest of the planet. Humanity had survived the ravages of its Second World War only to consummate the marriage of commodity heaven and neo-Stalinist hell. Oh, there had been some instability until the Marshall Plan got Western Europe back on its industrious bourgeois feet again, and a few militarist loonies in the States had even rumbled about "rolling back" the Red Army's conquest of Eastern Europe. But that was old news. The balance of terror had stabilized.[19] The contrived drama of the Cold War was losing interest. Ike golfed. Nikita loved Disneyland. The Americanization of Europe was in full swing.

And while the Left busied itself with these macropolitical events, or cried "New Depression!" at each miniscule dip in the economic indicators, a new old friend took center stage: everyday life.

Billboards smiled serenely on commuters snarling their way through rush-hour traffic. An emerging "new class" of gray-collar functionaries could neither work up an honest sweat nor bask in the dubious aura of the faded professional caste. A breathtaking new technological wonder called television entitled everyone to memorize a million haunting jingles they'd rather forget. In all, a small price to pay for the bountiful fruits of progress.

Even the nightly reports of stress and strife in the outlands, that mythic Third World of so many humanitarian appeals, could not shake the suspicion that everyone, eventually, was headed the American Way. *De te fabula narratur*, Marx had been fond of quoting, "of *you* the story is told!" And if America was setting the standard for ubiquitous "modernization," who was to say that the last extant primitive culture wouldn't be stumbled on somewhere near an offramp from the L.A. Freeway?

Enter the Situationist International. Like gangbusters.

"Modern youth has been given the choice between love and the garbage disposal unit. It has chosen the garbage disposal unit." Or: "The situationists will execute the judgment that contemporary leisure is pronouncing against itself." Or: "Ours is the best effort so far toward *getting out of the twentieth century*."

Colossally arrogant, boundlessly presumptuous, not at all modest.

Boredom was the burr under their hides, a slow strangulation, a creeping terror that today was a Xerox of yesterday, and infinity would stretch out *just like this*. "If we are not surrealists it is *because we don't want to be bored*."

So they flailed around for something, anything, that would lead them out of this impasse. Maybe putting it that way makes it sound like they weren't terribly bright. On the contrary, they were much *too* bright to invest hope in Norman Mailer's "hipsters," C. Wright Mills' "new left," Beatnik mysticism, existentialist resignation, senescent surrealism, or Dada's cul-de-sac. In fact, the S.I. disdained to place *hope* anywhere. As Raoul Vaneigem was later to write: "Hope is the leash of submission." Such an extremity of tough-mindedness is only suited for those who can make a career of contemplation, and neither careers nor contemplation held the least interest for the S.I.

The gambits which the S.I. then toyed with (e.g., "psychogeography" and the "dérive")[20] were not so different from old surrealist pastimes or, for that matter, from the thumb-sucking postures that Laurie Anderson and her crowd so lucratively perpetrate today.

Overall, the S.I.'s most politically fecund "aesthetic" concept, the one that was to outgrow their infancy with them, was that of *détournement* (literally: "diversion"). Nowadays among visual artists, "appropriation" seems to be the password on many a lip, though it is often just a poor nephew of *détournement*. Known by either name, the process is to lift preexisting elements out of their original contexts and, by montage, modification and/or insertion of text, reassemble them into a "new coherence." In most instances, one also intends thereby to "reveal," to get to the root of, the latent content—the "real" essence—of those original elements.

So far, so good. But since *détournement* is, in every sense, a profane[21] technique, no one can protect it from inept use or willful abuse. One can only denounce such abominations after they occur, or set forth criteria for judging motives and methods.

Among some trendies on the current art "scene," for instance, it seems that the whole thrust of "appropriation" is to entrench even further the insularity of an aesthete subculture. All these chic creatures seem to want is another excuse to snicker at the corny imagery (usually from the fifties) that "straight" people used to produce/consume with heartfelt conviction, thus raising themselves up a notch in smug superiority.[22]

That ladder leads nowhere.

On the contrary, as a technique of popular agitation, *détournement* has even now barely tapped its available reservoir which, if not infinite (by its very nature), is still far from depleted. The raw materials for *détournement* are cheap, commonplace, and enable anyone to (as the matchbook covers advise) "strike anywhere." Thus the S.I. could conceive of "the critique that feels at home everywhere"—not just on picket lines, at factory gates, or other places to which orthodox militants trek to feel politically engaged.

"In the spectacle," Debord wrote, "the true is a moment of the false." This maxim has decisive implications for strategy and tactics.

It's fairly simple, really. The spectacle is a monopoly of appearances.[23] Most people believe what they see because they never have *occasion* to see anything else. Nothing in the patterns of their daily routines will ever snap them out of the lockgrip of

Ward: *The Situationists Reconsidered*

conformist thinking. The whole way that cities are designed, workplaces are structured, traffic is routed—and especially the way that electronic media broadcast from a controlled center to a dispersed, atomized mass—conspires to reinforce this setup. So radical literature collects dust on the bookshelves, radical films are seen only by aficionados, and so on. No one else even sees such things because they *think* they already know what to expect—and want no part of it. So there is a perfectly closed circle joining expectation to result to expectation . . . ad infinitum. For instance, most people in the West have received, from the schools and media, an *image* of socialism; namely, "what they have in Russia"—and, quite rightly, they want no part of it.

The object, then, is to jolt: to interrupt the continuum of everyday experience *and* expectation in such a way that people are forced to confront the familiar from an altered perspective (one they'd never otherwise consider).[24] Such is the political purpose of *détournement*, as illustrated throughout this essay, and as I'll examine in depth in the concluding section.

By 1966, EVENTS IN the outside world had been heating up: Berkeley's Free Speech Movement, the Watts riot, the putsch in Algeria, escalation in Vietnam, etc. C. Wright Mills' yearned-for New Left was now *visibly* on the move, albeit in directions the S.I. found confused, contradictory, or worse. What mattered was that isolated outbursts were reverberating into a kind of chain reaction, and the placid image of permanent stability had been shattered. It was time to get serious. The S.I. intensified its critical study of other political tendencies.[25] Not that the S.I. turned its attention *away* from daily life or its avant-garde experiments, just that priorities couldn't help but shift.

The next two years would see the culmination of their theory and practice. In 1966: the "Strasbourg scandal," putting them on the map, so to speak. In 1967: the publication of books by Debord and by Vaneigem, the two major works of S.I. theory. Then, the S.I.'s hour of triumph in

May–June 1968: a movement that took a form and raised demands which verified the S.I.'s analysis, while disproving the assumptions of almost everyone else.

In one dizzying decade, the S.I. had evolved from a tiny coterie of suicide-prone existential desperadoes to become the widely acknowledged instigators[26] of the most far-reaching social *contestation* in a Western nation since the Spanish Civil War—yet with almost no numerical increase in membership! And lest I leave the impression that the S.I. merely sat around writing, I should stress that at least some of these theoreticians eventually proved themselves to be fierce streetfighters and tireless troublemakers as well.

Yet at the same time, one should avoid mythologizing the S.I.-as-organization. Talent and initiative were hardly spread evenly throughout its membership, and some of their most fabled escapades should in fact be credited to persons "in accord with" but outside the group.

The 1966 disruption at the University of Strasbourg, for instance, started when a handful of malcontents got themselves elected, thanks to default-by-apathy, to head the student government. Next, they called on Mustapha Khayati and other S.I. members for advice and aid, then proceeded to stage hashish orgies in the student center, to close down the psychiatric service ("a tool for adjusting people to a sick society"), and to (mis)appropriate funds for a subversive comic strip and a scabrous text, "On the Poverty of Student Life."[27]

Similarly, the *enragés* at Nanterre (Gérard Bigorgne, Réne Riesel, et al.) were younger and more "activist" than the S.I.'s own members (though Riesel later joined). These incorrigibles were expelled from the university for the mounting series of disruptions and broadsides that comprised the now-infamous detonator for May '68. During these preliminary skirmishes, the S.I. mostly theorized from the sidelines (which they did, I should add, with greater cogency than most).[28]

But once the chips were down, during the May–June upheaval itself, the S.I. members comported themselves about as admirably as could fairly be asked of fallible mortals. They were prolific at a pace only adrenaline could explain and, more important, were consistent with their own announced principles. (Some were ar-

rested, exiled, etc.) At the point of their weightiest influence (viz., Riesel's popularity in the Occupied Sorbonne), they disdained any power play and stayed true to the slogan: "All power to the general assembly." On May 17, once the power plays of *others* had vitiated the Sorbonne's democracy, the S.I. merged, on an ad hoc basis, with some thirty other revolutionaries to form the Council for Maintaining the Occupations (CMDO). This CMDO went on to produce and disseminate as many as 200,000 copies of an astounding stream of posters, *détourned* comics, etc.[29]

In Nanterre (by André Bertrand of the *enragés* group).

That May '68 was, for the S.I., the proverbial "tough act to follow"; that the intoxication of 1968 ("from Prague to Mexico City . . .") unsettled the group's normal composure; that the S.I. didn't handle sudden notoriety as ably as it had endured obscurity; that May '68 itself has receded in importance and interest—all of this, with the benefit of hindsight, is obvious enough. What's no less obvious, to me, is that some people would too gladly conceal behind such "knowing" remarks their own failure even to approximate the level of accomplishment the S.I. attained in that hour.

I hesitantly approach the hornets' nest of the S.I.'s bad reputation. But a number of people have constructed, then circulated, superficial impressions based on rumor, cursory reading, or someone's jaundiced recollection.[30] Such impressions serve to discourage others from making the effort that's needed *now*—long after the tempest-in-a-teacup acrimony has subsided—to retrieve the valid distillate from the S.I.'s theory and practice.

First, the oft-heard "sectarianism" charge is usually invoked by those who need to play down *real* differences. Hence, the constant Stalinist ruse of the "popular front," that notorious foot-in-the-door trick designed to silence criticism until it's too late to voice it. True, the S.I. was called "sectarian and dogmatic" even by other self-avowed "anarchists." But the S.I. was alert to the danger of "nonsectarian" coalitions in which authoritarians could maneuver with impunity, and the gullibility of libertarians who joined such "action alliances."[31] The S.I. also differed from Trotskyists, etc., in that they had *no* desire to lure people away from coalitions in order to "recruit" them. To quote directly:

We are not a power *in society, and thus our "exclusions" only express our freedom to distinguish ourselves from the confusionism around us or even among us. . . . We have never wished to prevent anyone from doing what he/she wants. . . . We merely refuse to be ourselves mixed up with ideas and acts that run contrary to our convictions and our tastes.*[32]

The matter of the S.I.'s insulting arrogance is vastly more complicated. To some extent, the sneering tone is *très* French—or at least in one French tradition—and some degree of sublimated, intellectualized sadomasochism seems undeniable. Regrettably, some of the types who've been attracted to the S.I. find that tone titillating, and strain to mimic it. A chronology of the S.I.'s work even devotes an entire chapter to "an index of insulted names."[33]

One has to look past all this to determine whether there is substance to a given criticism or insult. Moreover, quite apart from gratuitous sadism, the unpleasantry of *ad hominem* assault seems inherent in political struggle. In other words, if you confront a well-paid or high-status individual, you can't very well divorce "ideas" from the personal circumstances that largely explain why he/she holds such ideas.

Still, I think that by expending too much energy in dreaming up imaginative insults (admittedly an art form), rather than methodically unraveling opponents' arguments, the S.I. made the going needlessly rough for itself.

And the going could get rough enough as it was. . . .

APPLIED THEORY: INTO THE AMERICAN CRUCIBLE

To realize radical imagination requires a varied knowledge, but this knowledge is nothing without the style with which it is handled.

—Raoul Vaneigem

The style is the man. And how! The law allows me to write, but on the condition that I write in a style other than my own. . . . I am a humorist, but the law orders me to write seriously. I am bold, but the law orders my style to be modest. Grey and more grey, that is the only authorized color of freedom.

—Karl Marx

The old problem of knowing if men as a whole really love freedom finds itself superseded; because now they are going to be compelled to love it.

—Guy Debord

The centrality of the French-American connection dates back to the two great bourgeois revolutions of the eighteenth century. For then both America's 1776 and France's 1789 appeared as two closely aligned moments within the same dawn of an epoch. And yet the splits that wedged in soon thereafter have since widened to where they could now be said to divide the planet into warring camps: Leninists the world over, claiming to carry the torch of the French (via the Russian) Revolution, versus the conservative Americans who behave as if our first Revolution—or rather, the official interpretation of it—were sufficient and valid for all time.[34]

I discussed earlier the meaning of Europe's turning-point years (1917–1923). But the decisive juncture for America came right after 1945, as Henry Luce's "American Century" took shape. It was then that the U.S. for the first time could boast all the advantages: a nuclear monopoly, a revved-up economy, four-fifths of the world's intact industrial plant, a longstanding hegemony in the Western Hemisphere now extending throughout Asia and Africa (as the older colonizers evacuated), and so on. Of course, the U.S. had to reckon with other new extrusions on the geopolitical map—viz., an expanded

Soviet sphere, various Third World upstarts, etc.—but Mother Europe, ravaged and humbled, would come begging for junior-partner status in any reconstruction scheme.[35]

Before 1945, "progressive" people elsewhere looked to America with a mixture of admiration and puzzlement: a beacon of hope, as it were, that sent out conflicting, unreliable signals. (Latin America, of course, had seen our worst ever since the Monroe Doctrine.) But since 1945, the prevalent sentiment everywhere has become more and more that blend of derision and mortal dread you feel toward a clumsy, walleyed giant who wants to win your love, and could crush you in the process. (Feelings toward the U.S.S.R. have become not so different.)

Likewise, before 1945, some radical analysts, both in the U.S. and abroad, stressed the importance of "the American question" but were ultimately exasperated by America's bewildering knack for eluding old or imported intellectual models. Besides, it was understandable to concentrate on areas of the globe that conformed more recognizably to the set scenarios (Marxian class struggle in Europe, Lenin's anti-imperialism elsewhere) so long as those areas seemed to

Ward: *The Situationists Reconsidered*

betoken the impending wave of the future.[36]

Since 1945, America can no longer be shunted onto radical criticism's back burner. But it's the U.S. role in the arms race and in Third World counterinsurgency that has riveted the orthodox Left's attention. Only the S.I., Marcuse, and a few others have grappled with subtler, more insidious factors: the new techniques of social control, so dazzling in sophistication, so overwhelming in complexity, as to make the heavy-handed fascisms of Europe between the World Wars seem but crude forerunners in comparison.

In this light, then, S.I. theory was to some extent a French[37] response to American-led developments, requiring of its creators an imaginative leap out and "in advance" of the backward French setting that the Gaullist regime, through its web of archaic institutional buttresses, labored stubbornly to hold intact. Bearing in mind these retardant factors, not to mention the self-serving anti-Americanism of the French Stalinist Left, one is all the more impressed by the S.I.'s degree of advancement—and enabled to measure its limitations.

The S.I.'s effort to "keep abreast of reality" was, to be sure, not altogether successful. Their analysis of the 1965 Watts riot was, to me, a glaring example of their unfamiliarity with much of the American scene.[38] Still, not unlike Marx despairing of his German compatriots while expecting great things from "advanced" Britain, Debord and friends, at least for a time, were highly intrigued by the potentials of an historical encounter between S.I. theory/praxis and American conditions.

This sanguine trans-Atlantic outlook didn't last long.

The U.S. New Left fizzled, and the New York section (1968–1970) of the S.I. appeared ineffectual; meanwhile, growing movements throughout Europe (though not, ironically, in France itself) were intensifying, maturing, and making appreciable impact among industrial workers.

By 1971, Debord felt no more desire to embellish the façade of an "organization" that had been glutted by sycophants and, finally, superseded by history. Ever since Debord and the Italian G. Sanguinetti announced the S.I.'s "dissolution" in *The Veritable Split in the International* (1972),[39] their gaze has been fixed almost exclu-

"Taxi! Taxi! (by anonymous in Portugal).

sively on European tendencies: in Spain, Portugal, Poland, but above all, in Italy. "Being for the moment the most advanced country in the slide towards proletarian revolution, Italy is also the most modern laboratory of international counter-revolution." Thus wrote Debord in 1979; and also: "It is in the factories of Italy that [*Society of the Spectacle*] has found . . . its best readers."[40]

So I can proceed no further without a balanced critique of the S.I.'s "Euro-centrism." The latter neologism was coined during the sixties, most notably by Black Power advocates and "Third Worldists," to expose the cultural narrowness that neglected—and, the argument ran, *slighted*—a whole range of nonwhite, non-Western experiences (e.g., the "Great Books of the Western World" approach in university curricula). This line of criticism, like most, has produced better and worse expositors, so I want here to distance myself from the moralizers who merely reciprocate such ignorance (as if there weren't also long *dissident* and antiracism traditions in the West, as if liberatory prospects elsewhere wouldn't have gleamed brighter if such tendencies had won out, etc.).

In fact, during the latter half of the sixties, a series of S.I. journal articles thoughtfully analyzed the promising

currents in Algeria, China and elsewhere, while taking to task the unthinking long-distance emulators of Mao, Frantz Fanon, Che Guevara, et alia.[41] The S.I. then began, but never carried far enough, the kind of clear-eyed, guilt-free assessment of the Third World that is still in such miserably scarce supply among radicals in the West. The trouble is that in the dozen years since the S.I.'s break-up, it would seem that its ex-members, and far too many of their epigones, have not kept pace with new developments outside Europe: neither OPEC's oil-rich sector, high-tech "islands" like Taiwan or South Korea, Japan's managerial methods, nor the militant and quite "advanced" actions of workers in Bolivia, Jamaica, and elsewhere.[42] For example, the profound turmoil in Portugal (1974–1975) drew inspiration from Italy, Poland, May '68, and even a certain "situationist" trace. But it was begun by young soldiers who sympathized with the anticolonial movements they were sent to suppress in Africa, and many Portuguese were acutely aware of the recent bloodbath in Chile when Allende, just two weeks before the September 1973 coup, disarmed the worker and peasant *consejos* (councils) that had sprung up around—and sometimes against—his wavering social-democratic government. Hence the Portuguese watchwords: "Watch out, workers! You have too many friends!"[43]

Nor am I persuaded that Italy *alone* has been "the most modern laboratory of international counterrevolution" (though this may have been true "for the moment" of the Moro kidnapping in 1978). More accurate to say that national elites, East and West, all learn from each other, and that these rulers are light-years ahead of the ruled at the game of transnational coordination. Indeed, for chilling efficiency and thorough planning, what could rival the Jaruzelski coup in Poland in December 1981, as coached by Western bankers and the KGB?

Still, it *is* true that guilt-ridden "Third Worldism," lack of information, or the sense of urgency over nukes, Central America, and the like, have prevented Americans from learning a fraction of what they might about some remarkable currents among European youth and workers.[44] Then again, some Eurocentric ex-situationists seem to have lost interest in the last decade of U.S. history—because it doesn't conform so recognizably to the S.I. scenario?—and left us to fend for our ourselves . . . .

THE AMERICAN (New York) section was spawned in March 1967, when the S.I. dispatched their roving delegate, the Dutch-born Tony Verlaan, to agitate and make contacts in the U.S. Since the S.I. always and wisely had insisted on some manifestation of "autonomous activity" before admitting new members into the group, Robert Chasse and Bruce Elwell later that year formed the "Council for the Liberation of Daily Life." Chasse wrote *Hall of Mirrors* (on the 1967 urban riots) and then, in April 1968, *The Power of Negative Thinking or, Robin Hood Rides Again*, which was a brief but lucid critique of SDS, SNCC, Black Power, etc. Insofar as Chasse wrote in a clearly American idiom, and didn't mechanically graft S.I. constructs onto these particulars, his texts endure even now—better than much of what followed.

Meanwhile, Verlaan gadded about the States, spreading the Strasbourg legend among SDS activists and prevailing upon "underground" newspapers to reprint S.I. comic strips and "On the Poverty of Student Life" (which, often in bowdlerized form, some were only too happy to do). In the confused delirium of New Left activism's peak years, one found, as in the classroom disruptions of the Radical Action Co-operative, an imagined mimicry of the Nanterre *enragés* coexisting with all manner of Maoist and "Americong" fantasies.

By June 1969, Verlaan, Chasse, and Elwell, along with Jon Horelick—now S.I. members—published the first and only journal of the American section. In it, the critiques of the "modernist ideologues" Marcuse and McLuhan mostly miss the mark. The swipes at assorted Left luminaries, and the chronicle of the New York section's earlier activities, are somewhat better, but of little interest today.

These New Yorkers then suffered the distinct misfortune of meeting their European counterparts on the downslide of disintegration; viz., at the September 1969 Venice conference, of which Debord wrote: "There were fourteen situationists present, but they had the spirit of two." In any case, the Americans resigned or split from the S.I. in 1970 with a rather sour aftertaste. Verlaan and Chasse have preferred "private" life ever since, while Elwell has done his best work since leaving the S.I. Only Jon Horelick has bothered to continue in a constricted, arcane pamphlet medium of dubious value.[45]

IT WAS OUT OF WHAT Chasse and Elwell had dubbed "the gelatinous sea of Bay Area 'oppositions'" that the most impassioned efforts to Americanize S.I. theory or *tactique* next emerged. The New Yorkers weren't wrong, but the slippery nature of ideologies, and of the character-structures that could juggle grotesque inconsistencies inside the same skull, was only most *pronounced* in California vis-a-vis the more clear-cut sectarian procedures among some East Coast politicos. (Vis-a-vis Europe, such blithe and casual incoherence was all American.)

In *The Totalitarian Temptation* (1976), the Trilateral Commission publicist Jean-Francois Revel used the terms "pidgin Marxism, or unofficial Stalinism" to describe the mentality that was coming to prevail on the post-1968 European Left: "A mishmash of Marxist-Leninist as well as Marcusean and [ultra-] leftist ideas, accompanied by third-world postulates."[46] My point here is that such "pidgin Marxism"—with some populist, countercultural, and other ingredients tossed in—was *always* endemic to the U.S. New Left, and persists unclarified to this day. (Rare the American neo-Stalinist who is even aware of being one, much less ready to cop to it.)

The reasons are historical. There was an almost unbroken continuity in the European Left, with each "parent" Stalinist, Trotskyist, and anarchist group sprouting its "youth branch," while traditional formality (drafting "position paper," enunciating "program," and so on) remained the prevalent mode right up until 1968. We might recall that the S.I. was, with certain reservations, quite impressed by the freewheeling style of Berkeley's 1968 Free Speech Movement, and that the "new spirit" they commended in May '68 took a longer time bursting through the stodgier European atmosphere.

Back in the U.S.A., the Old Left had virtually vanished after 1948, so that the next crop of young rebels very much had the sense of starting from scratch. Most were too busy in their blind rage against "war, poverty and racism" to scrutinize musty texts. Even for the more serious-minded and the "red diaper babies," the dim memories of sterile Trotsky-vs.-Stalin disputes just seemed to threaten the freshness, the sweet excitement of those heady days.

Obviously, a deluge of pop sociology and other demeaning crap has been written on that period, the motive often being the envy of older New York literati for sex-crazed California kids (cf. Lasch or the neoconservatives), the result being to trivialize "the children of Mao and Coca-Cola." My purposes here are quite different. I'd almost argue that the oft-lamented "ignorance of history" was, in the case of the sixties radicals, a blessing in disguise—or at least a neutral phenomenon. If it gave rise to all kinds of ghastly and laughable contradictions, it also unleashed a vitality that most Frankfurt School worshipers—and some S.I.-influenced Americans—have yet to fully appreciate.[47]

*I*N *AT DUSK* (1975), DAVID Jacobs and Chris Winks charted two broad courses taken by the S.I.-influenced Americans: "the popularizers," as against those of "a more theoretical inclination, being involved with a particularization of situationist analysis to the specific context of American capitalism."[48] I heartily agree with much of *At Dusk*, but the bit just cited could not be more misleading. What they *mean* to say, as is evident from the rest of the text, is that the "popularizers" proceeded as if S.I. theory were a nicely finished and perfect import, obviating the need for any further homework. Since I was, and shall remain, one of those damnable "popularizers," I can attest that this insinuation just wasn't true of me, or of any of my favorite collaborators. (There were some unfortunates who produced crude, ill-considered work, but this was mostly due to their personal shortcomings; in principle, they had nothing against "particularizing" or improving on the S.I.)

Besides, it is pointless to use "popularizer" in this pejorative sense. It is a neutral term, while "vulgarizer" is the pejorative one. What's needed are stipulative criteria for determining when and how an attempt at popularization slips into vulgarization. Meanwhile, more serious problems are *dilution* and *recuperation*, such as when a "pidgin Marxist" like Stanley Aronowitz borrows a few ill-digested S.I. notions to liven up a soporific book or to modernize the image of his Democratic Socialist Alliance.[49] (We will surely see more such monstrosities, if popularizers like myself have greater success.)

On the other hand, *At Dusk* is closer to the bull's-eye when it discusses those who began their S.I. apprenticeship in the Bay Area's Contradiction group, for whom "a collapse of theory as social criticism" led to "theorizing about theorizing," to a "narrowing of the scope of critical inquiry," and to "mere commentary on secondary issues in situationist theory." *At Dusk* is also close to correct in speaking of a "situationist etiquette . . . in the stylized comportment of groups toward each other." But what's missing there is the fact that my friends and I *never* played along with such silliness. Even though Ken Knabb, Isaac Cronin, et alia had nary a single gracious word to say about us, we opted to address the wider world, and left it to them to hurl charges of "behindism" or "counterfeitism" or the quasi-mandatory "pro-situ" back and forth at one another.[50]

To be sure, I don't wish now to resume this not-so-merry minuet. As I've noted, Knabb performed an invaluable service for English-speaking radicals by publishing his meticulous *S.I. Anthology*. Also recently, Isaac Cronin (with Terrel Seltzer) has pioneered the situationist use of videotape in *Call it Sleep* (1982). (I'm not terribly impressed with the result, but I'm sure others will benefit from it.)

What interests me more is the perennial question of the target audience for any agitation. Reading back over the Knabb/Cronin pamphlet literature of the early seventies, I am most struck by its cloistered feel. To care about it, one would have to accept that being a "pro-situ" is the most grievous sin that any knave could commit, and that being the Rightful Inheritor of the S.I. is the *summum bonum* of life itself. Clearly, some kind of perceptual warp occurs when one assumes that "the burning questions" for one's handful of friends hold the slightest interest for the population at large.

At the same time, I've come up against the limits of public statements which are

Alienation (by Collective Inventions).

A L I E N A T I O N

In capitalist space no one can hear you scream.

© 1979 TWENTIETH CENTURY FIX

TWENTIETH CENTURY PRODUCTION REPRESENTS **A L I E N A T I O N**

STARRING YOU AS YOURSELF, AT WORK, AT HOME, OUT SHOPPING, IN YOUR LEISURE TIME
CO-STARRING WAGE LABOR, SURPLUS VALUE & COMMODITY CULTURE

EXECUTIVE PRODUCER WORLD CAPITALISM   PRODUCED BY HIERARCHY, COERCION AND SEDATION   DIRECTED BY PROFIT MOTIVE
STORY BY MILTON FRIEDMAN & J.K. GALBRAITH   SCREENPLAY BY WALT DISNEY   MUSIC BY NATIONAL CASH REGISTER   NORMALVISION®   ARTIFICIAL COLORING®

 PAIN BY DELUXE®   MOTION PICTURE SOUNDTRACK PLAYING CONTINUOUSLY EVERYWHERE

EDUARDO CALDERON

155

Ward: *The Situationists Reconsidered*

too "at large," aimed like scattershot toward a hypothetical Average Person who may or may not exist. *At Dusk* explores the pitfalls of approaching "the proletariat" as a singular (rather than plural) entity, and of failing to "explicate the various categories and subdivisions within this class."

The challenge, then, is to find the means to speak not only to other revolutionaries, nor to an amorphous mass, but to specific groups, or subgroups, with a precision and insight that acquires the resonant power of recognizability. For instance, to the extent that "On the Poverty of Student Life" played *effectively* on the status-anxiety and self-image of a certain kind of student—viz., one with the "humanist" illusions of a liberal-arts orientation—one can see why it was the most popular S.I. text (half a million copies in nine languages). So, too, one can grasp why the same text would have far less impact among the more cynical-pragmatic students in the U.S. today.

In the narrative arts, one speaks of a novelist or playwright "having an ear"—or lacking one—for the nuances of dialect within specific milieus. To bring radical theory from the general clouds back down to particular patches of Earth—or from the margins into the mainstream—one must likewise "have an ear" for whomever one encounters: in one-to-one conversation, in *détournement*, in local actions, or in the more ambitious "texts." By this standard, the most telling thing one could say of a poor effort is: "What are they talking about? I've never met anyone *like* that..." (remarks I've often muttered when reading the worst S.I.-influenced stuff).

To cut through all the bullshit, to make others say: "Yes, this is how it is, how we live"—that's how real dialogue begins....

THE *AT DUSK* authors themselves had once been members of Point-Blank, some of whom began as a gang of insolent brats at Palo Alto High School with a lively, if raw, pronunciamento on *The End of High School*. Point-Blank made its mistakes, such as calling for a *situationist* revolution, whereas the

S.I. itself had only set about advancing the *social* revolution. (Most other Point-Blank errors are adeptly reappraised in *At Dusk*.)

But Point-Blank, to its credit, also maintained a fairly high level of graphic quality—not for them the excuse that "we haven't got time to make this look better."[51] Their *détournement* of the U.C. Berkeley student paper was, in many respects, exemplary. Several thousand copies of *The Last Daily Cal* were, in May 1972, surreptitiously deposited at all the campus distribution points where somnambulant students routinely picked up the dreary rag it parodied. The front page revealed why this was to be the *last* issue— complete with a letter from the Chancellor "thanking" the staff for having been such well-behaved liberals—while inside was a scathing assault on some cozy assumptions of the Berkeley scene. This "intervention" certainly had the desired, disorienting effect. Not only was the paper read with more avid curiosity than usual, but the "real" *Daily Cal* staff was compelled to make an embarrassed public denial— which, of course, was feeble and too late.

Still, there is a useful lesson here on the limits of *détournement*. Both the *At Dusk* authors and Point-Blank ex-member Chris Shutes[52] later downplayed the value or impact of this and other would-be "scandals." Yet such disappointment itself is the result of having had an inflated expectation of what might have been accomplished in the first place. My comrades and I later spoke of "The Myth of the Magic Bullet;" i.e., the unstated but operative assumption in those days was that if some single project were just potent enough, just timely enough, then people would run right out and commence the social revolution—or at least a healthy-sized insurrection—the very next day. If *détournement* doesn't work—Are we being too coy? Is the joke going over everyone's heads?—then we'll try a direct "statement-in-the-positive."

Obviously, we needed a more sober, deflated set of criteria for how to ascertain whether or not something "worked." We had read our Debord on "not expecting miracles from the working class," on approaching our own activity with "a certain fatigue." But it has to be admitted that, as late as 1975, our youth and our ambivalence toward the Bay Area Left— hating its Maoist, mystical, and reformist deformations, but unready to let go of the

presumption that the underlying rebellious impetus could still, somehow, be set right—kept us from taking to heart what we saw perfectly well. Not only did the pursuit of "The Magic Bullet" repeatedly end up in the "postpartum depression" that made so many of us unduly hard on ourselves, it also—along with the aforementioned "situationist etiquette"—made all concerned brutally harsh with each other. In surroundings where no one else was about to utter a peep of encouragement, this pins-and-needles bitchiness did nothing for the morale. Only the hard way would we relearn the meaning of comradely consideration, of the senses of proportion and of humor (about *ourselves*), and of "knowing how to wait."

MY FEELINGS ARE ME

Here is your chance to write how you feel. There can be no "right" or "wrong" feelings. Your feelings are very important because they are yours. Finish these sentences.

1. Today I feel <u>but tomorrow I might not be so lucky</u>.
2. I get mad when <u>I consider the enemies who will predecease my revenge</u>.
3. I feel bad when <u>I get caught</u>.
4. To me school is <u>work without wages</u>.
5. Most of my teachers are <u>poor parodies of complete human beings</u>.
6. My parents are really <u>not to blame for what work & moralism did to them</u>.
7. I would rather <u>make history</u> than <u>read about it</u>.
8. I know I will never <u>go along to get along</u>.
9. Most people think I <u>don't understand what I know only too well</u>.
10. I get scared when <u>I wonder why they let me run loose</u>.
11. I am happiest when <u>I'm dead drunk, ejaculating or fast asleep</u>.
12. I would like to <u>own a hand-held Exocet missile</u>.
13. My future is <u>the plaything of evil fools</u>.
14. To me, a job <u>is self-sale on the installment plan</u>.
15. I will finish school when <u>I can no longer postpone the inevitable</u>.
16. Working and going to school is <u>having your shit and eating it too</u>.
17. School without a job is <u>proof that half-loafing is better than none</u>.
18. Money in my pocket is <u>the best place for it till we burn it all</u>.
19. I like to get money from <u>out of thin air like the Government does</u>.
20. Looking for work sounds <u>almost as bad as finding it</u>.
21. My friends are <u>filling in while my enemies are otherwise occupied</u>.
22. I am studying for <u>the Civil Service exam for Surgeon-Genital</u>.

My Feelings Are Me (by Bob Black).

On a happier note, I can report that, by the later 1970s, the more sensible attitude was widely in evidence. For instance, former members of Point-Blank, regrouped as Collective Inventions, were inclined to collaborate amicably with some of their old adversaries. Indeed, it seemed that *no one* had much appetite for picayune internecine squabbles; at any rate, the pamphlets stopped.

IT WAS IN THE SUMMER of 1972 that a rakish fellow named Stephen Duckat began slipping me sundry S.I. materials. Quite an eye-opener. I was twenty-four years old, and enough of a "pidgin" radical to be simultaneously drawn to Wilhelm Reich and Murray Bookchin, yet swallowing the purportedly "non-doctrinaire" apologetics for Third World Stalinism in *Ramparts*, *Monthly Review*, and just about the entire Left press. I was then working with the "eclectic" Berkeley paper *New Morning*, which was not without its own mild critiques of the more lunatic excesses of the sacrificial and other-directed Left.

From the outset, then, S.I. theory was a bracing tonic for me, but I was dissatisfied with the formulaic transplanting of these ideas into the American setting. I was even more put off by the needlessly precious and convoluted prose style, yet eager to see the valid core of this perspective reach beyond the hermetic "milieu" where it was festering, to little effect.

I was destined to get it from both sides: the purer situ epigones gave me nothing but shit, while the ostensibly "open" and "nonsectarian" forums were closed off to me *tout de suite*.

I relied on my political instincts. What was true of France's Stalinist Left was not so readily applicable to U.S. New Left writers like Carl Oglesby; to older mavericks like Dwight Macdonald, Noam Chomsky or Norman Mailer; or to the "revisionist" historians like William Appleman Williams and his protegés. (Some Europhiles wouldn't even make time to read anyone who didn't bear the right European pedigree.) Since it was these people that I had previously—and since!—respected, and not cardboard buffoons like Tom Hayden, Jerry Rubin, and Bob Avakian, I always stayed wary of the too hastily adopted French import.

I knew there was a great deal more to the counterculture than the "squalid hippie crash pads" my friends so snootily dismissed in their first "theoretical" pamphlet[53] and, for the matter, something far more knotty and elusive about the New Left than a few people joining some preposterous outfit like the Progressive Labor Party. Hence, my participation in "the group" I then met always remained peripheral, guarded, qualified, ad hoc. (Some of them had their doubts about me as well.)

Still, I had a high old time helping Negation (later, For Ourselves) disseminate ingenious posters like "Jesus Loves You—Kill Yourself," "Don't Change Life—Change Leaders" (on the 1972 elections). For later episodes, such as when repentant radical Rennie Davis came to promote his newfound guru, there was

not only a leaflet ("Forget Your Life—Contemplate Mine") but an occasion to heckle, disrupt, and generally make a circus of what threatened to be a deathly serious gathering. Such targets were too easy, of course—as a comrade later quipped, "as broad as a preacher's ass"—but dammit, we had *fun* in those days. It was no less a pleasure to push the *New Morning* paper "past the point of no return" by exposing Berkeley's hippie-Maoist "red Mafia" for what it was. (In retaliation, funding for the paper was promptly terminated.)

No doubt the most exhilarating moments of all were the night-riding graffiti blitzes, a form of adult delinquency so incomparable that I pity anyone who hasn't savored it. (To take up radical critique *solely* by way of polite forums and lonely perusal of texts just isn't the same.) At a time when the writing on Berkeley's walls was descending from the trite to the necrophiliac (from "Free Huey" to "Che—or whoever's dead—Lives"), we deemed it quite the public service to grace the shopping districts with "SHUT UP AND BUY!" and "HURRY UP AND PARK! YOUR BOSSES ARE WAITING!" Another popular item was "MURDER THE ORGANIZERS OF YOUR BOREDOM." There were many others. Isn't it heartwarming how a dozen malcontents can redecorate a city? All it takes is two or three inconspicuous vehicles, a planned itinerary, synchronized watches, and at each stop, two to stand lookout, one to drive the getaway car, and one to inscribe the spray-paint poetry. Billboard modification is a bit trickier, but the resourceful find ways. One brainstorm we never took far enough was the Name the Terrain Game, whereby all public spaces in a given perimeter would have their true identities pinned on them. But "Bureau of Slow Death" on a welfare office and "Museum of Separate Thought" at a university made for a good start....

Above all, it was the intersubjective richness of working/playing with such a remarkable affinity group that is the hardest to convey, and yet made the most vivid impression on me. There were a few dullards hanging around, but nothing—not even subtle peer pressure—was forcing me to befriend them. Moreover, for the first time, I had come across a more or less coherent belief system that enabled me to join in on serious political work while simultaneously indulging my deepest, not-so-secret personal preference: i.e., for sexy intellectuals with a flair for the outrageous. (Not for nothing were we called "elitist";

Jesus Loves You — Kill Yourself

The humiliation and joyless vapidity of daily existence, where life is only survival, is part of the *necessary* suffering, in accord with His plan, that will cleanse your soul for the after life to come.

So, brothers and sisters of the Cross; you who have accepted the Lord Jesus Christ into your hearts, who have forgiven your trespassers, and who regard the daily plate of shit as the Holy Sacrament of Fate — give that final testimony of Faith and

Leap For the Lord

POINT OF DEPARTURE

Come, Children of God, to the Golden Gate Bridge, Sunday, October 8th, 1972, 6 AM to the first annual *Meet-Your-Maker Marathon* and punctuate your life of rigorous devotion and conscientious self-denial with the *supreme* sacrifice:

Jump For Jesus !

(With regard to those sociopathic heretics who feel that boredom *isn't* the Will of God, but the necessary product of a society in which time is money; who say that it's the commodity economy, and its capitalist pimps (forgive them Jesus!), that reduces men and women to mere objects in the order of things, and who have *not yet* recognized the impossibility of changing life on earth: *they* might be better off writing to those God-less malcontents at NEGATION (P.O. Box 1213 Berkeley, Ca. 94701) to discuss such blasphemous matters.)

So as to dispel any unintended illusions let us, as a great Christian once said, make a few things perfectly clear:

It's not because we fear our own freedom that we'll submit to any degradation and to the authorities who enforce it, but because it is only in the *acceptance* of our destiny that any freedom can be found.

The amoral advocates of unbridled passion and world revolution are just *hellbound hedonists* who don't know that self-less renunciation is the only path to heavenly bliss. They say that our move-ment for spiritual rediscovery is an "emotional plague" that infects those whose daily squalor and anaemic will-to-live has made them despair about ever changing life. But how can it be: it's our only hope! Furthermore, let us rectify once and for all that *Satanic Untruth* that the religious excitation we get from being close to Jesus is only a sublimation of our repressed sexuality. After all, *every good Christian knows that genitals are TOOLS OF THE DEVIL and that orgasms are just revolting SEIZURES OF SIN experienced by those into whom the love of God has not penetrated.* And when the atheistic anarchists of today's wayward youth say that God only represents the projected image and repository of *man's* own alienated powers, the supreme but suppressed possibilities of people themselves, they mouth an *irredeemable sacrilege.*

For those who *do* know the Lord, the Kingdom of Heaven awaits you. Jesus died for *you.* You owe Him *at least* your life. So don't forget to join your enlightened brethren October 8th for The-Big-Baptism-In-The-Bay. See you there!

And the Meek Shall Inherit the Earth

EDUARDO CALDERON

Power to the Passive !!

Central Committee
Christian World Liberation Front

Jesus Loves You—Kill Yourself (by Negation).

I'm strongly in favor of any elite that doesn't constrain anyone else, and in which one *earns* one's aura of distinction.) Truly, almost every one of the men and women who were dear to me then are dear to me now. There were never enough of "us," of course, and we never shook the earth as much as we intended to. But we were grand.

THE YEAR 1974 brought the "energy crisis," deep recession, the SLA madness, events in Portugal, plus two very influential texts from Detroit's Black & Red group: *Eclipse and Re-emergence of the Communist Movement* and *Lip and the Self-Managed Counterrevolution.*[54] At the time, the aggregate impact of these and other factors made certain pet "situ" arguments rattle hollow indeed. It's now clear enough that the prolonged contraction in the world economy does *not* signify a "simple return" to the 1930s. Besides, the crux is always how one *responds* to an economic crisis. Yet there was no denying that S.I. predictions of increasing "abundance" had become somewhat embarrassing. We knew it was time, without succumbing to economism or "workerism," to resume the critique of political economy.

Likewise, the Black & Red texts of that year made us more hesitant than ever to trumpet "the Councils" and "self-management" in the parroting manner of some S.I.-influenced people. For the record, it should be added that the S.I. spoke of *generalized* self-management, and always disdained localized "self-management" of the sort attempted in 1973 by the Lip watch-factory workers. Still, the overall thrust of these new critiques was well taken.

In retrospect, most from our "group" would now concur that we then *over-reacted* to the perceived deficiencies of our 1972–1975 phase. Those of us who could sustain the sense of now-or-never urgency about a revolution that was just around the corner, or *had better* be there, spent the next few years in Marxist recantations of childish situationism—hence, the journal *Red-Eye* (1978).[55] The rest of us "responded" to the economic crisis in a

Le Tank Solaire (by Processed World and the Union of Concerned Commies).

more bourgeois fashion; i.e., by taking our own job/career prospects seriously for the first time.

Yet before Negation/For Ourselves gave up the ghost, some of the prime movers completed its two major projects: *The Right To Be Greedy: Theses on the Practical Necessity of Demanding Everything* (1974), and a three-hour radio montage of readings, skits, music, and discussion named *The End of Prehistory* (1975–1976).[56] *The Right to Be Greedy* was a worthwhile but flawed *oeuvre* on the ethical implications of "communist egoism," while the radio project was the one in which I was most centrally involved. It is sprawling, disjointed, and of uneven quality, but even now it deserves a listen from anyone interested in the "situationist" use of electronic media.

Too bad, though. It wasn't The Magic Bullet, either.

IN 1979, SOME OF THE veterans of Point-Blank, Negation/For Ourselves, and related groupings joined forces with some younger anarchists and antinukers to form "The Union of Concerned Commies" (U.C.C.). Preparing for the "No Nukes Is Not Enough" conference, in November of that year, provided the context for libertarian socialists in the antinuke movement to link up with those, like myself, who preferred "the critique of everyday life" to

> "Under the visible fashions that disappear and reappear . . .
> the obvious and secret necessity of revolution."
> G. Debord *Society of the Spectacle*

EDUARDO CALDERON

THE FUNKTIONARIES — Monday, June 9th; 9:30 p.m.

Funktionaries with Debord text (by Melinda Gebbie and By Any Other Name).

issue-oriented politics. For those of us with a "situ" past, it was during these meetings that the degree of maturity became obvious (but a *playful* maturity, nonetheless). We could by then take S.I. theory and *tactique* in stride, so to speak, and we were meeting a new "generation" of radicals, who came of age with feminism, punk rock, and antinuke activism, and among whom the moralism, hysteria, and illusions of sixties diehards were not nearly so thick.

Then, Carter's jittery response to events in Iran and Afghanistan precipitated a brief revival of antidraft and antiwar activities. The U.C.C. donned mock uniforms (as "the John Wayne Peace Institute") and worked up a series of loosely related street-theater skits that linked macropolitical themes (jingoism, militarism, etc.) to the hierarchy and commodification of daily life. Just to make sure that lefties couldn't applaud too easily, the U.C.C. also lampooned Barry Commoner, bourgeois feminists, vegetar-

ians, Leninists, Jane Fonda's opportunist husband, and assorted noxious creatures. In April 1980, a spinoff contingent from the U.C.C. (baptized "The Theater of Operations") shared the stage with my band, The Funktionaries, for an extravaganza called "Blame God It's Monday!" (thus ensuring that the club owner wouldn't invite us back, even though we packed the place).

A few of the U.C.C. perpetrators have since been active in the collective that publishes the quarterly *Processed World*,[57] which certainly "has an ear" for the information-handling and clerical-work sector of the proletariat in which most of them happen to find themselves employed. (A vicarious fascination with the shrinking "industrial" sector had always been a weakness of earlier S.I.-modeled efforts.) *Processed World* is not yet as analytically rigorous as its more experienced detractors would like it to be, but I think it has so far served its limited function adroitly.

Basic Principles of Resistance
(Bulletin #8 — Solidarity)

The following is some practical advice for workers in any job or country. It was published underground by the Warsaw chapter of Solidarity, dated December 30, 1981.

1. During a strike or other form of protest, stay with your colleagues.
2. Do not establish Strike Committees. Protect your leaders and organizers. Basic principle of action: the entire crew goes on strike — there are no leaders.
3. In contacts with the police or the military you are uninformed, you know nothing, you have heard nothing.
4. Do not denounce ordinary people. Your enemies are: the policeman, the eager conformist, the informer.
5. Work slowly; complain about the mess and incompetence of your supervisors. Shove all decisions, even the most minor, into the lap of commissars and informers. Flood them with questions and doubts. Don't do their thinking for them. Pretend you are a moron. Do not anticipate the decisions of commissars and informers with a servile attitude. They should do all the dirty work themselves. In this way you create a void around them, and by flooding them with the most trivial matters you will cause the military-police apparatus to come apart at the seams.
6. Eagerly carry out even the most idiotic orders. Do not solve problems on your own. Throw that task onto the shoulders of commissars and informers. Ridiculous rules are your allies. Always remember to help your friends and neighbors regardless of the martial law rules.
7. If you are instructed to break mutually contradictory rules, demand written orders. Complain. Try to prolong such games as long as possible. Sooner or later the commissar will want to be left in peace. This will mark the beginning of the end of the dictatorship.
8. As often as possible take sick leave to care for an ''ill'' child.
9. Shun the company of informers, conformists and their ilk.
10. Take active part in the campaign to counter official propaganda, spreading information about the situation in the country and examples of resistance.
11. Paint slogans, hang posters on walls and distribute leaflets. Pass on independent publications — but be cautious.

Down Time! (by Solidarinosc and Processed World).

Ward: *The Situationists Reconsidered*

CONCLUSION

Every philosopher. . .participates in the impure reality of his age.
—Paul Nizan

We are going to die one day, soon. Let us therefore not be unworthy of our pride and our ambitions. This, I believe, is Guy Debord's message.

—a *Le Monde* reviewer

The 1980s present a host of novel challenges for radical critique. If one observes Reagan or Thatcher domestic policies, legitimized by recuperation of right-wing "libertarian" populism, one sees a pattern of *selective* economic recovery, favoring high-tech sectors to the detriment of dying "smokestack" industries, resulting in all kinds of dislocations, regional discrepancies, etc. Thus, unlike the 1930s, the hardships do not fall as evenly across the entire labor-selling class—a fact which powerfully impedes classwide solidarity, already undermined by racism, suburbia, and false consciousness. Also, these brave new adjustments in the organic composition of capital are being prettified, for the "hip" young intelligentsia, by variants of Alvin Toffler's "third wave" ideology. Meanwhile, parts of the Third World enjoy the opulent influx of petrodollars, while a so-called "fourth world" sinks into a wretched abyss of International Monetary Fund indebtedness.

In the "cultural" sphere, ludicrous but not ineffective attempts to resuscitate the most archaic forms of conditioning (patriotism, Cold War paranoia, fundamentalist religion, *ad nauseam*) manage to coexist with a cocaine-drenched Wall Street and Culture Industry, the flagrant pornification of television, and other completely incongruous phenomena.

In response, the sad little Left seems irretrievably locked in on automatic pilot: the fight against cutbacks, voter registration for black mayors, the rearguard defense of a discredited Welfare State, and an anti-imperialist rhetoric as super-annuated as the now-fading U.S. hegemony.

What, if anything, can S.I. theory and tactics contribute to the elucidation of the *present* situation?

One can begin to answer by recalling that, in terms of program and (lack of) vision, most of the Left is bogged down in even earlier time frames. One can also note that it is only in this decade that competent translations and editions of the major S.I. source texts, along with serious critical discussion of them, are being made widely available in our language.[58]

But it will probably be up to those who newly "discover" S.I. theory, and who then try their own hands and imaginations at S.I. tactics, to provide any adequate answer.

There is a missing link between theory and tactics, of course. It's known as *strategy*. The S.I. never really formulated one. For that reason, the S.I. *as organization* has little to teach us that we couldn't learn better through devising our own strategy —and *program*. (Questions of "organization" could only be broached further down the road.)

On the brighter side, we can at least feel relieved that many of the obstructions which hobbled previous generations no longer loom so large today. There is no massive, popularly respected Communist Party—nor, in the U.S., even a social-democratic one—to corrupt political discourse and to stand guard as intermediary between radical minorities and the rest of the proletariat. Even the minor nuisances of the sixties and early seventies—white guilt, Third World romanticism, reformist naiveté, and the more male-hating and moralizing strains of feminism[59]—are not nearly as pervasive as they once were.

We face, then, something like a clear field or, as the S.I.'s Raoul Veneigem defined it, an "interworld. . .a completely public realm, open to every kind of experiment, an exposed battlefield between creative spontaneity and its corruption." This is not to underestimate the enormity of the obstacles still standing. Indeed, so far the proletariat has known *nothing but* failure and defeat. This means that even the most Promethean efforts of centuries amount to so much piss in the wind. And no one should rule out the alarmist scenarios of nuclear and/or ecocidal Armageddon. But the adventures of the dialectic are *still* not over. Tom Paine knew: "We have it in our power to begin the world again." Just as the Wobblies knew that those who work the machines *always* have the potential to bring them grinding to a halt.

Still, I wouldn't quibble if someone suggested that our situation really is hopeless. Hope, after all, is a treacly Christian sentiment, and a poor substitute for intention, determination, resolve. Ultimately, we need no better answer to the glib pessimists and the unadventurous whiners in our midst than the one that Christopher Columbus gave to a disgruntled crewman who complained, just eight days before the momentous landing, that they were all risking their lives for "a mere speculative opinion."

Columbus retorted: *So it is: I cannot deny it. But consider a little. If at present you and I, and all our companions, were not in this vessel, in the midst of this sea, in this unknown vessel, in a state as uncertain and perilous as you please; in what other condition of life should we pass these days? Perhaps more cheerfully? Or should we not rather be in some greater trouble or solicitude, or else full of tedium? I care not to mention the glory and utility we shall carry back, if the enterprise succeeds according to our hope.* Should no other fruit come from this navigation, to me it appears most profitable inasmuch as for a time it preserves us free from tedium, makes life dear to us, and makes valuable to us many things that otherwise we would not have considered. (Emphasis added.)

Guy Debord completed that line of thought: "And as passivity makes its bed, so shall it lie in it."△

NOTES

The following notes are far from exhaustive. Highly motivated individuals who wish to know more can direct inquiries to me, c/o The Real Comet Press.

1. My use throughout of "S.I.-influenced" is a bit awkward, but to fairly treat *non*members of the S.I. I wanted a more neutral, less loaded term than the old "pro-situ" epithet. (On the other hand, "S.I.-inspired" would have been too flattering a designation for some awfully uninspired efforts.)

2. No one should suppose that such a brief introductory survey could exempt them from the rigors of a thoroughgoing scrutiny of the S.I. corpus of theory. After all, there are only half a dozen major texts (i.e., it's not like tackling the complete words of Marx or Freud). These include: *Society of the Spectacle* by Guy Debord; *The Revolution of Everyday Life* by Raoul Veneigem; René Viénet's unpublished (in English) book on May '68; Knabb's *Anthology*; *The Veritable Split in the International* by Debord and G. Sanguinetti. Also, for other evaluations of the S.I.-influenced Americans, compare mine with *At Dusk* (cited below) or *The American Situationists* by Isaac Cronin.

3. Walter Benjamin, "Theses on the Philosophy of History," in *Illuminations* (New York: Schocken Books, 1973), 255.

4. *Situationist International Anthology*, edited and translated by Ken Knabb (1981), available from: Bureau of Public Secrets, P.O. Box 1044, Berkeley, CA 94701. Also, on the early S.I., see the Greil Marcus review of Knabb in the *Voice Literary Supplement*, May 1982.

5. Thesis #191 from Guy Debord, *Society of the Spectacle* (1981), the revised 1977 English translation by Black & Red, P.O. Box 02374, Detroit, MI 48202.

6. I discussed Wolfe/Hughes a bit further in an earlier draft of this "Antecedents" section, which appeared in the *San Francisco Review of Books*, May–June 1983, as "After Modernism: The End of Politics, the Realization of Art."

7. See Marian Kester's reflections on Kandinsky in *Passion and Rebellion: The Expressionist Heritage* (South Hadley, Mass.: J. F. Bergin, 1982), as well as Charles Jencks on the Bauhaus in relation to the 1918 German Council movement in *Modern Movements in Architecture* (New York: Anchor/Doubleday, 1983).

8. The joke here is that the S.I. wrote a lot of pamphlets/articles about the need to get beyond writing pamphlets/articles. Of these, the best are Debord's "Cinema and Revolution" and Viénet's "The Situationists and the New forms of Action Against Politics and Art." Both are in Knabb's *Anthology*.

9. Debord, *Society of the Spectacle*, #100.

10. I opt to use "Marxian" instead of "Marxist"—a merely semantic distinction, of course, but still a useful one.

11. See Murray Bookchin, Fredy Perlman, E. F. Schumacher, John Zerzan, or a host of other regressive thinkers which Detroit's *Fifth Estate* reveres regularly.

12. See especially Debord, *Society of the Spectacle*, #79–95.

13. Ibid., #118.

14. From the anarchist side, see Daniel Guerin's *Anarchism* (New York: Monthly Review Press, 1971). Meanwhile, from the recently burgeoning literature on the older council-communist and "libertarian Marxist" currents, I'd suggest: Dick Howard's *The Marxian Legacy* (New York: Urizen Books, 1977); Richard Gombin's *The Radical Tradition* (New York: St. Martin's, 1979); Raya Dunayevskaya's *Marxism and Freedom* (Atlantic Highlands, N.J.: Humanities Press, 1982); and Russell Jacoby's *Dialectic of Defeat* (New York: Cambridge University Press, 1981). Each book is flawed—and only Jacoby can *write*—but the research is substantial.

15. Reich's books are now widely available, Breton is taught in any decent art school, and Marcuse needs no plug from me. The quote is from Dwight Macdonald's 1946 essay, *The Root is Man*. For some surprising similarities between the midforties Macdonald and some later S.I. themes, see my article, "The Mercurial Mind of Dwight Macdonald" in the *Soho Arts Weekly* (27 June 1984).

16. Debord, *Society of the Spectacle*, #191.

17. Webster's distinguishes "artistic" as "an urge to create" from "aesthetic" as "delight in contemplating that which has been created."

18. Consider Breton's quixotic concern with "honor" and other moralistic sludge, or his gushing, sycophantic tone when describing his meeting with Trotsky. Franklin Rosemont just carries on this tradition, without blinking.

19. See "The Geopolitics of Hibernation" in Knabb, *Anthology*, 76–82. (This 1962 critique should be mandatory reading at all nuclear freeze rallies.)

20. Consult the "Definitions" on page 45 of Knabb, *Anthology*.

21. In other words, it is "not sacred" and can also be "debased by a wrong, unworthy, or vulgar use."

22. As you can gather, I've seen too much Lower Manhattan "performance art" recently.

23. Guy Debord uses this one, along with about three chapters worth of other definitions in the opus cited.

24. Warning: anyone can play this game—Larouche's loony Labor Party has already done so twice, with counterfeit *New York Times* supplements—and, at some forseeable point, a glut could have a numbing effect.

25. Note the qualitative leap in seriousness and sophistication that separates the 1966 S.I. journal from the first nine numbers.

26. At the time, amusingly enough, the French CP's nightmare was that several "thousands of these situationists" were out to torment them. Therefore I'm amazed that René Viénet's documented history of the May–June events has yet to be published in the U.S. Until it is, glean what you can from Alfred Willener's *Action-Image of Society*, Vladimir Fisera's *Writing on the Wall*, Bernard Brown's *Protest in Paris*, Richard Gombin's *Origins of Modern Leftism*, or my own "Fifteen Years After May '68" in *The Village Voice*, May 1983.

27. Knabb, *Anthology*, 319–337.

28. See Viénet's own testimony, or "Our Goals and Methods in the Strasbourg Scandal" in Knabb, *Anthology*, 204–212.

29. Some of these can still be seen in *The Penguin Book of Political Comics* (New York: Penguin, 1982). However, the translations are execrable, as is Steef Davison's accompanying text.

30. For instances of each, see the quotes Knabb compiles in "The Blind Men and the Elephant," in *Anthology*, 381–392.

31. See Viénet on Cohn-Bendit's March 22nd Movement in Knabb, *Anthology*, 375.

32. Ibid., 178.

33. Jean-Jacques Raspaud and Jean-Pierre Voyer, *L'Internationale Situationniste: protagonistes, chronologie, bibliographie* (Paris: Champ Libre, 1972).

34. Compare with the more idiosyncratic conservative view in Hannah Arendt's *On Revolution* (New York: Viking, 1963). Disdaining the French Revolution in favor of the American, she links ours to the later Council movement in Europe. Contrarily, see Dunayevskaya, *Marxism and Freedom*, lauding the direct democracy of the 1793 *enragés*.

35. See Gabriel Kolko, *The Limits of Power: The World and U.S. Foreign Policy, 1945–1954* (New York: Harper and Row, 1972).

36. In retrospect, it's clear that FDR's New Deal anticipated the Keynesian social-democracies of postwar Europe, inserting a solid center across the Continent's Great Fascist/Communist Divide.

37. The truth, of course, is that this grand "International" was Paris-centered, class-privileged, and male-dominated to a fault—but not because they preferred to be.

38. Knabb, *Anthology*, 153–160.

39. A wretched translation was published in London by "B. M. Piranha" in 1974.

40. Guy Debord, *Preface to the Fourth Italian Edition of "The Society of the Spectacle"* (London: Chronos, 1979), 7.

41. See the relevant S.I. journal articles from #10 and #11 in Knabb, *Anthology*, 148–224.

42. Some recent developments are reported/analyzed in *Processed World* and in *No Middle Ground*, 495 Ellis Street, #781, San Francisco, CA 94102. Also, a 1973 "Caribbean Situationist" record album, *None Shall Escape*, plus a journal, *Caribbean Correspondence*, can still be obtained c/o: K. Collins, 224 Elsie Street, San Francisco, CA 94110.

43. See Phil Mailer, *Portugal: The Impossible Revolution* (New York: Free Life, 1977).

44. Exceptionally good in this regard are recent Italian and German issues of *Semiotexte(e)*, 522 Philosophy Hall, Columbia University, New York, NY 10027—also, the journal *Midnight Notes*, 12 Parkton Road, Jamaica Plain, MA 02130. Likewise, check the sources cited in my piece on the 1981 U.K. riots, "Broken English: We Have Seen the Future, and It Refuses To Work," in the *Voice Literary Supplement*, December 1983. Sorely lacking, by the way, is an adequate history of the *British* situationist milieu.

45. Horelick's prose style reads like a stilted translation from the French. *Il n'est pas français.*

46. Revel, of course is an utter Ubu, yet even he can make mincemeat out of the common beefs of most leftists. This is one reason I drink to excess.

47. Norman Mailer's *Armies of the Night* still conveys that vitality, remarkably well. You won't find it in *Telos*.

48. David Jacobs and Christopher Winks, *At Dusk: The Situationist Movement in Historical Perspective* (Berkeley: Perspectives, 1975), 60. This out-of-print text ought to be reissued.

49. See his book *False Promises*, and see what I mean. More recently, Aronowitz has decided that Samuel Gompers wasn't so bad after all. He should know.

50. They denounced and misquoted us but never supplied an address whereby others could inspect our work and form their own judgments. Knabb's address is given above. Cronin's is: Suite 270, 1442A Walnut Street, Berkeley, CA 94709.

51. The quote is a lame excuse I used to hear from my comrades. I never liked it.

52. Chris Shutes (with Gina Rosenberg) wrote *Disinterest Compounded Daily*. More recently, he has written *On the Poverty of Berkeley Life*. His address: P.O. Box 4502, Berkeley, CA 94704.

53. *The State and Counterrevolution: What Is Not To Be Done* (Berkeley: Negation, 1972).

54. Contact: Black & Red, address above.

55. A copy of this one-shot magazine may still be available c/o Louis Michaelson at *Processed World*. Jean Barrot's "critique" of the S.I. is featured therein.

56. *The Right To Be Greedy* was recently reprinted by Loompanics Unlimited, a right-wing libertarian outfit at: P.O. Box 1197, Pt. Townsend, WA 98368. (True to caveat emptor principles, they've botched the typesetting and jacked up the price.) *The End of Prehistory* may still be requested from: D. S. Crafts, c/o Lutra Recordings, 2000 Center Street, Box 1200, Berkeley, CA 94704.

57. The *Processed World* address is: 55 Sutter St., Suite 829, San Francisco, CA 94104.

58. As we say in my neighborhood: about fucking time.

59. Women Against Pornography is lately taking a beating from some highly lucid, fun-loving feminist critics in *Heresies*, *Processed World* and *The Village Voice*.

60. Columbus is thus quoted on pages 22–23 of the 1925 classic, *In the American Grain*, by William Carlos Williams (New York: New Directions Paperback, 1956).

ARCHIE SHEPP:

We Must Move toward a critique of American Culture

An interview with the musician conducted by Kofi Natambu, editor of Solid Ground: A New World Journal, *in Detroit in September 1981.*

Solid Ground: Archie, you, along with people like Duke Ellington, Lester Young, Charles Mingus, Max Roach and many others, have long been recognized as one of the most politically conscious and socially responsible black artists in the history of black creative music. I'd like to ask you in terms of today's scene, do you think younger musicians are aware of this responsibility?

Archie Shepp: Oh yes, I think we would find a good deal of sensitivity in these areas. But then you would have to define that, because what do you mean by younger people? Which area? Now if you're talking about kids who listen to "soul music," I don't think they're too aware. And they haven't demonstrated either a great deal of political responsibility or sensitivity, social responsibility or sensitivity; and furthermore, I think they're in a syndrome which is taking them downhill. For the few African-Americans who have listened to the music of Coltrane, Ellington, Lester Young, Hawkins, on through to the modern era Chicago, the AACM, Chico (Freeman) and

those cats, it is an entirely different story. I think that those guys represent a different sensibility and a different area of consciousness. They're coming *from something* that is rapidly disappearing among the great majority of our youth. In other words, what I'm saying is that black youth, if we really want to get into it, are very complex. I taught in the New York City school system for two years, from 1961 to 1963. I teach at the University of Massachusetts now. I've taught a wide spectrum of black youth. I've taught pre-school youngsters in the Bronx and in Brooklyn when I was just a kid out of college. So I kind of know what happens to black youth. I mean what goes with "rock 'n roll" as far as I'm concerned is a kind of plantation mentality.

Solid Ground: In terms of your experiences in the past ten years or so, teaching in higher education institutions like U-Mass at Amherst, can you share with us some of your feelings about that experience and how you feel that is contributing to a deeper or broader understanding of social responsibility in the arts?

Archie Shepp: Well, let me put it this way: I asked a group of young people recently in a class of black and white students—Who was Sidney Bechet? None of them knew who he was. Neither Negroes or whites. And then in my lecture, I asked: Who was Paul Robeson? And none of them knew who he was... well, one, a white student. So at that point I reflected on the need for the professional at the level of academia, that is to say: Does the artist have a role to play, particularly the black artist? And I say: *You damn well right! He's got to have.* Because if I go to France, say I go to the town of Nancy. They built a big statue there to Sidney Bechet, one of the greatest clarinetists, soprano saxophonists, and proponents of the blues this country has ever known. In France, they built a statue to him—every school kid knows who this man is. Here in the place of his birth (United States), knowledge of him has completely disappeared. We may look at these people somewhat as role models as well. Role models are not only successful TV personalities or successful musicians. They represent the entire spectrum of our people who achieve some degree of success in whatever their life endeavor is. In this case Bechet was a musician, but I think he represents something important to black youth they should be hip to. So what's the need for me at that level, what is the need to proliferate people like me? I'd say we are *essential* to raise the level of consciousness in respect to culture. I think also of people like Harold Cruse who teaches at the University of Michigan. He is a very essential person because he is a *critic of culture*. Negroes know nothing about their culture. They just boogeying baby. That's why you have the present administration in Washington. Sad, man. . . .

Solid Ground: In terms of what we can do today, I know that people like Jackie McLean at Hartford, Max Roach at U-Mass, Larry Ridley at Rutgers, Clifford Thornton at Wesleyan, etc., are trying to educate black youth throughout the country, but it seems to me that there's some difficulty in terms of that filtering down process in communicating to black youth some of the aesthetic values of the culture that have been developed in creative music. What do you feel is going to be important in the future for black scholars and musicians to do to rectify this problem?

Photograph of Archie Shepp by Deborah Ray.

Shepp: We Must Move Toward a Critique of American Culture

Archie Shepp: Well, I think again I would call Cruse's statement to mind, the challenge he raises to the intellectual, and to the artist to forge a dialog, a *critique* of American culture. At a certain level it cannot be left to the musician. I don't think we can just rely on B. B. King or Muddy (Waters) to begin to form those kind of slick, sophisticated alliances: Neo-Quasi-Marxist-Post-Socialist-Renaissance ideas that really don't belong to their chain of experiences. Or musicians, per se. Musicians of course have their role to play, but you see I've often challenged young students, black students: Why haven't you studied and organized? The Chinese have discussed black culture, the Russians have talked about it. They say it's decadent, they say we play the blues because of slavery. And a lotta niggas believe that! That's how ignorant they are. They've never really even thought about the fact that the blues is the basis of their identity. The basis of the identity of their music, of their *being*, it's a *metaphor* if we understand it. So first the black youth, the students, etc., they have to come together and say: What is it to be black? How do we *define* that? First, they would have to go to their music. After all, Nat Turner is the reputed author of the song called "Steal-Away," one of the Negro spirituals. So it shows us that there is an intrinsic alliance between our politics and our music, because Turner also forged one of the great rebellions in our history. There is an intrinsic relationship between our politics and our culture, specifically our music. Sojourner Truth and Harriet Tubman were very close to music and used music to help people escape from slavery. This is part of the whole African "Song of Allusion," if we get into some musical history. This is how our people carry on these various forms and spin them off into certain meaningful political statements.

So first the black youth must begin to forge a dialog and discuss exactly what is their culture—what does it *mean* to be black? What are the essential components of our culture? What is the blues? What is "jazz"? Should we describe these realities with these old terms that have been handed down to us from slavery? The Africans changed the names of their countries; can't we change the names of our cultural experiences? We're still relating to our music through slave symbols: disco, rock 'n roll. All this is done to keep Negroes from realizing that their music represents the whole (African) diasporic entity. If they could *understand* that what they're doing down in those places, in Haiti and Brazil and Cuba, Condomble, Lucimi...is very close to the syncretism of Afro-Christianity which is the source of so-called jazz music. So first of all what should we do as, say, an "intellectual-academic" constituency? We should confab and dig what it is we are. Maybe when we're listening to Stevie Wonder we're also listening to a Shango rhythm....

Solid Ground: In light of that, some sixteen years ago you made a very famous statement to the effect that the art of black America, and particularly the art of black creative musicians, will serve as the foundation for the development of a true America, an America that is actually responsive to, and reflective of, the different *peoples* that make up this country, and that this is the actual revolutionary legacy of the art. In light of everything you've said thus far, and considering the tremendous problems that we're having in 1981, do you think black artists, scholars, and political people can begin to take that particular sentiment to a higher level of understanding for youth? Given their lack of educational experience in terms of the social values of the art, and because of their ignorance of the history of the art and the culture, do you think this coalition of interests in the black community can unite? Do you think it is possible at this time to bring those people together and educate them?

Archie Shepp: Well, of course it's possible to educate them, but I think we have to consider various approaches. I mean we all constitute certain constituencies, you know, the teacher, the musicians, the activists and so on. But really part of the answer to our problems today has to be seen as *political*. I mean the fact that many of the cities are becoming predominately black is a major factor that we should control and understand. We should also try to spin off into certain kinds of power to secure our position and to make us less vulnerable in an increasingly tentative capitalist context. So I think that's certainly something we should do. In other words, to begin to look at ourselves as an economic and political constituency and entity, and begin to think about how we can perhaps join other groups. And I think they will be particularly from the industrial working classes of the northern urban areas who are becoming disaffected with the tactics that are being used by the current administration in D.C. *And I think that black people will have to develop a much more sophisticated and cohesive political answer.* We were caught totally off-guard by Reagan, and I say Ree-gun, I don't say Ray-gun... because I'm an ex-slave.

Solid Ground: Let's talk a little bit about some of your recent creative contributions in terms of your artistic collaborations with people like blues pianist/composer Horace Parlan. Some of the records that you've made and that have been released in this country in the past three to four years have been of particular interest because they speak to a concern with the history of the music. There's a great emphasis on spiritual and gospel music and also traditional blues. I've noticed that a number of black artists in a number of different idioms are going back to that particular source today. First of all, what do you think accounts for that, and secondly, in your exploration of these forms, what use do you think we can make of them today?

Archie Shepp: Well, the blues: We got that. A nigger, he's the blues, he's "jazz." Niggers gonna play the blues because if you walk into any bar, you're gonna have the blues. The arrangements are slicker today, they do different things. They've borrowed elements of so-called jazz music. They use very sophisticated arrangements, but it's *the blues*. If it's The Delphonics, if it's Donna Summer, somewhere they got to sing that minor third or that flatted seventh that identifies the idiom. Somewhere there's got to be that beat, that *thing* that James Brown says "make you wanna get up and dance." So we got the blues, I think that'll be there. The blues ain't the question; it's that synthetic form that was put together, the combination of ragtime, and the blues that we call "jazz," that some people call "jazz." I call it *great diasporic music* because I feel it's a part of a much larger entity that we need to understand. That I feel we need to comprehend and preserve. It's our classical music, but Negroes don't seem to care much.

Solid Ground: In terms of your own excursions into these areas, do you think that at some point black artists will be able to seriously begin the process of self-determination so that these particular aesthetic forms are made available and more accessible to people?

Archie Shepp: Well, not until black artists begin to make saxophones, drums, automobiles, etc. I think we've got the bull by the tail, really. We can't start with musicians when what we're dealing with is power in its most naked sense. Neutron bombs, etc. All that's rather academic and silly. I don't see why Frank Sinatra should make more money than a plumber—he can't fix a toilet. That's Marx's analogy, but I agree with him. If the toilet breaks down. . . . So I think our whole value system needs to be rearranged. So that's why I say we have to begin with *a people* who understand themselves as *a body politic.* As an entity. A people who get together and say: This is how we're gonna fix our toilets. This is how we're gonna build our buildings. This is how we're gonna play our music. That's how everybody else does it. That's why when you go to college, you don't learn about Ellington, you learn about Beethoven and Brahms. Because those things are pre-arranged. They're arranged by Mr. Ford, they're arranged by Mr. Reagan, they're ordained for us. We are *really*, in a sense, *a captive population* here! I wouldn't say colonial but certainly captive. We need to alter our circumstances greatly while the chance is in our hands. Because I think our condition's being altered through certain psychological states, through the whole element of class and the alienation of the working people from the so-called middle classes of Negroes. Our leadership has been filtered out and killed off. The Martin Luther Kings, the Malcolm Xs, the John Coltranes. All these people constitute a power base that has evaporated.

Solid Ground: One thing that's troubling me, and this is a conversation that I've had many times with many different artists and scholars, is: How do we move beyond theoretical abstractions and the necessity for analysis and for study, into some concrete proposals, practical programs that we can begin to implement today? Because you've very eloquently documented the reasons for our present plight. I'm asking in terms of your own experience, how do you think we can begin to talk about, for example, the education of black youth to change American priorities?

Archie Shepp: Without being redundant, I think there's a necessary first step which begins long before we try to educate youth to these priorities. I think it begins at the academic level, in fact, since I'm so much in touch with African-American youth at the college level. The various black studies departments and programs, other types of cultural apparatus like perhaps even areas of the black news media, "intellectuals," artists should critique, on a national level, the question of culture in several major areas. First to define it in terms of its history, its socioeconomic component and then to divide it in its respective areas of ritual, dance, music and religion.

Solid Ground: Today people are concerned about the direction of America and the rest of the world. When we examine the problems in the Middle East, South Africa, Europe, etc., we see that people are bewildered by their own personal responsibility for what is currently taking place or puzzled by what response to take in these "crises." In terms of your own experience, what do you think is now necessary for a black artist specifically to do as our priorities begin to meet the challenges of the immediate future?

Archie Shepp: Well, it's a big question and I want you to sort of break that down.

Solid Ground: Just pick up on the idea that Harold Cruse often projects: That a cultural revolution is a necessity in the Western world, especially in the United States. Obviously black artists have always played a major role in that struggle. What do you think is going to be our role in that struggle in terms of responding to the situation today?

Archie Shepp: You mean the national or international?

Solid Ground: National and international.

Archie Shepp: Well, again I think it puts the onus on the so-called artist, when I'm not so sure that our artists, per se, are artists in the sense that white people mean, or when we give a white Western definition of an artist. Of course our B. B. Kings and Lester Youngs have always been a part of the audience, in that their role is as an active aspect of the community. So when we put the onus on them as artist, meaning leader, they are only quasi-leaders in a sense because the black musicians are still the Griots. He's buried outside the village. Niggers forget. Then they say what should "an artist" do? What is an artist? That's a big fat white word. Let's define what an artist is, then we'll go on. Let's define what a nigger artist is . . . .

Solid Ground: Let's look at it in terms of the tradition. The Griot, which is a very important concept spiritually and socially. Let's look at it in terms of that. It's clear to me that telling the history of our people in this part of the world has been the primary function of the Griot, both in terms of transforming our consciousness of what's going on in the world, and what we are doing for ourselves. So let's talk about it in terms of that traditional function of the Griot. In terms of today, and the crisis that we've been talking about, what do you think is the function or priority of the traditional black artist?

Archie Shepp: Well, it carries on the "Song of Illusion" like the carnival. We still choose our King and maybe he's B. B. and he says, "I went down to the welfare department to get some grits and stuff, and the woman told me I hadn't been 'round long enough." Well, that's a major statement—that's a Griotic statement. It's illustrative. It speaks for all of us who know the problem, which is most of us. So that's what the black artist is doing. Some of them are "getting over." Look at Motown. How they made millions of dollars off the black community and put nothing back. Even moved out to a bank in California. If black people didn't buy records, they would have nothing. Motown returned none of that money. As I pointed out recently at the National Endowment (and Orrin Keepnews, a major record producer agreed with me on this), though Negroes are reputed to make music and dance, there is not a single "jazz" club owned by a negro in the United States. To me, that is ironic. Italians have Ronzoni spaghetti, the Chinese have a big bank in California, and the niggers don't even have a jazz club. And we talk about the role of our artists?!? That's absurd. I think we are in a very confused and ambivalent state now. Politically speaking, I think that people among us who fancy that they are intellectuals and politically sophisticated should really begin to emerge and begin to develop answers to some of these questions. I mean really forge the dialog itself. Because that's in need of doing as well.

Shepp: We Must Move Toward a Critique of American Culture

Solid Ground: The concern is still, be they artists, scholars, pseudo-intellectuals or activists, the problem remains, and I think this is crucial. I don't think we can bypass this very easily; the problem remains whatever category a person puts themselves in, or are put in, in the black community there's obviously not the kind of unity that is necessary to begin to do all the things that you've outlined. And this is a recurring kind of problem historically in the black community. To risk sounding redundant, how do you think we begin to do what is necessary in terms of the things that you've outlined? I think as far as the 1980s and 1990s are concerned, that is going to be the crucial issue.

Archie Shepp: Well, I was talking to a friend of mine today. And I was saying that the first thing is we ought to nationalize our music. That's where I would start. Cruse has really put forward an idea like that. If we read between the lines. I raised the question about Motown advisedly, the fact that it was a privately run corporation that developed sort of on a shoestring, you might say, on a street corner with a guy with a piece of paper telling a bunch of kids, "I can make you a star." And in fact Gordy made them "stars" through hard work and so on. Which any inner-directed person could do. But we've never looked at this from a whole community standpoint. How come it's we who make our Nat Coles, our Charlie Parkers, our Coltranes, and we never reap the benefits of any of these rewards? We should begin to own these artifacts. We should have publishing companies, not only nightclubs, not only dances—these abound in our communities, it's our thing but we don't own it. I say nationalize our cultural product.

Solid Ground: In terms of the issue of nationalization of resources in the black community, in your view, how do you begin to do that?

Archie Shepp: I'd start by nationalizing my cultural product and the rest of it I wouldn't even talk about...that's purely from an economic point of view. And in that I think we can take a lesson as a people from Jews and Italians, people who have a very "inside" phenomenon that nobody else knows nothing about. And they don't talk about it on television and that's their thing.

Solid Ground: A lot of people are concerned about the ongoing controversy involving multinational recording outlets. The relationship of black musicians to these institutions and the paucity of black institutions that could conceivably serve as some alternative to this situation. In that area, the area of production and distribution, in terms of cultural independence, what do you think is necessary?

Archie Shepp: Well, once again, I think nationalization is necessary. If we begin there, there's no problem. You see I'm a music publisher as well as a songwriter. When I formed my company (called Dawn of Freedom Publishing Company) it cost $7.50 for a business certificate in New York about fifteen to sixteen years ago. That makes me a licensed publisher. That means even though I don't sell sheet music, I am able to publish my songs when I record them. I can retrieve mechanical licenses for those songs. And as a result, I'm paid a certain royalty. As a writer of a song I'm paid only a penny. As a publisher of a song I can be paid from sixty to ninety-nine cents. So it's not only a question of should we own the artifacts of our artistic community, but look at all the spinoffs. Look at if we had a Detroit Motown Publishing Co., Inc., which belonged to the people. The answer to me seems to be that he felt if Stevie Wonder sold a record, we sold a record. Sixty-forty, seventy-thirty. He'd still be rich, and we'd be rich. Then we'd spin that off. We'd begin to produce the kinds of music, "art music." You might then say an artist could really exist. Music that didn't *have to* make money, that's art music. Artists are like John Coltrane who play music that we listen to because it *belongs* to us. Some of us understand it, some of us believe in it, some of us try to understand it, maybe some of us will understand it later on. We realize it has a certain value to us because it contains musical information that comes out of our tradition. Maybe white people come in a club and don't understand it because they're not part of the whole ritual atmosphere in which this phenomenon was created. I'll give you an example. I was at the National Endowment recently with Chico Freeman and several others, and applicants applied for a grant on the basis of a spiritual song or a gospel piece that he played on the piano. And it was a piece that I thought I might of heard in church as a boy, but Chico recognized it

immediately and began to sing some of the words to it, and so did Frank Foster. And I stopped him and I said, "You know, Chico, that's it, that's what you have that no white Coltrane imitator has." It's the Afro-Christian experience which is fundamental to us and to our community because we bring it all the way from Africa. So I define ritual as a fundamental aspect of our success.

Solid Ground: Some artists have expressed the idea that because of the problems that face us politically and economically, it's not going to be possible for us to develop that ritual aspect of the culture that you speak of, and that because of the intrusions of advanced technology in a capitalist society, black people have not developed a counter-force, or countervailing force to begin to move beyond that. In your view, do you think that under present circumstances, we can develop ritual forms that actually speak to the experience of an urban people?

Archie Shepp: Yes. If we look at music as a form of language and if we look at it as a unifying factor in our historical tradition which keeps the experience of slavery before us, which reminds us of the hardship of our people through the songs that have been played right on up through the 1960s, like (John) Coltrane's music, which tells us about the struggles of our people. There's many ways in which this music could be edifying to us, and a *teaching force*.

Solid Ground: If you look at the contributions of groups like the Art Ensemble of Chicago and that whole AACM development—Muhal Richard Abrams, etc.—there seems to be a very healthy and positive response to that issue. So in that respect, at least, it seems that advances are being made....

Archie Shepp: Oh, I think so, yes.

Solid Ground: In terms of your ongoing relationship with people like Max Roach, do you think you're going to be able to convey that particular message to musicians coming up who may not be aware of their responsibilities in that area? For example, those musicians in the so-called pop and rock fields, etc. What do you think is going to be the spillover effect of the kind of contributions the Art Ensemble of Chicago has made, you have made, Max Roach, etc., in terms of educating these younger musicians and artists to their cultural and social responsibility?

Archie Shepp: None at all. In fact, I hope there's not too much spillover the other way (laughter). . . . I've been trying to make a "rock and roll" record myself man, I need some money! (Everyone cracks up.) You kidding?!? Who's educating who? "Success" is the norm, you know, it's all "Sanford and Son," man. "The Jeffersons." (Sarcastic grin) You gotta git over, you know? That's how you got to do it. And I think these are the standards, like it or not, by which many of our youth live today. Many of our people are forced to live this way. . .it's frustrating.

Solid Ground: But Archie, in the meantime. . .you're still putting out great records, with people like Max Roach, Horace Parlan, etc. Despite the pervasive feeling that black youth and artists are totally apathetic about these issues, people like you remain. You're still out here, playing in different places. . . . What I want to emphasize is that I think it's important for people like yourself to make these younger people aware, in spite of themselves, about their responsibilities in these areas, because obviously I don't think you're going to change. . . .

Archie Shepp: Well, thank you for those kind words, but you know man, I'll tell you why the situation has changed. You see, Bill Cosby and I went to school together and I had a nice conversation with him about this, you know about the influence of a program like "Sesame Street" on our youth. And I raised a question, I said, "Well, Bill, how come you have so much rock 'n roll and disco type music on a show like that, and you don't hear more of the kind of music you and I grew up with, like Bird and 'Trane because I know you know all about this music." And it's a real inside part of his (Cosby's) style. Because I know Bill from when he was a kid when he used to do that kind of stuff in the lunchroom, and crack cats up, twenty-five guys laughing like crazy. But a lot of that comes out of the music that he heard and he does little bits on Miles (Davis) etc., that are very inside, very ritual. So I said, "Why don't you use more of this kind of material for the kids, you know, scat-singing 'ornithology' and these kinds of things that communicated something." And his answer to me seemed to be that he felt the establishment had already taken this thing another way. That he wouldn't have enough of an audience. It wouldn't be commercially successful. So even teaching devices have to have a certain commercial success when we put them in the context of television. So let's say the kind of music you're talking about died out when television came in. That's really my feeling about that, that this sort of music called "jazz" is more or less a museum piece, and it's a forgotten issue.

Solid Ground: Do you feel that way about your own music?

Archie Shepp: Oh, for sure, I think it's becoming more and more what you call an artistic medium. Which means it's becoming more and more for white people, it's becoming more of a kind of museum piece for collectors who have the records. You hear it in Europe. You have to go to places where it's expensive to hear it. In other words, what I'm saying is that it's no longer a viable, dynamic aspect of Negro life. We're not continuing to create Coltranes and Charlie Parkers. That's over with. Now we're creating James Browns and Stevie Wonders. That development is integrally bound up with television. I'm a follower of (Marshall) McLuhan in that respect.

Solid Ground: In light of all that, do you think the possibilities are there for people who still want to pursue the area that you are still pursuing?

Archie Shepp: No. No, I don't. Because this all came through an oral tradition which was very much alive during the era of radio, which could be communicated from a would-be teacher or quasi-guru to some guy watching how he made a chord to some guy watching how he held a horn or a guy relating how you run a minor seventh chord, but that doesn't go down like that anymore. They do that at Berklee (School of Music) today, and you pay $5000 a semester to learn that stuff. And it still doesn't make you what they *try* to make you. Well, that came out of our oral tradition, our post-slave experience here in Babylon, but that's all through, because now the people who played it are either playing something else or dead.

Solid Ground: Mr. Archie Shepp, thank you very much.

Archie Shepp: Thank you, brother. Peace.△

171

The Power of Communal Song

by
Bernice Johnson Reagon

I remember a revival meeting at Mt. Early Baptist Church. Rev. Onsley was preaching. He was a whopper.

He would start his sermon in a talk presentation rhythm and then shift into another gear, a slow chant, and a third gear which was the more heated rapid-fire rhythmic preaching. It was like prose-poetry, where the lines were marked by a breath made visible because it was blended with a wheezed cry. Most preachers had three cadences, but Rev. Onsley had one more gear that he put on top of that which was like a song. The church fell apart. People were shouting everywhere. When we were leaving my mother said to the pastor, "Ain't this some kind of meeting?" They talked about the singing and the power. I had felt it. It felt like the walls of the church would come off!

It was the kind of singing where everybody was singing, patting their feet and clapping their hands, where you threw all of the life that was available to you in that moment into the song you were helping to create. It was a very physical, spiritual, and emotional experience. Everything about you was affected. Your whole body felt raised up. I remember feeling, as I walked outside the church, like I was sort of coming down to earth but, in another way, would never be the same because the power of the experience had been etched into me. Those experiences gave me rest and relief from my regular routine, and each new one would touch those same places more deeply.

In high school, it was singing "The Heavens Are Telling" in the chorus. Miss Anne Elizabeth Wright would hit the opening chord and we would explode. She would say sometimes, "Children, you don't have to scream it." But we weren't screaming; we were just exploding. There is a way that singing in a group transforms the human being you are. In college, it was "The Battle Hymn of the Republic," the arrangement with full orchestra. Then the Movement came. There was singing in jails and mass meetings.

All of the singing I had experienced before was put in shadow compared to what we did through song in those mass meetings.

I'm trying to talk here about my experience with congregational-style singing, or singing with a group of people. It is a discussion of power—the creation, celebration, and unleashing of communal power.

Black traditional songs, especially the call-and-response ones, are structured to be boundless and limited only by the ability or facility of the group to express itself as a sound force. Slow songs, the lining-out hymns and dirges, create a different force because of the way their melodic line and pacing takes the time to seep inside the singer, encircle and intertwine with hidden, untapped feelings, and release them in the slow-moving, mournful wail of what is, many times, soft sound—growing hot and heavy—very, very heavy. The call-and-response songs hit you like a butt-head truck, if you're listening or not listening.

Oh-let me ride, Jesus
   let me ride
Let me ride Jesus
   let me ride
Let me ride Jesus
   let me ride slow you
   chariot and let me ride
            —Traditional

The slow ones creep over their sound range, dripping in between spaces you never knew were there.

Lord revive us, Lord review us
All our help must come from thee
Lord revive us, Lord review us
All our help must come from thee
      —Black traditional verse to "What
        A Friend We Have in Jesus," by
        Joseph Scriven, 1855

When we began to blend the African-influenced traditional songs with Western song forms, the concept of rehearsal and arrangement entered. Quartet and gospel choral songs are marked by the need to practice and rehearse them. This also goes for rhythm and blues, and jazz. They are Black because they continue to be designed so that there is always a way to get to the boundlessness. Because of the exaltation written into the arrangements, these pieces were able to lend themselves to the expression of Black communal power in song.

In the Movement, we had both songs in the traditional congregational and rehearsed styles. Singing served in Movement structures as it had always served. That is, you sang when you needed to sing, when you needed to treat yourself. If you were in jail and needed some self-healing, you sang:

This-a little light of mine,
   I'm gonna let it shine,
(oh) This little light of mine,
   I'm gonna let it shine,
(oh) This little light of mine,
   I'm gonna let it shine,
Let it shine, let it shine, let it shine.
            —Traditional

If you needed some preparation, an infusion of energy for the next activist step, you could use a song. All formalized gatherings were set up so that songs came at various points to address the communal need for nurturing, mourning, and explosive power displays.

The idea of the Freedom Singers—worked out between James Forman, executive secretary of SNCC (Student Nonviolent Coordinating Committee), and Cordell Reagon, a SNCC field secretary in Albany, Georgia (whom I later married)—was based on the songs and the musical experience of the Albany movement. The Albany Movement began as a series of demonstrations against segregated bus facilities. It was the first Movement to take on the entire power structure that maintained segregation. The struggle was marked by massive arrests beginning December 1961, when over seven hundred people were jailed over a three-day period for peacefully demonstrating at City Hall. Everybody was talking about Albany singing and old and new songs.

SNCC was faced with a media blackout of its field work; news cameras were not yet coming to rural communities where it was conducting voter registration. There was a discussion: could there be a group of singers that would begin to identify and pull together people outside of the action areas as support groups, as well as raise funds to continue the work and the building of SNCC as an organization? When the Freedom Singers began, in the fall and winter of 1962, there had already been a group of CORE singers who performed for Congress of Racial Equality chapters, as well as song leaders and groups like the Almanac Singers and the CIO Singers, who did for earlier movements those things that songs seemed to be able to do.

The first Freedom Singers were Cordell Reagon, Rutha Harris, Charles Neblett, and myself; at various times, we were also joined by Chico Neblett and Bertha Gober. We tried to get people to feel, through song, their support of Civil Rights Movement issues. These people, sometimes mostly white, would often come up and ask us how they did in the singing

Reagon: *The Power of Communal Song*

because Cordell would really fuss at them if they didn't let go. Sometimes the reserved audience was middle-class Black or from a church background. I think the style may have been too familiar and too close to something they had left, something they did not want to return to, even for the length of two or three songs.

efforts of Guy Carawan. I remember Bessie Jones talked to us about songs that we'd been singing all of our lives and told us what they meant. Through her teaching, and that of John Davis, old songs would turn new in our hands. Most of the time, they had political and struggle definitions.

There were also singers, dancers, and artists involved. Floyd Coleman, Chairman of Art at Clark College, designed the poster; and Kofi Bailey, a Black American painter who had just come back from Ghana, put up his paintings on the walls of Magnolia Hall in Vine City. Wendall Whalum, head of music at Morehouse College, taught a small group of students "Tain't But Me One," a William Lawrence James arrangement of a traditional song, which was led by Liz Spraggins. I taught work songs to the same group. Georgia Allen, who was in charge of dramatics, brought in her high school students, LaTanya Richardson and Charles Mann. Doris Dozier told me her sister had sung in the Montgomery Bus Boycott; that's how I met Mary Ethel Jones, who brought in Mattie Casey. We asked people to donate money so that we could charge a penny for admission.

This was in 1967. There were riots all over the place. We were stocking up survival provisions, practicing self-defense, and meeting with a group of Black women called the Harambee Sisters. After the Penny Festival, Mary Ethel and Mattie came to my house and asked if we could keep singing. The singing group that evolved was called the Harambee Singers. We were Black nationalist, Pan-Africanist. We did not want to sing to white people. We did not want recordings of our concerts to be made because of the CIA (maybe today they have the only recordings of this group). We sang at the developing Black studies departments in colleges, national Black conventions, community programs, and the independent schools which were springing up all over the country at that time.

Because we were Black women with families, I was concerned that the group not be a financial burden. If these women could get support from their families to come to rehearsal and go out of town for concerts, then we should provide enough to take care of expenses for transportation, babysitters' fees and costumes. That was done. This concern that socially conscious artists be supported by the communities we serve has remained a major point with me.

Our repertoire consisted of traditional Black songs, songs I wrote, African songs, and a little later, songs Mary Ethel wrote. The topical songs ranged from "Joe Willie," my love song to Black men, a parody of the blues song "Corinna," to "Had, Took, Misled," based on a speech by Malcom X called "The Ballot or the Bullet":

Freedom Singers of the Student Nonviolent Coordinating Committee: Charles Neblett, Bernice Johnson, Cordell Reagon, and Rutha M. Harris, in 1963.

You see, Black congregational-style singing has a memory bank that goes beyond your life span. It hooks you into the collected memory of your people. You feel an experience, wounds and burdens, you may have sworn you would never bear again. There are certain sounds you can make with your voice that, like a computer, will bring up these collective memories. There are Black people and Black singers who stay away from those triggers with a passion because these songs and sounds echo underneath the skin.

Today, when I see people who heard the Freedom Singers, they talk about how much they always loved those songs. The songs allowed them to join the community of fighters in a way that humanized and personalized their support efforts as the crucial dollars and telegrams could not.

One of the most important experiences of being a singer in the Movement was meeting the Georgia Sea Island Singers and Bessie Jones, as well as the Moving Star Hall Singers; this was through the

Juba! Juba! Juba dis and Juba dat!
And Juba killed the yellow cat
Bent over double-trouble Juba

Sift the meal, give me the husk
Cook the bread and give me the crust
Eat the meat, give me the skin
That's where my mama's trouble begin—
—Traditional

Coming out of that experience with the Freedom Singers, I went back to Atlanta and began to organize with Guy Carawan and then later alone, and still later with Anne Romaine, conferences, festivals, and concerts that brought traditional and contemporary singers together to southern audiences. One of our most important efforts was a Penny Festival sponsored by a preschool in which I was a parent. I was put in charge of the program. We used traditional and gospel songs, rhythm and blues, and arranged spirituals in a production narrated by Vincent Harding, with a script by Charlie Cobb and Julius Lester.

Don't you know, we been had,
Don't you know we been took,
Don't you know we been misled.
We been had, we been took, we been misled.

Well, the food on our table,
For a long time we done grown.
Now, we're packed in the cities.
Where no seeds can be sown.
Don't you know...

—Bernice Johnson Reagon

Vantile Whitfield. Although we did a little rhythm and blues and gospel, our major focus was to work out the musical structures of congregational-style songs and introduce the artists to the community created through this singing. It was the community and experience with power that had Mary Ethel and Mattie knocking on my door for more singing. It was that same need that made Carol Maillard and Louise Robinson come to me, along with

STAFF PHOTOGRAPHER, UNIVERSITY OF GEORGIA, ATHENS

Harambee Singers (from left to right): Gail Jordan, Mattie Casey, Mary Ethel Jones (front), Jacqueline Howard (back), and Bernice Johnson Reagon, 1969.

The Harambee Singers did not do a lot of congregational style (unrehearsed) singing. The repertoire extended beyond the Freedom Singers in that we embraced a contemporary concept of a sufficient Black community. My approach in working with a group of singers, no matter where they are from and what their experience is, is to shove them into new areas. This has caused problems in every group I've been in. In the Freedom Singers, I fought to keep the group unaccompanied. When the second group finally reorganized, they were all male and used a guitarist.

I left Harambee Singers in 1970 (too much pushing) and moved to Washington, D.C., in 1971, where I soon was teaching vocal techniques to the D.C. Black Repertory Company, a theater group founded by Robert Hooks and directed by

Smokey and Letari, to ask for more singing. Sweet Honey In The Rock was the answer, initially a group of about eight people, men and women, and finally taking real root the fall of 1973 as a group of four women singers.

At this time, I was in graduate school, doing the workshop with the theater and working at maintaining a home with my children Toshi and Kwan. It was not one of my seeking stages; I responded to requests. So when I was asked about pulling together a group to focus more on singing, I said, "Okay, let's try it." That first night, there were about eight people. The sound was good, like a smaller workshop. Since this was a new group, I taught them a new song, "Sweet Honey in the Rock." When I heard the song, I said, "That's the name of the group," and everybody agreed.

Reagon: *The Power of Communal Song*

We met several times, with new people coming in and others dropping out. But we never found a working chemistry, and I sort of let it drop. Louise and Maillard came to me one day to say, "Let's get together again." I called another rehearsal; Maillard, Louise and Mie showed up. After working with six to ten people, it felt like a sort of letdown. But I had this thing that if rehearsal was supposed to start at six o'clock, it started at six o'clock. We started singing, and it was right.

Since the beginning, Sweet Honey In The Rock has been a process, always defining itself by whatever part of the path it happens to be traveling at the time. Little about the group was clear to me before it happened. I did not know initially that it was a group of Black women singers. I did not know at the time a women's movement was going to affect my life.

I had had two contacts with women's consciousness-raising groups. Both were all white. The first was when I was asked to talk with a group of women who thought my experiences would be helpful to them. I asked them what women's liberation meant, because I'd heard about it but didn't know much about the theory. The answer was slightly condescending: "It's like when you don't wash diapers and dishes. Women want to do more than housework." At the time, I was sole support of my family with two small children. I told her I would really love to have someone sit me down so I could wash diapers and clean the house and therefore didn't think I had anything to say to the group. The next time was when I visited a consciousness-raising session in New York. I cannot tell you clearly what went on. There were women and I remember a stroller with a baby in it. I remember not being able to connect.

The idea of Sweet Honey being a Black women's singing group grew on me. The first time a friend of mine talked to me about feminine and masculine responses in men and women, I got scared because I did not know what she was talking about. I asked her to describe it, but it was difficult for her to find the words to convey it. I suddenly felt I had missed this thing that everybody else knew about. I called Maillard and asked her if she knew what it was about. She said, "Yeah." That scared me more. I said, "Maillard, I don't know what that is." she said, "I know you don't." "Why don't I know about it?"

"Because you've never paid it any attention. You are already beyond that. You ignore sexes when you deal with people." That was the beginning of trying to learn what I meant when I said "woman."

Early Sweet Honey sound was mixed. We did traditional songs in arranged spiritual and arranged quartet styles and then what I called "blues harmonies":

Traveling shoes, Lord,
    Got on my traveling shoes
Traveling shoes, Lord,
    Got on my traveling shoes
I can travel now, Got on my traveling shoes
I can travel now, Got on my traveling shoes

Death come riding by my mother's door
He said Come on mother
    are you ready to go?
Well my mother stooped down
And she buckled up her shoes
She counted up her cost and began to move
She moved on down by the Jordan stream
Cried Oh Lord, I have been redeemed.
She said, Lord, I done my duty,
Got on my traveling shoes

—Traditional

Then we did new songs. The political songs I wrote:

Who is this girl,
And what is she to you?
Joann Little, she's my sister.
Joann Little, she's our Mama.
Joann Little, she's your lover.
Joann's woman
Who's gonna carry your child.

I've always been told
Since the day I was born,
To leave them no-good women alone.
Keep your nose clean,
Keep your butt off the street,
You gon' be judged
By the company you keep.

Said I always walked
By the golden rule,
Steered clear of controversy,
I stayed real cool,

Til along came this woman
Little over five feet tall,
Charged and jailed
With breaking the law.
Then the next thing I heard
As it came over the news

First degree murder
She was on the loose.
Who is this girl?. . .

—Bernice Johnson

I also wrote a few personal songs, but a lot of them were written by Diana Wharton and Maillard.

I don't care how I get there,
but I gotta make this journey
He called my name out loud
and lord knows I heard him
So I packing up my bags gonna
leave my worries on the doorstep
'Cause a life all alone,
it ain' even worth the ride

Hey I'm going, going to see, see my—
going to see my baby. . .

It's been years since I seen him
but my love grows stronger and stronger
I'm gonna keep on moving
with my eye on the north star shining
So I'm saying good-bye to these
four cold walls that surround me
I'll be right by his side

Hey I'm going, going to see my—
going to see my baby. . .

—Carol Lynn Maillard

We sang to the community that was coming to the D.C. Black Repertory Theater productions. At our first performance, in November 1973 at Howard University, we sang for Stephen Henderson's conference on blues in honor of W. C. Handy. Over the next two years, we sang in schools in Washington, D.C., and slowly began to travel. Our performance in summer 1974, at the Smithsonian's Festival of American Folklife, led to invitations to the Toronto and Chicago folk festivals, which later led to the first recording on Flying Fish, a Chicago-based record company. We later began doing a few programs for political gatherings.

By this time, the personnel was changing (Evelyn Harris came into the group in the fall of 1974). I kept wanting people to stay when they needed to leave. It was trying for me, and for Evie, who kept being there when the dust cleared.

Sweet Honey in the Rock (clockwise from the top): Evelyn Maria Harris, Aisha Kahlil, Yasmeen Bheti Williams, Ysaye Maria Barnwell, and Bernice Johnson Reagon.

Reagon: *The Power of Communal Song*

We were always building repertoire and teaching people to sing. The repertoire was traditional and contemporary. The contemporary was split between topical issues, people building, and personal individual statements. Then it began to dawn on me that one of the consistent things about Sweet Honey would be our unique repertoire and sound, and that people would move in and out.

A real leap in our community occurred in 1977 when Holly Near and Amy Horowitz organized a tour of California for the group. They also wanted us to back up Meg Christian on an album but, since she was a political lesbian, told us we should make sure we were ready for that. I remember Pat Johnson asking, "What's a political lesbian?" I explained that, according to Amy, political lesbians were women who were probably involved with women sexually but in a broader way chose women as the basis from which they did everything. It went beyond homosexuality, when you looked at the development of record companies, local producers, women who tried to support women politically, socially, financially; there was a whole network developing. We decided that we could do it. It was a shock to go from Washington, D.C., where we sang for Black people, churches, schools, theaters, folk festivals, and political rallies to the radical, separatist, white women–dominated, lesbian, cultural network in California.

There were immediate and constant conflicts. Most of the time we felt as if we were in alien territory and had to protect our identity and the integrity of who we were, and who we were was different from who they were. A lot of conflicts came from racism. A lot of the conflicts came from their radicalism—the community wanting to be sure that they protected themselves and that they were dealing with women-identified women. In spite of the tensions, the community took an extraordinary risk to present us to the public that would come to events they sponsored. There was clearly a Movement energy I understood. People turned over their houses and cars and lugged around sound equipment. In two cases that I will never forget, all-women establishments that had never allowed men—Artemis in San Francisco and a bar in Albany, California—changed their policy when we sang. We were fierce about our need to be accessible to men and women, as well as to "women-only" spaces, but I was very aware of the trauma some of our early sponsors went through to organize a platform we would accept; a platform that was life-threatening to them in many ways. It was coalition work of the riskiest kind.

The women's cultural network provided the structure that made it possible for Sweet Honey to begin addressing a national constituency. I say "begin" because our audiences have been restricted when we are brought to a local community by a predominantly white, female, usually lesbian organization, both because of racism and because there continue to be tremendous fears and bigotry around homosexuality within the Black community. The bigotry is usually not as overt as Jerry Falwell's brand; homosexuals are allowed to exist and function as long as they do not articulate their identification and assert a sense of integrity (if you call that existence).

The issue of homosexuality has been one of the cutting lines of Sweet Honey's radicalism both for its members and for its audiences. In Sweet Honey, you have a group of Black women singers constantly struggling to stand in support of the right of this and all communities who are oppressed, exploited, and discriminated against. I have grown to hold in high regard these women who, standing with me, lend their voices to sing "Every Woman":

Every woman who ever loved a woman
You oughta stand up and call her name
Mama-sister-daughter-lover
Every woman who ever loved a woman
You oughta stand up and call her name

Mama holds me in my joy and pain
Mama walked heavy in my life
Mama labored so that my road
could be longer and fuller than hers
And I love—you woman

Mama-sister-daughter-lover
Every woman who ever loved a woman
You oughta stand up and call her name
    —Bernice Johnson Reagon

And they have come. It has been both a frightening and interesting process to watch people's reactions when we offer so much of what they need but also offer aid and comfort to something they detest.

Sweet Honey is the most courageous performing group in this country today because of our success in maintaining a political and social stance that placed us both within and, at times, beyond our base community. We sing to a constituency that embraces the commonness of human life, a constituency that takes a stand against the Klan, the draft, nuclear energy and weaponry, unemployment, rape, drugs, child abuse, homelessness; against forces in the world driven by greed and not committed to the needs of human beings.

Echo
Echo
Echo
Nothing but an echo of the past
Nothing but an echo of the past

The brothers you lynched a few years ago
The sister you raped just the other day
the babies you starve
every day of the week

Nothing but an echo of the past
Nothing but an echo of the past

The sounds from the jail cells
of the Wilmington 10
Are echoes of a massacre
keeping Black freedom locked in
The sounds of struggle you hear
That are filling your world today
Are echoes of the voices your father killed
and smothered away
You can steal my tongue—go on
and try to hush my song
of your children centuries unborn
Nothing but an echo of the past
Nothing but an echo of the past

Believe I'll run on (alternate lines)
(sing, shout, fight, love...on)
See what the end's gonna be
Believe I'll run on
See what the end's gonna be
Believe I'll run on
See what the end's gonna be
Believe I'll run on
See what the end's gonna be
    —Bernice Johnson Reagon

This constituency is not unified. There are some people who are against racism but use drugs profusely, some people who are against rape but are very racist, some people who are against the Klan and rape, but also against poor people. Many times our audiences spend the period before the concert reconsidering their presence because they would not be caught dead with the other people present. They have stayed and grown, and our job, in the too brief time we have, is to make some sense out of the bubbling community. We struggle with this all of the time, believing fiercely that we must affirm the constituencies in this society that speak for sanity. We also believe that it is right that we should be here at this time as Blacks and as women, the two groups of human beings that have carried the burden of building and maintaining the fabric of this society without pay, and too often without ruffling the surface. We have been most awarded by the dominant power structure when we have held our positions silently, but we have moved forward when we have been most outrageous!

The sound is important. Sweet Honey creates a wall of sound. It is a wall like falling water, and it is powerful the way the songs in church were powerful. It breaks the rules for what women are supposed to sound like. I have to give credit to powerhouses like Tina Turner and La Belle and Betty Carter, who seem to understand so well the process of using your voice so that your life becomes a song for a little while.

Three years ago, Sweet Honey began to sing consistently to people who could not hear, the deaf. Again, the credit goes to Holly Near, who had begun working with her sister Timothy to have concerts interpreted in sign language. I did not want to go through the work required to sing to the hearing-impaired and the deaf. I was especially insulted when our sponsor consistently could not come up with Black interpreters. This changed when Ysaye Marie Barnwell came into the group. She hammered into my head that this audience could hear our music if we were willing to work with an interpreter long enough so that she could sing the songs through her body and hands. When you see Sweet Honey perform with Shirley Childress Johnson, you'll see how this works. The deaf community had told us that the concept in our repertoire, affirming who you are and expressing that stance against forces that ignore you and keep you down, is important for them. The opportunities to share in the culture of resistance and struggle are too rare and not always included in information accessible to them.

When we went to Japan, we were told that they get all of the modern Black music and love it: jazz, rhythm and blues, soul, gospel. But they had never heard the power of the choral sounds produced by Sweet Honey. They had never heard the harmonies in our songs, and they had never witnessed a concert of music by women who sang about being women on the same level and with the intensity that they sang about being Black, about being for peace and against nuclear weaponry, about our struggles against racism and imperialism.

Sweet Honey is an important personal forum. It has allowed me to begin to understand that it is safe to be vulnerable and that, no matter what your individual political stances are, it is the process of trying to manifest your beliefs in a community, in a group—for me, Sweet Honey— that connects you to the history of struggle, change, and love, which must be carried through the present, alive and well, to be available—tomorrow—in the morning.△

Committee Against Fort Apache

by *Richie Perez*

The Bronx Mobilizes Against Multinational Media

ON 1 MARCH 1980, FILMING FOR THE MOVIE *FORT Apache, the Bronx* began in the South Bronx. Financed by Time-Life Films (a division of Time Incorporated), the movie was made by a team with impeccable liberal credentials: executive producer, David Susskind; producer-in-the-street, Dan Petrie (who had also worked with Susskind on the widely-acclaimed 1961 movie version of *A Raisin in the Sun*); and stars Paul Newman and Ed Asner, both long associated with social causes. However, the film soon became the focus of a major controversy amid charges of racism made by a formidable community coalition.

By the time the film opened in February 1981, organizing efforts against it had spread around the country. Massive demonstrations and threatened protests forced one New York theater to close the movie and delayed its opening in Philadelphia and Jersey City. The film was also the target of protests in Hollywood, Rochester, Miami, Albuquerque, and Boston. To fully understand the events that occurred between March 1980 and February 1981, it is necessary to understand the historical and social context in which this situation developed.

Photographs by Jerry Kearns

Perez: Committee Against Fort Apache

The South Bronx

Over the years the South Bronx has become an international symbol for urban decay, evoking images of burned out and abandoned buildings and idle, bitter groups of unemployed blacks and Puerto Ricans. Although the rate and scope of devastation in this area are unmatched, it is not unique; its problems are repeated in declining urban centers around America. Solutions proposed for the South Bronx are clearly presented with one eye on the rest of America, and residents of urban ghettos throughout the U.S. watch closely, knowing that for most of America and the world, there is little difference between the South Bronx, the Lower East Side, Bedford-Stuyvesant, Chicago's South Side, and Watts.

Between 1969 and 1979, the South Bronx lost ten percent of its housing, with some districts losing as much as twenty-seven percent. Disinvestment by banks, landlord and industry abandonment, and the scorched-earth arson-for-profit schemes, coupled with white flight and "planned shrinkage" of essential government services, led to a forty-two percent drop in population and a forty percent drop in manufacturing jobs.

In 1972, the South Bronx Model Cities Neighborhood Office, a municipal agency, reported that housing was generally deteriorating and that infant mortality was fifty percent higher than the national rate.[1] In 1977, the New York Department of Health used areas of the South Bronx to make the point that communities with the *most* health problems had the fewest doctors and the fewest health facilities.[2] And in 1978, the American Friends Service Committee reported that conditions in the South Bronx paralleled those in the underdeveloped nations of the Third World: "Thirty percent of the eligible work force is unemployed. The infant mortality rate is higher than that of Hong Kong. Average life expectancy is lower than that of Panama. The average per capita income in 1974, according to HUD, was $2,340 or forty percent of the national average."[3]

But this is only one side of the picture. With the largest concentration of Puerto Ricans in New York, this area is also known for its long history of community organization and struggle. In the 1960s, it was one of the focal points for the struggle for community control of the schools. Both the Young Lords Party and the Black Panther Party had active branches in the area and often worked together, consciously striving to build black and Latin unity. In the early seventies it was the scene of the historic campaigns for better health care and the internationally-recognized Lincoln Detox program, which pioneered the use of acupuncture to combat the heroin plague (and was subsequently closed by the city government). It was a community where residents successfully opposed the closing of a community college and where groups of black and Puerto Rican construction workers fought to break into the racially-exclusive construction trades.

These and many other struggles left the area with not only an activist historical legacy but also with many highly politicized groups and individuals who would later become the core of the movement to stop the movie *Fort Apache, the Bronx.*

Police–Community Tensions

In the nine months preceding the first announcements that *Fort Apache* was going to be filmed in the South Bronx, twelve unarmed blacks and Puerto Ricans in New York City were shot or beaten to death by police, including:
—Peter Funches, a black Vietnam veteran who died on a Bronx street on 17 June 1979. Police said Funches ran through a red light, crashed into several parked cars, rammed a concrete wall, and then attacked them with a knife. Witnesses said six policemen pulled Funches from his car and beat him in the street. Two months later, the medical examiner superseded the original autopsy report and said Funches had died from a police beating that had inflicted "multiple blunt force injuries to the face, head and other extremities."[4]
—Luis Rodriguez, who was arrested on July 17 after an argument with a Bronx grocer. Eyewitnesses testified that Rodriguez was unarmed when he was arrested. He died three hours later in a Bronx precinct. The medical examiner

ruled that the blows Rodriguez suffered while being arrested "directly contributed to this death." Ten policemen refused to cooperate with a grand jury investigation of Rodriguez's death.[5]

—Luis Baez, a recently released mental patient whose mother had called the police on August 22 to take him back to the hospital because she thought he was suffering a relapse. When they arrived, Baez was cutting his mother's carpet with a small scissors. The police chased him to a fire escape and knocked him down to the pavement below. During this scuffle, witnesses later testified, Baez dropped the scissors. Baez, who suffered from paranoia, tried to run. As Mrs. Baez and neighbors watched, the police opened fire. One policeman emptied his revolver, reloaded, and fired once more.

—Arturo Reyes, who, according to a Bronx policeman, was stealing two containers of orange juice from a parked car. The officer said the seventeen-year-old attacked him with a knife, and he fired in self-defense. However, a doctor's report revealed that Reyes had been shot in the *back* of the neck. Paralyzed from the neck down, he died three weeks later.

—Elizabeth Mangum, a black woman who was shot once through the heart inside her Brooklyn apartment. Police claimed she resisted an attempt to evict her and attacked them with a knife.

In *none* of these cases were any police officers even suspended.

The day after Baez was killed, black and Puerto Rican demonstrators clashed with police outside the 79th Precinct in Brooklyn. Two days later, over three thousand demonstrators rallied and marched through the streets of Bedford-Stuyvesant in protest. Police drove cars into the crowd and beat dozens of demonstrators and community residents who were watching the demonstration. A week later, over four hundred people attended a community speak-out where victims of the police attack testified publicly.

Sparked by the Baez killing, the Black and Latino Coalition Against Police Brutality was formed by groups from around the city "to unite our communities to fight the rise of police brutality and killings." This group linked the rise in police beatings and killings to the "poverty, unemployment, slum housing, racist education, and deadly hospitals that we are forced to live with." The police, said the coalition, exist to maintain the status quo and thus deserved to be categorized as "hitmen for the rich."

The police of the 41st Precinct, or "Fort Apache" as it was named by the police who worked there, had a long reputation of racist abuse in the South Bronx. In 1978, it was identified by officials in the police department itself as a "problem precinct." Police officials noted that it was one of the precincts that had a history of 'nonacceptance' of civilian complaints alleging that officers used excessive force, were discourteous, or abused their authority." It also 'flunked' a department integrity test, according to the report.[6]

Selling the Movie to the Public: The Community Responds

For Time Inc., *Fort Apache* was part of a much larger plan. The movie, according to an article in *Variety*, was part of a three-film package that marked the entrance of Time-Life Films into the film production business and was linked to their plan to produce movies that could be recycled later on television through cable, network, public broadcasting, and station syndication. Their ownership of both cable and other television outlets, of course, made this feasible.

The film's financers and producers began to utilize their vast media resources to prepare the public for *Fort Apache* months before filming even began. As early as January 1980, gossip columnists were beginning to mention the upcoming film. During the first week in March, stories appeared in the *New York Post* about the search for the actress who would play opposite Newman. One columnist described how a young Puerto Rican actress got the part as "a Cinderella story."[7] In the following days, numerous pictures of Newman in a police uniform appeared in gossip columns, feature stories, and in photo spreads. Newman's co-star, Ed Asner, also popped up in a number of newspaper spots.

Much of this was the work of the publicist hired by Time-Life, Bobby Zarem. The New York *Daily News*, in a full-page feature, described Zarem as the "super-flack" responsible for the "I Love New York" campaign, which Zarem called "the most successful public relations campaign in history. It singlehandedly put New York back on its feet."[8]

The Community Responds: First Steps

Many community activists, especially those who had previously been involved in organizing against police brutality, had already heard of the book, *Fort Apache*. It was written in 1976 by Tom Walker, a fourth-generation New York cop who, after fourteen years on the force, was made a lieutenant and "promoted" to the 41st Precinct in the South Bronx. The book presented the South Bronx and its people as seen through the eyes of the police.

The Union of Patriotic Puerto Ricans, one of the groups that had formed the Black and Latino Coalition Against Police Brutality, did a ten-page analysis of the book and concluded that it was "anti-Puerto Rican and anti-Black" and that the community had ample reason to be concerned about a film based on this book's theme. They circulated a flyer that listed the objections to the book and called for the formation of a Committee Against Fort Apache (CAFA).

By the time CAFA was two weeks old, it had grown to include the Black United Front, the Black and Latino Coalition Against Police Brutality, the United Tremont Trades (construction workers), the United Bronx Parents, the Coalition in Defense of Puerto Rican and Hispanic Rights, and the Union of Patriotic Puerto Ricans, as well as many unaffiliated individuals. Many of CAFA's members had been active in the 1973 protests that closed down the racist film *Badge 373* and the more recent protests against anti-Puerto Rican slurs that had appeared in *Swank* and in the *New York Post*.

In its first meeting, CAFA agreed to send telegrams requesting an immediate meeting with Susskind, Newman and Time-Life officials. Recognizing the power of the mass media to reinforce existing stereotypes and prejudices, as well as to promote new ones, CAFA decided to set into motion a multipronged strategy. The group wanted to explore all possible avenues but believed that only a *mass movement* would have any effect. From the beginning then, community outreach and preparation for mass demonstrations were seen as a priority. The guiding principle was that only an educated and organized community could successfully fight this film or any other abuse.

CAFA set the following goals:
—to demand a temporary halt to filming

AUTO GLASS
FORT APAC
INSULTS
BLACK & LAT
WOMEN
PACHE
PAUL NEWMAN
LIBERAL

while copies of the script were circulated to community groups, agencies, and churches for their input;
—to educate the community about the effects of media stereotyping and show the links to the overall situation we face, the deterioration of our living conditions, and the rise of racism and police brutality;
—to organize community resistance;
—to build higher levels of unity between the Puerto Rican and black communities through common struggle; and
—to develop our communities' ability to use the media.

Selling the Film to the South Bronx Community

While we were getting organized, Time-Life was already moving into the South Bronx. They began contacting community agencies to ask for help in recruiting extras and gaining access to facilities for shooting and staging areas. At this time, no one had yet seen the actual screenplay. One of these community agencies, United Bronx Parents, a well-respected educational institution with a fifteen-year history of service, asked for a copy of the screenplay. When they received it, they turned it over to CAFA and requested a meeting with Time-Life on March 13.

CAFA's preparations for the meeting included an in-depth analysis of the screenplay and a comparison with the book. Although Time-Life had denied any connection between the book and the screenplay, CAFA concluded that, although changes had been made, they were only "cosmetic surgery." That cops break the law is justified "because they only do it with pimps and pushers—not with decent people. As a matter of fact, there are no decent people in the South Bronx according to this film."[9] Every woman was portrayed as either a "loose woman," a prostitute, a junkie, a homocidal maniac, or some combination of all these. All the Puerto Rican and black characters are portrayed as either criminals or victims. They are not characters per se but are caricatures of evil. They pimp their own sisters; sell heroin to their children or sit passively by and watch it happen. (After the protests began, a few "decent" bit

roles were written, but they were insignificant.)

The movie shows drugs in the South Bronx coming through Lincoln Hospital (although it is given another name in the film, it is the only hospital in the area), and the doctors and the hospital workers themselves as heroin users. It portrays community activists as buffoons and misguided kids who "make a lot of hate cop noises, preach armed revolt and all but spend most of their time ballin' chicks from Scarsdale."[10]

Although CAFA was not trying to deny that there are serious problems in our communities, this film presented a one-sided, biased picture—selecting consciously the most sensational things, dehumanizing and degrading us, and ignoring the causes of these problems: high unemployment, the heroin plague, overcrowded and understaffed hospitals, abandoned buildings. The CAFA analysis pointed out that this leaves "the viewer with the impression that the people themselves create the poverty of the South Bronx. Thus, rather than win people to support our continuing struggle to change our conditions, the film will turn other people against us."

The movie romanticized the police: "Fort Apache is shown, not as a police station, but as a fort in hostile territory. . .[where] the police can do what they want because they're dealing with savages. It excuses their brutality while at the same time denying our humanity."[11]

"I Love Rice and Beans More than Spaghetti"

On March 13, fifteen representatives from CAFA (including myself) met with Tom Fiorello, associate producer of *Fort Apache*, and Kip Watkins, a Time-Life executive. The meeting was taped with the knowledge of everyone present; we insisted on this to protect ourselves against any phony charges that we were trying to extort money from the corporation. We presented our analysis of the screenplay and our demands: that production of the film be stopped for one month and that Time-Life provide copies of the screenplay for broad distribution and review by groups and individuals in the black and

In the summer of 1980, over 1,000 people marched several miles through the streets of the South Bronx to the real "Fort Apache," demonstrating against the film and showing the depth of the movement in the community.

Perez: Committee Against Fort Apache

Puerto Rican communities. If they agreed to this demand, we would return in one month with comments and suggestions. Time-Life refused and argued that the movie was bringing jobs into the community.

Fiorello (who, as it turned out, had a bit role in the movie) told us not to get excited: "I have the same kind of feelings you guys have. I understand. We have to talk right to each other. . .I personally feel hurt. I would like to see the Bronx develop. I want to buy property here. I love rice and beans more so than I love spaghetti [sic]." When this appeal to interethnic solidarity failed, Watkins, a Kennedy-type liberal, took over. He couldn't understand why we were protesting. True, he said, the book *was* racist, but the film had *nothing* to do with the book. It had to be seen *not* as something political, but as a "piece of art." He said it was a benevolent act to let us see the script because "artists" rarely do that. Finally, he told us that if we didn't think there were "tender and humane Puerto Ricans and blacks" in the film, we were "looking at the script through jaded eyes."

After we answered that they were looking at our communities through racist eyes, they told us they would not postpone production. "It will never happen," said Fiorello, "but maybe we could sit down and talk some more. . . . We'll call."

They never did call, and we never expected them to. On the same day we were meeting with them and they were telling us about all the positive images in the film, Time-Life ran a two-page ad in *Variety* describing *Fort Apache* as: "A chilling and tough movie about the South Bronx, a forty-block area with the highest crime rate in New York. Youth gangs, winos, junkies, pimps, hookers, maniacs, cop killers and the embattled 41st Precinct, just hanging in there." We didn't see the ad until the next day. It confirmed our fears and showed us that the representatives that were sent to meet with us were lying all along and were just trying to buy themselves time.

After this CAFA intensified its work. We circulated copies of the ad and a transcript of the meeting with Time-Life, prepared for the first demonstrations, called a press conference for March 22, and stepped up work on the lawsuit that we were going to use to break the press blackout of our movement.

Taking It to the Streets

To avoid demonstrations against the film, Time-Life did not publicize their shooting schedule in advance. Even reporters were unable to obtain this schedule. Without advance notice, community mobilizations became very difficult. However, the week after our meeting with Fiorello and Watkins, workers in stores along Third Avenue in the Bronx (a shopping center called "The Hub") notified CAFA that the filmmakers had offered to pay storekeepers $100 to keep their stores open until midnight that Friday, March 21.

With less than two days' notice, we called people out for 7:00 P.M. There was no sign of any filming when we got there, although people who lived in the area reported seeing film crews earlier in the day, and extra security guards were patrolling the area. It was raining, and some people got tired of waiting and went home. Then at about nine-thirty, a caravan of cars and panel trucks with film equipment began to move down Third Avenue. A lone police car drove well ahead of the caravan and turned the corner at 149th Street.

Thirty CAFA members surrounded the first car in the caravan and blocked the street. We chanted "Fort Apache, Racist Movie" and carried posters that said "Fort Apache is Anti-Puerto Rican and Anti-Black," "Paul Newman—From Liberal to Racist for $3 Million," "Indians Are Not Savages—Neither Are We," and "End Media Stereotyping of Black and Latino People."

It wasn't until after the demonstration had started that we realized that Paul Newman was the driver of the car that we had stopped. Rachel Ticotin, the young Puerto Rican woman who played the junkie-nurse, was with him. She sank down in her seat. As we blocked the windshield with posters and banged and rocked the car, Newman sat frozen at the wheel, looking straight ahead. Finally, the two policemen in the squad car realized what was happening and ran back towards us, swinging their clubs and pushing. They rushed Newman out, running alongside his car, with us running alongside and behind them, still chanting our opposition to the film.

Our prevention of filming partially cracked the press blackout. The *Post*

called the confrontation "Uprising at Fort Apache,"[12] and our press conference the next day received considerable media coverage. We issued a statement summarizing our meeting with Time-Life and our objections to the film; we also announced the filing of a $1 billion lawsuit against Time-Life Films for "group libel." We knew that we would not win the lawsuit but also knew it would draw the filmmakers out for public debate and would receive considerable publicity.

Time-Life's Dirty Tricks Offensive

Time-Life's publicity campaign faltered temporarily as they were thrown on the defensive. Besides hiring a second law firm, one that specialized in First Amendment cases, they also responded by quietly withdrawing the ad campaign they had begun on March 12 in *Variety*.

Understanding the clout of Time Inc., we knew our challenge to *Fort Apache* would not go unanswered. The community grapevine had already produced numerous stories of individuals and poverty groups accepting money in return for helping to "sell" *Fort Apache* to the Puerto Rican and black communities. However, it was not until the day we filed our lawsuit in the state supreme court, when we also held a demonstration and press conference outside, that we had concrete evidence of Time-Life's "dirty tricks offensive" against community opposition to their film.

While we were demonstrating, about sixty Puerto Rican and black high school students approached, carrying signs that read: "Pro-Fort Apache," "Fort Apache Will Help the Community," and "Don't Mix Our People's Progress with Communist Political Advancement." It was obvious to us that a confrontation had been set up. We quickly sent representatives of CAFA to talk to the students and read them portions of the screenplay (which none of them had seen). The students told us they had been hired through members of a South Bronx storefront church, headed by a white minister from Tennessee. They had been promised fifteen dollars an hour for three hours, plus five dollars for lunch—as well as roles in the movie—in return for demonstrating.

They had also been told that CAFA members were "communists that were against the community."

Before the day was over, CAFA's lawyers (William Kuntsler and Anthony Roman) and reporters had the sworn testimony of the people who had hired the students for Time-Life, as well as those of the students themselves. They told of how, guided by Tom Fiorello, they signed phony press releases with the names of non-existent organizations, recruited the high school students, and wrote up the slogans for the picket signs and the press releases.

In an interview with *El Diario-La Prensa* and NBC-TV, Eddie Perez, a member of this storefront church, told of being sent to observe CAFA activities and meetings. (Interestingly, NBC, which had conducted an exclusive television interview with Perez and other church members who acted as go-betweens for Time-Life, never aired the interview. Later it was announced that NBC had purchased the television rights for *Fort Apache*.)

Before the day was over, the students had switched sides and joined the CAFA demonstration. Meanwhile, they spotted "superflack" Bobby Zarem, who said he

had come to court to watch the demonstrations (although he couldn't explain how he knew there would be more than one demonstration). After he was identified as working for Time-Life, the students confronted him and demanded that he pay them the money they had been promised. A heated exchange followed, Zarem's cowboy hat was knocked off, and the angry students chased him out of the courthouse. Zarem fled into a taxi as riot police were called to hold back the angry crowd.

Time-Life's plan had backfired badly. The exposure of their "dirty tricks"

received wide coverage in the media. CAFA publicly denounced Time-Life's attempt to manipulate the poverty of our youth and to set up a confrontation. Had they succeeded, seventy-five "pro–Fort Apache" demonstrators would have been trying to occupy the same space at the same time as fifty "stop Fort Apache" demonstrators. A clash between the two groups could have been interpreted as a split within the community over the merits of the film, and the CAFA demonstrators could more easily have been labeled an "isolated, violence-prone fringe group" which did not represent the community.

The Filmmakers Defend Themselves Publicly

After the fiasco at court, some of the people involved with the movie began to defend their motives. Susskind and Newman, defendants in the lawsuit, submitted affidavits arguing that the film would help the South Bronx. Both asserted their history of involvement in social causes. Both expressed outrage at being called "racists."

At a carefully staged press conference in April—held on a small hill in an abandoned lot, against a backdrop of burned-out buildings—Newman accused the *Post* and *The Village Voice* of "irresponsible journalism." He reiterated that "I have spent my whole life caring about what happened to the underprivileged," adding, "This is a tough movie. It's tough on whites, blacks, Puerto Ricans and on lousy white cops." He implied that the demonstrators were troublemakers and asked why we weren't fighting for better health care instead of opposing the film.

However, the Time-Life public relations campaign to dust off the movie's and Newman's image was undercut at every turn. The *Post* ripped the script in a full-page article, "What Paul Didn't Tell Us About Fort Apache."[13] Newman's press conference itself was disrupted by four CAFA protestors who received almost as much coverage as Newman himself. Finally, even the police attacked the film. The head of the Patrolmen's Benevolent Association (the police union) publicly

called Newman a "money-hungry mongrel" and a "bigot" for referring to "lousy white cops" in his defense of the movie. Later, the Hispanic Society of city police officers, including some who were assigned to guard the film site and others who were sent undercover into CAFA, attacked the film publicly, saying it presented a "one-dimensional" and "slanted view" of Hispanics and blacks. Tom Walker, the author of the book *Fort Apache*, accused Time-Life of stealing the plot for their movie from his book, and he filed a multimillion-dollar lawsuit.

But what set the context and gave all this real impact was the continuous opposition to the film in the streets of the Puerto Rican and black communities. Hundreds continued to march in "Stop Fort Apache" protests. Thousands signed petitions against the film. Tens of thousands of leaflets were distributed at beaches, community block parties, and at any activity where people gathered. Musicians and poets staged a "Stop Fort Apache Cultural Arts Festival," attended by hundreds. Physical disruptions occurred whenever protestors were able to find out the shooting schedule in advance.

When a hospital scene was filmed in East Harlem (after Time-Life was refused access to Lincoln Hospital by outraged workers and administrators), eighty demonstrators crashed the film site, and filming was only able to continue after hundreds of police were called out. This confrontation was reported and shown on television news. Despite Time-Life's continuous claims that there was no "real opposition" to the film, protests and growing opposition kept breaking into the news.

Moreover, while producers hinted (in a magazine article) that the problems were due to local gangs trying to extort money,[14] they were offering to buy off protestors by suggesting, through a well-known figure in the Puerto Rican community, that CAFA should be realistic and try to get something out of all this that would "benefit the community"—such as a writers workshop funded by Time-Life. (This offer was angrily rejected by CAFA.)

Following this, Time-Life and its *Fort Apache* team seemed to have made a decision by the end of April to take a low profile. Time-Life, Susskind, and Newman all turned down offers to debate CAFA on Herman Badillo's local TV program "Urban Journal." They also refused to attend a city council hearing where the General Welfare Committee was consider-

The CAFA demonstration against the film culminated with a rally at the real "Fort Apache." Richie Perez, on the podium, addressed the assembled crowd.

Perez: Committee Against Fort Apache

ing a resolution to withdraw permits for the film. (The committee passed a resolution condemning the racism of the screenplay and calling on all New Yorkers to boycott the movie.) Although demonstrations and opposition continued, Time-Life was silent. By June, they had finished filming and left New York.

Some Reflections on the Media Battleground

From the beginning, we understood the necessity of dealing with the electronic and print media. We were very conscious of presenting CAFA as a broad, community-based coalition. In every press conference, for example, we chose representation that would reflect our composition: Puerto Rican and black, women and men, young and old. Although our membership included every sector within our communities— including workers, students, parents, professionals, clergy and politicians—we were described as "black and Puerto Rican militants." In press conferences and interviews, many reporters became impatient with our explanation of how we saw the issues. They only wanted to know if we were going to use violence to stop the movie.

Besides a preoccupation with violence, we found that the structure of television news itself worked against us. In-depth analysis is, for the most part, absent on the nightly news. We could prepare a ten-minute press statement, explaining carefully *why* we opposed the film and answering the arguments of our opponents, but only a very small fragment would ever be televised. A sympathetic television reporter once told us, right before the cameras were turned on, "Say everything you have to say in sixty seconds because that's the most you're going to get on the air." Other reporters told us that without any violence or any arrests, their assignment editors "just weren't interested."

Despite these and other difficulties, we were determined to, as much as possible, "use the media." To keep our public statements consistent, CAFA chose specific people who would represent us to the media. Others were assigned to develop and cultivate contacts in the media and to stay abreast of moves by Time-Life in this area.

At the end of March, Time-Life hired a second public relations firm, Lisboa Associates, to offset the favorable coverage we had received from the Spanish-language press. They succeeded in getting two full-page articles of favorable coverage in *El Diario*; the exact process by which this came about became the source of considerable controversy in that newspaper. We later demanded and got "equal time." In an important victory for us, *El Diario* eventually published an editorial condemning the movie.

The "Freedom of Speech" Controversy

CAFA came under attack from civil libertarians as our efforts to stop the movie mounted. Nat Hentoff, in *The Village Voice*, called us "thought police," comparing us to the Nazis. The ACLU filed a "friend of the court" brief to oppose our lawsuit—as if we had the power to deny Time-Life's freedom of speech.

While we did not pretend to have all the answers to this complex question, we were not deterred by these attacks. We were fighting against the vilification and slander of our people. *Fort Apache* imposed on us, and most importantly on our children, negative racial stereotypes that incite hatred towards us, reinforce existing prejudices, and thus contribute to the denial of our civil and human rights.

To the absolutists who said freedom of speech means people can say anything, we raised a number of questions. Does freedom of speech mean that someone has the right to infringe on our rights? Does this mean our right to live free of libelous stereotyping and racial attacks is subordinate to the right of multinational corporations like Time-Life to make more money? Does freedom of speech mean that huge corporations that control the mass media have the right to portray us as less than human, thus denying our children positive role models and simultaneously

Teenagers, recruited on their schoolyard with the promise of payment by the film company, came down from the Bronx to disrupt the CAFA demonstration in Foley Square. Upon their arrival, however, CAFA members quickly won them over and they joined the demonstrators instead. When the film executive arrived to see how his planned disruption was going, the teenagers gave chase and he literally ran for his life. The demonstration played a major role in discrediting the filmmakers and the New York newspapers ran major pieces on the event the next day.

Ringed by the state and federal courthouses of Manhattan's Foley Square, Richie Perez speaks with lawyer William Kuntzler and the press during the CAFA demonstration in March, 1980. Mr. Kuntzler was a member of a team that filed a class-action suit on behalf of the Latino community to bring an injunction to stop the film.

"teaching" white children about "black and Puerto Rican inferiority"? Do those with a lot of money have more freedom of speech than those who are poor and cannot buy it?

The Movement Against *Fort Apache* Grows

The attacks on us by civil libertarians had no effect on our support within our own community. While grappling with this question in forums and in interviews, we continued the fundamental work upon which our campaign was built—educating, uniting, and mobilizing our people. CAFA members spent much of their time organizing on a one-to-one basis; literature tables were set up, and periodic community leafleting and door-to-door offensives were carried out. We had also selected certain groups for special outreach, including community planning boards, district school boards, parents associations, day care centers, educators groups, church groups, unions, rank-and-file groups within unions, student organizations, media and arts groups, and health workers.

On April 12, Bronx City Councilman Gerena Valentin conducted a public hearing on the movie attended by over 125 people, including more than thirty who spoke in opposition to the film. A week later, 350 people marched through the streets of the South Bronx in a concrete reflection of the growing opposition to the movie. At the rally that followed the march, Rev. Neil Connolly, the Roman Catholic Vicar representing twenty-four churches in the area, read a statement that condemned *Fort Apache* as "obsessed with scars only," never mentioning "the thousands of church-going people, dedicated community workers, self-sacrificing parents. . . . We are outraged at the Time-Life Films for continuing to beat the drums of racism and classism for the price of a dollar."

The next week, the state supreme court threw our case out of court. Without reading the screenplay upon which our complaint was based, the court dismissed our charges as "speculative connotation" and "ideological innuendo." Because we had not expected the court to rule in our favor, we considered it a victory to have kept Time-Life in court for weeks and forced them to defend themselves publicly and hire a second law firm.

While the struggle against *Fort Apache* was sharpening in New York, links were being made with other groups across the country. Forty chapters of the Chicano student group MECHA (*Movimiento Estudiantil Chicano de Atzlan*) passed a resolution against the film during a California-wide conference and vowed support in any boycott or other actions taken if it was produced and released. Representatives of CAFA also met with activists in San Francisco's Chinatown who were protesting derogatory Asian stereotyping in a new "Charlie Chan" film. In New York, a representative of the black groups that had been protesting NBC's "Beulah's Land" addressed a meeting of CAFA and called for better communication and coordination among groups fighting media racism.

Preparing for the Opening

After the filmmakers quietly left New York City in June, we prepared for the next phase of the struggle: consolidating the groups and individuals that had already become part of CAFA, broadening our outreach to bring in new forces, and preparing for the boycott itself.

We developed an internal newsletter, the CAFA bulletin, which kept people informed of new developments, provided analysis of Time Inc. and research on Time's push into the movie and cable arenas (thus placing *Fort Apache* in a larger context), and mobilized people for pickets and call-in protests. We also made presentations and showed a slide show on media racism to as many organizations and groups as possible—each time enlisting further support for the planned boycott of the movie when it opened.

During the summer of 1980, we also emphasized setting up literature tables and poster-photo exhibits at large outdoor gatherings in the Puerto Rican community. We put out a special leaflet which answered common questions about our opposition to the movie and stressed the growing broad unity against it. Significantly, CAFA had grown by this time to include over twenty organizations, community agencies and institutions. In addition, the film had been condemned publicly by several public officials, media outlets, religious leaders, professional

Perez: Committee Against Fort Apache

associations and other organizations. The momentum *was* growing.

In November 1980, there were signs of a new Time-Life publicity offensive. A sneak preview was held in St. Louis, Missouri, an area with few if any Puerto Ricans. Liz Smith, the *Daily News* gossip columnist, reported that Newman got "rave reviews." A week later, she reported that he was "coming up strong as a contender" for an Academy Award for his role in the film.[15]

In December, *New York* magazine ran a feature story about the two policemen whose real-life exploits supposedly provided the basis for the movie. The thrust of the article was that the film's story was a good, tough, and *true* one, and that Newman's presence would guarantee its box office success. The article, quoting the cops, repeated the racist stereotypes of the South Bronx and generally trivialized protests against the film (although it flippantly mentioned that "There were so many protestors even the press agents had to have a bodyguard").[16] In another interview with the *National Star* the two cops justified the "street justice" they had meted out in the South Bronx.[17]

CAFA recognized that it could not respond to every step in Time-Life's extensive publicity campaign but called on supporters to seek ways to demand equal time. The November 1980 bulletin announced a demonstration at the Grand Hyatt Hotel in New York, where David Susskind was to be honored by the Chamber of Commerce and Industry for his "contributions to the revitalization of New York's film industry;" two call-in protests to ABC and CBS opposing Newman's appearance on the Barbara Walters and Mike Douglas shows; and the first press conference to be held by the newly formed Philadelphia CAFA.

In January 1981, Time-Life Films and Twentieth Century Fox (TCF), which was now handling the distribution of the movie, held a special screening of *Fort Apache* in Atlanta, Georgia, for reporters from around the country. As part of an all-expenses-paid "press junket" to win favorable reviews, reporters were flown to the Atlanta Hilton where they were wined and dined by a TCF publicity team. Because CAFA did not have enough money to send a group, it was decided to send one person and arrange for some local backup. A group of black activists in Atlanta

agreed to provide transportation, a command post outside the Hilton, and legal support if necessary. Despite pressing security concerns of their own—they had been targeted by local racists—they risked exposing themselves to further police "attention" and, by their actions, advanced the cause of black and Latino unity.

CAFA's representative registered at the Atlanta Hilton for one night. Friendly reporters tipped him off to the publicity party's schedule. After an extended "cocktail hour" the reporters were to board a bus that would take them to the screening itself. The CAFA rep, in suit and tie, stood outside the bus and distributed CAFA press packets which included press releases, newspaper clippings, statements of opposition to the film, and leaflets. Most of the reporters thought he was part of Twentieth Century Fox and gladly accepted the packets.

When the woman in charge for TCF finally realized what was happening, she threatened to have CAFA's representative arrested. By the time hotel security arrived, however, the CAFA "publicity team" was back in his room, reporting in to the outside support group. On the bus, sympathetic reporters confirmed that there was a lot of discussion as the press people went through the CAFA material. After the screening, there was continued discussion and some debate among reporters over dinner.

The next day, a major press conference with Paul Newman was held in the hotel, half of which was taken up by questions about the protests and the extent of community opposition to the movie. CAFA's representative was followed from the moment he left his room by a team of plainclothes detectives. When reporters left the press conference, he was waiting in the lobby with press packets. As the reporters recognized and moved toward him, their tape recorders ready, a squad of plainclothes Atlanta police surrounded him and used their massed bodies to strong-arm him away from the reporters. Threatened with arrest, despite his arguments that he was a registered guest in the hotel, he retreated after giving the room number to interested reporters. The CAFA representative got to talk with reporters from several newspapers, many of whom confided that they risked losing the privilege of these junkets to important screenings if they gave TCF a hard time.

The Opening

A month before the announced opening, CAFA began to focus on theaters that had announced they had booked *Fort Apache*. After an unsatisfactory meeting with a representative from United Artists and the manager of U.A.'s Gemini theater in midtown Manhattan, we hit the Gemini with an unannounced pre-boycott demonstration. One hundred people participated in five-degree weather. Less than a dozen people crossed our militant picket line, and police were called in. During a tense confrontation inside the theater, we told the Gemini's manager that he would have to surround his theater with police to show *Fort Apache*.

On 22 January 1981, Time-Life and TCF made their final attempt to divide the community by holding a screening at Lincoln Center for some South Bronx community groups and leaders. CAFA got hold of the invitations, reproduced them, and sent members to the screening. We distributed leaflets outside (and inside) the screening and held a community meeting immediately after in nearby offices of Channel 13.

The press had hinted that the screening would be an opportunity to have some community leaders endorse the film and attack CAFA as a "small, unrepresentative group." Afterwards, however, more than forty representatives of community planning boards and educational, media, religious, and civil rights groups angrily denounced the movie and its promoters. They publicly endorsed CAFA's efforts and threw their support behind the boycott. This was a *major* victory for us and meant that when the movie opened, a *united* Puerto Rican community would respond.

In the final weeks before the opening, CAFA stepped up its efforts: thousands of "Boycott Fort Apache" stickers were printed and distributed; leafleting was carried on around the city; and we continued to get press coverage. During this period, committees to oppose the movie were also formed in Jersey City, Boston, and Albuquerque.

Fort Apache opened in 800 theaters across the country on 6 February 1981. In its first week:

—In New York, the Gemini theater cancelled the movie, and fourteen blocks

Perez: Committee Against Fort Apache

away, 350 people picketed the Orpheum on opening night. Hundreds of people marched in ten demonstrations over a three-day period, and *extensive* media coverage educated hundreds of thousands more about the protests.

–In Philadelphia, the opening was postponed for a week because of militant pickets. Philadelphia CAFA was so effective that eventually it was hit with an injunction that said we could only have four pickets 100 feet away from the theater.

–In Jersey City, the *threat* of demonstrations postponed the opening of the movie. When it did open, CAFA members from New York joined the Jersey City CAFA on the picket lines.

–In Hollywood, a demonstration was organized by the Chicano group MECHA on opening night.

–Organizing efforts and protests took place in other cities as well, including Rochester, Boston, Miami and Albuquerque; students at SUNY-Binghamton and SUNY-New Paltz also stopped showings of the film.

Accomplishments

CAFA recognized that it was fighting, not only the giant media conglomerates which financed, produced and distributed *Fort Apache*, but also the growing right-wing sentiment in America. We were demanding respect and reaffirming the strength and beauty of our history and culture—at a time when our past gains were being eroded and we were increasingly being used as scapegoats for the nation's economic and social failures, at a time when many American liberals were embracing the "solutions" of the reactionary Right.

Recognizing this reality, our goals were primarily educational and organizational: to educate our community about the effects of media stereotyping and show its links to the overall situation we face—the deterioration of our living conditions, the destruction of survival programs like bilingual education, the rise of racism and police repression—and to challenge with

our presence and strength the movie's racist messages that we were inferior peoples, incapable of organizing ourselves for change.

The secondary focus of the boycott organized by CAFA was economic. While we realized that we did not yet have a movement that could shut this movie down nationwide, we could have some impact at the box office—and we did! *Fort Apache* made $13 million in domestic rentals, but *Variety* reported that even this was "way below expectations for the costly, controversial picture."[18] After this (and the failure of their other two films), Time-Life Films went out of the movie business.

The education conducted around *Fort Apache* was tremendous and invaluable. Hundreds of thousands of people were alerted to our charge that this movie was anti-Puerto Rican and anti-black, that racist films like it feed into the rising right-wing tide in America, and that these films have a detrimental effect on our people's fight for survival and advancement.

The year-long struggle created a context within which *Fort Apache* had to be evaluated by the people who insisted on seeing it. Our community's collective efforts turned it into an important social issue and made it easier for viewers to recognize the racism in the film. We also set the framework for movie reviewers—many of whom borrowed directly from CAFA's analysis in writing their reviews—and had a strong impact on filmmakers. Another exploitation movie about heroin wars in the South Bronx was cancelled, and a television documentary about "cops fighting crime in the South Bronx" was shelved in what the *Daily News* called a reaction "to the backlash from the controversial movie 'Fort Apache, the Bronx.' "[19]

Beyond that, we are encouraged that some filmmakers have taken progressive positions. The producer of *Ragtime* told *The New York Times* that when he was filming on the Lower East Side, he consulted community groups because "I didn't want another 'Fort Apache.' "[20] In a more critical statement, Constantin Costa-Gavras, director of *Missing*, said in a *Rolling Stone* interview, "Recently I went to see *Fort Apache, the Bronx* and I was surprised to see two actors in there who are considered ideologically left . . . . I think

Fort Apache was racist—anti-black, anti-Puerto Rican."[21]

CAFA was a broad coalition which united different sectors of the community and different political perspectives around a single issue and utilized a wide range of tactics. We widely challenged the film's racist explanations of poverty, unemployment, arson and police brutality. We publicized and defended the community's justified concern about "street justice" at the hands of racist policemen. We challenged the movie's degrading images of Puerto Rican and black women with the reality of proud and militant women of all ages in the movement.

The organizing against *Fort Apache* also contributed to the unity of Latin, black, Asian and white activists for social change. In addition, it helped us identify many progressive media activists, as well as people inside the establishment media, and formed important bonds of unity for future struggle. Finally, this struggle helped deepen our community's understanding of the media and showed how we can deal with it effectively.

We believed that the best way to build on this movement was to deal with media racism on an even higher level. This included strengthening existing groups like the Puerto Rican Institute for Media Advocacy (PRIMA) and carrying out ongoing community education around this issue. CAFA officially dissolved itself in March 1981, after voting to work with the First National Puerto Rican Convention (held in the South Bronx on April 25–26, 1981). The National Congress for Puerto Rican Rights, a permanent body formed at the convention, resolved to form a Mass Media Task Force to continue the struggle for change in the mass communications industry.

The campaign against *Fort Apache* was a genuine mass movement which understood that the fight against media racism is part of our overall struggle to change our conditions. It was a fighting movement which engaged the enemy on a number of fronts, added to the historical legacy of past battles, and advanced the starting point for the next struggles against media racism and for freedom.△

The National Congress for Puerto Rican Rights can be contacted at: NCPRR, Post Office Box 453, Williamsburg Station, Brooklyn, New York 11211.

Notes

1. *Neighborhood: The Journal for City Preservation—the South Bronx*, August 1982.

2. Ronald Sullivan, "A Virtual Lack of Doctors Found in Some Slum Areas of New York," *The New York Times*, 13 December 1977.

3. American Friends Service Committee, "The Third World Here at Home: The South Bronx," *Actionletter*, April 1978.

4. Earl Caldwell, "Widows Have Grisly Pictures and Stories to Match," *New York Daily News*, 9 November 1971.

5. "10 Cops Refuse to Testify in Fatal Beating of Rob Suspect," *New York Daily News*, 16 November 1979; Daniel O'Grady and Don Gentile, "Quizzes 10 Cops with 1 Lawyer," *New York Daily News*, 1 December 1979; Earl Caldwell, "It Matters That the Eyes of the Law Keep Justice in View," *New York Daily News*, 24 November 1979.

6. Leonard Buder, "Police Find 7 Pre-cincts Brush Forth Public Complaints About Officers," *The New York Times*, 6 March 1978.

7. "Late Night with Martin Burden: Cinderella Story," *New York Post*, 6 March 1980.

8. Jan Hodenfield, "A Life in the Day of Bobby Zarem," *New York Daily News*, 25 September 1980.

9. Committee Against Fort Apache, "Analysis of the Screenplay 'Fort Apache, The Bronx,'" 12 March 1980.

10. From the screenplay, quoted in CAFA, "Analysis."

11. CAFA, "Analysis."

12. Eli Teiber, "Uprising at Fort Apache: Angered Residents Demand Newman Film Be Stopped," *New York Post*, 22 March 1980.

13. Joe Nicholson, "What Paul Didn't Tell Us About Fort Apache," *New York Post*, 28 March 1980.

14. "Intelligencer: All Quiet on the Newman Front," *New York*, 31 March 1980, 6.

15. Liz Smith, *New York Daily News*, 4 December 1980.

16. Marie Brenner, "City Lights: Stardom in the South Bronx," *New York*, 1 December 1980, 14.

17. "'Fort Apache' Cops Tell of Real Exploits in New York Jumble," *National Star*, 3 February 1981, 17.

18. Lawrence Cohen, "40 Features Await Spring Debuts: Hope to Beat Poor '81 Record," *Variety*, 27 January 1982.

19. George Maksian and Brian Kates, "PBS Cancels 'Bronx Detectives—Rap Program's 'Negative View,'" *New York Daily News*, 2 April 1981, 7.

20. Richard F. Shepard, "Filming of 'Ragtime' Restores 1906 to Block on E. 11th St.," *The New York Times*, 28 July 1980.

21. Peter S. Greenberg, "Art, Lies and Reality: An Interview with Costa Gavras," *Rolling Stone*, 13 May 1982, 15.

Our BUGA UP Is Here. The beer can was readily changed into a spray can.

ABOVE-GROUND ORGANIZATION OF AUSTRALIA'S UNDERGROUND BILLBOARD ACTIVISTS

Photographs by Sigrid Daube

The Art of Billboard Utilizing

by Peter King

ORIGINS

The last decade has seen an unprecedented growth in the environmental awareness of Australians. Concerned individuals have come together to form active movements around issues ranging from preservation of wilderness to nuclear disarmament. These movements have ranged in size from massive pressure groups with thousands of members to determined individuals, fighting solitary battles to change society in some way.

In October 1973, three such "crusaders" came together to form an unusual alliance. One was an artist who was outraged by the indiscriminate rape of the visual environmental by outdoor advertising, another a student who was studying the media and advertising, and the third an ex-smoker concerned about the growing number of children who smoke. They had been expressing their views through direct action by adding graffiti to billboards. Graffiti has traditionally been a cheap and effective medium of self-expression for those who do not have access to the commercial media. The added dimension of using billboards is that ads can be turned against themselves, so that advertisers fund their own "demotions" (anti-promotions).

However, because these three activists had worked individually, their actions had been perceived by Sydney people as fairly random outbreaks of graffiti. They decided that it would be advantageous to form a movement with a unique identity and, from that point on, concentrated their joint attacks on unhealthy promotions, including ads for unhealthy products and ads which promoted products in an unhealthy way (such as through sexist stereotypes). The work was signed with the mysterious letters BUGA UP, an acronym for Billboard Utilizing Graffitists Against Unhealthy Promotions. (In the Australian vernacular, BUGA UP is pronounced just like "bugger up," meaning much the same as "screw up.") Whenever possible, BUGA UP graffiti was artistic and witty, capturing the imagination and sympathy of the public. A movement was born.

GETTING STARTED

Several support activities were established. Since individual activists had to maintain a low profile—in order to avoid arrest—a post office box was used for contacts with the press and public (which required some creativity when it came to filling in the forms). The address was easily and effectively publicized on blank billboards in key locations. Because several months had elapsed since the first appearance of the BUGA UP acronym, there was a flood of letters from journalists and people wanting to become actively involved; suitable arrangements were made for telephone contacts or personal meetings.

Before long, graffitists who had been arrested on the job were willing to make public appearances because they no longer needed to keep their identity secret. Media outlets were keen to offer free publicity for what they considered to be a couple of harmless eccentrics—although as time went on advertisers began to threaten withdrawal of business if glorification of BUGA UP continued.

King: The Art of Billboard Utilizing

At one time, a supporter ran an advertisement in a national newspaper which explained the movement's motivation and called for financial support. Donations ranging from one to one hundred dollars were received in response. BUGA UP itself brought out a number of publications, the most popular of which was *Catalogues*. This collection of photographs of cleverly refaced billboards included accompanying text which described the movement and explained how to become actively involved. About forty thousand copies have been sold over the last three years by mail order and through alternative bookstores.

A bank account was opened, and revenue from publications, as well as donations received from sympathizers, went into a "fighting fund" to pay half the fine for anyone found guilty of billboard utilization. (It has rarely been drawn on, since most activists accept their own financial responsibilities.) The fund is not used to pay compensation for any alleged "damage."

TIPS FOR GRAFFITISTS

Before attacking a billboard, plan how the wording (if there is any) and the overall message can be used most effectively. The objective is to expose the manipulative process used in the ad with a minimum of alteration. By changing a few letters or suitably enhancing an image, the whole message can be turned against itself. Start by rejecting the assumption that the advertiser has a monopoly on communication, and consider the potential for two-way communication. If the ad asks a question, provide an answer. If it promises an answer, pose the question.

Humor can be used to ridicule the pretensions of advertising, and BUGA UP's good public image has been maintained by the wit of their graffiti. People will seek out graffiti if it entertains them; however, both the media and the public prefer to ignore "doomsday" messages.

Of course, it is essential that your work be noticed at a distance. The altered message must be at least as bold and readable as the original, which usually means enormous lettering in contrasting colors. If the background of the poster is too complex to achieve good contrast, you may try outlining the graffiti in a contrasting color (for example, silver with a black outline).

Spray cans are the graffitist's best friend. Although they are ecologically undesirable, many alternatives have been tried and found lacking in versatility and

effectiveness. Brushes and paint have good potential from an artistic point of view, but they are messy and slower, make it difficult to change colors, and require a ladder for reaching high areas. With a spray can, however, colors can quickly be changed as dictated by poster design and aesthetic considerations. (Australian experience has shown that the most versatile colors are black, white, red and silver.) The top of posters can be reached with the "extension," a simple but effective device using a can on the end of a long pole. If a billboard is too high even for an extension, it can be suitably "de-glamourized" with "paint-bombs": children's balloons or blown-out eggs filled with thinned paint.

There are no hard and fast rules about the best times to attack billboards, but generally the dead of night is the *worst* time. Late at night police patrols are more intense, and people lurking around billboards are more conspicuous. Graffitists working during the day are generally ignored by passersby, either because they don't care or they assume that if what you are doing were illegal, you wouldn't be doing it openly. Nighttime does have an advantage in that you are much less likely to be identified; it is also easier to disappear under the cover of darkness.

Most graffitists prefer to work between sunset and about ten o'clock.

Because it only takes about one minute to extensively reface an average billboard, your chances of being caught red-handed are fairly slim. To date, there has been about one arrest for every four hundred refaced billboards in Australia. Of course, some people are unlucky enough to get caught on their first foray, while others go on for years with no problems.

It's a Bore. Two graffitists spent an hour and a half refacing this one in broad daylight. The crowd that gathered in the street was too intrigued by what was evolving to call the police.

SOME FURTHER TIPS

—Don't park your car within sight of the target; most arrests have resulted when license numbers were reported to police.
—Decide exactly what you will do, which colors you will need, and whether an extension will be required before arriving at the site. Pick your moment and go for it. Don't lurk around looking nervous.
—Once you have started, don't be distracted. People may honk horns, shout encouragement or stop to chat, but your goal is to get the job done quickly.
—Work on your own or with one person as lookout. Large groups only attract attention.

LEGALITIES

Contact with the law is inevitable in any campaign involving civil disobedience. Although time consuming and expensive, court cases make an excellent forum for public debate of the issues.

BUGA UP's activities have precipitated about forty court cases, ranging from ten minutes to two days in duration. In most

Let's Forsake All and Follow Jesus. A group of radical Christians refaced this ad so effectively that no one would ever suspect it was once a cigarette ad. The Bible covers the Sterling pack, and the caption once read, "Let's stow away for a night or two."

"Let's forsake all and follow Jesus." "What a Sterling idea."

The Chauvinist Charade. The brand name of the car has been completely covered. The original lettering was traced for size and typeface, and the replacement word was painted at home on prepasted wallpaper, which was then soaked and stuck on. A very neat and quick operation.

THE GREATEST CHARADE EVER MADE

CHAUVINIST CHARADE

We are Witless Nits. A comment on the way television news is packaged and sold. The billboard originally read "Eyewitness News, Always First."

WE ARE WITLESS NITS: ALWAYS ARE ...

WITH CLOWNS MANDY & ANDY, NIGHTLY AT 6 PM.

King: The Art of Billboard Utilizing

Smile While You've Still Got Teeth. A favorite with the kids.

Masturbation Fantasy.

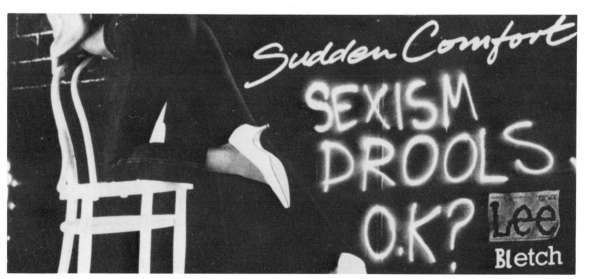

Sexism Drools O.K.?

cases it is best to plead innocent to the charge, which in Australia is usually "malicious injury to a billboard." If you plead guilty, the case is over very quickly, and you have little opportunity to present the reasons for your action. There is also no chance of being acquitted by a sympathetic judge.

By pleading not guilty, graffitists reaffirm their belief that their actions are morally justified, although the law may not be able to distinguish their actions from vandalism. Some cases have been dismissed for lack of evidence, such as the inability of witnesses to identify the accused positively. It is essential that you admit to nothing if you are charged or questioned by the police.

Several defenses have been tried. The most fruitful of these has been the "defense of necessity," which claims that a minor wrong was committed to prevent a much more serious one—such as harm to people who might otherwise have believed that smoking and drinking would improve their sex life. BUGA UP has called witnesses to testify that the promotion in question was indeed unhealthy. Expert witnesses have also been used to argue that the billboard was not damaged but in fact was improved; the alterations enhanced its truthfulness and transformed it into a unique work of art.

Although legally unsuccessful, these arguments have attracted media attention and won the movement widespread sympathy. So far, three out of four graffitists have been found guilty; penalties have ranged from a stern reprimand to a fine of about two hundred dollars. From this point of view, civil disobedience has proved to be an extremely cost-effective way of raising public consciousness.

ACHIEVEMENTS

The central issue in most BUGA UP trials has been the inadequacy of a legal system designed to protect property, not people. On some occasions, judges have openly expressed their sympathy for the accused, much to the delight of the press and despair of the advertisers.

By constantly keeping the issue of morality in advertising under public scrutiny, BUGA UP has forced the industry to take the rights of the consumer much more seriously. So far, the campaign has focused on the worst offenders, the cigarette industry; the government has finally

responded to the widespread pressure to prohibit all tobacco promotion by introducing new controls which will soon lead to a total ban. Other industries, such as liquor companies, now fear for the future of their advertising. Attacks on sexist advertising have caused designers to think twice about using sexist imagery and choose less offensive alternatives.

Paint Bombing. The harder they are to paint-bomb, the harder they are to clean off.

Sometimes it seems that the victories are small and progress frustratingly slow. BUGA UP can rarely claim direct responsibility for specific gains, but the Australian experience has shown that the visibility and provocative nature of billboard utilization is an extremely important social catalyst.△

HANS HAACKE:

Where the Consciousness Industry Is Concentrated

An interview with the artist conducted on 24 June 1983 by Catherine Lord, formerly the associate editor of Afterimage magazine and currently dean of the School of Art of the California Institute of the Arts.

Lord: I want to focus on strategies in making political art and changes in your work—your strategies in relation to other peoples'. I'm curious because I have a sense that things shifted for you in the very late sixties and early seventies, that there was a real leap.

Haacke: I don't view it as much of a break. Not only is there a gradual transition, but there is, I think, already a foundation laid in the sixties, insofar as I was not as interested in fixed objects fitting a particular stylistic mode as in processes, situations, open systems which communicated with their environments. I was quite taken by a book by Ludwig von Bertalanffy, *General Systems Theory.* It helped to clarify my thinking and reinforced semiconscious aspirations. Working with physical and biological phenomena is only dealing with one aspect, although a very large aspect, of the world; if one wants to deal with the world as a whole— and I think artists should do that—then, of course, the social aspect is an integral part of it. So it was a natural outgrowth of this kind of thinking that I expanded into the social and political field. It provided a theoretical base.

Then, of course, like many people, I was affected by the increasing politicization of the United States and, in particular, of the art world, toward the end of the sixties. I felt more and more that it is artificial to separate what the artist does in his or her studio and what they do as civic beings: the two belong together. You are a whole person.

Most artists have political and social convictions, but these often do not transpire in their work. The more you become aware of this almost schizophrenic separation, which is normally not perceived as such, the more you have to deal with this problem.

Lord: In regard to the ways you have focused your strategies from 1969 on, can you talk about the shifts in what you are doing?

Haacke: It's hard to pinpoint. One thing, of course, is essentially different when you are dealing with physical or biological phenomena: they have a more factual character. When you move into the sociopolitical field, you are dealing primarily with attitudes, opinions, history, ideology, and so forth. That, obviously, has consequences.

Lord: What kind of effect do you have in the art world? Do people argue back or are you presenting things in situations where people say, "Yes of course?"

Haacke: Well, that varies a great deal; it depends on who looks at it. There are, of course, people who agree with me before they have even seen it and their counterparts who reject it out of hand in an equally knee-jerk fashion because it conflicts with their views. There are other people who come with no fixed opinions. For them, the works may provide information and can challenge them to reconsider their attitudes. As you know, there is also the contingent that argues that political and social subject matter should be left to the "experts," to the politicians, and that artists shouldn't meddle with it. And lots of variations in between.

Lord: How does the "mass" media treat it? How do the companies you criticize react?

Haacke: The companies ignore it officially. How they react behind the closed doors of the executive suite is hard to determine. I do know, though, that some of them are aware of what I'm doing; in one or two cases, corporations appeared to be quite nervous and tried to contain the good news.

Lord: What do you mean?

Haacke: In the case of Alcan, I was told the company tried to prevent the show from traveling to the region of Quebec where most of their factories are located, which is far away from Montreal. According to my informants, Alcan supposedly threatened that money the company normally gave to a locality for some sports event would no longer be forthcoming if it mounted the exhibition.

But my "target group," to use advertising jargon, is not the company executives. It doesn't matter what they think about my work. I don't believe they could be moved. It takes pressure from an alert public and politicians responding to that pressure to effect changes. A long and indirect process.

Lord: Do you think of that public pressure coming from an art audience or the workers' audience?

Haacke: Where the Consciousness Industry is Concentrated

Haacke: In the first place, of course, that is the art audience. But my hope is—and I have some evidence to be confident—that it spreads beyond that circle. It is much easier in areas where the art world is not as densely packed as in New York. In smaller places, your chances of getting coverage in the press is much greater than in New York. In areas where nothing much seems to be happening, it can become big news.

Lord: Do you try to use or steer that?

Haacke: As far as possible. In Montreal, it so happened that the art journalists of the two big Quebec dailies had a direct interest in this subject and were sympathetic. They used their entire space in the weekend edition for the discussion of my show, with reproductions of the works. That helped a great deal. It apparently reached the farthest corners of the province. In New York, this is absolutely inconceivable. Most art journalism here is focused almost exclusively on the "art" aspect of things. The writers are probably nervous about dealing with things that are not strictly confined to what they perceive as art issues, because it would require them to take a position. And that could mean making enemies. Political journalists usually do not pay attention to what is happening in the art ghetto.

Lord: New York is a small town.

Haacke: It's a very small town. If you get on the wrong side, it can mess up your career. So you'd better ignore troublesome subjects. London, by contrast, is more open. For example, the Tate Gallery, even though reluctantly, did put on works critical of the British government and the prime minister. And the press did not hold back with coverage.

Lord: You don't seem to show much in New York.

Haacke: I show at the John Weber Gallery every two years, almost ritually. Occasionally, I participate in a group show outside the museum circuit. Museums in the U.S. don't touch me.

Lord: Why are museums in Europe more apt to take you on?

Haacke: Because European museums are structured differently. They have different kinds of boards of trustees, not dominated by people from the business and financial world. They are public institutions; the employees are civil servants. They usually have tenure. Therefore, if they do something that doesn't sit well with their supervisory bodies, they are not putting their job on the line. Much depends on the prevailing political climate, of course. The worst that can happen, however, is that the show will not go on. What is important is that the curator does not risk his or her job. As you know, in some cases my works are indirectly or directly a critique of the world represented by the board of trustees. Most of the people working in museums in the U.S. don't have tenure; many of them don't even have a contract and can be dismissed from one day to the next. Therefore, I cannot blame them for not getting involved with my stuff. Self-censorship is rampant.

Lord: Which puts you straight into the gallery system here.

Haacke: Yes. The commercial, profit-making world, contrary to what one would assume, is one of the few outlets I have here.

Lord: Does your work sell here?

Haacke: Not well. The gallery that continues showing my work does not make much of a profit from it.

Lord: I noticed, looking through your catalogues, that a lot of things are still your property.

Haacke: I couldn't possibly do this without a teaching job. I think one can state as a general rule that anyone who is dependent on the sale of his or her work, or *hopes* to live off it, will to a large degree sign away his or her freedom of movement. Dependence on the market can be crippling.

Lord: Which makes it even odder that you're pushed into the gallery system. You have tenure?

Haacke: Yes.

Lord: Did your work change when that happened? In terms of what you were saying and the risks you were willing to take?

Haacke: No, not really. When I moved into work with direct social implications, I didn't have tenure. I must say, however, after I got tenure, I did feel much more secure.

Another peculiar phenomenon is the shifting coverage of my work in the art press. There was quite a bit in the late sixties and early seventies. Later I had two or three shows with no coverage *whatsoever* in any of the New York magazines. *The New York Times* has never reviewed a show of mine. It is only during the past few years that coverage is picking up again.

Lord: Do you think that is because political art is getting chic, rather than that the art world itself is changing? A lot of stuff is being called political.

Haacke: It seems so. I'm told it is because some younger artists are moving in a direction that, in one way or another, can be interpreted politically. They view themselves or others view them as being related to the world I am coming from, although they are, in fact, doing different things.

Lord: One of the things which strikes me as odd is the amount of work that purports to be a political critique—particularly the ever-expanding postmodernist stable. I find much of that world *extremely* problematic when called "political." The range of the critique is miniscule. It's the sort of work that can easily be recuperated. However, some of what I've been reading lately about your work is blurred into the same sort of "quotation" as, say, Sherry Levine or David Salle.

Haacke: People are very eager, for reasons that I cannot quite figure out, to read political intent into all sorts of things which, in my view, have little or no relation to politics, other than perhaps on a theoretical level. The mere reference to something in our contemporary environment is already interpreted as a political act. In those terms pop art was highly political, which, of course, it wasn't. The only interpretation I could offer is that, up until not too long ago, our everyday world was totally excluded as a worthy subject for an artist.

Lord: What's excluded from what's now termed political—work like good old straight documentary photography with text—isn't embraced in this new movement of "political" art. It's not seen as political, and the rationale given is that it's not a critique of form.

Haacke: Much of what gets a political reading now lacks directness. I see it as a rather arcane discussion, bottled up within a small segment of the art world, a purely theoretical discourse. In that sense, it becomes academic, divorced from the real world, even though some of the theoretical issues alluded to are not without interest. The insights gained could, in fact, be put into practice. Naturally, all products of the consciousness industry have political implications, whether they are done with a political intent or not. But that is a discussion at a different level.

Lord: One of the arguments I have with people who call themselves postmodernist and political comes from the belief that their audience is limited, their statements are limited, the analysis is limited. The answer is often: "I am an artist. I am a member of the art world. That is my real audience and that's where I'm going to start," which is close to what you said. How do you make it clear what *you* are doing? How do you continue to do what you're doing in a system which seems to be trying hard to recuperate *any* critique?

Haacke: I think the differences are apparent. And I don't want to waste my energies on how to "position" myself within the art world. I have no time or patience for such marketing strategies that seem to occupy a lot of people in Soho. I am not afraid of being recuperated. On the contrary. As long as one remains alert, aware of what is going on, "recuperation" can be one of the ways of infiltrating the mainstream consciousness. It is wrong to see the art world as totally isolated from the rest of our social environment. There's a lot of spillage into the political culture. Even though it happens on a relatively small scale in places like New York, possibly in London and a few other big metropolitan places where the consciousness industry is concentrated, the mental and emotional climate is, to some degree, affected by what people hear, see, or take in by osmosis from the art world. At that level, I think it matters what happens in the art world. It affects the social atmosphere. That's why the big corporations are so eager to get control over it. I think it also matters to what kinds of things younger artists and art students are exposed while they are forming an idea of the world and the field into which they are moving. It is not preordained that everyone who goes to art school eventually is going to perpetuate the parochial habits of the contemporary art world. And I would say that the viability of art as a form of communication and interpretative expression, over the long run, depends on how far it can transcend this parochialism. If it doesn't, it could easily deteriorate into nothing but a hobby, without significance beyond tenuous self-gratification and money for a few.

Lord: But your strategy still seems to be to stay within the art world in order to transcend it, to use its mechanisms of communication. For example, you don't do subway posters, that I know of.

Haacke: I have nothing against doing subway posters. But it's an expensive affair if they are to be more than an honorable gesture. In England I did a poster, jointly sponsored by the Museum of Modern Art in Oxford and the anti-apartheid movement, using one of the panels of a work I showed in the museum. I don't know if it had any impact. We also placed ads in the Oxford newspaper, reproducing some of the panels. Because of the financial limitations, the ads were so small that even I had difficulty finding them. You must be able to pay for at least a half page. That easily costs you between five and ten thousand dollars a shot.

Lord: It may be awkward to keep asking this, but I am interested in the audience you choose to reach: to show in a commercial gallery because you can show there, not to show in a museum because you can't show there, and then to use mass media journalistic art coverage to get the work out again to other people who ought to see it.

Haacke: I believe discussions about the audience often do not take the real world into account. Very few people have the choice of their audience. One often assumes artists can, in fact, choose between the art audience, the television audience, the subway audience, etc. In practice, I

(Interview text continued on page 210)

Haacke: Where the Consciousness Industry is Concentrated

LUCIA DI LAMMERMOOR, produit par l'Opéra de Montréal avec des fonds d'ALCAN.

Photo: André Lecoz

La filiale d'ALCAN en Afrique du Sud est le plus important producteur d'aluminium et le seul fabricant de tôle d'aluminium laminée en Afrique du Sud. Sur une main d'oeuvre de 2300 ouvriers de couleur la compagnie forme huit ouvriers spécialisés.

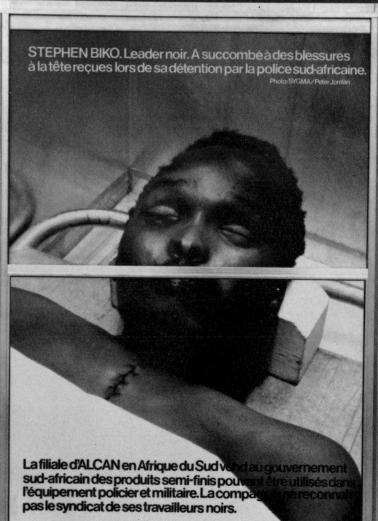

STEPHEN BIKO. Leader noir. A succombé à des blessures à la tête reçues lors de sa détention par la police sud-africaine.

Photo: SYGMA / Peter Jordan

La filiale d'ALCAN en Afrique du Sud vend au gouvernement sud-africain des produits semi-finis pouvant être utilisés dans l'équipement policier et militaire. La compagnie ne reconnaît pas le syndicat de ses travailleurs noirs.

BRIAN MERRET

BRIAN MERRET

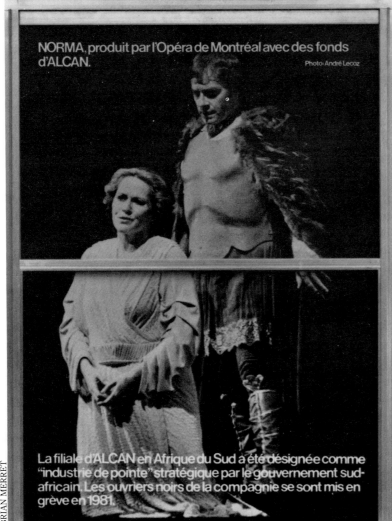

NORMA, produit par l'Opéra de Montréal avec des fonds d'ALCAN.

Photo: André Lecoz

La filiale d'ALCAN en Afrique du Sud a été désignée comme "industrie de pointe" stratégique par le gouvernement sud-africain. Les ouvriers noirs de la compagnie se sont mis en grève en 1981.

BRIAN MERRET

Voici Alcan, 1983
Three panels, each 86½ x 41 inches.
Two sepia photographs, one color photograph, lettering, aluminum windows, acrylic plastic with silver foil.
First exhibited in one-man show at Galeria France Morin, Montreal, February 1983.

Translations:

Left: *Lucia di Lammermore*, produced by the Montreal Opera Company with funding from Alcan.

Alcan's South African affiliate is the most important producer of aluminum and the only fabricator of aluminum sheet in South Africa. From a nonwhite work force of 2,300, the company has trained eight skilled workers.

Center: *Stephen Biko*, black leader. Died from head wounds received during his detention by the South African police.

Alcan's South African affiliate sells to the South African government semi-finished products which can be used in police and military equipment. The company does not recognize the trade union of its black workers.

Right: *Norma*, produced by the Montreal Opera Company with funding from Alcan.

Alcan's South African affiliate has been designated a strategic "key point industry" by the South African government. The company's black workers went on strike in 1981.

Haacke: Where the Consciousness Industry is Concentrated

don't think it is that easy. If you want to work in television, you must have paid your dues to the industry before you get to do something yourself. And you must have made your peace with all the constraints of the institution. What I'm doing certainly would not have a chance to get on the air. If you think you want to reach large audiences through journalism, you have to work within the constraints of the industry—you have to put in many years as a rookie—and you are obviously no longer a visual artist. Video is mostly closeted in the art world, and mass audience films require resources that are outside my reach.

Lord: But on the other hand, there are people—I'm thinking of Les Levine or Michael Lebrun—who work by getting grants or a set amount of money from someone to do subway posters. I know what you're saying about the realities of audiences and limited choices, but I also think there are ways to reach a bigger audience, albeit in a very limited way for a short time.

Haacke: From Michael Lebrun, I know that his poster, which had very limited exposure, cost him something like four thousand dollars. That's more money than I usually spend on a show. He cannot spend four thousand dollars several times a year. I am glad that he did his project. But it is unwise not to recognize the limitations. You get grants for this kind of stuff only if it is mild and innocuous. I can't see anybody giving me a grant to put my poster on Reaganomics into the subway.

Lord: It would be wonderful to have it up there at Grand Central.

Haacke: Oh, I'd love to do that, but it just costs an awful lot of money. Don't forget that we are implicitly talking about competing with the advertising of big corporations. Klaus Staeck, in Germany, is the only one with really tough work who has succeeded. It took him many years. And he could not have done it without a solid distribution network for his posters, i.e., a great variety of political organizations who take enough copies to warrant the expenses for editions of several thousand each. Recently Group Material mounted an exhibition of some twenty-five hundred subway advertising panels by a

hundred-odd artists on the IRT trains. A beautiful idea, and also many good pieces. But when the participating artists were looking for their posters to photograph them, they had a hard time finding them. What we often overlook is that the mere presence of an artwork or poster in a public place does not automatically mean that people will actually see it and think about what they have seen. It must survive next to Preparation H. Particularly in New York, that is a problem. It is easier in a small town. In an overcrowded visual environment, where messages are hitting you whichever way you look, much gets overlooked. It may be talked about in an art magazine or in a newspaper, because a press release drew attention to it. But the audience that is supposedly addressed rarely notices it unless it is large and all over the place. It has to survive among the general visual clutter. There are notable exceptions, like Keith Haring. I believe people did see his work. What they made of it is another thing. But in most cases we are talking about a potential audience at best.

Lord: What about the idea of access to an audience through cable television?

Haacke: Theoretically, there appears to be this tremendous opportunity to reach an awful lot of people by way of cable television. We have the public access channels, because the law stipulates that, on a first-come-first-served basis, everyone can use the medium. In practice, of course, it's a bit different. Since everyone can use the channel, the quality of the programs is usually very low. The general audience does not watch because they have learned how television is to look from the big networks; public access cable television programs do not live up to these criteria. They get viewed only by those who produced the program and those who happen to be alerted to it because they have a common interest in the subject. It remains an in-group affair.

Lord: Would you say the same thing about the artists' cable enclaves?

Haacke: As is only natural, one gets announcements in the mail, like invitations to an opening, telling when one should switch on to view this particular artist's work. It is essentially the same as showing

The Right to Life, 1979
50¼ x 40¼ inches.
Color photograph on three-color silkscreen print.
First exhibited at John Weber Gallery, New York, 1979.

American Cyanamid has required the sterilization of female employees of child-bearing age if they want to continue in certain jobs. Other large chemical companies have also practised "protective discrimination," usually restricted to moving women of child-bearing age into often lower-paid jobs within the company, where they are not exposed to toxic substances. Reported among these companies are Dow Chemical, Monsanto, Du Pont, General Motors, Bunker Hill Smelting, St. Joseph Zinc, Eastman Kodak, and Firestone Tires and Rubber.

AMERICAN CYANAMID

AMERICAN CYANAMID is the parent of BRECK® Inc., maker of the shampoo which keeps the Breck Girl's hair clean, shining and beautiful.

AMERICAN CYANAMID does more for women. It knows: "We really don't run a health spa." And therefore those of its female employees of child-bearing age who are exposed to toxic substances are now given a choice.

They can be reassigned to a possibly lower paying job within the company. They can leave if there is no opening. Or they can have themselves sterilized and stay in their old job.

Four West Virginia women chose sterilization. **AMERICAN CYANAMID...**

WhereWomen have a Choice

Portrait of BRECK Girl by James Donnelly Text   by Hans Haacke. 1979.

HANS HAACKE

211

Yes, my son collects unemployment, too!
REAGANOMICS

in a gallery. It remains an in-group affair and should be understood as such. No claims are justified to have broken out of the confines of the art world, to have addressed the *people* of popular leftist myth. It could be that out in the country there are places where public access cable television is not as far removed from the general audience as it is in New York.

Lord: What about other strategies to reach an audience directly like using things such as labor publications?

Haacke: Principally, that's fine. Wherever I have an opportunity that seems viable, I use things that I've done as posters, postcards, or in other ways. For my show at the Tate, a photo of my Reagan installation from *documenta* served as a poster in the London subway. I think one should explore this more but also be quite realistic about its potential. Aside from the problems already mentioned, such a project also requires considerable managerial skills and sometimes a legal backup. Klaus Staeck is a lawyer, and he has been sued a number of times. It takes quite a bit of trial and error.

One has to be very pragmatic, not come with a hard theoretical approach that has no relation to the real world. For instance, if you want to work with unions, you have to establish a relationship with the people in charge, the people who are to put money aside for your proposals. They must be convinced that what you have in mind is useful for them. That cannot be done from one day to the next. It can take years. I've tried a couple of times to get involved with such organizations. While they were sympathetic to what I proposed, they either didn't have the time or they couldn't quite imagine how one could apply it. One specific example is the piece I did on American Cyanamid's requiring women to be sterilized if they wanted to continue working in jobs where they would be exposed to toxic substances. I offered it as a poster design to the Oil, Chemical, and Atomic Workers Union and the Coalition for Reproductive Rights. Eventually word came that people didn't quite understand my mock ad, and therefore it wasn't done. The first time it got large exposure was in *The Village Voice*. I was quite happy about that, but that was five or six years after I actually did the piece. When I had the show in which the piece was exhibited, the *Voice* didn't publish a line, let alone reproduce it.

I also tried to "market" my *Reaganomics* piece through the union of Hospital and Health Care Employees (District 1199). Even though the union has a radical history, and a vital cultural program, I got no place with it. The same with the Institute for Labor Education.

Lord: Since you think so hard and so carefully about where you show, about how and what the form will be, I wonder how, at this point, you think about your strategies in the art world?

Haacke: We should not lose sight of the general social and political climate. Obviously, we have moved into quite a conservative period. This is not because of one or two events, or a few posters here and there; it is the result of a combination of millions of elements that came together. To move into a different direction, in turn, requires an awful lot of little steps. Seen from such a somewhat removed point of view, I think it doesn't matter so much in what circles or under what circumstances you participate in trying to affect the climate. The art world is, as I said earlier, not as isolated a circuit as one normally thinks. It radiates out and, in an indirect fashion, affects the general ideological climate. Therefore, what happens in the art world is not negligible. As you know, we have this big wave of romantic expressionist painting right now. It fits perfectly with the conservative mood of the moment. If we had, instead, a different kind of art, I believe we would be better off, because it would not reinforce the prevailing conservative attitudes. I am a bit afraid of what is purported to be an irreconcilable opposition between working inside or outside the institutions of art. In both areas, consciousness is being shaped, and it is useful to participate in this process wherever one sees a promising opportunity. The rest is sectarian bickering. Oskar Negt once said one should not leave the bourgeois media to the Right.

Lord: Given all that, how important is it to you to work politically with groups of other artists? How important is your direct influence on students?

Haacke: The transition in my work took place in 1968/1969, at a time when I was active in the Artworkers Coalition. That lasted for two or three years until the group took an exclusively feminist direction. That was where I got my political

Reaganomics, 1982/1983
Color transparency in black wood frame, four fixtures with fluorescent tubes, 72 x 49 inches.
Designed by Hans Haacke, © 1982.
First exhibited in one-man exhibition at the John Weber Gallery, New York, 1983.
Photograph of Ronald Reagan by Michael Evans/The White House.

Haacke: Where the Consciousness Industry is Concentrated

education in the art world, as many others did at the time. We learned on the job, by trial and error. There was a second coming, in the middle seventies, with the publication of *The Fox* and Artists Meeting for Cultural Change. In the beginning, I participated. But since, to some degree, it was a rerun of what I had experienced before, I didn't have the patience and energy anymore to go through the weekly "group therapy" sessions. That sounds degrading, but it is not meant so. It was a valuable process. Currently there are a couple of groups that do very valuable work in this area, such as PADD and Group Material. I am friendly with them, but I'm not actively involved. As far as teaching is concerned, possibly some of my students get a bit of a political education. But I'm not pushing it; I don't want to indoctrinate them. I like to prepare the ground so that they can gain insights on their own rather than providing ready-made answers. I don't believe that would stick, anyway. If you buy political attitudes wholesale, you discard them the next year.

Lord: This is the "right" stance.

Haacke: "Politically correct," supposedly. "PC"—that's abdicating the responsibility to think for yourself and to reexamine things. I enjoy working with images and language, and I think the audience should also get a kick out of it. A discussion like this takes the risk that my work may be viewed one-dimensionally, as nothing but political activism. I am an artist, working within the art world, with all its contingencies. These are, in fact, an essential element in the work. If you go outside the art world, the work takes on a different character.

Lord: It's interesting to show your work to people who aren't art world people.

Haacke: It's actually very peculiar. . . . Non-art world people usually pay attention to the content, and often bring to it knowledge that the denizens of the art world don't have. However, they often do not get the more art world/art historical allusions and miss some of the formal qualities. On the other hand, art world people, even if they pay attention to the content, sometimes run away with the art references and either don't understand the

other aspect or don't particularly care for it. It's a peculiar split. However, such selective viewing is not unusual in human communication.

Lord: Some of your work strikes me as absolutely hilarious, but nobody ever seems to talk about that. It's not just irony, it's also a comic edge.

Haacke: I hope the comical, sarcastic, ironical—or whatever you want to call it—helps to make the work accessible and interesting. It also alleviates what can easily turn into melodramatic seriousness. I don't like the raised finger. There should also be fun. Usually, people get hung up on the political seriousness (the assumption is that politics is very serious—which it is, of course). But one can also deal with it in a way that is funny and serious at the same time. Bertolt Brecht, for example, is someone who was able to combine the two. His work is luxurious and hilarious and funny, and it also drives the point home. But politics, for some odd reason, has this church seriousness about itself. That's devastating; it turns people off. A positive example is the Bread and Puppet Theater. Maybe also Keith Haring.

Lord: Do you think about the comic when you write the scripts, for example, in the Mobil piece? You said before you worked more or less on one thing at a time, getting into the "mind of Mobil," the public relations mind-set, and you can see it in that piece—it's perfectly plausible "Mobilese."

Haacke: They're speaking a language of their own.

Lord: Except what's in it is utterly reversed.

Haacke: If you adopt Mobilese or some other such PR language, and take it out of its normal context, it becomes very comical. Then it reveals its true nature.

Lord: My sense looking back over your work is that it has become more and more crystallized. The things being produced are more and more succinct.

Haacke: It's true. In many of the more recent things, I reduced the verbal information to a minimum. The one notable

exception was the Ludwig piece. To a certain degree, the amount of text necessary depends upon the subject. I don't know how to condense the Ludwig piece; it just requires quite an extensive text to convey to an uninformed audience what the Ludwig phenomenon represents. But I do try more than in the past to reduce the amount of text. I know from my own experience how uncomfortable it is to read long stories on the walls of galleries. It's not an ideal way of communicating. It also risks making the work dry and unsensuous, almost bureaucratic. The less text, the more you have a chance to make it "juicy."

Lord: Yet the Ludwig piece interests me because there is more of an explanation, more text. It could have been done more easily on a simple level as a short version of the economics of collecting.

Haacke: It's more complex than that. One cannot rely, as in other subjects, on prior knowledge. Take the example of Reagan; everybody knows him and has opinions about him. Unless one unearths something really new, there's no point in telling a long story over again. So it's more a question of putting Reagan into a new perspective. Ludwig is only known to insiders, and even the art world insiders have little, if any, knowledge of the industrial aspect of his operations. So the long text gave indeed new information.

Lord: How do you pick topics to work on?

Haacke: Usually it is circumstantial—that is to say, I know I'm going to participate in this exhibition, and I have assumptions about the locale, the audience, and the time when it is to take place.

Lord: About the corporations in the locale?

Haacke: Yes. In the case of the show at the Stedelijkvan Abbemuseum in Eindhoven, for example, I knew that Philips is, in fact, running the town. It is the largest employer in Eindhoven, and the largest nongovernmental company in Holland. So that was a subject that lent itself immediately. With the Reagan piece in Kassel, at *documenta*, there were a couple of things I knew beforehand: Reagan was visiting Germany, to promote the deployment of the cruise and Pershing missiles, almost simultaneous to the opening of *documenta*; painting was to play a particular role in that exhibition, as it does in the art world in general today. And I knew a bit about the public of *documenta*, which is really very large, some two to three hundred thousand people. It's not just an inside art world event.

Lord: What about the Ludwig piece? Was that done for a specific show?

Haacke: Yes and no, i.e., I knew that the *Westkunst* exhibition would take place in Cologne, in 1981, and that it would be a big international exhibition of modern art, including contemporary art. There was a possibility that I would be invited to participate. But irrespective of my participation, I knew that a great number of people who deal professionally with art would be in Cologne for the opening. I also knew, of course, that Ludwig is the "King of Cologne," i.e., he runs the art world there. These were the circumstantial elements that provided the groundwork.

Lord: How long was the piece in the making?

Haacke: I worked about two years on it. That's the thing: if you deal with complex subjects like this one, you have to do an awful lot of research. For the Reagan piece, you hardly have to do any. Now, the sculpture *We Bring Good Things to Life - General Electric* required some research. I wanted to do something about nuclear arms. So I got in touch with one of the research organizations here in New York that monitor corporate conduct. They have a department dealing exclusively with weapons and nuclear arms. Speaking to those people and looking through their material, I became aware that G.E. is heavily involved in the development and manufacture of nuclear warheads. Then I remembered that G.E. was the employer of Reagan in the fifties. He did commercials for the company. It occurred to me that the term "warhead" makes reference to the "head," and a rocket can also be a pedestal in the shape of a column. And I thought of the religious fervor with which Reagan called the Soviet Union the "empire of evil" when he addressed a fundamentalist conference. Thus, the mixture of hope and anxiety in his look to heaven. I probably don't have to explain why the head is gold-leafed.

And so the combination of elements developed. It's a very disorganized process.

Lord: It actually doesn't sound disorganized at all.

Haacke: I imagine, to a certain degree, it resembles research and development in corporations.

Lord: In the Alcan piece, how did the window framing come about?

Haacke: In retrospect, it becomes clearer and clearer that I am often concerned about frames, both in the literal sense of the term—frame for an object—as well as the frame, the circumstances, the context in which something takes place or is exhibited. After some preliminary research on Alcan I went to Montreal to snoop around, and I learned that the company was sponsoring the Opera of Montreal. So I went to the opera's public relations department and asked for photographs of these productions. I picked two in which a man is in a dominant position and a woman the victim or subordinate to the male. Then I looked for a photograph that encapsulated the problems blacks face in South Africa. I went to picture agencies here in New York and looked through every picture they had of South Africa. And there I found the slides from the morgue showing Steven Biko bashed up. I knew, "This is it." The combination then suggested itself almost automatically. Alcan, of course, is an aluminum company. One of the daily encounters we have with aluminum is aluminum window frames. A window is also, metaphorically speaking, a window on the world. This is, in fact, how people thought of painting in the old days.

Lord: That's why the painting is in there?

Haacke: That's why the painting is also in the aluminum frame. So it's really lots of circumstantial, chance encounters with elements that finally come together.

Lord: Just before the deadline. It must be nerve-racking to work that way.

Haacke: Oh yeah, it is. Not to speak of all the problems that might occur with the institution that is supposed to show it. Sometimes they get cold feet.

Lord: Does that happen often?
(Interview text continued on page 224)

Prof. Dr. Dr. h. c. Peter Ludwig
Aufsichtsratsvorsitzender der
Leonard Monheim AG.

Kunstbesitz in Dauerleihgaben ist vermögensteuerfrei

Peter Ludwig wurde 1925 in Koblenz als Sohn des Industriellen Fritz Ludwig (Kalkwerke Ludwig) und Frau Helene Ludwig, geb. Klöckner, geboren.

Nach dem Wehrdienst (1943–45) studierte er Jura und Kunstgeschichte; Promotion 1950 über *Das Menschenbild Picassos als Ausdruck eines generationsmäßig bedingten Lebensgefühls*. Die Dissertation stützt sich auf Bezüge zwischen zeitgenössischer Literatur und dem Werk Picassos. Historische Ereignisse werden kaum berücksichtigt.

1951 heiratete Peter Ludwig Irene Monheim, eine Mitstudentin, und trat in die *Leonard Monheim KG.*, Aachen, seines Schwiegervaters ein. 1952 wurde er geschäftsführender Gesellschafter, 1969 Vorsitzender der Geschäftsleitung und 1978 Vorsitzender des Aufsichtsrats der *Leonard Monheim AG.*, Aachen.

Peter Ludwig ist Aufsichtsratsmitglied der *Agrippina Versicherungs-Gesellschaft* und der *Waggonfabrik Uerdingen*; er ist Vorsitzender des Bezirksbeirates der *Deutschen Bank AG*, Köln-Aachen-Siegen.

Seit Anfang der 50er Jahre sammeln Peter und Irene Ludwig Kunst, zunächst alte Kunst. Seit 1966 konzentrieren sie sich auf moderne Kunst: Pop Art, Photorealismus, Pattern Painting, Kunst aus der DDR und die *neuen Wilden*. Seit 1972 hält Peter Ludwig als Honorarprofessor der Kölner Universität kunsthistorische Seminare im *Museum Ludwig* ab.

Dauerleihgaben moderner Kunst befinden sich im *Museum Ludwig*, Köln, der *Neuen Galerie-Sammlung Ludwig* und dem *Suermondt-Ludwig-Museum* in Aachen, den *Nationalgalerien* in West- und Ostberlin, dem *Kunstmuseum Basel*, dem *Centre Pompidou* Paris, und den Landesmuseen in Saarbrücken und Mainz. Im Kölner *Schnütgen-Museum*, im Aachener *Couven-Museum* und in bayrischen *Nationalmuseum* befinden sich mittelalterliche Werke. Das Kölner *Rautenstrauch-Joest-Museum* beherbergt Objekte aus dem präkolumbianischen Amerika, aus Afrika und Ozeanien.

Das Kölner *Wallraf-Richartz-Museum* erhielt 1976 als Schenkung eine Pop Art-Sammlung, (jetzt *Museum Ludwig*), das *Suermondt-Museum* in Aachen 1977 mittelalterliche Kunst (jetzt *Suermondt-Ludwig-Museum*). Dem *Antikenmuseum Basel* (jetzt *Antikenmuseum Basel und Museum Ludwig*) wurde 1981 eine Kollektion griechisch-römischer Kunst geschenkt, die Dauerleihgaben aus Kassel, Aachen und Würzburg einschließt. In eine *Österreichische Stiftung Ludwig für Kunst und Wissenschaft* wurde 1981 eine Sammlung moderner Kunst eingebracht.

Peter Ludwig sitzt in der Ankaufskommission der *Landesgalerie Düsseldorf*, im International Council des *Museum of Modern Art*, New York, und im Advisory Council des *Museum of Contemporary Art*, Los Angeles.

LOTHAR SCHNEPF

Der Pralinemeister
(The Chocolate Master), 1981
Seven diptychs. Each of the fourteen panels 39½ x 27½ inches. Multicolor silkscreen prints into which photographs and packaging of assorted chocolates and chocolate bars are pasted; in brown farmes under glass.
First exhibited in one-man exhibition at the Galerie Paul Maenz at the time of *Westkunst*, a major survey of art since 1939, in Cologne, May 1981.

Translation:
Art Objects on Permanent Loan are Exempt from Property Taxes
Peter Ludwig was born in 1925 in Koblenz, the son of the industrialist Fritz Ludwig (Cement Factory Ludwig) and Mrs. Helen Ludwig (neé Klöckner). After his military service (1943–1945), he studied law and art history. In 1950 he received a doctorate with a dissertation on "Piccaso's Image of Man as an Expression of his Generation's Outlook on Life." The dissertation focuses on relations between contemporary literature and the work of Picasso. Historical events get little attention.

In 1951 Peter Ludwig married a fellow student, Irene Monheim, and joined Leonard Monheim KG., Aachen, the business of his father-in-law. In 1952 he became managing partner, in 1969 president, and in 1978 chairman of the Leonard Monheim AG., Aachen. Peter Ludwig is represented on the boards of directors of Agrippina Versicherungs-Gesellschaft and Waggonfabrik Uerdingen. He is the chairman of the regional council of the Deutsche Bank Ag. for the district Cologne-Aachen-Siegen.

Peter and Irene Ludwig have been collecting art since the beginning of the 1950s. At first they collected old art. Since 1966 they have been concentrating on modern art: Pop Art, Photo-Realism, Pattern Painting, art from East Germany, and the "New Expressionists." Since 1972 Peter Ludwig has been an adjunct professor at the University of Cologne and holds seminars in art history at the Museum Ludwig.

Permanent loans of modern art are located at the Museum Ludwig, Cologne, the Neue Galerie-Sammlung Ludwig and the Suermondt-Ludwig-Museum in Aachen, the National Galleries in West and East Berlin, the Kunstmuseum Basle, the Centre Pompidou in Paris, and the state museums in Saarbrücken and Mainze. Medieval works are housed at the Schnutgen Museum in Cologne, the Couven Museum in Aachen and the Bavarian State Gallery. The Rautenstrauch-Joest Museum in Cologne has pre-Columbian and African objects, as well as works from Oceania.

In 1976 The Wallraf-Richartz-Museum of Cologne (now Museum Ludwig) received a donation of Pop Art. The Suermondt-Museum in Aachen (now Suermondt-Ludwig Museum) was given a collection of medieval art in 1977. A collection of Greek and Roman art, which includes permanent loans located in Kassel, Aachen and Würzburg, was donated to the Antikenmuseum Basle (now Antikenmuseum Basle and Museum Ludwig). In 1981 a collection of modern art was brought into the "Austrian Ludwig Foundation for Art and Science."

Peter Ludwig is a member of the Acquisitions Committee of the State Gallery in Düsseldorf; the International Council of the Museum of Modern Art, New York; and the Advisory Council of the Museum of Contemporary Art, Los Angeles.

Translation:

Regent International

Under the Regent label the Monheim Group distributes milk chocolate and assorted chocolates, mainly through the low-priced Aldi chain store and vending machines.

The production takes place in Aachen, where the company employs 2,500 people in two factories. It also has its administrative headquarters there. About 1,300 employees work in the Saarlouis plant, some 400 in Quickborn and approximately 800 in West Berlin. As it did ten years earlier, Monheim had in 1981 a total of some 7,000 employees (sales tripled over the same period); 5,000 of these are women. The blue-collar work force numbers 5,400, of which two-thirds are unskilled. In addition, the company employs approximately 900 unskilled seasonal workers.

The labor union Nahrung-Genuss-Gaststätten negotiated wages ranging from DM 6.02 (scale E = assembly line work, under 18 years) per hour to DM 12.30 (scale S = highly skilled work). According to the union contract, the lowest salary amounts to DM 1,097 per month, and the highest salary scale stipulates a minimum of DM 3,214.

The overwhelming majority of the 2,500 foreign workers are women. They come predominantly from Turkey and Yugoslavia. However, foreign workers are also hired by agents in Morocco, Tunisia, Spain, and Greece (price "per head": DM 1,000 in 1973).

Another contingent of foreign workers crosses the border daily from nearby Belgium and Holland. The company maintains hostels for its female foreign workers on its fenced-in factory compound in Aachen, as well as at other locations. Three or four women share a room (the building of hostels for foreign workers is subsidized by the Federal Labor Agency). The rent is automatically withheld from the worker's wage.

The company keeps a check on visitors to these hostels and, in fact, turns some away. The press office of the Aachen Diocese and the Caritas Association judged the living conditions as follows: "Since most of the women and girls can have social contacts only at the workplace and in the hostels, they are practically living in a ghetto." Female foreign workers who give birth reportedly have to leave the hostel because Monheim does not have a day care center, or they must find a foster home for the child at a price

Arbeiterinnen in einem Werk der Leonard Monheim AG.

Die Monheim-Gruppe vertreibt Tafelschokolade und Pralinen der Marke Regent zu Niedrigpreisen vor allem über Aldi und Automaten.

Die Fertigung erfolgt in Aachen, wo das Unternehmen mit rund 2500 Arbeitern und Angestellten in 2 Werken die größten Produktionsstätten und seine Hauptverwaltung betreibt. Die Zahl der Arbeiter im Werk Saarlouis beträgt ca. 1300, in Quickborn ca. 400 und in West-Berlin ca. 800.

Insgesamt hat Monheim in Deutschland 1981 wie vor 10 Jahren rund 7000 Beschäftigte – bei verdreifachtem Umsatz. Davon sind 5000 Frauen. Die Zahl der gewerblich Beschäftigten beträgt 5400. Darunter sind zwei Drittel ungelernte Arbeitskräfte. Zusätzlich werden ca. 900 meist ungelernte Saisonarbeiter eingestellt.

Der von der Gewerkschaft Nahrung-Genuß-Gaststätten ausgehandelte Tariflohn bewegt sich zwischen DM 6,02 (Tarifgruppe E – Fließbandarbeit unter 18 Jahre) und DM 12,30 (Tarifgruppe S – qualifizierte Facharbeit). Das niedrigste Gehalt, gemäß Tarifvertrag, beträgt DM 1097,–, das der höchsten Gehaltsstufe mindestens DM 3214,–.

Die überwiegende Mehrzahl der 2500 ausländischen Arbeitskräfte sind Frauen. Sie stammen vornehmlich aus der Türkei und Jugoslawien. Aber auch Gastarbeiterinnen aus Marokko, Tunesien, Spanien und Griechenland sind angeworben worden («Kopfpreis» 1973: DM 1000,–). Ausländische Arbeiterinnen kommen auch täglich aus dem

belgischen und holländischen Grenzgebiet.

Das Unternehmen unterhält in Aachen auf seinem umzäunten Betriebsgelände und an anderen Orten Wohnheime, in denen Gastarbeiterinnen zu dritt oder viert in einem Zimmer untergebracht sind (der Bau von Unterkünften für ausländische Arbeitskräfte wird von der Bundesanstalt für Arbeit subventioniert). Die Monatsmiete wird vom Lohn einbehalten.

Besuche werden von der Betriebsleitung kontrolliert und zum Teil abgewiesen. Das bischöfliche Presseamt und der Caritasverband in Aachen beurteilten die Wohnverhältnisse folgendermaßen: «Da die meisten dieser Frauen und Mädchen lediglich am Arbeitsplatz und innerhalb der Wohnheime menschliche Kontakte knüpfen können, leben sie praktisch in einem Getto.»

Da Monheim keine Kindertagesstätte habe, müßten Gastarbeiterinnen, die ein Kind bekommen, das Heim verlassen oder für ihr Kind eine für sie kaum erschwingliche Familienpflegestelle suchen, oder aber sie müßten das Kind zur Adoption anbieten.

«Es dürfte für eine große Firma, bei der so viele Mädchen und Frauen beschäftigt sind, ohne weiteres möglich sein, eine Kindertagesstätte zu errichten.»

Die Personalabteilung antwortete darauf, Monheim sei «eine Schokoladenfabrik und kein Kindergarten». Für eine Kindertagesstätte könne kein Personal beschafft werden. Die Firma sei kein Sozialamt.

LOTHAR SCHNEPF

they can hardly afford. Another option would be to offer their child for adoption. "It should be no problem for a big company which employs so many girls and women to set up a day care center."

The personnel department retorted that Monheim is "a chocolate factory and not a kindergarten." It would be impossible to hire kindergarten teachers. The company is not a welfare agency.

Haacke: Where the Consciousness Industry is Concentrated

Toch denk ik, dat U mij neit de juiste motieven toeschrijft
(But I think you question my motives),
1978/1979
Triptych of lightboxes in black formica.
Left and right boxes 60⅞ x 41 x 9⅞ inches
with black/white transparency. Center box
79¾ x 54 x 11¾ inches with color
transparency. Background to images and
texts blue silkscreen printing on plastic.
First exhibited in one-man exhibition at
Stedelijk van Abbemuseum, Eindhoven,
Netherlands, January 1979.

Translations:

Left: We are businessmen and we look
for business opportunities, which is the
only factor governing our decisions.
Political considerations don't come into it.
Nobody is going to help South Africa
unless he is paid for it, and obviously you
need know-how from abroad. We are here
to stay.
Jan Timmer, Managing Director of Philips
in South Africa.

Center: But I think you question my
motives. You see me just as a man of
capital. However, above all I really would
like people to have the freedom to develop
themselves as much as possible, to create
opportunities for themselves, to take
initiatives and carry the responsibility
for them.
Frits Philips, in his autobiography,
45 Years with Philips.

Right: The Employee Councils are
advisory bodies. They are precluded from
negotiating minimum wages or conditions
of employment, and in fact wages are
rarely discussed. The average black
worker earns 229 rand a month. Blacks
are excluded from apprentice training for
radio and TV technicians by the Job
Reservation Act.
Photo of installation in *Kunst in Europa na
'68*, Museum van Hedendaagse Kunst,
Ghent, 1980.

**Oelgemaelde, Hommage á Marcel
Broodthaers**
(Photographs follow on pages 220 and 221)
(Painting, Hommage á Marcel Broodthaers),
1982
Installation. Overall dimensions variable.
Oil painting on canvas in gold frame,
picture lamp, brass plaque, brass
stanchions with red velvet rope, red carpet
and photo mural.
Painting 35½ x 29 inches (including
frame).
First exhibited at documenta 7, Kassel,
1982.
Translation of banner inscription: Reagan
get lost. Neither NATO nor WARSAW.

Haacke: Where the Consciousness Industry is Concentrated

Caption on previous page.

UDO REUSCHLING

Haacke: Where the Consciousness Industry is Concentrated

FRED SCRUTON

We Bring Good Things To Life, 1983
Overall height 110 x 35½ inches, height of bust 27 inches.
Marbled wood pillar with fins, lettering, copper plate, gilt plaster bust, circular fluorescent tube.
First exhibited in one-man show at John Weber Gallery, New York, May 1983.

In the 1950s Ronald Reagan appeared on television in promotional programs for General Electric. The company is a large defense contractor and performs major work on the nuclear warhead for the MX and other missiles. MARK 12A is the code name of these warheads. "We bring good things to life" is the advertising slogan of GE for its electrical appliances.

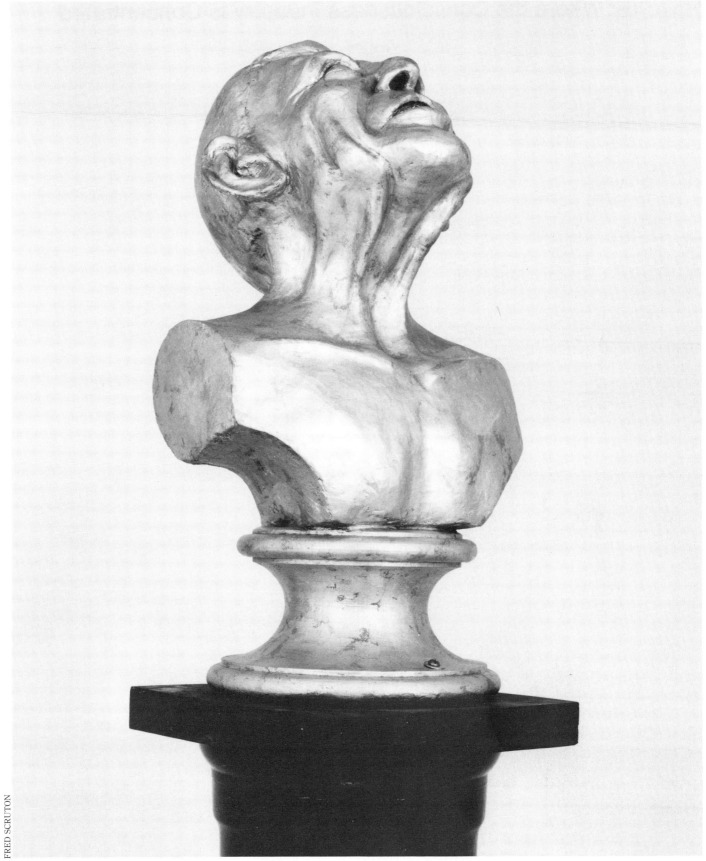

Haacke: Where the Consciousness Industry is Concentrated

Haacke: It has happened a couple of times. Whenever I go into a big thing, I have to reckon with that possibility and think of fallback positions. I learned my lesson with the Guggenheim Museum.[1] That was my introduction to the world of museum politics. So when it looked as if there would be trouble with the Wallraf-Richartz Museum in Cologne, in 1974, I made arrangements with the Paul Maenz Gallery in Cologne.[2] Fortunately, one could say, the gallery had had no dealings with the museum, that is, the museum had never bought work and there was no prospect that they would buy something in the future. So the gallery had nothing to lose and could show the work there concurrent to the big show in the museum for which it was originally made. The audience of the opening could see what had been censored. We got quite a bit of press coverage, too. It was similar with the Ludwig piece. Again, Paul Maenz came through. One can plan how to publicize such an event. These are the fallback positions. The exclusion from a work's intended venue does not necessarily mean it's all over. If you can't publicize it, however, it is the end. It's as simple as that.

Lord: Have there been pieces that haven't been shown and disappeared?

Haacke: So far not, with the exception of the Guggenheim.

Lord: Which got more publicity after that happened than it would have ever gotten had they at least put it up.

Haacke: For quite a number of years, I had no place to show the Guggenheim pieces in New York. I didn't have a gallery at the time. And there's some sort of camaraderie among the museums; they don't rebuke each other publicly. Galleries also do not like to antagonize a potential client. And museums, of course, are buying in galleries. So there was no way. It really came out in the press; the work itself was never visible. The press at the time worked very well. Around 1971, the art world and the art press were still quite sensitive. It was the time of the Vietnam War. Everybody was alert. If it had happened five years later, probably no one would have reacted. So, in a way, I was very lucky. I think we always underestimate the climate of the times.

Lord: Let's talk in more detail about your work in the last five or six years. How did the British Leyland work start?

Haacke: I was invited to have a show at the Museum of Modern Art in Oxford. Like everybody else, I knew that there's the university. Then I learned that British Leyland is the other big industry that keeps people in bread in Oxford. Leyland is the largest British automobile producer. It is a government-owned company. That made me curious. So I looked a little bit into Leyland's operations. And I stumbled across Leyland's involvement in South Africa. I went over to England and got in touch with the anti-apartheid movement and other organizations that monitor British companies' relations to South Africa. I found a lot of material. And then I went out to solicit stuff on my own. I wrote to Leyland, both in England as well as in South Africa, asking for promotional brochures. I presented myself as a potential client for a Leyland car, a Jaguar. Then I inquired with Leyland South Africa about a few things down there. I got a letter back, from the head of public relations in South Africa, telling me that South African law prevents them from giving information to any foreigner about business affairs in South Africa.

There are a great number of things in South Africa which in other countries are public information; down there they are state secrets because it would allow people outside to understand how the South African apartheid system functions. It also serves as a fantastic smoke screen for any non-South African company operating in South Africa to ward off scrutiny of their operations. During the research period, I got a call from a South African student, inquiring whether I wanted to do a guest teaching stint down there. I asked him whether he could get something for me, picture material and so forth, without endangering himself. In fact, he did send me photos and clippings from South African newspapers. Two of the pictures I actually used in this work: panel three and panel seven. Both were taken during the Soweto riots in 1975. The reproduction quality is a little poor because they were Xerox copies of newspaper prints. But it works nevertheless.

(Interview text continued on page 232)

A breed apart, 1978
Seven panels, each 36 inches square.
Photographs on hardboard (three in color), framed under glass.
First exhibited in one-man exhibition at the Museum of Modern Art, Oxford, November 1978.

Land-Rover
South Africa

No other vehicle ever produced can claim the international admiration and fame that surround the Land-Rover; overseas military authorities, in particular, continue to rely on this famous cross-country vehicle despite ever-increasing competition from motor manufacturers worldwide.

British Leyland, Press Release, Aldershot 1976

Leyland Vehicles. Nothing can stop us now.

Leyland advertising slogan

Haacke: Where the Consciousness Industry is Concentrated

Jaguar
a breed apart

An employee may have an incentive to remain with his employer, no matter how he is treated, in order to qualify for urban residence: and it has been argued that contract workers' rights to work in urban areas are so tenuous that, regardless of how uncongenial their employment or how poor their pay, they are forced to stay in their job for fear of being endorsed out of their area and back to the homelands.

UK Parliamentary Select Committee on African Wages, 1973

 **Leyland Vehicles. Nothing can stop us now.**

Leyland advertising slogan

Photo: John Paisley, Argus

The Security Council decides that all States shall cease forthwith any provision to South Africa of arms and related matériel of all types, including the sale or transfer of weapons and ammunition, military vehicles and equipment, paramilitary police equipment, and spare parts of the aforementioned, and shall cease as well the provision of all types of equipment and supplies, and grants of licensing arrangements, for the manufacture or maintenance of the aforementioned.

United Nations Security Council Resolution 418, 1977

 **Leyland Vehicles. Nothing can stop us now.**

Leyland advertising slogan

Haacke: Where the Consciousness Industry is Concentrated

Jaguar
a breed apart

Photo: Leyland

JAGUAR

Jaguar, a breed apart. The new-generation Jaguar Executive has been born. And it has opened the door to a new world...a world that, because of its sophistication and sheer class, only a select few will enter.

It is a world that has been created for the leader, not the pack. For those who have made it and stand apart from the masses. For those whose success demands, and deserves, a quality of life that spells luxury, elegance, perfection.

Leyland South Africa

 Leyland Vehicles. Nothing can stop us now.

Leyland advertising slogan

HANS HAACKE

228

Land-Rover
South Africa

No British Leyland military display could be complete without the world-famous Land-Rover. In 28 years of production the Land-Rover has become one of the United Kingdom's greatest export winners, opening up areas of the world previously inaccessible to ordinary vehicles and playing a major role in the development of many overseas territories.

British Leyland. Press Release. Aldershot 1976

 **Leyland Vehicles. Nothing can stop us now.**

Leyland advertising slogan

HANS HAACKE

Jaguar
a breed apart

It is only with great reluctance that we have concluded that Leyland South Africa cannot at this point in time reasonably recognize an African trade union for bargaining purposes—outside of a more general move towards recognition by progressive South African employers—without setting our business and employment at risk.

J. P. Lowry, Director of Personnel, British Leyland, 1976

Leyland Vehicles. Nothing can stop us now.

Leyland advertising slogan

Photo: Alon Reininger, Contact Press Images

The Protection of Business Act of 1978 is a piece of legislation specifically enacted to restrict this company and other organizations in South Africa from divulging information concerning their activities to overseas entities.

A. E. Pitlo, Leyland South Africa, 1978

Leyland Vehicles. Nothing can stop us now.

Leyland advertising slogan

HANS HAACKE

Haacke: Where the Consciousness Industry is Concentrated

Lord: The press photos are black and white, and the Jaguars are color.

Haacke: Yes.

Lord: What was the reaction in Oxford?

Haacke: I don't know all of it. As it often happens, I left immediately after the opening because I had to go back to New York to teach. However, at the opening there were a number of union people from Leyland, the head of the union of Leyland workers in Oxford and a couple of shop stewards. It could be that they recommended that their members go and look at the show. They, themselves, were all the way for it. It was interesting that they did not respond so much to the South African subject matter, although they did not remain indifferent. What they particularly reacted to was the center panel with the Jaguar and the text addressing the Jaguar clientele, the "breed apart," their classiness, the "select few" bit. They said, "This is exactly how these fuckers talk to us."

Lord: You should definitely talk about how the carpet piece came about.

Haacke: Well, I knew that the world headquarters of the Philips company was in Eindhoven. Philips is the fifth largest non-American multinational. They produce electrical household goods and work in sophisticated electronics. The company projects an image of liberalism and enlightenment—in tune with the rest of Dutch politics. I went to Amsterdam to look at the files of a research organization which is, I believe, related to the Institute for Policy Studies in Washington, D.C. Sure enough, they had a big file on Philips. I went through five big folders and, among all sorts of things, found this clipping which reproduced an advertisement that had appeared in a daily newspaper in Teheran in 1975. The ad was a eulogy of the Shah by Philips. I made a Xerox copy and then tried to reconstruct the advertisement, because the quality of the image was very poor. Its decorative border was relatively easy to do, because I had full control over it. However, I didn't understand the Arabic script. I had to divine how it could possibly look. Then I searched for Iranians in New York who could check the script and also whether

the translation was accurate. I went through several stages until it was acceptable to the experts. Then I made stencils, bought a carpet, and sprayed the image onto the carpet. And I supplied a translation from the Farsi original into Dutch, so that people in Eindhoven could read what their company was doing in Iran.

Lord: Has that ever been shown here?

Haacke: No. It probably wouldn't make too much sense here, because in the States the Philips name is practically unknown, although they also operate here. Magnavox belongs to Philips, and they are involved with Philco and Sylvania. But Philips is not known as an electronics giant in this country. Nor have people been exposed to the moral rearmament rhetoric flowing from Philips in Holland.

As it often happens, a piece can be savored fully only by people who are familiar with the situation. Just as the Philips piece doesn't mean much here, when the Mobil piece is shown in Europe, you have to provide a lengthy explanation about what Mobil means in the cultural world of New York. However, I found Australians understand it perfectly, because Mobil has moved very aggressively down there.

Lord: You seem to lose automatically whole sections of your audience.

Haacke: That's another thing about audiences. There's not just one audience; there are national audiences, there are local audiences, there are audiences that break down along educational lines, and so forth.

There is an additional problem with the Philips rug now. The piece could be taken at face value, because the Ayatollah has certainly not established anything remotely resembling a free society.

Lord: Carpet spraying seems a switch from the techniques you usually employ.

Haacke: I use a lot of different techniques. Lately I painted an old-fashioned portrait of Reagan. I also did a painting of an industrial landscape, the smelters of Alcan, in Canada.

Lord: You often pick out corporate materials and formulas—metal, glass . . . .

De oneindige dankbaarheid
(Everlasting Gratitude), 1978.
Silkscreen paint (night-blue and cobalt) sprayed on beige wool carpet, 127 x 144 inches.
Translation from Persian to Dutch in black frame under glass, 15½ x 80 inches.
First exhibited in January 1979 in one-man show at Stedelijk van Abbemuseum in Eindhoven. The Shah left Iran three days after the opening.
Translation from Persian into English: Philips of Iran expresses its everlasting gratitude to His Imperial Majesty, the Shah of Iran, who secured national unity by founding the Iranian Resurgency Party. Advertisement in the Iranian newspaper *Keyhan*, 5 March 1975.

Philips is the fifth largest non-American multinational corporation. The number of its 383,900 (1977) employees is surpassed worldwide only by General Motors, Ford and ITT. Corporate headquarters are located in Eindhoven, Holland. It is the largest private employer of that country.

In Iran, Philips maintains production facilities and a sales organization. During the Shah's regime, the Iranian military received, among other material, 210 Tiger and Phantom fighter-planes, sixteen Super Frelon helicopters and 15,000 heavy Chieftain tanks equipped with radio-altimeters, UHF radios, and/or night vision equipment from Philips. When the Shah left the country in January 1979, twelve vessels of the "Kaman" class were under construction for the Iranian Navy. Their missile guidance systems were produced by Hollands Signaalapparaten BV in Hengelo, a Dutch subsidiary of Philips.

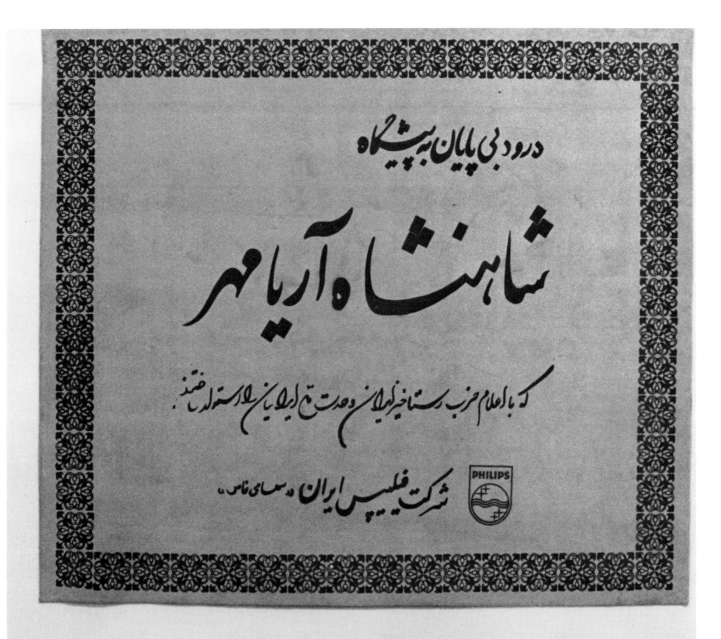

De Iraanse vestiging van Philips getuigt van haar oneindige dankbaarheid jegens zijne Keizerlijke Majesteit, de sjah van Iran, die met de proclamatie van de Iraanse Herrijzenispartij de nationale eenheid veilig heeft gesteld.

Advertentie in het Iraanse dagblad *Keyhan*, 5 maart 1975

Haacke: Where the Consciousness Industry is Concentrated

Haacke: It's really the nature of the message which determines what form the work should take. When I casually speak in such terms, I make the mistake of distinguishing between message and form. One should be very careful about that, because the form is a very integral part of the message. For example, if I use aluminum frames for the Alcan piece, the frames mean something; so do light boxes, or the medium of oil painting.

Lord: The Philips light boxes in Eindhoven?

Haacke: I looked at the annual reports of Philips. In each report, as is customary, there's a picture of the chairman. I also read Fritz Philips's autobiography. Then I discovered an article and an interview with people from Philips in a South African business journal, a periodical similar to *Forbes*, "the Capitalist Tool." I picked a few sentences from that. A technique I employ frequently is to present the contradictions between official, very noble sounding pronouncements on the one side and actual company policies on the other. For that, I rely on sources which are not suspect of a leftist bias, in this case a South African business journal.

Lord: Indisputable in the sense that they are credible?

Haacke: Not that they are indisputable, but they do not reek of a leftist bias, and therefore, in the popular mind, do not lack credibility. That, I think, is important.

Lord: Do you ever find yourself searching out information that you already know from leftist periodicals?

Haacke: Aside from the church groups that conduct valuable research work, some of the research organizations from whom I obtain my material have leftist sympathies. However, they usually have reliable source material. They have every clipping that *The Wall Street Journal*, for instance, has on a given subject. And they subscribe to most bona fide capitalist publications. Sometimes I have to double-check something. It is not wise to rely on interpretative articles; they are good to get you into the subject, but when it comes to the veracity of certain facts, it's good to check.

Lord: You're very careful not to leave yourself open.

Haacke: It's very important that you retain your credibility. As soon as you lose that, whatever you do is for the birds. If *The New York Times* were generally questioned about the accuracy of its reporting, it wouldn't have the power it has. Then, of course, there is the other aspect; if you present something as fact that is not true, and is damaging to the reputation of a company or an individual, you are in legal trouble. I have no ambition to get into that.

Lord: Or to be caught on a stupid mistake.

Haacke: It can happen that you make a stupid mistake. It could be that I've made a stupid mistake along the line of which I am unaware. So far, nothing has happened.

Lord: In terms of the circumstances and difficulties of getting things out in New York, what were you thinking about when you chose Paine Webber for a New York show?

Haacke: Somewhere or other, I found a Paine Webber annual report. I don't remember how it got into my hands. It was quite incredible: a stock brokerage house using a depression photo of an unemployed man to drum business from its investor clients. I learned around the same time that one of the principals of Paine Webber is a trustee at the Museum of Modern Art and is an art collector.

Lord: Did you think it would be more likely to get picked up by the New York press because it was Paine Webber?

Haacke: It didn't, but of course it had that potential. The more one deals with these things, the more one understands how fickle and unpredictable the press is. There are so many things that can keep a story from being published—any kind of story: a news event like an earthquake might preempt the attention; the reporter who is most prone to do something might be on vacation; there might be social connections between people in the editorial office and my "target"—anything from the trivial to the sinister. It's really quite unpredictable. It's probably easier outside New York. New York is so saturated with news or stuff that has sufficient clout to be published. It's very difficult to get through unless you have a big PR campaign going, and that requires money and connections.

Take the building of the image of the Mary Boone Gallery: that is a fantastic phenomenon. There's a lot of money invested and a lot of clever maneuvers. After a while it goes on its own momentum. Obviously, I don't have such resources. What I am doing is not as glamorous as Mary Boone.

Lord: Do you always visit the place you're going to show?

Haacke: I usually go there. Once I was in an awkward situation. I was to have a show in Zagreb, Yugoslavia. I didn't have an opportunity to go there before and, of course, I didn't speak or read Serbo-Croatian. It was also kind of touchy to do something there. So I thought about how to extricate myself from this dilemma and, at the same time, hint to the audience in Zagreb what they could have expected had I been able to do what I do in other places. There was a staircase leading up to the exhibition rooms with a large mirror at the top landing. Everyone going into the museum saw himself or herself in the mirror. So I put one or two sentences on the mirror, in blue letters, explaining that I do not speak Serbo-Croatian, that I don't know the situation there well enough and that, therefore, I'm not producing something in this show as I do in other places where I deal specifically with the context of the exhibition place. I put my name underneath, with a red star. So the blue, the red star, and the white ceiling reflected in the mirror made up the Yugoslav flag. And the viewers saw themselves in the mirror. I hoped everybody could read between the lines, which they did.

Lord: It's a beautiful solution.

Haacke: We have talked a lot about audiences. This is important for anyone who is concerned about how their communications are received. For good reason advertising agencies spend a fortune on finding out more about the people whom they want to address and who would potentially be receptive to their persuasive efforts. As much as one might despise the Madison Avenue mercenaries, they are sophisticated professionals. One can learn a lot from them. After all, they are often trying to reach the same audience. Although infinitesimally small, like them, I am part of the consciousness industry. The mythical aura of the artist compensates, to some degree, for my lack of resources, particularly when the battleground is the art world. I think it is politically as important to continuously challenge the association of culture with big business as it is to make the population aware that the goals of corporations are, by definition, in conflict with the public interest. It would be disastrous if it were generally accepted that culture's best friend is big business. And, I think it would be equally harmful if the opposition failed to develop a culture that, due to its sectarianism, could not radiate beyond its congregation.△

Notes

1. In 1971, a one-man exhibit of Haacke's work at the Guggenheim Museum was cancelled six weeks before the scheduled opening. Thomas Messer, the museum's director, objected to the inclusion of three works that were especially made for the show. When Haacke did not agree to withdraw these works, the show was called off. Two of the works dealt with New York real estate by way of photographs of the facades of buildings and documentary information culled from the city registrar's files on their owners. The third work was to have been a poll of the museum's visitors. Through answers to a multiple-choice questionnaire, the visitors would have provided a demographic profile of themselves and would have taken a position on art-world and sociopolitical issues of the day. When the curator of the exhibit, Edward F. Fry, defended the censored works publicly, he was fired.

2. In 1974, Haacke was invited to participate in an international exhibition of contemporary artists organized by the Cologne Wallraf-Richartz Museum to celebrate its hundredth anniversary. Haacke produced a work on the provenance of Manet's *Bunch of Asparagus* in the museum's collection. The director of the museum objected to the documentary portrayal of the German banker Hermann Josef Abs (Abs had been instrumental in the purchase and donation of the painting to the museum) and excluded Haacke's work from the exhibit. Daniel Buren, an artist who had also been invited, collaged a reduced-scale version of the censored work over his own, thereby making it a part of his work. The museum's director then had all the parts of Buren's piece that originated from Haacke pasted over.

LOS ANGELES LESBIAN ARTS

by Arlene Raven

UNTIL THE EARLY 1970S, there was nobody of work that could be called lesbian art—the result of a painful conspiracy of silence between fearful lesbians and a homophobic society. When lesbian artists gathered together in feminist art-political groups and took courage to name themselves, their art came into focus for the first time as a creative expression of self-consciousness and a common sensibility.

The work emerged in fragments and pieces over a number of years of talk, collaboration, and public exposure. None of it was developed exclusively in the rarefied world of art; rather it grew out of and was influenced by activism on behalf of ethnic minorities, the economically disadvantaged, women, and other oppressed groups. The political literature of the Left and the women's movement also influenced lesbian art, and lesbian-feminist theories, rather than only art theories, were applied. No matter what its theme or style, any work made by a woman-identified woman was considered lesbian art. This new perspective challenged us to question our protective invisibility in the masculinized

"neutrality" of art and artist. In the earliest critiques and exhibitions, we sought to identify specific themes and forms in our work; we were our own audience, critics and supporters. At the same time, we addressed feminist, art and general audiences in these public events, exposing many people to a body of work that expressed creative pride and beauty about a subject long veiled in secrecy and shame.

Womanhouse, a collaborative project of the feminist art program at the California Institute of the Arts, contained no specifically lesbian content. Exhibited in a condemned house in midtown Los Angeles early in 1972, environments and performances expressed the suburban, white middle-class housewife's dissatisfaction with her roles and life-style. Although a number of lesbians participated in the project, most of the women in the United States—including lesbians and women of color—remained invisible in *Womanhouse*.

We have to look very closely at *Womanhouse* to see evidence of the bonding which was taking place among women; only in the performance *Birth Trilogy* was there any expression of woman-identifica-

tion. But the community symbolized in *Birth Trilogy* was real—an ongoing group of women who created Womanspace, which opened in January 1973. Although by no means exclusively lesbian, they nevertheless identified with each other in an all-women environment, and support of lesbians was visible.

One of the first Womanspace activities, Lesbian Week, included an exhibition, entertainment, dancing, lectures about lesbian heritage, and workshops. For some participants, this event was a first coming out. In a slide presentation (and subsequent article in *Womanspace Journal*,[1]) Christina Schlesinger described her reaction to the working-class lesbians in a neighborhood bar who fit the "butch" stereotype. Despite her initial alienation, she nevertheless felt a need to identify with them and thus claim parts of herself and her heritage. Stereotypes were not in the people at this bar but in the social structure itself.

Dara Robinson, Lesbian Visibility Series, 1979.

Raven: Los Angeles Lesbian Arts

MY OWN EXPERIENCE with lesbian art and artists is most closely connected with the Woman's Building, which opened in 1973 and is today one of the oldest surviving feminist cultural centers. Within the Woman's Building, lesbians could participate in gallery exhibitions, take classes, attend dances and lectures, the cafe or Sisterhood Bookstore, join NOW or other women's organizations. It was a positive place where women could meet and work with feminists who had political and artistic interests.

The ongoing dialogue and support among lesbians and feminists resulted in a variety of events, workshops and other projects that combined art, education and action to deal with issues ranging from an anti-homosexual bill pending in the California legislature to incest, the exclusion of women from Los Angeles museum exhibitions, and the threat of nuclear war. Throughout the decade, the network of people and organizations working on these social issues contributed to the growth of lesbian art—which in turn inspired the expansion of the feminist political community.

MARIA KARRAS PHOTOGRAPHY

The Feminist Studio Workshop and LALALA

In the fall of 1973, women from all over the country gathered in Los Angeles for the first Feminist Studio Workshop (FSW), the educational component of the Woman's Building and the only independent feminist art institution then in existence. Thirty to forty-five students attended the full-time program annually, working together from one to three years, often collaboratively.

Two projects by FSW students were both typical and exemplary: *Victim to Victory* (1974) and *Family Portraits* (1975). Cheryl Swannack and Marguerite Elliot, who had been beaten by police while locking the Woman's Building one evening, created *Victim to Victory* as a combined ceremony, environment and art performance to publicly exorcise and heal this experience. They cast a circle spread with fine-colored sand and, with Anne Philips acting as shaman, painted their bodies, chanted, and invited their friends for a feast. Their performance was also an

affirmation of lesbianism as the source for their art making and a magical agent of transformation. In *Family Portraits*, Elliot, Marcie Baer and Diane de Vine "played" with life-sized dolls, parodying various art historical modes—such as the picnic, the anatomy lesson, or Grant Wood's *American Gothic*—as a way of fashioning art in their own images.

Family Portraits was exhibited in the LALALA (Los Angeles League for the Advancement of Lesbianism in the Arts) group show at the Woman's Building in 1975. LALALA also included a weekend of events and celebration for hundreds of women. Although the work varied in media from Nancy Fried's bread dough sculptures to Lili Lakich's neon constructions and Dara Robinson's photo collages, much of the art was made with a conscious "lesbian perspective"—which had clearly shifted in a few years from that of an outsider to one of belonging.

From Victim to Victory. **Marquerite Elliott, Anne Philips, and Cheryl Swannack, 1974.**

Live Lesbian Art, **by Lili Lakich, neon, porcelain, and steel, 11′ × 8½′ × 12′.**

Raven: Los Angeles Lesbian Arts

Eating more, but enjoying it less?

whatever you do, DON'T diet.

Eating More, But Enjoying It Less? **Postcard by Sue Maberry, 1982, produced as part of the Art & Life Postcard Project at the Women's Graphic Center, Los Angeles.**

When Nancy was a child, her grandmother told her the story of the difference between Heaven and Hell. In Hell, a long banquet table is piled high with sumptuous food and all the people are desperately trying to feed themselves with four-foot-long forks. Heaven is exactly the same scene – the long banquet table and the sumptuous meal. The difference is that in Heaven, people are using the four-foot-long forks to feed each other.

Heaven or Hell? **An art performance by the Feminist Art Workers, presented November 21, 1981, for Thanks, But No Thanks, a week-long citywide public art event. Postcard design and photograph by Sue Maberry.**

The Lesbian Art Project and An Oral Herstory of Lesbianism

The most comprehensive journey into lesbian art and culture at the Woman's Building was the Lesbian Art Project (LAP), which I began as part of the FSW in 1977 and continued in partnership with Terry Wolverton. We used our own experience to provide concepts which were then translated into images and words of lesbian life. Consider these examples:

–Bia Lowe's poster for a Family of Women Dance reflects our sense of women as a basic social unit as important as the nuclear family.

–Sue Maberry's postcards proclaim joyful lesbian messages and romanticism in a startling new view of universal feelings.

–The Feminist Art Workers perform as amazons to recall a tradition of history and myth infused with lesbian strength.

–Clsuf's mail art poster, *HERSHE-KISSESHER*, takes apart male-oriented English and puts it back together in the feminine gender.

These works bring the special quality of female intimacy into public territory, where it may be strange or difficult for some people but is always educational, enlightening, politicizing, even trans-forming.

An Oral Herstory of Lesbianism was a collaboration of LAP conceived by Terry Wolverton and performed by thirteen lesbians for small, all-female audiences during May 1979. It was the fullest synthesis of research and work in the project as well as its most artistically complex artwork. Songs, dialogue, dance and multimedia vignettes were presented in an oval "stage" separated from the audience by only a line on the interior floor. The program, designed by Bia Lowe and printed by Clsuf, contained a solarized photograph by Tee Corinne of two women making love; it served as an equivalent of all that the audience would hear and see in *Oral*—shocking or uncomfortable material presented with grace and beauty. The stories told by the performers—composites of lesbian identity, relationships and community—dramatized issues that brought sighs of recognition among both lesbian and heterosexual members of the audience—such as anger between lovers— as well as those particular to lesbian life, such as "coming out" or the triple burden of being queer as well as female and black/

brown/yellow/Jewish/poor. The experience helped women better understand one another and thus put to rest divisive issues that can impede political action.

GALAS and Woman*Woman*Works

The Great American Lesbian Art Show (GALAS), a national invitational exhibition curated by Bia Lowe, included some of the most developed and successful lesbian artists in the U.S. *Woman*Woman*Works*, curated by Sue Maberry, Betsy Bloser and myself, was an open exhibition in which artists and nonartists expressed their relationship to other women in a standard format. Held together at the Woman's Building in 1981, the exhibits were documented by Terry Wolverton's *GALAS Guidebook* and my catalogue essay for *Woman*Woman*Works* (published in the Woman's Building's newsletter, *Spinning Off*).

I have described some of the works and activities in Los Angeles that made the most direct contribution to the evolution of forms and ideas we call lesbian art. I have often speculated about the real power and effectiveness of such activity. Once I believed that the larger and more diverse the audience, the more accessible an action for change can be; now I see that the internal changes and small group or one-to-one communications can have a spiraling pattern, which may in the end prove more powerful an agent of change than larger organized efforts. More than ever aware of the repressive power of governments, religions, and the media, I also see how human understanding is buffeted back and forth in cycles rather than in logical or linear progression. But I do believe in the power of art to change consciousness. And I know that simple persistence and the will to go on working, declaring oneself visible and accountable each day, is the only sure practice through which we can live and keep alive our goals and visions.△

Notes

1. Christina Schlesinger, "The Image of the Lesbian in Contemporary Society," *Womanspace Journal*, 1 (2) (April/May 1973): 21.

Sheela-na-gigs, by Sue Maberry and Cherie Chaulke, 3½ × 7".

Sheela-na-gigs are prehistoric symbols of female sexuality from a time when people worshipped the Earth Mother.

Sheela-na-gigs were placed on churches built by Christians on pagan worship sites. As the cult of the Virgin Mary grew, the church succeeded in replacing the pagan Earth Mother.

▼

Sheela-na-gigs on Christian churches are thought by some to have been a symbol to ward off evil spirits. To modern feminists, Sheela-na-gigs represent a time when female sexuality was worshipped, not feared. They remind us that women's sexuality & spirituality coexist inseparably even today.

◆

HEADLINES, HEARTLINES, HARDLINES

One of the saddest cases is that of the critic Lucy Lippard ... There was every reason to believe that a writer of this quality would one day become one of our leading historians of the modern movement. Yet in the Seventies Miss Lippard fell victim to the radical whirlwind. The scholarship and discrimination that won her the respect of the art world is a thing of the past. Nowadays she writes in defense of ideas that, if triumphant, would require all her earlier work to be placed under a permanent ban. This, to be sure, is an extreme case. The descent into straightout political propaganda is not usually so crude.
—Hilton Kramer, The New Criterion, 1982.

In reading this article it should be recognized that the authors are advocates of their deeply held beliefs. Artforum is printing this article as an opinion of the writers and as a matter of public interest affecting the arts. —Artforum *editors' disclaimer prefacing "Cashing in a Wolf Ticket," by Kearns and Lippard, October 1981.*

Advocacy Criticism As Activism

by Lucy R. Lippard

WITHIN THE MAIN-stream of Western visual art, criticism is seen more as a reviewing service to the market, or a superior intellectual commentary, than as a socially engaged activity. The *Artform* disclaimer above indicates that writing from a base of "deeply held beliefs"—a euphemism for left politics—is suspect. "Good criticism" is supposed to provide an objective look at specific objects, bodies of work, or trends, not to reflect in any direct or god forbid subjective way the writer's political views; certainly not to focus on the social, economic, and cultural forms in which the art is located.

What I'm calling an advocate critic, on the other hand, works from a communal base to identify and criticize the existing social structures as a means to locate and evaluate the social and aesthetic effect of the art. Ideally such a critic avoids star making or promoting any single style; openly supports art that is also critical of, or openly opposed to, the political powers that be (whether through experimental form, visual analysis, community outreach, or directly agitational imagery); and perhaps most importantly, tries to innovate the notion of "quality" to include the unheard voices, the unseen images, of the unconsidered people.

It may be that the notion of an advocacy *criticism* is a contradiction in terms. I see it, like activist art, as an organizing tool as well as the source of aesthetic expression or provocation. It is for me a means by which to raise public consciousness about the role of art in social life and to affirm the connections between artists and the Left and a variety of cultural communities. Advocacy means taking a stand, arguing for an aesthetic or a value system. It denies neutrality and false objectivity and forces the hands of those who prefer to take no position. As we know from so many other contexts, "apolitical" stances simply reinforce the status quo.

Mainstream Western criticism also advocates, but it does so by burying its political agendas in a cocoon of accepted values, by limiting its range of choices to the neutral array of styles laid out by the dominant culture, and by carefully rejecting any taint of what I call advocacy— forthright belief, focused anger, direct opposition to the ways art, and therefore people's voices, are disempowered. The best left and feminist criticism does not limit itself to any single style, nor does it claim any particular piece of turf within the mainstream. On the contrary, it makes its selections of "good art" from many different levels of cultural production, and from a cross-racial, cross-cultural, cross-class reservoir, respecting the locality from which it comes rather than trying to wrench it into the dangerous flow of the fashionable. In the process, this art is frequently and inaccurately assumed to be "bad art," as though good politics automatically destroyed formal achievements.

LIPPARD: HEADLINES, HEARTLINES, HARDLINES

The distinction, then, between progressive and mainstream advocacy would be the degree of overt and covert support. The disadvantage of overt opposition to the status quo is that the critic is identified (in fact identifies her/himself) primarily in relation to the opposition. Covert advocacy, because it is supposedly neutral, can pose as *not* advocacy, as *not* the product of "deeply held beliefs," but as just another "original," individual contribution to society.

Thus the leftist or advocate critic's major dilemma is how do we define ourselves not through the opposition but through our own positive goals for an empowered, democratic art? Having analyzed the meaning of individualism in relation to different cultures, different times, how do we reinstate the role of the creative individual within our wider definition of culture? Some possible models are emerging from "minority" and feminist art, from Cuba and Nicaragua, where revolutionary culture is not defined as what we would call "political art" but as any "good art," with any (or no) content, executed within the revolution—a subject beyond the scope of this article, but crucial to the future of its arguments.

I AM GOING TO HAVE TO USE myself as an example here because by definition, advocacy criticism is rooted in specific experience. I write free-lance, choosing my own subjects, because it fulfills an ideological need. I was first attracted to art because it represented rebellion within the middle class where I was raised. After years spent gradually learning how individual rebellion alone fails to fulfill the potential power of art, I was led into an active exploration of the relationship between individual work and social rebellion, and from there into group work.

In a monthly column for *The Village Voice*, and in other alternative publications, I write journalism about art I can support politically and aesthetically—a far wider range than one would suspect. For specialized or trade magazines, where I can reproduce much more art and thus be

more specific, I sometimes try to apply my politics to work that does not overtly share them, but that has roots in social concern (such as the abstractions of Harmony Hammond or Kes Zapkus, the surreal naturalism of Ellen Lanyon, the public art in nature of Pat Johanson, to cite some recent articles).

Advocacy doesn't preclude a critical viewpoint, but I tend to leave the criticism up to the art itself. My audience is artists, and people involved in left culture or in the issues the artists deal with. I guess I'm advocating *with* artists *to* other artists as a way of opening up the public notions of what art can be, of the impact of images, and of what images mean to different audiences. I make a point of spreading my efforts out. In writing or in organizing a few exhibitions a year, I try not to cite the same artists and I try to expose art that is often peripheral or unfamiliar to the mainstream. It's a strategy to get a more multi-faceted art *seen*, and it's a means of networking, of showing artists how many other artists are making challenging varied work on social issues. As a consequence, I can spread myself pretty thin, and I'm often told that my supportive stance makes me uncritical, or makes me not a critic, period. That's okay with me, since I've never like the term anyway. Its negative connotations place the writer in fundamental antagonism to the artists, whereas I prefer to work in an indirect (at times direct) partnership with an artist or group.

The lines between advocacy, promotion, and propaganda are thin. My dictionary defines an advocate as "one who pleads the case of another or argues in behalf of a proposal"; a promoter is "one who promotes or furthers any movement or project and advances another in dignity or position"; and a propagandist is "one who devotes himself to the propagation of some creed or doctrine." Is there a place for creed (belief) in art? At what point does the word one is spreading become separated from one's beliefs and one's audience and become dogma? At what point does an expression of commitment *to* become negatively propaganda *for*? (My positive use of the word propaganda in itself is forced on me by the opposition's negative use of the term for aspects of my work that I find positive.)

Advocacy criticism, like activist art, is defined by a communal base. It is also, paradoxically, defined by its opposition to

the community the critic is supposed to be part of—the mainstream art world. Part of this paradox is the hardly concidental fact that the dominant culture encourages a false dichotomy between critic and artist. We are theoretically pitted against each other instead of acknowledging our common manipulation. For the same reasons that artists can't be unionized ("too individualistic"), solidarity is anathema. In the early sixties, *New York Times* critic John Canaday went so far as to decree that critics and artists should not even know each other socially, since such intimacy with the enemy threatened critical objectivity. This bizarre viewpoint took on a distinctly sexist tone when he used it as an excuse to fire Dore Ashton from the *Times*; she "knew" artists too well—was in fact married to one of them. So was I at the time, and I took it personally. Since I began to write about art in the mid-sixties, my ideas have consistently emerged from direct contact with artists, from studios rather than from galleries and magazines.

In the late sixties–early seventies, when I began to understand more about the structures in which art is made and then manipulated, and when I began to make occasional streetworks and other bits of "art" myself, my notion of criticism extended from the work of individuals to include those structures. Its form emerged from political dissent and from rage at the exclusion of so much art that moved me. Feminism was a crucial factor, empowering many of us not only to revise the patriarchal history of art, but also to embrace subjectivity as opposed to the prescribed objectivity, to approach art more personally, to take a more honest look at the sources of our aesthetic standards and values.

By the mid-seventies, I was trying to acquire, belatedly, a theoretical armature for my socialist-feminist practice. Perhaps due to an overdose of undigested Marxism, in the late seventies, I went through a painful period of passionate disillusionment with artists themselves. I blamed them for the opportunism, competitiveness, and impotence that the art world forces on them; I was outraged by the lack of responsibility and reluctance to communicate with any audience that I found in some quarters. I did a slide performance called *Propaganda Fictions*, in one section of which I shouted spitefully and repeatedly at my friends in the audience (because, of course, the people I was aiming at weren't there), *"You lousy artists!"*

Having divested myself of that particular layer of my authority problem, I began again to organize with socialist artists. We started PADD (Political Art Documentation/Distribution) in spring 1979, began to meet seriously in February 1980, and got our act together in the fall of 1980. One of our platforms is to combat the insidious notion imposed by conventional art education—that you must choose between making art and being politically active. We insist not only that you can do both, but that social action can be incorporated into our art practices. An element of this fusion is a deliberate confusion of the traditional roles. Since the avant-garde stopped trying to shock the bourgeoisie and dived under its wing for economic protection, it has been in the interests of those who buy and sell art (and everything else) to keep us all in our places. You are supposed to be either an artist or a critic, either a painter or a performer, either a critic or a curator. You are making either art or craft, high or low culture; you are either a professional or an amateur artist, and so forth.

PADD attracted not only so-called political artists, but also those interested in working politically as artists, whatever the style and content of their work in the studio. Over the last three years, we have debated whether even our organizational work—postering, magazine production, fund-raising, demonstrating, envelope licking—might not be integrated into our definition of activist art. For example, artist Jerry Kearns and I see our long-term collaborative work of curating, organizing, writing, designing, and performing together as part of *his* work as a painter and *mine* as a writer.

Collaborative and collective work is one way activist artists have challenged the divisiveness and compartmentalization that are capitalism's prime props. The notion of critic as parasite on the artist disappears when criticism is redefined in terms of various levels of collaboration and exchange (though the disproportionate *power* of the critic remains a problem). In the mainstream, there are also younger artists defiantly ignoring their job descriptions. A case in point is Thomas Lawson—painter, critic, and editor of *Real Life* magazine. He suffered an *Artform* disclaimer in the same issue Kearns and I did, not because he "believed too deeply," but because he illustrated a critical article

with the work of artist friends whose art is shown in the same gallery as his own is. In other words, he advocated the work of artists whose aesthetic and commercial interests he shared, thereby violating market etiquette. A year later, he replied to the disclaimer, decrying "the tyranny of specialization" in art as "the white collar equivalent of the division of labor." He cited his "refusal to settle down and be one thing or another" as central to his activity as an artist, "for it is precisely through the expediency of naming and categorizing that the culture entraps us, gives us an identity that can then be monitored."[1]

Lawson sees the task of "his generation" as searching "the ruins of a discredited ideology for a renewed sense of purpose and authority. This search has typically taken the form of an investigation of text and context, of the impure situation in which art finds itself, and of the means it uses to represent itself." Actually this "impure situation" (the phrase was initiated by Jasper Johns some twenty years ago) stems from another "discredited ideology"—the advocacy/activist approach that originated in the sixties and was not entirely co-opted by the pluralism that dominated the mainstream seventies. Blurring of boundaries is still looked upon with suspicion, although for well over a decade the lines have repeatedly been crossed, more often by artists than by critics.

In the mid-sixties, the innovative writings of Ad Reinhardt, Robert Smithson and Dan Graham, among others, were joined by so-called conceptual art. Artists claimed the text as a valid medium for visualization, bypassed their "critics," and reclaimed the right to speak for themselves. This was a political strategy, if not a highly successful one, that emerged from the social consciousness-raising taking place in and out of the art world at that time. During the seventies, an increasing number of avant-garde artists were influenced by left media analysis which had surfaced, and later made it into the mainstream, through those sixties radicals in sociology and communications and other nonart fields who managed to hang onto their university jobs. This in turn led some artists to define their pictorial strategies in relationship to the mass media and to the popular culture that had in fact formed their ways of seeing. Among the most effective practitioners today are artists/critics Martha Rosler, Hans Haacke, Alan Sekula, Lisa Steele, Doug Kahn, and

LIPPARD: HEADLINES, HEARTLINES, HARDLINES

the late Kenneth Coutts-Smith. New lines are still being crossed, most notably and controversially by the young graffiti artists invading the mainstream from the barrios and the ghettos, and by the alienated young middle-class artists going in the opposite direction. In these cases music, dancing (as opposed to dance), performance, and film are the vehicles of changeover.

ADVOCACY CRITICISM has two major problems. The first is avoiding a moralizing or preaching tone that the converting don't like any more than the unconverted. The second is "conflict of interest." For example, I am in the peculiar position of being practically the only journalist writing regularly on activist art from the inside. I often find myself writing about friends and/or people I work with, about groups and events which I have supported or helped organize. My life is centered on the development of a responsible and responsive left culture, but if I exercise my expertise (that is, if I write about what I'm doing as well as what I'm looking at), I'm caught in a bind between conviction and promotion, advocacy and "self-interest," learned rhetoric and experiential enthusiam. If I'm critical of the more naive art, I'm seen from the left as unsupportive, incorrect, or—worse still—a formalist! From the center and right (the mainstream), I'm accused, sometimes justifiably, of preaching to the converted. And I hate writing about progressive group shows—inevitably having too little space to do them justice, and ending up just listing names and objects. But if I don't nobody else will cover these often obscure and unpublicized events whose ratios of "good art" are usually as high as most museum shows. How else can I fulfill my function of communicating what is being made, how well, where, and how?

The conventional view of the critic's role is an arbiter of taste, market researcher, or messenger from high culture handing down The Word to unsuspecting consumers. Like all critics, my tastes are subjective. I also choose to write primarily about what "I like"—by which I mean not just the personal or educated taste and conditioning that influence my aesthetic standards, but also the ethics and values, intent and effect of the artist and the work. My criteria for quality (I prefer the term "aesthetic integrity") include the political compoents of race, sex, age, and geography as well as style, subject, and visual compatibility. As an advocate, I like to see myself as a medium through which a dialogue or exchange is facilitated, resulting in an indirect collaboration between artist, writer, and reader/viewer. An integral part of this task is "to forge words that even children can understand," to abandon, often reluctantly, the intricacies of obfuscatory language, to escape the specialist's corner into which criticism has backed itself.

But when the *vox* of advocacy becomes too clear, too vociferous, it is dismissed as propaganda—a term I've embraced because I find it poetic. To propagate means to seed, to spread the word—functions I want very much to fulfill in my writing. The word originated in the church and still implies *belief* as dogma. At the same time, I intend no disrespect for my audience, and its negative sense of propaganda is assumed to be aimed at a nonthinking, nonquestioning audience; most of us who see outselves as advocates are motivated by the opposite intention. Activist art and advocacy criticism hope to provide unpredictable and sometimes unpleasant jolts out of the ruts into which the dominant culture has lulled us. Both must include a constant awareness of the insidiously subtle propaganda that pervades everything we see and do and think—hegemony.

It's significant that one gets called a Stalinist, a propagandist, or a "victim of the radical whirlwind" (à la Hilton Kramer), not when one "pushes" a single style or the work of a single artist, but when one begins to advocate specific ways in which art can challenge the status quo, when one insists on relating art to what exists in society—racism, classism, sexism. I've also found that if one writes from one's convictions, and if those convictions are shared by an identifiable number of other people, then one's writing is perceived as dogma, a "line," by the ruggedly individual art world which has a low tolerance for passion, militancy, and directness.

Now and then, someone in PADD complains that as a group we "don't deal with theory," being too taken up with our current activities. My own experience is that everything I write is informed by the theory (ideas) that arises within collaborative and collective work with PADD, with the *Heresies* collective (which since 1976 has published a feminist magazine on art and politics), and with Kearns, my working partner (as well as with friends who read more than I do and are better informed on current ideas and events or come from different cultures). I find that even the most rambling intramural discussions in meetings or the most minute socialist small talk can open up areas I can learn from, and I call that theory. (The word comes from the Greek *theoros*—"to watch a spectacle.")

Similarly, the networking that goes on between feminist, leftist, and community artists is invaluable. From often different bases, we are trying to develop an activist art that doesn't simply illustrate existing theory or history, but evolves its own theory organically, as it goes along, through discussion, public forums, public art projects, studio art, and personal and political life. PADD's exhibitions, monthly Second Sunday forums, and projects such as the recent *Not For Sale* against gentrification and displacement on New York's Lower East Side, are developed within a workshop or mini-study group format, so at best the process is in true feminist fashion as important to the participants as the product.[2] When I write about a PADD project (which I'm not "supposed" to do because of conflict of interest, but which I do anyway, on principle, if I haven't been totally immersed in it), I've done my homework and am able to incorporate diverse viewpoints, sometimes to the point of virtually plagiarizing my colleagues' ideas.

So organizing work, frustrating as it can be, is my school of continuing education. Through work with District 1199's Bread and Roses program, I've had to consider the role of culture in the labor movement; through *Heresies'* issue on racism, I had to confront my own stereotypes and prejudices and incorporate into my other work unfamiliar tastes and approaches; through work with the Institute for Arts and Letters of El Salvadore in Exile (INALSE), I've had to try and envision the life of an exile and the role of art in the various stages of a revolution; through making protest art for political demonstrations, I've seen the possibilities for new forms of public imagery, and the need to recharge some old forms; through making decidedly amateur comic strips and posters, as well as page and performance art of my own and with Kearns, I have gained increased respect for the professionals; the same goes for the minimal amount of teaching I've done, which made me realize the major contribution of those providing alternatives within the constricting towers of learning. Grass-roots community organizers, in particular, offer models for visual art strategies as yet uninvented.

The groups I work with give my criticism a context and support system, allowing me to define and develop my ideas in a dialectical relationship to a community that both nourishes and takes issue with them. But the weeds of contradiction and conflict run rampant. The problem of the perceived (if often illusory) power of the critic over the artist's fate remains a divisive factor, as do the varying levels of success, talent, and political experience within any group. These problems can be analyzed in terms of the broader situation, but they remain specific, local, and nagging; not to mention the endless cycle of powerlessness and protest, burnout and regeneration, the endless conflicts between public and personal life, art making as an individual and a group activity. And time, always time—*Time, Life, Fortune*, even *Good Housekeeping*, and their inroads into our aspirations. I hope I've avoided sounding like everything's rosy in the progressive art gardens. Still, all that shit helps keep the seeds of cultural democracy growing.△

NOTES

1. *Artforum*, November 1982.
2. See issues 5-7 of PADD's publication, *UPFRONT*.

For further information on PADD, write 339 Lafayette Street, New York, New York 10012, or call 212-420-8196.

Beware Art!

Photomontage as Political Intervention

by
KLAUS STAECK

Klaus Staeck: Art & the Public Arena

This text originally appeared in Klaus Staeck's newsletter and catalog, *Staeckbrief*, as a statement to accompany exhibits of his work. The translation was provided by John J. Neumaier, with editorial assistance by Elizabeth Gjelten. Captions for the visual materials were supplied by *Praxis* and Hans Haacke.

For over ten years Klaus Staeck has gone beyond the narrow confines of galleries and museums to produce mass art—by now about ten million posters, postcards, bumperstickers, flyers, and other documentation. His posters have been distributed in many cities and shown in more than 3,000 exhibits in West Germany and abroad.

A self-taught artist, Staeck had, until 1967, produced mainly abstract oil paintings, watercolors, and wood carvings, and had exhibited in galleries with modest success. Later he turned to silkscreen prints, collages, and objects with sociopolitical themes. However, the galleries weren't interested in political work, and his small-edition prints were not suitable for broad public distribution. Unable to gain public notice in the traditional artistic framework, Staeck turned to mass-produced posters in an attempt to extend the concept of art.

It all began in 1971 during the celebration of Dürer's anniversary in Nüremberg. At his own cost, Staeck had posters put up on the city's advertising kiosks with a portrait of Dürer's mother and the words "Would you rent a room to this woman?"—a satirical commentary on old people's housing problems.

Through this experience, Staeck found that he could speak directly to a large public. During the 1972 election campaign for the Bundestag, his posters were distributed on a mass scale, mainly by groups of grass-roots activists favoring the social democratic–liberal party coalition. Although the first edition of the Dürer poster amounted to only 500 copies, the poster entitled "Workers of Germany! The SPD will take away your villas in Tessin!" quickly reached an edition of 70,000.

This image, as forceful and hallucinating as anything produced by John Heartfield, Richard Huelsenbeck, or any of the other masters of photomontage, is accompanied by the line, "And the shark has teeth!" (from Brecht's *Threepenny Opera*: "See the shark with his teeth like razors/All can read his open face/And MacHeath has got a knife, but/Not in such an obvious place . . ."). Black and red postcard, 1975.

Photographs of postcards by Eduardo Calderon.

Und der Haifisch der hat Zähne

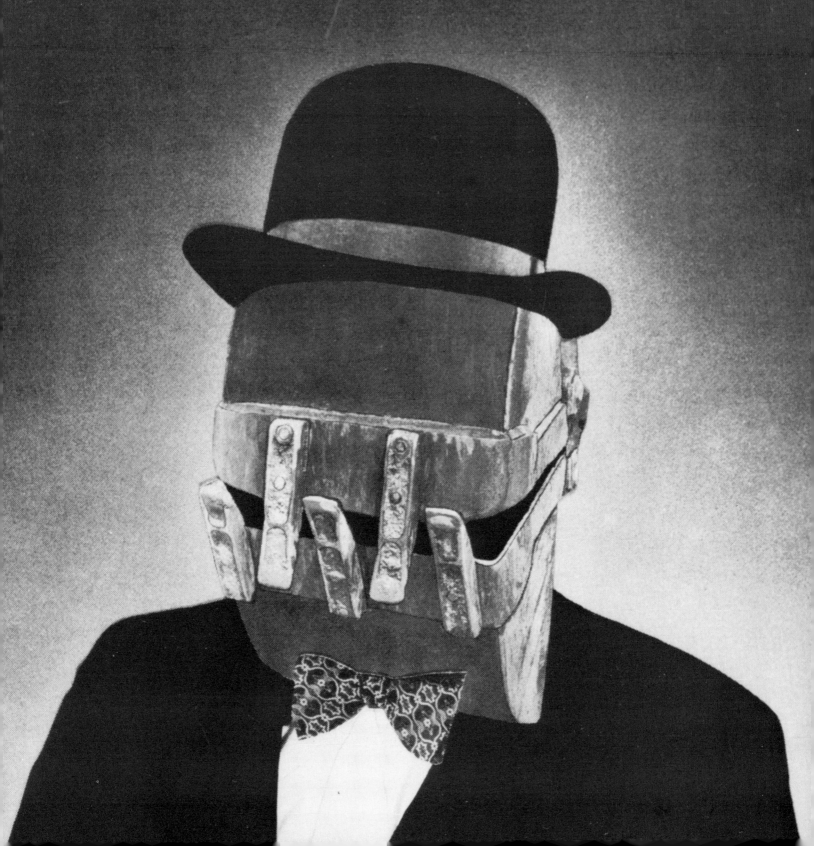

STAECK: Beware Art! Photomontage as Political Intervention

Art and Politics

Ever since Staeck's first posters, the bourgeois art public and those in the business of art have argued whether his work is art or politics. Since this issue seems to be their main interest in the pieces, Staeck feels the question should be left open as long as possible. Never exclusively art or politics, his works represent a balancing act between the two.

When somebody sees a poster on a kiosk, he or she does not think primarily about art as such but is concerned with the subject at hand, with the content—as well as with the aesthetic form. Thus the viewer is not intimidated, as often happens with other works of art. Staeck sees this as an opportunity to address important social issues, which otherwise are brought into the open only with great difficulty. In contrast to his opponents—who try to squeeze him out of the arts because he does not operate primarily in the traditional art context—Staeck never uses art as a mere vehicle; rather, he sees in it a dimension of freedom and openness that permits him to present his concerns—concerns that he believes are shared by many others.

Working Method And Stylistic Devices

Almost all of Staeck's works are photomontages, because most people see the photograph as the truth, and because lies can be unmasked most easily through pictures. Staeck uses the techniques invented in the twenties by John Heartfield, and tries to develop and adapt them to our times. His text-picture montages generally embody a dialectical contradiction, employing irony to generate curiosity in the viewer. However, since the Germans are not really talented when it comes to irony, they don't always understand the point.

Designed to be suitable for mass reproduction, the works are generated without the aura usually attached to art. There is never an "original"; the posters and postcards are created directly in the machine. With his friend Gerhard Steidl, Staeck produces everything, beginning with the idea and following through to the

film, to the engraving plates, and to the offset printing. This technical independence is an important precondition for the political work he pursues within the framework of his poster art.

Distribution

In the beginning it was very difficult to get Staeck's works out to people, since there was no special distribution network. The main problem was to construct a completely independent apparatus free from outside interference. Although Staeck has been a member of the SPD (Social Democratic Party) since 1960, he likes to remain independent of the party so that he can criticize it at any time. Therefore, rather than disseminate the posters through party channels, he has sold his output to all individuals who might be interested. It has taken considerable time and imagination, but a far-reaching distribution network has made the work possible even in difficult times. The large editions have kept prices low, and all profits are used to subsidize the continuing work.

Themes

Staeck's work deals with freedom of speech, the environment, social problems, and the fight against hypocrisy and reactionary thinking. Though he does not accept direct commissions, he does take many suggestions from groups such as grass-roots activist organizations, Amnesty International, and Terre des Hommes. For economic reasons, he devotes himself to themes with long-range significance rather than to topical political concerns.

Effect

The posters are primarily designed to further communication. The like-minded feel supported in their beliefs and supplied with fresh arguments; those who think differently feel challenged and try to refute them. Above all else, Staeck wants to stimulate thought, shake prejudices, and further the critical capacity of as many people as possible. All that is doctrinaire is foreign to him; he mainly poses questions and, in association with others, searches for solutions. Staeck has always thought of (Article text continued on page 257)

The worker holds a placard that says: "The air belongs to everyone!" The capitalist replies: "But we'll determine the poison content!" Red, brown, and black postcard, 1973.

STAECK: Beware Art! Photomontage as Political Intervention

Satirizing the right wing's scare campaign concerning the alleged horrors of nationalization, this poster, which enjoyed an enormous distribution (according to a survey, 9.1 percent of the total population of the Federal Republic saw this poster and responded to it in one way or another), states: "Workers of Germany! The Social Democrats will take away your villas in Tessin." Tessin, actually called Ticino, is a posh Alpine ski resort in the Italian part of Switzerland where many industrialists and right-wing politicians have villas. Blue, yellow, and black postcard, 1972.

Referring to the enormous difficulty that old people have in securing decent accommodations in the Federal Republic (as elsewhere in the capitalist world), Staeck asks, in the context of Dürer's mother (a potent cultural icon, incidentally, of the German bourgeoisie): "Would you be willing to rent a room to this woman?" This discrimination is especially directed at southern European old people, called "guest workers," who come to Germany to do menial labor. This poster was Staeck's contribution to the Dürer quinquacentary in 1971. Silver and red postcard, 1971.

Würden Sie dieser
Frau ein Zimmer
vermieten?

STAECK: Beware Art! Photomontage as Political Intervention

"Class struggle . . . For our children, no class is too big!" This is a poster agitating for smaller school classes and more personalized education. Red and black postcard, 1974.

"The true Germans stand behind Reagan. The Society for Living with the Bomb, Inc." Full-color postcard, 1982.

himself as a kind of interpreter: someone who transposes complicated facts into a simple picture or one question, the answer to which is found in the tension between text and picture.

His works always serve to enlighten. At a time in which irrationality threatens to spread like an epidemic, especially among young people, it is more important than ever to engender critical thought without falling into a vocabulary of slogans and stereotyped thinking. Since he works visually, Staeck would like to teach a new way of seeing. The montage technique is especially suited to exposing hypocrisy. Instead of trying to refute all advertising lies, Staeck feels it is enough to make people look behind the colorful pictures and be suspicious.

Staeck's art is used by political groups as a basis for debate. It reaches out to the viewer, not in an art context, but in the everyday environment: on kiosks, billboards, bumperstickers, flyers, or postcards. This broad dissemination carries the risk that some of the meaning might be lost. Unlike party propaganda, Staeck's works often make high demands on the viewers; he does not seek instant comprehension or depend on gags. What matters is not that every poster be immediately understood, but that it be so designed as to make understanding possible without a political or aesthetic education. Through humor and wit, Staeck has successfully awakened the curiosity of even the politically disinterested, speaking not just to youth or students, but to all segments of the population.

The Public Arena

Staeck's work serves as a kind of counter-propaganda. The more that public opinion is dominated by a few information monopolies, the more necessary it is to permit the voicing of uncomfortable, displaced, and suppressed views. Since all satire rests on truth (otherwise it would really be defamation), those who have no interest in truth are constantly trying to deprive the public of his art.

There is an increasing inclination to blame the seismograph for the earthquake. During election years, conflicts over the posters increase; in 1976, there were over a hundred serious incidents, including disrupted city council meetings, smashed windows, torn-down posters, closed-down exhibits, filing of legal charges, and various other types of interference. (Most of the difficulties have occurred in Bavaria.) Staeck's training as an attorney is becoming increasingly useful; although his opponents have tried everything from lawsuits (over thirty-six so far) to ripping down his posters from exhibitions, no poster has ever been legally banned. Until now, at any rate, these continual attempts have failed to criminalize or consumerize his work—both fairly effective means by which our society reacts to everything that's uncomfortable and by which it defends itself in order to isolate or at least neutralize it.

Since democratic controls still function effectively in West Germany, it has almost always worked to gain broad exposure for the conflicts. To be sure, this becomes ever more difficult and requires ever new resourcefulness, since cowardice and self-censorship in the media have taken on epidemic proportions. But thanks to the misjudgment of his political opponents and the attendant publicity, these political attacks have made Staeck's work very popular. Staeck has no respect for the Left's often-observed self-pity in the face of opposition; even though the conflicts have been forced upon him, he has used the exposure to his advantage. His opponents must be given credit for having significantly contributed to the wide propagation of his works.

Since Staeck's posters are part of public political discussion, their effectiveness is in part subject to changes in the prevailing climate. The growing interference with the work, in terms of reaching a broad public, is more disturbing than being branded, on one pole, as an agitator, political pornographer, corrupter of children, and communist traitor; and, on the other, as a fascist agitator, etc. The posters themselves are only part of a campaign, the focus of which is a broadly based debate concerning the problems they portray. A poster has been successful when it has triggered a fundamental discussion about critical conditions and possibilities for improvement. In spite of the difficulties, there have always been opportunities to familiarize many people with uncomfortable ideas. It remains to be seen, in future elections, if this will continue to be possible.△

Staeck comments here on the media monopoly by the Right with the ironic statement: "We guarantee pluralism through a balancing of opinion." The images that fill the television screens are, clockwise from top left: Gerhard Lowenthal, right-wing television commentator; Dr. Hans Filbinger, ex-Nazi Naval Court-Martial judge who was CDU Ministerprasident (Governor) of Baden Württemberg; Helmut Kohl, CDU leader, currently Chancellor; Franz Josef Strauss, right-wing CDU party leader and currently Minister-prasident of Bavaria; Ludwig Erhardt, ex-Chancellor of the Federal Republic; and Strauss again. Blue, yellow, and black postcard, 1975.

"Soldiers of all lands! The antimilitarists are after your jobs." Full-color postcard, 1981.

This poster refers to British party politics. Tan, black, and red postcard, 1974.

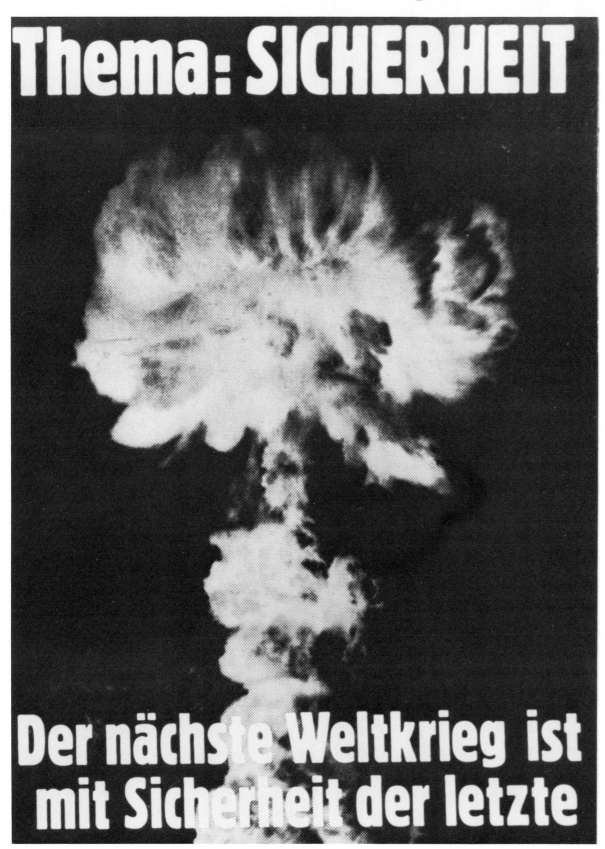

This image depends on a German pun. The German word "Sicherheit" means "security" in the sense of "certainty" or a "guarantee." Superimposed on the mushroom cloud of a nuclear blast, the poster reads: "Subject: SECURITY. The next World War, with certainty, will be the last." Brown and yellow postcard, 1981.

"NO to the Missile Republic of Germany." Black and red postcard, 1981.

KATHERINE YOUNG

General Antonio de Spinola

An introduction to Günter Wallraff's "The Coup Merchants," the article which scuttled plans for the rightist coup in Portugal. The Wallraff article follows this one.

The Portuguese Revolution *and the* German Connection

by
Albert J. Camigliano

Merci, but no coup!

FTER A MILITARY COUP HAD ENDED PARLIAMENTARY GOVERNMENT IN PORTUGAL ON 17 June 1926, the army became the sole possessor of true power. However, lacking both the expertise and desire to administrate, the soldiers entrusted the business of government to Antonio Salazar. In 1932, satisfied with his ability to stabilize the economy as finance minister since 1928, the army appointed Salazar prime minister. For nearly four decades he ruled Portugal with dictatorial might, but always mindful of his dependence on the military.

Relations between Salazar and the army became strained in the 1960s because of the increasingly unpopular colonial wars in Mozambique, Angola, Guinea, and Guinea-Bissau. Salazar, dedicated to colonialism, vehemently opposed any consideration of independence. Many of the younger army officers, however, began to question their role in these seemingly fruitless struggles. This gulf widened when Marcello Caetano became prime minister in 1968 after Salazar's retirement. To attract recruits, Caetano issued a decree in July 1973 that facilitated promotions for conscript officers. This action angered the young

career officers and served to alienate them further from the regime and its conservative military supporters. On 9 September 1973, a group of the more militant officers in what had become known as the *Movimento das Forcas Armadas*—the Armed Forces Movement (MFA)—met in Evora in southeastern Portugal to formulate their military grievances and opposition to the wars. It soon became obvious that the Caetano government was not interested in dialogue with the officers. Thus the coordinating committee of the MFA, led by Colonel Vasco Goncalves, Major Melo Antunes, and Captain Otelo Saraiva de Carvalho, began preparations for a coup. To provide their movement the legitimacy and appeal needed to gain the support of the entire officer corps, the MFA leaders turned to the charismatic and popular General Antonio de Spinola. No longer in Caetano's favor because of his belief in progressive autonomy for the Portuguese colonies, which was articulated in his book *Portugal and the Future* (1974), Spinola had recently lost his position as deputy chief of staff. He therefore agreed to support the MFA. The coup took place on 25 April 1974, as planned, and in early evening Caetano formally surrendered to Spinola.

Camigliano: The Portuguese Revolution *and the* German Connection

The new power structure in Portugal consisted of President Spinola, a six-man Junta of National Salvation, the Council of State, and a provisional government headed by Palma Carlos. In reality, the seven-man MFA coordinating committee, part of the Council of State, soon assumed control of policy, and Spinola found himself isolated. In late September Spinola planned both a mass demonstration by the "silent majority" to show support for him and a counter-coup against the MFA extremists. Both undertakings failed miserably, and on September 30 he resigned. General Francisco da Costa Gomes, army chief of staff, became Portugal's new president.

In the following months the left-wing faction of the MFA succeeded in strengthening its position of power by institutionalizing itself through a complex structure of governing committees and councils. Many feared the country was headed toward a left-wing military dictatorship that would prove more disastrous than the right-wing regime that had ruled Portugal for nearly fifty years. Spinola again felt compelled to intervene on behalf of the spirit of 25 April 1974. His coup attempt on 11 March 1975, ended once more in failure. Spinola fled first to Spain and then to Brazil, where he was granted political asylum.

After this the pace of the revolution quickened. The power structure of the 1974 coup was replaced by the Supreme Revolutionary Council, in essence an extended MFA coordinating committee comprising only left-wing members. On April 11 the political parties signed an agreement that gave the military control over the country's future for three to five years. At the urging of the Portuguese Communist Party (PCP) under Alvaro Cunhal, the MFA banned almost all right-wing parties. Although elections to a constituent assembly were held on April 25, the MFA announced that the results would have no impact on political realities. Economically, experimentation replaced policy: the MFA nationalized most banks and industries; worker unrest resulted in widespread strikes; an expanded money supply fueled a growing inflation rate; and foreign investments stopped. Public rallies against the MFA began during the summer and increased when the Catholic Church under the Archbishop of Braga openly opposed the MFA and the Communists. At the same time the right-wing

Democratic Liberation Movement of Portugal (MDLP) under Spinola's direction began a series of bombings on left-wing targets in the north. In short, chaos was the order of the day in Portugal.

In an attempt to appease the people and stop the right from gaining control, President Costa Gomes dismissed pro-communist Prime Minister Goncalves and appointed Pinheiro de Azevedo on August 29. Although well intentioned, this move did nothing to ameliorate political realities, for in the fall conditions deteriorated steadily. The army became hopelessly factionalized. Left-wing, moderate, and right-wing groups acted independently of each other and struggled constantly for power. Rumors of coups by both the Left and the Right abounded. In November, Cunhal's Communist Party again instigated a series of paralyzing strikes. On November 20 Prime Minister Azevedo announced that his government would be forced to strike because it simply could not function amid the chaos without military backing. On November 25 far-left paratroops attempted their own coup, but they were repelled by loyalist forces led by General Antonio Ramalho Eanes.

The leftist uprising did mark a turning point in Portuguese affairs. With the government under the control of Eanes as army chief of staff, a semblance of normalcy returned. Power shifted from the Revolutionary Council to the political parties. A socialist constitution was adopted on 2 April 1976, and later in the month parliamentary elections were held. On June 27 Eanes easily won the presidential election. Mario Soares, leader of the Socialist Party (PS), was appointed prime minister on July 16.[1]

The political, military, and civilian disorder that ensued after the unsuccessful coup on 11 March 1974, could only be viewed as a positive sign by one man: Antonio de Spinola. He realized that the chaos and disenchantment of the people would facilitate his return as Portugal's savior. He was encouraged by his MDLP's success against leftist organizations in the north, the church's open opposition to the MFA, and the left-wing defeat in November. Other events, however, added a sense of urgency to his mission. The replacement of Goncalves by Azevedo and Eanes' actions signaled a more moderate turn and a firmer entrenchment of the Socialists in government.

During the fall and winter of 1975 Spinola tried to obtain political and financial backing for his planned coup. To this end, he made various trips from Brazil to Europe and even to America. After finally being expelled from Paris on 7 February 1976, Spinola took up residence in Geneva, Switzerland. It became known after the fact, through the efforts of the West German journalist Günter Wallraff, that Spinola had traveled to Munich, Germany, on February 15. He went there to discuss the possibility of receiving political asylum and to share his political strategy with Franz Josef Strauss.

Spinola's choice of Strauss as a possible source of help was indeed not arbitrary. A member of parliament since 1949 and chairman of Bavaria's conservative Christian Social Union (CSU) since 1961, Strauss is an extremely vocal anti-communist. As defense minister (1956–1962) responsible for rebuilding the German army, he was an unrelenting advocate of an independent offensive atomic capability for Europe and nuclear weapons for the German army. His resignation in December 1962 was forced in no small way by his role in the now famous "Spiegel Affair." In its issue of 8 October 1962, the weekly news magazine *Spiegel* featured a highly critical cover story on Germany's defense policy and its Defense Minister Strauss. The author and associate editor, Conrad Ahlers, was accused of publishing state secrets that might endanger Germany's security and the people's well-being. As a result, Ahlers and publisher Rudolf Augstein were arrested. The Hamburg and Bonn offices of *Spiegel* were searched and files impounded on October 26. Because of Strauss's active role in the arrest of Ahlers, ministers from the Christian Democratic Union (CDU) government's coalition partner, the Free Democrats (FDP), resigned from Chancellor Adenauer's cabinet on November 19. Strauss's reputation has never fully recovered from the incident.

Although he served as minister of finance from 1966 to 1969 in the "grand coalition" government—CDU/CSU and Social Democratic Party (SPD)—Strauss bitterly opposed the planned association with the SPD at first. His rejection of the Social Democrats' policies was later fully manifested in his outspoken opposition to Chancellor Willy Brandt's *Ostpolitik* and his government's eastern treaties with the Soviet Union (12 August 1970) and Poland (7 December 1970). Strauss's vitriolic attacks on liberal policy found no favor among voters in his unsuccessful attempts to become chancellor in 1976 and 1980. His demagogy is, however, warmly received in Bavaria, where he has served as minister-president since 1978.[2]

Spinola's last attempt to secure funds and arms is detailed in the following pages of "The Coup Merchants." In a word, Günter Wallraff posed as a representative of a right-wing German group willing to support Spinola's plans for a coup, successfully infiltrated the organization, and met with Spinola himself in Düsseldorf, Germany, on 25 March 1976, to discuss the exact terms of their agreement. Satisfied that the negotiations had gone well and his coup now had the necessary backing, Spinola returned to Switzerland. Wallraff, however, added a third party to the discussions: the public. On April 7 he held a press conference in Bonn in which he revealed Spinola's plans and the Spinola-Strauss contacts. The next day the popular magazine *Stern* published a Wallraff story that again detailed the events. On April 12 Wallraff was featured on the television news magazine "Panorama." He offered viewers tangible proof of the facts: portions of taped conversations with Spinola, weapons lists and documents supplied by Spinola or his confidants, and photographs of the Spinola-Wallraff meeting in Düsseldorf. Because of Wallraff's disclosures, Swiss authorities expelled Spinola and sent him back to Brazil. Strauss called on his rhetorical genius to defend his actions in parliamentary debates and media interviews in order to weather the political storm.

Günter Wallraff's role in the exposure of the Spinola conspiracy did not represent anything extraordinary for him. By 1976, Wallraff had had over ten years experience in "exposing" reality. His first major publication was a collection of industrial reportages entitled *We Need You—as a Worker in German Industries* (1966). It documents the miserable working conditions in German firms which Wallraff himself had experienced as a laborer from 1963 to 1966. His *13 Undesirable Reportages* (1969) deals with a much broader spectrum of reality. Among the topics are the treatment of patients in mental institutions, the care of the homeless in hostels, the existence of paramilitary units at Germany's large industrial complexes, and the tyrannical,

for-profit-only work atmosphere at the Melitta coffee filter firm. His joint effort with Bernt Engelmann, *You Up Above— We Down Below* (1973), details the differences in life-styles between owners and employees at a number of Germany's largest concerns, such as Krupp, Gerling, Melitta, Horten, and Oetker. One of his most sensational works is *The Front Page Story* (1977). This publication discloses how the Axel Springer-owned newspaper *Bild*, comparable to America's *National Enquirer*, presents and represents the "news." To gain first-hand knowledge of the inner workings of *Bild*, Wallraff posed for four months as the reporter Hans Esser.

Almost all of Wallraff's collections of industrial, political, and social reportages have been bestsellers. The aforementioned volume *We Need You—as a Worker in German Industries* sold 50,000 copies within three months of its appearance in paperback in 1970. By 1978 the number had reached 350,000.[3] To date, nearly two million copies of Wallraff's works have been sold. Both his methods and mission have not only endeared Wallraff to millions of West German workers, students, and professionals alike, but brought him international acclaim as well. The Swedes, for example, have coined the terms *Wallraffen* and *Wallraffiade* to describe unusual methods of research.[4]

Born on 1 October 1942, near Cologne, Wallraff decided not to finish his secondary education at the *Gymnasium*, but instead chose to serve an apprenticeship in the booksellers trade (1957–1961). Shortly thereafter he received his induction notice from the army. Having filed his petition for conscientious objector status too late, Wallraff was soon called up but served only ten months. After a period of observation in the psychiatric ward, he was declared unfit for military service and discharged. His army experience, however, marked a turning point in his life: it had brought him face to face with a kind of reality he had never thought existed. From that point Wallraff began to think politically, to realize that an individual's problems are determined and conditioned by society, and the the solution as well must come from society, not the individual.

Wallraff's exposure to the real world through both the military and industry helped form his concept of the writer. For him, most contemporary writers are little more than the court jesters of a feudalistic age, the privileged voices of the privileged classes. He urges the writer, whom he

Camigliano: The Portuguese Revolution *and the* German Connection

prefers to call a "worker of words," to be a spoilsport, a rule breaker, not an entertainer who accepts money to avoid telling the truth rather than to propagate it. Wallraff's intention is sociopolitical. He favors the expression of "social truth," the exposure of problems, failures, and shortcomings in society that go all but unnoticed or to which one grows callously accustomed. His works indicate how things really are as opposed to how they are said to be. Yet the meaning and thrust of his reportages do not lie in the disclosure of individual instances. Wallraff's intention is to show the cause of the symptoms he documents, to expose the social mentality that allows such conditions to persist, and to indicate that they are representative of an entire social structure. Success for Wallraff can only be measured by the degree to which his works affect reader consciousness and in turn produce a desire for change.

Wallraff's insistence on social change should not be construed as an adherence to a revolutionary political ideology, however. He is anything but an ideologue. In his writing Wallraff presents himself as an opponent of the system responsible for the conditions he has witnessed, not as an outspoken proponent of the other side. Although his most frequent and severe critiques concern the injustices, inequities, and inhuman conditions created by capitalism, Wallraff has also been a harsh critic of life in East Germany and the Soviet Union. His association with the West German Left results as much from his operational pragmatism as from his political bent. He is simply willing to work with any organization helpful to his cause—and in West Germany, it is almost always the Left.

The role of participant-observer employed in "The Coup Merchants" is indeed Wallraff's favorite methodology. In addition to having worked three years as a laborer and four months as a *Bild* reporter, Wallraff has committed himself as an alcoholic to an institution, joined a monastery, posed as a government official, and assumed numerous other roles. As Michael Töteberg has pointed out, through his methodology Wallraff succeeds in offering the reader more than just socially critical literature. By placing himself as an active participant at the center of his works, rather than merely presenting a montage of documents, Wallraff affords

readers a person with whom they can identify.[5] The popularity of Wallraff's books and his own notoriety, however, have proved to be ironic obstacles to his working methodology. To avoid detection, he has been forced to disguise himself. Although his disguises have not been elaborate—he sometimes wears contact lenses instead of his normal glasses or shaves his mustache—they have allowed him to gain access as an insider to information otherwise unobtainable. In response to accusations of deception and foul play with respect to his "disguises," Wallraff states that it is a matter of deceiving in order not to be deceived. He justifies his method by the substance of the material he has obtained.

Although Wallraff's concepts and methodology may set him apart from most other contemporary German writers, they are not without tradition. His works are similar in many respects to those produced by members of the Worker Correspondents movement and the Union of Proletarian-Revolutionary Writers in the 1920s. Wallraff acknowledges that one writer, Egon Erwin Kisch—the self-described "peripatetic reporter"—served as a model for him and his thinking. A prominent member of both movements, Kisch became a master of the reportage. He too attempted to present a truthful and realistic depiction of prevailing social conditions through facts and documents. In Kisch's opinion, it is the writer's claim to verifiable truth that makes his work so dangerous.[6] And like Wallraff, Kisch employed the working methodology of the participant observer in gathering information for his reports on factories, jails, asylums, and other institutions.

Given the popularity of Wallraff's books, his own notoriety, and the volume of correspondence and unsolicited offers of help he receives, there can be little doubt that his reportages have raised the consciousness of his readers. When judged according to the widespread social changes they have effected, however, his works fall rather short of the mark. There are many factors responsible for this apparent lack of success. Most can be divided into two interrelated categories. The first entails the obstacles placed in Wallraff's way with respect to his methods. The many lawsuits brought against him as a result of his reportages are symptomatic of the consequences of such opposition. In all of the

Photograph of Günter Wallraff, in front of the SPRINGER Building, by Günter Zint, printed by permission of PAN-Foto, Hamburg, Germany.

Wexstraße
Kaiser-Wilhelm-Straße
Erste Nachricht der Entführer
Schleyer
14 Terroristen
frei - Oder er
Bild

Camigliano: **The Portuguese Revolution** *and the* **German Connection**

court cases, emphasis and publicity have been misplaced. Wallraff's repeated attempts to discuss the substance of his work have been unsuccessful. Arguments by both the prosecution and defense have centered exclusively on the means by which he has gathered his information. Wallraff himself—the man of many faces—and his methodology have become the cause célèbre. Ironically, the content of his reports, the initial cause of concern, has been skillfully defused.

The second category pertains to content. Many critics have objected to the absence of systematic analysis in his works and the lack of solutions to the problems he documents. (The implication is that change would be more immediately effected if he offered solutions.) The calls for analysis and solutions miss the point of Wallraff's intention, however. His writing is not meant to be a handbook of ideological or sociological tenets. As Ulla Hahn points out, documentary literature does not guarantee social action, a smooth transition from the textual reality to social reality.[7] Wallraff's purpose is to provide the reader not with a plan for opposition to abuses

but rather a reason for opposing the abuses. Opposition should result from the reader's confrontation with the documented issues. The reader's role must not be forgotten or underestimated. Significant and lasting change can be occasioned only by those concerned readers and organizations who can direct their efforts to the establishment of change. Wallraff's works are only the initiator of a process. Their force must be centrifugal, not centripetal.

In a sense, then, both Wallraff's ability to effect change and the immediacy of that change, through the successful outcome of the Spinola trap depicted in "The Coup Merchants," are untypical but also ironic. Unlike most of his undertakings, the Spinola reportage was not planned. To escape what he termed "the reality of the Federal Republic," Wallraff had gone to southern Portugal to work on an agricultural collective for three months. He first became aware of the Spinola conspiracy during a brief trip to northern Portugal toward the end of his stay. Thus, almost purely by chance, Wallraff unearthed a part of Portugal that proved to be much more fertile than he had anticipated!△

Notes

1. This summary of the Portuguese Revolution is based in part on Robert Harvey, *Portugal: Birth of a Democracy* (London: The MacMillan Press LTD, 1978).
2. The proof of Strauss's reputation and prowess as a champion of conservative causes is documented in "The Coup Merchants." When asked about his organization's leadership, Wallraff states, "There's only one major politician in Germany who could possibly give his full support to such an organization." No further questions are asked!
3. Ulla Hahn and Michael Töteberg, *Günter Wallraff* (Munich: C. H. Beck, 1979), 26.
4. Christian Linder, ed., *In Sachen Wallraff: Berichte, Analysen, Meinungen und Dokumente* (Hamburg: Rowohlt, 1977), 132.
5. Hahn and Toteberg, 75.
6. Ibid., 49. (Remarks from his speech in Paris to the Congress for the Defense of Culture.)
7. Ibid., 42.

Glossary

Bundestag (House of Representatives). The popularly elected federal legislative body in Bonn, its members serve four-year terms. In addition to writing legislation and controlling government, the Bundestag elects the federal chancellor.

Bundeswehr (Federal Armed Forces). Consisting of the army, air force, and navy, the Bundeswehr is strictly a defensive unit under the command of the minister of defense. The external security of West Germany is a function of NATO. All males can be conscripted to fifteen months of military duty. At present, the Bundeswehr numbers approximately 500,000.

Caetano, Marcello. Portugal's prime minister from 1968 to 1974, when he was ousted by the coup that signaled the start of the Portuguese Revolution.

CDS (Center Democratic Party). Actually a right-wing party with close ties to many European Christian Democratic parties.

CDU (Christian Democratic Union). Founded as a party for Christians of all faiths, it is conservative and supports a social market economy. For the first twenty years of the Federal Republic's existence (1949–1969), the CDU, either alone or in a coalition government, was the party in power.

CSU (Christian Social Union). A sister party of the CDU, this ultra-conservative party under the leadership of Franz Josef Strauss is found only in the state of Bavaria. In Bonn, the CDU and CSU have formed one joint parliamentary group.

ELP (Portuguese Liberation Army). An extreme right-wing organization whose tactics against communist and leftist opponents were often more brutal than those of the MDLP.

FDP (Free Democratic Party). Smallest of the four major political parties in West Germany, it stands in the tradition of German liberalism that was shared by many parties before World War II. It has served as the opposition party or a coalition partner of the larger parties.

Federal Intelligence Agency (Bundes-nachrichtendienst, BND). Charged with the responsibility of collecting intelligence and documentation in the case of subversive activities coming from abroad or the GDR, this agency is responsible to the head of the federal chancellery.

Konrad Adenauer Foundation. Named for West Germany's first chancellor, it was founded in 1964 and is headquartered in Bonn. Its goals are the promotion and furtherance of political consciousness, international understanding, and educational and social structures in developing nations. One of the foundation's main agencies is the Institute for International Solidarity in Bonn.

MDLP (Democratic Movement for the Liberation of Portugal). A Spinola-backed underground organization responsible for hundreds of attacks on communist and leftist organizations in Portugal.

MFA (Armed Forces Movement). This group of militant and discontented officers was responsible for the coup on 25 April 1974, that overthrew the Caetano government. The MFA coordinating committee controlled the government for the next two years.

PCP (Portuguese Communist Party). Founded in 1921, its membership grew after the revolution from 15,000 to around 150,000 under the leadership of Alvaro Cunhal.

Pinochet. The strong-arm general and president of Chile since 1973 who came to power through a right-wing military coup that ousted the Marxist government of Salvador Allende.

PPD (Popular Democratic Party). In October 1976 it became the PSD, Social Democratic Party. A middle-class party usually right of center, it was represented in all but one of the many provisional governments after the revolution.

PS (Portuguese Socialist Party). Founded in 1967 as a Marxist-socialist party, in reality its politics have been more closely aligned with those of European Social Democratic parties. Its leader is Mario Soares.

Salazar, Antonio. Portugal's prime minister from 1932 to 1968, who together with the military ruled with absolute authority.

Soares, Mario. Leader of the Portuguese Socialist Party (PS). Instrumental in drafting Portugal's socialist constitution, he has served as Portugal's foreign minister and prime minister.

SPD (Social Democratic Party of Germany). A labor-oriented party whose roots lie in the worker unions of the nineteenth century, the SPD developed into a "people's party" after the war. Its emphasis on welfare and social legislation, progressive educational systems, and detente in foreign affairs has made it the party of the worker and liberals.

Strauss, Franz Josef. Leader of the West German conservative Christian Social Union.

The
Coup
Merchants

PRIMATE ARCHBISHOP FRANCISCO Maria da Silva, the highest ranking bishop of the Iberian peninsula, resides in Braga, an historic old episcopal town. His diocese is the richest in the country in worldly possessions as well as in its number of priests. He has authority over as many priests as all the other dioceses of the North put together. The newspapers of the region are his, as well as printing firms, publishers and holdings in industrial companies. Monte Sameiro near Braga which, after Fatima, is the second largest shrine of pilgrimage in Portugal with its own restaurant and hotels, is in his diocese and in his charge. The reduced demand for crutches, corsets and bandages and the drop in the number of letters of thanks being sent in show that the number of 'miraculous cures' there has gone down noticeably since 25 April 1974.

Some months ago the Archbishop publicly swore an oath that he intends to lead a pilgrimage of his whole diocese to Monte Sameiro if communism (i.e. what he considers to be communism) is overthrown in his country by the end of 1976. (For him the Portuguese Communist Party [PCP] is synonymous with marxism-leninism; the Socialist Party [PS] with marxism.) Time is running out. He has just proclaimed in a pastoral letter that he will have communists excommunicated.

How does one go about getting an audience with an Archbishop who is the most powerful prelate in the Church of Portugal, who, to say the least, prepared the psychological climate and gave his blessing to more than three hundred bombings, burnings and lootings of communist, socialist and trade-union offices? The Archbishop has a reputation for being shy of the press and for more than six months now he has refused to give any interviews. By referring to my friendship with Dr Nikolau, the influential industrialist and friend of the Archbishop, I manage to get an interview in the episcopal palace.

The Archbishop comes straight to the point. Ecclesiastical matters are just a pretext to bring up political subjects. There is no trace of Christian principles in a word he says. The solid gold cross on his breast reminds me of a souvenir from a Spanish shrine. A sharp blade shoots out when you press a button.

ARCHBISHOP FRANCISCO DA SILVA: 'The communists began a battle against the Church to win over the masses. The Church must accept this struggle, not as man against man, but as Christ against Satan. Religion, the family and property are the main targets which communism attacks. A defensive battle is not enough, we have to go right over to the attack in factories, offices, markets, banks, in the administration and public institutions, in schools and in sport—everywhere. We have been called to do battle for or against God. Retreat would be a betrayal. And this betrayal would be death. Communism challenges us to fight. We know its tactics and we know what ours have to be. What are we waiting for?!'

Finally, as we are going, the Archbishop gives us another secret as a parting gift: 'What we have just been talking about is not yet for public consumption. We have just formed a new movement, the "Movement for the Defence of Basic Human Rights." Its purpose is to help us in the political struggle.'

DAY 2, BRAGA. How does one come into contact with bombers? Braga, a peaceful town surrounded by hills, has a population of 40,000. 617,000 people, almost ten per cent of the population of Portugal, live in the town's administrative district.

Apart from three burnt-out cars which no one has towed away yet and the completely gutted two-storey CP office, where boarded-up windows hide worse damage, there is nothing in this episcopal town—which could be compared with Regensburg or Passau—to remind one of violence and terror. It was here, according to Professor Giacometti, the curator of the local Folklore Research Institute, that his friend was beaten up in a pub one day because he had refused to tell some ELP men which party he had voted for in the last election. (ELP is short for 'Portuguese Liberation Army,' a secret terrorist organisation.) When his friend explained the cause of his injury to the doctor, the doctor refused for over half an hour to treat him, saying that in that case he must be a communist. The friend, a PS voter, then emigrated to the South of Portugal with his family—as many other prominent left-wingers had done before him.

DAY 3, BRAGA. On the surface there is nothing in my appearance to indicate that I have left-wing sympathies. Signet-ring, attaché-case, hair which had not been cut for three months now cropped short, suit and tie instead of leather jacket.

I ask a taxi-driver where in Braga I could find the brave men who had begun to get rid of the communists once and for all. The taxi-driver is inscrutable. He does not let on what he thinks. He mentions

by
Günter Wallraff

Translated by Paul Knight

271

Wallraff: *The Coup Merchants*

the 'Idolo' snack bar. His manner is off-hand. 'There are always people from the CDS sitting around there,' he says.

I spend a whole afternoon waiting around getting nowhere. Towards evening, purely by accident, I establish contact. A German alsatian wagging its tail brings it about. Someone calls him: 'Kaiser.' 'Are you a monarchist?' I ask, turning to the dog's owner who is slouching against the bar. He pushes his peak cap back on his head. 'No, why should I be?' He had adopted the stray dog which obviously belonged to German businessmen who had fled the country. He asked if we were tourists and said his name was Eduardo. 'We're not here for fun, I reply significantly, putting my hand on the black attaché-case. Eduardo da Costa Leite or Eduardo da Costa Pereirra, twenty-six, small, wiry, with a hard, childish face and swaggering manner drops his defences as soon as he hears I am acting on behalf of a right-wing organization.

He turns the lapel of his jacket round so that I can see the CDS party badge. 'Why do you make a secret of it, the CDS is the ruling party around here, isn't it?'

'They think that's the best way of doing things. They told me they were right behind me, but I didn't need to advertise it.' Then he goes into detail: 'Lots of people here in Braga know I've got a machine-gun and I don't keep it just for fun. They know I worked for the ELP before and now I work for the MDLP [Democratic Liberation Movement of Portugal]. They're all afraid of me because they think I'm a tough-guy. But I'm not. All I do is defend the people who pay me. And I hope they'll see me all right for it one day. Or else... (he motions as if firing a machine-gun). Take yesterday evening. There's a communist a hundred yards down the road from here. He's got a bookshop where these left-wing books are always on display. So I went in there and drilled away for a bit. That was yesterday evening about eleven. You can still see the bullet holes. That is the second warning. He knows it was me. If he still has those books in his window next week, he'll get it. I'm not afraid of anyone. I say what I think, straight to anyone's face, the police and all. I had a chat with the Chief of Police a while back. He told me he couldn't do what he liked either, he had to watch it. He said I should be a bit more careful driving around in my red Volvo

sports. It was asking for it. But I'm not going to give that up, nobody can catch me when I'm driving it.

'Here in the North all the influential people are on our side. Lots of factory owners support us. I know a lot of these higher-ups personally, who would never be seen with me officially, those from the CDS for example; they pay, but it's all secret, and there are well-known factory owners like Dr Nikolau who pay my wages and the others,' but that is all done on the quiet too. The government mustn't get to know about it. Galvao de Melo [CDS Presidential candidate] and Freitas do Amaral [Chairman of the CDS] support us, too.'

'How many of you are there in Braga?'
EDUARDO: '700 to 800.'

'Was it the enraged townspeople who burnt down the CP offices, as our newspapers said?'

'No, that was me, with someone else. A petrol bomb. You have to drop it and then start running. I'm not afraid. I even go into CP and union offices and look around for the best place—to put the bombs. Me and a few friends put some in union buildings last week. People are afraid now. Most of the communists have already made themselves scarce—gone to Lisbon or the South. Those who have stayed behind know what they've got coming to them.'

'Where do you get your arms?'

EDUARDO: 'Before, when I was in the ELP, we had American automatics. The MDLP gets them through its people in the commandos and the forces. They insist that we should use the weapons that are used in the army. In May 1975 we in the ELP even got arms direct from the CIA once. But nowadays we don't know where we are with them, whether they're for us or against us.

'What is the strategy at the moment, will you go on here in the North or switch operations to the South?'

EDUARDO: 'I don't know for sure. I'd have to ask the bosses first. I can't do anything without asking the bosses first. But I've heard the nationalised banks are going to be the next targets. All I need is the go-ahead. We've already got lists of dangerous left-wingers who'll be killed when we've won. They'll be rounded up and then grrtch' (he accompanies the sound by a motion as if he is strangling someone). Pause.

'The best move now is for us to make contact with the bosses,' I say. 'We haven't got much time and we've got to find out what help is needed.' Eduardo volunteers to make contact. 'I'll put you in touch with a paratroop captain from Braga, he's usually in Povoa de Varzim, and he's in contact with the central command.'

Eduardo races in his Volvo along the winding 45km road to Povoa de Varzim. (A number of place names along the way have been sprayed 'ELP' or 'MDLP.') I drive behind and I am hard pushed to keep up with him. At two o'clock we arrive in Povoa, an exclusive seaside resort, but now, in the off season, it is dead. The sea is roaring. 'Pelintra,' on the promenade, is a bar which stays open till early morning. The landlord is called Luis, an officer half-way up the ladder of command. A pasty bouncer lets us in and closes the door behind us. The bar is full. 'They're all friends,' someone says. The paratroop captain is away on assignment at the moment. A meeting is arranged for the afternoon of the next day.

A customer holds out a newspaper to Eduardo. It is the *Jornal de Noticias* and its headline reads: 'Shots Fired At Braga Union Leader's Car.' 'That's your work,' he says to Eduardo appreciatively. And then Eduardo, turning to us, says: 'The fifty shots I fired at the union secretary's car were just a warning. I know he hasn't got enough money to buy a new car and I hope it'll teach him a lesson.'

'And if it doesn't?'

'Then he'll get it.'

Teixeira, the paratroop officer, arrives. He is a rough, mercenary type, maybe thirty years old and as good-natured a a teddy-bear. Talkative and guileless like Eduardo. This may be because here in the North they can move about freely and show their allegiance openly, as if they were in a 'liberated area.' He too is playfully naive, but this naivety can quite unexpectedly turn into aggression and brutality. We are to go to Guimaraes, about sixty kilometers from Povoa.

'Is the MDLP better or worse organised than the ELP?'

TEIXEIRA: 'Better, I think. We've got a larger number of contacts, and more important contacts, with officials in the government and beside we've got Spinola as President. We work together with the ELP from time to time, but they've got no ideology any more, they're just desperadoes. We've got 50,000 active members all over Portugal. Our people even work without pay. All the bombings that have been done in the last six months were organised by us. We like to make co-ordinated attacks: in Braga, Povoa, Coimbra, Oporto, all at the same time. That makes a great impression, and people respect us.'

'What does the MDLP need most of all, money or arms?'

'Both, but we'll go into all the details of that when we talk to the men in charge tomorrow. The atmosphere here in the North now is good, the communists are intimidated. We want it to be the same in the South, but there are too many of them down there. Here it's enough for us to drive them out. But down there we want to exterminate them.'

'It must be tough, the kind of work you have to do.'

'We're sick and tired of just planting bombs. The time is ripe. We want to kill now. Planting bombs solves nothing, but killing does. You see what I mean?'

'When are you going to extend operations to the South?'

'You'll have to ask the bosses about that. I'm a specialist in the practical side of things, I'm not political at all. They only call me when they want me to make or plant bombs.'

'What party does the MDLP work with?'

'Mostly with the CDS. In my opinion all the really important people in the CDS are with us, it's just that they can't admit it openly, for the moment at least. Without us the CDS would be lost. We in the MDLP keep order, do security checks and provide body-guards at CDS meetings. As far as we're concerned, there are only two parties. The CDS and the PPD [Democratic People's Party]. But the PPD is not so reliable. They split again only a short while ago.'

'What kind of contacts have you got with the Church? Do you get moral support from it?'

TEIXEIRA laughs: 'Moral support—I like that. Not all of us are religious, but Francisco the Archbishop is one of us. I know him very well. He let us use his seminary for the first joint meeting between the ELP and the MDLP in the autumn when Copcon (the security force under General Carvalho) still existed and there was danger of being arrested. They were looking for First Lieutenant Benjamin Abreu, for the part he had played in our President's last coup. He had hidden under the bed. He is one of our most important men, we need him for the South. He is still in prison in Caxias.

We've already got a plan to spring him. He is going to fall ill soon and he'll have to go to hospital. When he's there we'll get him out and one of us who looks like him will go back to prison. I've heard that someone on the prison governor's staff is collaborating.'

'Does the Archbishop give you financial support as well?'

TEIXEIRA: 'Yes. Everything goes through our special delegate Conego [Canon] Melo. He is a member, one of us. Francisco the Archbishop arranges everything with him. And Melo then provides the money for us.'

'What about your contacts with the police?'

TEIXEIRA: 'Oh, they're excellent. To give you an example: usually when I'm planting bombs I wear gloves. A short while back I forgot my gloves and of course that turned out to be the day the bomb didn't go off. So my finger-prints were on it. The police came and wiped away all traces before the commission of enquiry got there. So they didn't find out who did it this time either.'

Two days later. Meeting with MDLP Northern Section bosses in Povoa de Varzim. Teixeira's flat in a new high-rise block, 657 Rua casa dos Poveiros do Rio. A commando captain with close-cropped hair (his name is Duarte, as we find out weeks later) is the spokesman. At first he is suspicious and cautious. He seems to be a military man through and through, one of the dangerous kind, cool, arrogant, ambitious, self-satisfied; I have a picture in my mind of him giving the order for mass liquidation with a slight motion of the hand. Then a subordinate of his, Lieutenant Pedro (his name is Menezes as we later find out in Germany), jeans-suit, unkempt wiry brown hair, bright-eyed and smiling. And then an *éminence grise* with a very wrinkled face, who looks at us very closely and says nothing—he is treated as if he were one of the MDLP's most important backers.

I describe our assignment, saying that we are representatives of a right-wing German organisation who have been sent here in strict secrecy to get a picture of the situation for ourselves and then to make arrangements for financial aid and the supply of arms. In the discussion it becomes clear that the MDLP is planning a coup before the Presidential elections in May or June. This coup will re-establish a right-wing dictatorship in Portugal, with all active left-wing forces liquidated.

There is a lot of whisky being poured

Wallraff: *The Coup Merchants*

out and we are encouraged to drink as much as we want. After this meeting I am absolutely shattered. Constantly having to keep up this act. The nervous tension. Being forced to join in with a happy laugh when someone drinks to the killing of political 'opponents.' We are accompanied back to the four-star Vermar hotel on the sea-front. After that I lose control. It is a kind of nervous breakdown, with prolonged bursts of crying.

The next evening there is another meeting with Captain Duarte, Lieutenant Menezes and Teixeira.

PEDRO: 'The period of isolated actions is coming to an end. The North is firmly in our hands, we've got our members or sympathisers in influential positions in the army, the Church and the police. We have to carry out one more large-scale operation with a clear goal. It would be wrong to carry on with guerilla tactics. If we go on like this, people will end up feeling sorry for the communists, they'll say the poor communists can't defend themselves and we'll be making them into victims, martyrs. The long-term effect abroad is not so good either—especially as up to now we've always managed to present our actions as the will of the people.'

DUARTE: 'And at the same time we have to find a physical solution to the problem. These activists have got to be eliminated. But that can't be done by us, the people who are carrying out the coup, we mustn't do anything to alienate international opinion. We have to have men all over the country who drag these fellows out of bed when the rising takes place and liquidate them. Our task is to ensure that these parallel operations run smoothly. The rebel forces must not get their hands dirty in the eyes of public opinion. And if we throw them into prison that will be the same as in the old days as far as public opinion is concerned. If we liquidate them openly, they'll say we're like Pinochet. We'll have to do things like the "death squads" [*esquadrao da morte*] in Brazil, only we'll have to adapt our action to our own circumstances and do it on a larger scale. We have already got one of these groups together (note, liquidation group), on the lines of the proverb: "A light that goes on ahead is worth two." '

PEDRO: 'We have to set up legal strongholds in Alentejo, which is full of communists. The CDS has already started operations there, they've opened offices

and launched an ambitious advertising programme. The most important thing about any operation we start now is to win. 28 September and 11 March [1975, dates of General Spinola's abortive coups] must not be repeated. If they are then all the left forces will unite and take to the streets, armed and ready for anything.'

DUARTE: 'We are an ideological force and many people share our way of thinking, even though they don't belong to the movement. For example we've got three men in the Revolutionary Council on our side.'

Duarte names Morais e Silva, Air Force Chief of Staff, Pires Veloso, Commander of the Northern Military Region, and 'strong man' General Ramalho Eanes, Army Chief of Staff and NATO commissioner for Europe, who recently lectured at a conference in Munich organised by the Bundeswehr magazine *Military Science*. (Another invitation to come to the Federal Republic was turned down at short notice by Eanes after it had been leaked in *Stern* magazine.)

After so much communicativeness and loquacity on his part, the captain now asks, with a threatening undertone: 'And who is behind your organisation?'

Now I have to come out with it. I can no longer claim the backing of a powerful, mysterious organisation which they might take to be the CIA or the Federal Intelligence Service [*Bundesnachrichtendienst*].

'There's only one major politician in Germany who could possibly give his full support to such an organisation.'

The terrorist chiefs exchange a short glance of understanding and approval. Trust has been restored. Duarte tells me that they are already in contact with a German organisation. The next meeting would establish to what extent we were connected with them. We arranged our next meeting for 25 March at the Hotel Liaberny in Madrid. There we would talk with leaders of the Madrid MDLP and go into more detail. We leave them a telephone number in Munich through which we can be contacted and ask them, whenever they are talking about arms to use the words *Cortiza* (cork) or *Peixe* (fish) because 'even in Bavaria—our South is like your North—it is best to play safe.'

On 22 March at 4.45 p.m. there is a call from Geneva at the Munich number we left. 'Luis' is on the line. He says that he is phoning about the cork exports on

behalf of General Walter, and as he is coming to Germany on business anyway, he could combine both. It is extremely important to fix an earlier date for the discussion.

Wednesday, 24 March, 3.30 p.m., the bar of the Düsseldorf Park Hotel. Two respectably dressed gentlemen, Dr Jose Valle de Figueiredo (about thirty-five) and Dr Luis Oliveira Dias (forty-four). They show their credentials as Spinola's adjutants with full negotiating powers and, at the same time, the former President's Brazilian passport, to prove the authenticity of his signature.

WALLRAFF: 'May I show this authority to our President?'

LUIS: 'Of course. Our President the General is also prepared to come here or to receive you in Geneva, if our negotiations should make it necessary. Whenever you want, wherever you want.'

WALLRAFF: 'This is very important in view of the sums of money involved. The main thing is to solve the problem of the General's safety.'

LUIS: 'If we have to take risks, we simply have to take risks. The decision as to whether a meeting between the General and your President should take place is yours.'

WALLRAFF: 'Could he come as early as tomorrow?'

LUIS: 'Any time. Perhaps you could tell us something more precise about your organisation and your impressions in the North.'

WALLRAFF: 'We have adopted this unusual method of making contacts from below instead of at the highest level because we've had bad experiences with the ELP in the past, when our money didn't always get into the right hands. We wanted to get a picture for ourselves of the ordinary members' activities. We didn't want to be let down a second time. Also we wanted to take a closer look at members who were in the ELP and are now in the MDLP.'

LUIS: 'Ah yes. Now we understand. That's a good way of gathering information. And what conclusions have you reached?'

WALLRAFF: 'We were very pleased—and that's why we've made this offer of help.'

At 12.45 the next day, Thursday 25 March, the former Portuguese President, now President of the MDLP, General Antonio Ribeiro de Spinola, is to arrive from Geneva via Zurich at Terminal Two of Düsseldorf airport.

The problem now is: how can I find a 'President' who is prepared to sit down and negotiate with the former President of Portugal? I spent three hours that night phoning around. I tried to persuade a vicar, a publisher, a lawyer, a doctor and a member of the *Bundestag* to play his part. But in vain: they all agreed with me that it was morally and politically right and even necessary to stage this gigantic deception. But they all have pressing reasons for not doing it: either they have commitments or they don't think they could go through with it. Not one of them is prepared to give up his own role and take on a new one, even for an afternoon, to help prevent a right-wing coup and possibly even a second Chile. Yet I can say from my own experience that it is a hundred times easier to play the part of a President, with the prestige and respect that surround him, than for example to lead a production-line worker's life for any length of time. The next morning another two hours phoning round. Friends phone up friends for me. Real actors whom I want to persuade to take the part cannot be got hold of so quickly. So there is no President. We drive to the airport in Dr Meinecke's Mercedes. Dr Meinecke is a lawyer and FDP [Free Democratic Party] man and President of the World Association for Human Rights [WAHR]. He agreed without hesitation to be present as a neutral witness at this historic meeting. At 12.58 we reach the arrival hall. The plane was ten minutes late. But there is no sign of Luis, Jose or Spinola.

Suddenly we see Luis and Jose behind the barrier talking to an elderly man in sunglasses. A thought rushes through my mind: 'Someone from the *Verfassungs-schutz* [State Security] who is going to warn him.' We walk towards the group. Jose and Luis introduce 'Our President, the General.' (Spinola is accompanied by his niece.) We walk to Dr Meinecke's car with him and talk about the weather until we arrive at the exclusive *Schnellenburg* restaurant. It is cool and rainy.

Everything in the *Rheinsaal* is appropriate to the occasion—flower-decor and champagne reception. As a patriotic German I am wearing a black, red and gold striped tie and I also have a number of ridiculous status-symbols on me, such as a gold-plated cigarette-lighter and similar junk. (The scene which follows is so unreal, the kind of musical comedy situation you find in poor German films, that it would have been dismissed as pure invention and utter exaggeration if it had

not been authentic and proved to be true. This is a case where reality outstrips the author's powers of imagination.)

LAWYER: 'I would like to welcome you, General, on German soil in the name of men and organisations who are determined to see to it that law and order is maintained internationally and in Europe in particular.'

SPINOLA: (Who has now replaced his sunglasses with a monocle.) 'I would like to express my gratitude for the reception you have given me here in Düsseldorf in these circumstances and I would like to thank you for your words of welcome. This is my first visit to Germany since the second world war. And I come here full of hope. Germany has a great part to play in the future or Europe. I have always been firmly convinced that we have to combine forces within Europe to fight against Soviet imperialism. We need a Western Alliance against the Soviet Alliance. And Germany is in the best position to bring this Western Alliance about.'

WALLRAFF: 'We would like to thank you, General, for these encouraging words. The General will appreciate that we have kept the number of people taking part in these discussions to an absolute minimum, for security reasons. But we, too, fully appreciate the importance of this historic moment and this meeting is, I believe, in all our interests.' (Although he is a tee-totaller the General drinks champagne at this reception, for the first time in years. The Busum crab soup was very much to his taste and as a former huntsman he was absolutely delighted with the venison. He did not have any dessert.)

WALLRAFF: 'Did you have any difficulties with the immigration author-ities, General?'

SPINOLA: 'None at all. Everything was quite straightforward.'

WALLRAFF: 'If you had more time we could arrange some more meetings tomor-row with any German politcans you care to name to us.'

SPINOLA: 'Am I really flying back today?'

JOSE AND LUIS (together): 'I am afraid so, General.'

WALLRAFF: 'When can we expect you to return to Portugal?'

SPINOLA: 'In general terms I would say whenever it is best for the country as a whole. As soon as I am free to engage in political activity. Certainly not before the elections. And only when I decide that the time is ripe.'

WALLRAFF: 'Your wife is already

expecting you and getting the house ready in Lisbon.'

SPINOLA: 'Next Sunday my brother and nephews are going back to Portugal.'

WALLRAFF: 'Do you think that the CDS will get about twenty-five per cent of the votes at the next election?'

SPINOLA: 'No, I don't. But in the present confused state of things the last week before the elections can have a decisive effect on the results. The CDS will have the largest increse in votes in relation to all the other parties.'

WALLRAFF: 'Are there any reliable political allies in the PPD?'

SPINOLA: 'This party has no programme to offer which can come anywhere near solving the problems of the Portuguese people. The PPD is very divided, which means that we could hardly consider them as coalition-partners—although I agree that they do have reliable people. The three most important parties, the PPD, the CDS and the PS are all at one another's throats now during the election campaign. They are fighting a life or death battle. But of course this is only a very superficial analysis of the election.'

LUIS AND JOSE: 'On the contrary, General.'

SPINOLA: 'The few worthwhile political principles still to be found in Portugal today are all within the PPD and the CDS. And to a small extent also in the PS. But in the final analysis you can't depend on the right wing of the PS, their ties with their party are too strong. They are nothing but opportunists in my opinion. The PS ministers even have PC secre-taries of state working in their ministries and seem to find this quite acceptable. How can they remain credible after that?'

The venison is served.

WALLRAFF: 'That is German venison, General. Do you have deer like this in Por-tugal?'

SPINOLA: 'Yes, but only on one estate, fifty kilometers north of Lisbon, in Torre Bela. It belongs to the Duke of Braganza, he often gives hunting parties there.'

LUIS: 'He used to give them, General. It is a co-operative now.'

WALLRAFF: 'Well, are there still deer in Torre Bela or not?'

LUIS: 'Not a single one.'

JOSE: 'They've all been slaughtered.'

THE GENERAL'S NIECE: 'The venison is very tender.'

WALLRAFF: 'Do you see any possibility, General, of these stolen lands soon being returned to their lawful owners?'

SPINOLA: 'Mmmmm (chewing). The

Wallraff: *The Coup Merchants*

moment for this depends partly on you.'

LUIS: 'The last time the General was in Germany was during the war as an observer in the German army.'

SPINOLA: 'That was the year Leningrad fell. 1939.'

LUIS: 'It is called Stalingrad today. And it was 1942.'

SPINOLA: 'No, it was 1940 in Leningrad. I have got a photograph from then, with me and two German officers on it. It shows me wearing German uniform and the Iron Cross, and they are in Portuguese uniform. I would like to exchange uniforms again today.'

THE GENERAL'S NIECE: 'It is twenty to four. Shouldn't we take a rest now?'

LUIS: 'If your President is coming at four o'clock perhaps we ought to take a break now.'

WALLRAFF: 'No need to hurry. When our President comes, he'll have time.' (Frantic phone calls to find a 'President'—again in vain.)

WALLRAFF: 'The President asks us to work out an agenda. He says he will come when it gets dark, for security reasons.'

A last attempt to get hold of a President. I get through to an old friend, B., in the publisher's office where he works. I beg him: 'Look, you've got to help me. I've got to the end of exhaustive researches and I just need one more link in the chain—the clinching proof.' I tell him what he needs to know, giving him only the absolute essentials. 'What does a President need to do but look important and say "yes" and "no" in the right places? Have you got a tie on. Go out quick and buy yourself an attaché-case, it'll make you look busy and important.' B. is ready. Returning to the *Rheinsaal*, I declare: 'Our President, like the General, has decided to take the risk of coming here. He realises that the General's time is short. In spite of everything he'll be here in half an hour. There are a few things which have to be seen to here first, to make sure everything is safe, and he'll have a few men posted in front of the restaurant. Just in case. I'm afraid that's German perfectionism with its good and its bad sides.'

The 'President' arrives about 5.30 p.m., grey-haired, unassuming, composed. Sprightly and relaxed after his siesta, Spinola comes into the room after him. The two Presidents greet one another cordially.

'PRESIDENT': 'We are already agreed of course about basic principles. Your Excellency will understand that I came here to get an overall impression. You have convinced me that we can't wait any longer, that we have to act quickly to save Portugal—as a first step.'

SPINOLA: 'What you have already discussed and decided with my two most trusted adjutants is assured of my agreement in advance. We have been discussing this for months and whatever you say and do will have my complete approval. I am only too glad to answer any further questions or deal with any further criticisms you may have.

'We have to intensify our work now and concentrate on the people's consciousness. That is why we want to establish our Institute of National Recovery as soon as possible.'

WALLRAFF: 'Of which you will be the Director, I presume?'

SPINOLA: 'Yes, and as Director I will be counting on economic aid from your country. Portugal needs something like a German economic miracle. And in any event we are firmly expecting technical aid from Germany. We are sure that once it has been set up our Institute will be a magnetic centre of attraction for all of Portugal. (The Konrad Adenauer Foundation has donated DM 500,000 to an 'Institute for National Renewal.') And beyond our borders I put my hopes on Germany after the next *Bundestag* elections. The decision of the German people is a life or death decision for Portugal and the rest of Europe. Have you any further questions?'

'PRESIDENT': 'Allow me to make one little observation. I am deeply impressed by your readiness to act and your decisiveness. And I certainly appreciate the privilege of meeting your Excellency here in person. Our assistants can work out and decide the details of our arrangement. I do not wish to promise too much at the moment, but I can certainly say one thing: you will not be disappointed, your Excellency.'

WALLRAFF (to the 'President'): 'And the question of arms?'

'PRESIDENT': 'Perhaps your Excellency could tell us how the problem of arms can most satisfactorily be solved?'

SPINOLA: 'Either by sea, with the cargo being unloaded in the Algarve—I have already worked out a plan for this. Or directly through the Supreme Command of the Portuguese Army.'

WALLRAFF: 'But Captain Duarte suggested that the weapons should be delivered in the North.'

SPINOLA (disconcerted, getting excited): 'Of course it could be done in the North but I know the South better. Both ways are possible. The next possibility would be air-transport, which is policed by the Portuguese army. Officially it would be for the Portuguese forces or the National Guard and then . . . we would get it.' (He laughs.)

WALLRAFF: 'And how are these arms to be used? The North has already been pacified, what is going to happen now in the South, which is still firmly in communist hands?'

SPINOLA: 'We are mainly interested in highly sophisticated automatic weapons.'

WALLRAFF: 'Your people in the North spoke of unloading the arms at sea from a large ship on to fishing boats.'

SPINOLA: 'That is exactly what I had in mind in the Algarve. Unfortunately we can't count on Spain at the moment. The situation in Spain is even more difficult than in Portugal. The political process in Portugal is coming to an end, while in Spain it is just developing.

'PRESIDENT': 'Extremely interesting, extremely interesting.'

SPINOLA: 'You will certainly be pleased to hear that we've got over 100,000 working underground for us, and they have a well-organised network. These people are not beginners, they've already been through some stiff tests. Our main enemy is the CP—and we are the only ones who are on the offensive against them. Unfortunately the number of fully-trained special-duty anti-communist units is still too small.'

WALLRAFF: 'But the commandos?'

SPINOLA: 'Yes, everything is all right there. The military mission of the MDLP is the *annihilation of the International Brigades.*'

WALLRAFF: 'You mean physical?'

SPINOLA: 'Yes. But we've got to see how the masses react to this. We have quite deliberately only asked you for a small quantity of weapons. We only want to replenish our stocks.'

WALLRAFF: 'The President would like to know (at this the 'President' nods) what guarantees you can give that the weapons will be used for the right purposes so that the communist movement will eventually be smashed. From what we have heard, it is not a matter of isolated actions in the North, but of moving into the South in a big way. Do you expect the complete extermination of all communists in Portugal?'

SPINOLA (agreeing): 'Mmm. Well, that is our ultimate objective, our overall objective of course. What we are aiming for is the total elimination of communism in Portugal. I won't accept any theories about democracy being possible with communists in the government. We are further ahead than other European countries in this respect.'

LAWYER: 'There are powerful forces here too working towards a prohibition of the Communist Party.'

SPINOLA: 'Prohibition is the very least that must be done. But it is not just communists, it is socialists too. On a European level the socialist and social-democratic parties are a much bigger danger than the communists. Many social democrats and of course all socialists are just communists in disguise.'

'PRESIDENT': 'And how can one deal with these socialists, your Excellency? In the most subtle way, I mean, of course.'

SPINOLA: 'That depends on the means you put at our disposal.'

LAWYER: 'How can the CDS, as an official party, support the MDLP?'

SPINOLA: 'Well, there are many connections between the CDS and the MDLP. As for official pronouncements, no party will risk admitting its connections. Besides, the parties are all suffering from one complex at the moment, they are afraid of communism. They don't dare to admit that they are anti-communist and right-wing. On the other hand we are known as a strong anti-communist movement of the far right.'

WALLRAFF: 'Do you mean to say that the PPD and the CDS are so cowardly as to decribe themselves as "moderate parties"?'

SPINOLA (excitedly): 'That's just it. Secretly they accept our objectives and show solidarity with us but in public they are afraid of compromising themselves. And that is why they lie. But they can't tell the truth at the moment.'

'PRESIDENT': 'One doesn't always have to tell the truth, your Excellency.'

WALLRAFF: 'What guarantees can you give that after the weapons have been delivered they will in fact be used and lead to the desired end? When can we expect results?'

SPINOLA: 'I will let you into a secret. Our organisation in the South is considerably better than in the North. And your arms are intended for the South.'

'PRESIDENT': 'That is exactly what I had been thinking. I am glad to hear this confirmed.'

SPINOLA: 'Have you heard of the Organisation of Small and Medium Farmers? Do you know what Rio Major and Coruche mean?' (Rio Major is the centre of the reactionary Farmer's Associations. In Coruche there were bomb attacks by these associations.) The German hosts nod. 'Then I need say no more. We have a few things up our sleeves in the South.'

'PRESIDENT' (in a low voice, to Wallraff): 'I really have to be going now. I have an important appointment.'

SPINOLA: 'Our main plan as you already know is to mobilise the masses and be in a position to support their "spontaneous uprisings," their "outrage." Blowing up party offices here and there leads nowhere in the long run. They are just gestures of intent, the communist structures remain the same. (Spinola demonstrates what he means on the green felt tablecloth, flicking away a box of matches.) First of all we have to have the masses behind us, then we can raze these places to the ground. (Enthusiastically.) Yes, our organisation in the South is tactically much sounder. You'll see.'

'PRESIDENT': 'As I now have to bring our extremely interesting talk to a close I would like to ask you to do as I do and leave the working out of concrete details to our assistants. I would like to thank you again for your brave efforts in our common cause and to express my respect and admiration for you.'

WALLRAFF (to the 'President'): 'Did you know that the General has invited you to Geneva?'

'PRESIDENT' (in a low voice): 'No, really? (Aloud.) I will be only too delighted to accept your invitation.'

SPINOLA: 'We can guarantee maximum security for you in Geneva. It is good that our two organisations already exist and all we need to do is co-ordinate them. But we have to act quickly.'

We have to hurry. Luis and Jorge keep pressing us to finish. The plane leaves in forty minutes, at 20.05. Spinola will not be rushed, he starts going into detail about weapon systems, giving data and numbers. Luis warns: 'And don't forget boarding gear for helicopters.'

Finally the two Presidents take cordial leave of one another. The 'President' takes his empty new attaché-case and leaves the room gravely.

Wallraff: *The Coup Merchants*

LUIS: 'He is a good man, your President.'

WALLRAFF: 'Yes, he gives us a completely free hand.'

The next day we continue our discussions with Spinola's two plenipotentiaries in the Restaurant Bobino, Burgplatz 7, Düsseldorf. Here we are told the account number for our financial 'contribution.'

WALLRAFF: 'When and how is the first installment to be paid?'

LUIS: 'It is a matter of DM 11 million altogether, excluding arms. DM 4,400,000 for the first three months. Apart from the arms, of course.' And now the account number. The account is in three names: mine, Luis' and the General's. Two have withdrawal rights.

WALLRAFF: 'There is one difficulty, in connection with the second phase of our financial aid, which our President mentioned. What contribution are the big Portuguese industrialists going to make to all this?'

LUIS: 'The industrialists want to see success. And there are two kinds of success. The first is when they see we are actually getting support from abroad. And the second is that they are men who are always taking risks, so they want to get something out of it, too. I don't think we need worry about their support, especially after our victorious return. We would like to thank you for your help. And of course Portuguese industry will be the main beneficiary of our political activity, after all.'

'Dr Strauss phoned me...'

It was the day before the President of the MDLP, General Spinola, arrived in Düsseldorf. (Wednesday, 24 March. The Conference Room in the *Schnellenburg*). Before going into details of our 'financial and arms aid,' Dr Luis Dias, one of Spinola's personal advisers and plenipotentiaries, asks an unexpected question: 'Has Dr Strauss been informed of our meeting?'

WALLRAFF: 'He doesn't know we're sitting here at this moment, but you can be sure that he'll be told about it very soon.'

LUIS: 'I rang his secretary Miss Haase from the *Bayrischen Hof* (Munich) yesterday and asked her to let him know we were in Munich and would be flying on to Düsseldorf. He is preparing for a fact-finding tour to the North of Portugal, where he's going to have talks with the CDS in Povoa de Varzim. The General and I were with Strauss a month ago—he had invited us to a meal—and I didn't think we'd be contacting him again so soon.'

JOSE: 'Meetings like this, among people of the same political views, are always going on.'

WALLRAFF (turning the pages of my diary, as if I had a note of this, too): 'What was the reason for the talk again?'

LUIS: 'About four weeks ago we talked with Dr Strauss about the possibility of the General living in Germany if there were any difficulties in Switzerland. Strauss assured him he would be able to live in Bavaria and with no restrictions on his political activity. So the moment there are any difficulties in Switzerland, we'll go to Munich. We've had offers from Austria, too.'

WALLRAFF: 'Did you let Strauss know you were making contact with us?'

LUIS: 'We met Dr Voss in the Bonn office of the CSU about three weeks ago. [Note: Dr Voss is Strauss's personal adviser.] We gave him plans explaining our strategy. He told us from Strauss that we had to act quickly and we shouldn't contact anyone but him. That was during the carnival. Now he'll be able to get a good picture of things in Portugal for himself, as you did. And we were going to make contact again afterwards...

'I really don't understand what I'm meant to be doing sitting here at the moment. Dr Strauss phoned me in Geneva a short while ago and I wasn't there. Do you think the CSU will operate on a federal level in the next election? The problem with the CDU is that their leaders have got no international standing.'

WALLRAFF: 'Right, but Strauss is capable of leading both parties...'

After I had revealed the connections between Strauss and Spinola at the press conference in Bonn, Strauss's personal adviser Dr Voss issued a denial. Two hours later Strauss admitted that he had had a meeting with 'this historic personality.' And the guest he had once welcomed with open arms suddenly becomes 'an obstacle to Portugal's democratic development.' 'That is why I broke off my connections with him.' (Note: after the February meeting.)

This repudiation of Spinola was only for the sake of public opinion. Strauss and Spinola in fact remained in touch according to Dias.

LUIS: 'Whenever I left the place I was staying I always gave Miss Haase a phone number at which I could be contacted.'

JOSE: 'Our contacts with the German Embassy were made through Dr Oberacker, whom we know well from Brazil.' (Dr Oberacker, a link-man between German and Brazilian industry, always prided himself on being a preserver of German national interests. In 1955 he wrote a book entitled: *The German Contribution to the Brazilian Nation*, in which he even includes Sweden as part of the Pan-German Empire.)

Jose's contacts with Oberacker proved very useful when he was arrested after the first abortive Spinola coup on 28 September 1974. (Copcon, then the Portuguese Security Service, had discovered lists of weapons and plans for revolution in the offices of the 'Progress Party' which Jose and Luis had founded. Jose had been sentenced to eight months.)

JOSE: 'When I was in prison he was in contact with me all the time and he made sure I got help. He even used his diplomatic connections to get me out early. When our four officers took refuge in the German Embassy after the second unsuccessful coup, Oberacker did all he could to help....And we've got him to thank for putting a stop to the Director of the German Institute's subversive cultural relations work.' (Curt Meyer-Clason, the well-known translator of Latin-American works, had gained a reputation for liberal, progressive cultural work during the Salazar and Caetano dictatorships. He was removed from his post at the end of July 1976, after constant intrigues against him within the German Embassy.)

JOSE: 'It was our friend Oberacker who put us in touch with Kurt Ziesel and the *Deutschlandstiftung* [German Foundation]. I've got a nice photo taken at the Chiemsee, with me in the middle, Kurt Ziesel and Georg von Studnitz, the last person to be granted an interview with Salazar before his death.'

(There is no way of establishing whether Oberacker also arranged the contacts between the MDLP and the *Bundesnachrichtendienst* [Federal Intelligence Service].)

LUIS: 'Between us, the CIA works closely with the German Secret Service. We made contact with the BND through a good friend, who asked the Federal Government if there was any possibility of giving us support. That was when Galvao de Melo was in Paris. The SPD/FDP coalition turned down his request. That was a really difficult period for us.'

Soares: *'Spinola can be trusted'*

We asked Spinola what he thought of Mario Soares, the socialist leader. He did not think as highly of Soares as Soares thought of him.

WALLRAFF: 'What do you think of Lopes Cardoso, the Minister of Agriculture?'

SPINOLA: 'He is a communist. Of course it's very difficult to tell the difference between marxists and pseudo-marxists in the PS. They are always attacking one another. We can't trust the PS at all, they want to go ahead with the historic compromise in Italy. And Mario Soares is no good at all to us, he's one of the worst.'

WALLRAFF: 'Is Soares' anti-communism credible?'

SPINOLA: 'No, it's nothing but a tactical move.'

LUIS: 'We mustn't forget that Soares was a member of the PC himself.' (Note: as a young man.)

SPINOLA: 'I remember that Soares and Cunhal were very friendly in the first months after 25 April, in Palma Carlos' government. And I could tell you a tale about that.'

LUIS: 'But not now please, General.'

SPINOLA: 'No? (Sulkily.) (Intellectually.) Soares is only average. He can't even solve a simple equation.'

JOSE: 'Since 25 April he's been nothing but a fabrication of *The New York Times*.'

(In an interview with the French magazine *Le Nouvel Observateur* Soares gives the General and his supporters the stamp of political approval. -*Nouvel Observateur* interviewer: 'Carvalho and Fabiao had to go. But now officers such as Firmino Miguel, Lieutenant-Colonel Almeida Bruno and Major Manuel Monge are being appointed to important posts. Is the return of these Spinola men a good thing for democracy?' -Soares: 'These men had been very unfairly treated. The time had come to rehabilitate them. I have absolute confidence in them.')

WALLRAFF: 'What is your opinion of the PCP/ML and the MRPP?' (Note: The MRPP is one of the 'maoist' parties in Portugal, by far the richest, and at one stage it even had its own daily newspaper.

Along with the PCP/ML, which is also 'maoist' it is openly anti-communist. The PCP/ML advised its supporters to vote for the conservative 'social-democratic' PPD, which it considered to be the most effective anti-communist force.)

LUIS: 'I think very highly of them, they always used to come to us in the Progress Party to ask our advice. It is important to have them on the so-called left-wing. But our main support comes from the Church. The bishop of Aveiro for example. There was an anti-communist demonstration there in July 1975, a month before Braga, and he led it . . .'

WALLRAFF: 'Can you see any possibility of bringing Soares and the right of the PS into a future CDS/PPD government as a unifying factor?'

LUIS: 'He'd be stupid enough to go along with that, too. The only political leader I have any respect for is Cunhal. He's brave and sticks to his ideas. I'd kill him if I could but I still respect him.'△

CONTRIBUTORS

Nancy Angelo has worked in community arts in Los Angeles since 1975. She received her art training at the San Francisco Art Institute and Goddard College, and has worked in video and art performance. Her art has been concerned primarily with community organizing and feminist issues. She is an arts administrator, focusing for the past several years on developing funding for social art projects. She lives in Los Angeles.

Judith Francisca Baca is an artist, muralist, and founder of the Social and Public Art Resource Center (SPARC), in Venice, California, and is currently serving as its artistic director. She is also assistant professor at the University of Southern California at Irvine in the Department of Studio Arts. Her work has been exhibited internationally, appeared in numerous periodicals and journals, and has been documented in several films. She was a member of the National Endowment for the Arts Task Force on Hispanic Arts, and has received numerous awards and recognition for her work from community groups, state assemblymen, the U.S. Army Corps of Engineers, and Los Angeles Mayor Tom Bradley. She makes her home in Venice, California.

Albert J. Camigliano is assistant professor of German at the University of Missouri in St. Louis. He received his Ph.D. from the University of Wisconsin–Madison, in 1974. His current research concerns the theory and function of contemporary documentary prose in America and West Germany. He lives in St. Charles, Missouri.

Father Ernesto Cardenal is a Trappist monk and founder of the Solentiname contemplative community and artists' workshop in Nicaragua. He is the author of several books of poetry, and is currently Nicaragua's Minister of Culture.

Peter Dunn lives in London and teaches part-time at the Architectural Association and in the Art Department of East Ham College. He has collaborated with Loraine Leeson on various projects since 1976; they are currently working together on the Docklands Community Poster Project.

Honor Ford-Smith is artistic director of SISTREN. She has worked with SISTREN since 1977, when she organized the original training program at the Jamaica School of Drama. She is a poet, actress, and teacher of drama, and currently lives in Kingston, Jamaica.

Martha Gever, former editor of *Afterimage,* is currently editor of *The Independent,* a magazine for independent film and video makers. She is the author of a number of articles on independent video, publishing, and film, and lives in Brooklyn, New York.

Hans Haacke was born in Cologne, Germany. He has had numerous one-man shows in both the United States and Europe. His works have been exhibited at the Venice Biennale, the Tokyo Biennale, the Sydney Biennale, and at Documenta. He currently teaches at Cooper Union, and lives in New York City.

DeeDee Halleck has for several years been thoroughly involved in every aspect of communication and independent filmmaking. She is currently producer of *Paper Tiger TV,* a live, low-budget weekly cable television show, and is also working on a feature documentary on U.S. intervention in Latin America in the early twentieth century. She lives with her family of four in New York City.

Abbie Hoffman came to national prominence in 1968 during the anti-Vietnam war demonstrations outside the Democratic National Convention. A defendant in the Chicago conspiracy trial, he shocked the nation by bringing his guerilla theater tactics into the courtroom. He went underground in 1973, although he managed to stay politically active, organizing a successful grassroots campaign against the Army Corps of Engineers' plan for a year-round barge canal for the Thousand Island region of New York State. He currently works with several environmental groups throughout the Great Lakes and the Northeast, works to mobilize opposition to U.S. policy in Central America, and organizes tours of Nicaragua.

Douglas Kahn is a writer and audio artist, whose tape work involves "high-tech ventriloquism"—the rearrangement of audio tracks to present to the listener the true meaning of the speaker's statement. His book, *John Heartfield: Art and Mass Media,* will be published this year by Tanam Press. He lives in Seattle, where he is currently at work on a mode of composition for mass media appropriation and subversion.

281

Ross Kidd is a popular educator and community organizer who has spent several years (1966-1978) in Africa, working on literacy campaigns, radio-based mass study group campaigns, popular theater, and community education. He has played a key role in the development of a Third World popular theater network, and is currently completing a work tentatively entitled, "Popular Theater and Social Action in the Third World." He is a member of the Participatory Research Group in Toronto and is the interim coordinator of the International Popular Theatre Alliance. He lives in Toronto.

Peter King is an independent consultant to the building industry. His involvement in the environmental movement over the past ten years influenced his critical view of much urban development, which in turn lead to his active participation with various advertising reform movements, especially B.U.G.A. U.P. He has "refaced" hundreds of billboards over the past four years, been apprehended by police only twice, and never charged. He lives with his wife and family in Melbourne, Australia.

Tetsuo Kogawa is a writer, media and culture critic, and editorial associate for *Telos* (U.S.A.). He teaches philosophical criticism at Wako University, and lives in Tokyo.

Leslie Labowitz has devoted her professional efforts to her business, SPROUT TIME. Incorporating her philosophies of life, death, and woman's role as survivor, she has to date produced four performance pieces and art installations by the same title. She advises women's groups on media strategy and has appeared on national television in this capacity. She currently lives with her family in Venice, California.

Suzanne Lacy is a Los Angeles artist, well-known for her large-scale performance pieces involving non-professionals in meticulously orchestrated visual scenes. A recent piece is *Whisper, the Waves, the Wind,* (San Diego, 1983-1984), the culmination of a year-long series of art and public information events on aging women. She writes, teaches, and lectures nationally on mass culture implications of performance art, and lives in Los Angeles.

Loraine Leeson teaches at the University of Leeds and has collaborated with Peter Dunn on various projects since 1976. She is currently working with him on the Docklands Community Poster Project and lives in London.

Lucy R. Lippard is the author of twelve books on contemporary art, and one novel. She is co-founder of *Heresies,* Printed Matter, PADD (Political Art Documentation/Distribution), and Artists Call Against U.S. Intervention in Central America, and is on the board of the Alliance for Cultural Democracy. She writes a monthly column on art and politics for the *Village Voice* and lives in New York City.

Fred Lonidier is associate professor in the Visual Arts Department at the University of California in

San Diego. His photographs have been exhibited nationally and internationally, in both one-person and group shows, and have been widely published in such periodicals as the *Village Voice, LAICA Journal, In These Times, Praxis* and *Obscura*. He lives in La Jolla, California.

Catherine Lord, formerly the associate editor of *Afterimage,* is dean of the School of Art of the California Institute of the Arts. She has written extensively about photography, and continues to write essays of cultural and institutional criticism. She lives in Hollywood.

Gabriel Garcia Marquez was born in Arcata, Colombia, but has lived most of his life in Mexico and Europe. He attended the University of Bogota and worked as a reporter and film critic for the Colombian newspaper, *El Espectador.* He received the Nobel Prize for Literature in 1982 and is perhaps most famous for his novel *One Hundred Years of Solitude.* He currently lives with his wife and family in Mexico City and Cartegena, Colombia.

Kofi Natambu is a poet and journalist. His reviews of literature, music, and cultural and social history have appeared in *Downbeat,* the *Pan-African,* and *The New World,* among others. He is founder, editor, and publisher of *Solid Ground: A New World Journal,* a quarterly magazine of the arts, culture, and politics, and his book of poetry, *Intervals,* was published by the Post Aesthetic Press in 1983. He lives in Detroit.

Holly Near left a budding acting career in 1971 to join the anti-war movement fulltime as an activist and cultural worker. She is a singer and songwriter as well as an actor, and is dedicated to coalition politics and high quality music, both of which are reflected in her work. She tours nationally and internationally and has released eleven albums on her own independent alternative label, Redwood Records.

Diane Neumaier is a photographer and writer. Her writing focuses on criticism and contemporary culture, while her current photographic work investigates the similarities between advertising and fine art. She teaches photography, and lives and works in New York City.

Richie Perez is a lifelong resident of the Bronx, and for the last fifteen years has taught various courses on mass media in the colleges of metropolitan New York City. A community activist, he is a past member of the Young Lords Party, the Anti-Bakke Decision Coalition, the New York Committee to Free the Puerto Rican Nationalist Prisoners, and the Committee Against Fort Apache, to name but a few, and is a founding member of the National Congress for Puerto Rican Rights. He currently teaches in the Department of Black and Puerto Rican Studies at Hunter College, and directs a voter registration/community organizing project in the Bushwick section of Brooklyn.

Arlene Raven, Ph.D., is an art historian specializing in American and women's art. She is a founder of the Woman's Building and Feminist Studio Workshop in Los Angeles, and a founding editor of *Womanspace Journal* and *Chrysalis* magazine. A political activist for twenty-five years, she has participated in civil rights and student protests, as well as women's actions for social change. She lives and works as an art writer in New York City.

Dr. Bernice Johnson Reagon is a writer, teacher, and performing and recording artist. She is a founding member of Sweet Honey in the Rock, and performs as a solo artist as well. She is currently director of the Program in Black American Culture, Division of Performing Arts, at the Smithsonian Institution, and lives in Washington, D.C.

Archie Shepp is an internationally renowned composer and a recognized master of the tenor and soprano saxophones. He is also an accomplished poet, actor, and playwright, and a dedicated political activist. He has performed and recorded with John Coltrane, Cecil Taylor, Max Roach, and Bill Dixon, among many others. He is a professor of music at the University of Massachusetts at Amherst.

Klaus Staeck has, for the past fifteen years, concentrated his art in the form of posters, postcards, fliers, and documentary pieces. His posters have appeared in over 3000 exhibitions, both in West Germany and abroad. He lives and works in Heidelberg, Ingrimstrasse 3, West Germany.

Günter Wallraff is among the most celebrated and intrepid investigative journalists writing today. He is famous for his methods of assuming false identities to infiltrate industry, government, religious institutions and newspapers, intending and most often succeeding in exposing corruption in high places. His experience recounted here in "The Coup Merchants" is perhaps his most daring, dangerous, and effective escapade. He is rumored to live somewhere in West Germany.

Tom Ward has been a journalist, political activist, and performing artist for twenty years in Chicago, the San Francisco Bay area, and now in New York. The Situationists, about whom he writes here, have been a strong influence in much of his work—street theater, radio montage, essays, pamphlets, graffiti, and his current band, the Funktionaries. He is a freelance contributor to the *Village Voice* and the editor of "Reality Sandwich," a political supplement to the *Aquarian Weekly*. He lives in New York City.

SELECTED READINGS

Camigliano, Albert J., *Friedrich Schiller and Christian Gottfried Korner: A Critical Relationship,* (Akademischer Verlag Hans-Dieter Heinz, Stuttgart, 1976).

Cardenal, Ernesto, *Apocalypse and Other Poems,* (New Directions, 1977); *The Gospel in Solentiname,* (Orbis Books, 1982); *Love,* (Crossroad, New York, 1981); *Zero Hour and Other Documentary Poems,* (New Directions, 1980).

Haacke, Hans, *Werkmonographie,* Introduction by Edward F. Fry, (Dumont Buchverlag, Cologne, 1972); *Framing and Being Framed,* with essays by Jack Burnham, Howard S. Becker and John Walton, (Nova Scotia College of Art and Design Press, Halifax, and New York University Press, 1975). *Hans Haacke* - Vol. I, (Museum of Modern Art, Oxford, and Stedelijk van Abbemuseum, Eindhoven, 1978). *Hans Haacke* - Vol. II, (The Tate Gallery, London, and Stedelijk van Abbemuseum, Eindhoven, 1984).

Hoffman, Abbie, *Soon to Be a Major Motion Picture,* (Berkeley, 1982); *Square Dancing in the Ice Age,* (South End Press, 1983).

Ford-Smith, Honor, contributor to *Focus,* (1983 and 1984, Caribbean Authors Publishing Company Limited, Kingston, Jamaica); and *An Anthology of African and Caribbean Writing in English,* (Figueroa Heinemarn, London, 1982).

Kahn, Douglas, *John Heartfield: Art and Mass Media,* (Tanam Press, 1985).

Kidd, Ross, *Popular Theatre and Popular Action: Experiences from the Third World,* (International Popular Theatre Alliance, Toronto, 1985); co-editor, *Tradition for Development: Indigenous Structures and Folk Media in Non-Formal Education,* (German Foundation for International Development, Bonn, 1982); co-author, *Radio Learning Group Manual,* (Friedrich Ebart Foundation, Bonn, 1978). Contributing editor, *Theaterwork,* (U.S.A.), *New Theatre Quarterly,* (England), and *Convergence,* (Toronto).

Kogawa, Tetsuo, *This Is Free Radio,* (Shobunsha, Tokyo); *Walking Cities,* (Tojusha, Tokyo); *The Prison of Mass Media,* (Shobunsha, Tokyo); *Paradoxes of New Media,* (Shobunsha, Tokyo); *Memory of the City,* (Sorinsha, Tokyo); *Husserl's Phenomenology,* The Japanese Translation from L. Robberechts, K. Held and E. Paci, (Serika Shobo, Tokyo). Editorial Associate, *Telos* (U.S.A.).

Lippard, Lucy R., *Get the Message? A Decade of Art for Social Change,* (Dutton, 1984); *Overlay: Contemporary Art and the Art of Prehistory,* (Pantheon, 1983); *From the Center: Feminist Essays on Women's Art,* (Dutton, 1976). Monthly contributor on arts and politics to the *Village Voice.*

Lonidier, Fred, *Foto Folder,* (self-published, 1977). Contributor to *Red Herring 2, Praxis,* and *Obscura.*

Marquez, Gabriel Garcia, *Chronicle of a Death Foretold,* (Alfred A. Knopf, 1983); *In Evil Hour,* (Avon, 1980); *Leaf Storm and Other Stories,* (Harper & Row, 1979); *No One Writes to the Colonel and Other Stories,* (Harper & Row, 1979); *Autumn of the Patriarch,* (Avon, 1977); and *One Hundred Years of Solitude,* (Avon, 1971).

Natambu, Kofi, *Intervals,* (Post Aesthetic Press, 1983), and *Nostalgia for the Present,* (Post Aesthetic Press, 1985). Regular contributor to *The Metro Times,* Detroit.

Neumaier, Diane, contributor to *Exposure* and *Afterimage.*

Raven, Arlene, AT HOME, (Long Beach Museum, 1984); *The New Culture: Women Artists of the Seventies,* (Indiana University, Terre Haute, 1984). Author of the introductory texts for *William Morris* and *Wiener Werkstaette,* (Gift Wraps by Artists Series, Harry N. Abrams, 1985). Contributor to *Anonymous Was a Woman,* (St. Martin's Press, 1979), and *Feminist Collage: Educating Women in the Visual Arts,* (Teachers College Press, 1979). Contributor to *Arts, MS., High Performance, New Art Examiner,* and *LAICA Journal.*

Reagon, Dr. Bernice Johnson, contributor to *Radical America, SING OUT,* and *Southern Exposure.*

Shepp, Archie, contributor to *Downbeat, Black Talk, Face the Music,* and *The Black Scholar.*

Staeck, Klaus, *Staeck's Umwelt,* (Steidl-Verlag, 1984).

Wallraff, Günter, *Wallraff: The Undesirable Journalist,* translated from the German by Steve Gooch and Paul Knight, (Overlook Press, 1979).

Ward, Tom, contributor to the *Village Voice;* editor of *Reality Sandwich,* (supplement to the *Aquarian Weekly).*